RELIGIONS OF TIBET IN PRACTICE

PRINCETON READINGS IN RELIGIONS

Donald S. Lopez, Jr., Editor

TITLES IN THE SERIES

Religions of India in Practice edited by Donald S. Lopez, Jr.

Buddhism in Practice edited by Donald S. Lopez, Jr.

Religions of China in Practice edited by Donald S. Lopez, Jr.

Religions of Tibet in Practice edited by Donald S. Lopez, Jr.

RELIGIONS OF
TIBET
IN PRACTICE

Donald S. Lopez, Jr., Editor

PRINCETON READINGS IN RELIGIONS

PRINCETON UNIVERSITY PRESS

PRINCETON, NEW JERSEY

Published by Princeton University Press, 41 William Street,
Princeton, New Jersey 08540
In the United Kingdom: Princeton University Press, Chichester, West Sussex

"Daily Prayers" consists of the following texts: "Dedications of Merit"; "Fulfilling the Aspirations of Gyalwang Karmapa"; "The Aspiration Prayer of Choggyur Lingpa"; "Meal Chants"; "The Sūtra of the Recollection of the Noble Three Jewels"; "Short Feast Offering" by Jigme Lingpa; and "Concluding Request to the Protectors."

Library of Congress Cataloging-in-Publication Data

Religions of Tibet in practice / edited by Donald S. Lopez.
p. cm.—(Princeton readings in religions)
Includes bibliographical references and index.
ISBN 0-691-01184-2 (cloth : alk. paper). — ISBN 0-691-01183-4
(pbk. : alk. paper)
1. Buddhism—China—Tibet. 2. Tibet (China)—Religion.
3. Buddhist literature, Tibetan—Translations into English.
I. Lopez, Donald S., 1952– . II. Series.
BQ7620.R45 1997
294.3'923—dc20 96-31592

This book has been composed in Berkeley

Princeton University Press books are printed on acid-free paper and meet the guidelines for permanence and durability of the Committee on Production Guidelines for Book Longevity of the Council on Library Resources

Printed in the United States of America by Princeton Academic Press

1 3 5 7 9 10 8 6 4 2

1 3 5 7 9 10 8 6 4 2
(pbk.)

PRINCETON READINGS IN RELIGIONS

Princeton Readings in Religions is a new series of anthologies on the religions of the world, representing the significant advances that have been made in the study of religions in the last thirty years. The sourcebooks used by previous generations of students, whether for Judaism and Christianity or for the religions of Asia and the Middle East, placed a heavy emphasis on "canonical works." Princeton Readings in Religions provides a different configuration of texts in an attempt better to represent the range of religious practices, placing particular emphasis on the ways in which texts have been used in diverse contexts. The volumes in the series therefore include ritual manuals, hagiographical and autobiographical works, popular commentaries, and folktales, as well as some ethnographic material. Many works are drawn from vernacular sources. The readings in the series are new in two senses. First, very few of the works contained in the volumes have ever have made available in an anthology before; in the case of the volumes on Asia, few have even been translated into a Western language. Second, the readings are new in the sense that each volume provides new ways to read and understand the religions of the world, breaking down the sometimes misleading stereotypes inherited from the past in an effort to provide both more expansive and more focused perspectives on the richness and diversity of religious expressions. The series is designed for use by a wide range of readers, with key terms translated and technical notes omitted. Each volume also contains an introduction by a distinguished scholar in which the histories of the traditions are outlined and the significance of each of the works is explored.

Religions of Tibet in Practice is the fourth volume of Princeton Readings in Religion and the first substantial anthology of Tibetan religious literature to appear in English. The seventeen contributors are leading scholars of the religions of Tibet, each of whom has provided one or more translations of key works, most of which are translated here for the first time. Each chapter in the volume begins with an introduction in which the translator discusses the history and influence of the work, identifying points of particular difficulty or interest. The works they have translated here represent many genres; they are drawn from a millenium of Tibetan history and from many regions of the Tibetan cultural domain.

In addition to acknowledging the cooperation and patience of the contributors to *Religions of Tibet in Practice*, I would like to thank Zeff Bjerken for his assistance in the initial editing of the manuscript.

Religions of Japan in Practice is currently in press. Volumes nearing completion are devoted to *Islam in Asia*, *Islamic Mysticism*, and the *Religions of Latin America*. Several volumes on Judaism and Christianity are also planned.

Donald S. Lopez, Jr.
Series Editor

NOTE ON TRANSLITERATION

Unfortunately, there is no commonly accepted system for phonetically rendering Tibetan words. The editor has attempted to represent the sound of Tibetan words as accurately and consistently as possible, while respecting the preferences of the individual translators. After the first occurrence of a name or title, the Tibetan transliteration follows in parentheses, using the Wylie system but with the first letter of a proper name, rather than the root letter, capitalized.

CONTENTS

Prayers and Sermons

Dealing with Death and Other Demons

CONTRIBUTORS

Yael Bentor teaches in the Department of Indian Studies at Hebrew University of Jerusalem.

José Ignacio Cabezón teaches Buddhist Studies at Iliff School of Theology.

Hubert Decleer is academic director with the Kathmandu-based Tibetan Studies program of Academic Semesters Abroad, for the School of International Training.

David Germano teaches in the Department of Religious Studies at the University of Virginia.

Janet Gyatso teaches in the Department of Religion at Amherst College.

Toni Huber is an independent scholar living in Berlin.

Roger Jackson teaches in the Department of Religion at Carleton College.

Matthew Kapstein teaches in the Department of South Asian Languages and Civilizations at the University of Chicago.

Anne C. Klein teaches in the Department of Religious Studies at Rice University.

Richard J. Kohn is a research associate at the Center for South Asian Studies at the University of California, Berkeley.

Robin Kornman teaches in the World Literature program at the University of Wisconsin in Milwaukee.

Per Kvaerne teaches in the Institute for Comparative Research in Human Culture at the University of Oslo.

Donald S. Lopez, Jr. teaches in the Department of Asian Languages and Cultures at the University of Michigan.

The Nālandā Translation Committee is based in Halifax, Nova Scotia.

Françoise Pommaret teaches in the Institut de Recherche sur le Sud-Est Asiatique at the Université de Provence.

Cyrus Stearns is a graduate of the Department of Asian Languages and Literatures at the University of Washington.

David Templeman is an independent scholar living in Victoria, Australia.

RELIGIONS OF TIBET IN PRACTICE

INTRODUCTION

Donald S. Lopez, Jr.

The religions of Tibet have long been objects of Western fascination and fantasy. From the time that Venetian travelers and Catholic missionaries encountered Tibetan monks at the Mongol court, tales of the mysteries of their mountain homeland and the magic of their strange religions have held a peculiar hold over the European and American imagination. Over the past two centuries, the valuation of Tibetan society and, particularly, its religion has fluctuated wildly. Tibetan Buddhism has been portrayed sometimes as the most corrupt deviation from the Buddha's true dharma, sometimes as its most direct descendant. These fluctuations have occurred over the course of this century, as Tibet resisted the colonial ambitions of a European power at its beginning and succumbed to the colonial ambitions of an Asian power at its end.

Until some thirty years ago, knowledge of the religions of Tibet in the West had largely been derived from the reports of travelers and adventurers, who often found the religions both strange and strangely familiar, noting similarities between Tibetan Buddhism and Roman Catholicism, calling the Dalai Lama the Tibetan pope, for example. It is only since the Tibetan diaspora that took place beginning in 1959, after the Chinese invasion and occupation of Tibet, that the texts of the religions of Tibet have begun to be widely translated. Until this point, however, there has been no attempt to gather a wide range of Tibetan religious texts into a single volume. The present volume, therefore, unlike others in this series, is not intended as a supplement or a substitute for past anthologies (no such anthologies exist), but is a first attempt to represent the contours of Tibetan religious practices through Tibetan texts.

This volume is thus testimony to the vast scope of religious practice in the Tibetan world, past and present. It does not follow a chronological sequence or attempt to represent systematically the various Buddhist sects. Instead, it offers a selection of texts, in the broadest sense of that term, in order to provide the reader with a sense of the remarkable diversity and range of the practices of persons who have inhabited the Tibetan cultural domain. The chapters highlight types of discourse (including ritual texts, epics, prayers, accounts of visits to hell, sermons, pilgrimage manuals, and autobiographies) and voices (vernacular, esoteric, clerical, prophetic, and female) that have not been sufficiently represented in previous accounts of Tibetan religion. The selections juxtapose materials from different "sects," historical periods, and geographical regions in an attempt to broaden the range of what we understand the religious practices of Tibet to encompass.

Because this volume, like the others in the series, is organized thematically, it is perhaps useful here to provide a brief historical overview of the religions of Tibet, with repeated excurses into some of the presuppositions and foundations of Tibetan religious life that are represented in the chapters of this book.

The history of Tibet prior to the seventh century C.E. is difficult to determine. According to a number of chronicles discovered at Dunhuang dating from the seventh through the tenth centuries, Tibet was ruled by a lineage of kings, the first seven of whom descended from the heavens by means of a cord or ladder. Each king ruled until his first son was old enough to ride a horse, at which point the king returned to heaven via the rope. (Buddhist historians say that the first king in the lineage was an Indian prince who arrived by crossing the Himalayas; when the Tibetans asked where he had come from he pointed up, and the credulous Tibetans assumed he had descended from the sky.) These kings founded a system of law that reflected the cosmic order of heaven. As a literal descendant of heaven, the king was the embodiment and protector of the cosmic order and the welfare of the state. The king's stable presence on the throne thus ensured harmony in the realm.

It was only when the eighth king lost his protective warrior god (*dgra lha*, see chapter 26) in battle that the sky rope was severed and the king was slain, leaving his corpse behind. To deal with this crisis, according to later sources, priests were invited from an area called Shangshung (Zhang zhung, the precise location and extent of which is unknown but is assumed to include much of western Tibet) to perform death rituals and bury the king. The story reflects the popular notion of Tibet as an untamed and uncivilized realm, with civilization arriving only from the outside. Recent scholarship thus does not assume from this account that foreign priests were actually summoned, seeing it instead as a creation myth meant to explain the origin of the elaborate royal mortuary cult. A class of priests called "reciters" (*bon*) performed a range of sacerdotal functions in service of the divine king, such as officiating at coronation ceremonies and in rites of allegiance to the king. There was also another class of priests, called *shen* (*gshen*), who seem to have performed divinations.

The cult of the divine king included the belief that he was endowed with both magical power and a special magnificence. There was a trinity of the king, the head priest, and the chief minister, with the active power of government in the hands of the head priest and the minister who represented the priestly hierarchy and the clan nobility. The king represented the continually reborn essence of the divine ancestor, who was reincarnated in each king at the age of maturity and remained incarnated in him until his son reached the same age of maturity and ascended the throne as the consecutive link of the ancestral reincarnation. This procedure applied also to both the priest and the minister, so a new trinity was instituted at the accession of each king. The king also had a special guardian called the "body spirit" (*sku bla*) who protected the king's power, encompassing everything from his body to his political authority to the order of the universe. One of the primary responsibilities of the royal priests and ministers, then, seems to have been the maintenance of the king's health, for if the king became ill or if the body spirit was determined otherwise to be displeased, the safety of the kingdom and even of the universe was in jeopardy. Epidemics and droughts were interpreted as signs of this displeasure.

The notion of *la* (*bla*), generally translated as "soul," "spirit," or "life," dates from the ancient period and remains an important component in the religions of Tibet. The *la* is an individual's life force, often associated with the breath. It is seen as the essential support of the physical and mental constitution of the person but is mobile and can leave the body and wander, going into trees, rocks, or animals, to the detriment of the person it animates, who will become either ill or mentally unbalanced. The *la* is especially susceptible during dreams and can be carried off by demons, who particularly covet the life forces of children. There are thus rites designed to bring the *la* back into the body, known as "calling the *la*" (*bla 'bod*).

Even when the *la* is properly restored to its place in the body, it may simultaneously reside in certain external abodes, most often in a particular lake, tree, mountain, or animal. The person in whom the *la* resides stands in a sympathetic relationship with these phenomena, such that if the *la* mountain is dug into, the person will fall sick. The Tibetan epic hero Gesar (see chapter 1) in his attempt to conquer a certain demoness cuts down her *la* tree and empties her *la* lake; he fails because he does not kill her *la* sheep. The identity of these external *la* are thus often kept secret, and portable abodes of the *la*, usually a precious object of some kind (often a turquoise), are kept in special receptacles and hidden by the person who shares the *la*.

There were thus regular offerings made to the king's body spirit at the site of the king's sacred mountain, the physical locus of his power. Of particular importance to the royal cult, however, were the funeral ceremonies. A king was still expected to abdicate upon the majority of his son and retire to his tomb with a large company of retainers, although whether this entailed the execution of the king and his retinue or simply their exile into a tomb complex remains unknown. The royal funerals were apparently elaborate affairs, with food and other necessities provided for the perilous journey to the next world, a bucolic heaven called the "land of joy" (*bde ba can*). Animals, especially yaks, sheep, and horses (see chapter 25), were also offered in sacrifice. Chinese sources suggest that humans were also sacrificed, perhaps to serve as servants to the departed king, perhaps to be offered as gifts or "ransoms" (*glud*) to various spirits who otherwise would block the king's route. This concern with death and the fate of the dead has continued throughout the history of Tibetan religions, as evidenced by the chapters in the section entitled "Dealing with Death and Other Demons."

Although Buddhism was flourishing all around Tibet in the first centuries of the common era, there is no mention of Buddhist elements in the chronicles apart from the account of a small stūpa and an illegible Buddhist sūtra falling from the sky into the palace of one of the prehistoric kings. The formal introduction of Buddhism to the Tibetan court seems to have occurred during the reign of King Songtsen Gampo (Srong btsan sgam po, ruled c. 614–650), at a time when Tibet was the dominant military power of Inner Asia. According to later chronicles, as a result of treaties with the courts of China and Nepal, the king received two princesses as wives. Each was a Buddhist, and each brought a precious statue of the Buddha with her to Lhasa, the capital. They are credited with converting their new husband to the dharma, although what this meant in practice is difficult to say. The king dispatched an emissary to India to learn Sanskrit and then return to design a written language for Tibet. Among the many purposes to which such a script could be put, it is said that the king's pious motivation was the translation of Buddhist texts from Sanskrit into Tibetan.

The script invented was modeled on one current in northern India at the time. Tibetan is, like Sanskrit, an inflected language, with case endings used to mark grammatical functions. Words are made up of combinations of independent syllables, each of which is constructed by grouping letters in various combinations. The simplest syllable can be made up of a single letter while the most complex can have as many as six, with a prefix, a superscription, a root letter, a subscription, a suffix, and an additional suffix, not to mention a vowel marker. Historical linguists speculate that originally all of these letters were pronounced, but over the centuries the auxiliary letters became silent, such that there is a vast difference today between the way a word is written and the way it is pronounced. To render the spelling of a Tibetan word in English requires that all of the letters be represented. The result, however, appears to be utterly unpronounceable to someone who does not already know Tibetan. For that reason, phonetic renderings (for which there is no widely accepted convention) must be provided. For example, the name of the current Dalai Lama in transliteration is Bstan 'dzin rgya mtsho, but it is commonly written in English as Tenzin Gyatso. Although the same script is employed throughout the Tibetan cultural domain, dozens of regional dialects have developed, many of which are mutually incomprehensible.

The conversion of Tibet to Buddhism is traditionally presented as a process of forceful but ultimately compassionate subjugation (rather than destruction) of native Tibetan deities by the more powerful imported deities of Buddhism, often invoked by Indian yogins. The profoundly chthonic nature of Tibetan religion is evident even from the traditional chronicles, which represent the conversion of Tibet to the true dharma not so much as a matter of bringing new teachings to the populace but of transforming the landscape by bringing the myriad deities of place—of valleys, mountains, hills, passes, rivers, lakes, and plains—under control. Thus Songtsen Gampo was said to have ordered the construction of Buddhist temples at key points throughout his realm, each temple functioning as a great nail impaling a giant demoness (*srin mo*) lying supine over the expanse of Tibet, immobilizing her from impeding the progress of the dharma, the symmetry of a Buddhist maṇḍala superimposed over the unruly landscape of Tibet.

But all this derives from chronicles composed centuries after the fact by authors concerned to promote Buddhism and link the introduction of the dharma to Tibet's greatest king, the king who unified Tibet and led its armies in victory against Chinese, Indians, Nepalese, Turks, and Arabs. The few records surviving from the period make no mention of Buddhism, nor even of the Nepalese princess. The historicity of the emissary to India is questionable. Songtsen Gampo seems to have remained committed to and even to have developed further the cult of divine kingship, a cult that involved both animal and human sacrifice (an anathema to Buddhists), while continuing to worship local deities and supporting his own ministers and priests of the royal mortuary cult. At the same time, it seems unlikely that the Tibetan kingdom, surrounded as it was for centuries by Buddhist societies, should have remained untouched by Buddhist influence until the seventh century, as the traditional histories claim.

The first king to make a choice between Buddhism and the native religion of the Tibetan court was Tri Songdetsen (Khri srong lde btsan, ruled 754–797). Both later Buddhist and Bönpo chronicles report that he promoted Buddhism and suppressed the practices of priests of the native cult; his support of Buddhism may have been motivated by the desire to escape the restricting bonds of the feudal clan nobility who supported the priests. Contemporary inscriptions, however, also indicate that he continued to have rituals performed that involved animal sacrifice. During these ceremonies, the old oaths of loyalty between king and servant were sworn. Before taking the oath, it was the custom for the participants to smear their lips with the blood of the sacrificial animal, a practice from which the Buddhist monks who were present apparently demurred.

Tri Songdetsen invited to Tibet the prominent Indian Buddhist abbot Śāntarakṣita, whose presence angered the local spirits sufficiently for the Indian abbot to request the king to invite a tantric master to aid in the further subjugation of the local spirits. The great master Padmasambhava was invited and proved equal to the task, after which it was possible to establish the first Buddhist monastery at Samye (Bsam yas) circa 779. The further activities of Padmasambhava and the duration of his stay are unknown, but he remains a figure of mythic significance in the history of Tibet, often referred to simply as Guru Rimpoche, the precious guru. The stories of Padmasambhava's defeat and conversion of the local spirits and demons of Tibet are pervasive and popular, and they figure prominently in the descriptions of specific sites found in pilgrimage narratives (see chapters 5, 6, and 24).

Buddhism is famous for its ability to accommodate local deities into its pantheon. In the case of Tibet, most of the local deities became regarded as "mundane gods" (*'jigs rten pa'i lha*), that is, deities who are subject to the law of karma and cycle of rebirth, who, after a lifetime as a particular god, will take rebirth in some other form. The vast pantheon of deities imported from India included such gods, as well as "supramundane gods" (*'jigs rten las 'das pa'i lha*), that is, deities who—although they appear in horrifying forms, such as the protector of the Dalai Lama, the goddess Belden Lhamo (Dpal ldan lha mo, the "Glorious Goddess")—are in fact enlightened beings already liberated from the cycle of birth and death. Still, the process of the Buddhist conversion of Tibet should not be understood to mean that Buddhism was not also converted in that process; indeed, many deities cannot be identified as simply Indian or Tibetan.

The deities that Padmasambhava subdued and converted were often identified with mountains, rock formations, and other prominent elements of the topography of Tibet. The Tibetan plateau stands at 12,000 feet, with the surrounding mountains rising yet another mile above the plateau. The northern region is a vast uninhabited plane, but there are also dense forests and fertile valleys that are cultivated to produce barley, the staple crop. It is thus misleading to characterize Tibet as a desolate place, or to suggest (as Western travelers have) that the bleak landscape and vast sky (with its thin air) have turned men's minds toward the contemplation of a rarefied world of gods and demons, their unconscious releasing vivid hallucinations that appear in sharp relief against the distant horizon.

Yet it is difficult to overestimate the importance of the land in Tibetan religion. From early times Tibetans have held a belief in numerous local spirits, demons, and gods, who lived in lakes, rivers, creeks, wells, trees, fields, rocks, and mountains. Deities inhabited unusually shaped mounds; rocks shaped like animals; hills shaped liked sleeping oxen; burial mounds; juniper, birch, and spruce trees; and any anomalous geologic formation. Various types of demons roamed mountains and valleys and chose abodes in rocks, forests, ditches, and overhanging rocks, all places that could be disturbed by humans, to whom they sent both physical affliction (such as leprosy and smallpox) and social affliction (such as gossip; see chapter 34). The atmosphere was the domain of another class of spirits, demons who appeared in the form of warriors who would attack travelers. Beneath the surface of the earth and in rivers and lakes lived a class of demons named *lu* (*klu*), who would become enraged if the earth was disturbed by digging, plowing, or laying the foundation for a house. Unless they were properly appeased, they also would inflict disease on humans and livestock. There are also *tsen (btsan)*, "rock spirits"; *sa dak* (*sa bdag*), "lords of the earth"; *ma mo*, "demonesses"; and *dre* (*'dre*), *drip* (*sgrib*), *dön* (*gdon*), and *gek* (*bgegs*). The Tibetan pantheon (although the term pantheon suggests a clearer system than in fact exists) of both benevolent and, especially, malevolent spirits is large and complex, and English lacks sufficient terms to render their names, beyond things like "demon" and "ogress." (For a useful list of some of these deities, see chapter 15.) Even the terms "benevolent" and "malevolent" can be misleading, since many horrifying deities, despite an awful demeanor and testy disposition, can provide protection and aid if they are not offended or disturbed, but properly propitiated (see chapter 3).

As mentioned above, Buddhist chronicles describe the Tibetan landscape as itself a giant demoness who must be subdued. There are gods of the plain and gods of the mountains; an entire mountain range is a god (see chapters 3 and 24). This animated topography is itself further populated by all manner of spirits who must be honored to avoid their wrath (see chapter 15). But the landscape is not only a domain of danger, it is also an abode of opportunity, blessing, and power. (In chapter 3, one of these spirits mates with a human, and the two serve as progenitors of a fierce Tibetan tribe.) Thus, pilgrimage is an essential element of Tibetan religious life, with pilgrims seeking to derive power and purification by visiting those places believed to embody a particular potency, either naturally—as when the place is the abode of a god or the god itself—or historically—as when the place is the site of the inspired deeds of a great yogin such as Padmasambhava or Milarepa (see chapters 5 and 6). The topography even contains hidden countries (*sbas yul*), ideal sites for the practice of tantra, the most famous being the kingdom of Shambala; there are guidebooks with directions to such destinations. It is also the land that yields the treasures (*gter ma*), the texts left behind, hidden in rocks, caves, and pillars by Padmasambhava himself, left safely within the earth until the time is right for them to be discovered and their contents made known to the world. Thus, the landscape is not simply an animated realm of fearful demons and ogresses, but above all the abode of power for those who know where to seek what lies within.

During the reign of Tri Songdetsen, not long after the founding of the Samye monastery, a politically charged doctrinal controversy erupted in Tibet. In addition to the Indian party of Śāntarakṣita, there was also an influential Chinese Buddhist contingent who found favor with the Tibetan nobility. These were monks of the Chan (Zen) school, led by one Mohoyen. According to traditional accounts, Śāntarakṣita foretold of dangers from the Chinese position and left instructions in his will that his student Kamalaśīla be called from India to counter the Chinese view. A conflict seems to have developed between the Indian and Chinese partisans (and their allies in the Tibetan court) over the question of the nature of enlightenment, with the Indians holding that enlightenment takes place as the culmination of a gradual process of purification, the result of combining virtuous action, meditative serenity, and philosophical insight. The Chinese spoke against this view, holding that enlightenment was the intrinsic nature of the mind rather than the goal of a protracted path, such that one need simply to recognize the presence of this innate nature of enlightenment by entering a state of awareness beyond distinctions; all other practices were superfluous. According to both Chinese and Tibetan records, a debate was held between Kamalaśīla and Mohoyen at Samye circa 797, with King Tri Songdetsen himself serving as judge. According to Tibetan accounts (contradicted by the Chinese accounts), Kamalaśīla was declared the winner and Mohoyen and his party were banished from Tibet, with the king proclaiming that thereafter the Middle Way (Madhyamaka) school of Indian Buddhist philosophy (to which Śāntarakṣita and Kamalaśīla belonged) would be followed in Tibet. Recent scholarship has suggested that although a controversy between the Indian and Chinese Buddhists (and their Tibetan partisans) occurred, it is unlikely that a face-to-face debate took place or that the outcome of the controversy was so unequivocal. Furthermore, it is probably important to recall that, regardless of the merits of the Indian and Chinese philosophical positions, China was Tibet's chief military rival at the time, whereas India posed no such threat. Nonetheless, it is significant that from this point Tibet largely sought its Buddhism from India; no school of Chinese Buddhism had any further influence in Tibet. Mohoyen himself was transformed into something of a trickster figure, popular in Tibetan art and drama.

The king Ralpajen (Ral pa can, ruled c. 815–835) seems to have been an even more enthusiastic patron of Buddhism, supporting numerous Indian-Tibetan translation teams who continued the formidable task of rendering a vast corpus of Sanskrit literature into Tibetan. Translation academies were established and standard glossaries of technical terms were developed during the ninth century. The relatively late date of the introduction of Buddhism to Tibet compared with China (first century C.E.) and Japan (fifth century) had important ramifications for the development of the Tibetan Buddhist tradition, the foremost being that the Tibetans had access to large bodies of Indian Buddhist literature that either never were translated into Chinese (and thus never transmitted to Japan) or had little influence in East Asia. This literature fell into two categories: tantras and śāstras.

The origins of tantric Buddhism in India remain nebulous, with some scholars dating the early texts from the fourth century C.E. Its literature, including all manner of ritual texts and meditation manuals, continued to be composed in India for the next six centuries. This literature offered a speedy path to enlightenment, radically truncating the eons-long path set forth in the earlier discourses attributed to the Buddha, called sūtras. To this end, the tantric literature set forth a wide range of techniques for the attainment of goals both mundane and supramundane, techniques for bringing the fantastic worlds described in the sūtras into actuality. Tantric practices were considered so potent that they were often conducted in secret, and aspirants required initiation. The practices themselves involved elaborate and meticulous visualizations, in which the practitioner mentally transformed himself or herself into a fully enlightened buddha, with a resplendent body seated on a throne in the center of a marvelous palace (called a maṇḍala), with speech that intoned sacred syllables (called mantras), and with a mind that saw the ultimate reality directly.

A second body of literature, more important for Buddhist philosophy per se, were the śāstras (treatises). Buddhist literature is sometimes divided into sūtras—those texts traditionally held to be either the word of the Buddha or spoken with his sanction—and śāstras—treatises composed by Indian commentators. In the case of Mahāyāna literature, sūtras often contain fantastic visions of worlds populated by enlightened beings, with entrance to such a world gained through devotion to the sūtra itself. When points of doctrine are presented, it is often in the form of narrative, allegory, or the repetition of stock phrases. The śāstras are closer to what might be called systematic philosophy or theology, with positions presented with reasoned argumentation supported by relevant passages from the sūtras and tantras. East Asian Buddhism was predominantly a sūtra-based tradition, with schools forming around single texts, such as the *Lotus Sūtra* and the *Avataṃsaka Sūtra.* Although many important śāstras were translated into Chinese, the major project of translating Indian texts into Chinese virtually ended with the work of Xuanzang (596–664), by whose time the major East Asian schools were well formed. Consequently, works by such figures as the Middle Way philosophers Candrakīrti (c. 600–650) and Śāntideva (early eighth century) and the logician Dharmakīrti (seventh century), who flourished when the Chinese Buddhist schools had already developed, never gained wide currency in East Asia but were highly influential in Tibet. The works by these and other authors became the basis of the scholastic tradition in Tibet, which from the early period was a śāstra-based Buddhism. Sūtras were venerated but rarely read independently; the śāstras were studied and commented upon at great length.

To undertake the task of translation of the sūtras, tantras, and śāstras, a whole new vocabulary had to be created. To render an often technical Sanskrit vocabulary, hundreds of neologisms were invented. In some cases, these were relatively straightforward translations of folk etymologies; in other cases, rather unwieldy terms were fabricated to capture multiple denotations of a Sanskrit term. When these eighth-century exegetes came to decide upon a Tibetan equivalent for the Sanskrit term for teacher, *guru*, a term classically etymologized in India as "one who is heavy (with virtue)," the translators departed from their storied penchant for approximating the meaning of the Sanskrit and opted instead for the word lama (*bla ma*). Here they combined the term *la* ("soul") with *ma*, which has as least three meanings: as a negative particle, as a substantive indicator, and as the word for "mother." Subsequent Buddhist etymologies, drawing on the meaning of *la* as "high" rather than its pre-Buddhist usage as "soul," were then construed, which explained *la ma* as meaning either "highest" (literally, "above-not," that is, "none above") or as "exalted mother." Although the original intention of the translators remains obscure, lama came to be the standard term for one's religious teacher, a person of such significance as to be appended to the threefold refuge formula: Tibetans say, "I go for refuge to the lama, I go for refuge to the Buddha, I go for refuge to the dharma, I go for refuge to the saṅgha."

It would be impossible to summarize the contents of the myriad sūtras, tantras, and śāstras translated into Tibetan, but it might be appropriate at this juncture to review some of the basic elements of Indian Buddhism that were important in Tibet. Tibetans, both Bönpo and Buddhist, conceive of a beginningless cycle of birth and death, called *korwa* (*'khor ba*, a translation of the Sanskrit *saṃsāra*, "wandering"), in six realms of rebirth: gods, demigods, humans, animals, ghosts, and hell beings. The realms of animals, ghosts, and hell beings are regarded as places of great suffering, whereas the godly realms are abodes of great bliss. Human rebirth falls in between, bringing as it does both pleasure and pain. The engine of saṃsāra is driven by karma, the cause and effect of actions. Like other Buddhists, Tibetans believe that every intentional act, whether it be physical, verbal, or mental, leaves a residue in its agent. That residue, like a seed, will eventually produce an effect at some future point in this life or another life, an effect in the form of pleasure or pain for the person who performed the act. Thus Tibetans imagine a moral universe in which virtuous deeds create experiences of pleasure and nonvirtuous deeds create experiences of pain. These latter are often delineated in a list of ten nonvirtuous deeds: killing, stealing, sexual misconduct, lying, divisive speech, harsh speech, senseless speech, covetousness, harmful intent, and wrong view (notably belief that actions do not have effects). The ten virtues are the opposites of this list: sustaining life, giving gifts, maintaining sexual decorum, and so on. Much of Tibetan religious practice is concerned with accumulating virtuous deeds and preventing, through a variety of ritual means, the fruition of negative deeds already committed. These deeds determine not only the quality of a given life but also the place of the rebirth after death. Depending on the gravity of a negative deed (killing being more serious than senseless speech, and killing a human more serious than killing an insect, for example), one may be reborn as an animal, as a ghost, or in one of the hot or cold hells, where the life span is particularly lengthy. (For an excellent example of a sermon on these topics, see chapter 21.)

As in India, karma is not concerned simply with what might be termed in the West moral and immoral deeds. There is, in conjunction with the belief that virtue brings happiness and nonvirtue sorrow, a powerful system of purity and pollution, generally concerned with one's behavior not toward humans but nonhumans, the various gods and spirits that inhabit the world. In determining the cause of some affliction, there is often an attempt by the afflicted or his or her ritual agent to determine both the karmic cause (some nonvirtuous deed in the past) and polluting acts (such as associating with a blacksmith, building a fire on a mountain, or accepting food from a widow) that contributed to that past evil deed coming to fruition in the form of a particular misfortune.

Rebirth as a god or human in the realm of desire is the result of a virtuous deed and is considered very rare. Rarer still is rebirth as a human who has access to the teachings of the Buddha. In a famous analogy, a single blind tortoise is said to swim in a vast ocean, surfacing for air only once every century. On the surface of the ocean floats a single golden yoke. It is rarer, said the Buddha, to be reborn as a human with the opportunity to practice the dharma than it is for the tortoise to surface for its centennial breath with its head through the hole in the golden yoke. One is said to be reborn as a god in the realm of desire as a result of an act of charity: giving gifts results in future wealth. Rebirth as a human is said to result from consciously refraining from a nonvirtuous deed, as when one takes a vow not to kill humans.

Although the various sects of Tibetan Buddhism derive their monastic regulations from the Indian schools known pejoratively as the Hīnayāna ("low vehicle"), all sects of Tibetan Buddhism identify themselves as proponents of the Mahāyāna, both in their practice and in their philosophy. Mahāyāna, a Sanskrit word that means "great vehicle," is the term used to distinguish a rather disparate group of cults of the book that arose in India some four hundred years after the death of the Buddha and continued in India into the twelfth century. During these centuries, the followers of the Mahāyāna produced a vast literature of sūtras that purport to be the word of the historical Buddha, as well as commentaries upon them. Among the factors characteristic of the Mahāyāna are the view of the Buddha as an eternal presence, associated physically with reliquaries (stūpas) and with texts that embody his words, a belief in the existence of myriad buddhas working in multiple universes for the benefit of all beings, and an attendant emphasis on the universal possibility of enlightenment for all, monks and laypeople alike. It is from this last tenet that the term "Great Vehicle" is derived: the proponents of the Mahāyāna believed that their path was capable of bringing all beings in the universe to buddhahood, whereas the earlier teachings were capable only of delivering the individual disciple to a state of solitary peace.

Perhaps the most famous feature of the Mahāyāna is its emphasis on the bodhisattva, a person who makes the compassionate vow to become a buddha in order to lead all beings in the universe out of suffering and to the bliss of enlightenment. The Sanskrit term *bodhisattva* was rendered into Tibetan as *jang chup sem ba* (*byang chub sems dpa'*), "one who is heroic in his or her aspiration to enlightenment." The path of the bodhisattva is portrayed as one of extraordinary length, encompassing billions of lifetimes devoted to cultivating such virtues as generosity, ethics, patience, effort, concentration, and wisdom, the so-called six perfections, all of these deeds motivated by the wish to liberate all beings from the beginningless cycle of rebirth.

A common tenet of Buddhism is that all suffering is ultimately the result of ignorance. This ignorance is defined as a belief in self. Mahāyāna philosophy expands upon earlier teachings to see ignorance not simply as a misconception concerning the nature of the person, but as a misunderstanding of all things. According to the Middle Way school, the fundamental error is to conceive of things as existing in and of themselves—independently, autonomously, possessed of some intrinsic nature, some inherent existence. Wisdom, the sixth of the perfections to be cultivated by the bodhisattva, is the understanding that all things, including persons, are utterly devoid of such a nature and are, in fact, empty of an independent status, although they exist conventionally. To say that things exist conventionally means, for example, that cause and effect remain viable and that things perform functions; one can sit on a chair and drink tea from a cup. Emptiness, then, does not mean that things do not exist at all, but rather that they do not exist as they appear to the unenlightened.

To become enlightened, then, the bodhisattva must develop not only this wisdom but infinite compassion as well, that is, must dedicate himself or herself to work forever for the welfare of others while simultaneously understanding that all beings, including oneself, do not exist ultimately, that they do not exist as they appear.

The practice of the Mahāyāna generally may be said to take two forms, both focused on the bodhisattva. The most influential of the Mahāyāna sūtras, such as the *Lotus Sūtra*, proclaim that all beings will eventually become buddhas, and that, consequently, all beings will traverse the bodhisattva path. Thus, one form of Mahāyāna belief emphasizes practices for becoming a bodhisattva and performing the bodhisattva's deeds. As bodhisattvas advance along the path, they become increasingly adept at allaying the sufferings of sentient beings who call upon them for aid, often through miraculous intercession. Consequently, the other major form of Mahāyāna practice is concerned with devotions intended to procure the aid of these compassionate beings. The bodhisattva who is said to be the physical manifestation of all the compassion of all the buddhas in the universe, Avalokiteśvara, is the particular object of such reverence in Tibet, as discussed below (see also chapters 2 and 17). Avalokiteśvara is invoked by the famous mantra *oṃ maṇi padme hūṃ*, which might be rendered as, "O you who hold the jeweled [rosary] and the lotus [have mercy on us]." (It certainly does not mean "the jewel in the lotus.") Avalokiteśvara is depicted in a wide variety of forms in Tibetan art, two of the most frequent being with one head and four arms (two of which hold a rosary and a lotus evoked in the mantra) or with eleven heads and a thousand arms. The multiple arms are said to represent the bodhisattva's extraordinary ability to come to the aid of suffering sentient beings. Paintings of the thousand-armed Avalokiteśvara often show an eye in the palm of each of the hands. The bodhisattva thus serves as both role model and object of devotion in Mahāyāna Buddhism, functions that are by no means deemed mutually exclusive; it is quite common for persons who consider themselves to have embarked on the bodhisattva path to seek the assistance of more advanced bodhisattvas in their long quest for enlightenment.

In the realm of Buddhist practice, the Tibetans were able to witness and assimilate the most important development of late Indian Buddhism, Buddhist tantra. Tantra, known also as the *vajrayāna*, the "Diamond Vehicle," and the *mantrayāna*, the "Mantra Vehicle," was considered an esoteric approach to the Mahāyāna path whereby the length of time required to achieve buddhahood could be abbreviated from the standard length of three periods of countless aeons (reckoned by some as 384×10^{58} years) to as little as three years and three months. One of the chief techniques for effecting such an extraordinary reduction in the length of the path was an elaborate system of ritual, visualization, and meditation, sometimes called deity yoga, in which the practitioner imagined himself or herself to be already fully enlightened with the marvelous body, speech, mind, and abode of a buddha. In addition to the ultimate attainment of buddhahood, tantric practice was said to bestow a wide range of lesser magical powers, such as the power to increase wealth and life span, to pacify the inauspicious, and to destroy enemies, both human and nonhuman. Yogins who developed these powers were known as *mahāsiddhas*, "great adepts"; they are popular subjects of Tibetan Buddhist literature (see chapter 7).

Among the elements of tantric Buddhism most commonly identified in the West are its erotic and wrathful motifs, where male and female are depicted in sexual union and bull-headed deities, adorned with garlands of human heads, brandish cleavers and skullcups. In Mahāyāna Buddhism, as already mentioned, wisdom and compassion (also referred to as method, that is, the compassionate means whereby bodhisattvas become buddhas) are the essential components of the bodhisattva's path to buddhahood. Wisdom, especially the perfection of wisdom, is identified with the female. In tantra, the symbolism is rendered in more explicitly sexual terms, with wisdom as female and method male, their union being essential to the achievement of enlightenment. Buddhist tantra is said to be the "Diamond Vehicle" because wisdom and method are joined in an adamantine and indivisible union, bestowing buddhahood quickly. This is the chief symbolic meaning of depiction of sexual union. However, part of the unique nature of the tantric path is its capacity to employ deeds that are ordinarily prohibited in practices that speed progress on the path to enlightenment, hence the great emphasis on antinomian behavior, such as the consumption of meat and alcohol, in the hagiographies of the *mahāsiddhas*. One such deed is sexual intercourse, and many tantric texts, especially of the Unexcelled Yoga (*anuttarayoga*) variety, prescribe ritual union as a means of unifying the mind of the clear light and the immutable bliss (see chapter 29). Whether this intercourse is to be performed only in imagination or in fact, and at what point on the path it is to take place, has been a point of considerable discussion in Tibetan tantric exegesis.

Wrathful deities also populate the tantric pantheon. Despite claims by nineteenth-century scholars that continue to be repeated, the most important of these deities are not of Tibetan shamanic origin, added to Indian Buddhism after its arrival in Tibet. It is clear from Indian tantric texts that these deities derive directly from India. Some are buddhas and bodhisattvas in their wrathful aspects, the most famous of these being Yamantaka, the wrathful manifestation of the bodhisattva of wisdom, Mañjuśrī. His terrifying form is said to be intended to frighten away the egotism and selfishness that are the cause of all suffering. Other wrathful deities have the task of protecting the dharma; others are worldly deities with specific powers that may be propitiated. Despite such explanations, Western scholars of Tibet have yet to engage adequately the issue of the apparent presence of the demonic in the divine that confronts the observer so richly in Tibetan religious iconography.

Tantric Buddhism places especial emphasis on the role of the teacher. The teacher-student relationship was always of great importance in Buddhism, providing the means by which the dharma was passed from one generation to the next. In tantra, however, the teacher or guru took on an even more important role. The practice of the Vajrayāna, the rapid path to enlightenment, was regarded as a secret teaching, not suitable for everyone. For that reason, the teacher was both the repository of secret knowledge and the person who was to judge the qualifications of the student as a receptacle for that knowledge. Once the student was deemed ready, the teacher provided the student with an initiation, serving as the surrogate of the Buddha (see chapter 17), and one of the basic practices of Buddhist tantra is thus to regard one's own teacher as the Buddha (see chapter 23). In fact, Tibetans are fond of saying that the teacher is actually kinder than the Buddha, because the Buddha did not remain in the world to teach us benighted beings of this degenerate age. This great emphasis on the importance of the teacher was inherited from India, as the accounts of Tibetans' sojourns to India make clear (see chapters 8 and 9). Because of this importance of the teacher, or lama, during the nineteenth century Tibetan Buddhism was dubbed "Lamaism," a term that continues to appear today. Tibetan Buddhists regard this as a pejorative term, because it suggests that whereas there is Chinese Buddhism, Japanese Buddhism, Thai Buddhism, and so forth, the Buddhism of Tibet is so different that it does not warrant the name "Tibetan Buddhism" but should be called "Lamaism."

In the Vajrayāna, rituals called *sādhanas* (literally, "means of achievement") are set forth in which the practitioner, through a practice of visualization, petitions a buddha or bodhisattva to come into his or her presence. Much of the practice described in tantric sādhanas involves the enactment of a world—the fantastic jewel-encrusted world of the Mahāyāna sūtras or the horrific world of the charnel ground. In the tantric sādhana, the practitioner manifests that world through visualization, through a process of invitation, descent, and identification. Tantric sādhanas generally take one of two forms. In the first, the buddha or bodhisattva is requested to appear before the meditator and is then worshipped in the expectation of receiving blessings. In the other type of tantric sādhana, the meditator imagines himself or herself to be a fully enlightened buddha or bodhisattva now, to have the exalted body, speech, and mind of an enlightened being. In either case, the central deity in the visualization is called a *yi dam*, a word difficult to translate into English (and left untranslated in this volume). It is sometimes rendered as "tutelary deity," but the *yi dam* offers much more than protection. The *yi dam* is the tantric buddha with which the meditator identifies in daily meditation and whom he or she propitiates in daily rituals. Some *yi dams* take peaceful forms, adorned with the silks and jewels of an Indian monarch. Others appear in wrathful forms, brandishing weapons and wreathed in flames.

Tantric sādhanas tend to follow a fairly set sequence, whether they are simple and brief or more detailed and prolix. More elaborate sādhanas may include the recitation of a lineage of gurus; the creation of a protection wheel guarded by wrathful deities to subjugate enemies; the creation of a body maṇḍala, in which a pantheon of deities take residence at various parts of the meditator's body; etc.

In many sādhanas, the meditator is instructed to imagine light radiating from the body, inviting buddhas and bodhisattvas from throughout the universe. Visualizing them arrayed in the space before him or her, the meditator then performs a series of standard preliminary practices called the sevenfold service, a standard component of sādhanas and prayers (see chapters 17, 23, and 27) that developed from an Indian Mahāyāna three-part liturgy (the *triskandhaka*). Prior to the actual sevenfold service, the assembled deities are offered (again, in visualization) a bath and new clothing and are treated just as an honored guest would be in India. The sevenfold service is then performed. The first of the seven elements is obeisance, an expression of homage to the assembled deities. Next comes offering, usually the longest section of the seven parts. Here fantastic gifts are imagined to be arrayed before the buddhas and bodhisattvas to please each of their five senses: beautiful forms for the eye, music for the ears, fragrances for the nose, delicacies for the tongue, and sensuous silks for the body. The offering often concludes with a gift of the entire physical universe with all its marvels. The third step is confession of misdeeds. Despite the apparent inexorability of the law of karma, it is nonetheless believed that by sincerely confessing a sin to the buddhas and bodhisattvas, promising not to commit it again in the future, and performing some kind of purificatory penance (usually the recitation of mantra) as an antidote to the sin, the eventual negative effect of the negative deed can be avoided. The fourth step, admiration, also relates to the law of karma. It is believed that acknowledging, praising, and otherwise taking pleasure in the virtuous deeds of others causes the taker of such pleasure to accumulate the same merit as that accrued by the person who actually performed the good deed.

The fifth step is an entreaty to the buddhas not to pass into nirvāna. A buddha is said to have the ability to live for aeons but will do so only if he is asked; otherwise, he will disappear from the world, pretending to die and pass into nirvāṇa. Indian sūtras recount the Buddha scolding his attendant for not making such a request. In Tibet this entreaty to the buddhas to remain in the world developed from a standard component of daily prayers to a separate genre of literature, called *shap den* (*zhabs brtan*); the term literally means "steadfast feet," suggesting that the buddhas remain with their feet firmly planted in this world. However, in Tibet these prayers were composed and recited for the surrogate of the absent Buddha, the lama. Prayers for "steadfast feet" or long-life prayers are hence composed for one's teacher. (For such a prayer to the current Dalai Lama, see chapter 12 in *Buddhism in Practice*.) The sixth of the seven branches follows naturally from the entreaty to remain in the world; it is a supplication of the buddhas and bodhisattvas to teach the dharma. The final step is the dedication of the merit of performing the preceding toward the enlightenment of all beings.

The meditator then goes for refuge to the three jewels, creates the aspiration to enlightenment, the promise to achieve buddhahood in order to liberate all beings in the universe from suffering, and dedicates the merit from the foregoing and subsequent practices toward that end. The meditator next cultivates the four attitudes of love, compassion, joy, and equanimity, before meditating on emptiness and reciting the purificatory mantra, *oṃ svabhāvaśuddhāḥ sarvadharmāḥ svabhāvaśuddho 'haṃ*, "Oṃ, naturally pure are all phenomena, naturally pure am I," understanding that emptiness is the primordial nature of everything, the unmoving world and the beings who move upon it. Out of this emptiness, the meditator next creates the maṇḍala.

The meditator here creates an imaginary universe out of emptiness. The foundation is provided by the four elements wind, fire, water, and earth (represented by Sanskrit syllables). On top of these, the meditator visualizes the maṇḍala. The Sanskrit term *maṇḍala* simply means circle, but in this context within a tantric sādhana, a maṇḍala is the residence of a buddha, an extraordinary palace inhabited by buddhas and their consorts, by bodhisattvas, and protectors. A maṇḍala may be quite spare, an undescribed palace with only five deities, one deity in the center and one in each of the cardinal directions. But usually maṇḍalas are much more elaborate. The Guhyasamāja maṇḍala, for example, is articulated in great detail, with five layers of walls of white, yellow, red, green, and blue. It has a jeweled molding, archways, and a quadruple colonnade. It is festooned with jewels and pendants and is populated by thirty-two deities, each on its own throne, arrayed on two levels. The maṇḍala is the perfected world that the meditator seeks to manifest and then inhabit, either by identifying with the central deity or by making offerings to him or her. It was said to be essential that the visualization be carried out in precise detail, with each item of silk clothing and gold ornament appearing clearly. It was also necessary for the meditator to imagine the fantastic palace of the buddha, the maṇḍala, which he or she inhabited, noting the particular bodhisattvas, protectors, gods, and goddesses located throughout the multistoried dwelling. Part of this visualization was accomplished through the description of the details in the tantric text itself. However, meditators were typically advised to study a visual image of the particular buddha and maṇḍala, and this was one of the uses to which paintings and statues were put by those involved in meditation practice. Paintings and statues were not considered to be functional in any context, even as the object of simple devotion, until they were consecrated in a special ceremony in which the dharmakāya was caused to descend into and animate the icon. (Such a consecration ceremony is translated in chapter 14.)

The next step in the sādhana is for the meditator to animate the residents of the maṇḍala by causing the actual buddhas and bodhisattvas, referred to as "wisdom beings" (*ye shes sems dpa', jñānasattva*), to descend and merge with their imagined doubles, the "pledge beings" (*dam tshig sems dpa', samayasattva*). Light radiates from meditator's heart, drawing the wisdom beings to the maṇḍala where, through offerings and the recitation of the mantra *jaḥ hūṃ baṃ hoḥ* ("Be summoned, enter, become fused with, be pleased"), they are caused to enter the residents of the maṇḍala. The residents are then often blessed with three syllables: a white *oṃ* at the crown of the head, a red *āḥ* at the throat, and a blue *hūṃ* at the heart.

With the preliminary visualization now complete, the stage is set for the central meditation of the sādhana, and this varies depending upon the purpose of the sādhana. Generally, offerings and prayers are made to a sequence of deities and boons are requested from them, each time accompanied by the recitation of appropriate mantra. At the end of the session, the meditator makes mental offerings to the assembly before inviting them to leave, at which point the entire visualization, the palace and its residents, dissolves into emptiness. The sādhana ends with a dedication of the merit accrued from the session to the welfare of all beings. (For an example of a brief sādhana, see chapter 16.)

From this brief survey of Buddhist doctrine and practice, several distinctive elements of Tibetan Buddhism become apparent. First, Tibetan Buddhism is the last of the major national Buddhisms to develop, having access to a larger corpus of Indian Buddhist literature than reached China or Japan, for example. As discussed above, this literature included the śāstras and the tantras, such that Tibetan Buddhism can generally be characterized as śāstra-based in its doctrine and tantra-based in its practice. It is important to note, however, that certain central elements of practice, such as monastic regulations and the techniques for creating the bodhisattva's compassionate aspiration to buddhahood, are delineated in śāstras.

Furthermore, all sects of Tibetan Buddhism developed sophisticated scholastic traditions of tantric exegesis.

Second, the Tibetans had sustained contact with major figures of the late Indian Buddhist tradition for over a century, and the legacies of these figures, such as Atiśa (see chapter 8) and Niguma (see chapter 9), remain powerful elements of the tradition. Third, Tibet was perhaps the least culturally evolved of the major Buddhist nations at the time of the introduction of Buddhism, when culture is measured in terms of written language, literature, and structures of state. The introduction of Buddhism encountered resistance, as noted above, but with the demise of the royal line in 842, the way was left open for Buddhism to provide the dominant ideology for the entire Inner Asian cultural area. Finally, Tibetan Buddhism is the only major form of Buddhism to continue in a fairly traditional form into the second half of this century.

The evidence of the early records indicates that, despite their patronage of Buddhism, Ralpajen and his two predecessor kings gave numerous public testimonies to their attachment to principles irreconcilable with Buddhism, principles pertaining to the highly structured politico-religious system of divine kingship (called *gtsug lag*), while at the same time propagating the new religion. The translation of Indian Buddhist literature, the sūtras, tantras, and śāstras, from Sanskrit into Tibetan was interrupted by the suppression of Buddhist monastic institutions in 838 by the king Langdarma (Glang dar ma, ruled c. 836–842). Although Langdarma is represented as the embodiment of evil in Buddhist accounts, persecuting monks and nuns and closing monasteries, recent scholarship indicates that his persecution, if it took place at all, amounted to a withdrawal of state patronage to the growing monastic institutions.

Nevertheless, his reign, which according to later Buddhist accounts ended with his assassination in 842 by a Buddhist monk (an event some scholars question), is traditionally seen as the end of what is called the early dissemination of Buddhism in Tibet and the beginning of a dark period of disorder, at least in central Tibet. It marked the beginning of the end of the royal line and the eventual disintegration of the Tibetan empire. Although it is the case that the status of Buddhist thought and practice during the next century and a half remains only vaguely understood by modern scholars, its representation in traditional Buddhist histories as a time of degradation and chaos may be something of an exaggeration, motivated to provide a striking contrast with the glorious renaissance that was to follow. Nevertheless, little of "pre-Buddhist" religion of Tibet survived intact after this period. This religion, which Tibetans call "the religion of humans" (*mi chos*), as opposed to the "religion of the gods" (*lha chos*, identified with Buddhism and Bön) is all but impossible to identify, with much of its content assimilated by Buddhism and Bön after the eleventh century, leaving only a few legends, aphorisms, and folk songs.

After the so-called dark period a Buddhist revival began in western Tibet in the eleventh century, a period of active translation of numerous philosophical texts and the retranslation of texts, especially tantras, first translated during the period of the earlier dissemination. The eleventh century was also a time of active travel of Tibetan translators to India, where they studied with Indian Buddhist masters in Bihar, Bengal, and Kashmir. Many of the sects of Tibetan Buddhism trace their lineages back to these encounters.

The most famous Indian scholar to visit Tibet during what came to be called the second dissemination was the Bengali master Atiśa (982–1054). (For an account of the invitation of Atiśa to come to Tibet, see chapter 8.) A Tibetan named Dromdön ('Brom ston pa) was Atiśa's first and closest Tibetan disciple. He urged Atiśa to visit central Tibet and organized his tour of the area, where Atiśa taught and translated until his death in 1054. Dromdön devoted the rest of his life to preserving Atiśa's teachings, establishing the monastery of Rva sgreng in 1056 and founding the first Tibetan Buddhist monastic order, the Kadampa (Bka' gdams pa, which is traditionally etymologized as "those who take all of the Buddha's words as instructions"). Although Drom was a respected scholar and translator, he is best remembered for the rigor and austerity of his Buddhist practice. He seems to have been wary of the potential for abuse in tantrism and imposed on his followers a strict discipline and devotion to practice for which they became famous. They abstained from marriage, intoxicants, travel, and the possession of money. Although later Tibetan orders were not as strict, the Kadampa provided the model for all later Tibetan monasticism.

The monastery was an institution of fundamental importance for all sects of Tibetan Buddhism. The first monastery was constructed around 779 under the direction of the Indian paṇḍita Śāntarakṣita and the tantric master Padmasambhava. From the outset, Tibetan monasteries were modeled on the great monastic centers of late Indian Buddhism, where the monastic code was maintained in conjunction with scholastic education and tantric practice. With the growth in lay and state patronage, some monasteries grew from small retreat centers to vast monastic complexes. The largest of these, such as Drepung (which, with some 13,000 monks in 1959, was the largest Buddhist monastery in the world), functioned as self-sufficient cities, with their own economy (with farms worked by sharecroppers), government, and police force. Tibetan monks were not fully supported by the monasteries, receiving only a small ration of tea and roasted barley for their subsistence; they had to rely on their families or their own earnings (from trade or performing rituals) for anything more. Monks did not go on begging rounds, like their counterparts in Southeast Asia, but engaged in a wide range of occupations. It is therefore inaccurate to imagine that all Tibetan monks spent their days in meditation or in debating sophisticated points of doctrine; only a small percentage were thus occupied. Furthermore, the majority of the occupants of Tibetan monasteries remained as novices throughout their lives, not going on to take the vows of a fully ordained monk (*dge slong*, *bhikṣu*).

To be a monk was to hold a respected social status in the Tibetan world, and monkhood provided one of the few routes to social advancement. Monks who distinguished themselves as scholars, teachers, or meditators commanded great respect and attracted substantial patronage, especially those considered to be effective in performance of rituals and divinations. (On patronage, see chapters 21 and 22.) Such monks could rise through the monastic ranks to positions of great authority as abbots or (among the Geluk) as government officials.

Each of the sects, both Buddhist and Bönpo, had large monasteries that drew monks from all over the Tibetan cultural sphere, which extended from as far west as the Kalmyk region between the Caspian Sea and the Black Sea, from as far east as Sichuan, from as far north as the Buryiat region near Lake Baikal, and from as far south as Nepal. Some came for an education and then returned to their home regions, while others remained for life. However, the majority of monasteries in Tibet were isolated places (as the Tibetan term for monastery, *dgon pa*, suggests), populated by a few dozen local monks who performed rituals for the local community and were supported by their families. Monastic life, whether in a major center or a remote hermitage, was not so much a matter of doctrine or belief, but of behavior, a behavior that creates the identity of the monk. That behavior was governed by a monastic code inherited from India but adapted for each monastery in its constitution called a *ja yik* (*bca' yig*); a portion of that of Sera monastery is translated in chapter 20.

Although a substantial segment of the male population of Tibetan was monks (estimated between 10 and 15 percent), the community of nuns (*a ni*) was much smaller (perhaps 3 percent). They lived in some six hundred nunneries, the largest of which, a Kagyu institution called Gechak Thekchen Ling (Dge chag theg chen gling), housed approximately one thousand nuns. Whereas Tibetan monks could eventually receive the full ordination of the gelong (*dge slong*), the order of full nuns was never established in Tibet, such that nuns could advance no higher than the rank of novice. (There have been efforts in recent years, led largely by Western women who have become Tibetan nuns, to receive full ordination from Chinese nuns in Taiwan and Singapore). Being a nun carried little of the status held by a monk; there is a Tibetan proverb that if you want to be a servant, make your son a monk; if you want a servant, make your daughter a nun. Unmarried daughters often became nuns (sometimes remaining at home). Other women became nuns to escape a bad marriage, to avoid pregnancy, or after the death of a spouse. The educational opportunities and chances for social advancement open to monks were generally absent for nuns, whose chief activities involved the memorization and recitation of prayer and the performance of ritual.

The role of women in Tibetan religions was not, however, limited simply to the order of nuns. There are many important females divinities, both peaceful and wrathful, benevolent and malevolent. The goddess Tārā stands with Avalokiteśvara as the most commonly invoked of Buddhist deities (see chapter 36). The wrathful tantric goddess Belden Lhamo is the special protectoress of the Tibetan state. Among the many malevolent female forms, one finds the "gossip girl" (see chapter 34) who sows discord in the community. Women have also played significant roles in various meditation and ritual lineages, such as the Indian yoginī Niguma (chapter 9), the wife of king Tri Songdetsen and consort of Padmasambhava, Yeshe Tsogyal (Ye shes mtsho rgyal, see chapter 10 of *Buddhism in Practice*), and the tantric master Majik Lapdön (Ma gcig lab sgron). There are lines of female incarnations, the most famous of whom is Dorje Pamo (Rdo rje phag mo, the "Diamond Sow"). Beyond these famous figures, Tibetan women have played important roles as mediums for deities (see chapter 3) or as messengers for bodhisattvas (such as the weaver girl in chapter 8). The majority of those who return from the dead to bring messages from the deceased and exhortations to observe the laws of karma are women (see chapter 32). Despite the disproportionate investment of religious power and authority in the males of Tibetan society, women enjoyed a greater economic and sexual autonomy in Tibet than generally was the case elsewhere in Asia. Many of the rituals and practices described in this volume would have been practiced by women as well as men.

With the decline of the monarchy, both political and religious authority (although the strict distinction between the two should not be immediately assumed in the case of Tibet) shifted gradually to Buddhist teachers. Since many of these were Buddhist monks who had taken vows of celibacy, the problem of succession eventually arose. In some cases, authority was passed from a monk to his nephew. However, by the fourteenth century (and perhaps even earlier) a form of succession developed in Tibet that, although supported by standard Buddhist doctrine, seems unique in the Buddhist world. This was the institution of the incarnate lama or *tulku* (*sprul sku*).

In Mahāyāna literature there is a doctrine of the three bodies of the Buddha. The first is the *dharmakāya*. Prior to the rise of the Mahāyāna, this term meant the "body of [uncontaminated] qualities," those qualities of the Buddha, such as his wisdom, patience, and fearlessness, that were not subject to suffering and decay. It was this body that was deemed the true object of the practice of refuge. Thus, the term "body" came to shift its meaning from the physical form of the Buddha to a collection of timeless abstract virtues. In Mahāyāna literature, the dharmakāya is often represented as almost a cosmic principle, an ultimate reality in which all buddhas partake through their omniscient minds. For this reason, some scholars translate dharmakāya as "Truth Body." After the dharmakāya comes the enjoyment body (*saṃbhogakāya*), a fantastic form of a buddha that resides only in the highest pure land, adorned with thirty-two major and eighty minor physical marks, eternally teaching the Mahāyāna to highly advanced bodhisattvas; the enjoyment body does not appear to ordinary beings. Many tantric deities are depicted in the enjoyment body form. The third body is the emanation body (*nirmāṇakāya*). It is this body that appears in the world to teach the dharma. The emanation bodies are not limited to the form of the Buddha with which we are familiar; a buddha is able to appear in whatever form, animate or inanimate, that is appropriate to benefit suffering sentient beings.

Tibetans chose the term for the third body of a buddha to name their notion of incarnation. That is, the next incarnation of a former great teacher is called a tulku (*sprul sku*), the Tibetan translation of nirmāṇakāya, "emanation body." The implication is that there is a profound difference in the processes whereby ordinary beings and incarnate lamas take birth in the world. For the former, rebirth is harrowing process, a frightful journey into the unknown, a process over which one has no control. One is blown by the winds of karma into an intermediate state (*bar do*) and then into a new lifetime. There is a strong possibility that new life will be in the lower realms as an animal, hungry ghost, or hell being; Tibetans say that the number of beings in these three lower realms is as large as the number of stars seen on a clear night and the number of beings in the realms of gods and humans is as large as the number stars seen on a clear day. The fate of the denizens of hell is particularly horrific, and Tibetans recount the journeys of those who are able to visit the lower realms of rebirth and return to tell the tale (see chapter 32). The process of powerless rebirth is a beginningless cycle and can only be brought to an end by the individual achievement of liberation and enlightenment through the practice of the path. (Common attitudes toward death and the fear of rebirth and the appropriate responses to death can be found in chapters 28, 29, and 30.)

The rebirth of an incarnate lama is a very different matter. As "emanation bodies," incarnate lamas are technically buddhas, free from the bonds of karma. Their rebirth is thus entirely voluntary. They need not be reborn at all, yet they decide to return to the world out of their compassion for others. Furthermore, they exercise full control over their rebirth. For ordinary beings, rebirth must take place within forty-nine days from the time of death. Incarnate lamas are under no such constraints. For ordinary beings, the circumstances of the rebirth—the place, the parents, the form of the body, and the capacity of the mind—are all determined by karma. For the incarnate lama, all of these are a matter of choice and are said to have been decided in advance, so that a dying incarnation will often leave instructions for his disciples as to where to find his next rebirth. (For a famous incarnate lama's memories of past life, see chapter 12.)

Since the fourteenth century, all sects of Tibetan Buddhism have adopted the practice of identifying the successive rebirths of a great teacher, the most famous instance of which being of course the Dalai Lamas. But there some three thousand other lines of incarnation in Tibet (only several of whom are female). The institution of the incarnate lama has proved to be a central component of Tibetan society, providing the means by which authority and charisma, in all of their symbolic and material forms, are passed from one generation to another. Indeed, the spread of Tibetan Buddhism can usefully be traced by the increasingly large geographical areas in which incarnate lamas are discovered, extending today to Europe and North America.

A common use of the term "lama" is as the designation of incarnations. In ordinary Tibetan parlance, such persons are called "lamas" whether or not they have distinguished themselves as scholars, adepts, or teachers in their present lives. The ambiguity in usage between "lama" as a religious preceptor and "lama" as an incarnation has led the current Dalai Lama in his sermons to admonish his followers that a lama (as one's religious teacher) need not be an incarnation and that an incarnation is not necessarily a lama (in the sense of a fully qualified religious teacher).

The period of the thirteenth through fifteenth centuries was among the most consequential for the history of Tibetan Buddhism, with the development of distinct sects that evolved from the various lineages of teaching that had been initiated during the previous periods. These sects are traditionally divided under two major headings: those who base their tantric practice on texts translated during the period of the first dissemination and those who base their tantric practice on texts translated or retranslated during the period of the second dissemination. These two groups are referred to simply as the old (*rnying ma*) and the new (*gsar ma*), with the old obviously including the Nyingmapa (Rnying ma pa) sect and the new including the Kagyu, Sakya, and Geluk. The Nyingmapa sect traces its origins back to the first dissemination and the teachings of Padmasambhava, who visited Tibet during the eighth century. "Treasures," called *terma* (*gter ma*), believed to have been hidden by him, began to be discovered in the eleventh century and continue to be discovered even into the twentieth century; the fourteenth century was an especially active period for text discoverers (*gter ston*). According to their claim, these texts were sometimes discovered in physical form, often within stone, or mentally, within the mind of the discoverer. Often ignored in the old-new categorization are the Bönpos, who seem to have appeared as a self-conscious "sect" in the eleventh century, along with new sects, but who represent themselves as even older than the old (Nyingma), predating the introduction of Buddhism into Tibet.

The various institutional entities of Tibetan Buddhism are referred to in Tibetan as *chos lugs*, literally, "dharma systems." This term is generally rendered into English with one of three terms: order, school, or sect. Each of these translations is misleading. "Order" implies a monastic unit with its own code of conduct, whereas in Tibet all Buddhist monks followed the same Indian monastic code. Furthermore, many adherents of the Tibetan groups are not monks or nuns. "School" implies a group distinguished on the basis of philosophical tenets, and although there are differences among the Tibetan Buddhist groups, there is much more that they share. "Sect" carries the negative connotation of a group dissenting from a majority that perceives it as somehow heretical. If that connotation can be ignored, however, "sect" provides a serviceable translation and is used here. What is perhaps more important than the translation used is to understand that central to each of these groups is the notion of lineage (see chapter 6). Like other Buddhist traditions, the Tibetans based claims to authority largely on lineage, and in their case, they claimed that the Buddhism taught in Tibet and by Tibetan lamas abroad could be traced backward in an unbroken line to the eleventh century, when the founders of the major Tibetan sects made the perilous journey to India to receive the dharma from the great masters of Bengal, Bihar, and Kashmir, who were themselves direct recipients of teachings that could be traced back to the Buddha himself. (For accounts of such journeys and the teachings received, see chapters 8 and 9.) Moreover, this lineage was represented as essentially oral, with instructions being passed down from master to disciple as an unwritten commentary on a sacred text. Even those sects that could not so easily list a successive line of teachers stretching back through the past, such as the Nyingmapas and Bönpos, were able to maintain the power of their lineage through the device of the hidden and rediscovered text, the *terma*, designed to leapfrog over centuries, bringing the authentic teaching directly into the present. These texts thus provided the present with the sanction of the past by ascribing to their ancient and absent author (usually Padmasambhava) the gift of prophecy.

Nyingma (Rnying ma)

The Nyingma sect traces its origins back to the teachings of the mysterious figure Padmasambhava, who visited Tibet during the eight century. The Nyingmapas include in their canonical corpus a collection of tantras (the *Rnying ma rgyud 'bum*) as well as these discovered texts, all works that the other sects generally regard as apocryphal, that is, not of Indian origin.

The Nyingma sect produced many famous scholars and visionaries, such as Longchenpa (Klong chen rab 'byams, 1308–1363, see chapters 18, 19, 30), Jigme Lingpa ('Jigs med gling pa, 1729–1798, see chapter 22), and Mipham ('Ju Mi pham rnam rgyal, 1846–1912, see chapters 1 and 26). Nyingma identifies nine vehicles among the corpus of Buddhist teachings, the highest of which is known as Atiyoga or, more commonly, the Great Perfection (*rdzogs chen*) (see chapters 18 and 19). These teachings, found also in Bön, describe the mind as the primordial basis, characterized by qualities such as presence, spontaneity, luminosity, original purity, unobstructed freedom, expanse, clarity, self-liberation, openness, effortlessness, and intrinsic awareness. It is not accessible through conceptual elaboration or logical analysis. Rather, the primordial basis is an eternally pure state free from dualism of subject and object, infinite and perfect from the beginning, ever complete. The Great Perfection tradition shares with certain Indian Buddhist schools the view that the mind creates the appearances of the world, the arena of human suffering. All of these appearances are said to be illusory, however. The ignorant mind believes that its own creations are real, forgetting its true nature of original purity. For the mind willfully to seek to liberate itself is both inappropriate and futile because it is already self-liberated. The technique for the discovery of the ubiquitous original purity and self-liberation is to engage in a variety of practices designed to eliminate karmic obstacles, at which point the mind eliminates all thought and experiences itself, thereby recognizing its true nature. The Great Perfection doctrine does not seem to be directly derived from any of the Indian philosophical schools; its precise connections to the Indian Buddhist tradition have yet to be established. Some scholars have claimed a historical link and doctrinal affinity between the Great Perfection and the Chan tradition of Chinese Buddhism, but the precise relationship between the two remains to be fully investigated. It is noteworthy that certain of the earliest extant Great Perfection texts specifically contrast their own tradition with that of Chan.

Unlike the Geluks, Kagyu, and Sakya, the Nyingma (along with the Bönpo, with whom they share much in common) remained largely uninvolved in politics, both within Tibet and in foreign relations. They also lacked the kind of hierarchies found in the other sects. Although they developed great monasteries such as Mindroling (Smin grol gling), they also maintained a strong local presence as lay tantric practioners (*sngags pa*) who performed a range of ritual functions for the community.

Kagyu (Bka' brgyud)

The Kagyu sect derives its lineage from the visits by Marpa the Translator (1012–1099) to India, where he studied under several of the famous tantric masters of the day, including Nāropa (the disciple of Tilopa, see chapter 7) and Maitrīpa. Marpa's disciple Milarepa (Mi la ras pa, "Cotton-clad Mila") is said to have achieved buddhahood in one lifetime (an achievement usually considered to require aeons of practice) through his diligent meditation practice in the caves of southern Tibet, despite having committed murder as a youth through the practice of black magic. His moving biography and didactic songs are among the most famous works of Tibetan literature. (For a story of another cotton-clad yogin, see chapter 11.) Milarepa's most illustrious disciple was the scholar and physician Gampopa (Sgam po pa, 1079–1153), who gave a strong monastic foundation to the sect. His own disciples, in turn, are regarded as the founders of the four major schools and the eight minor schools of the Kagyu. The most important of these is the Karma Kagyu, led by a succession of incarnate lamas called the Karmapas, headquartered at Tshurpu (Mtshur pu) monastery. Among the prominent philosophers of the Kagyu sect are the eighth Karmapa, Migyö Dorje (Mi bskyod rdo rje, 1507–1554), Pema Garpo (Padma dkar po, 1527–1592, see chapters 5 and 7), and Kongtrül (Kong sprul yon tan rgya mtsho, 1813–1899, see chapter 9).

The defining doctrine of the Kagyu sect is the Great Seal (*phyag rgya chen mo, mahāmudrā*), which Kagyus regard as the crowning experience of Buddhist practice. The Great Seal is a state of enlightened awareness in which phenomenal appearance and noumenal emptiness are unified. Like the Great Perfection of the Nyingmapas, it is considered to be primordially present, that is, not something that is newly created. Rather than emphasizing the attainment of an extraordinary level of consciousness, the Great Seal literature exalts the ordinary state of mind as both the natural and ultimate state, characterized by lucidity and simplicity. In Kagyu literature, this ordinary mind is contrasted with the worldly mind. The former, compared to a mirror, reflects reality exactly as it is, simply and purely, whereas the worldly mind is distorted by its mistaken perception of subject and object as real. Rather than seeking to destroy this worldly mind as other systems do, however, in the Great Seal the worldly mind is valued for its ultimate identity with the ordinary mind; every deluded thought contains within it the lucidity and simplicity of the ordinary mind. This identity merely needs to be recognized to bring about the dawning of wisdom, the realization that a natural purity pervades all existence, including the deluded mind.

Sakya (Sa skya)

The Sakya sect looks back to another translator, Drokmi Shakya Yeshe ('Brog mi Shākya ye shes, 993–1050), who studied in India under disciples of the tantric master Virūpa (see chapter 10). Khon Gonchok Gyalpo ('Khon dkon mchog rgyal po), a disciple of Drokmi, founded a monastery at Sakya ("gray earth") in 1073. This monastery became the seat of the sect, hence its name. The most influential scholars of the Sakya sect in the twelfth and thirteenth centuries were members of the 'Khon family, the most notable of whom was Gunga Gyaltsen (Kun dga' rgyal mtshan, 1181–1251), better known as Sakya Paṇḍita. He studied under one of the last generations of Indian Buddhist scholars to visit Tibet, notably Śākyaśrībhadra. Sakya Paṇḍita claims two important achievements in the history of Tibetan philosophy. First, he defeated a Hindu paṇḍita in formal philosophical debate. Second, his master work on logic, the *Treasury of Reasoning* (*Rigs gter*), was so highly regarded that it is said to have been translated from Tibetan into Sanskrit and circulated in northern India. In his other writings, Sakya Paṇḍita insisted on rational consistency and fidelity to Indian sources in all branches of Buddhist theory and practice. This conviction resulted in often polemical evaluations of the doctrines of other sects, particularly the Kagyu.

In 1244 Sakya Paṇḍita was selected to respond to the summons to the court of the Mongol prince Godan, who had sent raiding parties into Tibet 1239. He impressed the Mongols with his magical powers as much as with his learning and offered submission to Godan on behalf of Tibet in return for freedom from military attack and occupation. He remained at Godan's court as regent, sending orders to officials in Tibet. For roughly the next century, the head lamas of the Sakya sect exercised political control over Tibet with Mongol support. Sakya Paṇḍita's nephew, Pakpa ('Phags pa blo gros rgyal mtshan, 1235–1280?), became the religious teacher of Qubilai Khan.

The early Sakya tradition was concerned primarily with tantric practice, especially the "path and fruition" (*lam 'bras*) tradition associated with the *Hevajra Tantra*, but there was very soon a move to balance and harmonize tantric studies with the study of scholastic philosophy (*mtshan nyid*). Sakya scholars wrote extensively on Mādhyamika philosophy but are particularly famous for their work in logic and epistemology (*tshad ma, pramāṇa*). It was the Sakya scholar Budön (Bu ston, 1290–1364) who systematized the various collections of Indian Buddhist texts circulating in Tibet into the well-known Kanjur (*bka' 'gyur*, literally, "translation of the word [of the Buddha]") and the Tanjur (*bstan 'gyur*, literally "translation of the śāstras").

Geluk (Dge lugs)

Unlike the other major sects of Tibetan Buddhism, the Gelukpas do not identify a specific Indian master as the source of their tradition, although they see themselves as inheriting the tradition of Atiśa, the Bengali scholar who arrived in Tibet in 1042 (see chapter 8). The preeminent figure for the sect (who may only retrospectively be identified as the "founder") is Tsong kha pa (1357–1419). While known in the West primarily as a reformer, apparently because of his commitment to monasticism, Tsong kha pa was also a creative and controversial interpreter of Buddhist philosophy, especially of Mādhyamika. His stature, which seems to have been considerable during his lifetime, was only enhanced by the subsequent political ascendancy of his followers through the institution of the Dalai Lama, the first of whom (identified as such retrospectively) was Tsong kha pa's disciple Gendundrup (Dge 'dun grub, 1391–1474). Tsong kha pa founded the monastery of Ganden (Dga' ldan, named after the Buddhist heaven Tuṣita) outside Lhasa in 1409, and his followers were originally known as the Gandenpas (Dga' ldan pa). This eventually evolved to Gelukpa, the "system of virtue." The Gelukpas established large monastic universities throughout Tibet, one of which, Drepung ('Bras spung), was the largest Buddhist monastery in the world, with over 13,000 monks in 1959. The third of the "three seats" of the Geluk, in addition to Drepung and Ganden, is Sera monastery, just outside Lhasa. A portion of Sera's monastic constitution is translated in chapter 20.

Bön

Some scholars regard Bön as a heterodox sect of Tibetan Buddhism that began (or a least developed a self-conscious identity), like the other sects (with the exception of Nyingma), in the eleventh century. This is a characterization that both Buddhists and Bönpos would reject. There has been a long antagonism between the two, with Buddhists regarding Bönpos as the descendants of benighted performers of animal sacrifice who plagued Tibet prior to the introduction of the true dharma. For Bönpos, Buddhists are adherents of a heretical alien religion whose interference deprived Tibet of its past glory (see chapter 4). The Buddhists look back to India as the source of their religion, portraying Tibet prior to the introduction of Buddhism as an amoral and even demonic realm. The Bönpos look back to Tibet and to Shangshung as their source, seeking to establish a link with the religious tradition(s) of Tibet prior to the seventh century, a link that most scholars regard as tenuous. Both Buddhist and Bönpo chronicles suggest that there was strong opposition to Buddhism among certain factions of the Tibetan court during the seventh and eighth centuries, especially among the priests who were called *bon*. But with the eventual triumph of the Buddhism, those priests seem to have completely disappeared. Little more than the name remained, to be taken up in the eleventh century by those who claimed to represent the continuation of that lost tradition. However, the pre-Buddhist practices centered around a royal funerary cult dedicated to assuring the arrival of the king in a pastoral heaven. The practices of post-eleventh-century Bönpos represent a fully elaborated path to enlightenment ending in liberation from rebirth and buddhahood (see chapter 31).

Both Buddhists and Bönpos regard a buddha as their founder. For the Buddhists, he is the Indian Śākyamuni; for the Bönpos, he is the great teacher Shenrap (Ston pa Gshen rab), from the land of Tazig (Stag gzig, identified by some scholars with Persia and Tadzhikistan) to the west of the kingdom of Shangshung. When Shenrap arrived in Tibet, he subdued the local demons and converted them to the true religion, much like Padmasambhava did. (Indeed, recent scholarship has shown that some of the accounts of Padmasambhava's conquests are based on Bönpo accounts of Shenrap.) Bönpos themselves regard their religion as having been imported by the teacher Shenrap, the true Buddha, long before the arrival of Indian Buddhists. Unlike the Indian Buddha, Śākyamuni, Shenrap was enlightened from birth and lived the life of a layman (eventually becoming a monk late in life). Thus, his extensive biography is not simply a version of the life of the Indian Buddha (although he also is said to have performed twelve major deeds) but tells a very different story. In an attempt at reconciliation and appropriation, later Bönpo texts state that Śākyamuni was actually an emanation of Shenrap.

Buddhists and Bönpos have different names for their traditions; Buddhists call theirs *chö* (*chos*) while Bönpos call their *bon*. The terms are equally untranslatable and multivalent, ranging from "law" to "truth," but their use is perfectly parallel in the two traditions. Each has its own canon, containing similar genres of texts, each believes in karma and rebirth, each has a bodhisattva path, and so forth. Like the Nyingmas, Bonpos have continued to rediscover treasure texts since at least the eleventh century. (However, rather than being texts left by Padmasambhava to be revealed at an appropriate moment in the future, the texts the Bönpos discover are said to be as those hidden to escape destruction during the persecutions of Bön by Tri Songdetsen.) Like Nyingma, the highest teaching is the Great Perfection (and the lines of influence are uncertain). Like the Geluks, Bönpo monks engage in formal debates on points of doctrine.

Because Bönpos do things in an opposite direction to Buddhists (they circumambulate and turn their prayer wheels counter-clockwise, for example), Bön has been long regarded as simply a "backwards Buddhism" that plagiarized everything from Buddhism, only substituting the word *bon* wherever the term *chö* occurred. Recent scholarship has demonstrated that this is inaccurate, that despite the protestations of both parties there has been significant mutual influence between the two, such that it is often very difficult to regard any Tibetan ritual as purely Buddhist or purely Bönpo (see chapter 33). It is also not the case, as was once assumed, that all non-Buddhist Tibetan religion is by default Bönpo. Both Buddhists and Bönpos regard their lineages as self-conscious traditions with specific histories. And again, despite their protestations, both partake fully of rituals, beliefs, and pantheons that predate either of them. However, whereas Buddhists insist on the Indian origins of those practices, Bönpos appropriated pre-Buddhist Tibetan cosmologies, deities, and terminology, all of which were employed to establish the historical priority of Bön in Tibet and thus to demarcate their traditions from those of the Buddhists. Thus Bön is not the pre-Buddhist religion of Tibet, not Tibetan "folk religion," and not a primitive animism. It is perhaps best described as a heretical sect of Tibetan Buddhism, with its own creation myths, cosmology, and pantheon (sometimes with obvious Buddhist correlates, sometimes without), which does not accept the teachings of Śākyamuni Buddha and his tradition as the true dharma. It must be noted, however, that such a characterization could be taken to imply both a devaluation of Bönpo innovation and a capitulation to the anti-Bön polemics of Tibetan Buddhists. It may be, as some scholars have postulated, that Bön is a form of Buddhism that entered Tibet from Central Asia rather than from India. Regardless, the Bön tradition that exists today is difficult to trace back beyond the formation of the other sects of Tibetan Buddhism in the eleventh century.

As is clear from the foregoing description of the major sects, Tibetans (usually Buddhist or Bönpo monks or lamas) have produced a large corpus of what might be termed philosophical literature. Due to the generally technical nature of these writings, which often involve the detailed exegesis of Indian scholastic works and the refutation of conflicting exegeses, such philosophy (works on logic, on epistemology, on emptiness) has not been included here, although the works of some of Tibet's most famous authorities on these topics (figures such as Longchenpa, Tsong kha pa, Mipham, and Kongtrül) are to be found in this volume. What is clear from their works is that the Buddhist or Bönpo philosopher was also a Buddhist or Bönpo and thus a participant in rituals and institutions that provided the setting for his writing. Thus, what we might term "philosophy" was but one concern of these authors; a perusal of the titles in the collected works of any of Tibet's most revered scholars reveals that among the commentaries on Indian logical treatises and expositions of emptiness are works devoted to tantric initiations and consecrations, propitiations of deities, biographies of Indian and Tibetan masters, and instructions for drawing maṇḍalas, making rain, stopping smallpox, and manufacturing magical pills. Hence, the contents of this volume should not be mistaken as a compendium of the popular or lay practice of the common folk in contrast to what the philosophers did. Rather, this volume is intended to represent a wide spectrum of the religious practices of Tibetans, some of whom also composed philosophical treatises.

As mentioned above, during the Mongol Yuan dynasty (1260–1368), Tibetan Buddhism played an important role at the court of Qubilai Khan, where the emperor's Buddhist preceptor was the famous monk Pakpa ('Phags pa, died 1280) of the Sakya sect. When Pakpa's uncle, Sakya Paṇḍita, was summoned to the court of the Mongol prince Godan in 1244, he took his young nephew with him. As a result of Sakya Paṇḍita's influence, the head lamas of the Sakya sect were given political rule over Tibet with Mongol patronage. With the founding of the

Yuan dynasty, the new emperor of China, Qubilai Khan, wished to keep an important member of the Sakya hierarchy at his court to ensure Tibet's continued submission to Mongol rule. Pakpa thus went to the Chinese court as a hostage. He soon so impressed the emperor with his learning and magical powers that he was asked to bestow tantric initiation on the emperor and his consort and later converted the members of the court to Tibetan Buddhism. Their interest seems to be have been based less on an appreciation of Buddhist doctrine than on the fact that Tibetan medicine and magic proved more efficacious than that of the court shamans. Qubilai Khan appointed Pakpa as teacher to the emperor (*dishi*) and teacher to the state (*guoshi*), making him in the process the vassal-ruler (in absentia) of Tibet. Their relationship provided the model for the subsequent relationship between Tibet and China, at least as perceived by the Tibetans. In this relationship, known as "patron and priest" (*yon mchod*), the leading lama of Tibet (in subsequent centuries, the Dalai Lama) was seen as spiritual adviser and chief priest to the emperor, who acted as patron and protector of the lama and, by extension, of Tibet.

With the decline of Mongol rule, there occurred a new sense of Tibetan national identity, especially under the rule of Jangchup Gyaltsen (Byang chub rgyal mtshan, 1302–1364). A nostalgia for the ancient Tibetan empire and its military dominance of Inner Asia was manifested in festivals in which officials dressed in the garb of the ancient kings. Native Tibetan deities, even those tamed by Buddhism, such as the *dapla* (*dgra lha*, see chapter 26), are depicted as fierce warriors clad in armor and riding battle steeds. During Jangchup Gyaltsen's reign, many terma texts were unearthed that told of the glory of the imperial age.

Jangchup Gyaltsen and his descendants ruled Tibet for over a century. After that, rule came into the hands of the princes of Rinpung (Rin spung) and then the kings of the western province of Tsang (Gtsang), both groups being patrons of the Karmapas. Meanwhile, in China, the Ming (1368–1644) emperors continued to confer gifts and titles on lamas of the Kagyu, Sakya, and Geluk sects. The Gelukpas received important patronage from the Tümed Mongols when the third Dalai Lama, Sonam Gyatso (Bsod nams rgya mtsho), was summoned to the Altan Khan in 1578. It was actually the Altan Khan who bestowed the appellation "Dalai Lama" on the third incarnation of Tsong kha pa's disciple by translating part of his name, Gyatso ("ocean"), into Mongolian; Dalai Lama means "Ocean Lama." The Mongols converted to Tibetan Buddhism and proved powerful patrons of the Geluk, especially when, after Sonam Gyatso's death, a grandson of the Altan Khan was identified as the fourth Dalai Lama. Another Mongol leader, Gushri Khan of the Qoshot, supported the fifth Dalai Lama against his Kagyu rivals, eventually establishing him as the ruler of Tibet in 1642. This consolidation of religious and secular power in a single figure was an important moment in Tibetan history, a consolidation that received strong ideological support through the promotion of the cult of Avalokiteśvara.

In a treasure text discovered in the twelfth century (but with significant additions apparently made in the fourteenth century) called the *Hundred Thousand*

Words of Maṇi (*Maṇi bka' 'bum*, see chapter 2), Avalokiteśvara, the bodhisattva of compassion, was retrojected into Tibet's past as both Tibet's protector and the central agent in Tibetan history. Thus, in the prehistoric past, the bodhisattva was said to have taken the form of a monkey and mated with a ogress; their offspring were the first Tibetans. The illegible text that fell into the king's palace was none other than the *Kāraṇḍavyūha,* which tells many tales of Avalokiteśvara. And the three great "dharma kings" (*chos rgyal*) who oversaw the introduction of Buddhism into Tibet were none other than incarnations of Avalokiteśvara. The great epic hero Gesar of Ling is an emanation of Avalokiteśvara (see chapter 1). Finally, the fifth Dalai Lama identified himself not only as the fifth incarnation of Tsong kha pa's disciple but as the present incarnation of Avalokiteśvara. From that point on, the bodhisattva protector of Tibet was believed to take human form as the Dalai Lama, thus establishing an unbroken link with Tibet's prehistoric past and exalting the religious lineage of one of many lines of incarnation to the level of kingship through identification with Avalokiteśvara; the Dalai Lama was both Tsong kha pa's historical successor and the human embodiment of the transhistorical bodhisattva of compassion. The fifth Dalai Lama also declared his own teacher to be an incarnation of Amitābha, the Buddha of Infinite Light, and Avalokiteśvara's teacher, bestowing upon him the title of Panchen Lama, establishing a new line of incarnation, which was to have its seat at Tashilhunpo (Bkra shis lhun po) monastery in Tsang province, the former center of his opponent's power. (See chapters 23 and 29 for works by the first Panchen Lama.) The Dalai Lama moved the capital back to Lhasa, the seat of the ancient kings, and built his palace there, a massive edifice called the Potala, taking its name from Potalaka, the name of Avalokiteśvara's palace. Thus, the power and authority that had once descended in the form of the ancient kings, which had then devolved to local incarnate lamas, was now arrogated (at least in part) back to a single divine figure, the Dalai Lama.

During the eighteenth and nineteenth centuries, the Gelukpas maintained their political control over central Tibet, with the occasional aid of the Manchu rulers of China's Qing dynasty. Especially from the time of the Kangxi emperor (ruled 1661–1722), imperial favor was directed especially toward the Gelukpas. Under the Qianlong emperor (ruled 1736–1795), for example, the entire Tibetan Kanjur was translated into Manchu under the direction of the Geluk hierarch Janggya (Lcang skya rol pa'i rdo rje, 1717–1786, see chapter 29).

With the fall of the Qing, Chinese influence in Tibet dwindled through the Second World War (during which Tibet remained neutral). In 1950 Tibet was invaded and occupied by troops of the People's Liberation Army. The situation deteriorated over the next decade. A popular uprising against the Chinese began on March 17, 1959. When it became clear that the Chinese intended to arrest the Dalai Lama, he escaped to India, eventually to be followed by some 250,000 of his people, one-fourth of whom arrived safely in India and Nepal. Today there are over 100,000 Tibetans living in exile, while Tibet, much of its territory divided among Chinese provinces, remains a Chinese colony.

Since 1959 the practice of Tibetan religion has taken place in two very different domains. In Tibet, Tibetan religion has been severely proscribed, as have all forms of traditional Tibetan culture. The violent suppression reached its peak during the Cultural Revolution when all but a handful of the thousands of monasteries and temples that existed in Tibet in 1959 were destroyed. From 1959 to 1979 it has been estimated that one million of the six million ethnic Tibetans died as a result of Chinese policies. Since 1979 there has been some relaxation of the strictest constraints, and a number of monasteries and temples have been rebuilt, although whatever Chinese funds have been provided for this purpose seem directed ultimately toward the promotion of Western tourism. The monastic population has been reduced drastically, as has the program of monastic education.

The other domain of Tibetan religious practice is in exile, with most refugees living in India and Nepal. Of the approximately 70,000 Tibetans who successfully followed the Dalai Lama into exile in 1959 and 1960, an estimated 5,000–7,000 were monks, a tiny fraction of the monastic population of Tibet. But a disproportionate number of the monks who escaped (and remained monks in exile) were from the ranks of incarnate lamas and the scholarly elite, and they worked to reestablish their monastic institutions (of all sects) in exile. Their presence and accessibility has attracted the attention of a large number of Western scholars and enthusiasts, and the last three decades have seen an explosion in interest in Tibetan Buddhism, with a wide variety of translations of Tibetan Buddhist texts.

Indeed, a certain reversal in the perception of Tibetan religion has taken place since 1959. During the Victorian period and lasting well into this century, representations of Tibetan religions generally fell into one of two categories. By some it was portrayed as the most depraved deviation from the Buddha's true teaching, an abomination born from mixing superstition and animism (identified with Bön) with the decrepit remnants of original Buddhism, the remnants named Mahāyāna and tantra. By others, Tibet was seen as the abode of Atlantean masters who held the secrets of the universe; Tibet was a land of "magic and mystery," a Shangri-La.

The Victorian representation of Tibetan Buddhism as the most corrupt and therefore least truly Buddhist of the Asian traditions reached its inevitable antipodes. In the 1960s and 1970s, the earlier Buddhological valuation of Tibetan Buddhism was reversed, as a generation of young scholars came to exalt Tibet, just at the moment of its invasion and annexation by China, as a pristine preserve of authentic Buddhist doctrine and practice. Unlike the Buddhisms of China, Japan, and Southeast Asia, Tibetan Buddhism was perceived as uncorrupted because it had been untainted by Western domination. The value of Tibet to scholars of Buddhism was no longer simply as an archive of the scriptures of Indian Buddhism. The Tibetan diaspora after the Dalai Lama's flight to India in 1959 made widely available to the universities of Europe and North America (largely through the efforts of the Library of Congress office in New Delhi) a great flood of autochthonous Tibetan Buddhism literature, heretofore unstudied. This literature, scorned by scholars at the end of the last century as "contemptible mummery," was now hailed as a repository of ancient wisdom whose lineage could be traced back to the Buddha himself. Much of the scholarship and more popular translations produced since the Tibetan diaspora have, as if, sought to counter the prior negative valuation of Tibetan religion as polluted by representing it as pristine, reflecting largely the normative Buddhism of the scholarly elite, such that the essential ritual practices of Tibetan religions have been ignored to a great degree. In Bönpo studies, Bön has moved from being dismissed as a primitive animism to being hailed as the authentic and original source of Tibetan culture. Works on meditation, compassion, and the stages of the path to enlightenment are certainly famous in Tibet and hold an important place in the histories of the traditions. But without placing such works within their larger ritual context, the religions of Tibet can be misconstrued as merely a sophisticated philosophy divorced from the concerns of the everyday. This attitude is sometimes found among modern Buddhist clerics who see Tibetan Buddhism as entirely of Indian origin, free from any pollution by the pre-Buddhist past. One of the purposes of this volume is to provide the materials for the foundation of a middle ground between these two extreme views of Tibetan religion by presenting a wide range of Tibetan religious literature, derived from many different centuries, regions, and sects, with no attempt to occlude those elements that some might construe as "magical," while attempting to demonstrate how those elements are designed most often to address the most quotidian of human concerns.

Since 1959 the bulk of scholarly attention has been focused on two periods: that of the dissemination of Buddhism to Tibet from India (which, as discussed above, occurred in two waves, in the ninth and eleventh centuries) and that of the "classical period," generally seen to run from the fourteenth through the sixteenth century. Relatively little attention has been paid to the "medieval period," from the sixteenth to the late nineteenth century, a period dominated politically by the Gelukpas. This period has generally been characterized as one of hermetic scholasticism, much as the entire Tibetan Buddhist tradition had once been portrayed, but here with the scholars of the major sects represented as devoting much of their attention to the interminable exegesis of the works of the creative geniuses of the fourteenth and fifteenth centuries. Of the modern period, to the extent that such is recognized, histories usually make mention of the largely unstudied revivalist movement known as the "Unbounded" (*ris med*), of Nyingma, Kagyu, and Sakya scholars against the Geluk orthodoxy. Otherwise, the modern period is portrayed as an even more stultifying period of abstruse philosophical mechanics among the Geluk. But Tibetan religion has not been static since the sixteenth century, as the many selections of works from subsequent centuries contained in this volume testify.

Rather than being organized chronologically, or according to sect, or by a division into Buddhist and Bönpo, the chapters of this volume are organized thematically, in an attempt to juxtapose the selections in interesting and illuminating ways. (Like any system of organization, there is an inevitable element of randomness, and some of the chapters could easily fit under another of the categories.) There are indeed works here from each of the major sects, but the purpose of the volume is not to be representative in that sense. Instead, works from different sects are organized thematically to illustrate the continuities that all forms of Tibetan religious practice share. The doctrines, prayers, and ritual forms of the sects of Tibetan religion share much in terms of both content and structure; it is often only by the lineage of lamas listed at the beginning or end of a text that one can easily identify the sectarian source. In important ways, Tibetan sects are affiliations based on such lineages. What is perhaps more interesting to observe is the ways in which the same aspirations, the same fears, the same strategies for success, the same logics of representation recur in works from sects that sometimes seem so different from each other, and how points of contestation and change must somehow be confronted in order that lineages may represent themselves as a self-identical transmission. The contents of this volume offer much to ponder in this regard.

The first section, "Accounts of Time and Place," offers examples from an early Tibetan chronicle in which the great king Songtsen Gampo, himself considered an incarnation of the great bodhisattva, sets forth the mantra of Avalokiteśvara. Here there also pilgrimage guides, showing again the pivotal importance of place in Tibetan religions. There is an excerpt from the great Tibetan epic poem about the warrior king Gesar of Ling, a Bön history that counters the claims to authority of Indian Buddhism, and a portion of the history of a Tibetan tribe whose name means "Upside Down Heads."

The second section, "Remarkable Lives," brings together a number of life stories, hagiographical accounts that are such a popular and pervasive element of the religions of Tibet. Some of the accounts tell of great tantric saints of India whom the Tibetan founders of the major sects traveled so far to meet or who were the previous incarnations of later Tibetan lamas. Others recount events from the vivid and sometimes humorous biographies of Tibetan yogins.

The third section is called "Rites and Techniques." Here are found a number of tantric practices, from a fasting ritual to a meditation to overcome attachment to clothes. The meditation texts are placed here to emphasize the importance of thinking of meditation as a ritual act; in some of the chapters, meditation is better understood as a programmed visualization, punctuated by the recitation of mantra. Elsewhere, it is a reflection on the nature of awareness itself, but everywhere it comes with precise instructions directed toward a specific goal. This is followed by a selection of prayers and sermons, some of which are recited daily, some of which are the centerpieces of solemn rituals, some of which are accompanied by feasting and merrymaking.

The book concludes with techniques for confronting the unwanted, whether it be the hail that can destroy a barley crop, the gossip that divide a village, or that most unwelcome of intruders, death. Because of the inordinate popularity in the West of the so-called Tibetan Book of the Dead, there is a general impression that Tibetans are obsessed with death. It is unlikely that Tibetans are more concerned with death than is any other culture, but they have developed a wide range of sophisticated responses to it, some of which are presented here.

Taken together, the contents of the volume dispel the old views of Tibetan religion as either depraved superstition or disembodied philosophy, as a repository for Indian Buddhist texts or a blank landscape onto which the contents of the unconscious are projected. The volume provides a wealth of voices that together may lead to a new and more nuanced understanding of the religions of Tibet.

Further Reading

For general surveys of Tibetan religion and culture, see David Snellgrove and Hugh Richardson, *A Cultural History of Tibet* (Boston: Shambala, 1968); Giuseppe Tucci, *The Religions of Tibet* (Berkeley: University of California Press, 1980); R. A. Stein, *Tibetan Civilization* (Stanford: Stanford University Press, 1972); Geoffrey Samuel, *Civilized Shamans: Buddhism in Tibetan Societies* (Washington, D.C.: Smithsonian Institution Press, 1993); and the articles "The Religions of Tibet" by Per Kvaerne and "The Schools of Tibetan Buddhism" in *The Encyclopedia of Religion*, ed. Mircea Eliade (New York: Macmillan, 1987). For an encyclopedic survey of Tibetan literature, see José Ignacio Cabezón and Roger R. Jackson, eds., *Tibetan Literature: Studies in Genre* (Ithaca, N.Y.: Snow Lion Publications, 1995).

Accounts of Time and Place

—1—

Gesar of Ling

Robin Kornman

The oral epic *The Gesar of Ling* can be considered the *Iliad* or *Odyssey* of Central Asia, so popular and well known is it there. This ancient epic is still sung across Asia wherever dialects of Tibetan are spoken. Versions of it also exist in other languages, including several dialects of Mongolian, and in Chinese, but the Tibetan version has the most extensive tradition. The epic narrates the heroic adventures and campaigns against demonic enemies by the divine King Gesar, a name linked etymologically with kaiser and Caesar. Like the eulogies composed by the Romans to praise Caesar, this epic extolls the greatness of King Gesar, but there are significant differences in the various epic traditions about what made Gesar so great, why he reigned so successfully, and how he acquired his divine power to conquer his enemies. In the Tibetan versions there is some debate as to whether it is proper to characterize Gesar as a Buddhist hero or to say that his story is even a "Buddhist epic." Many of the versions discovered actually refer very little to Buddhism but evoke more explicitly native Tibetan religious beliefs and the non-Buddhist religion of Tibet called Bön; in fact, there appear to be both Buddhist and Bön versions of the Gesar epic.

The version discussed here is explicitly Buddhist, having been edited under the direction of a Tibetan Buddhist scholar of the nineteenth century, Mipham Gyatso (Mi pham rgya mtsho). Mipham is most famous as a philosopher and a master of the most abstract metaphysical texts in the Buddhist tradition. But he was also an avid aficionado of the Gesar epic, and, in addition to editing the epic, he wrote numerous ritual practices dedicated to Gesar as a heroic protector of Buddhism and the Tibetan nation. There are hundreds of such practices in the cult of Gesar throughout Tibet, but Mipham's have become popular in recent years and have even begun to be translated into Western languages (see chapter 26). Mipham's edited version of the Gesar epic was based on manuscripts found in the library of the King of Ling, a man who actually claimed to be descended from the family of Gesar.

The epic tells the story of a divine hero named Gesar who begins as an enlightened deity in a Buddhist heaven. There his name is "Good News" (Thos pa dga', literally "joyful to hear") or in some versions of the epic "Accomplishment of Actions" (Skt. Siddhārtha, Tib., Don 'grub). The epic begins with a crisis: everything is going badly on Earth because of an infestation of dharma-destroying demons. These demons in previous lifetimes were powerful magicians and enemies of the Buddhist teachings. Some were simply enemies of Tibet, bent on invading and capturing the country; others were actually Buddhist practitioners gone bad, especially tantric adepts who developed great powers through their yogic practices, but later turned these powers against their teachers. Their evil aspirations and perverted karma have resulted in their rebirth as kings of countries that surround and threaten the Tibetan Buddhist kingdom of Ling.

Avalokiteśvara, the bodhisattva of compassion, requests the buddha Amitābha to send down a hero to Ling in order to rid the world of these "beings with perverted aspirations." This leads to a meeting in heaven of the buddhas and gods, much like the Olympian councils of the gods found at the beginning of many Western epics following Homer. The council of Buddhist divinities decides that one of their number should incarnate on Earth to become the magical warrior hero Gesar, who will take over Ling and conquer one-by-one all the enemies of the Buddhist teachings in Asia. After selecting the individual who will become Gesar, the gods and buddhas next try to convince him to leave his place of bliss and enter the worldly realm of action. In some versions of the epic the future Gesar is not anxious to become a human being and fight demons, so the gods must pursue him throughout the universe, confront him, and finally persuade him of the seriousness of the problem. In other versions, the future hero's vow of compassion as a bodhisattva instantly occurs to him and he makes the sacrifice. In still other non-Buddhist versions of the epic, Gesar's willingness to abandon heaven for the benefit of humankind marks him as a favored son of the gods. Whatever the religious framework, the tradition of Gesar narratives explores the mystery of incarnation, what the Hindu epics call the *avatāra*, meaning literally the "descent" of the divine to Earth.

When the hero agrees to enter the flesh, the action of the epic proper begins. A magical mother is found among the race of dragons (*nāgas*) and chosen to receive the hero in her womb. She leaves her kingdom at the bottom of the sea and travels to Ling where, because of her great beauty, she becomes a member of the king's retinue. Many other enlightened beings and magical servants are born into the tribe of Ling to assist Gesar in his future quest. Gesar's miraculous birth and childhood are featured in an entire book of the epic. Although perfect in form and completely enlightened, the child Gesar disguises himself as an ill-favored hunchback, which is intended to deceive his opponents of his true identity as an incarnation of the Buddha. Nevertheless, the forces of evil attempt to destroy him even though he is a deformed child, and he uses magic and deception to elude them and defend himself. When Gesar reaches young manhood he finally reveals himself in all his glory and power, being transformed from a deformed trickster into a splendid version of the Central Asian knight. In a scene typical of

Turkish and Mongolian epics, he enters a special horse race, competing with the warriors of Ling, which he wins easily, and as a reward he gains the hand of the Princess of Ling in marriage. Through such contests Gesar becomes King of Ling and thus begins his righteous reign and campaigns against the evil foes of the dharma.

One of Gesar's first deeds as a king is to recover the magical weapons and armor, left by the gods for the people of Ling buried in the mountain range of Magyel Pomra (Rma rgyal spom ra). Magyel Pomra is both an actual mountain in eastern Tibet and one of the most powerful native Tibetan deities, who in the epic becomes a great friend and supporter of Gesar (see chapter 3). Once armed with the magical weapons and shielded with wondrous armor, Gesar and his troops become invincible. The rest of the epic is devoted to a lengthy recounting of his martial adventures, as he subjugates demons and invades one by one the many kingdoms that threaten Tibet. In the early versions of the Gesar epic, there were probably only four major enemies in the cardinal directions, to the north, south, east, and west of Ling. But as bards across Inner Asia elaborated on the story, additional sagas were added, with new enemies being located in the intermediate directions, until in some versions Gesar conquers the great historical empires of Asia. In fact, episodes are still being composed. Sometimes a Tibetan bard will seem to "remember" more material than the previous generation sang. Often it is clear that the epic is being elaborated on the spot for the audience's entertainment, after the manner of storytellers across the world. There are also additional chapters added to the Gesar by Tibetan literati. For example, during World War II word reached Tibet that a demon king named Hitler was trying to conquer the world. A famous Buddhist lama named Kamtrül Rinpoche actually composed an additional book of the epic entitled *Gesar Conquers the Kingdom of Jarman*. In this episode Gesar travels to Germany and assassinates Hitler for the benefit of all sentient beings.

The selection translated below is excerpted from the first chapter of the first book of Mipham's Gesar. The central figures in the action of the first chapter are Avalokiteśvara, the bodhisattva of compassion, and Padmasambhava, both of whom are considered the special protectors of Tibet. According to Tibetan mythology, Padmasambhava was an all-powerful enlightened magician who brought the tantric teachings to Tibet and tamed the local deities into defenders of the dharma. After he had done his work he departed to another continent, the demon island of Cāmara, where a race of cannibal demons called *rākṣasas* dwell. The epic opens with Avalokiteśvara's mission to the island continent of Cāmara, which is entirely inhabited by these dangerous, shape-shifting demons and other occult monsters. They all surround Padmasambhava's palace Luminous Light on the Copper-Colored Mountain of Cāmara. The scene of Avalokiteśvara's mission to the demonic land of Cāmara is a commonplace of epic literature, but it is also reminiscent of a Tibetan literary genre called *delok*, in which male and particularly female yogins describe their out-of-body journeys to the netherworld and to mystical lands (see chapter 32).

Avalokiteśvara tries to enter Padmasambhava's palace but is blocked by an ignorant demon minister with seven heads, in a scene that is quite humorous, for both the bodhisattva and Padmasambhava are enlightened beings, who are well aware of each other's presence and what cosmic issue brings them together. The exchange between Avalokiteśvara and the demon minister is thus a deceptive charade performed for the enjoyment of the reader and the edification of the minister. Avalokiteśvara plays with the mind of the minister, puzzling and challenging him and generally leading him into confusion. Avalokiteśvara's skillful use of tantric methods may have been intended to serve as an example of enlightened diplomacy and politics; the play of phenomena and political power is transformed here into an occasion to sing songs about the Buddhist teachings.

But one important point is made again and again, almost as a second level of meaning in the text. Avalokiteśvara sings songs to the demon minister to convince him that he should be escorted immediately into Padmasambhava's presence. He argues his determination with countless metaphors about what it means to have an important goal or a serious case or a profound meaning to one's actions. A person with such strong determination is thought to have a strong life-energy force or soul (*srog*), a crucial notion for understanding the Tibetan sense of selfhood. Understanding the role of this occult energy is also an important key to understanding native Tibetan literature, especially the popular stories about warrior heroes. The warrior must know how to guard and nourish his life-energy force, to ensure his strength, endurance, and determination. It is believed that when a person's life-energy force leaves them, often caused by a feeling of sudden fright, that person will display a number of symptoms, such as becoming depressed or susceptible to outside influence, gullible, easily fooled, and vulnerable to demonic attack or possession. Once weakened by the loss of one's life-energy force, if a demon invades or possesses the susceptible person, he or she may be driven to suicide, severe depression, or death by destruction. But a person with a strong life-energy force can easily repel the demonic forces and indeed any negative external influence, and that person displays strength, full of confidence and determination.

Gesar is the ultimate symbol of this determination. Completely empowered by the five buddhas, hardened and honed by aeons of training as a bodhisattva in heaven, called forth by the determination of the bodhisattva of compassion and the tantric yogins of Tibet, he is beyond the possibility of depression or suicide. In addition to having a strong life-energy force, he possesses a consummate aura of power that surrounds and infuses his being, making him nearly invincible. There are many Tibetan terms for this charismatic quality: it is called "windhorse" because it can be ridden like a horse as a personal sense of energy; it is called "field of power" because in the best warriors it forms a globe around them that radiates a sense of effectiveness; it is also called "the aura of merit," which is connected to one's karmic store of life-energy. When it has been drained away by a lifetime of action, then not only does a person become ill, but Tibetan methods of diagnosis, which are based in part on readings of this aura through the pulses, are unreliable or report nothing. The songs sung by the characters in this first chapter seem straightforward, but all of them are full of references to this philosophy of determination and life-force.

Finally, to the utter confusion of the demon, Avalokiteśvara transforms into a gigantic lotus, the Mahāyāna symbol of compassion, which, when brought into the presence of Padmasambhava, dissolves into his heart center. This symbolism of Avalokiteśvara's lotus and its dissolution into Padmasambhava's heart center may be interpreted as representing the two protectors of Tibet embodying the symbols of the Mahāyāna and the Vajrayāna or tantric path, respectively, which are actually inseparable.

The next scene shows Padmasambhava actually creating the god Good News, who will live in heaven and then be reborn into the human realm as Gesar of Ling. In other, less metaphysical and overtly Buddhist versions of the epic, Good News already lives in heaven and is merely sought out by the other deities. But in this Buddhist edition of the epic, he is constructed by Padmasambhava. He is a composite deity, formed out of a combination of native Tibetan gods and famous Buddhist tutelary deities. This illustrates the occult meaning of the Gesar legend in Mipham's version—that it is, in a sense, a transmutation of a Central Asian war epic into a sermon on the Buddha dharma. It shows in its symbolic language exactly how local gods are tamed and transformed into Buddhist deities. In other words, the rough and warlike elements of Tibetan culture, which once combined to form an Inner Asian empire, have now been tamed and reformed into a nationwide instrument of moral instruction and contemplative training. The Tibetan empire has been refashioned into a Buddhist pure land.

The moment Good News is born, he sings a song of moral admonition. Then, a few days later, he is given the all-important ritual empowerment of *abhiṣeka* by the "five buddha families." This section requires a somewhat lengthy explanation. Tantric Buddhism employs colored diagrams called maṇḍalas as a basis for its sophisticated visualization practices. These maṇḍalas are representations of palaces occupied by five buddhas who sit at the four gates and in the center of the palace. Each buddha represents one aspect of reality in the tantric fivefold analysis of the energies of the world. The most elaborate tantric practices are those in which the disciple identifies with one of these energies and becomes inseparably joined with the corresponding buddha. To do such practices, one must first receive a ritual consecration in which the energy of the buddha associated with the practice is assumed by the practitioner. This is done by invoking the maṇḍala of that deity and blessing the disciple with symbols of that deity's power, enabling the disciple to enter into the buddha's maṇḍala palace. Usually these ceremonies are highly secret and the texts of their practices are rarely seen except in the recondite societies of tantric practitioners. Here though, in the last section of the first chapter of the Gesar epic, we see something like a public and generic empowerment that can be described to a general readership without breaking oaths of secrecy.

The empowerment section is a strange but interesting passage. Even Tibetan lay people and novice yogins, who are not advanced meditators with the skills to visualize the maṇḍalas in all their intricate detail, nevertheless go to receive empowerments if they can. They regard them simply as elaborate blessing ceremonies and rarely understand the ritual acts being performed. Perhaps Mipham inserted this ritual into the text as a way of explaining this ceremony to the untutored faithful. Or perhaps it is a way of introducing young Tibetans and inexperienced practitioners to the empowerment liturgy. In any case, its presence in a text meant for a universal readership provides us with a rare opportunity to discuss the main ritual of Vajrayāna without violating its laws of secrecy.

The *abhiṣeka* is organized in a special way, based upon the pentad structure of the maṇḍala. Each of the five buddhas will be called upon to grant Good News his special brand of empowerment. Each has his own color, his own single-syllable "seed mantra," and each transforms a certain moral flaw into a specific form of buddha wisdom. Also, each is associated with a certain aspect of life: body, speech, mind, quality, or activity. Thus when Padmasambhava invites the five, he does so with appropriate lights emanating from the five centers of his body, which represent respectively these five dimensions of sentient existence.

Padma's song invoking the five lists the usual sets of mystical correspondences by which the family of five buddhas can be mapped across all of enlightened and unenlightened reality. But he adds a section that is actually a form of political commentary, when he mentions the various classes of society: "It is a poor ruler who has no supporters to honor and magnify him / And poor lower classes who have no respect." And there is a stanza that mentions weapons, herbal medicine, and agriculture. All these are subjects that concern the Tibetan laity and mark this empowerment as a work related to folk poetry, not simply a normative religious ritual meant for the Buddhist clerics alone.

This chapter of the epic contains many different examples of poetry found in Tibetan literature. The first few pages of verse are typical of the tightly constructed classical Indic poetry known in Sanskrit as *kāvya.* This Sanskrit court poetry is full of complex figures and multiple layers of meaning, and it is a favorite vehicle for the Buddhist literati, who use it in lyrical poetry and also in the highly formal language of ritual. But when the demon minister begins to sing to Avalokiteśvara, we shift to a heroic song, a form of poetry native to Tibet. This indigenous form is sung to tunes known by the particular bard who performs the work. It seems that each character had his or her own signature tune. The melody would actually be given in the opening lines with the Tibetan equivalent of "tra-la-la": *lu a la lu tha la.* Tibetan epic ballads begin with a half-line of alliterative nonsense syllables that give the tune of the song. A literal rendering would be "*lu a la*, the song is sung with this tune. . . ." *Tha la* are the same sort of musical sounds, like "tra-la" in English. These songs are the heart of the epic, written in a racy, humorous style of colloquial speech. Tibetans enjoy the moral or heroic sentiments evoked, as well as the cleverness of the songs, which are filled with two-line proverbial expressions and tricky analogies. The twisty quality of the songs delights the

Tibetan audience and challenges their understanding. The alternation of prose sections with these songs and verses is typical of almost all Tibetan narrative literature. The prose sections are usually written in a careful, concise, but highly ornamented language, sometimes in elegant parallel prose couplets. But when we enter the world of the empowerment ceremony, the prose changes to the high church language of Tibetan liturgies, with its rich baroque symbolism, which requires some explanation.

The empowerment proceeds as ordinary *abhiṣeka* rituals do, beginning with the figure of Vairocana, the white buddha at the center of the maṇḍala, who represents the transformation of the moral fault ignorance into the enlightened wisdom of all-encompassing space. Each of the five buddhas has a "sceptre." Vairocana's sceptre is the wheel of dharma. The wheel is an ancient Indian symbol for sovereignty, and here it is the symbol for the buddha family at the center of the maṇḍala. *Oṃ*, the mantra of enlightened body, is his seed syllable. The empowerment he gives is directed to the body of Good News, and the verses speak of the virtues of his body. The wheel finally dissolves into Good News's forehead, the center of which represents the body among the five centers of body, speech, mind, quality, and activity. These are the correspondences that constitute the empowerment of the first family. But in the midst of them is a sermon composed in the epic mode and recited by this buddha Vairocana. It speaks of the moral flaws that arise in society because of ignorance, and it suggests that Good News, having received the *abhiṣeka* of body, which transforms ignorance into wisdom, should cleanse society of these flaws.

Each day during the consecration ritual of Good News, another buddha in the fivefold maṇḍala presents his blessing and gives his sermon. The language of these passages is quite innovative and marks Mipham's version of the epic, combining both classical discourse and folk poetry. Epic passages like this illustrate the syncretic character of Tibetan Buddhist practice, for we see a representation of Buddhist and native elements combined, which is rarely admitted in more strictly orthodox canonical texts. At the same time, it must be noted that the construction of this chapter shows the hand of a great scholar. The heroic songs may indeed be transcriptions of songs sung by itinerant bards. But the careful construction of the empowerment section is too learned to have been composed whole cloth by an itinerant storyteller. For example, each of the songs sung by the empowering buddhas begins with two lines drawn from an Indian tantra, the *Mañjuśrīnāmasaṃgīti*. (For a translation, see chapter 4 of *Religions of India in Practice*.) The Sanskrit mantras of empowerment, such as *padma abhiṣiñca hrīḥ*, the sceptres, and body-centers are correctly presented according to the exacting rules of Tibetan ritual. Only a scholar could do this.

The translation is from *Lha gling gab tse dgu skor: An Episode from the Tibetan Epic of King Gesar of Gling*, reproduced from Szechuan People's Publishing House ed., 1980 (Gantok, Sikkim, 1983).

Further Reading

A summary of the epic was written by the French explorer Madame Alexandra David-Neel and Lama Yongden, *The Superhuman Life of Gesar of Ling,* (New York: Claude Kendall Publisher, 1934). There are two interesting versions that may be more primitive versions of the epic: A. H. Francke, *A Lower Ladakhi Version of the Kesar Saga,* in *Biblioteca Indica, n. 1543,* (Calcutta, 1904), and Francke, *The Epic of Gesar,* vol. 29 (Thimbu, Bhutan, 1981).

The most complete study of the *Gesar Epic* to date is in French. It is by R. A. Stein, who also wrote a partial translation of one version of the epic: *L'épopée tibétaine de Gesar dans sa version lamaïque de Ling* (Paris: Presses Universitaires de France, 1956). There is also an English translation of Stein's excellent study of native Tibetan culture: *Tibetan Civilization,* trans. J. E. Driver (Stanford: Stanford University Press: 1972). This work provides a good anthropological background for understanding the epic, since it explains the system of gods that occur in *The Gesar.*

Geoffrey Samuel has done a book-length study of the cults associated with the Gesar epic: *Civilized Shamans: Buddhism in Tibetan Societies* (Washington, D.C.: Smithsonian Institution Press, 1993). Samuel has also produced a number of articles on Gesar, and they provide a good bibliography of Gesar studies: "Gesar of Ling: Shamanic Power and Popular Religion", in *Tantra and Everyday Religion,* ed. Geoffrey Samuel (New Delhi: Aditya Prakashan). Here are two other good articles by Samuel in the anthropological mode: "Gesar of Ling: The Origins and Meaning of the East Tibetan Epic," in *Proceedings of the 5th International Seminar on Tibetan Studies,* Narita, Japan, 1989, and "Music and Shamanic Power in the Gesar Epic," in *Metaphor: A Musical Dimension,* ed. Jamie Kassler (Sydney: Currency Press).

The notion of a shamanic epic is explored by a specialist in the European Renaissance, Thomas Greene. His most famous book, and a good introduction to the kind of epic studies that would apply to the *Gesar of Ling,* is *The Descent from Heaven, a Study in Epic Continuity* (New Haven: Yale University Press, 1963). There is a fascinating essay by him on poetry and magic in a collection: *Creative imitation: new essays on Renaissance literature in honor of Thomas M. Greene,* ed. David Quint (Binghamton, N.Y.: Medieval & Renaissance Texts & Studies, 1992).

Chapter 1 of *Gesar of Ling Epic: The Divine Land of Ling, the Nine-Squared Divination Board: The Epic of the King of the War Gods, Gesar the Jewel, Tamer of Enemies*

Oṃ svasti
Within the essence of dharma (*dharmatā*), your

Unobstructed compassion gave rise to
The impartial awakened mind (*bodhicitta*), which benefits beings.
Never abandoning that, you took the vajra-like oath
To perform the four-fold spontaneous buddha activity,
The hundred points of the adamantine sceptre.

Once when perverted ambitions piled high into a mountain of evil merit
And pride rose up to a rocky peak of haughty arrogance,
To show the teaching of cause and effect you crushed it with this vajra [adamantine sceptre].
Greatest of heroes, supreme being, jewel tamer of
Enemies, may you be victorious.

The noble Supreme Compassionate One's moonlight
Dissolves into the heart center of the One Whose Splendor Tames the Phenomenal World.
The five families of the blessed victorious ones
Grant empowerment to Good News.

Now in this time when the five corruptions are rampant and increasing, it is difficult to liberate from evil karma these savage sentient beings through the causal path of characteristics, the Mahāyāna alone. It is even difficult to ripen them through tantra, the fruition path of the secret mantra. For their minds are hard as rock and stone: if you do not carve its hard surface with a chisel, even if you soak it in a stream, it will not give way. Even if you rub it with butter and oil, it will not become flexible. They are too stiff to be bent by the teachings on this life and the next. They will not submit to the restraint of the temporal and spiritual laws.

Formerly, during the lives of the three dharma kings [of Tibet's imperial period, namely, Songtsen Gampo, Tri Songdetsen, and Ralpajen], the ancestor and his descendants, when the land of Tibet passed from Bön to Buddhism, in order to pacify naturally the temperamental demons of Tibet, Lotus Skullgarland [i.e., Padmasambhava], the mantra holder, bound them by oath. If he had managed to make them swear their oaths of fealty to the Buddha dharma three times, then the dharma kings would have been long-lived.

But even though the sovereign and their subjects shared bliss and happiness, devilish ministers, noblemen, and warlords turned the subjects from the commands of their lord king. [Faced with such opposition, Padmasambhava failed to complete his taming of the native spirits of Tibet.] Padmasambhava's failure to bind the spirits of Tibet more than twice led to disordered conditions in the state, and the auspicious coincidence of the glorious gateway, the perfect astrological conjunction, was missed. As a result there was the turmoil of weapons in the four directions, the foreign borderland demons wandered into central Tibet, and the dynasty of the dharma kings fell down to the level of commoners.

The whole world in general, and the land of Tibet in particular, became oppressed by suffering. The noble excellent Great Compassionate One [Avalokiteśvara] gazing on all this with unbearable compassion, supplicated the lord of the Happy Land [Sukhāvatī], Amitābha:

Oṃ maṇi padme hūṃ.
I pay homage to the refuge, the lord of countless realms,
Amitābha, lord of the Happy Land in the West.
Even though your compassion is truly unbiased,
Look down on the world of impure saṃsāra.
In the vast whirlpool ocean of suffering
You are skilled in killing the crocodiles of evil deeds.
Have compassion for sentient beings in endless cyclic existence.
Surrounded by the ocean waves of the five poisons,
The mirror of their minds is blinded by the obscurations.
Circling endlessly in cyclic existence, they are truly to be pitied.
Out of compassion please show supreme skillful means.

With these words he reverently supplicated. The blessed one Amitābha answered with these words:

Good, good, O son of noble family.
For sentient beings ignorant and confused,
If they are not fortunate enough to be tamed, it is difficult to pull them
From the ocean where they drown.
Thus, if beings near and far
Have no iron ring of faith,
Even the teacher who pulls beings out of the three worlds
Has no way of catching them with the iron hook of compassion.
Nevertheless, in the divine buddhafield of the Thirty-Three [a heaven where gods who study the dharma dwell]
The father, the great god, Lord White Luminosity
And the supreme mother Mandā Divine Beauty
Had a son, Supreme Bliss Good Nature.
He and the divine princess Illusory Beauty
United as *e* and *vaṃ* [together meaning "thus"] and gave miraculous birth
Through the radiance of their unwavering compassion
To the magical child whose blessings accomplish all purposes.
He is joyful to hear and delightful to see.
If he were to transfer into a human body in Jambudvīpa
That heroic bodhisattva would tame the difficult to tame.
Sentient beings in the land of Tibet would experience bliss and happiness.

There is no doubt they would be free from rebirth in the lower realms.
Therefore go to the continent of Cāmara.
And request Padmasambhava Skullgarland Power for this.
Strive for the benefit of beings, supreme warrior of the mind.
Remember this! *e ma ho*! [an exclamation of jubilation]

He praised and complimented Avalokiteśvara with these words of prophecy and confirmation.

Then, in a single instant, the greatly compassionate lord [Avalokiteśvara] went to the blissful, spontaneously arisen Limitless Palace of Lotus Light on the subcontinent of Cāmara. Around it was the city of the terrifying *rākṣasas* [cannibal demons], his subjects—a place so horrible that it frightens even the death gods and makes the lord of life himself, Brahmā, withdraw—a land so terrible that even the Vinākayas [obstructing spirits] shun it, not to mention ordinary men, who cannot even stand the sight of Lotus Light Palace. In this place, in order to effect the measureless benefit for beings, Avalokiteśvara manifested as a cannibal-demon child, his head surrounded by oysters and enveloped in a halo of glimmering white light. He went to the eastern Gate of All-Pervading Mercy (*maitri*). There he met a demon minister *rākṣasa* with seven heads who said:

Wondrous indeed, your inner reality and outward appearance.
I would say you are a god, but you look like a demon cub.
I would say you are a demon, but for your aura of light.
Within the walls of this blazing lotus land
We sentient beings, confused by ignorance,
Have never seen, would be lucky even to hear,
Of the coming of such a unique individual.

With this speech he asked Avalokiteśvara for what great purpose he had come. Then the demon minister sang to the lord this miraculous song:

Lu A La Lu, the song is sung; in case you do not understand,
Tha La, this is the melody of the song.
Surrounding this land of Cāmara, the country of the demons is
The place of the impure *rākṣasas* and demons
And the field of the pure wisdom holders and ḍākinīs.

This morning, young child, you landed here.
From what place and from what direction do you come?
What aims can you have that are such great matters?
If you do not have in mind great matters,
Then it is meaningless to pursue ends of no great importance.
Only a person possessed by the evil spirits (*gdon*) of great suffering
Would drown himself in the river!
If you have not become involved in a great quarrel,
There is no great cause for you to bring to court.

In Cāmara's Blood Lake of Sin
The food of the cannibal demons is hotter than fire.
The reach of the cannibal demonesses is longer than a river.
The *tramen* [wrathful naked women with animal heads] seek you out faster than the wind.

Why have you come to this place?
Who are your father and mother, their race and religion?
Keep back no secrets; be straight in your speech.
In the monastery our commerce is all straightforward speech.
Straight arrows strike the target yonder.
If your path is straight, the road between central Tibet and China is not long.

If you understand, you are a superior man: a single sign is enough.
If you do not, you are an aging ox and only understand the stick.
If that is what you need, then look to your red-blooded life.
If you understand, these are the words of my song.
If not, I'm not going to sing it again.

Thus he sang and the lord answered: "Oh yes, I understand sir:

The secret meaning of the essence of speech like yours must be clarified
Or else the profound and secret meaning of the words will be silenced.
If the meaning of the words does not place the fruition in your hands,
Then all those words are just bubbles of spit.
If the earth in early spring is not first fed with water,
Then the spirits of weather, the southern turquoise dragon and the venomous serpent, will be silent.
In the sky Mount Meru is circled by the sun and the moon.
If they do not benefit the plains of the four continents,
Then Meru is of no benefit or harm.
Then the sun and the moon would just be distractions for the spinning heads of brainless dupes.
Then there would be no gratitude for the good done by the Sun and Moon.
It is impossible that things should be that way.
For the black earth is thick with settlements
And the measureless white clouds float freely above.
If my cause is great, China and Tibet are circled by the heavenly bodies each day.
If my cause is important, then these words carry great weight.

"I realize that most cases are brought by petitioners to the court of the chief, the majestic Lotus Skullgarland, and heard by the great ministers in the imperial assembly hall. But just as it is pointless to plant seed anywhere else but in a plowed field, so the nature of my discourse is too great to explain before the plenary council and I must see Lotus Skullgarland himself. The tale I must tell is like this," and he sang this song:

Oṃ maṇi padme hūṃ hrīḥ
I supplicate the dharma of the six perfections.
Just rest in your own place, ultimate emptiness.

In case you do not recognize me,
I am known as the All-Benefiting, Compassionate, Beloved Child.
My father is Enlightenment Mind Sovereign Lord.
My mother is Emptiness Dharma Torch.
This morning I came from the Plain of Great Bliss [Sukhāvatī].
The benefit I seek is the benefit of both self and other.
My goal is the Isle of Cāmara, that goal.
My supplication is to supplicate the Master Skullgarland.
Thus, the ancient proverb says
If you travel back and forth, as a merchant, between China and Tibet,
It is not that there is nothing of value in one's own home valley:
This is the mental relationship of trust that unifies China and Tibet.
The master transmits to the disciples empowerments and teachings.
Passing them down does not mean the teachings are not precious,
But that they are a connection of aspirations and commitments.
Between the people and the ruler the great minister travels back and forth.
It is not that without him there is no way of conducting government.
He connects the two ranks of the law-giver and the subjects.
These words of information I offer to you.
Please intercede on behalf of my humble self,
And tell the master the essence and inner meaning of my message.
Initiate the all-pervading activity of your compassion.

My import is not small, it is of great importance.
Of great import is the welfare of all beings.
If it were meaningless, why would I explain to you why I have come?
Those who pointlessly travel around in distant lands
Purchase for themselves thirst and famine.
Those who suffer not, yet throw themselves into deep gorges,
Have let their life force be carried away by demons.
The wealthy who bear the burden of material goods
Will be carried away by profit and loss.
The powerful with their many evil reports
Will cast themselves down in self-humiliation.
The poor who utter proud words

Will bind themselves to false friends.
Things such as these are indeed without point.

But into the entrance hall of Lord Rakṣa Skullgarland
I have had no choice but to enter.
May I be seized by his compassion.
Taking the form of a dragon-being, this song is my offering.
Please let my words enter your heart and hearing.

Thus he requested and the demon minister answered, "Hey, you! [The minister's speech is thick with colloquialism and clever folk sayings. His language would be absurd and incongruous in any other situation. But we must remember that this man-eating demon does not necessarily realize that a buddha in wrathful aspect has taken over the government of his country.] According to ancient history, our demon king Rakṣa Skullgarland's royal lineage is terribly strict. In court they strike with the accuracy of hot lightning bolts. Their sovereignty covers the country, more vast than the blue sky. Their clout is mightier than Rāhu [a planet that can eclipse the moon]. What can a little gypsy kid like you hope for? Even people like me, the interior minister, when we stand before such kings we are just waiting to be punished, even when we have done nothing wrong. They are ready to jump on us for no reason or arrest us for no real cause. They are ready to gobble up the flesh of a living man and gulp down the blood of a live horse. In this lineage there have been such men. In recent generations, however, their guts seem to have broadened somewhat and their minds, which are empty in nature yet full of mercy, unite all three temperaments: peaceful, wrathful, and relaxed.

"In recent generations they have all been the same that way, like sleeves all cut from the same pattern or beads all chosen from the same rosary. In the strictness of our monastic law, we don't let anything get swept under the carpet.

"We must formally request that you be allowed the kindness of entering. Otherwise the two of us will be just like an old ox leaping into the river when it is thirsty, or an old cow heading for grass, or an old donkey driven by rain and wind. No one has ever dared to break in upon him like that. Generally when you visit a temple, you offer the guru there a white scarf. So what do you have as a presentation offering to give to the ruler?"

Avalokiteśvara answered: "I have the thirty varieties of formal offerings to present. If you want to count them they are: as dharma, the six syllable *maṇi* mantra; as path, the six perfections; as the six objects of outer appearance, the six consciousnesses of inner knowing, and the six gates of the sense faculties that lie between these. Are these suitable offerings to present?"

When he said this, the minister answered, "I can't really say they will be okay. The more the poor man values food, the more the rich man tightens his stomach for him. The more the rich man values a horse, the more stubborn-headed the merchant becomes on his selling price. If you don't have one, then a dzo [a cross between a yak and a cow] is like a horse. But for a great band of robbers, the dzo is nothing but a quick snack on the road. The jackal who usually eats horses sometimes wonders, "Perhaps this sheep's body would do?" Who knows what will be satisfactory as a presentation offering?

"At the same time I cannot say that these presentation offerings would not do: the sacred symbol, the souvenir of a pilgrimage to Tsari Mountain, is really nothing but a nine-node bamboo stick. To harvest Chao Hsi Mountain's tea, you must find your way across hill and dale. But anybody with money can have it if they want.

"Generally speaking, you can say that these things are at the same time both rich and abundant, and tiny and insignificant. Indeed, they are not great, for these precious qualities of being free and well-favored [that is, being reborn as a human with the opportunity to practice Buddhism] all fit within the two spans and four cubits of the human body. On the other hand, they are not tiny, because if you possess analytical [intelligence], they are the inexhaustible provisions for this life and the next, the materials that fulfill all wishes in the cycle of existence, the wish-fulfilling gem, so difficult to acquire. But if you do not possess an analytical mind, then these things are the anchor of the three poisons in the ocean of cyclic existence; the stick that drives us with happiness and sadness; a sack full of impure substances.

"Well now, whoever you are, I will go and request permission for you to enter into his presence. Wait here for a moment," he said and entered the palace.

There on top of a wrathful seat of corpses, on a dazzlingly beautiful throne of gold, sat Lotus Rākṣasa Skullgarland [Padmasambhava] himself, his mind resting in meditation on the great nature of phenomena. Even though he already understood that Avalokiteśvara was outside, he feigned ignorance and said to the great rākṣasa minister with seven heads:

"Hey you! This morning you were singing pointless songs, chanting unlovely melodies with imbecilic words! Who sang in response to you? What great goal does he aim to attain? To whom does he pay homage? In whom do his mind and heart trust? In whom do his body and skull take refuge?"

The minister thought to himself, "He seems to be sitting here on his lordly throne, but his fine bright eyes see the bridge outside. His sight must be like the proverbial royal parasol of the Sun traveling across the sky, its light pervading the world, or like the southern clouds piled high in the mid-heavens, raining all across the dense earth." He uttered these sayings thinking that Padmasambhava in his chamber had probably seen everything that had just happened outside.

He said to Padmasambhava, "Oh precious crest jewel, in the multicolored demon village, Hundred Thousand Great Blisses, at the second gate in the iron mountain wall, the eastern gate named Great Garden of Mercy, a little boy, who is neither human, demon, nor god, but who has an aura of white light, says that he has an essential matter of importance to impart. He says this with words clear, bright, concise, and lovely to the ear. Please do not wander, but listen carefully." With these words he prostrated three times and then sang this song:

> *A la la* sing the song this way.
> Above in the Palace of Padma Rāga,
> Amitābha of Uḍḍiyāna, know me!
> May I and all sentient beings filling space
> Attain the deathless state of a wisdom holder.
> On a peaceful and wrathful jeweled corpse throne
> On a blazing lotus,
> Leader in this life, dear lord and chief, listen.
> Guide in the next life, O guru, listen.
>
> Today at the moment when the golden rays of the royal parasol
> Struck the peak of the glorious mountain
> At the eastern gate of the Garden of Great Mercy
> In the middle of the Plain of All-Pervading Great Bliss
> Appeared a little boy made from beautiful rays of light,
> Wrapped in garlands of light rays and rainbows.
> His name is Compassion Benefiting All.
> His great aim is the limitless benefit of others.
> He says: "There is an urgent need to see you.
> There is no time to spare."
>
> Whether you condescendingly praise your gift as "alms"
> Or elegantly call it "offerings,"
> It really makes no difference at all.
> It still goes to the erudite guru who has mastered the ten sciences.
>
> It may be payment to purify one's sins,
> Or else the extortion exacted by a minister.
> It really makes no difference at all.
> In any case it is a fine, the punishment meted by the mighty chieftain.
> Clouds in the sky may be a storm front coming in,
> Or else the gaping mouths of the eight classes of demons.
> It really makes no difference at all,
> For in both cases the rain will help to ripen the eight fruits.
> A beggar's prayers for your good health may be altruistic aspiration prayers.
> Or else he calls you friend just to get some food.
> What does it really matter?
> Either way, his stomach's hunger is pure as a white silk scarf.
>
> I couldn't grasp him, but I said that I would ask the favor.
> Please grant whatever he requests with his long white scarf.

Do not make a minister such as myself wander back and forth about the monastery.
Please let him make his request personally before your golden throne.
These rocklike words of a stupid, prideful person
You have heard. He should not just wander in before your golden throne in the monastery.
However, if the affair is important, it is your honor's business!

If you listen to my song, it is an offering up to you.
Then please give your reply to what he has requested.

Then the magnificent Skullgarland Lotus answered: "Oh, excellent! These sayings are good. As for what you give the guru who is a guide and a teacher, he is more pleased by the abandonment of evil deeds than by a hundred offerings. As for what you give to the chief whose sovereignty is vast, he is more pleased by the straight truth than by a hundred offering gifts. When you begin to practice dharma and accumulate merit, he is more pleased by one auspicious sign of success in meditation than by a hundred measures of provisions for travel.

"Today, in the Fire Monkey year, the eighth day of the first moon, on the glorious Mount of Auspicious Coincidence, whatever of the eight orders of beings he is, whether god (*lha*), mountain spirit (*gnyan*), serpent, or man, let him now enter the audience hall and stand before me."

The minister went out to the gate, but the little boy had disappeared without the least trace. Like the track left by a bird in the sky when it makes its way in the paths of the winds, just so were the traces of the little boy on the ground—nothing, not even an indentation in the soil. But straight ahead was a golden lotus with eight petals and a white *hrīḥ* on its anthers. On the petals were *oṃ maṇi padme hūṃ hrīḥ āḥ*. These eight syllables were repeating their own sounds. He thought, "How strange! What shall I declare to the chief? How will I explain this to the ministers? What will I say to the servants? What will I proclaim to the people?"

Then he began to strategize. In his mind he went through his strategy twelve times; he worked out twenty-five tricks and tactics. Finally he thought, "I must decide. Since the mind, being by nature empty, is inexhaustible, the intellect of a superior man is inexhaustible as well. If you do not clamp down on your little tongue, there is no end to the speech of a learned man. If you do not control the measure of your little step, the long white strip of road will stretch out endlessly before you. If you do not touch it with blue water, what will control the red fire?"

Then he had the thought, "This thing might be meaningless, like relic pills from the grave of a pig, which have no blessings. But what can I say in answer to Padma's command? Like the mute trying to explain the taste of brown sugar, I have no words of reply to him. But even though it may be pointless to try to describe this with my mouth, maybe I can carry it in my hands.

"I guess the person that I saw this morning must have been some kind of transformation. So it seems that this flower here is the child's magical transformation. If that's so, then why not carry the flower in and place it before the king? It's a sign of something and signs are necessary—like the auspicious signs [of visions and experiences of insight] that are so necessary for the practitioner collecting merit [while performing religious practices]. And after all, the king gave me orders, saying: "Whether it is a god or a demon, bring it in!" This thing is not solid; it is a form like that of a rainbow. Maybe it is a magician's illusion? Or perhaps the flower is all there ever was and I have been hypnotized. Whatever it is, I am certain that it is a miraculous thing!

"On top of that, whatever this thing is, I cannot talk to it. But since it is all I have to show for this morning's events, I will carry it in and just present it. Just as white snow is pleasing to the mind and colored ornaments are lovely to the eyes, so this is probably an auspicious sign." Then he picked up the lotus and carried it to the door of Lotus Self-luminosity's living room. The flower in his hand turned into a white light the size of the moon and dissolved into the heart center of the demon king Rākṣasa Skullgarland. At that moment the noble supreme Greatly Compassionate One [Avalokiteśvara] told Padmasambhava to invoke and call forth from the self-luminous thought stream the mind of Gesar. His words were poured into a song so that they were easy to understand. [The "thought stream" is a technical term in Buddhist psychology that refers to the stream of impressions and self-transformations that make up an individual. When the thought stream is evoked from the breast of Padmasambhava, it will arise as the mind of Good News, the deity who will later be reborn as Gesar. The song that follows is an invocation designed to "call forth" the deity who will become Gesar of Ling. The "calling forth" is an important aspect of the technology of tantric ritual. The idea is that by singing this song Avalokiteśvara can provoke, and stimulate Padmasambhava to action, arousing him to generate the deity Good News. The deity is an emanation of Avalokiteśvara, who is himself an emanation of the buddha of the Lotus Family, Amitābha. Thus we have a complex series of emanations. First, Amitābha confers authorization on his bodhisattva emanation, Avalokiteśvara, who transforms himself into a magical demon-child. The demon-child becomes a lotus, the symbol of Mahāyāna compassion, and then dissolves into the heart center of Padmasambhava. Now, Avalokiteśvara, even though he has evolved into rays of light, still exists in an absolute sense outside this series of transformations. Thus his voice can sing the following invocation, which asks Padmasambhava to call forth Gesar.]

Oṃ maṇi padme hūṃ hrīḥ
From the pure land of the flaming lotus
Blessed one Amitābha, know us.
And you who are supreme in the Lotus Family, omniscient treasury.
Miraculous king, I ask you to give thought to me.

It is difficult to tame the wilderness of Tibet.
When they passed away in the Snowy Kingdom,
Nine oath-breaking demons uttered perverted aspirations [that is, these demons are the individuals who violated tantric vows]
And so were reborn as the nine evil kings and ministers:

The eastern devil, Lotri (Lho khri) Tiger Eye,
The southern devil, Sadam (Sa dam) Poison Tree,
The western devil, Lutsen (Klu btsan) of the Mu Clan,
The northern devil, White Tent The'u Rang Cub.

[Next we have the demons of the intermediate directions]
Turquoise Peak Luminous Child,
Earth lord King Nyenrawa (Snyan ra ba),
The lion devil Ase Khyilpa (A bse 'khil pa),
The borderland devil King Shingtri (Shing khri),
And the general demons of the world such as black bear, etc.

Each one of them is surrounded by an innumerable retinue—
The enemies who have form and the obstructing spirits without form.
They lead the land of Tibet into suffering.
They treat the teachings of cause and effect, the rare and precious three jewels, with contempt.
They guide all sentient beings on the path to the lower realms.
They plant deep down [in sentient beings] the seed of rebirth in hell.

[Now Avalokiteśvara directly addresses Good News, who still exists as a potentiality in the breast of Padmasambhava; but he is "calling him forth" at the level of his thought stream:]

"Oh pity the ignorant in saṃsāra!
You are the Great Powerful One who defeats those difficult to tame—
Great Being, god child, Good News,
Primordially pure, All Good, self-liberate them.
And grant them the empowerments of the five families of the Buddha.
Grant them the blessings of the three protectors [Mañjuśrī, Vajrapāṇi, and Avalokiteśvara].
The time has come to fulfill your sacred vow
And evoke the transformation body to tame the vicious.
Therefore, don't be idle, protector of beings."

Thus he supplicated. And then He Who Overpowers the Phenomenal World with His Brilliance [Padmasambhava] smiled brilliantly, his heart glad, he said, "Good," and sang these words in a sweet melody:

"*Kye ho*, good, supreme bodhisattva;
Your striving for the benefit of beings is good.

In the limitless sky of your enlightenment mind
The White Luminous One is your compassion which benefits others.
The innumerable constellations are your aspiration prayers.
Your kindness eliminates the darkness of ignorance.

Like the Moon shining in the midst of the moving stars
Are you, child who will master the phenomenal world.
A great bodhisattva, hearing you, rejoices and liberates sentient beings.
You are the lord who embodies the activity of all the buddhas.

For all the buddhas are one in the space of wisdom.
The buddha nature pervades all sentient beings.
Beings in cyclic existence, not understanding this,
Must be liberated. Thus the buddhas
Never abandon their vows to benefit beings.
Protector, whatever thoughts you have for the benefit of others
Will come true for all sentient beings.
So may your practice of the perfection of aspiration be perfected."

This was his utterance of an aspiration prayer that confirmed the invocation of the mind vow of all the buddhas of the ten directions. Through it and the wondrous liberation through seeing, that demon minister of the enjoyment body buddha field of disciples was established in bliss. Then the Greatly Compassionate One returned to Potala Mountain.

[Here begins the section in which Padmasambhava initiates the process by which Good News is miraculously born as a deity in heaven. Miraculous birth is a technical term for the method by which gods come into being. The entire process of emanating and gathering lights, sounds, and tantric symbols that is depicted in this passage could be regarded as a technical description of the birth of a deity.]

Later, on the holy day when the ḍākas and the ḍākinīs especially gather, the tenth day of the month, deathless Lotus Skullgarland himself was surrounded by a vast assembly performing a tantric feast. At that time he was dwelling in the meditative absorption of the all-pervading dharmakāya. From the top of his head he emitted a green ray of light that invoked the mind stream of the dharma realm Samantabhadra. Then from the heart center of the dharma realm Samantabhadra there emanated a five-pointed blue vajra marked in the center with the syllable *hūṃ*. It flew to the garden of the Heaven of the Thirty-three and entered the top of the head of the godling White Supreme Bliss. He experienced inexpressible bliss and his appearance transformed into that of the warrior buddha Hayagrīva, the neighing horse.

From the heart center of the supreme mother Opulent Goddess of the Space Element emanated a red lotus with sixteen petals, the anthers marked with the syllable *āḥ*. It entered into the top of the head of the goddess Illusory Bliss

Beauty. An indescribable meditation experience blazed within her, and her appearance transformed into that of the adamantine sow, Vajravārāhī. Horse and pig joined in passionless union.

The sound of their union of bliss and emptiness invited the mind streams of the sugatas of the ten directions. From the heart centers of the blessed ones, the victorious ones of the five families, various colored lights emanated in the ten directions, cleansing the obscuratons of the five poisons of all sentient beings. The lights gathered back here and transformed into a crossed double vajra, the essence of the activity of all the buddhas of the ten directions.

That vajra entered into the top of the head of White Supreme Bliss where it was melted by the fire of great bliss, flowed through his body, and entered into the space of Illusory Divine Beauty as wisdom wind. This wisdom wind was blessed into the transformation body. A little while after that it miraculously appeared in her lap as a god child blazing with such a magnificent dignity and splendor that, like all good news, to see him would bring illumination and to hear him would bring joy. As soon as he was born he began to produce the sound of the hundred syllable mantra of purification. He was floating in the air in vajra posture at the height of an arrow-length above an eight-petaled golden lotus. He produced this song, which teaches the meaning of cause and effect.

[This song by the newly born Good News presents a traditional sermon to exhort people to practice with great diligence, describing the horrors of sickness, old-age, and death. Realizing the impermanence of ordinary human life and the certainty of suffering should motivate the proper detachment.]

Oṃ maṇi padme hūṃ hrīḥ
From the buddhafield of the Akaniṣṭha dharma realm
Blessed ones of the five families of the victorious ones, know me.
For I and all sentient beings like space
Please naturally pacify discursive thoughts of the five poisons.
May we meet the five wisdoms of the five bodies [i.e., body, speech, mind, quality, and activity].

The single generative essence drop dharma body—
If you see it, buddhahood is delivered in the palm of the hand.
Nevertheless, for ignorant sentient beings
Even if you explain it, it is difficult to understand.

According to the provisional meaning, gods and men
Are protected from fear of cyclic existence
By seeking refuge in the three rare and supreme ones.
Suffering is naturally pacified
By giving birth to the mind of enlightenment, which holds others dearer than self.

Beings of the three lower realms, border tribes, and erring gods,
Those of perverted views, inhabitants of buddhaless lands, and the mute:
When you are free from the faults of these negative eight states of being [in which you do not have the opportunity to hear and practice the Buddha's teachings]
And when you are born in the central land, with sense organs whole, with faith,
Free from evil intentions in your actions, inclined to virtue—
Then if you do not practice the holy dharma in the present,
What will happen when he comes, the one known as the Lord of Death [Yama], the sharp and swift?
He comes to friend and foe alike, to good and bad.

The high ones famed as the "Sun" and the "Moon"
May seem to pervade the four continents with their rays.
But there is no way they can overcome the eclipsing planet Rāhu with their light.
Even so are the high kings; think about them!

The distant red rock cliffs are high and strong.
Only the vulture can make his way to them.
And yet there is no way they can beat their rival, the lightning meteoric iron.
Even so are the mighty unrivaled ones; think about them!

In the third month of summer, tiny creatures emerge above ground.
At harvest time one speck of frost alone will destroy their precious lives.
The poor and feeble are humble and weak; think about them!

Generally, at first you are born in your mother's lap.
You are fed with soft food, the delicious three sweets.
You are dressed in soft clothes, Chinese silk.
In the middle time, you wander in worldly activities.
You turn the wheel of friends and enemies, passion and aggression.
If you are high up, not satisfied with your station in life, you suffer fear of falling low.
If you are low, you suffer from taxes, war, and corvée labor.
The strong suffer, worrying about how to avoid an evil end.
If they lose out, then they suffer fear of others' contempt.
If you are rich, you suffer because you cannot manage to keep up the level of your livelihood.
If poor, you cannot feed your face or clothe your back.

The suffering of human life is endless, suffering is inexhaustible.
The four hundred diseases are stirred by sickness as the wind.
Many will die because of sudden obstacles.

When you are old, you cannot bear up against sickness.
An old body is like dry sticks on the river bank.
Few are those who listen to the words of old speech.
When the mind is old it gathers all the suffering in the kingdom.

When you catch a long fatal illness:
The nine sweets and the ten delicious flavors nauseate you.
Your soft and warm bed becomes harder than stone.
You are fed up with taking beneficial medicines.
The sleep guardian [someone who prevents the ill from sleeping, which is believed to be unhealthy] makes you angry.
Your grunts and groans are inexhaustible.
A day and a night take forever to pass.
The divinations mislead, the incantations no longer work.
This short life, so dear to you,
Is now without pure dharmas; it is too late to plant virtuous roots;
For the avaricious who held back generosity,
It is too late to hope for help in the forty-nine days [during the intermediate state].

On the day when death has finally come,
Feeling for the pulses is like poking a stone.
On the day when you are facing Yama,
Averting ceremonies is like a lamp with water for fuel.
Your aura of merit sinks and
The more you try the worse it gets.
Your field of power and windhorse are expelled and
Your strength is like a water bubble.
The castle of the wargods [i.e., the deities who protect you] is turned away.

Now your fortress against enemies threatens your own life.
All your heroic champion's brave accomplishments
Are just a mound of earth piled on top of you.
The rich man's avaricious inner stores [where long-term provisions are kept for emergencies]
Are just a wooden stake of attachment driven into the ground.
You wasted your life in confusion about food and clothes.
When you die you are naked with empty hands.
Even the high king on his golden throne
Must pillow his head that day on cold earth.

And the queen with silken robes on her back
Burns in an oven, clothed in red flames.
Even the youthful tigers in their prime [i.e., young warriors], with their six attributes of a warrior [arrow, sword, spear, etc.],
Are dragged around by the king of birds, the vulture.
And the mothers and aunts with their six accomplishments
Are bound tightly hand and foot by the black rope.
In the red charnel ground of stupefying fear
On the day when the corpse is cut to pieces, showing the round white marrow,
It is all over—too late for regret.

The hot and cold of hell are unbearable.
The hungry ghosts are starving and parched.
The animals are bound and stupid.
The jealous gods struggle and die by the knife.

And we gods of the higher realms suffer in our own way:
Even if we avoid sickness and old age, we are carried away by sybaritic distractions.
Seven days before death the portents of a god's death arise:
The brightness of their lovely palaces fades.
Their dear wives withdraw far away.
Their sweet-smelling garlands of flowers wither.
Their bodies start to stink, rhinoceros skinned, their light now obscured.
The negative force of cause and effect blazes up in terrible suffering.
The regret of a dying god is useless—just a cause of further suffering.

All you thoughtless and crazy beings of the six realms
Do not wander, turn your mind within!
Lord gurus, resolve us about the nature of mind.
Imperial rulers, make no mistake about cause and effect.
Mighty ones, do not disturb the king's political plans.

Rich men, offer up and give down most generously.
Ordinary people, do prostrations, circumambulations, and say the *maṇi* mantra.
The more exertion and mindfulness you practice,
The more you will not fail to be free and well-favored.
I am the great indestructible being, Vajrasattva
The primordially pure dharma realm Samantabhadra.
O beings pervaded by impure illusions,
Listen to this song's words and put their sense into practice!
Carefully guard that understanding, the gem of great price.

If you do not understand the song, I will not repeat it anyway,
For our communication has failed.

Thus he proclaimed this dharma in a great voice which was heard by all sentient beings, either moving or unmoving, each in their own language and each according to his or her own capacity.

Then, knowing that the time had come to grant empowerment (*abhiṣeka*), from the glorious Copper-colored Mountain on Cāmara, the master, Lotus Skullgarland, called forth the mind stream of the buddhas. From his forehead white rays of light invoked the mind stream of the buddha Vairocana in the Akaniṣṭha buddhafield. From Padma's heart center blue rays of light invoked the mind stream of Akṣobhya in Abhirati. From his navel yellow rays of light evoked the mind stream of Ratnasambhava in the buddhafield of Glorious Beauty. From his throat center red rays of light invoked the mind stream of Amitābha of the Happy Land [Sukhāvatī]. From his secret center green rays of light invoked Amoghasiddhi of Supreme Action buddhafield.

Then he raised this song in order to supplicate for the fruition of the truth.

Oṃ The five poisons purified are the wisdoms of the five buddhas.
I invoke the mind stream of the buddhas from unborn space.
The five elements purified are the five goddesses
Arising from unceasing space for the benefit of beings.
From within the union of supreme skillful means and the nature of phenomena, which is emptiness,
Has appeared the self-existing form of wisdom and compassion.
To this transformation body who will rescue beings from the flood,
Grant empowerment so that he may conquer the hosts of Māra.
This is the meaningful song of self-luminosity.

According to the traditional worldly proverbs,
It is a poor guru who has neither empowerment nor textual transmission.
It is a poor student who has not taken the sacred vows of the tantric pledge;
It is a poor ruler who has no supporters to honor and magnify him,
And poor lower classes who have no respect.

Weapons that are neither sharp nor tempered,
Even if they have both handle and sheath, cannot handle the enemy.
If you have the main six herbal ingredients, but not the additives,
Even if the medicine is fragrant, shining, and wholesome, it will not heal.
Finally, a field that has not been fertilized,
Even if it sprouts, will not ripen to the six fruits.
So therefore enthrone him, praise him, and compliment him.
For the weapon of compassion cuts off the lives of enemies.

The medicine of blessings heals the six realms.
And buddha activity makes the field of disciples flourish.

Fulfilling the aspiration to liberate all beings,
May the auspiciousness of complete fulfillment of goals be present.

Thus he invoked the compassionate mind streams of the five buddhas and their consorts with these words.

Then from Akaniṣṭha, Vairocana's forehead light rays streamed out in the ten directions. They purified the obscurations of ignorance of all sentient beings and gathered back here in the form of a syllable *oṃ*, the embodiment of the body blessings of the buddhas of the ten directions. This became a white wheel with eight spokes. The wheel traveled in the realm of the mid-heavens and hovered before the divine child. From it came the self-proclaiming sound resounding with these words:

Oṃ. From the self-existing wisdom of the realm of dharma
Lord of beings, you were just born.
You are the king who possesses various magical transformations.
You dispel delusions from deluded minds.
It is sad to see the unhappiness of sentient beings.
The border tribes, because of doubt and delusion,
Mental obscuration and ignorance—
If they have free time, still wander in the activities of cyclic existence.
Even though they are well-favored, they are too lazy for the dharma.

When the time for death finally arrives,
Though the dharma-less guru has a big golden hat,
Though he radiates majesty and seems quite high,
He will have trouble showing the path to the next life.

The ruler who has no gentle mind,
Although he looks great when he mightily executes the law,
Throws his karma in the air, like a child throws a stone.

The disciple who has taken no sacred vow of the tantric pledge,
Even though he is learned and seems widely read,
His explanations are like a mist of spit.

The ungenerous rich man,
Even though he has collected bribes through avarice,
At the time of death will be naked and empty-handed.
These are the philosophers of cyclic existence.

On this learned child is bestowed
The name "Good News."
Because he is full of blessings, this buddha
Is joyful to hear and exhausts sin.

This ruler who is sovereign of a vast area,
If he remains will make the kingdom happy.
May his body defeat the enemies of the four directions!
May everyone who has relations with him be free from rebirth in the lower realms!
May everybody who sees him be purified into the buddha land!
buddha abhiṣiñca oṃ

After the wheel had uttered these words, it dissolved into the child's forehead. From this day on he was known as Good News.

At dawn the next day from the pure land of Abhirati, from the heart center of Akṣobhya, light rays streamed out in the ten directions. They purified the obscurations of aggression of all sentient beings, gathered back here in the form of a blue five-pointed vajra, the embodiment of the mind blessings of the buddhas of the ten directions, and then dissolved into the heart center of the divine child. As a result he mastered the treasury of the meditative absorptions. Then he was offered a bath by the entire assembly of the five families of deities, who bathed him with nectar poured from a precious vase and this song was sung:

Hūṃ. From the great vajra space of emptiness
Flows forth the nectar of mirror-like wisdom.
May the weapons of vajra aggression
Conquer the hosts of enemies, the poisons!

The ignorant angry sentient beings of saṃsāra:
The guru who has no compassion,
Even though he exerts himself in mantra recitation and retreat practice,
He will still not become a buddha.
The ruler who has no gentle mind
May be strict in the law, but still his people will leave the country.
The hero who has no restraint,
May be both hearty and brave, yet he will die by the sword.
Therefore, in the savage minds of sentient beings
May no sinister thoughts of aggression arise!

Supreme being, divine child, Good News,
Even though you are not obscured by the three poisons,
I grant you the empowerment of the completely pure three bodies.
May you spontaneously accomplish the buddha activity of pacifying!
vajra abhiṣiñca hūṃ

Thus they bathed him with nectar.

Again, from the Beautiful pure land, from the navel of Ratnasambhava light rays streamed out, purifying the obscurations of pride of all sentient beings. They gathered back here as all the qualities and merit of the victorious ones of the ten directions in the form of a blazing jewel and dissolved into the navel of the divine child. He was then adorned by the bodhisattvas of ten levels with priceless precious ornaments: jeweled crest ornaments; throat, shoulder, hand, leg, and ear ornaments; rings; the long and short necklaces of crystal; the divine clothes of silk; and so forth, ornaments worthy of a great being—with all of these he was clothed and enthroned. And then this auspicious song was raised:

> *Traṃ*. The precious wisdom of equanimity,
> The noble jewel who completely purifies pride,
> The meritorious one, the accumulator of all merit,
> And the great source of jewel wisdom, Ratnasambhava,
> In order to tame those difficult to tame, you are granted empowerment,
> So that your compassion may achieve the benefit of beings.
>
> In the sky of your merciful compassion
> May the auspiciousness of unbiasedness be present!
> For disciples who are like constellations,
> May the auspiciousness of your limitless and fast buddha activity be present!
> For your life span which is like a vajra,
> May the auspiciousness of indestructibility and deathlessness be present!
> For the swastika of your vows to benefit beings,
> May the auspiciousness of unchanging spontaneity be present!
> By these beautiful ornaments, the precious jewel crown,
> May the auspiciousness of exalted majesty be present!
> By these earrings and rich golden necklaces,
> May the auspiciousness of the sweet sound of your fame pervade space!
> By these silken, soft, and broad vestments,
> May the auspiciousness of conquering the hosts of Māra be present!
>
> Great being, precious Good News,
> Although you are not attached to conventional ornaments,
> You are granted the empowerment of these five precious qualities.
> May your vast buddha activity be spontaneously accomplished!
> *ratna abhiṣiñca traṃ*.

Thus he was enthroned with auspiciousness.

Again, from the pure land, the Happy Land [Sukhāvatī], from the throat center of Amitābha light rays streamed out, purifying the obscurations of passion of all sentient beings. They gathered back here as the embodiment of the blessings of the speech of all the buddhas in the form of a red lotus and dissolved into the throat center of the divine child. He was then empowered with the sixty limbs of speech and singing. Furthermore, the symbol and support of the sacred vows of all the buddhas, a golden five-pointed vajra fell from the sky into his hand:

> *Hrīḥ*. From the space of passion purified as discriminating awareness wisdom
> Great desire, great bliss,
> Lord of dispassionate lotus speech,
> You are the supreme skillful means of coemergent wisdom.
> This vajra is the symbol for your sacred vows.
> Until the ocean of cyclic existence is emptied,
> You will free the ocean of sentient beings.
> Having realized the ocean of wisdoms,
> May you fulfill the ocean of aspiration prayers!
>
> Receive the empowerments of the gods above.
> Remind the *nyen* in the middle of their previous vows.
> And below open the treasury of the dragons.
> From Ling, the country of desire, look after the benefit of beings.
> The black devils and the golden Hor [untamed demons and nations]
> Those with form and those without—bind them all by oath.
>
> Although the bodhisattva who looks after the benefit of beings
> Needs no encouragement to keep these vows,
> Nevertheless we ask: please take care to save them from the ocean of cyclic existence.
> May you spontaneously accomplish the activity of magnetizing!
> *padma abhiṣiñca hrīḥ.*

This song was heard, pronounced in the mid-heavens.

Again, from the pure land of Completely Accomplished Action, from the secret center [at the genitals] of the blessed one Amoghasiddhi, light rays streamed out, purifying the obscurations of jealousy of all sentient beings. They dissolved into the secret center in the form of a green double vajra, the essence of the activity of all the buddhas. He received empowerment in all the vast buddha activities. Furthermore, a silver bell fell into his left hand: it represented the spontaneously accomplished four karmas of all the buddhas.

> *Āḥ*. Jealousy is purified into Amoghasiddhi,
> The completely pure wisdom of all-accomplishing action.
> The greater voice of the great wrathful one
> Overpowers the self-proclamation of the five poisons,
> Tames the five dark ages, subjugates them with its skillful means.
> The great powerful one, the tamer of all others,
> Conquers the great mountain of the phenomenal world.
> You who have perfected all buddha activity,
> From great billowing clouds of your peaceful compassion

Flash out the terrible thunderbolts
Which conquer the rock mountain of the pride of great sinners.

The guru who is full of attachment to rich offerings
If he is not converted by the philosophical systems of the learned,
Then his chest is filled with nothing but words!

The ruler who is full of pride,
If karma does not strike him in the face,
Then it will ripen as agony for the kingdom and people!

Like the callow youth, full of himself, the tiger of the east [a healthy young man who is brave, proud of his physical prowess],
If a real warrior does not knock him out
Then his hollow bragging will be like the roaring of a dragon.
Like a stuck-up young girl, full of pride,
If famine does not exhaust her arrogance,
Then her brash self-centeredness will be high as the sky.
Therefore in this time of the dark age
The tough guys full of black thoughts
Have disrespect for cause and effect and pile-up perverted aspirations.

Let not your compassion abandon them; liberate them into the pure lands!
Strike down the aggregates of the self with the vajra weapon.
Dissolve their consciousness into this vajra of the dharma realm.

Your warriorship is the embodiment of compassion.
Even though you do not hesitate to apply your buddha activity,
May your wrathful buddha activity be spontaneously accomplished.
karma abhiṣiñca āḥ.

Thus he received *abhiṣeka.*

All the assemblies of great, supreme wrathful deities enthroned him completely with the four empowerments. Then the divine child, Good News, himself was full of learning, good qualities, splendor, and dignity unrivaled in the world.

COLOPHON

This was the chapter on the empowerment and the chapter on the birth by magical transformation, known as "Blessings Flaming Continuously Like a Stream." It has been composed in ordinary language, easy to understand.

2

The Royal Way of Supreme Compassion

Matthew Kapstein

The reign of King Songtsen Gampo (Srong btsan sgam po, 613/14–649/50) marks the beginning of the age of Tibetan imperial power, when for some two centuries Tibet vied with China's Tang dynasty for the control of what is today northwest China. Relentlessly pursuing the expansionist policies of his father, Namri Songtsen (Gnam ri srong btsan), the lord of the small Yarlung valley, Songtsen Gampo consolidated his rule over most of the Tibetan plateau and then proceeded to move into the surrounding countries in all directions. In tandem with the growth of the empire, Songtsen Gampo concerned himself too with the problems relating to the administration of his vast territories, and so it was under his rule that the Tibetan system of writing was developed and the creation of a legal and administrative code was begun. Following the arrival of the Tang Princess Wencheng, who was certainly accompanied by her own court when she came to wed the Tibetan monarch, elements of Chinese learning began to make inroads in Tibet at this time as well. Scholars at present debate whether Buddhism was in fact adopted in Tibet under King Songtsen, but a considerable body of tradition suggests that some presence of the foreign religion was at least tolerated during his reign.

This, in brief, summarizes our rather scanty historical knowledge of Songtsen Gampo, but Tibet writers have woven around such threads a rich tapestry of legend and tradition. In many respects, Songtsen Gampo, Princess Wencheng, and the other members of the king's family and court figure in Tibetan literature and folklore much as do Arthur, Guinevere, and the Knights of the Round Table in the medieval traditions of England and France. In recent years the Chinese government has even sought to manipulate the popularity of this lore for its own ends, by promoting the notion that Tibet's modern "marriage" with China had its origins in the union of the Tibetan emperor with the Tang princess. For the Tibetans, however, King Songtsen is an enduring emblem of Tibetan sovereignty and power, a conception reinforced both by history and by legend.

Perhaps the most influential of the popular traditions connected with Songtsen

Gampo are those associated with the collection of texts called the *Maṇi Kambum* (*Maṇi Bka' 'bum*). The writings found here originated as *terma* (*gter ma*) or "treasures," texts said to have been concealed by ancient masters and rediscovered during a later age by prophetically designated "treasure-finders." Their discovery is attributed to three such persons who lived during the twelfth and thirteenth centuries, and by the fourteenth century the *Maṇi Kambum* was already in circulation in a form close to that which we have today. According to the tradition contained here, Avalokiteśvara, the bodhisattva of compassion, is the special divine protector of Tibet and in fact is to be identified with the fundamental principle of enlightenment throughout the universe as a whole. This principle, which is also the name preferred by Avalokiteśvara as he appears in the *Maṇi Kambum*, is Supreme Compassion (Skt. *Mahākāruṇika*, Tib. *Thugs rje chen po*). Supreme Compassion is the basis for love, kindness, and nurturing among all living creatures, but it is much more than a positive sentiment alone; for Supreme Compassion is none other than the open and creative power of mind or spirit, whose infinite potentialities for self-actualization constitute the very basis for creation itself. The bodhisattva Avalokiteśvara, therefore, is in effect the concrete embodiment of the abstract and unlimited principle of Supreme Compassion.

In his special relation with Tibet, Avalokiteśvara is said to have taken birth as the monkey who, having united with an ogress, became the progenitor of the Tibetan people. When the Tibetans later mature to the point at which they are receptive to the Buddha's teaching, Avalokiteśvara takes birth among them once more as none other than King Songtsen Gampo. The *Maṇi Kambum*, then, represents the collected teachings of this figure, who is at once the father of the Tibetan people, the highest spiritual principle, the bodhisattva of compassion, and the king of Tibet.

According to the *Maṇi Kambum*, the king marries two foreign princesses, the second being Tritsün (Khri btsun), daughter of the ruler of Nepal. Both princesses are themselves the emanations of goddesses, and both bring with them, as part of their dowries, sacred images of the Buddha Śākyamuni, which are installed in temples specially built to house them. The tale of the king and his brides, as it is told here, is the drama of Buddhism's introduction to Tibet. The image said to have been brought by the princess of Wencheng, and known as the Jowo or "Lord" (*Jo bo*), and the Jokhang temple constructed for it in Lhasa became Tibet's greatest center of pilgrimage, which virtually all Tibetans aspire to visit. The *Maṇi Kambum* played a crucial role in the promotion of the cult of the Jowo, and the pilgrims who flock to it find there Tibet's ancient ruler and his court always present before their eyes in the statuary of the temple itself. Text and monument together engender a uniform vision of Tibet's imperial past and its enduring spiritual presence. This perspective is strengthened in popular belief by strong associations with the living figure of the Dalai Lama, who, as a contemporary emanation of Avalokiteśvara, is also identified with King Songtsen.

The title *Maṇi Kambum* literally means the "Collected Pronouncements [concerning] Maṇi," referring here to the famous six-syllable mantra of Avalokiteśvara, *oṃ Maṇipadme hūṃ*. As early as the seventeenth century, European visitors noted the importance of this formula in Tibetan popular religion—it is often uttered aloud while a "prayer-wheel," containing the mantra written many times on a paper scroll, is turned. The recitation of the "six-syllable mantra" is indeed a ubiquitous devotional act, and even a 1992 popular song in Lhasa used it as a lyric, expressive in this modern context of a Tibetan national prayer, and hence a prayer for the Tibetan nation. The mantra is to all intents and purposes the central teaching of the *Maṇi Kambum*, as indeed its title suggests (see chapters 16 and 32).

Since the nineteenth century Western writers on Buddhism have frequently asserted that the six-syllable mantra may be translated as "Hail to the jewel in the lotus!" This expression has even become, for many, emblematic of Tibetan Buddhism as a whole. It is ironic, therefore, that not only would such a translation require that the mantra be composed in grammatically incorrect Sanskrit, but the popular Western interpretation of it is not supported by any known Indian or Tibetan sources. The Indian interpretation, known also to Tibetan scholars trained in the study of Sanskrit grammar, understands *Maṇipadme* to be a term of address for Avalokiteśvara, meaning "[possessor of] jewel and lotus," for these indeed are the objects most frequently held by the bodhisattva in his iconographic representations. *Oṃ* and *hūṃ* are purely symbolic expressions, not capable of translation, but commonly used in the formation of mantras. They are interpreted in many ways, according to context, but are generally taken as utterances bridging the gap between mundane and sacred planes of experience.

The *Maṇi Kambum*, however, is not at all interested in Sanskrit grammar and treats each of the six syllables as being purely symbolic. It elaborates literally dozens of ways of understanding their symbolism, intending that the devotee should incorporate this rich field of meaning into his or her meditations while reciting the mantra. Thus, for example, the six syllables represent the six states of being (gods, demigods, humans, animals, tormented spirits, and creatures in the hells) that Avalokiteśvara seeks to liberate through compassion; they are the six psychological poisons (pride, envy, lust, stupidity, greed, and anger) that must be pacified in meditation; they are the six basic colors (white, green, red, blue, yellow, and black) of which visual experience is constituted; and so on. The devoted religious practitioner, who will sometimes aspire to recite the six-syllable mantra one hundred million times during the course of a lifetime, by contemplating such associations thus endeavors to find Supreme Compassion permeating all possibilities of experience.

The *Maṇi Kambum* is a large work, occupying two thick volumes in most editions. It has three major sections concerned, respectively, with the legends of Avalokiteśvara and his emanation in Tibet as King Songtsen, with the rituals of Avalokiteśvara according to the "royal tradition" associated with the king, and with the ethical and meditational teachings that the king is said to have delivered. In the selections that follow, the first and third sections are represented.

The first text is drawn from a recent history of the ancient Nyingma school of Tibetan Buddhism by the late head of the school, H. H. Dudjom Rinpoche (1904–

1987). In summarizing the traditional story of Songtsen Gampo, he bases himself primarily on the accounts given at length in the *Maṇi Kambum* and includes a brief discussion of its discovery. The second and third texts are taken from the third section of the *Maṇi Kambum* itself, where they are said to be the king's teachings to his own son and daughter regarding the way of Supreme Compassion. See *Maṇi bka' 'bum: A Collection of Rediscovered Teachings* (New Delhi: Trayang and Jamyang Samten, 1975), vol. 2.

Further Reading

For a more detailed introduction to the *Maṇi Kambum*, refer to my article "Remarks on the *Maṇi bKa'-'bum* and the Cult of Avalokiteśvara in Tibet," in Steven D. Goodman and Ronald M. Davidson, eds., *Tibetan Buddhism: Reason and Revelation* (Albany: State University of New York Press, 1992). On the cult of Avalokiteśvara in the Tibetan Nyingma tradition, see Dudjom Rinpoche, Jikdrel Yeshe Dorje, *The Nyingma School of Tibetan Buddhism: Its Fundamentals and History*, vol. 1, trans. Gyurme Dorje and Matthew Kapstein (Boston: Wisdom Publications, 1991), pp. 510–12. The selection on "The Legend of King Songtsen Gampo" has been made available for the present publication, with minor editorial emendations, by permission of the translators and Wisdom Publications. The story of Songtsen Gampo's construction of temples over the supine ogress is discussed in Janet Gyatso's "Down with the Demoness: Reflections on a Feminine Ground in Tibet," in Janice D. Willis, ed., *Feminine Ground: Essays on Women and Tibet* (Ithaca: Snow Lion Publications, 1987), pp. 33–51.

The Legend of King Songtsen Gampo

There is a prophecy in the *Root Tantra of Mañjuśrī:*

> In the place called the divine land,
> Surrounded by snowy mountains,
> A king called "God among Men" will be born
> Into the Licchavi race.

The fifth hereditary monarch after Lha Totori was the religious king Songtsen Gampo, an emanation of Avalokiteśvara in the form of a mighty lord of men, who began to rule the kingdom at the age of thirteen. When he was fifteen the emanational monk Ā-kar Matiśīla brought him a self-created image of the Sublime One [Avalokiteśvara]. Then, the king commanded the religious minister Gar, an emanation of Vajrapāṇi, to invite the Nepalese princess Tritsün, an emanation of Bhṛkuṭī, and the Chinese princess of Wencheng, an emanation of Tārā, both of whom were agreeable to the people, to be his two consorts.

This he did in order to introduce two images of the Teacher, representative of the Buddha himself, which were, respectively, the size of an eight-year-old and a twelve-year-old. The princesses came to be known as the two "Lotuses of the Lake."

While the Trülnang Temple [i.e., the Jokhang, the "Cathedral of Lhasa"] was being constructed, the building-work was disrupted by nonhuman beings. Therefore, the king and his two consorts went into retreat in the palace known as Maru, at Nyangdren Phawongkha in the valley of the Kyichu. They attained accomplishment by propitiating their meditative deity, on whose advice the king built the temples to tame the borders, frontiers, and districts, which were situated on geomantic sites on the body of the supine ogress [that is, Tibet]; and so it was that he exorcised the malignant earth spirits. He then erected Trülnang and Ramoche temples and the images they housed.

Songtsen Gampo invited the master Kusara and the brahman Śaṅkara from India, the master Śīlamañju from Nepal, and the master Hoshang Mohoyen from China. With others, they translated many sections of the tripiṭaka and of the tantras and thus introduced the teaching to Tibet. Though no actual teaching or study took place, the king himself secretly gave instruction on the peaceful and wrathful forms of Supreme Compassion to many fortunate beings, who then practiced these teachings. No one was ordained [as a monk] prior to the "seven men who were tested," but it is said that there were always about a hundred long-haired yogins engaged in the practices of Supreme Compassion at Nyangdren Phawongkha. At that time the scriptures that formed the king's testament were collected and hidden in separate treasures. Later, these treasures were revealed by the accomplished master Ngödrup, Lord Nyang, and the teacher Śākya-ö. Today they are renowned as the *Collected Works of the King Concerning the Mantra "Oṃ Maṇipadme Hūṃ,"* the first Tibetan doctrinal work.

The king also sent Tönmi Sambhoṭa, an emanation of Mañjughoṣa, to India to study grammar and writing. On the basis of the Indian scripts he created the forms of the Tibetan letters, and he composed eight treatises on Tibetan grammar. Before Songsten Gampo's time there had been no proponents in the Land of Snows of a code of conduct in accord with the doctrine, but thereafter the great door of the true doctrine and of theories in accord with the doctrine was opened for the first time. The king innovated the just spiritual and temporal laws, as illustrated by the ten divine virtues and the sixteen pure human laws. In these ways, King Songtsen Gampo blessed the country of Tibet to become a prosperous and luxurious source of the true doctrine.

TWO SELECTIONS FROM THE MAṆI KAMBUM

Oṃ Maṇipadme hūṃ!

King Songstsen Gampo, who was himself an emanation of Supreme Compassion, gave these precepts to his son Kungsong Kungtsen:

Meditation upon the body of Supreme Compassion may be associated with the six bodies of enlightenment:
His *body*, endowed with the signs and attributes of the fully enlightened Buddha, is like the Sun.
It is the body of perfect spiritual rapture.
His *speech*, a union of sound and emptiness, which arises with incessant variety, is like the Moon, which has many varied reflections.
It is the emanational body.
His *mind*, abiding without change, birthless and empty, is like the sky.
It is the body of all that is real.
The *qualities* of his enlightenment, whereby he acts on behalf of living beings without interruption, are like the planets and stars.
They are the body of essential being.
His *enlightened activity*, which teaches beings throughout the three realms in accord with their particular spiritual needs, is like a panacea.
It is the body of actual awakening.
And *Supreme Compassion* itself, which remains one-pointed, without change or transformation throughout the three times, for the sake of living beings, is the vajra-like body, the body of indestructible reality.

Thus Supreme Compassion is fully endowed with the six bodies.

They are not something that is attained by meditation or practice directed to anything outside of yourself.
When you cultivate the realization that your own mind is Supreme Compassion they arise by themselves.
Thus his body, which is free from birth and death, is like a reflected image: it is free, it appears, but it is devoid of substantial existence.

Speech as Supreme Compassion is like an echo, and is incessant.
Oṃ Maṇipadme Hūṃ, the natural voice of reality, is uninterrupted:
Oṃ stills pride, purifies the heavens of the gods, and cuts off birth among them.
Ma stills jealous rage, purifies the realms of the demigods, and cuts off birth among them.
Ṇi stills lust, purifies the world of human beings, and cuts off birth among them.
Pad stills stupidity, purifies the habitats of animals, and cuts off birth among them.
Me stills greed, purifies the lands of tormented spirits, and cuts off birth among them.
Hūṃ stills hatred, purifies the hells, and cuts off birth within them.

When the six afflictions are thus stilled, and the realms of the six classes of beings thus are emptied,
You will realize that saṃsāra arises and subsides by itself.
And it is something that is not found elsewhere, but occurs when the six-syllable heart-mantra is uttered.

The mind of Supreme Compassion is clear like a mirror, free from the ideas and concepts, and endowed with the five modes of enlightened cognition.
Hence, it is pure intuitiveness that is free from conceptualization.
Because mind emerges by itself, arises by itself, it is the enlightened cognition of the foundation of all that is real.
Because it is clear and incessant, it is the enlightened cognition that is like a mirror.
Because it abides in equality, without divisions, it is the enlightened cognition of sameness.
Because it arises and subsides by itself, coming to rest at its point of origination, it is the enlightened cognition that distinguishes particulars as they arise and subside.
And because it abides as the indivisible union of clarity and emptiness, it is enlightened cognition engaged in action.
None of that is to be found elsewhere, for it emerges from mind itself and dissolves into the mind itself.
Therefore, it is enlightened cognition that is coemergent, the enlightened intention that arises and subsides by itself.

These are the precepts the king gave to his son, sixfold precepts introducing Supreme Compassion's body, speech and mind.

Oṃ Maṇipadme hūṃ!
Songtsen Gampo, the dharma-protecting king who was himself an emanation of Supreme Compassion, gave these precepts to his daughter Trompa-gyen ["the ornament of the town"]:

The *view* of Supreme Compassion is the indivisible union of appearance and emptiness and is like the sky.
External appearances, the incessant appearing of whatever may be, is nonetheless the appearance of mind, which appears by itself. The essential character of mind is that it is empty.
And the essential character of appearance is that it is empty in being apparent, but without substantial existence.

The *meditation* of Supreme Compassion is the indivisible union of clarity and emptiness and is like a rainbow appearing in the sky.
You must cultivate the realization that the essential character of mind,

which is clear and unobscured, and which emerges by itself, arises by itself, is that it is empty.

The *action* of Supreme Compassion is the indivisible union of awareness and emptiness and is like the sun rising in the sky.
Action is freedom from hankering after whatever there is that arises incessantly in mind, whose nature is pure awareness.
Though you act, you act in emptiness, not grasping at entities as real.

The *fruit* of Supreme Compassion is the indivisible union of bliss and emptiness.
Mind itself, without contrivances, is blissful within the expanse that is the foundation of all that is real.
Being empty and free from grasping, it is like the moon reflected in water.
Being free from all superimposed limits, it is without features that serve to define it.
And because it has forever abided within you, it cannot be achieved.

The *spiritual commitment* of Supreme Compassion
Is emptiness of which the core is compassion.
Its characteristic being just that,
You will grasp all living beings in all three realms
With unqualified compassion.
Being equal, you will act without "levels."

The *enlightened activity* of Supreme Compassion
Grasps beings with a snare of compassion in which
Buddhas and sentient beings are no different.
It slaughters their pain with the weapon of emptiness,
And draws sentient beings to the level of bliss supreme.

These are the precepts he gave to his daughter, six precepts introducing Supreme Compassion.

3

A Tribal History

Robin Kornman

The *History of the Goloks* appears in the autobiography of the nineteenth-century master of meditation, Do Khyentse (Mdo mkhyen brtse ye shes rdo rje). In theory, this text is a history of the family lineage of Do Khyentse, a reincarnation of the famous Nyingma teacher, poet, philosopher, and text-revealer Jigme Lingpa ('Jigs med gling pa, 1730–1798, see chapter 22); but actually it is the fabulous story of the development of his tribe, the Golok, from their mythical origins to the magical birth of Do Khyentse himself. We begin with the story of a short-term marriage between the daughter of a mountain god and a particularly inept human being, the first Golok. The narrative style used to describe their misadventures is pithy, informal, and quite humorous. Much of the humor comes from the fact that Khyentse Rinpoche has written this passage in the earthy Golok dialect of Tibetan—giving the story an informal, at times highly colloquial tone—quite different from typical, elegant, classical Buddhist prose. It is interesting to note the particular tribal origins of such a learned teacher, connected, as he is, with a subtle philosopher like Jigme Lingpa, for the Golok were and are still today a rough, extremely proud ethnic group who live and fight in their mountain country. They are lovers of songs and epics like the Gesar of Ling story, and one of Do Khyentse's special points in telling *The History of the Goloks* is to show the natural relationship that exists between the origins of the Golok tribe and the hybrid religious world of the Gesar epic (see chapter 1). The *History* thus consciously combines the Indic teachings of philosophical Buddhism with themes from native Tibetan religion.

The Goloks are a fascinating people, notorious for their aggressiveness and fierce independence, who inhabit a sparsely populated territory of eastern Tibet. Located at the heart of the territory that they control lies the mountain range of Magyel Pomra (Rma rgyal spom ra), also known as Amnye Machen. As both an imposing mountain and a powerful deity, Magyel Pomra is second only to Nyenchen Thanglha in importance as a mountain deity of Tibet (see chapter 24). Magyel Pomra also acquires special significance from his association in the Gesar of Ling epic as the site where Gesar's magical weapons and the marvelous war implements destined for his warriors of Ling were all buried; Gesar is said to have left his miraculous sword behind, and local legends claim it is still buried in Magyel Pomra, making the mountain a source of power for the Golok.

J.F. Rock, an American scientist who spent many years living in the region during the late nineteenth century, explored as much of the Golok region as he could safely visit before writing his fascinating monograph on the Amnye Machen range. In characterizing this rough nomadic group, he tells stories that one hears quite often when discussing the Golok with other Tibetans, reminding us of the cowboys of the Wild West:

> Although murder was said to be outlawed within the sanctuary of the Am-nye Machen, the Go-log attack anyone approaching the region west of the Yellow River. They acknowledge no one's authority except that of their chiefs, and as the Shing-bzah incarnation told us their word could not be trusted. They enjoy attacking anyone, especially foreigners who penetrate their mountain fastness. They have always been thus, and will probably remain so. . . . Their life is spent on horseback, always ready for battle and even among themselves they squabble to the point of combat.
>
> . . . I quote a speech made by a Go-log: "You cannot compare us Go-log with other people. You obey the laws of strangers, the laws of the Dalai Lama, of China, and of any of your petty chiefs. You are afraid of everyone; to escape punishment you obey everyone. And the result is that you are afraid of everything. And not only you, but your fathers and grandfathers were the same. We Go-log, on the other hand, have from time immemorial obeyed none but our own laws, none but our own convictions. A Go-log is born with the knowledge of his freedom, and with his mother's milk imbibes some acquaintance with his laws. They have never been altered. Almost in his mother's womb he learns to handle arms. His forebears were warriors—they were brave fearless men, even as we today are their worthy descendants. To the advice of a stranger we will not hearken, nor will we obey aught but the voice of our conscience with which each Go-log enters the world. This is why we have ever been free as now, and are the slaves of none—neither of Bogdokhan nor of the Dalai Lama. Our tribe is the most respected and mighty in Tibet, and we rightly look down with contempt on both Chinaman and Tibetan."

Even today, under the rule of the People's Republic of China, the area around Machen Pomra is still a dangerous place to travel, and the Golok people are considered a problematic presence.

According to the chronicle excerpted here, at the time of its founding the Golok region was a thinly populated, mountainous district, only gradually settled by human beings. When humans first arrived, they discovered that the territory had been inhabited since time immemorial by a society of deities, who had their own politics and a form of social organization associated with the physical structure of the land. Each district was thought to belong to a lord or proprietor, who is the god of that land. These deities are called "earth lords" (*sa bdag*), "ground lords" (*gzhi bdag*), "place lords" (*gnas bdag*), or sometimes just "the lord" (*bdag po*). They are of various "races" (*rig pa*) or types of beings. For example, Nyenchen Thanglha is said to be of the "race" of the "cannibal demons," the *rākṣasas* of Indian storytelling and epic traditions, but here it simply means "intelligent and fanged monsters." Each earth lord is thought to have sovereignty over a certain amount of territory, extending out from a center where he dwells when he is in the ordinary world of humanity. This center is called his "gateway," which leads to another divine realm where the god truly dwells. Buddhist and native Tibetan liturgies refer to these realms as "palaces." In this account we actually see the interior of one of these palaces described, when the future mother of Do Khyentse is kidnapped by gods. From this description we learn that the true home of the gods is a separate realm, where spatial and temporal relationships are profoundly altered.

Most of the gods in this account are "wrathful," meaning that they appear in an angry, martial manner, wearing ornaments of bone and human skin, with fierce features, long fangs, and talons. In the language of Buddhist iconography, "wrathful" is a technical term, indicating how the gods are depicted, in distinction to the other two iconographic categories of "peaceful" and "semiwrathful." Often the wrathful aspect is interpreted philosophically as representing the principle of transmutation, while the peaceful aspect would represent the serene state of enlightenment. In this text, however, we see the special jargon of tantric Buddhism used colloquially in a social context to tell a story, and the technical vocabulary takes on a more direct, less alchemical meaning. Here, if the deities should appear to the characters in their peaceful form, it is not because they are manifesting the fundamentally serene nature of their enlightenment, but because they "have made friends" with humans or have "promised to be friendly."

Similarly, the gods are wrathful not in the symbolic sense, but in the conventional meaning of the word: they are irascible and easily angered. They tend to regard human beings as invaders of their land and become infuriated by what we would regard as ritual pollution. For example, at one point in the narrative the father of the saint-to-be considers moving to Yutse but then decides against it because Yutse is a sensitive and reactive land (*phug thog shor ba*). There, a person could all too easily make a mistake and harm the local spirits of the soil, for example, by urinating in the wrong place (and "pissing them off," as we might say), or by inadvertently moving a stone that is the power spot of a dragon (*nāga*), or by polluting the atmosphere while cooking rotten meat and sending out stinking, impure smoke. Any such actions might infuriate the local deities and attract catastrophe, illness, and death. In short, the deities have their own organic approach to ecology, if you will.

A word should be said about the *nāgas*, or dragons, which are very important mythical beings in Inner Asian religious lore. They usually do not appear in an actual snakelike form, as Indian nāgas do, but they may appear in any number of manifestations, often marked by signs of the water element. For example, in this story there is a boy in the second generation of Goloks, whose father is the first Golok man but whose mother is from the race of gods. Periodically, this boy is favored by a *nāgi*, a dragoness, who arises out of the lake to offer him gifts of wealth, blessings, and prophecies. She appears as a woman with blue-green hair and feeds him milk, the very substance used as an offering to propitiate the nāgas themselves. Like serpent spirits throughout the world, the nāgas are possessors of great wealth. To high lamas they give secret Buddhist texts they have held in trust at the bottom of the ocean or in their mountain lakes. To the nomads in this story the nāgas give gifts of wealth, specifically horses and cattle and the valued domestic property of a Tibetan encampment.

In the beginning of the story the first Golok man allies himself with gods who also appear in the great Tibetan national epic, *The Gesar of Ling*. These are the local deities of a certain region of eastern Tibet, the home of the shamanic hero Gesar. The *History* shows them to us in peculiar detail—in effect, we see the daily life of the local gods. Like humans, they are constantly engaged in territorial conflicts; like humans, they have marriages and the usual contractual agreements that accompany family unions; and, like humans, they must periodically go to war. The gods also interfere in human life in a particular way. They are specifically responsible for the origin and creation of each of the great tribes of Tibet, for like the Homeric heroes, the founders of tribal states are generally sons or daughters of local gods. Khyentse takes advantage of this fact to retell a story that refurbishes his Buddhist birth mythology in non-Buddhist ethnic particulars.

Khyentse's ethnicity is expressed in four aspects of the historical narrative: the gods are local rather than Indian Buddhist; the efficacy of religious practice is based on the dynamic of native Tibetan rituals rather than Buddhist contemplative practice; the ancestors are favored by providence and because of their compacts with local deities, not because of their Buddhist virtue; and finally, the liturgical performances described here come from the rituals and songs of epic bards, not from the Buddhist religion. Laid over the surface of these core native Tibetan elements is a veneer of Buddhist mythology, which accounts for all the various divine couplings as part of an overall plan to tame or convert Tibet to Buddhism, a plan initiated by Padmasambhava. The saint's magical rebirth is regarded as part of Padmasambhava's program to return his original disciples continually to Tibet as incarnations, so that they may propagate the subtle practices of Buddhism there.

One of the most interesting episodes of the narrative occurs during the pilgrimage of the Golok villagers from eastern Tibet to Lhasa in central Tibet, when we are given a picture of the religion of the people who live around Magyel Pomra. The description is filled with humor, for we see the villagers' naive beliefs and their quarreling, as they respond in ignorance to every miraculous foreshadowing of the coming birth of the saint. The pilgrims have two primary aims motivating their visit: to increase their merit by paying homage to the famous shrines in Lhasa, and to increase their good fortune by receiving the blessings of famous lamas. The lamas may be celebrated Buddhists, but within the framework of this narrative their powers are really little different from those of village shamans. For example, the pilgrims attend an audience with the eighth Dalai Lama, Jampel

Gyatso ('Jam dpal rgya mtsho, 1758–1804), who remains somewhat anonymous and mysterious. All we know of him is that he can see the true nature of Do Khyentse's holy mother, that she is a reincarnation of a goddess. He singles her out in a crowd of what must be thousands of peasants paying their respects and gives her a magical statue made of herbs. His aim is to create a "connection," so that he may have the "good fortune" to be reborn in her womb in his next incarnation.

The terms "connection" (*'brel pa*) and "good fortune" (*rten 'brel*) play an important role in Tibetan Buddhist popular religion. Both are technical terms used in Buddhist philosophy and psychology to indicate the presence of a karmic link and to describe the chain of cause and effect, respectively. But in this literature the terms have less philosophical import and more of a magical and ritualistic flavor. "Good fortune" applies to the auspicious events that happen to a person seemingly by magical coincidence. For example, if a person committed virtuous acts in a previous lifetime, their karma might make them wealthy in this one, although being so may seem effortless, resulting from an accident of birth or just plain luck. The word "connection" takes on a related meaning, often associated with notions of ritual purity and taboo. If a person has a connection with a saint in one lifetime, this creates the good fortune for them to be reborn near this saint in the next lifetime. In some Tibetan literature reminiscent of the inferno scene of Dante's *Divine Comedy*, there are depictions of Buddhist lamas and saints traveling through the hell realms, surrounded by the damned beings who had some previous connection with them. The lamas walk through hell, gather those with connections, and lead them out, which is referred to as the damned beings' "good fortune." In this way the abstruse Buddhist doctrine of karma and the chain of causal events is absorbed into the magical principles of practical religion (see chapter 32).

In the episode in which the Dalai Lama interacts with the holy mother, he recognizes that she is a pure vessel into which he may be reborn, for she has a divine nature. If she were just an ordinary person she would not be able to "sustain" his merit, and the reincarnated child would die. Tibetans believe that in order to assure the success of an emanated lama's rebirth, it is imperative that the mother be kept pure and clean. Even if she touches another person who is polluted, she will become ill because of her own purity and that of the child within her. If she has a connection with anything touched by the hand or mouth of an impure person, she will suffer. When the Dalai Lama gives her his little statue, then, her touching of it should create the positive connection. But inadvertently it is passed from hand to hand and so is touched by a "great sinner" and thus becomes impure. The connection is broken, and the lama loses the auspicious coincidence or good fortune to be reborn in her womb.

There are other requirements for the rebirth of an emanation or *tulku* (*sprul sku*). After the mother has been impregnated, the parents travel from country to country, seeking a land conducive to the birth of a *tulku*. There are countries that "cannot support" such a child, lands that would not be suitable or conducive to the upbringing of such an enlightened being. The baby would die if he were raised in such an impure environment. This message will be brought to the parents several times. It is a general belief of Tibetan Buddhists that *tulkus*, reincarnations of great lamas, must have very special families or else they will suffer irreversible mental and physical injuries in their childhoods. If they are not placed in an environment suitable for the study and practice of religion, they may go mad or die.

The assimilation of these Buddhist terms to a native context is a sign of the power of the narrative tradition in which it participates. Here we see not the assimilation of local tales into Buddhist philosophy, but the reverse assimilation of Buddhist teachings into indigenous beliefs. Notice, for example, that the prevalent ceremonies in this text are juniper smoke purifications (*lha sangs*) and offerings to the nāgas. At the time of Rainbow Body Vajra's (Do Khyentse's) birth, an invisible shrine is constructed on which offerings are made to the retinue of gods who attend the birth. It is not a Buddhist altar, however, but the special furnace used for the performance of incense offerings. The deities are described as wearing armor and blue silks in the fashion of the Tibetan martial spirits called "war gods" (*dgra lha*, see chapter 26). Like the war gods, these deities sing about the excellence of weapons and horses, not about Buddhist themes like the six perfections of the bodhisattva path. And most interestingly, the actual birth of the Buddhist saint is heralded not by Buddhist gods and bodhisattvas, but by troops of invisible bards chanting epics and wearing their special Gesar hats. The child is bathed just as the Buddha was bathed at his birth, but not in pure sanctified water; rather, he is bathed in a mixture of milk and water, one of the ritual materials offered in the native ritual fumigations. The practice of Buddhism is almost never separate from the worship or propitiation of local deities, but here the text is structured to place local gods in the foreground.

The native beliefs about the nature of divine forces require some commentary. Native Tibetan deities are sometimes called "the eight classes of gods" (*lha sde brgyad*). These include a famous triad: gods (*lha*), mountain spirits (*gnyan*, pronounced *nyen*) and dragons (*klu*, pronounced *lu*). The *lha* rule in the bright spaces of the sky and the tops of mountains. The *nyen* are the mountains themselves and the land. The *lu* or serpents inhabit bodies of water, clouds, and anything associated with water: wells, rivers, etc. These three classes of deities roughly match the ancient Chinese division of the world into heaven, earth, and humanity.

Magical creatures can give humans gifts of power and wealth, as in the *lha* and *nyen*, or they can cause illness, as when the serpents turn against one. A person possessed fully of the blessings and health that come from the gods is said to be "full of splendor" (*gzi brjid can*). This splendor, majesty, or, as it is pronounced in Tibetan, *ziji* is an actual radiant force that envelopes a healthy and prosperous being, whether god or man.

All of this is, of course, subordinate in theory to the highlight of the narrative, which is that the birth of Do Khyentse is an aspect of the ancient machinations of the founder of tantra in Tibet, Padmasambhava. Do Khyentse is a being of such vast wisdom and meditation power that he is called by many names. Sometimes he is called Rainbow Body Vajra, a name that refers to a sign of supreme accomplishment he can exhibit, which is that at the time of death his body does not undergo earthly corruption but slowly dissolves into a rainbow. A less beautiful image comes to mind with his name "the blood-drinking Heruka." This gruesome name is actually tantric code language, for there are wrathful buddhas called Herukas who represent the ability of enlightened beings to drink the blood of ego and thus destroy its essence.

But despite all this Buddhist jargon, the imagery that surrounds his birth is native to the Central Asian steppes rather than to India, and the long story of the development of his tribe, the Golok, makes this Buddhist saint into a native cultural hero. The fact that a great Tibetan philosopher, Do Khyentse, was willing to show this connection in his life story illustrates the reverence for local traditions that is part of Buddhism as it is actually practiced in Central and Inner Asia.

The translation is from Mdo mkhyen brtse ye shes rdo rje, *Rig 'dzin 'Jigs med gliṅ pa'i yan srid Snags 'chan 'Ja' lus rdo rje'i rnam thar* (*The autobiography of the knowledge holder Jigme Lingpa's later existence, the mantra-holder Rainbow Body Vajra*) (Gangtok: Dodrup Chen Rimpoche, 1974).

Further Reading

On the Golok people, see Joseph F. Rock's study *The Amnye Ma-Chhen Range and Adjacent Regions* (Rome: Istituto Italiano per il medio ed estreme oriente, 1956). For more historical material on Do Khyentse and his lineage, see, Tulku Thondup, *Masters of Meditation and Miracles* (Boston: Shambala Publications, 1996), and Dudjom Rinpoche, *The Nyingma School of Tibetan Buddhism* (Wisdom Publications, 1991). Two well-illustrated paperbacks give short biographies and icongraphic representations of Jigme Lingpa and the Khyentse incarnations: *Crystal Mirror VI: Indian and Tibetan Masters*, and *Crystal Mirror XI: Masters of the Ning*. They contain biographies of the great Nyingma gurus (Berkeley: Dharma Publishing).

History of the Goloks, from the Autobiography of Do Khyentse Yeshe Dorje

As for the great wisdom holder Jigme Lingpa ('Jigs med gling pa), he belongs to the lineage of the lord of secrets Garab Dorje, and he is an emanation and manifestation of Mañjuśrī, as well as an aspect of the play of the dharma king Tri Songdetsen (Khri srong lde btsan), who manifested in every lifetime only as a treasure finder, the last of the thirteen prophesied in the *Dgongs 'dus lung bston bka' rgya ma* (*The Confidential Prophecy of the Gong du*).

Now in this life, what was his race, his tribe, his maternal lineage, and so on? He was from the place known as Golok. It is the practice place of the buddhas of the eight great Heruka sādhanas, the practices of the eight logoi, a place blessed by Vajravārāhī, the place where the great master Padmasambhava practiced for six months and visited seven times. The lord of that place always maintained a powerful, black, wrathful form. His name was Nyenchen Thöpa Tsel (Gnyan chen thod pa rtsal). He was a great being of the tenth level [of the bodhisattva path]. He was always accompanied by his great consort, a goddess, a serpentess, and a lady mountain spirit (*gnyan*), these four, as well as his retinue of sons, his emanations, and the emanations of his emanations—a numberless retinue!

In that place there are eight great outer lakes. Among them are the upper and lower Blue Lakes, one known as the Lake of the Gods (*lha*) and one known as the Lake of the Devils. Near the upper lake there is a white boulder shaped like a crouching tiger, which is the great gateway of the chief earth spirit (*zo dor*).

Once a man unsurpassed in his skill at archery came up to the place of that mountain spirit and stayed there. His name was Longchen Thar (Klong chen thar, "Great Space Freedom"). One day while he was living there he saw two water buffaloes come out of the upper and lower lakes and start fighting with each other. They fought and fought—they did nothing but fight.

That evening the man slept next to the white boulder, and he dreamt that a white man riding a white horse came up to him and said, "Where do you come from?"

"I come from Upper Ngari," he said.

"What is your name?"

"Longchen Thar."

"What abilities do you have?"

"I am an archer of great power and ability," he said.

"Well then, listen! Tomorrow two bull yaks will leave the upper and lower lakes and will fight each other. The upper one is the life substance (*bla*) of the gods. [The *la* (*bla*) is a kind of soul that all people possess. When it leaves the body, death soon follows, for it is responsible for the life principle.] The one that comes out of the lower lake is none other than the life substance of the devils. If you pierce him and cut off his life, we gods will win and those devils will be defeated. You and I will become close friends, and we, the gods, will completely fulfill all your desires." With these words the god gave his promise.

But [on the following day], when two oxen emerged from the lakes and fought, their shapes were so similar that the man could not figure out which ox to slay. He stayed there all day but could not shoot his arrow. That evening the man on a white horse came and said, "Why did you not shoot the arrow?"

He answered, "I couldn't tell one ox from the other, they were so much alike."

"Well then, tomorrow there will be a mark on my life substance so that you can recognize it. Be alert! We will fulfill your every desire," he said and then left.

The next morning, once again the oxen fought. However, this time, after looking very carefully, the man saw that one of them had a brightly shining mirror hanging from among its nape hairs. He aimed straight at the heart of the other one who had no mirror and pierced him with an arrow. That ox jumped into the lower lake and disappeared. The water of the lake was stained with red blood and the hills, rocks, lake, and trees from the upper part of the valley all cried out, "*Ki ki so so*, the gods are victorious!" The sound of the victory cries was great enough to shake the earth. But everything in the lower part of the valley was full of groans and awful sounds.

That evening the same man came and said, "Now the white gods are victorious and the black devils are defeated—our wishes have been fulfilled! We will repay your kindness! Tomorrow morning at the foot of this boulder some kind of frightening animal will appear. [You must touch it!] The best way would be [to touch it] with your hand; the next best way would be to stroke it with the feathers of your arrow; the last and worst way would be to throw two handfuls of sand on its body." He said this and left.

The next morning when the sun rose, from the top of the boulder came a divine white yak, a frightening [sight], with its mouth open and its tongue sticking out into space and moving about. Steam issued from its mouth and piled up into clouds of mist. Its hooves pounded the boulder to rubble. The man was so frightened he could not even look at the creature, and he remained frozen that way, until finally it disappeared into the lake.

That evening the friendly deity came just as before: "You weren't much of a man, were you? But tomorrow another creature will come. Don't be afraid! All you need do is to act as I told you last time." He said this and left.

The next morning at dawn, from the top of the boulder appeared a fearful tigress, her mouth wide open, her eyes bulging, her fangs clenched. Her claws reduced the stones to rubble, and she crouched, as though ready to leap fiercely. The man was petrified with fear and remained that way, not daring to move, until the beast finally disappeared into the lake.

That evening the friendly deity came just as before. "You're the kind of blunderer who has exhausted his merit! Where is there another man like you who can't get anything done? It's really hard for us on our end to help you!"

The man said, "Now you're not going to keep your promise!"

"I'm not breaking my promise—it's you who can't perform! The divine yak who came the day before yesterday was my younger daughter, the goddess Luminous Glory Lady. Others have begged for her hand in marriage, but all have been rejected. She is superior to all others and therefore, if you had won her, your family lineage would have gained great merit in the dharma and would have certainly produced an uncorrupted line of wisdom holders descending through the family line. They would have subdued India and Tibet and their greatness and fame would have spread all across those lands. But you missed your chance for this good fortune!

"The tiger who appeared today was of the race of mountain spirits (*nyen*), named Merit Glorious Treasure. She is my middle daughter. There have been suitors and I have given her hand in marriage. If you had attained her, the religious rite that confers empowerment on your family lineage would have taken place; or you would have attained prosperity, might, glory, and the respect of all. But you missed your chance for that good fortune, too!

"Now there is my oldest daughter, Brilliant Superb Victorious Over Enemies. Although I have her, it has been decided to give her in marriage to Magyel Pomra. Nevertheless, I will allow her to be given to you once!

"We have been trying to help you for some time, but it is hard. When you win her, this is what you will receive: your family lineage will always thirst for sin; their work will be war and all sorts of thievery; they will make their living off the wealth and prosperity of others and only that way; they will kill living creatures and diligently strip the carcasses, taking the meat and red blood. As long as your human lineage lasts, you will never be dominated by others and your heads will never be lowered. This is the last good fortune I can grant to you!

"However, if tomorrow morning you cannot show your courage, there is nothing more I can do for you. In that case, leave this place in peace and find another country. I will give you as many cattle as you can take with you." He said this and left.

Next morning at sunrise, once again there came from the top of the boulder a fearful crocodile, its mouth yawning open, its eyes bulging, and its tongue sticking out. The man was not brave enough to rub it with his hand or with the arrow feathers, but he did manage to throw a handful of sand toward the creature's tail. In a moment it transformed into a lovely and charming woman, dressed in silken clothes with precious jewels, who offered her help and friendship.

Three days later the girl said, "Go today to the upper part of the valley. There is a little lake there. By its shores is my dowry, some of my herds. Drive the sheep down here!"

So he set out [to the lake and found the flock], and herding about a hundred head of sheep with different colors of wool, he came back down the valley. By the time he had arrived on the banks of Sky Lake it was already night. He found a fine yak hair tent set up and inside were all the property and belongings of a home. All the property and excellent wealth had been set up and neatly arranged.

He asked, "Where did we get all this stuff?"

"My brother brought it," she said.

"Is your brother the same as my friend from yesterday?" he asked.

"It's possible!" she said.

From then on, the two prospered together in comfort and happiness and sported together all the time. They had a male child. When he was a year old the wife said, "Now we have been friends for three years. All that time our life has been full of comfort and joy. Our son is one year old and we have never had a birthday celebration. Three days from tomorrow, let's have a big party, and we can present a huge offering for the family of his maternal uncle." The husband thought this was an excellent idea.

The woman said, "Sleep comfortably this evening—I will make all the preparations." In the middle of the night, many people and animals of all sorts assembled there. They bustled about, performing juniper smoke offerings and making ritual cakes for offerings. They butchered animals for food offerings, stripping away the meat and draining the blood. They made inconceivably vast offerings. They set out hundreds of thousands of ritual cakes as offerings to the nāgas and to various other deities. From moment to moment the offerings were enjoyed by countless troops of gods, mountain spirits, and serpents such as had never been seen before. After all of them had gone back to their own places, there remained the white man on his white horse.

"Hey, friend! Your wife, as I told you before, is the elder daughter of the king of the mountain spirits, and she was given to Magyel Pomra. Three days from now, he will come in all his power to take her back. At that time, do not look over at your son, your cattle, or any of your wealth. Just hold onto this girl with your left hand, hold this sword aloft in space with your right hand, and say these words: 'I am Great Space Freedom Victory Banner. The name of this sword is Resistless Blazing Blade. No one will take from me the woman whom I have found on this ground!' Say this, expand your bravery, and remain that way. They will not take your woman. You will once again be surrounded by everything—your son and your wealth." He said this and disappeared.

Three days later, a black cloud moved in from the north, sending forth a terrifying screaming sound. Terrible bolts of red lightning and stones rained down, and there were various frightening manifestations. The wife said, "The troops of Magyel Pomra are coming! Now whatever happens today depends on you!"

He seized his wife and held on to her tightly, just the way his friend had told him. He gripped his sword pommel and stood his ground. The tent, his possessions, his flocks—all were carried away by a mist and a wind. Nevertheless, he held his ground fearlessly. For a moment his son was also lifted by the wind. Then the man's heart was tortured by an unbearable sense of poverty, so he left his wife and ran quickly to grab his little boy. The moment he seized him, the howling and roaring, great red wind and the fog mixed together, enveloped his wife, and carried her away. Father, son, and sword—only these three were left. For three days they remained there in misery, unlike that ever experienced by anyone else.

Finally, he went back to the foot of the boulder and stayed there. Eventually two riders came. One was riding a supreme steed Turquoise Mane. He was a [*rākṣasa* and a] warrior of indescribable splendor. The other was the white man on the white horse. He said, "Soulless being, your spinning head is distracted and deceived! When you don't heed the commands I utter, your action and activities will be carried away by the wind just in this way. I've come here to take a look at my nephew; you just do whatever you like."

Since he now had neither wife, property, nor cattle, he thought they had come to steal away his son as well. He cowered there in fear. Then out of the lake there came a woman with turquoise locks of hair. She took the child in her arms and then poured out for him a small cup of milk, saying, "I pity the poor motherless little boy. I must give him a tiny portion of my wealth." She then leapt back into the lake.

The *rākṣasa* said, "Little child, [you are unlucky]. You lack merit in both dharma and wealth. Not only that, but since you are motherless, you also lack the good merit of a comfortable and happy life. May you be brave, skillful, and penetrating in your actions! Until the end of your family lineage, may your personal power and independence be great, and may your head never be lower than others!" Saying this he stroked his head.

To the father he said, "Even though you are a blundering idiot, since I have become your friend, I have no choice but to remain your boon friend. Therefore, I have no choice but to take revenge on Pomra for what he has done to you." He took back the sword and thrust it into the sheath at his waist. Mounting the horse, he disappeared. His earlier friend remained there before him. The man asked, "Who was that splendid man who was just here?"

"That was the *rākṣasa* Thöpa Tsel."

"Are you his son?"

"Oh no! How could that be? You mustn't talk like that. I am the inner minister godling Nyur Khyog. Now, return to your own bed and stay there. The child's portion of the wealth will arrive then." That evening he slept at home. The next morning when he awoke from his dream there was the little tent with all his things in it: the domestic utensils and provisions and the fifty head of sheep.

Then they went up and lived between the two lakes for three years. One day, when the boy was five years old, he was playing around the upper lake. Out of the lake came the blue woman who had appeared before. "Little boy, your horses are in the village over yonder. I confer on you the name Patsel Boom (Dpa' rtsal 'bum, Brave Power Myriads)."

The child said, "Did you say Patar Boom (Dpa' thar 'bum, Brave Freedom Myriads)?"

"No, and since you mispronounced your name, your merit will be small and your wealth nonexistent. Although your descendants will be brave (*dpa'*), if you always run away, you will be free (*thar*) from harm. Give them exactly the same name as yourself." She said this and disappeared into the lake.

The little boy went back down and said, "Father, I was wandering around that lake over there and met the blue lady again. She gave me the name Pathar

Bum. And my portion of horses is over in that village." His old father replied, "The day before yesterday [*sic*] when the troops of Magyel Pomra came, I was as brave (*dpa'*) as a man need be. If you are brave enough you will be called brave; if you are free enough you will be called free."

Then father and son went down into the village to see what was there. Near the white stone was a small blue horse wearing a saddle, blanket, and so forth. And there was the sword and panoply of a warrior. The old father began to perform sacred dances, crying out, "O great, O great, my young boy, all your wishes have been fulfilled!" Since that day that valley has been called "O Great" (O bzang). There at O Great Valley the father and son lived for several years, and the son became even braver and more effective in his skills.

There was a woman from the region around Nyarong named Iron Lady. She had been stolen away and taken off by the power of an earth lord [*sa bdag*, a kind of local spirit attached to a specific locality]. Now she had come to that place where the young man lived. The two met, and by the power of karma through the desire connection they fell in love. They became man and wife and settled in Upper Ma Thama. A boy was born, pleasing his grandfather, who said, "The land here is happy and with my grandson I am even more happy. Therefore I name this land Happy Valley (*dga' mdo*)."

When the little boy grew older, he first settled in a place called the Valley of Mar. The mountain valleys there were all under the control of All Glorious Shul, so the couple became subjects of Glorious Shul. After a while, however, all the tribes and people in the highlands there were gradually brought under the control of the young man. [Finally] even Glorious Shul could not hold his own seat and had to flee to Kha Khog. Since the one who bowed his head became himself the head [chief], the son of Iron Lady was given the name Golok, which means "Switch Heads."

He had three sons: the oldest was Great Power Myriads (Dbang chen 'bum), the middle one was Lotus Myriads (Padma 'bum), and the youngest one was A Kyong Myriads. They settled in Upper, Middle, and Lower Mar Valley, respectively. Their descendants spent all their time in war, banditry, stealing, and so on—only unvirtuous activities. This was all they did. . . .

In the fifth generation the father was Dharma Wheel Merit Benefit. Now, there was once a woman named Arrow of Praise who was famous for having descended from a Tsen spirit [*btsan*, gods who inhabit the sides of mountains and are often the gods of impressive boulders, usually red in color. In the iconography they appear in copper-colored armor]. Her youngest daughter, Garza (Mgar za), was different from other women: during her menstrual period, milk flowed out instead of blood. She had all sorts of different visions and dreams. Her daughter was named Life Power Maid (Tshe dbang sman), and Life Power Maid married Dharma Wheel Merit.

Once they [decided to] go on pilgrimage, and so they set out on the lengthy journey to Lhasa, in order to perform prostrations [there]. One day while they were there [in Lhasa], they approached the statue of the One Mother Glorious

Goddess (Ma gcig dpal lha). Out of the statue came two women, who grabbed Life Power Maid from among the large crowd there. A door appeared on the right side of the statue, which opened, and she was actually taken through it. Her senses became intoxicated and confused. She felt as if she were traveling down a long road, finally coming to the door of a miraculous palace. Held between the two women, she was taken inside, and they climbed a crystal staircase. Inside there was a vast court filled with many beings—some human, others with human bodies but with various nonhuman heads. Some were dancing. Some turned their faces away when they saw her. Some of them withdrew far away. Some hid to the side.

She asked the two ladies what these people were. The two women answered, "These are the retinue of the Great King. They are of the race of the gods, and they are playing and sporting. Some are of the race of mountain spirits and some are dragons. Most of them are poisonous and you could be harmed merely by seeing them, touching them, or through the poisonous vapor of their breath. So, out of fear that they might harm you, they went into a corner."

They continued on and came to a little door on the side. It opened and they told her, "You go in and stay there."

When she went in, two little boys led her upward. There she found a handsome, effulgent, youthful prince sitting on brocade cushions on top of a jeweled throne. He was clothed in brocade clothes and wore a silken head ornament and was adorned with many jewel ornaments. He said, "Come up, woman. You are not tired, are you? You used to live here and you were one of my lovers. Once, for certain reasons, you had to be reborn in eastern Tibet [Kham]. There is a reason that we have now met again."

He had her seated before him and offered her food and drink. In her visionary experience it seemed that they spent a whole night together in joy and pleasure. The next day that great being placed an excellent silk scarf on her neck: "I am the son of Zurpü ngapa—the divine child widely known as Godling Conchshell Topknot. You and I have a karmic connection from a previous life. In this life, through the play of Padmasambhava's buddha activity, you have entered into a womb. But actually, I am the son of a mountain spirit of the race of gods, and you are the flesh-eating ḍākinī."

When they were sporting in great bliss, during the union of the essence drops of the red and white elements [the sperm and the egg], Rainbow Body Vajra ('Ja' lus rdo rje), Do Khyentse, took birth in a body of flesh and blood.

"In the future may he blaze above the hosts of demons and dominate them," he said. Then the same two women as before came in and said, "Now you go back home!" That great being [the divine king] went so far as actually to escort her for three steps and took her before the door to the hall. He said, "In the future, when your time in the land of human beings has come to an end, return here."

She herself did not want to go for she was quite attached to him, but there was nothing she could do, and so she went out. There a blue woman arose and said [addressing the child in her belly]:

I am the mother of all your cycles of lives.
Child, in the space of the wisdom of awareness
You have been playing in complete enjoyment of great bliss.

That the time has come for you to benefit beings
Has been signaled by the sign ḍākinīs of space [wisdom ḍākinīs].
I will always help you.

She placed a white scarf around the woman's neck. Above Life Power Maid a little window opened in the wall, and out of it leaned a man full of splendor. He looked down and strew flowers on her, saying:

Once Lord Padma confirmed him
As the lord of the life force of the whole world:
In the future, at the end of the aeon,
He would take rebirth in a womb to perform benefit through various skillful means.
At that time I proclaimed and promised that I would function as his servant.
Now the time has finally come: it is marvelous, wondrous indeed!

Even if he does not offer to me, I will not be idle to protect him.
And even if he does not command me, I will still act for him.
I proclaim this: I will not break my promise! *Samaya* [let my oath be sealed!]
May the garden of the teachings flourish in Lower Do Kham [northeastern Tibet].
It is in the region of Rong where he will benefit beings, his disciples.
And ultimately he will be active in the field of disciples of Maha China.
May his life and activities be completely fulfilled!

He said this and closed the little window.

A woman with a dark brown body full of splendor placed a white scarf around her neck and said, "*A la la ho! Oṃ svasti*"; then, smiling, she went inside.

The two women took her between them and went outside. Next to the door was a frightening *bhante* [monk] with a long braid that coiled on the ground. He said,

O, this is the blood-drinking Heruka.
Great and wondrous that he takes birth among humans.
The girl is the flesh-eating ḍākinī.
The self-existing lord, emanation of the Sovereign [i.e., Tri Songdetsen],
Once again comes to the land of Tibet.
You are the woman who will give birth to him.

When she looked over at him her body became so numb that she felt as if she were going to fall to the ground. The two girls lifted her by her arms and stayed there for a while, waiting for her to come back to her senses. Then again they descended the staircase and went out by the great door. A wave of unsteadiness passed over her, like a person in a coracle boat [a Tibetan boat made of yak hide], and then in an instant she found herself before the door. She went through it and found herself again before the statue of the One Mother Glorious Goddess. Then she came out of the real door [of the temple].

Her husband, Merit Further Benefit (Bsod nams phan yangs [*sic*]), had also arrived there. The two women said, "Here is your woman back." She herself cowered there in shock and fear. Her husband said, "Three days have gone by since I lost you. I lost track of you when you were in front of the statue of the Glorious Goddess. After a day spent searching for you, I finally thought maybe you had fallen into the well over there on the left. But I didn't see any hint of the body of my wife there. [I almost gave up,] but I was ashamed and embarrassed. I thought, 'I will never be able to return to my own country without my wife.' It's really great that you're back! Where have you been? Who gave you all these scarves?"

She said, "There were two ladies who took me away. There were women, and many beings—they gave me food, and scarves, and all sorts of things." She told him vaguely and with some confusion about how she had been given things, but she could not explain everything in detail.

From that day on, she was not the same. Her body was light and her intelligence was greater. She had clear dreams and saw various visions from time to time; she would at times become possessed by a godlike being. At those times she would tell about things that were hidden from people's knowledge—and it would turn out to be the truth. The other people who were companions on the pilgrimage said [to the husband], "This girl has either been seized by a demon or else has gone mad. She's not going to be of help to you anymore."

They went to have an audience with the Sovereign Conqueror Jampel Gyatso [the Dalai Lama]. There were many people who went together to the audience. When they were all there, he said, "That woman over there, have her come here." He bestowed on her a medicine statue and a protection cord to wear. When they arrived at the hostel that evening, the whole circle of companions passed the statue from hand to hand to look at it. Unfortunately, it fell into the hands of a man who was a great sinner. This was a mistake, and because of it the Conqueror himself, who had wished to be reborn in her womb, missed his opportunity for that good fortune.

Gradually the pilgrimage journey returned to its starting point. When they had returned to their home in eastern Tibet, to the region called Dungbu Tra, they were surrounded by rainbows and snow clusters in the shape of flowers snowed down on them. The lady had a vision in which she saw thirteen horsemen riding across the land. Her traveling companions as well as she saw the thirteen horsemen ride around her three times and then speed off into the high country. This was Nyenchen Thanglha's way of seeing her off from his country.

In gradual stages they traveled the rest of the way to their own home, and arrived there easily.

Then it came to pass that the Only Mother, the protectress of mantra, Ekajati [the protectress of the Ati teachings, the ultimate and highest instructions in meditation practice, is depicted with one eye, one turquoise lock of hair, one breast, and one fang], suddenly descended on her, possessing her, and said [through her]: "Demons and devils are propagating in this land! People with perverted views, corruptors of vows, and people with perverted aspirations are gathering here. This land cannot support the birth of the little child! Both of you as a couple are just a hotel that has been rented for a while. In reality he is just like me, a child of the gods." She said that and showed many signs.

Then some people in the village said that she had been taken by the great king of the demons. Some said that he was a magical emanation, and they thought that maybe Gesar would be born from her; someone else said that a devil was going to be born who would bring about the degeneration of the country of Khams. And everyone quarreled with each other. In the village there was a seer who said that he saw from time to time visions near the house of the father and mother. He said that on top of their house, and in the field to the right of the house, and in other places as well, there were sometimes many people wearing the bard's sacred hat. And they had pitched tents and were invoking the gods and performing supplications to them, but only through the chanting of the melodies of epics. They would sing of horses and they would sing of weapons, and the seer saw that that was all they did. So he thought that they might be the demonic cause of the mother's sicknesses.

The father's attitude, however, was neither positive nor negative. He just listened and obeyed whatever the god possessing the mother said. So he asked the god: "Now to which country do we have to go?"

"Go southwest and then it will be clear," it said.

So they did not listen to the others and one night just went off. They went upland to the family of the maternal uncle. That turned out not to be a suitable place for them to stay either, and so they kept on going upward farther and farther. They then came to a place called Dothog. The mother was possessed by a god again, and while possessed she sang in the melodies of the epics:

> *Ki Ki So So* imperial god,
> Protector inseparable from the divine, rare, and precious three jewels.
> And the three roots of guru, yidam, and ḍākinī.
> Stay always inseparable as my crest ornament.
>
> Lord Uḍḍiyāṇa Padma, look on me with compassion!
> Lords of the five families of the victorious ones [buddhas], sing the accompaniment!
> The song is led by the mother ḍākinī.
> It is sure that I will not stay in this place.
> It is caught between the devils and *rākṣasas*.

It is the running ground of the *tsen* and the demonesses.
Here you will touch tantric pledge corruptors with hand and mouth [i.e., you will have contact with the corrupt through eating and touch].
Otherwise, go to Yutse Ja.
On the other side of lake Yutso Chugmo,
In a pond in the right corner called Dark Red Rakta,
There is a boulder that looks like a white tent.
In this place, mother, you can give birth to your little boy.
Or else, go to the country of Ma in Kham.
That is the place where the richness of the Indian dharma gathers.
That is the place where the richness of the laws of China gathers.
That is the place where the rich herds of the Yellow Mongols gather.
That is the place where the good fortune of the land of Tibet gathers.
Ma Yang Chug Mo, the land of Ling,
Fulfills the aspiration prayers of the gurus of the oral lineages.
That is the place where the *siddhis* of the tutelary deities (*yi dam*) enter the disciple.
All the auspicious coincidence of the mothers and ḍākiṇis will arise there.
The protectors and protectresses of the dharma perform their buddha activity there.
The eight orders of demons will help and protect there.
If the young child is born in that land,
He will be the jewel on the crest of the black-headed humans [Tibetans].

Then the father thought, "I don't even know where the land of Yutse is! If she had another divine possession, maybe we could find out? The local spirits of the land are so wrathful and powerful that if the child were born there, we might accidentally irritate them one day and excite their wrath and punishment, a thing not to be desired. So maybe the place of Murra Go Do in Ma Khog is better. There are a few communities of people living there. I think it would be advisable to go and stay there." So they went there and stayed a few days, but because of some really subtle negative conditions the mother became gravely ill. They did the practical rituals to cure her, but they had no effect.

Now, in that village there lived an oracle who was a medium for the oath-bound deity Vajrasadhu. In a trance he said: "I am the lord of half the sky and land of this world. I am the protector of the child who is in this woman's box. The many acts you have committed while living among these many communities have caused this reaction. Do not stay here! Go to a place where you will not touch with mouth or hand anything touched by other women. Go down now toward Mê. Tomorrow morning when the moon of the fifteenth day arises, a little circular light will arise. Near there are grasslands. On them you will find five-colored rainbows in a circle. Go stay there. It is certain that your aims will be fulfilled spontaneously!"

So they decided to do that, and early next morning they left. They arrived at the top of the mountain at night. When they looked down, they saw clearly manifesting all the signs the oath-bound deity had told them would be there. They went down and rented a small tent nearby. The father and mother, a sister-in-law on the father's side, and two servants all lived in that tent. All the others returned to their own country and the mother lived there touching nothing with her hand or mouth touched by anyone else.

Then on the eight day of the month that is in the Pleiades, the third lunar mansion, the mother was again possessed by a god:

The sixth buddha, the dharma body Vajradhara,
Full of the blessings of the buddhas of the five families,
Tārā goddess, long-life goddess,
Please grant this child the supreme empowerment.

If you do not know this place,
On the right is the waterfall of the Ma River.
On the left is the waterfall of the Kong River.
In front is the waterfall of the Golden River.
It is called Kong Ser Trashi Kha Do.

On the throne of the wish-fulfilling gem
If you don't know what woman I am,
Among the high rank of the imperial gods
I am the Queen of Practice, the life-holding mother of longevity.
I have come to grant long-life empowerment to this baby.
A mist of blessings piles layer on layer.
A rain of siddhis falls tinklingly.
A sheath of light rays of compassion flashes out.
May your indestructible body be clothed in vajra armor!
May your unchanging speech magnetize the three realms!
May your indestructible mind hold the treasury of dharma
Of the widom holder Padmākara!
May you be the ruler over the profound treasure texts (*gter ma*)!
May you hold the teachings of the Buddha!
And may it come to pass that you defeat the troops of Māra!
May you unite the eight tribes of Ling and
May your power and ability for the white [good] side be great!
May you establish sentient beings in bliss
And may you take their aspirations to the ultimate end!
May you unite the three realms
And subdue with your light the three aspects of the phenomenal world!
May the auspicious sun of dharma dawn
And may you completely enjoy bliss, happiness, and glory!"

When she had sung this, then from inside the mother's stomach a voice said, "Noble lady, it is good!" Everybody heard it.

Then on the tenth day of the month, a god possessed the mother: "Today the time has come for the child to be born." After a little while the god said, "O, the ḍākinīs still have not arrived! The planets and constellations have not come together in the appropriate pattern yet. The time has not yet come." And the god disappeared.

Again, on the fourteenth day, in the early morning the father had a dream in which he saw before their little tent many tents that had been put up. Many great beings and divine women gathered and set up a large ritual furnace altar in the middle, on which they arranged a feast with all sorts of foods. Above that, on a great throne sat a great being, wearing the sacred hat of a bard, invoking the gods with the melodies of epic songs. Some beings sang songs. Some did sacred dances on the dancing grounds. Some others were racing horses. Some were shooting arrows. Again, on top of the ritual altar, seated on a throne, was a woman adorned with many ornaments and full of splendor. She said, "This birthday celebration must go on for three days."

Others there were of the race of men, who seemed to speak a variety of different languages. They wore all sorts of different ornaments and numerous different styles of clothes. In his dream vision it seemed that the place was completely filled with all these beings.

Then on the fifteenth day at daybreak, the mother was again possessed, but by an extremely wrathful deity. He said "Hey you, set out a cushion quickly! Make offerings of barley and butter, drink, and the select offering. The time has come for the child to be born!"

The father was not used to taking orders from his wife, but he was afraid of the god who possessed her, so he put out the white wool cushion. He made offerings and sent up the juniper smoke. He sent the servants out of the tent, and then he too left.

When the sun struck the peak of the tent, that god shouted out "Ha, ha, you the man, come in here and if you do not serve this little boy I will indeed immediately destroy your life, for I do not care much about the actions and behavior of those who have a human form!"

The man was terrified and quickly went into the tent. The birth of the child had been accomplished, and he was sitting there in the vajra (lotus) posture. Rays of light came through a slit in the dwelling, and the son held them in his hand as he said, "*a ā i ī*," and so on as he sat there. [This is a Buddhist mantra of purification composed of all the letters of the Indian Sanskrit alphabet.] The god spoke various different languages and gazed up into the middle heavens. The father himself cut the umbilical cord of the baby and performed the other woman duties.

He handed the child into the arms of the mother. The mother, still in a state of possession, said, "Bring soft milk and water and wash his whole body carefully. Man, you come from the race of *rākṣasas*. We were connected by previous karma. Even then you were a mediocre servant! This time, be a good servant to this child! If you and the world have the merit to support this being, then it will be enough to benefit beings indeed." Then the god disappeared. And then it was morning.

4

Bön Rescues Dharma

Per Kvaerne

While the majority of Tibetans are Buddhists, a large minority are followers of a religion known by its Tibetan name, *Bön* (*bon*). This religion may, at first glance, appear to be nearly indistinguishable from Buddhism with respect to its doctrines, monastic life, rituals, and meditational practices. However, both Tibetan Buddhists and Bönpos (*bonpo*) ("adherents of Bön") generally agree that the two religions are entirely distinct. The basic difference above all concerns the issue of religious authority and legitimation. Although limited to Tibet, Bön regards itself as a universal religion in the sense that its doctrines are true and valid for all humanity. The Bönpos also believe that in former times their faith was propagated in many parts of the world, as conceived in their traditional cosmology. For this reason it is called *yungdrung bon*, "Eternal Bön." According to its own historical perspective, it was introduced into Tibet many centuries before Buddhism and enjoyed royal patronage until it was supplanted and expelled by the "false religion" (i.e., Buddhism) coming from India.

But before reaching Tibet, Bön, it is claimed, prospered in a land known as Shangshung (Zhang zhung), a country that served as the center for the religion before it was conquered by the expanding Tibetan empire in the seventh century C.E. and eventually assimilated into Tibetan culture and converted to Buddhism. There is no doubt as to the historical reality of Shangshung, although its exact extent and its ethnic and cultural identity are far from clear. But it does seem to have been situated in what today is, roughly speaking, western Tibet, with Mount Kailash as its center. Bönpos claim that the original homeland of Bön, however, lies farther to the west, beyond the border of Shangshung, in a land called Tazik (Stag gzig, or Rtag gzigs). Although this suggests the land of the Tajiks in Central Asia, the exact identification of this holy land of Bön cannot be specified at this point. For the Bönpos, Tazik is the holy land of religion (just as India is for the Buddhists), for it is the land of their founder Tönpa Shenrap (Ston pa Gshen rab), "The Teacher Shenrap," a fully enlightened being, the true buddha of our world age.

The Bönpos possess a voluminous hagiographical literature in which his exploits are extolled. Without delving into the many problems concerning the historical and literary genesis of this extraordinary figure, one may at least note that his biography is *not* closely related to the biographical traditions connected with Śākyamuni Buddha. For most of his career, Tönpa Shenrap was the ruler of Tazik and a layman, and he incessantly journeyed out from his capital in all directions to propagate Bön. His numerous wives, sons, daughters, and disciples also played significant roles in this soteriological activity, for which there is no parallel in Śākyamuni Buddha's life story. Their activity also included the institution of numerous rituals, some still performed by Bönpos today, which find their justification and legitimation in the exemplary action of Tönpa Shenrap. He is regarded as a fully enlightened being from his very birth, endowed with supernatural powers. His importance in the Bön religion is crucial; it is he who lends authority to the religious literature of the Bönpos and, indeed, to their entire religious tradition.

The Bönpos have a vast literature, which non-Tibetan scholars are just beginning to explore. Formerly it was taken for granted in the West that this literature was nothing but uninspired and shameless plagiarism of Buddhist texts, as the Buddhists themselves have argued. The last thirty years have seen a radical change in the view of the Bön religion. David Snellgrove initiated this reassessment in 1967, making the just observation regarding Bönpo literature that "by far the greater part would seem to have been absorbed through learning and then retold, and this is not just plagiarism." (*The Nine Ways of Bon* [London, 1967], p. 12). Subsequently, other scholars have demonstrated conclusively that in the case of several Bönpo texts that have obvious, even word-by-word Buddhist parallels, it is not, as was formerly taken for granted, the Bönpo text that reproduces a Buddhist original, but in fact the other way around: the Bönpo text has been copied by Buddhist authors. This does not mean that Bön was not at some stage powerfully influenced by Buddhism; but once the two religions, Bön and Buddhism, were established as rival traditions in Tibet, their relationship was a complicated one of mutual influence.

Bön tradition holds that the early kings of Tibet were adherents of Bön, and that consequently not only the royal dynasty but the entire realm prospered. This happy state of affairs came to a temporary halt during the reign of the eighth king, Drigum Tsenpo (Dri gum btsan po), who persecuted Bön and forced the Bönpos to flee, with the result that a large number of Bön texts were hidden away so that they might be preserved for future generations. As far as Bön is concerned, this was the beginning of the textual tradition known as *terma* (*gter ma*, "treasures"), concealed texts that are rediscovered at an appropriate time by gifted individuals called *tertöns* (*gter ston*, "treasure-revealers"). Although Bön was reinstated by Drigum Tsenpo's successor and flourished during the reigns of subsequent kings as it had done before, it was once again persecuted by King Tri Songdetsen (Khri srong lde btsan, r. 740–797). While this king is portrayed in mainstream Tibetan tradition as a devout Buddhist under whose patronage the first Tibetan monks were ordained (see chapter 24), Bönpo sources suggest that his motives for supporting Buddhism were questionable, both spiritually and politically: on the one hand, his conversion to Buddhism was based on the selfish belief that he could prolong his life, and on the other hand, he accepted the argument put forward by certain evil ministers at his court that the Bönpo priests, already equal to the king in power, would certainly take over the whole government of Tibet after his death. Whatever the truth of the matter may be, both Buddhists and Bönpos agree that during the reign of Tri Songdetsen, the Bönpo priests were either banished from Tibet or compelled to conform to Buddhism. Once again Bön texts were concealed, to be taken out again when the time would be ripe for propagating Bön anew.

In the vast body of literature that forms the Bön canon of sacred scriptures, most of it belongs to this class of terma, regarded as having been hidden away during the successive persecutions of Bön and duly rediscovered by tertöns in the course of the following centuries. Bönpos also claim that many of their sacred scriptures were transformed by the Buddhists into Buddhist texts, thus reversing the accusation of plagiarism. The Bönpos claim that the rediscovery of their sacred texts began early in the tenth century C.E. The first discoveries are said to have been made by chance. One account that has an authentic ring to it tells of wandering beggars who stole a box from the monastery of Samye (Bsam yas), believing that it contained gold; much to their disappointment, the contents turned out to be only Bönpo books, which they then exchanged for food. Another accidental discovery is described in the account of Buddhists looking for Buddhist texts, who, on finding only Bönpo books, simply gave them away. Gradually, however, the textual discoveries came to be surrounded by supernatural signs and prophetic circumstances. Discoveries of texts were frequently preceded by initiatory preparations, sometimes lasting several years, culminating in visions in which supernatural beings revealed the place where the treasure was hidden. Often the treasure was not a concrete book at all, but an inspired text arising spontaneously in the mind of the treasure-revealer.

Those texts considered by the Bönpos to be ultimately derived from Tönpa Shenrap himself were eventually collected to form a canon. This vast collection of texts constitutes the Bönpo Kanjur (*bka' 'gyur*, a current edition of which consists of approximately 190 volumes), as such forming an obvious parallel to the Tibetan Buddhist canon, likewise styled "Kanjur." While no precise date for the formation of the Bönpo Kanjur can be given, it is claimed that it does not contain texts that came to light later than 1386. A reasonable surmise would be that the Bönpo Kanjur (as well as the Bönpo Tenjur, *bstan 'gyur*, the collection of texts containing commentaries to the Kanjur) was assembled by around 1450. This collection, which in turn forms only a fraction of the total literary output of the Bönpos, covers the full range of this Tibetan religious tradition. Only a handful of Bönpo texts have been explored at all, and of these only one major text (the *Gzer mig*) has been partially translated. The Bönpo Kanjur (and Tenjur) is in all likelihood the last major textual collection from Asia to remain almost entirely unexplored by Western scholars.

A particularly significant genre within Bönpo literature is that of historiographical texts. The importance of this genre resides in the particular perspective on Tibetan history that it presents, a perspective that is radically different from that found in Tibetan Buddhist texts. In Buddhist texts, the introduction of Buddhism in the seventh and eighth centuries C.E. under the patronage of successive Tibetan kings is regarded as a great blessing, preordained by Śākyamuni Buddha and carried out by saints and scholars from the holy land of India. The Buddhist historical texts claim that only after the Tibetans' conversion to Buddhism did they acquire a higher ethical code, the art of writing, the subtleties of a sublime philosophy, and the possibility of reaching spiritual enlightenment: in other words, Tibet became a civilized nation.

The picture presented in Bönpo historical literature is altogether different, as is illustrated by the following passage taken from an unpublished Bönpo text, entitled *Grags pa rin chen gling grags* (a title that at present cannot be interpreted in a convincing manner and must therefore be left untranslated). The text, which traces the history of Bön from its very inception in Tibet until the banishing of the Bönpo priests during King Tri Songdetsen's reign (at the end of the eighth century), presents a picture of the early history of Tibet that differs radically from the standard Buddhist version. In this text Bön, as the national religion of Tibet, ensures the power of the king and the prosperity of the realm. In fact, the passage translated below claims that the Tibetan king also successfully rescued Buddhism in India from destruction at the hands of a "heretical" king. "Heresy" must be understood here in the particular context intended by the author, who distinguishes between "the doctrine of enlightenment" (which he also refers to as "the doctrine of the insiders"), by which he means the doctrine of Śākyamuni, and a false, evil doctrine of an unmistakable tantric type, which, as the text explains later on, was the religion brought to Tibet by Padmasambhava in a later period, thus causing the decline of Bön and, ultimately, the dissolution of the Tibetan realm.

The interesting point to retain in this passage is not whether it conforms in a strict sense to historical reality, but that it reflects a Tibetan sense, clearly formulated more than seven hundred years ago, of being a powerful nation with a significant role to play in the world.

The translation is from an unpublished manuscript in the Oslo University Library (Öst. As. II no. 14), fol. 48 ff.

Further Reading

For a general survey of Bön, with a special emphasis on art and iconography, see Per Kvaerne, *The Bon Religion of Tibet* (Boston: Shambhala, 1995).

How the Tibetans Came to the Rescue of Buddhism in India

First the creator, Sangpo Bumtri, and his consort appeared. Their son Sije Drangkar and his consort Lhaza Gangdrak had thirty-six male and female offspring. The youngest of the eighteen males, Sibu Logpachen, and the youngest of the eighteen females, Sicham Bhurema, donned the garb of ascetics and were expelled.

In Vārāṇasī in the land of India there is a place known as the Cave of Demons, facing toward the southwest. There the brother and sister practiced a perverted doctrine: they wrote letters on the ground; they sprinkled water; for food they ate mushrooms and scraps of vegetables; for clothes they wore yellow, rough shawls and cloaks without sleeves; and their hair was cut. As a sign of having renounced the world, they were given a vajra with a broken point, and a bell. From the incestuous union of the brother and sister, two offspring appeared: a brother and a sister, known as Marali and Matali. They in turn copulated, and a son was born; his name was Ngame Semladen.

In that country of India, starting from King Śuddhodana up to Prince Gedon, the doctrine of the Enlightened One [Śākyamuni] flourished. As for the doctrines of the heretics, there were 360 false views. Since there was no royal law in India at that time, everyone followed their own personal view. That evil-looking man, Ngame Semladen, created novel doctrines by mixing the Doctrine of the Insiders [of Śākyamuni] with the evil spells of heretics. That doctrine of his thereupon caused fierce controversy among the teachers in India, who consequently split into two parties, competing with each other in magic and philosophy. The upholder of Buddhism, Dharmarāja, and the heretic Lawa Nakpo ("Black Shawl") joined battle; the heretic hurled a great disc, breaking the neck of the king who upheld Buddhism, so that he died.

Since the Buddhists of India were almost destroyed, they conferred together and said: "Since this heretic cannot be destroyed by philosophical debate or by military might, we must ask the king of Tibet for help." They called on Tibet to send an army; Wa Kyesang Taknang, riding the steed Mukhen Khongma, soaring like a bird, was the general of the Tibetan army; he came with wonderful banners flying. Although the chief priest of India [the leader of the "heretics"], Lhadak Ngakdro, evoked the "enemy-gods" and subdued the "enemy-demons," the heretics were vanquished and the enemies of Buddhism in India were overcome.

That the "Insiders" [Buddhists] in the end were happy and fortunate was due to the favor of the Bönpos and priests and the military assistance of Tibet.

5

The Guide to the Crystal Peak

Matthew Kapstein

Among the characteristic religious activities in which virtually all Tibetans at some time or other participated, pilgrimage was particularly prominent. It may be said that pilgrimage was traditionally one of the central phenomena contributing to, and perhaps even to some extent engendering, the cultural unity of Tibet. Pilgrimage, among other things, promoted trade in both goods and information. It brought persons from far distant parts of the Tibetan world into direct contact with one another and thus militated to some extent against divisive regional tendencies. By ordering the cycles of pilgrimage according to calendrical cycles, by establishing the locations visited and the routes traversed, and by promoting specific religious teachings, historical narratives, and symbolic interpretations of the landscape and the events taking place within it, the Tibetan religious world constructed for its inhabitants a universe of shared meaning.

Among the many famous Tibetan places of pilgrimage, most Tibetans regarded it to be particularly important to visit the religious shrines of the Tibetan capital of Lhasa. There they could behold and be blessed by contact with the renowned image of Buddha Śākyamuni called the Jowo (*Jo bo*, "Lord") that resides in the central temple, the so-called Cathedral of Lhasa. The image itself was thought to have been brought from China in the early seventh century by the princess of Wencheng and so marked the beginning of Tibet's conversion to the Buddhist religion (see chapter 2). While in Lhasa, pilgrims could also make the rounds of the numerous important temples and monasteries in the vicinity of the capital and perhaps even attend a public blessing given by the Dalai Lama himself. The pilgrims who flocked to Lhasa brought offerings for the temples and monks and also frequently engaged in trade so as to finance their journeys. Pilgrimage thus came to play an important role in the Tibetan economy, besides its religious significance.

The capital, however, was not the sole center of pilgrimage. In fact, there was a sort of national pilgrimage network in Tibet, whose routes, extending the length and breadth of the country, joined great and small temples and shrines, as well as caves, mountains, valleys, and lakes that were imbued with sacred significance. In far western Tibet, the greatest pilgrimage center was undoubtedly Mount Kailash, regarded popularly as being substantially identical with the world-mountain, the axis mundi. As such, it was a major destination for both Hindus and Buddhists. The Tibetan pilgrims, who sometimes walked for months, even years, to reach the "most precious glacial peak" (*Gangs ri rin po che*), were often joined in the final stages of their journey by Indian holy men and devotees, who made the difficult trek from the Indian plains over the Himalayan passes.

Mount Kailash was thought to be the center of a sacred maṇḍala, around which, throughout an area extending for many hundreds of miles, all significant geographical features were arrayed in a well-ordered and meaningful fashion. Thus, the great Manosarovar and Rakshastal lakes, and the four rivers thought to have their sources near Kailash, all represented the symmetry and perfection of the natural maṇḍala of the landscape. Traveling south from Kailash to Nepal, one of the important landmarks encountered in this respect was the "Crystal Peak of Rong" (Rong Shel mo gangs), the pilgrimage guide to which is translated below. "Rong," a generic term in Tibetan for the deep valleys into which one drops after crossing to the south of the Himalayas, here refers to the specific district in western Nepal in which the Crystal Peak is located.

Guidebooks like *The Guide to the Great Pilgrimage Center of the Crystal Peak* were available describing all important centers of pilgrimage and many minor sites, too. Most pilgrims probably never read such works—in practice they were not used as the Tibetan equivalents of our Fodor's or Lonely Planet guides—but the traditions they contained were often repeated by word of mouth, and they certainly represent the attitude toward pilgrimage sites that religious Tibetans sought to inculcate. The present guidebook well exemplifies some pervasive themes relating to sacred places, emphasizing the symbolic significance of the landscape, specific sacred objects and "treasures" to be found there, and its legendary and historical associations with some of the great culture heroes of the Tibetan past. The configurations of stone, designs seen in the cliffs, and so forth are described as the naturally formed images of deities. Indeed, religious Tibetans were so accustomed to regarding sacred landscapes in these terms that it was in most cases unnecessary to state explicitly that the gods and their attributes as described here were in fact formations of rock. Uncanny occurrences, unusual features of climate and environment, were all interpreted as being imbued with profound spiritual meaning. Besides such topics, this guidebook, like most others of its type, is also concerned to enumerate the great benefits that accrue to pilgrims by virtue of their acts of devotion performed at the places described.

The text itself appears to be a recent work, though probably based in part on older guidebooks to Crystal Peak. It is clear, however, as will be indicated in appropriate notes, that this is in some sections a modern composition, seeking to establish authority by claiming to represent the words of great masters of the past. In this respect, the *Guide to the Crystal Peak* represents the deployment of declared antiquity as a means to achieve an aura of authenticity, a stratagem often used to foster some measure of innovation in an otherwise conservative religious culture. Nevertheless, as the references to the Crystal Peak in *The Sermon of an Itinerant Saint* (chapter 21) demonstrate, the sanctity of the site itself was widely accepted long before the present guidebook was composed.

The Tibetan manuscript of the *Guide to the Crystal Peak* was collected by Nancy E. Levine of the University of California, Los Angeles, and Tshewang Lama of Khor Gompa in Humla District, northwestern Nepal, during the course of anthropological fieldwork in ethnically Tibetan communities of Humla. The manuscript is often very irregular in spelling and grammar, so that its interpretation is sometimes uncertain. In editing this translation of it for the present publication, I have aimed to facilitate the reader's understanding and so have avoided lengthy discussion of many of the difficulties that would be of interest to specialists alone. Explanatory material has been added in square brackets.

Further Reading

For a detailed study of the Nyinba community of Humla, see Nancy E. Levine, *The Dynamics of Polyandry: Kinship, Domesticity and Population on the Tibetan Border* (Chicago: University of Chicago Press, 1988).

Here is contained a descriptive guide to the great pilgrimage center of the Crystal Peak, and a descriptive guide to its sacred relics, entitled: "Spontaneous Liberation by Seeing."

OPENING INVOCATIONS

Homage to glorious Cakrasaṃvara!

I do homage to omnibeneficent Vajradhara,
Who is the space embracing all buddhas of the three times, past, present, and future,
The glorious one, who, having overcome all the ignorance and emotionality of the three worldly domains [subterranian, terrestial, and celestial],
Establishes living beings of the three realms [desire, form, and formless realms] in buddhahood.

I do homage to the masters of the spiritual succession:
The peerless "Banner of the Śākyas" [Śākyamuni Buddha], endowed with ten powers,
Saroruhavajraśrī [Padmasambhava], who possessed the five miraculous abilities [including clairvoyance, telepathy, and the knowledge of past lives],
Tilopa, Nāropa, Marpa, Milarepa, and the rest [of the patriarchs of the Kagyü lineage].

I do homage to the body of Padmasambhava,
The consummation of the authentic masters—
the knowledge holders who are the roots of my practice,
and the past masters of the lineage—
And the consummation of all the sugatas [buddhas, literally "one who has fared well"],
including the myriad peaceful and wrathful deities.

THE SYMBOLIC SIGNIFICANCE OF THE LANDSCAPE

Now, concerning the condition of the especially great pilgrimage center at Crystal Peak: Its environment resembles the great world-system [of Mount Meru cosmology]. On the upper slopes dwell the masters who are the roots of one's practice, and also the past teachers of the lineage. On the middle slopes dwell the assembled meditational deities with whom one forms spiritual bonds. On the lower flanks the ḍākinīs of the three spheres [of body, speech, and mind] dwell like a mass of gathering clouds. The protectors of the teaching dwell all about. [The mountain is to be visualized as a "refuge tree," including the entire pantheon of teachers, deities, and protectors to whom the practitioner directs his or her devotions.]

On the left-hand side, as one approaches, in the "fortress" [a euphemism for the cliffs and outcroppings of rock that the deities are imagined to inhabit] that is like the mountain's jewel, dwell Lord Amitāyus, the buddha of longevity, and the deities of his retinue. At good times, a rain falls there, bringing forth the water of life: by drinking a mouthful of it all obstacles to life are removed. Beyond that place, in the "Iron-skillet Fortress" located at the rocky hill behind the hollow, there dwell the conquerors who are the lords of the three families, namely, the bodhisattvas Mañjuśrī, Avalokiteśvara, and Vajrapāṇi. To the west of that there are naturally manifest images of the eight aspects of the guru Padmasambhava. On the rocks above them there are naturally manifest images clearly depicting the five buddhas [Vairocana, Akṣobhya, Ratnasambhava, Amitābha, and Amoghasiddhi] called the "conquerors of the five families." There is a naturally manifest image of the goddess Uṣṇīṣavijayā on a stūpa-like rock, and on its southern edge is a naturally manifest image of guru Dorje Trolö (Rdo rje gro lod), the wrathful form of Padmasambhava riding a tiger. In front of that rock there is something resembling an infant in his mother's lap [a symbol of the yogin's meditation merging with emptiness, the metaphysical ground that is the "mother" of all that exists.] On that mountain there also dwell the meditational deities Hayagrīva and Vajravārāhī, seen as male and female consorts in union. If you desire the spiritual accomplishments of their son, seek them here. [The adept is metaphorically thought to be the son or daughter of the deities of the tantric tradition.]

To the right-hand side, in the rock fortress that is like a *paltor* [a type of large decorated offering-cake], there dwells the wrathful guru Kīlaya with the deities of his retinue. On the left are the ḍākinīs of the five families in the aspect of Siṃhavaktrā, the lion-headed goddess. Adjacent to Siṃhavaktrā are both a large and a small pile of corpses. To the south there are once again the lords of the three families. To the northwest of that place, where there is a pond, one finds a pass, the secret path of the ḍākinīs. Behind the pass is a skull-cup for the ḍākinīs' bath. In the first month of the year, the "eye" of the pond, its drainage stream, opens as a sign that the ḍākinīs are bathing. On the rock to the southeast there are naturally manifest images of the goddesses who bear offerings of worship. To its northwest, in the fortress of a rocky hill, that is off to the side, there is the glorious lord of pure awareness, Mahākāla, with his divine retinue. To the south of that spot, in the fortress of a jewel-like rock, is the divine assembly of the wealth-granting deity Jambhala. Below that, on a rock that resembles black Jambhala, is the divine assembly of Vaiśravaṇa, the lord of riches, who is riding a horse. If you want the accomplishment of wealth, there you'll find it.

On the lower part of that same rock there are the eight exalted sugatas. On the upper part there are the naturally manifest images of the sixteen exalted sthaviras, the arhats. Above that, in the rock fortress that is like a mass of light, there reside the twenty-one Tārās. If you supplicate them you will be liberated from the eight great fears [of fire, flood, earthquake, wind-storms, elephants, snakes, criminals, and kings].

In front of the Tārās there is the ḍākinīs' flower-garden. Behind it is the so-called Mirror Lake, the summer home of the Nāginī Anavataptā. On the boundary of water and wood is the cave called "Hidden Cave." That is an especially notable place of spiritual attainment. If you continue beyond that, you will reach a rock that is like a stūpa. Here there is a natural image of the black, wrathful goddess, Tröma Nakmo (Khros ma nag mo). Beyond that there is another pass. Descending from that pass there is the place called the "Great Cave at the Pass," the place of achievement of the venerable Milarepa, where there is a spring called the "Spring of Successful Meditation." That is the venerable Milarepa's "water of attainment," for the spring appeared as a sign of his success in meditation.

Coming this way from there, there is a cave called "Hayagrīva Cave," the meditation cave of Drukchen Pemakarpo ['Brug chen Padma dkar po, 1527–1592, a famous meditation master, scholar, and poet, and the fourth incarnate head of the Drukpa Kagyü order]. At the threshold of the cave there are the natural images of the domains of Hayagrīva, Vajrapāṇi, and Amṛtakuṇḍalin, the three deities of protection and purification. Above that is a place called "Cave of the Protector." That is where the venerable Blood-drinking Madman of Tsang [Gtsang smyon Heruka, 1452–1507] practiced the meditation of the Protector.

THE BLOOD-DRINKING MADMAN OF TSANG'S MEDITATIONS AT CRYSTAL PEAK

It is related that once upon a time a girl of pale bluish complexion [a protective deity of the Crystal Peak, identical to the ḍākinī mentioned at the end of the paragraph] called to him, saying, "Come out of your cave!" At that, when the venerable Madman of Tsang came outside, the head of the glacier melted and he saw an avalanche. He saw the lakes in front of him disappear. The venerable Madman then performed a miracle here. At the spot where he braced up the rock with his right foot there is still a footprint, even today. Though at that time there was an avalanche on the outer Crystal Peak, the "inner relic" of the mountain, a crystal stūpa, remained unharmed. The ḍākinī therefore asked him, "What is the meaning of this?"

The venerable Madman answered, "It is a sign that at this place there have been an early propagation, a middle propagation, and a later propagation of the teaching. The black entrance to the site of the Crystal Peak is a sign that the gateway of the place was opened by a Nyingma mantra-adept." [A sacred place is "opened" when a great adept first discloses its prospects as a place for contemplative practice. The ancient Nyingma school of Tibetan Buddhism depicts certain of its masters as black-garbed sorcerers; hence the symbolic reference here. Though the exact identity of the mantra-adept is not specified, the text seems to suggest that he is none other than Padmasambhava himself. The early, middle, and later propagations probably refer to the activities of Padmasambhava, Milarepa, and the Madman of Tsang at Crystal Peak.]

Then, he continued, "On this footprint of mine there is a sign that six protectors have opened the gateway to this especially distinguished place. Now, among them, if you wonder where the Speech-protector is to be found, then know that it is owing to my prayer that you can hear the sound of the waters of India's holy places in Kha-rang Cave.

"In the Lion Cave there is a natural image of a lion. In Eternity Cave there is an auspicious lattice-work. At Vajra-rock there is the Medicinal Cave of the Sun. Below Prostration Ridge there is the Fortress of Garuḍa. If lepers supplicate well there, they will be greatly benefited and will be freed of their illness. At the southeastern boundary is a Tiger-banner, above which is the Cool Grove Cremation Ground. On the southwestern boundary is the ḍākinī's lake and glacier. In Raling Cave there is a spring that brings about liberation naturally. If you bathe in it or drink or scatter some its waters about, all disease, demons, sins, obscurations, and obstacles will be removed. Above Prostration Ridge is the Gateway to Hell. If you enter it once, the gateway to rebirth in the vicious states of existence will be closed. Then you need not experience the vicious states. On the upper portal of the Gateway is the body-print of the revered Rechung Dorjetrak [Ras chung Rdo rje grags (d. 1161), the leading disciple of Milarepa, and the main heir to his yogic teachings]. By its blessing, too, you will be freed from the vicious states. This Crystal Peak is an especially great holy place, the place of attainment of the venerable Milarepa, master Padmasambhava, Drukchen Pemakarpo, and others."

PADMASAMBHAVA'S CREATION OF THE MEDICINAL PILLS

Concerning now the way in which the "cosmic medicinal pills" were created: Thinking that this especially exalted holy place should not be without an esoteric relic, Padmasambhava remained momentarily absorbed in that idea. Then, the dharma-lords and ḍākinīs, with the group of the five Long-life Sisters [*tshe ring mched lnga*, important protective divinities associated with some of the major peaks of the Himalayas] foremost among them, arrived altogether and said, "We have gathered together in a fissure in our side various earths and stones from Vajrāsana, where the Buddha attained enlightenment, and various stones from Mount Wutai in China, which is Mañjuśrī's earthly abode, as well as lake-stones from Pemaling, the lake of achievement, and also various earths and stones of the holy places of Mount Kailash, together with gemstones gathered from the many quarries, excepting none, as far as Tsari in Me [Smad tsa ri, a famous place of pilgrimage to the north of Bhutan], and also the various earths and stones of all the holy places of Jambudvīpa, with the jewels of gods, nāgas, humans, and others. These have been blessed by all the buddhas of the three times, and now we offer them before you, O master Padmasambhava."

The master kneaded together all that they had offered thrice with his feet and again kneaded it thrice with his hands. Having made two globes of equal size, he fashioned them into nearly identical "medicine pills," though in one there was also sparkling dew, as an auspicious token. In the medicine pills he placed physical remains of the Blessed Lord Śākyamuni and of Buddha Kāśyapa, and a lock of Nāgārjuna's hair, among other things, and in this way he made them not deficient in blessings. He shaped the pills in an oblong manner, and when he consecrated them rainbows immediately appeared in the sky. The conquerors of the five families, the lords of the three families, and others, surrounded by an immeasurable host of buddhas and bodhisattvas, then dissolved into those medicine pills that he had placed in front of him.

Again, it occurred to the master Padma that it would be well to conceal the medicine pills as treasures, whereupon he said to himself, "May these precious medicine pills, which subsume all buddhas, and which are like the wish-fulfilling gem, be indeed as is the wish-fulfilling gem in order to be the basis for the prayers of the defiled beings of the future, and so fulfill their yearnings and hopes!" He then concealed them in the middle part of a Jambhala-like rock. After doing this, Padmasambhava prayed: "May worthy persons come to encounter them in the future!"

MILAREPA OPENS CRYSTAL PEAK AS A PLACE OF PILGRIMAGE

Then, concerning the opening up of this holy place: When the venerable Milarepa arrived, he opened the holy place and brought forth the medicine pills from the Rock of Black Jambhala. In the Ḍākinī's Enclosure he placed them on top of a whole square of white linen placed upon a flat rock and, having offered prostrations before them, remained there for some time. The ḍākinīs, local divinities, and ogres were displeased, so to his right the rock split apart, and to his left there was a landslide. They hurled a boulder the size of a house onto both the venerable one and the pills. Milarepa immediately offered up an "oath of truth," and the boulder became fixed in place at roof-height, with the imprint of his body upon it. Nevertheless, the ḍākinīs still danced above it, so Milarepa went up to take a look. As if they had been treading on a mud hole, he found many footprints of the ḍākinīs and of the eightfold groups of divinities and ogres. Indeed, the divinities and ogres of the eight classes had already melted into that boulder.

Then pink water poured out from beneath the boulder. The venerable once again looked at his body-print on the outside of it and exclaimed, "My goodness! The boulder that crashed down on me is shaped like a stūpa!" Going back inside, he erected an image in his own likeness and sealed it up from bottom to top with a great stone slab. He prayed, "In defiled future times, may a 'vase' and a spire be affixed to that body-print stūpa!" ["Vase" and "spire" are here technical terms of stūpa architecture. The stūpa-like boulder, therefore, is an incomplete, natural stūpa that must be finished by human effort. As the line immediately following makes clear, it is regarded as an apt metaphor in this way for the site as a whole.]

Because of the fulfillment of his prayer, the place is at the present time a center of pilgrimage and of meditation caves. The great holy Crystal Peak is the outer shrine, the body-print of venerable Milarepa is the inner relic, and master Padmasambhava's pills are the secret relics. Homage to that holy abode of body, speech, and mind!

The section concerning the hermitage of the Crystal Peak, where master Padmasambhava was bodily present, has now been related.

[This perhaps marks the conclusion of an earlier version of the guidebook.]

SOME OTHER UNUSUAL FEATURES OF THE SITE AND ITS TREASURES

Above the body-print stūpa is the fountain of fluid from Vārāhī's womb. During the bright half of the month red menstrual fluid comes forth, and during the dark half of the month white fluid of the womb. At auspicious times worthy persons really meet ḍākinīs there.

To the east of Prostration Ridge is a golden mound, at the edge of which is a boulder. Beneath it is pressed the right foot of a demoness. That mound is the demoness's earth. If you scatter it on someone who is afflicted by divine, demonic, or elemental spirits it will be of benefit. Below Prostration Ridge, beneath the throne-shaped boulder, is pressed the left foot of the demoness. At that place there are four wild *tsen*-spirits (*btsan rgod*). [The *tsen* (*btsan*) are powerful and fearsome indigenous divinities, whose importance in ancient Tibetan belief is underscored by their association with the Tibetan emperor, the *tsenpo* (*btsan po*). In later times, however, the tsen came to be regarded as powerful, sometimes malevolent, godlings. When such spirits are called "laymen," it generally indicates that they were among the Tibetan deities subjugated by Padmasambhava, therefore assuming the vows of the Buddhist laity.] To the right is the white divine tsen, who is a layman, to the left is the brown demon tsen (*bdud btsan*). In front are the seven brothers who are the blazing tsen of Rong (*Rong btsan 'bar ba*). On the inside is the divine tsen Blazing Vajra (*Lha btsan Rdo rje 'bar ba*).

There are four treasures hidden in this place. The first is entrusted to the brown demon tsen. In front there is a copper treasure. That is entrusted to the seven blazing brothers. To the west is a grain treasure. It is entrusted to the white divine tsen, who is a layman. On the inside is a treasure of wealth, including gold and silver. It is entrusted to the divine tsen Blazing Vajra. It is not permitted for treasure-seekers to open those treasures; for if you do uncover them, then because of the oaths of the spirits to whom those treasures are entrusted, you will have to contend with them first!

Again, on the embankment a *kaṭorā* [a kind of brass bowl] is hidden. So long as the spire and "vase" are not yet affixed to the body-print stūpa, it is not permitted to uncover it either. Moreover, this holy place has many mines.

To the southwest of Prostration Ridge there is a secret compartment in a boulder. The treasure-keys are hidden in it. In Milarepa's cave there is the wind of India. Even if you try to cook rice there, the heat will not reach the pot. Again, in this holy place, there is a natural image of a vase, a natural image of a conch, a natural image of a stūpa, a natural image of a vajra, a natural image of a crown, and so forth. So it is an inconceivably holy place.

MILAREPA'S DECLARATION TO HIS DISCIPLE RECHUNG, CONCERNING THE BENEFITS OF THE MEDICINE PILLS

As has been described above, the venerable Milarepa dwelt there. He once said that to offer a butter-lamp in this especially holy place a stone lamp was needed, and so the venerable one brought forth a stone lamp from within the Jambhala-like rock. In that place Rechung rolled medicine pills, and after the venerable Milarepa examined their size and their weight, he compressed them, consecrated them, and hid them as treasures. He said, "In the future, the master called Pemakarpo must bring them forth from the treasure!" [The prophetic references, here and below, to figures living long after Milarepa's time suggest that these sections are of recent authorship. The long enumeration of the benefits of worship and other religious activity at Crystal Peak that follows appears to have been taken from another work, having nothing to do originally with the Crystal Peak in particular, and has been inserted here, attributed to Milarepa to lend it an aura of authority.]

Afterward Rechung dwelt there. He asked his master, "In this precious wish-fulfilling gem of a place, which is the gateway to the abode of the body, speech, and mind of the buddhas, what are the benefits of performing prostration, circumambulation, worship, and so forth, and of other acts of service?"

The great venerable Milarepa then made this declaration: "Listen and cultivate faith! If you pray to the precious medicine pills, the receptacles of spirituality into which the blessings of all the buddhas and bodhisattvas of the three times have melted, whatever you have prayed for will be effortlessly, spontaneously achieved. Whoever performs prostration, circumambulation, and worship with a pure, noble aspiration to such precious, wish-fulfilling gems should know the benefits are to be explained in this way:

Even all the buddhas of the three times cannot express it,
But in brief just in order to inspire their followers,
Then let it be said:
The medicine pills are the supreme spiritual receptacle of all the buddhas and bodhisattvas of the three times.
They are the field for the worship of the entire world with its ordinary beings and gods.
By supplicating them whatever you pray for will be effortlessly achieved!
They confer the supreme and common attainments.
For all beings who see with their eyes the "great pills," which are like precious wish-fulfilling gems,
The gates to rebirth in the vicious destinies will be closed.
Even if you just hear of them, the seed of supreme enlightenment will be planted.
All those who think of them will be freed from madness, fainting fits, and paralysis,
And special samādhi will arise in their minds.
All those who join their hands in prayer before them will find the authentic path.
All those who prostrate here will be born as universal emperors.
All those who circumambulate will acquire the seven virtues of heaven [i.e., the seven virtues of higher rebirths, namely, having a good family, physical beauty, longevity, good health, good luck, wealth, and wisdom].

All who supplicate will spontaneously achieve the two goals, of enlightenment for self and for others.

Whoever offers drinking water here will be born without afflictions of thirst.

Whoever offers washing-water here will be freed from emotional afflictions, sins, and obscurations, and will obtain the five modes of enlightened cognition [the cognition of the expanse of reality, mirror-like cognition, cognition of sameness, discriminating cognition, and accomplishing cognition—associated with the five buddhas].

All those who offer flowers will obtain the perfect liberty and endowment of human birth.

All those who offer incense will attain pure moral discipline.

All those who offer butter-lamps will be freed from all the darkness of unknowing.

All those who offer perfumed water will be liberated from all mental distress and suffering.

All those who offer foodstuffs will thrive on the food of samādhi.

All those who offer the music of large cymbals will sound the melody of the doctrine in the ten directions.

All those who offer the music of finger-cymbals will obtain profound and perfect intellectual brilliance.

All who offer the music of bells and miniature bells will obtain the authentic voice of Brahmā, a sweet voice, clearest speech.

All who offer maṇḍalas [symbolic offerings of the Mount Meru world-system] will fully perfect the provisional and ultimate goals, acquiring merit and wisdom.

All who offer maṇḍalas of the five gems [gold, silver, turquoise, coral, and pearl] will be relieved of all poverty and will come to possess the inexhaustible treasury of the sky.

All who offer maṇḍalas of the seven jewels [gold, silver, turquoise, coral, pearl, emerald, and sapphire] will provisionally enjoy the seven jewels of kingship and ultimately will attain the seven aspects of enlightened embodiment [the realization of the absolute truth in its ontological and epistemological aspects, and the enlightenment of body, speech, mind, attributes, and activity].

All who offer the five medicines [ginseng and other similarly valuable herbal remedies] will be freed from the illnesses of the four aggregated elements [earth, water, fire, and air] and from the consumptive illness of saṃsāra.

All who offer maṇḍalas of the five heart-mantras [*oṃ, hūṃ, traṃ, hrīḥ, āḥ,* respectively the "seed syllables" of the five buddhas Vairocana, Akṣobhya, Ratnasambhava, Amitābha, and Amoghasiddhi] will be liberated from all the sufferings of the five classes of beings [gods, humans, animals, hungry ghosts, and denizens of the hells] and will obtain the bodies of the five buddha families [Tathāgata, Vajra, Jewel, Lotus, and Action, corresponding to the five buddhas mentioned above].

All who offer maṇḍalas of the five grains [barley, rice, wheat, peas, and sesame] will obtain a fine harvest from whatever grains they plant.

Whoever offers maṇḍalas of the five kinds of incense will be fragrant, handsome, and pleasing to all.

All who offer maṇḍalas of the five perfumes [sandalwood, musk, jasmine, saffron, and camphor] will attain a pure abode and be freed from all taints.

All who offer maṇḍalas of the five "sights" [symbolic representations of the five sensory organs] will obtain an increase of all their merit, power, wealth, possessions, and enjoyment.

Whoever offers parasols and ensigns will obtain perfect, enjoyable possessions and be freed from the eight great fears [fire, flood, earthquake, wind-storms, elephants, snakes, criminals, and kings].

Whoever offers garlands and crowns will obtain the true happiness of gods and men, adorned with the seven jewels.

All those who offer lamps will really see the faces of the buddhas and bodhisattvas of the ten directions [the four cardinal directions, the four intermediate directions, and zenith and nadir].

All who offer the seven emblems of kingship [discus, wish-granting gem, queen, minister, elephant, horse, and military commander] will obtain the great kingdom of religion.

Whoever offers the eight auspicious emblems [eternal knot, lotus, parasol, conch, wheel, royal banner, vase, and golden fish] will obtain a body adorned with the signs and marks of a buddha.

All who offer the eight auspicious substances [mirror, curd, *durva*-grass, *bilva*-fruit, a conch with a clockwise spiral, the digestive stones of a ruminant, vermillion, and white mustard seed] will become fortunate and splendid and will enjoy the perfect glories of gods and men.

All who offer clothing will enjoy religious garb made of cast-off rags [signifying the purity of renunciation] and various clothes that are soft and comfortable.

All who offer white linen will obtain perfect complexion and luster and will overpower gods, demons, and men.

All who offer worship with the three white substances [milk, butter, and curd] will enjoy the plentiful feast of the ḍākinīs.

All who offer the three sweets [sugar, molasses, and honey] will enjoy the feast of divine food, all that is yearned for.

Whoever offers porridge will be free from hunger and will not be reborn among the tormented spirits.

All who offer worship with "grain juice" [alcohol] will enjoy an ocean of ambrosia.

All who offer worship with fruit will enjoy many-flavored food.

All who offer worship with a feast offering will attain the supreme and common accomplishments, and whatever it is they desire.

All who offer bathing water with the five fragrances [five perfumes, above] will obtain freedom from all pollution and obscurations and obtain taintlessness, pleasantness, and good complexion.

All who offer the supreme lotus-seat will be miraculously born atop a soft and beautiful lion-throne on a lotus flower. [This is to say that one will be reborn in a buddha paradise.]

Whoever acts as this site's treasurer will be liberated from all the sufferings of the vicious states of existence and will be endowed with all perfect attributes.

Whoever acts as a ritual attendant here will worship all the buddhas and will attain the enlightened activity of all buddhas.

All who wipe off dust and grime will obtain handsome and agreeable form.

Whoever sweeps away dirt and filth will uproot all sins and obscurations.

Whoever makes a spiritual commitment here will obtain the condition of a knowledge-holder of the *mahāmudrā*.

All who do recitations will obtain the condition of a knowledge-holder of spiritual maturation.

All who make this place their guru will obtain the condition of a knowledge-holder of spontaneity.

All who worship here will obtain the condition of a knowledge-holder of longevity.

All who repair the site will in this lifetime attain the four kinds of ritual action [pacification, enrichment, attraction, and sorcery] and all they desire, and also attain precious, unsurpassed enlightenment.

Whoever collects clay here will become a universal monarch as many times as there are particles in that clay.

Whoever carries loads of earth and stone will be freed from all obstacles to life and longevity and will enjoy long life, health, and beauty.

All those who assist virtue will, in all rebirths and lifetimes, enter the authentic path of the ten virtues, be inseparable from spiritual friends, and obtain whatever accomplishments are desired.

Whoever directs the work will be born as the senior disciple of all the buddhas of the ten directions and accomplish enlightened activity.

If one walks seven paces in this direction he or she will obtain a pure human body for seven lifetimes and will remember past lives.

All who do beneficial deeds vocally will become learned, adorned with virtues.
All who do beneficial deeds verbally will, whatever they say, be heard by all living beings in all rebirths and lifetimes.
Whoever writes down the histories and tales of liberation of the pills will in future lifetimes write down the entire canon of all the buddhas of the ten directions and three times.
All who pray that the pills remain intact for a long time will obtain the condition of a knowledge-holder of immortality.
All who repeat their consecration will be free, throughout the three times, from war and famine, will pacify epidemics and make the whole kingdom peaceful.
All who perform rites to protect people from harm will be freed from all fears of untimely death.
All who speak of their virtues and praise them to others will come to recite all the virtues of all the buddhas and bodhisattvas of the three times.
All those who study and teach will perform all the enlightened activity of all the buddhas of the three times.
Whoever rejoices will be born with all the many virtues of the buddhas of the three times.
All who receive blessing from them will obtain empowerment from all the buddhas of the ten directions.
All who go about while thinking of them will, when they pass away, be miraculously born on a lotus-flower in the Western paradise of Sukhāvatī.
All who harm them will experience various nonvirtues during this lifetime and in the next will be born in a great hell that is devoid of human riches; with no chance to escape, they will have no way to repent.
In brief, these great medicinal pills are like precious wish-fulfilling gems.
Whoever prays to them will obtain the supreme and common accomplishments and whatever things they desire according to their prayers.
Therefore, these pills are named the "Gems That Grant All One Seeks in Prayer."

So he spoke, and the retinue became amazed, awe-struck, and confident. Great faith being born, they wept. Hurling themselves to the ground, they offered a thousand prostrations. *Samaya gya gya gya*! [This exclamation indicates that the text is "sealed" as a treasure, concealed until the appointed time for its discovery. This convention is somewhat out of place in a discourse attributed to Milarepa and seems to reflect the heterogenous composition of the guidebook as a whole.]

FURTHER TESTIMONY ATTRIBUTED TO MILAREPA

At the order of translator Marpa of Lhotrak, Milarepa dwelt in isolated holy places, as he himself said:

> I stayed in rocky hermitages, glacier hermitages, and forest hermitages.
> Now, concerning those holy places:
> I meditated at Tögya Lasi (Stod rgya la sri) because it is a mountain that was blessed by the mahāsiddhas of India.
> I meditated at Mount Tise [Kailash] because it is the holy fortress surrounded by snow mountains that was prophesied by the Buddha.
> I meditated in Lapchi (La phyi) because it is the king of mountains, Wild Fox Peak, among the twenty-four glacial lands.
> I meditated at Mount Glory Blaze (Dpal 'bar) in Mar-yul and at Yo-'am snow mountain in Nepal because they were prophesied in the *Avataṃsakasūtra.*
> I meditated in Trinchi Chuwar (Brin phyi chu bar) because it is a place of residence and assembly of dharma-protectors and ḍākinīs.
> I meditated in the holy place Resembling a Crystal Dragon (Shel gyi 'brug 'dra) because it is the city of Vārāhī.
> I meditated at the holy Crystal Peak because it was blessed by the great guru Padmasambhava.
> Thus I meditated in whatever uninhabited places are favorable and raised up the banner of attainment!
> By just hearing of those holy places you will be released from saṃsāra and meet with the deities in person.
> You must cultivate meditation at them, doing prostrations, circumambulations, and such like.
> That way you will swiftly realize your own mind.
>
> On the glaciers I bound demonesses to oaths.
> In Powanamgo Cave (Bo wa rnams go phug) I bound a rock-ogress to oaths.
> To restrain them thus was an act of compassion!
> Then at Tso-lo-khar I bound a Nāga-demon to oaths.
>
> At the "water of attainment" and the "great snakehead" there is a natural image of Dzama Kaba (Rdza ma kab pa).
> At Phag-thang-yul there is my own jewel-footprint.
> There is also my "water of attainment."
> In Gyagrong (Rgyag rong) there is my venerable meditation cell and image.
> In Bar-khang valley there are handprints and footprints where I bound the spirit of the land to oaths.
> In the Hidden Cave (Sbas phug) there is the stūpa of the eight sugatas,
> And there are also many treasures.

Outside is the body-print of Orgyen Padma.
He went there miraculously and prayed for the spread of the doctrine in Tibet.
Above that is the spiritual hermitage of Vajradhara called Park of the Most Blissful Doctrinal Wheel,
Where Shabkar, my own rebirth, and the rebirth of the Indian master Javārīpa,
Will turn the wheel of the doctrine.
At this place there are upper, middle, and lower circumambulatory paths.
For the wrathful deities, they cross the summit pass;
While for Tārā, there is the summit path.
Nothing is incomplete in this holy place.
Various medicinal plants are completely present.
Various perfumes are completely present.
Various woods are completely present.
It is a place with the sweet songs of birds, large and small.
It is a place where monkeys and apes leap about.
It is a place where stag and doe play.
It is a place where various beasts of prey roam.
I take refuge in, and prostrate to, this wondrous place!

So he spoke, and at his words both gods and men rejoiced.

Venerable Rechung also dwelt there and constructed the blessed fountain. The venerable Milarepa then said to him:

This fountain, which brings natural liberation, is the water of attainment of guru Padmasambhava.
The Je-zur fountain is the water of attainment of Pumpa Dzagpa (Bum pa rdzag pa).
The Goddess fountain is the water of attainment of the Madman of Tsang.
The Tiger fountain is my water of attainment.
In the future, in Pendri (Pan 'gri), Pemakarpo's water of attainment will burst forth.

In the Yol-chab rock is the fortress of the five sisters of longevity.
There is a natural maṇḍala there.
On the rock in Phug-go-la there is a natural image of the Maṇi dhāraṇī [mantra].
I, Milarepa, declare all this.
And that on Sibri Rock (Srib ri brag) is the natural image of eight treasure vases.
In this place there are the natural images appropriate to a great holy place—none is lacking.

So saying, the venerable Milarepa praised the place. This place is also called Sukhāvatī. It is also called Copper-colored Mountain. It is also called Mount Potalaka. [These are the "pure lands" of Amitābha, Padmasambhava, and Avalokiteśvara, respectively.] It is called the "pass beheld by all." If you don't visit this place Crystal Peak, where else will you see Mount Kailash?

Homage and praise to this wonderful place! The Humla valley is like the passage to hell, and Crystal Peak is the obstruction to the entrance to hell!

COLOPHON

This eight-page catalogue originated with a brief declaration given by the five ḍākinīs, the sisters of longevity, to the venerable and great Madman of Tsang in a Dragon Year.

In the words of guru Padmasambhava, it is said, "Among the twenty-one great snow peaks there are hidden places, hidden treasures, and hidden lands. Especially in the great place Crystal Peak, all who pray, who offer feasts, who make material offerings, who perform beneficial acts of body, speech, and mind, will actually be guided by the mother goddesses and ḍākinīs to Sukhāvatī—no doubt about it! Even if the worst among you pilgrims is merely born in the mundane human world, that one will still avert all the harm of strife and violence, and the bad fortune of illness, war, and famine—there is no doubt!"

Guru Padmasambhava made this declaration to his Tibetan consort, the ḍākinī Yeshe Tsogyel, to benefit all beings in the future age of corruption. He hid it in Humla Cave for the time when people travel to foreign lands and the iron-bird lands in the plain of Le. It will be especially important then that men and women with pure spiritual commitments pray! [This reference to modern aviation further suggests the text to be a recent composition. Professor Levine was told that the "plain of Le" (Ble kyi thang) mentioned here is a slope above the Nyinba villages of Humla District. She says that the local people made much of the fact that the predictions have been nearly met by planes landing in Simikot, Humla's district capital and half a day's walk away from the Nyinba villages. Plane service began in the late 1970s or early 1980s.]

Again there is an extensive and clear history, catalogue, and guidebook concerning this place. He entrusted them to the five ḍākinīs, the sisters of longevity, to conceal them in 'Dongs Maṇḍala Rock, saying, "At some future time may some hidden yogin meet with them!"

So saying, he entrusted them to the protectors of the land, to the five longevity-sisters and to the other protectors of the doctrine.

—6—

Guidebook to Lapchi

Toni Huber

The translation that follows comprises the opening three chapters of a Tibetan pilgrimage manual, bearing the abbreviated title *Guidebook to Lapchi* (*La phyi gnas yig*). This example of noncanonical Tibetan literature serves to introduce a paradigmatic feature of Tibetan religious culture: the representation of interplay between the Buddhist belief system and the indigenous Tibetan world view. The opening narratives of the *Guidebook to Lapchi* are complex in terms of both space and time and invoke a host of cultural discourses and icons. These need to be briefly introduced so that the text can be appreciated from points of view that begin to reflect the Tibetan understandings and uses of the guidebook. But first, a few comments are in order concerning the type of document and associated cultural practices we are dealing with here.

The *Guidebook to Lapchi* is a modest text by Tibetan standards. Although guidebooks can vary greatly in style and content, several general features are worthy of particular note. Many are compilations of a range of materials, which might include anything from cosmology and points of formal doctrine to local songs, detailed travel instructions, or personal anecdotes. When reading guidebooks it is important to recognize that they are constructed and styled in particular ways in order to direct and to evoke certain responses from those who use them. They are actively advertising the sanctity of sites and promoting the powers and beliefs that play a significant role in controlling and shaping the lives of individual pilgrims. This is no less true today than it was in traditional times, and it should be noted that editions of the *Guidebook to Lapchi* are still being printed and are used by contemporary Tibetan pilgrims. As a genre, pilgrimage guidebooks have a very significant oral dimension, which sets them apart from many other types of Tibetan religious literature. Their contents are often publicly repeated by clerics, shrine-keepers, and local residents for the benefit of pilgrims, and they are always elaborated upon by oral traditions in different ways. Moreover, they are often composed on the basis of oral texts that their authors collect while on pilgrimage. Thus, in both oral and written forms, guidebooks constitute a popular and widely circulated type of religious literature in Tibetan culture. This reflects the fact that pilgrimage, the raison d'être of such texts, is one of the most widespread ritual ensembles practiced in the Tibetan world (see chapter 5).

Textual narrative and ritual journey or action are not separate modes for Tibetan pilgrims. Because oral and written guides present certain scenarios and then anchor them in the landscapes and features of pilgrimage sites, such texts become manuals for explaining and interpreting the very terrain that the pilgrim is negotiating and, indeed, experiencing. By relating the great events of the past that occurred at a site, guides do not simply direct one to ascend to the very same stage on which these dramas occurred in order to reenact retrospectively the roles that various divine and human superheroes once played there. They are also unequivocal in implying that what initially happened in bygone eras at a particular place remains both evident there and active in certain ways. Thus, the very details of topographical form are attributed to the results of battles of magic, struggles for power, or other acts, while the landscape becomes named and recognized on the basis of these events. Furthermore, the physical environment is regarded as being animated in various ways. Places, objects, and their substances are thought of as becoming purified or morally superior through a process of empowerment effected by the presence and actions of deities and saints. Many Tibetans conceive of empowerment in ways that are not too different from the nature and effects of the fields of energy or radiation posited by modern physics. An empowered site or thing is credited with the ability to transform subtly that with which it comes in contact. Aspects of both the natural and the human-made world are also considered as the abodes (*gnas*) of a wide variety of nonhuman beings. The Tibetan word for pilgrimage literally means "circling around an abode" (*gnas skor*), referring to the general practice of circumambulation as a way of relating to such places.

The specific environments, objects, and persons upon which pilgrimages focus, and the pattern of relationships between these and the pilgrims themselves, are what forms the basis of pilgrimage practice for Tibetans. Thus, although most Tibetans identify themselves and their culture as Buddhist, it is often misleading to justify—as outside observers and interpreters often do—aspects of Tibetan life primarily in terms of abstract Buddhist doctrines. This is a tendency shared to a certain extent by highly educated Tibetan Buddhist clerics as well. Explaining Tibetan pilgrimages in terms of a static system of Indic metaphysical imperatives, such as karma, saṃsāra, and nirvāṇa, not only lacks the explanatory power required to account for such complex phenomena, but it also negates the fundamental assumptions and categories Tibetans draw from their own worldview in order to construct and negotiate their social reality.

The fact that Indian Buddhist and indigenous Tibetan views of the world exist in complex relation to one another is well attested in the discourses operating throughout Tibetan cultural history. Our small *Guidebook to Lapchi* provides some specific local examples of this. The text was written by a learned lama named Tenzin Chökyi Lodrö (Bstan 'dzin chos kyi blo gros, 1868–1906), the thirty-fourth hierarch of the Drigungpa ('Bri gung pa) sect, a branch of the important Kagyü (Bka' brgyud) school of Tibetan Buddhism. He compiled his *Guidebook to Lapchi* from a number of sources after a pilgrimage to the area 1901. His text purports to offer a Buddhist account of the process of the introduction of Buddhism into a Tibetan-speaking zone of the high Himalaya. Its central narrative reveals a dramatic ideological struggle between the powers represented by Indian tantric Buddhism, and those identified with other Indian belief systems and the spirit forces that many Tibetans recognize as inhabiting and animating their physical environment. While this contest of powers is played out between divine beings on a cosmic level, it also comes down to Earth and involves human beings and their history, as our text situates the story at a geographical location, the place of Lapchi, in the actual landscape of Tibet.

Lapchi, or more fully in Tibetan, the "Snowy Enclave of Nomadic Lapchi" ('Brog la phyi gangs kyi ra ba), is an area of glaciated mountains and luxuriant alpine valleys located on the present border between Nepal and the Tibetan Autonomous Region of the People's Republic of China. It lies just to the west of the great Himalayan summit of Gaurishankar (7,150 m), or Jomo Tseringma (Jo mo tshe ring ma) as it is known to Tibetans. At present the region is inhabited by pastoralists and seasonally frequented by pilgrims and traders from both sides of the border. While today it is possible for people to locate the place on a map and visit it as a pilgrim or nomad, according to the *Guidebook to Lapchi* this has not always been the case. To explain the ways in which Lapchi became an empowered landscape worthy of performing pilgrimage at, and how human beings "opened the door to the place" (*gnas sgo phye ba*), the author resorts to two important narrative traditions. Both of these, the story of Rudra's subjugation in chapters 1 and 2 and the exploits of Milarepa (1040–1123 C.E.) in chapter 3, require some interpretive commentary.

First, the story of the subjugation of the evil Indian god Rudra by the virtuous buddha Vajradhara. Both main characters are referred to in the text under various names that mark their different manifestations and qualities, with Rudra also being called Mahādeva, Maheśvara, and Bhairava in places, while the buddha Vajradhara is identified as Heruka, Saṃvara, or Cakrasaṃvara as well. Both are also coupled with female consorts and served by their respective demonic or divine retinues. From a Buddhist point of view, Rudra can be seen to represent the powers and teachings of the heterodox Indian school of Śaivism, particularly as it developed in its tantric mode. The Tibetan area of Lapchi itself has a double Indian identity in the text, being equated with the tantric power place of Godāvarī. This is a site found listed in both Buddhist and Śaiva tantric literature and is associated with an area in the southern part of the Indian subcontinent. How, therefore, did Godāvarī come to be located in the high Himalaya by Tibetans, and become the setting for such a divine contest?

The answer to this question is complex and still not fully understood, but a few points seem clear. When Tibetan scholars and their Indian teachers began systematically to transfer late North Indian tantric Buddhism across the Himalaya into Tibet, they carried more than just texts, religious icons, and philosophies with them. They took with them a series of sophisticated narratives and rituals that related conceptions of the inner person to the ordering of the cosmos and the cult geography of the Indian subcontinent. As Tibetans began to engage in tantric meditation and yoga in their own land, many of the set of twenty-four or thirty-two famous tantric cult places of India gradually became identified with accessible locations in the high Himalaya and great plateau lands to the north. Some of the places at which Indian sites became duplicated were already significant to Tibetans as being the dwellings of powerful mountain gods and goddesses, along with a host of other local spirit forces. The Snowy Enclave of Lapchi is one such area.

The initial spatial setting for the story of the subjugation of Rudra at Lapchi is the universe itself, but more specifically our southern cosmic continent (Jambudvīpa), as it is conceived of in Buddhist cosmologies that have long been known in Tibet. The events unfold in the context of cosmic time, over the countless millions of years of the four world-ages (*yuga*). It was at the beginning of the present age of disharmony (*kali yuga*) that a cosmic drama unfolded in which two sets of divine forces competed for hegemonic power, and the control of the world changed hands. The fact that Buddhist gods are vanquishing those that represent other non-Buddhist Indian religious schools in the story in part reflects the themes in the earlier Sanskrit sources upon which Tibetan storytellers later based their own versions, and not necessarily any actual conversion struggle that took place in Tibet itself. As we shall see, there are other interpretations of this conflict to consider. On a grand scale, then, the entire world-system is converted in this drama, although during the process essentially the same scenario is played out locally at each of the twenty-four tantric power places located on Earth, Godāvarī (alias Lapchi) being one of them. The subtle operations by which this conversion takes place are of great importance if we are to appreciate the multiple implications of the story for Tibetans.

In the Buddhist tantras, one of the primary systems of representation is that of the cryptogram or psycho-cosmogram (maṇḍala). Essentially, a maṇḍala is a complex, three-dimensional system of organization or interrelations applied to reality at different levels. It can be conceived of as an elaborate, tiered palace inhabited by buddhas or their emanations, together with a divine host of beings all hierarchically assembled from top to bottom, and from center to periphery. For Tibetan Buddhists the universe is ordered in this way, with the Buddha dwelling upon the central cosmic mountain (Meru) and the world arranged around it in a great circle divided into different planes. The particular maṇḍala found in the *Guidebook to Lapchi*, that of Heruka or Saṃvara as a heroic emanation of the buddha Vajradhara, is organized on three planes: the celestial or "sky" zone, the surface of the Earth, and the subterranean or "underworld" zone. This threefold ordering of space (known as *tribhuvana* in Sanskrit or *sa gsum* in Tibetan) is pervasive in both Indian and Tibetan worldviews. The twenty-four tantric power places are arrayed within this system, with eight existing on each of the three planes. A further eight sites are included, these being a series of charnel grounds located around the circumference of the great circle of the maṇḍala itself, thus yielding a total of thirty-two locations often mentioned in the texts. Godāvarī or Lapchi is counted as existing on the celestial plane of the world-system maṇḍala, hence its designation as one of the "eight sites of celestial action."

For Tibetans, the organization of the maṇḍala is also repeated on various subcosmic levels. Thus, the *Guidebook to Lapchi* goes on to describe the conversion of the spirit powers at the site in terms of the establishment of a maṇḍala right there in the actual mountain environment of Lapchi, and the place becomes animated in a particular way as a result. This is one of the main reasons why Lapchi is regarded as empowered and important to visit by pilgrims, whether they be tantric yogins or lay worshippers. Many oral and written sources make it clear that to the ordinary observer such places appear mundane, as just earth, rock, sky, and water, although features of the landscape are often held to be shaped in certain ways as they reveal the form of another level of reality beneath their surface. To highly qualified meditators and enlightened beings who visit Lapchi, the true reality of the maṇḍala, as a celestial palace with divine inhabitants, is visible and accessible there.

Furthermore, on another, more esoteric level, the same maṇḍala is also repeated within the human body itself, particularly so when it is activated during the specialized meditation and yoga performed by advanced tantric Buddhist practitioners in Tibet. Thus, when the subtle psychic body of the meditator is generated in accord with this, it too has twenty-four related internal power points organized like the cosmic maṇḍala. This yogic network is often referred to as the adamantine-body (*vajrakāya*), and its internal points are homologized with the external tantric cult sites, such that the reality of the microcosm and macrocosm are equated. Thus, within the logic of this system we find that in the text the external power place of Lapchi is equated with, and said to correspond to, the left ear of the adamantine-body. Furthermore, it is to the external cult places like Lapchi, which had become established as natural maṇḍalas, the yogins made actual pilgrimages to develop and perfect their internal adamantine-body.

Bearing all this in mind, it is possible that the story of Rudra's subjugation can also be read as an implicit description of internal psychic transformations that the practitioner of tantric Buddhist yoga undergoes. In later parts of Milarepa's story we find these meditative processes explicitly referred to. Thus, the character of Rudra and his vile horde of demons also represent the negative predispositions that need to be overcome by the tantric yogin. The Buddhist Heruka and his potent and virtuous assembly are also the yogin's own overcoming of tendencies toward defilement. Attempting to understand such esoteric levels of meaning that the *Guidebook to Lapchi* may have is valuable as a key to how Tibetans might relate to the site itself as pilgrims. But it is also essential if we are to grasp the Tibetan significance of the character featured in the final part of the story of Lapchi, that is, the universally popular Tibetan saint and yogin Milarepa.

After its conversion into a Buddhist maṇḍala and subsequent empowerment, the place of Lapchi is finally fully opened to human beings by the bold activities of Milarepa. As his capsule biography in the text indicates, Milarepa wandered to remote tantric power places and through his meditative training became an accomplished yogin who was able to activate the adamantine-body within himself and identify with the powers and qualities of the divinities in residence. It is common knowledge for Tibetans that yogins attain many potent magical abilities, the so-called paranormal powers (*siddhi*), as a partial result of their practice toward enlightenment. From this point of view alone they are very highly regarded figures in Tibetan culture. Furthermore, as embodied representatives of realized divinity and the maṇḍala, they are personally empowered individuals whose psychophysical body is highly purified and morally superior. Given all these qualities, in our story of Lapchi, Milarepa is able not only to defeat successive waves of demonic attack with his superior tantric magic, but also at times seemingly to play with reality and leave miraculous traces behind, such as footprints in rocks, at the places he passes. For the Tibetan pilgrim at Lapchi these amazing traces of the saint, and the other places where he spent time in his supercharged body, are all empowered sites in their own right. They are important not only to witness as a record of his actions, but also to encounter and experience personally because of the spiritual transformations they are believed to be able to effect.

Finally, we should reflect on the general theme of subjugation and conversion that runs throughout the whole three chapters below. Discerning readers will notice that at no point are the forces of evil and perversity ever completely banished or totally annihilated by Buddhist deities or tantric yogins. Using the full force of Buddhist magical and moral superiority, divine residences are taken over and redecorated, the accessories and symbols of the vanquished are adopted and employed by the vanquishers, and identities and allegiances are changed and fixed with binding oaths. The benefits of Buddhist doctrines, including salvation, are available to those conquered and converted. In the case of Milarepa, the potent human conduit through which this process operates, he becomes the principal teacher or lama (*bla ma*) of the spirit world as well as that of the human one. We should note that while this tantric yogin wages magical warfare to battle male demons into submission, he conquers a feminine environment and its female spirit leader by means of ritual sexual penetration. The idea of the land of Tibet as a feminine ground tamed and converted by an introduced male Buddhist power is a recurrent theme in subjugation narratives surrounding the introduction of Buddhism to the high plateau.

Ultimately, then, there would seem to be no final or complete victory in the story of Lapchi. The indigenous forces of evil and perversity are still present in the world, although now pinned down, bound, or contained; they are neutralized and held in check by Buddhism in a variety of ways. Considering this, there is perhaps an important question that this small pilgrim's guide to Lapchi should provoke in its critical readers: Can we ever afford to assume that the Buddhist conversion of Tibetan culture was a historically or socially complete process? Or is it still an ongoing one; the maintenance of a balance between two sets of forces, which must be replayed or reconstituted continually by way of a welter of narrative and ritual scenarios developed and reproduced for the best part of a millennium? There is much in traditional Tibetan religious culture that is dedicated to this end, and this itself is a fact that has important social ramifications. As the powers of Buddhism must be continually employed to maintain this state of affairs and keep the balance, we find that they are channeled especially via its human representatives, that is, the high-status specialist figures of lamas, yogins, oracles, clerics, and various others, who occupy significant loci of social power in the Tibetan world. Such issues are surely worthy of continuing debate and inquiry in the study of Tibetan religion.

The translation below is based on two editions: Bstan 'dzin chos kyi blo gros, 34th 'Bri gung gdan rabs (1868–1906), *Gsang lam sgrub pa'i gnas chen nyer bzhi'i ya gyal gau dā wa ri 'am / 'brog la phyi gangs kyi ra ba'i sngon byung gi tshul las tsam pa'i gtam gyi rab tu phyed pa nyung ngu rnam gsal*. In *Dpal 'khor lo sdom pa'i sku yi gnas gangs ri ti se dang gsung gi gnas la phyi gangs ra gnyis kyi gnas yig* (Delhi: Damcho Sangpo Jayyed Press, 1983), ff. 261–402 (translation covers ff. 264–92 = 2b–16b); Bstan 'dzin chos kyi blo gros, 34th 'Bri gung gdan rabs (1868–1906), *Gsang lam sgrub pa'i gnas chen nyer bzhi'i ya gyal gau dā wa ri 'am / 'brog la phyi gangs kyi ra ba'i sngon byung gi tshul las brtsams pa'i gtam gyi rab tu byed pa nyung ngu rnam gsal (An account of the place of meditation known as Lachi in western Tibet)* (Gangtok: Sherab Gyaltsen, Palace Monastery, 1983) (translation covers pp. 1–16).

Further Readings

For more on the life and travels of Milarepa, see G. C. C. Chang, *The Hundred Thousand Songs of Milarepa*, 2 vols. (Boulder: Shambhala, 1977); and L. P. Lhalungpa, *The Life of Milarepa* (Boulder: Shambhala, 1984). For more on Indian and Tibetan conversion and subjugation narratives, see Ronald Davidson, "The Bodhisattva Vajrapāṇi's Subjugation of Śiva," in *Religions of India in Practice*, ed. Donald S. Lopez, Jr. (Princeton: Princeton University Press, 1995), pp. 547–55; Janet Gyatso, "Down with the Demoness: Reflections on a Feminine Ground in Tibet," in *Feminine Ground: Essays on Women and Tibet.*, ed. J. D. Willis (Ithaca: Snow Lion, 1989), pp. 33–51. On Tibetan tantric pilgrimage sites and the area of Lapchi, see Toni Huber, "Where Exactly are Cāritra, Devikota and Himavat? A Sacred Geography of Controversy and the Development of Tantric Buddhist Pilgrimage Sites in Tibet," *Kailash, a Journal of Himalayan Studies* 16, 3–4 (1990):121–65; Huber, "Guide to the La-phyi Maṇḍala: History, Landscape and Ritual in South-Western Tibet," in *Maṇḍala and Landscapes*, ed. A. W. Macdonald (New Delhi: D. K. Printworld, 1996); A. W. Macdonald, "Hindu-isation, Buddha-isation, Then Lama-isation or: What Happened at La-phyi?," in *Indo-Tibetan Studies: Papers in Honour and Appreciation of Professor David L. Snellgrove's Contribution* to *Indo-Tibetan Studies*, ed. T. Skorupski (Tring, UK: Institute of Buddhist Studies 1990), pp. 199–208.

An Elucidatory and Concise Analysis of Stories Concerning the History of Godāvarī, alias the Snowy Enclave of Nomadic Lapchi, One of the Twenty-four Power Places for Accomplishing the Secret Path

I
HOW THIS INANIMATE MOUNTAIN ITSELF WAS ORIGINALLY TAKEN OVER BY THE ARROGANT RUDRA

Long, long ago, after the elapse of a very great period of time following the creation of this very world-system, the lord of this world, the great god called Mahādeva alias Maheśvara, ferocious Bhairava [or Rudra], appeared in fierce and violent forms and then took up residence in and ruled over the country of Magadha in India. At the same time, there appeared four serpent deities and four demigods from the underworld, four bestowers of harm and four ogres from the surface of the Earth, and four gods and four gandharvas from the sky. These twenty-four fierce and violent spirits assumed control of their respective dwelling places in those twenty-four countries extending from Pullīramalaya to Kulutā in the southern cosmic continent and then took up residence in them. In particular, at that time the Snowy Enclave of Lapchi was known by the name Godāvarī. A certain fierce and venomous couple who were gods of the demon class, the gandharva Suravairiṇa and his consort Vīramatī, appropriated this place, establishing a palace there.

Thereafter, because of their excessive anger these twenty-four fierce ones consumed the life force of many sentient beings. Because of their excessive lust they made love at all times. Because of their excessive ignorance they accepted heretical views themselves and then imposed them on others. Having also taken Mahādeva as their ultimate refuge, they performed obeisance to him. As a result Maheśvara, after abandoning his own form and having manifested in the form of twenty-four stone phallic symbols (*liṅga*), dwelt thus in each of those places.

II
HOW THE PLACE WAS CONVERTED INTO A FIELD OF CELESTIAL ACTION, AFTER BEING SUBDUED BY AN EMANATION OF SAṂVARA

When the present cosmic age of disharmony issued in, following a passage of incalculable hundreds of thousands of years, after the completion of the cosmic age of perfection and the second and third cosmic ages accordingly, the great buddha Vajradhara saw that the time had come to descend and subdue those fierce ones. Having arisen in the form [of Heruka, a heroic archetype deity] with four faces and twelve arms, expressing highly enraged great wrath, even while his mind was not moved from objectless compassion, and assuming a dancing pose, he trampled ferocious Bhairava and his consort underfoot, as a result of which Bhairava attained great bliss, and gained complete awakening under the earth.

Thus, after conquering ferocious Bhairava, Heruka remained on the summit of the central cosmic mountain, at which time he was presented with a heavenly mansion provided with a throne by the buddha Akṣobhya, with twenty-four male and twenty-four female bodhisattvas by the buddha Ratnasambhava, with twelve goddesses by the buddha Amitābha, with armored gods by the buddha Amoghasiddhi, and with gods representing the magically empowered aggregates, constituents, and sources by the buddha Vairocana. After which, the maṇḍala of the sixty-two emanations of Saṃvara was completed.

At that time, the twenty-four pairs of male and female bodhisattvas, having also arisen in the form of wrathful father-mother unions (*yab yum*), subdued the twenty-four arrogant ones [and their consorts] living in the twenty-four countries of the southern cosmic continent. Eight of the wrathful father-mother unions, having manifested as eight guardians of the cardinal gates and intermediate points, subdued the eight wrathful goddesses of the cemeteries [surrounding the maṇḍala]. In particular, from among the aforementioned twenty-four pairs of bodhisattvas, both the male bodhisattva Vajrapāṇi and the female bodhisattva Vajravetālī, having arisen in the form of a wrathful father-mother union, subdued both of the couple of gandharvas who resided at the Snowy Enclave of Lapchi. The manner of their subjugation was as follows: Having seized the abode of those venomous ones, they transformed it into a palace; having taken away their power and strength, they rendered them powerless; having seized their elephant hides, tiger skins, and other garments, they dressed themselves in them; having seized their knives, skull-cups, ceremonial staffs, and other hand-held accoutrements, they used them as their own instruments; having appropriated their essential cries of rage, and so forth, they reempowered them as their own primary ritual formulas; having seized their meat, beer, and other edibles and drinkables, they performed circular feast offerings with them and then made their minds dissolve in the clear light and brought them to awakening. In particular, they empowered the receptacles of Mahādeva's emanations [i.e., the stone phallic symbols] so that the maṇḍala of the emanations of the sixty-two deities of Cakrasaṃvara was directly manifest there. And in that way, the maṇḍala of the emanations of Cakrasaṃvara as vanquishers was completed without abandoning the form of those to be vanquished. Regarding that, at the time when the twenty-four [external] countries were assigned to the internal adamantine-body, it was said: "The face was Pullīramalaya, the crown of the head was Jālandhara, the right ear was Oḍḍiyāna, and the neck was Arbuta." This place, Lapchi, was known as the left ear, Godāvarī, and nowadays the proof of this is so made as a self-manifest ear on a rock called Left Ear.

In brief, after the subjugation of ferocious Bhairava by glorious Heruka during the cosmic age of disharmony, the district known as Godāvarī, which is one of the eight sites of celestial action, was established as the physical field of Cakrasaṃvara. But it should be understood that before ferocious Bhairava was conquered, it was nothing but a heap of earth and rock, or an ordinary abode of nonhuman beings.

III
HOW THE ENTRANCE TO THE PLACE WAS OPENED BY THE MASTERS REALIZED IN TRUTH

Following glorious Heruka's magical transformation of it into a place of attainment of the powers of secret tantric Buddhism, for a long time after there were just flesh-eating celestial heroes and amazons roaming and playing there at will, and because of this there were no ordinary beings belonging to the human race there. But 336 years after the Buddha's passing beyond suffering and rebirth, in the holy land of India the great realized meditation master glorious Saraha appeared and initiated the vehicle of the Vajrayāna of secret tantric Buddhism, after which he visited all the twenty-four countries and thirty-two places. From that time on there is really no question that many of the great accomplished ones of India came to that place. Now, due to the vicissitudes of time, we can no longer be certain exactly who went there.

However, after the exalted Avalokiteśvara manifested as the king of Tibet, Songtsen Gampo (Srong brtsan sgam po), and acted as the protector of Snowy Tibet [see chapter 2], the flesh-eating celestial amazons became a little milder, whereupon Mangyül (Mang yul) and Nyanang (Gnya' nang) and other locations on the borders of this place began to be habitable by human beings. After that, because the great meditation master Padmasambhava visited the place and bound the flesh-eating celestial amazons by oath, they became even milder than before, and human beings could travel, to a certain extent, to the very center of Lapchi as well. Later on, because the learned and accomplished great Yuthogpa Dreje Badzra (G.yu thog pa 'dre rje badzra) went there, there are also various acknowledged meditation caves of Yuthogpa there nowadays. Finally, concerning the full completion of the entrance to the place, since the mightiest of yoga practitioners, the master Milarepa, is the one who opened it, I shall relate the brief account of that now.

As for the master Milarepa himself, he was born in Mangyül Gungthang (Gung thang) during the water-dragon year (1052) of the first sixty-year calendrical cycle (1027–1087), the time at which the translator Marpa (Mar pa) reached the age of forty. During his youth, he employed the black arts against his paternal relatives who had come forward as his enemies, and he destroyed thirty-five members of the enemy party. Having made it hail, he destroyed the harvest. Out of remorse for that, he came into the presence of Marpa the translator in the valley of Lhodrak Drowo (Lho brag gro wo). He won his favor by single-handedly erecting a nine-storied tower many times, as well as performing other deeds, and requested the teachings that had been handed down from glorious Nāropa. After he mastered them, on the occasion of his going to Latö, his lama prophesied to him the best meditation places at which to perform his practice, in particular:

> Because the Latö Gyelgiri (La stod rgyal gyi ri) is a mountain empowered by the great accomplished ones of India, meditate there. Because Tise (Ti se) snow mountain [Mount Meru] was prophesied by the Buddha to be the "snowy mountain" [in Buddhist scriptures] and is the palace of Cakrasaṃvara, meditate there. Because the Snowy Enclave of Lapchi is Godāvarī, one of the twenty-four countries, meditate there. Because Mount Pelbar (Dpal 'bar) of Mangyül and the Snowy Enclave of Yolmo (Yol mo) in Nepal are the places prophesied in the *Garland Discourse* (*Avataṃsaka Sūtra*), meditate there. Because Chubar (Chu dbar) of Drin (Brin) is the place where the celestial amazons who are field-protectors assemble and reside, meditate there. Furthermore, in any deserted place that is perfectly suitable, meditate and raise the banner of realization in each one.

Thus was his prophecy. After that, the master returned to Mangyül Gungthang and as a consequence of observing the condition of his homeland, his mind was softened by a liberating aversion to this world. Through the perfection of ascetic practices during his twelve years at Drakar Taso (Brag dkar rta so), he acquired special qualities, to the extent of being able to fly through the air. At that time, he resolved to go to open the entrance to the area of the Snowy Enclave of Lapchi and fully realize the instructions of his principal teacher. After he had traversed the Dringi Poze (Brin gyi spo ze) pass, he went to Drakmar Chonglung (Brag dmar mchong lung) and gained realizations there. As a result, at that time the king of the obstacle-making demons known as Vināyaka, who is at present the field-protector of Lapchi, transformed himself into seven iron festival clowns with hollow and sunken eyes and appeared looking for an opportunity to get at the master. Then Milarepa said:

> I, Milarepa, am not afraid of demons.
> If Milarepa was afraid of demons,
> There would be little profit in a knowledge of things as they really are.
> You! Hosts of obstacle-makers, demons, and evil spirits who have come here,
> How wonderful it is that you have arrived.
> Do not hasten to leave, but please stay here.
> Let us discuss this together clearly.
> Though you may be in a hurry, by all means stay here tonight.
> We should vie in skill of body, speech, and mind,
> And see the difference in greatness between the white and the black religions.
> Do not leave without having made a nuisance of yourselves.

If you leave without having made a nuisance of yourselves,
How shameful your coming here on this occasion!

Having said that, he raised the pride of his archetype deity and went directly for the festival clowns. The festival clowns, their eyes bulging in panic from their fear, fright, and terror, disappeared rapidly one into the other until the last remaining one, having formed itself into a whirling tornado, disappeared from sight. After, he performed a little meditation in that place. Following the field-protector's failure to get at him with this first magical trick, he resolved to go to the central place of Lapchi. He traversed the Drin Poze pass and the Nyanang Thong (Gnya' nang mthong) pass and went to the entrance of Lapchi, Nyanang Tashigang (Bkra shis sgang). Since the people of Tsarma (Rtsar ma) had already heard of the master's fame, there was a desire to meet him that coincided favorably with the master's arrival in Tsarma on this occasion. Because of that a wealthy resident of Tsarma, Shendormo (Gshen rdor mo), and his wife Leksebum (Legs se 'bum), and also Kyotön Shākya Guṇa (Skyo ston shākya guṇa) and others, were overjoyed when they realized that it was the master.

At that time, Lapchi was the nomadic pastureland of the residents of Nyanang Tsarma. But because it had become a physical field of celestial action, a land roamed by flesh-eating celestial amazons, there was a frequent occurrence of open attacks by goblins and demons against the people who went there. As a result, the name of Drelung Kyomo ('Dre lung skyo mo, "Discontented Demon Valley") was given to the region. They requested that the master go there to subdue the demons and open the entrance to the place. Then the master also went toward the Züleigang (Zul le'i gangs) pass of Lapchi, and from the top of the pass the nonhuman beings produced specters to frighten him. As soon as he reached the summit of the pass there were violent claps of thunder and flashes of lightning, and the mountains on both sides of the valley moved, so that the mountain torrent, diverted from its course and churned up in violent waves, turned into a lake. At this, the master gave a concentrated stare, took his staff and pushed it in, and the lake drained out from the bottom and disappeared. The place is known as Mudzing (Dmu rdzing, "Demon Pond"). From there, he descended a little way, and the nonhuman beings stirred up waves consisting of many boulders, to the point where the mountains on both sides were thrown down. The celestial amazons provided a safe path for him out of a hill running downward like a snake, between the sides of the valley. That "wave-stilling" path is known as the Khandro Ganglam (Mkha' 'gro sgang lam, "Ḍākinī Ridge Path").

Then, the nonhuman beings of lesser powers became calm of their own accord, while those of great powers, even though they did not find a point of attack, once again sought to get at him. The master, at the point where the Khandro Ganglam terminates, gave a concentrated stare causing reversion of their views and subjugation, whereby the magical tricks ceased completely, and after, in the spot where he stood, a footprint appeared on the rock. On a ridge a short distance from there, after the sky had cleared, he dwelt and cultivated the meditation of benevolence, and that spot is called Jamgang (Byams sgang, "Compassion Ridge"). When he went to Chuzang (Chu bzang) from there and stayed a short time, once again the field-protector of Lapchi the lord of obstacle-makers Vināyaka himself, in the guise of a Nepalese demon called Bharo with a demonic army as retinue, which filled the earth and sky of the valley of Chuzang, came and displayed many magical tricks, such as throwing mountains down on the master's head, pouring down fierce deluges of weapons, and so forth. The master said such things as:

> Due to the essential instructions of my supreme principal teacher,
> By the power of the firmly cultivated production and completion stages of meditation, and
> Because of an understanding of the causal nexus of inner being,
> In the outer world, I am not afraid of demons.
>
> In my lineage, that of Saraha,
> Are many yogins, effulgent as the sky.
> Having repeatedly meditated on the significance of primal mind,
> Illusory thoughts disappear into space.
> I see neither the hindered nor the hinderer.

And then he bound the nonhuman beings by oath. On that occasion they gave him various things, such as provisions for a month, and from then on they became the master's patrons. After that, when he stayed in a cave at Ramding (Ram sdings), many celestial amazons from Lapchi performed prostrations, gave him offerings of every kind of desirable thing, and circumambulated him, and as a consequence there appeared here on a rock the footprints of two celestial amazons. On the way down from there the nonhuman beings created the magical appearance of many enormous vulvas on the path before him. The master, his penis having become erect in anger, advanced on his way brandishing it, and through rubbing his penis on a rock in which was collected the quintessence of the place at a point past nine of the illusory vulvas, and by giving a powerful stare, the magic tricks were all brought to a stop. That place is called Lagu Lungu (La dgu lung dgu, "Nine Crests Nine Valleys").

Then, when he was close to arriving at the central place, again the field-protector, the lord of obstacle-makers himself, went to meet him and present offerings to him. After constructing a religious throne, he requested Buddhist teachings and finally was absorbed into a boulder in front of the throne, which is why nowadays in that place there is a ritual cairn of stones. Then, at the center of the place, which has the appearance of three matrix-triangles stacked one upon the other because the sky outside it is triangular, the ground inside it is triangular, and the rivers in between it are triangular; in the presence of Vajrayoginī, and other celestial heroes and amazons happily amusing themselves like the gathering clouds, he remained in meditation for one month in a cave known as the Dudül Phukmoche (Bdud 'dul phug mo che, "Great Demon Subduing Cave").

After that, he went to the place of his patrons from Nyanang and told them: "I have stayed at your grazing grounds in Drelung Kyomo. Since I have subdued all the demons it has become a place of practice, and I shall be the first to go there and meditate." Because of this they rejoiced and were filled with faith, and also this is said to be the beginning of the human practice of performing prostrations, making offerings, and circumambulating there. Then, many years later, after the master had converted the hunter Khyira Repa (Khyi ra ras pa), when he went into the presence of the ear of the Buddha glorious Cakrasaṃvara, which had arrived self-manifest on the rock known as Lapchi Nyenyön (Snyan g.yon, "Left Ear"), and stayed there, the five field-protecting celestial amazons, the Tsering Chenga (Tshe ring mched lnga), came to snoop and see what the master's meditative understanding was. At the time, the master was enjoying a low-caste girl in the forest of Sengdeng (Seng ldeng), and through looking in a white silver mirror he spotted them and finally disappeared into the sky. A year later, when he was staying in Chonglung, they came to snoop as before. At that time they saw the master riding on a lion, his body smeared with funeral ashes and blood, with a garland of flowers upon his head, wearing the sun and moon as clothing. In his hands he held a parasol and a banner. Finally he went, disappearing into the sky, so that they were unable to get at him.

Later on, in the year of the water-dragon (1112) when the master was age sixty-one, on the occasion of his sojourn in the Khyung gong (Khyung sgong) cave in the center of Menlung Chubar (Sman lung chu dbar) during the first summer month, one night an army of eighteen great demons, which filled the sky, the Earth, and the intermediate realm, came with these five at its head: a woman with a skeleton-like appearance, bearing the central cosmic mountain in her arms; a red jackal-faced woman, whose orifices were all gushing blood, who was disgorging an ocean by the mouthful; a fierce woman with the appearance of the lord of death, who was playing the Sun and Moon like a pair of cymbals; a black, terrifying woman, the color of coal, who was throwing the Sun, Moon, and stars to the ground, laughing out loud, "Strike, kill!"; and a woman as beautiful as a goddess, whose smile was seductive and coquettish. Even though they sought an opportunity, the demons failed to get at him, and once again they became faithful and earnest. As a result of that, they said, "You are a yogin who has attained a state of firmness. In our ignorance, we formerly ridiculed and hindered you, and because of this we are greatly ashamed and remorseful. From now on, we will obey whatever you command. We, the demons, will carry out all those actions and duties, whatever they are, that you command." Having promised this, they returned to their own abodes.

Later, in the water-female-snake year (1113) when the master was aged sixty-two, the queen of medicine deities, the auspicious Tsering Chenga, having come in the guise of five beautiful women, placed in the master's hands a full gemstone ladle, telling him it was wild-ox yogurt. After offering the five types of worldly paranormal powers, which are the powers of immortality, the divining mirror, food and prosperity, a treasury of jewels, and four-footed livestock, they requested to take the vow connected with conceiving the aspiration to highest awakening. Later, the five women made eye-viewed offerings consisting of incense, flowers, food, and drink, and as a result of their request he bestowed on them the teachings of definitive meaning and conferred the initiation of the goddess Tārā and the essence of the cycle of views of the Adamantine Path of Buddhism. He bestowed afterward the initiation of the goddess Kurukullā and advised them of the cycle of vows of the supreme ritual formula, and so forth.

Later, in the wood-horse year (1114), because some cowherds of Drin polluted their campfire with scraps of meat, the auspicious Tseringma became afflicted by a severe illness. When she invited the master himself from Chubar (Chu dbar), he arrived with the speed of flashing lightning on the path of magic light, Sa-manta tsa ri. On the left slope of the snow mountain Thönting Gyelmo (Mthon mthing rgyal mo), there was a tent of white silk, with golden walls, whose ropes were all made of precious stones. Inside, the center pole was a conch, and the tent pegs were of coral. Within this tent, looking gravely ill, was the auspicious lady Tseringma. She made a request, after which, from that evening, the master performed an ablution by means of the hundred syllable ritual, made an invocation to the principal teachers and precious ones, and prolonged her life by means of the Uṣṇīṣavijayā ritual.

She recovered gradually from the illness and gave thanks in gratitude to the master, her principal teacher. After that, the master gave her an explanation of the intermediate state between death and rebirth and the three bodies and led her on to the path of great awakening. The chief of the field-protecting celestial amazons, Tseringma, was accepted as his ritual sexual consort. Thus, as she was the chief and was now under his power, all the celestial heroes and amazons of the region of Lapchi perforce came under his power and were bound by oath. He took the life-force of all the eight types of demons and commanded that from then on they should not harm human beings. The various demons listened obediently. From that time up until the present day, there has never been any harm from the demons for us human beings who went there. This is due solely to the grace of the principal teacher and master Milarepa, his spiritual sons, and those aforementioned accomplished ones. Those narrations concern the manner in which the entrance to the place was opened.

Remarkable Lives

—7—

The Life of Tilopa

Nālandā Translation Committee

Tilopa was a Bengali yogin, crazy saint, and poet who lived during the tenth century. He was one of the most important figures in an antinomian movement that practiced tantric Buddhism in an especially colorful and vivid manner—the yogins known as the *mahāsiddhas* or "great accomplished ones." The mahāsiddhas believed that the essence of enlightenment was present throughout reality, and thus any ordinary activity could be transformed into a Buddhist practice by directing it toward awakening the mind itself. The mahāsiddhas sometimes chose professions and life-styles that ordinarily would have been considered a violation of the principle of "right livelihood" set forth by the Buddha. Their special method of transforming daily activities into meditation practices involved seeing mundane things as *mudrā*, as "seals" or "symbols" of deeper truths. For example, the mahāsiddha Saraha made arrows for a living, which might be considered an impossible profession for a Buddhist guru, since weapons enable violence to occur. But Saraha regarded the arrows as a mudrā, as a symbol: just as ordinary arrows kill people, so Saraha's arrows would kill ego-clinging itself.

The mahāsiddhas wrote religious songs in a popular style, some of which seemed to be about sexual subjects. Each line implied or evoked a special symbolic or "code" meaning. As a result, the biographies of these teachers are full of esoteric symbolism, making them very difficult to interpret or decode. At times they are downright obscure, and even great tantric scholars have trouble unraveling some of the allusive and elusive writings of Tilopa and his colleagues. An important and lengthy biography of Tilopa was written by Wangchuk Gyaltsen (Dbang phyug rgyal mtshan), a student of the "Mad Yogin of Tsang Province" (Gtsang myon Heruka, 1452–1507), a Tibetan yogin whose own life exemplifies the wildness and love of esoteric symbolism that marks the Bengali mahāsiddhas. This biography is a compilation of a variety of disparate stories about Tilopa, and when Pema Karpo (Pad ma dkar po, 1527–1592) summarized them in his abbreviated biography, he maintained the disparity. Thus, we have three biographies, directed, so Pema Karpo says, toward students of "lesser, middle, and greater" abilities. We have translated here the "lesser" and "greater" biographies and skipped the extremely obscure middle biography.

First we have "The Ordinary Biography" for students of "lesser capacity," even though the text is replete with obscure symbolism. This account tells the traditional Buddhist story of the rise of an ordinary person to fame and royal power through the magical assistance of a Buddhist hermit. Tilopa is a common oxherding boy with an extraordinary destiny. He meets the most famous philosopher in the history of Mahāyāna Buddhism, the master (*ācārya*) Nāgārjuna. The Tibetans believe that after Nāgārjuna gained enlightenment by means of Mahāyāna contemplative practices, he began to practice tantra and lived for hundreds of years as a yogin. At the outset of the story, Nāgārjuna has just gained mastery of the magical ability (*siddhi*) known as "the good vase," which enables him to fulfill all wishes. He makes Tilopa into a king and teaches him to rule through magical means. All of the tricks and illusions that Tilopa employs to convince his subjects of his power and to defeat his enemies are commonplaces of Indian storytelling. Like the Buddha, however, Tilopa becomes dissatisfied with the suffering in saṃsāra, so he renounces the world in order to become a Buddhist ascetic. After abdicating his kingship and establishing his son on the throne, he joins a religious community and begins to study Buddhist teachings.

Pema Karpo tells his story in a simple, straightforward manner, but it is full of tantric symbolism. It is almost as if this text were a primer in esoteric symbolism for people who have not been initiated into the secret and complex practices of tantra. An example of this would be the multiple meanings and functions of the vase. The vase plays a central role in the empowerment ceremony of tantric Buddhism known as *abhiṣeka* (see chapter 13). *Abhiṣeka* means "sprinkle and pour," and it originally referred to the annointing ceremony in which Indian princes were consecrated to become kings. The vase was placed over the head of the prince, and he would drink from it and then be bathed with the water. In this story we see the vase being used in its original function, as if Pema Karpo were introducing us to the history of the vase symbol.

A special feature in the biographies of the Kagyü saints like Tilopa is that their conversion to tantric practice occurs through the intercession of the same divine principle—a certain mother goddess—the fierce, passionate, and wrathful Vajrayoginī. She personifies transcendent wisdom (*prajñā*) as a vivid and intimate experience and can appear to practitioners in a variety of forms. To remind the ignorant that they have missed the point, she can appear as an ugly old woman or as a beautiful young girl. In every situation she embodies the energy of wisdom, untamed by conventional thought, social norms, or preconceptions. Often her name is not literally given in the biographies, perhaps because the practices that the name evokes are secret. Sometimes she is identified as Vajravārāhī, a name that literally means "Indestructible Sow," although no humor is intended by this curious appellation. The pig is often associated in Buddhist texts and iconography with ignorance, and Vajravārāhī, the Indestructible Sow, symbolizes the transmutation of ignorance into wisdom through tantric practices.

Vajrayoginī or Vajravārāhī is also a type of *ḍākinī*, a term that in Tibetan means literally a "sky-goer" (*mkha' 'gro ma*). In iconographic images, ḍākinīs fly through the sky into the world of the yogin or yoginī, bearing messages of enlightenment. Esoterically, they represent the phenomenal world to the practitioner. The meditator is to contemplate the nature of the self and the external world. But if he or she focuses too much on the self or becomes too intellectual, then the world as an external force, as a consort, will seduce or frighten the yogin back into awareness of the essence. Her buddha consort is Cakrasaṃvara, whose name means "binder of the psychic centers (cakras)" and refers to inner yogic practices. Often he is simply called "Heruka." In this version of his biography, when Tilopa abdicates his throne, he moves to a charnel ground where a huge stone has gradually changed shape, until it became a statue of Heruka.

Vajrayoginī first meets Tilopa after he has been ordained as a conventional Buddhist monk, while he is studying the famous Mahāyāna sūtras on emptiness called the Perfection of Wisdom Sūtras (*Prajñāpāramitā*). Although tāntrikas regard these texts as the profound word of the Buddha, they are difficult to practice and do not lead to enlightenment as quickly as their tantric equivalents. She initiates him into tantric practices, and so he begins his education in the Vajrayāna. This involves a system of practices in which one is introduced to the secret assembly of various tantric buddhas, such as Vajrayoginī's own consort Cakrasaṃvara, Guhyasamāja, Mahāmāyā, and many others. These practices include the use of liturgies, during which mantras are chanted and complex visualizations are performed, in what is known as the "developing stage" (*utpattikrama*). These developmental practices lead to a more direct experience of realization, without the mediation of chanting or visualization practices, called the "completion stage" (*sampannakrama*). Vajrayoginī explains both aspects of tantric practice to Tilopa in a marvelously succinct way. In story after story the ordinary biography continues to explain in subtle symbols and coded language the multifarious methods used in the Vajrayāna.

Tilopa was famous for combining four traditions of tantric practice in his own teachings, which were systematized and passed on to his disciple Nāropa, the next mahāsiddha in the Kagyü lineage. Here we see Tilopa meeting four different accomplished yogins and receiving one of these "special transmissions" (*bka' babs*) from each. These Bengali mahāsiddhas, such as Lavapa and Kṛṣṇācārya, are important for specialists in South Asian literature, for their songs in Apabhraṃśa and Old Bengali are some of the first vernacular literature ever written in India (see chapter 12). When their songs or *dohās* were translated into Tibetan, they were treated as esoteric instructions to tantric meditation, and they were given sophisticated commentaries. The practices recommended in the songs are still done to this day.

Biographies of Tilopa vary over what his true profession was once he abandoned his monastic robes and became a mahāsiddha. Many different forms of livelihood are presented here, as if Pema Karpo had collated and conflated the various accounts. Tilopa is perhaps best known for being a maker of *tila* or sesame oil, from which he gets his most famous name. Tilopa's song on sesame oil, unusual for being clearly expressed and unobscure, offers us an excellent example of the mahāsiddha's technique of transforming ordinary, mundane activities into subtle meditative practices. At the conclusion of these biographies, though, we will have seen Tilopa engaged in an amazing range of livelihoods. He was a king, a sesame-oil salesman, a pimp, a mendicant Buddhist monk, and a professional teacher. In another biography of his disciple Nāropa, Tilopa is presented as an unemployed street person, who survives by eating the leftover fish parts thrown away by fish merchants—the guts and scales. Based on this story, images of Tilopa often show him wearing rags, with an unshaven face, holding up a dead fish in his hand as if it were some sacred icon.

The last part of Tilopa's "Ordinary Biography" depicts his mission as a tantric guru, when he defeats and converts numerous Hindu heretics, most of whom then become famous Buddhist yogins themselves. These yogins tend to establish their permanent homes in charnel grounds or, as modern Indians call them, "burning grounds." These are areas where cremations are performed, the South Asian equivalent of a cemetery. Charnel grounds are considered both sacred and lawless places. Ghosts, demons, and wild animals live there, feeding on the remains of the dead who have not been totally consumed by the cremation fire. Criminals gather there too, because these sites are shunned by the citizenry as places of ill-omen. And so too do tantric yogins dwell there, for not only are these sites ideal places to meditate on life's impermanence, they also enable the tantric yogin to realize that such impure places are fundamentally sacred, that the entire nature of reality is equally beyond pure and impure. The charnel grounds named in the text, such as Cool Grove, are famous in Buddhist literature and recur constantly, in stories, tantras, and tantric practice texts.

Also worthy of note in this ordinary life of Tilopa are the peculiar pedagogical techniques he uses to introduce people to the Buddhist path. Tilopa tends to teach people by first irritating them and insulting them, a technique not so different from that of his irascible divine patronness, Vajrayoginī. This too is a special style of the mahāsiddhas. Whereas the Buddha was famous for first soothing and comforting his audience before giving them teachings, the tantric yogins are notorious for employing the opposite method. They first wake an audience up by exciting their ire and then give them teachings that will be all the more striking for having been delivered in such a violent manner. Tilopa's special magical powers (*siddhi*) enable him to revive the dead, defeat hostile armies, and conquer heretics in magical displays of power, thereby convincing his audience to place faith in him and change their own harmful habits.

The "superior biography" or "Biography in Accordance with the Capabilities of Superior Students" reads like an allusive tantric fairy tale. It symbolically represents the practice of receiving tantric empowerment with a story about how Tilopa became awakened to his true nature by Vajrayoginī. The story opens with Tilopa being confronted by the usual ugly old ḍākinī, and they sing verses back and forth to each other as they discuss the nature of the self. Tilopa claims that he is just an ordinary person with human parents, who is tending the buffalo. The ugly old woman, symbolizing transcendent knowledge (*prajñā*), retorts that he is actually a buddha by nature and his ordinary world is a sacred world full of deities and divine principles of insight. She tells him that if he wishes to "tend the buffalo of meditative experience in the forest of bodhi trees" (that is, tame his own mind and achieve enlightenment) he must first gain the teachings of the "hearing lineage of that without letter." The "hearing lineage," also known as the "ear-whispered lineage," refers to the transmission to the disciple of the essence of the Buddhist teachings through the enlightened teacher's spoken words. These teachings are secret and not written down, therefore they are "without letter." But in a deeper sense they are without letter because these ineffable teachings are meditative experiences and not mere discursive ideas. Although we can point to them with words, these meditative states are utterly inexpressible. As cryptic as this speech by the ugly old woman is, Tilopa understands its import immediately, and he sets off to gather the requisite materials for gaining access to the teachings beyond language.

These special teachings are held by a matriarchy of ḍākinīs who live in a magical palace, which the text describes as a *vihāra*, a center for religious practice. Vihāras usually have gardens, dormitories, rectories, and meditation halls, but this magical one is constructed like a maṇḍala, a palace that houses Buddhist deities. The palace is surrounded by moats and iron mounds that serve as walls, forming a maṇḍala pattern that expresses esoterically the sacred homological structure of the mind and the world. Some of these goddesses are lower-order beings, called "action ḍākinīs," while others are "wisdom ḍākinīs," female buddhas representing wisdom itself. The queen of this realm is "the mother of all the buddhas," but this ambivalent expression could also be translated as "the consort of all the buddhas." She embodies the transcendent wisdom that gives birth to the buddhas by turning ordinary people into enlightened beings: hence, she is the mother of all the buddhas. She is the consort of the buddhas because, as the female buddha who embodies wisdom, she is complemented by the male tantric buddha, Cakrasaṃvara, who embodies skillful means. Just as the goddess and Cakrasaṃvara appear iconographically in sexual union, so enlightenment itself is the union of wisdom and skillful means.

Tilopa, who now realizes his own innate nature as the buddha Cakrasaṃvara, meets some resistance at the palace from these ḍākinīs, but this dramatic conflict is merely a symbolic gesture used to test his confidence, for Tilopa's victory is assured since he is none other than Cakrasaṃvara. His determination to receive the teachings represents the ideal attitude of the advanced tāntrika. For tāntrikas, complete confidence in one's own innate buddhahood is the psychological key to gaining enlightenment rapidly. This doctrine is not without its dangers, since it can easily lead to false arrogance and a sense of entitlement. But in this allegorical tale Tilopa is the very embodiment of tantric confidence. And so, he does not meekly request the teachings, which might express his hesitation or doubt about his innate buddhahood. Instead, he demands them and takes them by force as he storms the palace.

Once inside the palace, he declares himself Cakrasaṃvara, the buddha king of this maṇḍala, but before he can take the queen as his consort and become satisfied with the oral teachings of the hearing lineage, he must first receive empowerment. The empowerment ceremony is described in cryptic terms, and it relies on the esoteric instruments of initiation: painted empowerment cards (*tsa ka li*), mantras, and mudrās. The empowerment cards are representations of divine principles that are transferred from guru to disciple during empowerment ceremonies (see chapter 24). Mantras and hand gestures known as mudrās are used in the same way.

From here on the language of the biography becomes so symbolic and esoteric that it is extremely difficult to understand. Almost every technical term has a code meaning. For example, Tilopa sings of the "path that ripens" and the "path that frees." "Ripen" and "free" are code terms for the conferring of abhiṣeka or empowerment and practical instructions. Through the power of the ritual, the guru communicates a direct experience of the fruition, and this is "ripening." Then, the guru transmits the special oral instructions (*man ngag*) for the student's practice, and this is "freeing." In principle this secret direct transmission of the truth can only be communicated to a disciple who is already bound to the empowering guru through *samaya* or "commitment." Thus, the commitment is considered to be a key to the entire process. Here it is represented concretely as a key made of grass. But how could such a seemingly flimsy thing work to open a real door? The answer is that one must have confidence in the power of commitment to bring enlightenment. With such confidence, even a key of grass can open the gate of the palace. This confidence is confirmed when the disciple receives his or her guru's prophecy that they will become enlightened. Such a prophecy was uttered to Śākyamuni Buddha by the then reigning buddha when he began the bodhisattva path in a previous lifetime. The ritual uttering of this prophecy for the disciple has become a key moment in the tantric empowerment ceremony. Often in esoteric biographies, the prophecy that confers indestructible confidence is communicated not by a male buddha, but by the goddesses of tantra, the ḍākinīs. This is the case with Tilopa.

The biography continues with more esoteric references to the secret practices of the Vajrayāna. Each line of the superior biography could receive a whole book of commentary. In fact, tāntrikas traditionally study each of these points—the nature of ripening and freeing through empowerment and instruction, the nature of commitment, the notion of prophecy and tantric confidence in one's own nature—for years. The ability to understand easily every line of this biography would indicate that one was indeed a student of superior capacities. Any reader, therefore, who finds this passage easily comprehensible is to be congratulated.

The biographies of Tilopa are important works in the literature of Tibet. And yet they do not present the story of a Tibetan teacher at all, but that of a Bengali mahāsiddha, one of the forefathers of the Tibetan Kagyü lineage. The strange names of these Bengali saints, the peculiar miracles they worked, the colorful stories of yogic contests, of kings, and of deluding sorcerors who would be king, and finally, the constant glorification of the country of Bengal—all these are narrative motifs that passed into Tibetan literature and became a part of their tradition. They evoke in the Tibetan reader a sense of the exotic Indian origins of their religion. One feels as if one has entered a time warp and received a magical, indeed fantastic, telescopic view of the long-vanished past.

The works below were translated from *Chos byung bstan pa'i padma rgyas pa'i nyin byed*, vol. 2 of the *Collected Works (gsuṅ-'bum) of Kun-Mkhyen Padma-dkar-po* (Darjeeling: Kargyud Sungrab Nyamso Khang, 1973), pp. 226:3–250:5. Subheadings have been added by the translators.

Further Reading

For Tilopa's relationship with his most famous disciple, Nāropa, see Herbert Guenther, *The Life and Teachings of Nāropa* (London: Oxford University Press, 1963) and *The Life of Marpa the Translator*, trans. Nālandā Translation Committee (Boulder: Shambhala, 1982). For a collection of songs and poetry by Tilopa and members of his lineage in Tibet, see *The Rain of Wisdom*, trans. Nālandā Translation Committee (Boulder: Shambhala, 1980).

The Life of Tilopa

The one who is unrivaled in the world for the taming of beings by means of the Vajrayāna, and whose name is as famous as the sun and the moon, is Tilopa. Teaching in accordance with ordinary students, the story tells how he trained on the path. In accordance with intermediate students, it tells how he manifested as a transformation body (*nirmāṇakāya*). In accordance with superior students, it tells how he manifested as a perfect buddha.

THE ORDINARY BIOGRAPHY: TRAINING ON THE PATH

Birth and Family

In the eastern region of Jago, Tilo's father was the brahman Radiance, his mother the brahman Radiant, and his sister was named Radiant Torch. Her brother, Tilopa, was named Radiant Light at birth. He was brought up lovingly.

First Meeting with Nāgārjuna: Tilopa Is Tested

Tilopa along with a group of young children tended oxen and played together. At that time the noble master, Nāgārjuna, had been living in the forest of Bharendra, where he was performing the practice known as "the good vase." This was a practice that was said to fulfill all one's wishes. He thought, "As a test, I will carry this vase as I go for alms." But before he had even picked it up, divine and delicious food appeared within the vase, and so he knew that he had indeed attained accomplishment.

After a while, the master came to eastern India. On the way he saw a group of children tending their cattle and playing. The master thought, "Is there anyone among these children who belongs to the Mahāyāna family and is a suitable vessel for the Mantrayāna?" In order to test them, he pretended not to know where to ford a small river that flowed between the forest and city. He took off his shoes and prepared to cross to the other side at a place where there were some rapids.

From among those children, one boy, Tilopa, came forward and said, "Master, stay there!" The young boy prepared to carry the master across and lifted him up. In order to test the boy, when they had reached the middle of the river, the master blessed the river to make it miraculously increase, and it rose until the boy was almost underwater. However, the young boy did not feel regret even for an instant. His only thought was, "No harm must come to the master."

At that point, the master said, "Whoever does not hold onto a corpse, root, or tree will drown in the middle of the river and never reach the other bank."

"Hold me by the neck and don't let go!" the boy replied. Thus the master knew that the boy had good karma, and so he caused the magically swollen river to subside. Then, the master went off on his business and the young boy remained with his friends.

Second Meeting with Nāgārjuna: Tilopa Becomes King

One day, the master Nāgārjuna returned. The young boy from before, Tilopa, was sitting on the trunk of a tala tree. Two young girls on his right and left acted as his queens. Three or four boys were his inner ministers, and about ten were his outer ministers. About twenty were there as his subjects.

The young boy descended from the tree, prostrated, and offered his respects, saying, "Are you well? Did you enjoy bliss and joy?"

The master was pleased and said, "Would you like to be a king?"

"Yes, I would, but because I lack fortunate karma, I was born as a commoner," the boy answered.

"I have the means for you to become a real king," said the master.

"Please grant it to me."

The master then consecrated his vase again for seven days. In accordance with the boy's desire, he wrote the words "king," "queen," "minister," "subject," "wealth," "vehicle," and "kingdom" and placed them in the vase. Bringing the vase near the young boy, he said, "Place your mouth in the vase and say three times, 'I shall be king of this country.' "

The boy did so, and through the power of the good vase, the king of that country came to desire to go to another country. Secretly he dressed as a commoner and left.

In the country that the king had left behind, there was an elephant named

Possessing the Power of the Sun who could read omens. Accordingly, if war was coming, he would scatter dirt. If sickness and the like were about to arise in the land, he would not eat his food and would shed tears. At auspicious events, he would gather flowers from the park with his trunk and scatter them about. When it was the right time to enthrone a king, he would bear aloft in his trunk the vase that would empower the king, and he would place it on the top of a person's head.

At this time, the elephant took the vase from the palace of the king and went in the direction of the forest where the children were playing. All the king's retinue were astonished. "Either our king will die or our kingdom will be lost! Who will become the king now?" they thought, and they followed the elephant into the forest. There the elephant placed the vase on the small boy's head.

All the ministers and the others then welcomed him. They placed him on the precious throne in the palace and empowered him as king. Afterward, however, many people of the palace would not carry out his orders. Consequently, people in the surrounding countryside thought, "This king is a fake, as even the people in his own palace will not carry out his orders." Thus it came about that no one would obey his commands.

Tilopa supplicated master Nāgārjuna, and he arrived, carrying his good vase. He said, "Don't be afraid. Ride your elephant, holding your shield and brandishing your sword. Go to the park with your retinue. Then, slap your hand against a tree and say, 'Vṛkṣa! ["tree"] Go to war!' In this way, you will tame those subjects." When Tilopa did all this, all the trees became soldiers, and everyone saw the park filled with men in armor. All his subjects then knew that Tilopa possessed great merit and felt the greatest respect toward him. Thus Tilopa reigned over the kingdom for a very long time.

One day, many Persians filled the plain in that country. Everyone thought they were merchants, but instead they opened the baskets on the backs of their horses and elephants and removed various kinds of armor and weaponry. Outfitted in their armor, the Persians then prepared to wage battle.

Everyone in the country was terrified. The king consoled them, saying, "Don't be afraid!" and took up his sword and shield. Going forth to meet them, he waved his shield around, and there arose a great light, at which the enemy soldiers could not bear to look. Tilopa took out his sword, and they saw the land filled with troops of soldiers. Thus the enemy fled and was gone. After this, Tilopa's subjects were filled with even more respect than before.

After a long time, Tilopa became depressed with saṃsāra, and so he enthroned his own son as king. At the charnel ground religious settlement of Somapuri, there was a spontaneously arisen statue of Heruka. Two religious communities dwelt there; Tilopa's uncle was the abbot, and his mother attended the nuns. Tilopa approached his uncle and received ordination from him.

While Tilopa was studiously reading one day, a dark-skinned woman appeared, who was bald but had a grey moustache. His attention was diverted to her for a little while, and she called to him, "Would you like to understand what you are reading?"

Realizing that she was a ḍākinī, Tilopa asked, "Please, I would like to understand."

"This philosophical method of the perfection of wisdom (*prajñāpāramitā*) that you are studying is a hard path to travel. It is very difficult, there are many obstacles, and so it is difficult to attain perfect buddhahood that way. With the fruitional Mantrayāna, however, it is easy to travel the path—the difficulties are small and the obstacles few. I will admit you into the gate of that teaching," she said.

She then emanated the maṇḍala of Śrī Cakrasaṃvara in the sky before him and gave Tilopa empowerment (*abhiṣeka*). She taught Tilopa the [visualization practices of the] developing stage so that he would abandon attachment to ordinary reality, and she taught him the meditation practices of the completion stage so that he would abandon any attachment to the deities.

"Now speak like a madman and, after throwing off your monk's robes, practice in secret!" she said, and then disappeared.

This was Tilopa's first special transmission. The exalted Marpa has said:

> As granted by the mother Excellent Good Fortune (Subhaginī)
> Whose river of blessings is continuous,
> The four empowerments were transmitted.

Although Tilopa acted according to her orders and exerted himself in his meditation, he did not attain anything special. Thus he desired to see the noble master Nāgārjuna again, and he traveled to the south. He asked some men of Bhedarbha [Vidarbha] where Nāgārjuna was, and they said, "He dwells at Śrī Parvata." On the road leading there, in a clearing of the forest, Tilopa saw a woven grass hut shaped like an umbrella. Approaching it, he saw a yogin seated inside with nothing around him. "What are you doing?" Tilopa asked.

"The master told me to expound the dharma to the gandharvas [divine musicians] and so I am dwelling here," the yogin replied.

"What is your name?"

"Matangi."

"Who brings you your food?"

"The forest goddesses."

"Where does master Nāgārjuna live?" Tilopa asked.

"He has left."

And so Tilopa asked him, "Please accept me as your disciple." Matangi assented, emanated the maṇḍala of the buddha Guhyasamāja, and gave him empowerment. Then he bestowed both the tantra itself and the oral instructions. "You should also receive this from Āryadeva," Matangi said. At that point, Tilopa perfected the developing stage.

When he was close to obtaining heat in the completion stage [an advanced stage, when the experience of fruition begins to occur], Tilopa returned to

Bengal in eastern India. While he was there, he went to Kṛṣṇācārya (Dark Master) and received all the oral instructions on the three traditions of Cakrasaṃvara. He also heard teachings from Vijayapāda, a disciple of Kṛṣṇācārya. It is said that Tilopa also obtained instruction from Dārikapa and Vajraghaṇṭa. During this time he completely mastered the signs of heat [that is, signs of tantric realization]. However, because he had not fully realized suchness, Tilopa went to meet a master in Uḍḍiyāṇa whose only garment was a blanket (*lava*). He received oral instructions on the heart teachings of the siddhas.

Thus Tilopa attended gurus of four special transmissions—Kṛṣṇācārya, Nāgārjuna, Lavapa, and Mati Subhaginī.

Twelve Years of Pounding Sesame Seeds: Tilopa's Realizations of Suchness

Then master Matangi said, "Go to Bengal and cultivate this realization for twelve years by pounding sesame seeds. When you have realized suchness, everyone in the surrounding country will attain the siddhi of the celestial realm." Thus he prophesied.

When Tilopa arrived at Pañcapaṇa in Bengal, a marketplace filled with delights of the five senses, he acted as the attendant of a prostitute. Because he also practiced by pounding sesame seeds, the wisdom of the path of seeing [reality directly] was born in him.

Then, at times, the people saw the attendant Tilopa as a mass of light surrounded by twelve lamps. Sometimes they saw him surrounded by nineteen women; at other times, they saw him as a fully ordained monk, or as a yogin. They related what had happened to the prostitute, who was filled with remorse and went to confess to Tilopa. Amazed by the news, all the people of the city gathered there. Master Tilopa said to the prostitute, "Because I purified my own evil deeds in working for you, there is no fault attributed to you." Then he sang this song:

> Sesame oil is the essence.
> Although this innate coemergent wisdom
> Exists in the hearts of all beings,
> If it is not shown by the guru, it cannot be realized.
> Although the ignorant know the oil is in the sesame seed,
> They do not understand the nature of cause and effect
> And therefore are not able to extract the essence, the sesame oil.
> One removes the chaff from the beaten sesame,
> And the essence, the sesame oil, appears.
> In the same way the guru shows the truth of suchness,
> And one should bring out what rests inside, just as with the sesame oil.
> All phenomena become inseparable in one essence.
> Kye ho!
> The far-reaching, unfathomable meaning
> Is apparent at this very moment! Oh how wondrous!

By merely hearing the sound of his song, the people's minds were blessed, and they traveled instantly to the celestial realm. Thus the country was emptied for the first time, and he became renowned as Tilopa.

Tilopa's Travels and Teaching

Tilopa said:

> I went to a hundred buddha realms.
> I appeared in ten thousand emanations.

Near Uḍḍiyāṇa in the west, there was a king who was so devoted to his mother that he would follow anything that she said. "What can be done to make you happy?" he asked his mother.

"If all the paṇḍitas and *kusulus* (ascetic yogins) were gathered together and were to perform a feast offering (*gaṇacakra*), that would make me happy," she replied.

Thus the king commanded, "For the sake of my mother, assemble all the paṇḍitas and yogins so they can now perform a feast offering."

Everyone gathered together and did their practice step by step to please their respective personal deities. Then they agreed that the yogin who had the greatest power would be made the leader of the feast. They tested each other's power, and the one with the greatest power was a yogin named Mati, who was designated the leader.

When everyone had taken their places, an old woman with eighteen marks of ugliness said, "Let me inside the feast!" They let her in, and she said, "You do not have a suitable leader of the feast."

"Who would be suitable?" they asked.

"My brother!" she replied.

"Where is he?"

"At the charnel ground."

"Call him here!"

The woman vanished. After a while, she reappeared, bringing a yogin with her. The yogin Mati said, "Let the one among us with the greater power be made the leader."

"Let it be done that way," the yogin agreed.

Both sat down on one mat. First Mati created a maṇḍala and its deities in the sky, and Tilopa destroyed it. Then Tilopa created another one, and Mati destroyed it. Next, Mati sent forth an emanation and brought back many corpses from the charnel ground—Tilopa made them disappear. Tilopa did the same thing, and Mati made them disappear. Then Tilopa rode on a lion and caused the sun and moon to descend to the ground. He turned his body inside out, and from each hair pore he emanated the four continents. Mati was not able to do this; therefore, Tilopa was appointed the leader of the feast, and everyone bowed to him. Tilopa accepted the yogin Mati as his disciple and he bore the name Śaktimati. Without abandoning his body, even now Śaktimati lives in Uḍḍiyāṇa in the west.

Now, in the southern country, there was a heretic teacher, a follower of Īśvara (Śiva), who was learned in the sciences. He debated with many Buddhist paṇḍitas and defeated them. Therefore it came to be said that the teachings of the Buddha were losing respect. Then master Tilopa, dressed like a fully ordained monk, traveled there and behaved disdainfully to the follower of Īśvara. The Śaivite said angrily, "You and I should debate and compete in power. Whoever is defeated must give up his own teaching."

"Okay!" replied Tilopa. Thrones were prepared for the questioner, the respondent, and the judge, and then they sat down. With the Śaivite as the respondent, the master refuted his philosophical system. Next they competed in magical power. The Śaivite stopped the sun, but the master pushed it and made the sun set. Then the master stopped the sun, but the Śaivite was not able to make it set. Tilopa prepared to cut off the Śaivite's long hair, but the Śaivite became angry and emitted flames from his mouth. The master emitted even more flames than the Śaivite and repelled his flames. Just before the Śaivite was about to be consumed by the flames, he took refuge. Tilopa gave him empowerment and oral instructions, and so he attained siddhi. He was called Kṛṣṇakalyāṇa (Dark Virtue) and even now lives in the Cool Grove charnel ground.

Later, many people gathered in the country of Bengal in the east, and it became as before. After a while, a magician from southern India, called Deceiver—who through the creation of illusions had managed to steal away the kingdoms of many lesser kings—desired to take over Bengal because it had such great wealth. Thus he created an illusory army and went there.

At that time, the people of the country did not realize that this was an illusion. They thought, "Several great kings have assembled together to fight us!" and they were terrified, as the magician controlled everything up to the capital city itself.

The king and his retinue then assembled together in the palace. While they were discussing what to do, an ugly woman appeared.

"What are you doing?" she asked.

"We are discussing who can expel this danger from Bengal," they replied.

"I have some advice," she said.

"What is it? Please tell us!"

"If you appoint my brother general of the army, he can expel them."

"Where is your brother?" they asked.

"In a charnel ground. He has tied a rope of fine horsehair on a branch of a shapa tree. It is a *yojana* [about a mile] high and corpses are attached to it. He holds them suspended and dances with them," she said.

They did not believe her, so they went to see for themselves, and they found him just as she had described. So they invited him to return with them. Tilopa then destroyed the illusory army through his meditative concentration. The magician was arrested and put in prison. When the magician learned who had done all this, he gained great faith in the master. The master taught him the dharma, and the magician and all the townspeople attained the rainbow body. The yogin Tilopa then dwelt in the great charnel ground called Resounding Laughter. It is said that all the others went to the celestial realm.

In the center of the country, at Śrāvasti, there was a woman called Sunlight, who sold liquor. Her liquor was famous for being equal to ambrosia, and thus everyone bought her liquor, which was very expensive. At that time, she was constantly occupied with her business.

One day, the young man who worked at the store went to gather wood. Tilopa, in the guise of a yogin, entered the deserted store, drank some of the liquor, and then began pulling out the stoppers, causing the liquor to run out. At that point the woman arrived, angrily beat him, and threw him out the door.

When the wood collector returned and found her weeping, he asked "What's the matter?"

"Look at what's happened!"

"He ought to be killed," the young man said.

Then Tilopa assumed the form of a cat and took out all the remaining stoppers. They tried as best they could to stop him but were unable to do so. Now there was no more liquor to sell, and they were very upset.

After a while, the yogin reappeared and said, "Why are you in despair?"

"First you took out the stoppers; then a cat did the same thing. Now there is no more liquor, and I have nothing to live on," she replied.

"You need not cry. Look inside. You have liquor again," he said.

"Is this true?" she wondered. She looked, and there was liquor of a higher quality and in much more quantity than before. She sold a lot of it, obtaining a high price.

Thus faith arose in her, and she supplicated Tilopa to accept her as a disciple. Tilopa gave her oral instructions, and she obtained spiritual accomplishment and was called Torch Holder. Even now, she dwells on the Sosa Island.

In the northern region, Tilopa found a butcher called Bliss Maker (perhaps Śaṅkara) who made his living slaughtering animals. When Tilopa went into his house to ask for some meat, the butcher did not want to give anything to Tilopa and so went out the door. So Master Tilopa killed the butcher's son, put his corpse into a pot, and departed.

When the butcher returned, his son was not there; when he opened up the pot to see if the meat was cooked, he saw his son's corpse and wept. Seven days passed, and he thought of neither food nor drink. He became extremely feeble and helpless.

Tilopa then approached the butcher, who was still weeping, and said, "What's the matter?"

"You killed my son!" the butcher accused.

"If you suffer so much because your own son is slaughtered, then other [animals] suffer just as much when their sons are slaughtered. Why do you kill them in order to make your living?"

"How true!" the butcher thought.

"If your son were to come to life now, would you stop slaughtering?" Tilopa asked.

"I would not slaughter any more," he replied.

Then the master revived his son. The butcher was happy and rejoiced. He prostrated to the master and was accepted as a disciple. He became the siddha Joy and now dwells on the island of the cannibal demons (*rākṣasas*).

At Śrī Nagara, there was a singer who was very arrogant. Everyone delighted in his songs while listening to them. Thus he made a great profit. One day, he was singing his song in the center of the marketplace when Tilopa appeared as a second singer and challenged him. He tried to rival Tilopa's singing, but he could not. "Is he a god? Is he a nāga? Who is he?" he wondered. The master appeared in his true form. The singer experienced faith in Tilopa's miracles and requested to be accepted as a disciple. He was accepted and so attained siddhi. He was called Melodious One and is still dwelling in that very city of Śrī Nagara.

In the south, the philosophical views of the materialists were spreading. One day, their foremost paṇḍita, named Jina, and the chief Buddhist paṇḍita were debating as to whether karmic cause and effect was true. At that point, Master Tilopa arrived and said to both of them, "You both should take hold of a corner of my robe."

As soon as the two paṇḍitas had done so, they all went below the ground to hell, where those who had committed evil deeds were being cooked in a giant cauldron of boiling molten metal. In another cauldron boiled molten copper, but there were no beings in it.

The heretic questioned the guardian of hell about the cauldrons, and the guardian replied, "These beings, who previously committed evil deeds, have been boiling in this cauldron since their death. Those heretics in Jambudvīpa who slander karmic cause and effect will be boiled in the other cauldron when they die."

The heretic became extremely terrified. He saw that it was true that appropriate effects would arise from his evil actions, the cause. "Perhaps I will not be taken right now," he hoped.

Then Tilopa took him to the realm of gods. There, other men were enjoying themselves with goddesses. At another place, several goddesses were gathered, but there were no gods. The heretic questioned these goddesses, and they said, "Those who practiced virtue previously were born here after they died. Now they are enjoying the fruits of their virtue. Those in Jambudvīpa who know the existence of karmic cause and effect and so abandon evil deeds will be born here after they die. Then they will enjoy playing with us."

When they returned to Earth, the heretic prostrated to the master. He was accepted as a disciple and so attained spiritual accomplishment. He was called yogin Jina, and even now he dwells at Śrī Parvata in the south.

In the city called Pāṭaliputra, "Child of the Pāṭali Flower," there was a heretic named Powerful One, who killed with his magical powers anyone who did not agree with him. Thus everyone was terrified of him and tried to please him.

Tilopa went before this heretic, insulted him, and then said some other things. The heretic became angry and set a time to kill Tilopa with his magical power. The master challenged him, saying, "Show your abilities." This made the heretic even more angry than before, but when he tried to practice his magical powers, their only effect was to kill all his relatives. He wept in grief.

The master came over and said, "I don't even have a toothache!"

The heretic felt extreme sorrow.

"Is it not the same for those others whose relatives you killed?" Tilopa asked.

"It is the same," the heretic replied.

"Now, if your relatives were to be revived, would you stop practicing your magical power in the future?"

"If remorse such as this arises for previous actions, how could I consider doing them in the future?" he repented.

Then Tilopa revived his relatives and taught the heretic about the dharma. Thus the heretic realized that Tilopa was a siddha and accompanied him as an attendant. He became the yogin Holder of the Sun and Moon and now dwells in the city Amicikali.

Then the master went to Bengal and built a woven hut in a charnel ground. While he was staying there, generally he was seen to be resting in meditative concentration in that place. At other times, his body resulting from the ripening of karma would confer with the perfect, complete buddha in the realm of Akaniṣṭha, great Vajradhara, sovereign of the six families. Afterward, he appeared to return to this world.

He brought with him the four and six aspects of all the development stages, the five levels of the completion stages of the father tantras, the four mudrās of the mother tantras, and in particular "the extremely wonderous tantra, which condenses the teachings into three words."

He proclaimed these to others, and he attained the supreme siddhi of mahāmudrā. In Bengal, Tilopa said:

> I have no human guru.
> My guru is the omniscient one.

He also said, "I have conversed with the Buddha." All worthy ones there heard him and attained the celestial realm. Thus the country of Bengal was emptied for the third time.

THE BIOGRAPHY FOR SUPERIOR STUDENTS: TILOPA MANIFESTS AS A COMPLETE BUDDHA

When Tilopa was a child in Jago practicing his letters under an akaru tree, a woman appeared and asked, "What is your country, who are your parents, and what is your name?" Tilopa answered:

> My country is Jago in the east.
> My father is the brahman Radiance.
> My mother is the brahman Radiant.
> My sister is the brahman Radiant Torch.
> I am the brahman Radiant Light.
> This tree is a shapa tree.
> For my herd, I am tending buffalo.
> After I learn my letters, I will practice the holy dharma.

The woman became angry and said, "That is not so!"

"Well, what is?" Tilopa said. The woman said:

> Your country is Uḍḍiyāṇa in the west.
> Your father is Cakrasaṃvara.
> Your mother is Vajrayoginī.
> Your sister is myself, She Who Bestows Bliss.
> You, my brother, are Pañcapana.
> If you desire to tend the buffalo of meditative experience
> In the forest of bodhi trees,
> The hearing lineage of that without letter
> Is in the hands of the stainless ḍākinī.

"Can I receive these teachings?" Tilopa asked. She replied:

> You are an emanation who possesses the prophecy and commitment for these.
> If you take them by force, you will get them.

"What is required to go there?"

"A crystal ladder, a jewel bridge, and a key made out of grass and burdock are all that is necessary," she said and then disappeared.

Tilopa returned home and told his parents what had happened. They gave him the three things he needed and told him to go ahead. Thus he departed, and in an instant he reached Uḍḍiyāṇa. There was a series of seven iron walls and seven moats there. In the center of these was the temple of the spontaneously arisen Heruka, also known as the Dharmagañja. First he came to the outermost wall. Devouring action-ḍākinīs were gathered there and said to him:

> We are devouring ḍākinīs.
> We eat flesh and thirst for blood.

Then they displayed various miracles. Tilopa said:

Because I am not frightened even by many ḍākinīs,
Not one tip of my hair has trembled!

He then subdued them with his overpowering brilliance. He set his crystal ladder against the iron walls and placed his jewel bridge over the moats. Thus he arrived in front of the monastery's door. The ḍākinīs there said:

Because we are weak, common women,
If we do not ask the assembly of lady ministers,
They will eat our flesh and drink our blood.
O holy man, consider our predicament with kindness!

They went to petition the enjoyment body (*sambhogakāya*) ḍākinīs, the assembly of lady ministers. Tilopa said:

Like bees hovering around a lamp,
How can the lady doorkeepers possibly conquer me?

He opened the door with his key and forced his way inside. The ḍākinīs who dwelt there appeared in terrifying guises and looked for an opportunity to harm him. However, Tilopa performed the gaze that overpowers body, speech, and mind, and so they asked their queen, the dharma-body wisdom ḍākinī, for permission to let him enter. She gave her assent. Tilopa entered into the center of the maṇḍala, but once there he did not prostrate respectfully to the Blessed Lady. The ḍākas and ḍākinīs said:

This manner is disrespectful
To the mother of the buddhas of the three times, the Blessed Lady.
Why don't we conquer him?

However, the Blessed Lady herself said:

He is the father of the buddhas of the three times, Cakrasaṃvara.
Even if a hail of vajras fell from the sky upon him,
He could not be conquered.

Then she asked Tilopa, "Why did you come here?" Tilopa replied:

I am Pañcapana.
My sister, She Who Bestows Bliss, sent me.
I request the hearing lineage, that without letter.

She showed him three signs: the empowerment card [pictures of sacred objects used in initiations] of the body, the seed syllable of speech, and the mudrā of mind. Tilopa said:

From the treasury of the empowerment card of the body
I request the wish-fulfilling jewel of the lineage.

From the treasury of the seed syllable of speech,
I request the wish-fulfilling jewel of the path that ripens.
From the treasury of the scepter of the mind,
I request the wish-fulfilling jewel of the path that frees.

The Blessed Lady replied:

In the treasury of the empowerment card of the body
Is the wish-fulfilling jewel of the lineage.
Because the lock of the commitments has been placed on it,
One who does not have the commitments cannot open the door.

In the treasury of the seed syllable of speech
Is the wish-fulfilling jewel of the path that ripens.
Because the lock of prophecy has been placed on it,
One who has not been prophesied cannot open the door.

In the treasury of the scepter of the mind
Is the wish-fulfilling jewel of the path that frees.
Because the lock of siddhas has been placed on it,
One who is not a siddha cannot open the door.

Tilopa said:

I have the key of the ḍākinī's prophecy!

The ḍākinīs all gave a horse laugh, and the Blessed Lady said:

Although a blind man looks, he does not see a thing.
Although a deaf man listens, he does not hear a sound.
Although a mute man speaks, he does not understand the meaning.
Although a crippled man runs, he does not get anywhere.
They are all deceived by Māra [the devil who creates obstacles], and there is no truth.

In reply Tilopa said:

The discipline of mind which is the secret words of the ḍākinīs,
The torch of wisdom that dispells the darkness of ignorance,
In itself, self-existing, self-illuminating:
I have the key to this self-existent commitment.

The nature of one's mind, in which all phenomena are unborn,
Is the nature of all phenomena, the truth body (*dharmakāya*).
In the great seal that prophesies this
I have the key to the experience of spontaneous presence.
Free from concept, free from any mental activity,
Free from even an atom of recollecting the past,
The mind itself experiencing itself is self-illuminating.
I have the key to the experience of an accomplished one.

Lest he commit an evil deed, he did not say anything untrue. The Blessed Lady said:

To you, my consort, the Blessed One,
Cakrasaṃvara, the supreme bliss,
Tilo Buddha, protector of beings,
I offer these three wish-fulfilling jewels.

Then she satisfied Tilopa by offering herself passionately. She gave him the oral instructions of the hearing lineage and appointed him master of all the tantras in the Dharmagañja. After this, Tilopa said:

Like a bird in the sky,
I soar unobstructed as excellent wisdom.

Thus, he became renowned by the name Excellent Wisdom (Prajñābhadra). The ḍākinīs requested:

O noble one, where are you going?
Please stay here for our sake!

Tilopa replied:

For the sake of my sons
Nāro, Riri, and Kasori,
I, the yogin, will go to Crown Jewel Monastery.

As he was leaving, a voice resounded from the formless realm and bestowed on him the teachings of the formless ḍākinī. Then Tilopa said:

When I teach others, I will do it like this.
In the gandola (vessel or palace) of the illusory body
I will place the secret of the formless ḍākinī.
Having fastened the lock of inexpressible speech,
The bird of my mind will soar in luminosity.

Tilopa went to stay at the monastery of Odantapurī. There he accepted worthy ones as his disciples, and he still remains there up to the present time. Tilopa said:

My body is Hevajra.
My speech is Mahāmāyā.
My mind is Cakrasaṃvara.
My sense organs are Guhyasamāja.
My main limbs are the *Black Yamāri Tantra.*
My secondary limbs are the great Vajrabhairava.
The hairs of my body are inseparable
From the body, speech, and mind of the buddhas of the three times!

—8—

Atiśa's Journey to Tibet

Hubert Decleer

Master Dromtön's account of Atiśa's travels, *The Dromtön Itinerary* (*'Brom ston lam yig*), is composed as an experiential account, to be read as a companion piece to the more stately, standard sacred biography of Dīpaṃkara Śrījñāna, better known by his honorific title Atiśa, the Outstanding or Supremely Genuine One (982–1054). The first part deals essentially with the complex reasons and circumstances that led to Atiśa's decision to leave his home in central India for, first, Nepal and, later, the inhospitable highlands of western and central Tibet; the second part recounts the actual journey.

The presumed author of the *Itinerary*, the lay disciple Gyalwe Jungne (Rgyal pa'i 'byung gnas), usually referred to as Dromtön ('Brom ston, the Master from the Drom clan, 1005–1064), met Atiśa shortly before the latter's near-departure from Tibet, at the close of a stay there as originally intended for "a maximum of three years." Dromtön was instrumental in making Atiśa instead choose the snowy land of Tibet for his main "sphere of taming"—a standard expression for leading capable candidates to the training—and remain there until the end of his life, for a full twelve years. As such, Dromtön is invariably depicted at Atiśa's feet as one of his two main disciples.

The Framing Tale of the *Itinerary*

At Bodhgayā's Vajra Throne, the very site where Śākyamuni attained enlightenment, Nagtso Lotsāwa (Nag tsho lo tsā ba), in the presence of his senior Tibetan colleague Gya Tsöndrü Senge (Rgya Brtson 'grus seng ge), presents Atiśa with an account of all the previous efforts made by the rulers of western Tibet to invite the great paṇḍita to their country. The first part of the *Itinerary* consists of one long flashback, starting with Nagtso first being drawn into the enterprise when he is awakened by a royal messenger at his own residence, within Tö ling's Golden Temple (Stod gling gser khang).

Nested within is another flashback, delivered by the princely monk Jangchub Ö (Byang chub 'od), in the course of which he reports the last wish of his royal uncle, King Yeshe Ö (Ye shes 'od), a most ardent appeal for Atiśa personally to come and resurrect the Buddhist teaching in Tibet. The king sacrifices his life for the great goal; later, his nephew and successor offers nearly the entire wealth of his country as the gift to go with a renewed request to Atiśa. The accompanying message represents serious ceremonial bargaining, worded in such a way as to make it virtually impossible for Atiśa to refuse.

Why were the royal "Uncle and Nephew" so set on inviting Atiśa? After the forced disbanding of the Buddhist community's monastic core under King Langdarma (Glang dar ma) one and a half centuries earlier, the newly acquired religion was in serious disarray throughout Tibet. Nagtso's royal patron sketches the desperate state of affairs in two short sentences: "All realized sages have passed away. The level of knowledge is enough to make one weep." In his view, the poor level of knowledge was often being compensated for by the improvisation of glib actors-turned-self-styled-gurus. Without the sure guidance of experienced mentors, the entire edifice of Buddhist theory and practice had lost its solid foundation. To the Uncle and Nephew, one thing was clear: either the full transmission was to be restored within their lifetime, or the Buddha's teaching in Tibet would, by the following generation, merely survive as a "dharma cult," the memory of a souvenir about an echo.

It was in western Tibet that, in reaction to a "bogged down" Buddhism, the preliminaries for a potential renaissance were thus being set in motion. It was not (and still is not) an easy place to live. The king does not fail to remind Atiśa of this, via the messenger Nagtso, when he compares the harsh conditions of his native Ngari (Mnga 'ris) to "Pretapuri City—the town of the hungry ghosts—where to raise a single yellow sheep already presents much hardship." It is nomad country at high elevation; endless desertlike steppe land crossed by rivers of melting snow, where within a twenty-four hour period one may suffer sunburn during the day and frostbite at night, and where travel, then as now, is likely to turn into an obstacle course and an endurance test very quickly. The exquisite Tsaparang frescoes that survived the Chinese Cultural Revolution—among the most sublime of all Tibetan painting—and pre-1950 photographs of the refined sculpture at the now ruined Tho ling (Mtho gling) monastery bear witness to the incredible cultural oases the rulers of western Tibet were able to create in these barely habitable barren wastes.

In the course of a royal alms tour to collect funds for sponsoring Atiśa's invitation, King Yeshe Ö was kidnapped and held for ransom by a neighboring ruler of the Qarlug Mongols. The text presents that nameless Mongol leader as ardently anti-Buddhist, without saying a word about his religious commitment. It was not for another two and a half centuries that some of the Mongol clans would begin converting to Islam, away from their original shamanistic and, later, Buddhist beliefs. At the time of the events recorded in the *Itinerary*, the Mongols probably just feared having to give up their wilder ways of adventurous raiding and kidnapping; if a large-scale Buddhist conversion were to occur among the Mongols, they might have to abandon the huge sacrificial events before ancestor-hero statuary and the exuberant feasting that were their traditional ways.

Of interest is the dialogue between the nephew, a rather tentative rescuer, and his imprisoned uncle. Jangchub Ö thinks he has to console the old king and mentally strengthen him with some dharma advice appropriate to the situation: "engage in some farming whereby to plant some compassion beneath your breast." Such advice is quite insulting, since King Yeshe Ö has previously been his own guru, as the text does not neglect to inform us explicitly. In his rebuke, King Yeshe Ö insists: do not bother about me; concentrate on the main issue, and settle for no one less than the best to restore Buddhism in Tibet.

Nagtso Lotsāwa's Journey from Ngari (Western Tibet) to Vikramaśīla (Northeast India)

In all of Buddhist India, Atiśa undoubtedly *was* "the best." In the words of the abbot Ratnākara of Vikramaśīla's monastic university, Atiśa was "the one who holds in hand the keys of all the vihāras of India," meaning not only was he the ultimate authority and "the incomparable" (Skt: Atiśa), but also he was thoroughly versed in each of the "eighteen philosophical schools," the views of each of which, at the corresponding colleges, he could expound as if they represented his very own.

Nagtso's task, therefore, was truly a mission impossible; a little as if a professor from the little University of the Andaman Islands set out to try and persuade Einstein to give up his prestigious Princeton post, after first having crossed the ocean by raft. The *Itinerary* allows us some glimpses of the dangers involved in a journey to India, circa 1037 C.E. Previous to Nagtso Lotsāwa's departure, Jangchub Ö makes a laconic remark about most previous messengers having "perished from either the heat or poisonous snakes." Nagtso is supposed to be already familiar with these forms of nuisance from an earlier study trip and residence in India—a major reason why the choice fell on him. He is less prepared for the threat of untrustworthy innkeepers and porters, all of them known as *atsaras*.

Nagtso survives the first attempt on his life—and, later, other dire situations—thanks to the intervention of a deus ex machina, who will manifest in ever-changing guises. Only in the last paragraph of part 1 will a weaver girl enter a trance and reveal to Nagtso this figure's real identity, which does not mean the reader cannot at least half predict the outcome. When the boatman who rows the party across the Ganges recites, by way of an answer to one of Nagtso's questions, "If the Ārya, as boat and boatman, does not *then*, in time of terror, [come to] escort [those in distress]," one is reminded of the famous Mahāyāna sūtra passage about the bodhisattva Avalokiteśvara appearing in whatever form happens to be the most efficient to inspire and guide fortunate disciples. Moreover, the fact that the boatman obliquely refers to himself in the third person as "the Ārya" ("Superior"; a common honorific for a bodhisattva) is a sufficient clue to fill in "Avalokiteśvara." As will be seen below, this is only half the answer.

In passing, the boatman (Ārya Avalokiteśvara) offers Nagtso a number of hints about the working of mantras in general and some direct instruction on the *maṇi* practice in particular, the famous mantra associated in Tibet with Avalokiteśvara as the national protector of Tibet (see chapter 2). An interesting minor trait in the depiction—Nagtso's eyewitness account—of Vikramaśīla's monastic university is the mention of "the common house of the Tibetans," showing that already in India (as later in Tibet) students were boarded in different houses according to their region of origin. By the eleventh century it was already an established feature for students to study abroad at Buddhist monastic universities, ranging from Taxila (present-day Pakistan) to far-away Wu Tai Shan in China, where Nāropa sent a student to study with a tantric master. Atiśa himself is a case in point, since at the time of Nagtso's arrival at Vikramaśīla he had still not returned from his twelve-year study trip to the Gold Isles in southeast Asia, a place identified variously by scholars as Sumatra, southern Thailand, or Java.

Nagtso's First Meeting with Lord Atiśa

As luck would have it, Nagtso is being informed about Atiśa's imminent return the very next day, when he will preside over a grand assembly of the saṅgha.

It is worth pausing here a moment to examine the author Dromtön's literary qualities. His account of Nagtso's first perception of the Master, seated high above the rows of the assembled monks (Nāropa among them!), is nothing less than majestic. The following scene of Nagtso's first, unexpected, face-to-face meeting with Atiśa achieves a clever crescendo in the sequences, with marked psychological finesse. Rather than vaunt Atiśa's sublime teaching skills, Dromtön allows the reader to view them in action when the Master corrects one error at a time, and he only points out the next one when the previous lesson has sunk in. Above all, the unsurpassed Atiśa is depicted as showing active interest in the hesitant progress of Nagtso, a relative beginner, here engaged in Sanskrit recitation and memorization of the *Heart Sūtra*, when all the other junior paṇḍitas had walked past without paying any attention.

Also intriguing is the secrecy maintained at Vikramaśīla about Atiśa's presence. Nagtso's monk neighbor in the assembly tells him an outright lie, denying the identity of Atiśa ("This is Vīra Hāsavajra!"), and so does a menacing beggar outside the vihāra ("Don't you dare take *our* Atiśa away from us!" followed by a gauche correction of this slip of the tongue: "This is not Atiśa anyway"). The explanation awaits the reader in the last chapter.

Signs and prophecies of Atiśa's impending departure for Tibet

Nagtso vaguely realizes that, throughout his own journey to India and his subsequent encounters there, "miraculous manifestations assisted me in an uninterrupted flow, but whether they meant anything definite I did not know." Not being a realized yogin, he wonders, in other words, whether it was not his imagination that had run amok; he never completely trusted these intrusions of the extraordinary. At the close of his long recollection of the antecedents to the invitation, he also inquires of Atiśa himself whether these *were* "miraculous manifestations," and, if so, whether they contained any prophetic value with regard to the possibility of Atiśa's willingness to make the long journey to Tibet. The Master refrains from any direct reply and instead sends him off to consult a professional in the arts of divination.

The diviner/weaver girl near Vikramaśīla scolds Nagtso for not having realized any earlier that—as we suspected, with the "Ārya" reference above—Ārya Avalokiteśvara has been acting as his guardian angel all along. But she precedes this explanation by another one: "it appears that all of these are Dromtön's miraculous transformations," and it is to Dromtön that Nagtso is directed to address his prayers.

It is of course bizarre, to say the least, that author Dromtön would thus interweave, in his account of Atiśa's travels, a strong streak of what is barely distinguishable from self-apotheosis (incidentally, the strongest argument *against* his authorship); entirely out of tune with the extreme humility, assumed at all times by Dromtön in Atiśa's presence, and about which all biographers are unanimous. The only possible explanation is related to the (postulated) function of the *Itinerary* as a corrective postscript to the sacred biography, in the sense that the mass of information therein tends to drown the one feature essential for Atiśa's lasting influence on the Buddhism of Tibet: the diffusion of his teaching of the "stages of the path" (*lam rim*) and the founding of the Kadampa sect, both of which were a direct outcome of the historic meeting between Atiśa and his prophesied disciple Dromtön. In "secret biography" style, author Dromtön, therefore, merely sets the record straight, albeit by means of a good dose of the supernatural.

This chapter marks the end of the framing tale: Nagtso concludes his lengthy monologue with a last plea to Atiśa to take up the burden of guiding the living beings of Tibet, the Snowy Fortress.

Nagtso's Final Interview with Abbot Ratnākara

Atiśa finally agrees, but in accordance with the vinaya rules he needs the official permission from abbot Ratnākara for a prolonged absence. He dispatches Nagtso as his official messenger. The plan is to set out on a pilgrimage "to show these Tibetan *āyuṣmans* (a respectful term of address used by a teacher for his monk students) the great sacred spots of India," i.e., those holy places associated with the major events in the Buddha's life and, then as now, the major target of foreign Buddhist pilgrims traveling to India. The intended subterfuge is somehow to extend that pilgrimage forever, even into Tibet. Through no specific blunder of Nagtso, Ratnākara, in an instant, sees through the game. The dialogue whereby Nagtso finds himself cornered, already fearing that all his (and Jangchub Ö's) long years of effort and their grand plan are about to fall apart, is again a masterly composition, a scenario worthy of stage performance. Nor is abbot Ratnākara much worried about political correctness: he squarely refers to Nagtso's Tibet as "that yak enclosure of yours."

Nagtso, guided by another vision (Avalokiteśvara as divine horseman, a manifestation of Dromtön), manages to reverse the situation overnight. This is also the moment when Ratnākara expresses the *major* reason for his reluctance to let Atiśa depart. It is no longer that the great paṇḍita holds the keys of India's vihāras and that he is desperately needed. Instead he brings up the lurking danger of Turko-Afghan raiders who, each spring, penetrate deeper into India; on the return journey to their native Afghanistan, loaded with plunder, they attract more volunteers to join them on another expedition to the fabulously wealthy country of India the next season. Ratnākara's apparent argument is that "many dharma centers have been destroyed, many vihāra complexes are becoming desolate, and many more are the Turuṣka armies that will come." Therefore, since the teaching centers have become few and are likely to become fewer still, the leading Buddhist institutions such as Nālandā, Vikramaśīla, Bodhgayā, and Odantapuri have to maintain their standards at all costs—impossible in the absence of the incomparable Atiśa.

But one wonders whether abbot Ratnākara does not also allude to another facet of Atiśa's multiple masteries. According to Tāranātha, in his *Transmission History of the Slayer of Death (Yamāntaka), King among Tantras*, the hidden reason why Buddhist North India eventually collapsed and suffered destruction from the Afghan raids was the absence of realized masters in the ferocious practices of the wrathful deities, specifically the Slayer of Death (Yamāntaka) and of the Lightning Terror (Vajrabhairava). That Atiśa possessed expertise in Yamāntaka is clear from the fact that he empowered Nagtso in the practice. In the autobiographical account of Atiśa's journey to the Gold Isles, there is explicit reference to that sort of intervention. Moreover, Atiśa's younger brother Vīryacandra, who accompanied them to Tibet, had also specialized in the same practice. All of this could provide a reason for abbot Ratnākara's conviction that, to counter the Turuṣka attacks by miraculous intervention of the wrathful type, Atiśa (and Vīryacandra) might be even more indispensable. This might account for the aura of secrecy about his person maintained by all those around him. Subjecting Atiśa to the fate that shortly before had befallen King Yeshe Ö in Tibet would be the dreaded ingredient that would accelerate the doom and "darkness all over India," so pointedly predicted by the abbot.

And thus, in 1040, Atiśa did set out for Tibet, with Ratnākara's (albeit reluctant) blessings. The total destruction of Vikramaśīla took place almost exactly two centuries later; but by this time, thanks to the protagonists of the *Itinerary*, the Buddhist transmissions had become firmly established in Tibet.

The selections translated below from *The Dromtön Itinerary* are based on the Zhöl edition, in the *Biography of Atiśa and His Disciple 'Brom ston (Bka' gdams glegs bam)*, ed. Lokesh Chandra, Shata Piṭaka series, vol. 311, (Delhi: International Academy of Indian Culture, 1982), 1:237–97. The first three sections of the *Itinerary* appear on pp. 238–53. The last selection on Nagtso's final interview with Abbot Ratnakāra is from pp. 258–61. To assist the reader in recognizing at what point in the recollections a particular monologue or dialogue takes place, indentations differentiate one framing tale from the next.

Further Reading

A translation by Hubert Decleer excerpted from *Dromtön's Itinerary* of Atiśa's twelve-year adventures in the Gold Isles of Sumatra appears in *Buddhism in Practice*, ed. Donald S. Lopez, Jr. (Princeton: Princeton University Press, 1995), pp. 532–40. For more on Atiśa's role in Nepal, see Hubert Decleer, *Jowo Atiśa in Nepal: The Tham Bahil and Five Stupas' Foundation according to the Dromtön Itinerary* (ZDMG, forthcoming 1996); on Atiśa's role in Tibet, see Alaka Chattopadhyaya, *Atiśa in Tibet* (Delhi: Motilal Banarsidass, 1967), as well as Sarat Chandra Das, *Indian Pandits in the Land of Snow* (Calcutta: Firma KLM, [1893] 1965).

The Itinerary

THE LAST WISH OF KING YESHE Ö

[At the Vajra Throne (Bodhgayā) Nagtso the Translator recalls the antecedents to the West Tibetan King Yeshe Ö's invitation of Master Atiśa. The main addressee of his long monologue is Atiśa himself, hence the not infrequent out-of-context switching back from "he" and "him" to "you, Lord (Atiśa)."]

In reaction to a strong influence from the enemies of the Buddha's teaching, the dharma kings Uncle and Nephew [King Yeshe Ö and his nephew successor Jangchub Ö], through some of their subjects, had come to hear about your renown. Judging by this, the dharma kings Uncle and Nephew—teacher and disciple, too—consulted an oracle as well as the astrological omens about a messenger ceremoniously to invite you, Lord [Atiśa]. The choice fell on me.

[I remember:] I was awakened from deep sleep at my residence in the Golden Temple, in the land of Gungthang, and conducted to the Ngari region of the king. The great monk-king [Jangchub Ö] had me seated on a throne and showed me great reverence, repeatedly calling me "learned," "accomplished," "of noble character," in terms of the utmost praise. Essentially, in his long address, he had this to say:

> Vinayadhara [upholder of monastic discipline], my ancestors, those bodhisattva kings and ministers, introduced the Buddha's teaching, passed it on as a tradition, then made it spread and increase far and wide. Yet, at present, the Buddha's teaching is on the decline, bogged down. Living beings of the demon race are the ones victorious in dispute. All realized sages have passed away. The level of knowledge is enough to make one weep. Now the two of us, uncle and nephew, have been asking ourselves: "Will this person [Atiśa] be useful and up to the situation? Is he reliable? Does he have his mind on the Buddha's teaching?" and next we decided to go ahead with it and donated the customary present to go with the ceremonial invitation. It was arranged for a hundred gold ounces to be carried to India in minimal amounts, and we sent these off, each time with just one principal messenger and a couple of attendants, in order to ceremoniously invite you, [Atiśa]. Most of them perished from either the heat or poisonous snakes, so that none of the wealth survived, and lives were lost. As for the little wealth that eventually *did* reach you, none of these major efforts could bring it about for you to accept our invitation.
>
> Yet without losing heart, this great divine being [that is, our King Yeshe Ö] went out to the regions bordering on Nepal in order to collect gold by means of which to ceremoniously invite the Lord [Atiśa].
>
> Now the [Turco-Mongol] Qarlug king came to know that the Dharmarāja was collecting gold for the paṇḍita, and he spoke: "Already before, his ancestors sponsored the diffusion of the Buddha's teaching too," and he had him captured, then ordered: "Once he has invited the paṇḍita, he is going to propagate the Buddha's teaching; therefore, caught as he is now, put him in jail!" and he had him tortured.
>
> When I came to hear about this, driven by the force of frustration I gathered a hundred horsemen and set out to get my uncle back. But the Qarlug king's clansmen outnumbered us by far, and I didn't manage to free him. Had I even declared war on the Qarlug and managed to beat them, it might have produced the reverse effect in the end. Not only would many humans and animals have perished in the process, but for ourselves as well, obstacles would thereby arise, [with negative karma such] that we might never be able to invite the Great Lord. And so, in agreement with one strategic expert, we negotiated. The Qarlug king replied:
>
> "Well, just postpone inviting the paṇḍita and come under my dominion. Either that or hand over to me the amount of gold equal to the king's weight. Only then will we release your king."
>
> From the gold thus far collected we picked one hundred ounces and brought it along; but even though we argued and tried everything, he would

not listen. Next, as we carried to him the amount equal to the prisoner's body weight and again negotiated, he insisted: "It should be absolutely the same, the complete amount," and he wouldn't listen any further. Then, having gone in front of the gate where my uncle stayed in prison and was having a hard time, I called out to him:

> Most kind one! Karma from previous lives has come down on us like lightning. Even if I beat him badly in war and get you out, still, we will thereby send many people to their destruction and will definitely be bound for an evil rebirth as a result. As for the Qarlug king's proposal—"Don't invite any paṇḍita and put yourself under my dominion!"—rather than dropping dharma from your mind and being held in sway by an evil king, I imagine it is far better if you stick to your course as a religious-minded person. He told us about the alternative: he wanted the amount of gold equivalent to yourself. So we set out for it and just managed to find the amount equal to your body. But he would not hear of it; so now, as soon we find the missing amount equal to your head, we shall bring it as the ransom. In the meantime you should recollect your previous karma and pray to the precious three [the Buddha, the dharma, and the saṅgha]; also, engage in some farming whereby to plant some compassion beneath your breast,"

thus I told him. My uncle laughed loudly:

> Am I perhaps your foster child, the dear little glutton who now needs some restraint? One unable to put up with hardship or devoid of courage—is *that* what you think? Once I am dead, you may look after me as part of the traditional rites for your ancestors! May you clearly understand this! As for myself, let things be the way they are! My sole concern is that if, in this Tibet of ours, the dharma tradition is not restored and I die, it will all have been in vain: *that*'s what *I* think. Even if cured from my present ills, this old man that I am will at the most have ten years to live—if I don't die this time, that is. Throughout previous lives in this beginningless cyclic existence, it never happened even once that I died for the dharma's sake. So if this time I do, that will be fine with me. Don't you give even a single grain of gold to that king! What hardship haven't you gone through to find gold just for my sake? So where are you going to find the extra gold, the weight of my head? You better carry all the gold to India and go to any lengths to invite a paṇḍita! And this is what I have to say for that paṇḍita to hear: "I, for your sake and for the sake of the Buddha's teaching, have offered my life and body to that nasty Qarlug king. Please, I pray you to accept me through your compassion in all future lives. Foremost in my thought is that after your coming to Tibet, you bring about the propagation of the Buddha's teaching. And I pray for your blessings so that this single thing may get done and that, throughout your

> lives after the present one, we definitely meet!" This is the message of mine to convey to him. In this way, all will be fine and you can forget about me and concentrate on the Buddha's teaching!"

So you, Vinayadhara, make sure that Lord Atiśa gets to hear these accounts of how my uncle was eliminated by the king of the Qarlugs. This compassionate uncle of mine, ah, the hardships that he went through!

Also, as I resisted going away leaving my uncle behind, through a chink in the door I looked inside and saw the bodies [of my uncle and his entourage] there, tied up with silk. Their voices had lost all luster; and all different in outward appearance from what they had been before, their bodies had now become like bees, [emaciated and] all alike. From the hole there came the sound: "And keep this in mind: for the sentient beings of Tibet and for the Buddha's teachings, there is none but the Lord [Atiśa]!"

Now since already we, ignorant beings of Tibet's border countries, have *that* kind of determination, what then must the determination be like of compassionate beings who are a source of refuge for transmigrators? Tell him [Atiśa] that too! Here are seven hundred ounces of gold. Carry these to India and offer them into the guru's own hands, with my message:

> I, here in this Tibet that is like Pretapuri City—the town of the hungry ghosts—where just to raise a single yellow sheep already presents plenty of hardship, I hereby "am one ahead of the guru" and have completely assembled all the human wealth [of the country]. If this time the Lord Protector, even in response to this gesture, does not set out for Tibet, [all we can say is:] Is *that* what the compassion of you holy ones is like? Even *I* manage to complete whatever task I have set my mind on!

Now you, Vinayadhara, tell the Lord about all these things, give him a full account. If as a result he still does not decide to come, it will deeply damage his reputation!

TRANSLATOR NAGTSO'S JOURNEY TO VIKRAMAŚĪLA IN NORTH INDIA

So we, master and attendants seven in all, loaded ourselves with the seven hundred ounces of gold; then, heading for the road to India, we set out. The princely monk escorted us over a long distance and then spoke these verses:

> Monk, you, about to achieve a task for my sake, for our benefit,
> This time, whatever great difficulties come your way,
> With the greatest perseverance, be ready even to sacrifice your life;
> And upon your return, once I know you've done it, I'll be forever thankful.

and with these words, looking back at me, he returned. One more time, though, he called out: "Please proceed while offering your prayer requests to Lord Mahākaruṇika [Avalokiteśvara], the Great Compassionate One."

As we approached "Nepal Fortress" [present-day Nuwakoṭ, northwest of Kathmandu], we met one solitary traveler who addressed us:

"You look as if you're setting out for some country far away, for some great purpose. . . ," so he said, ". . . now, as you go there, and also, having achieved your goal, are on your way back, you should keep on reciting:

> To the rare and precious three, I offer salutation with full prostration.
> In the land of Tibet, may the true dharma,
> Source of all the conqueror buddhas of the three times,
> Soon come to be diffused.

and no calamities will occur en route." I inquired:

"Please, who are you?"

"You'll gradually find out," he spoke, and made no further reply.

Then, as we arrived in the immediate vicinity of the Nepal Valley, we rented the residence of one atsara for our lodgings; and while caravan leader and servants were sleeping in a bamboo hut, the atsara came to know about the gold in our possession. He made a plan to put fire to the bamboo hut, then kill me and get hold of the gold. As I was the head of the group, my attendants were resting quite a distance from there. I suffered from fever, and just as I was desperate to get some sleep, next to my pillow a white human figure appeared, who pushed open the entrance of the bamboo hut, telling me:

> Don't sleep, don't sleep, get up, quickly!
> Don't go off to sleep, get up right now and get going!
> If you sleep now, your precious life will come to an end!
> [And as to your earlier question, know that] I am the *yi dam* deity of all of Tibet!

Offering a prayer to the compassionate Mahākaruṇika [Avalokiteśvara], we fled.

At daybreak we came across a Nepali prince who was on his way to Vikrama[śīla]. Having made friends with him, we traveled on together.

Upon our reaching the riverbank of the Ganges, the prince, being a person of importance, embarked on the ferry and went across. By that time the Sun had gone down. On our side there was no one, and the atsaras of the jungle regions [among our train] were behaving in suspicious ways. It is so that people from the Māra clans and the tīrthikas [non-Buddhists] hate the sacred dharma. As for us, with the Buddha's teaching foremost in mind, we had come here carrying a lot of gold, and now there was no place to hide it, nor anywhere to go. Totally disoriented in this unfamiliar country, we offered our prayers to Lord Avalokiteśvara and hid the gold beneath the sand at one spot while we went ourselves to stay and sleep elsewhere. A white boatman appeared, rowing his boat by moving the oars. As I inquired from him:

"How is it possible that you have come, [this late]?" He replied:

I have come to welcome master and servants with their entourage.
At the time when the snowlanders with great courage have arrived,
If the Ārya, as boat and boatman,
Does not *then*, in time of terror, escort them,
How then will these deluded beings ever reach their destination?
Quickly get in, "those seven hundred" [gold ounces] and all,
And I will get you across to [Vi]krama[śīla] at a leisurely pace.

After he had thus spoken we offered a prayer to the Compassionate One, dug up the gold from beneath the sand, and went aboard. I myself did one rosary of *[oṃ] maṇi padme [hūṃ]*. Said the boatman:

"I recite the *maṇi padme* mantra of this Great Compassionate One of the Land of Snows at length when there is plenty of time available; in brief only when there is little time," and next he recited the *maṇi padme* in a clear way, drawing out the syllables. Catching the melodious sound, my mind became happy, free from all worry, and the idea in me was born of viewing the boatman as a father.

"Who could he be?" I wondered, and as great doubts assailed me, I asked him:

"Please, who are you? There is just myself, this ordinary person. Please give a reply."

The boatman answered:

"All of you āyuṣmans, it has been said:

Early in an acquaintance, full reliance does not come about quickly.
Halfway acquainted, modesty and hesitancy become less.
When fully acquainted since long, it is no longer a casual friendship.

The benefit in times of utter helplessness and coming to the rescue, for someone long acquainted, is definite. You should know that it comes by stages, [the protection one receives] . . . ," thus he spoke, and any further reply to my original question did not come forth. He did, however, add:

"At present you have been saved from the imminent danger by approaching me as if your father. But since you did not simultaneously pronounce a prayer, you will not reach the guesthouse at the end of the journey tonight. In fact, that guesthouse, there it is, . . . " He said, ". . . Now we will get to the other side by midnight. Do not sleep on the riverbank nor on the farther away green slopes for fear of poisonous snakes. This night you should stay below the portal of Vikrama[śīla]. No robbers will come there tonight." So he spoke, then went off.

No sooner had we reached the portal of Vikramaśīla when from a lookout window in the gate tower there was the voice of Gya Tsöndrü Sengé telling us:

"Hey, you Tibetan āyuṣmans, where have you come from?"

"We're from Upper Ngari," we said.

He continued: "Fine, there is a boy gatekeeper to whom you may entrust all your luggage and valuables. As for yourselves, just make yourselves comfortable in the porters' lodge, and have some sleep. At present, the first dawn has been sounded. The gate will be opened starting from the second dawn onward."

So we entrusted the gold to that one boy present there as gatekeeper. That boy put the gold away in a niche, then said:

> Trust in wealth is like trust in an enemy;
> Trust in one's son is like trusting one's own heart;
> Someone trustworthy is the supreme companion.

"Thus it has been said. You look exhausted; better get some sleep!"

Overcome by fatigue, I wondered, "When such things come out of the mouth of a small child, how can he be an ordinary being?"

The next morning, as soon as the gate opened, a small boy appeared, wearing the common large nomad hat and double woolen clothes in nomad style, also carrying with him a small drinking bowl. He inquired:

"All of you look like Tibetans; where have you come from? Nothing frightening happened en route?" all of this clearly spoken in Tibetan nomad speech, so that it made me think he was bound to be of pure nomad birth. I replied, then asked in turn:

"We have come from Upper Ngari and 'the road was smooth.' As for yourself, where are *you* from and where are you headed?"

"Me too, I am a Tibetan and I'm about to go to Tibet. But by our loud talking here, we are being careless, and we talk too much. You should know that the wrong kind of talk will cause mistakes. For an important task one should act in secrecy. Gya Tsön Seng resides in the common house of the Tibetans. Come and discuss matters with him," he said and suddenly went away. Since we did not quite believe [what he had told us about being discreet], we did not lose our good mood.

After we had been going for a while through a narrow inner lane, we met an extremely old ṛṣi with long, blond hair, red eyes, all emaciated, and carrying a staff made of driftwood. He spoke:

"Where have you come from? And where are you going? And what have you come for?"

"We have come from Upper Ngari to ceremoniously invite Lord Atiśa. Oh, would you happen to know where the house of Gya Tsön Seng is?" we inquired. Supporting himself on his staff, he looked around from the corners of his eyes, then said:

"What the boy this morning said is true: Tibetans, rather than just shutting up, disregard all sense of discretion even to the first vagabond they meet in the tiniest lane. How can you possibly hope to achieve your goal this way? From now on, the best course to take is to stick close to my advice. As the Lord is not here right now, do not open your mouth about it to anyone else. Even to Gya, communicate about it only in whispers: that will be the right thing. I will show you the door to his place."

I started to walk behind him, but however slowly the ṛṣi proceeded, I could not keep up with his speed. I was utterly astonished and started to have some doubts, for there he was, waiting for me in the portal of the Tibetan boarding house:

"If you want to achieve a major task, you have to *hurry slowly*. If you hurry, do it at a leisurely pace, relaxed. For a distant goal, go about it slowly, stage by stage, like climbing a mountain. This is the house, by the way," so he said. I went in right away and present there was Gya Lotsāwa, looking into a number of scriptures. I offered him the present, in gold-embroidered cloth, and the Lotsāwa inquired:

"From what particular direction have you arrived?"

I told him the whole story in detail, and his comment was:

> You better act as my disciples and pretend we do not know each other. At present, do not pronounce one word about having come to invite Atiśa. What you *have* to tell everyone is that you have come for your studies. The elder Ratnākara is the one with the highest power here, to the point that he commands even Atiśa himself. What you have to do is listen to dharma from him and get him to develop a liking for you. Without him being able to sense your real intention, go and offer him now half an ounce of gold and inform him, "We have come from Tibet; not to invite a paṇḍita, though. What in your presence I would like to request is for myself to be accepted by, and connected with, a paṇḍita, just like any other disciple," thus you present your application. Then, without ever hurrying or expressing your intention, you move slowly, in the role of disciples. Eventually we will, in the most skillful way, present the request at the time of the Lord's coming back here.

Thus he spoke. Just to see the Lotsāwa's reaction, I inquired: "Now if somehow we fail to invite Lord Atiśa, which major great paṇḍita below him should we invite instead?" On the subject, the Lotsāwa had this to say: "Let no such thing come forth from your lips! Not just one but many more, some twenty paṇḍitas have gone there [to Tibet] on invitation, since last year. Haven't they all proved useless for the sentient beings of Tibet, for people with a behavior and temper like ours? Except for Lord Atiśa, there is absolutely no one to possibly tame the sentient beings of Tibet. Therefore it is Atiśa in person we must try to invite, by any means. . . ."

NAGTSO'S FIRST MEETING WITH LORD ATIŚA

". . . Tomorrow, at Vikramala[śīla]'s park, there will be a gathering of the 'highest, middle, and low,' with an attendance of some eight hundred saṅgha members, and you should come. Among them, most radiant, most outstanding, like a blaze, the sacred presence par excellence from whatever point of view, one wonderful to behold in whatever assembly row he may be seated, will be Atiśa. Direct your prayer wishes to him day and night!"

Next, both Gya Tsöndrü and I arrived in the presence of the elder Ratnākara. We offered prostrations, then presented him with half an ounce of gold and I made the request the way Gya had taught me. The elder spoke:

"That is most excellent. Āyuṣman, the situation is like this. It is not that I want to keep everyone here to ourselves. Other paṇḍitas cannot tame sentient beings the way he can. Without Atiśa here, in this India that is the source of the Buddha's teaching, all will come to naught, with an inevitable decrease in the general well-being of sentient beings. The one who holds in his hand the keys of all the vihāras of India is Atiśa—that is the reason. Apart from that, I have great love and much kindness for the living beings of Tibet. More in particular, I was greatly affected by the many lives lost and all the wealth spent by this dharma king of Tibet. Recollect their dedication to the Buddha's teaching, apply strong perseverance and the utmost willpower in your study, and gain vast knowledge in the Buddha's teaching. I will try to assist you in every possible way. Like this, you Tibetans will even amaze the Indian [scholars] here." This and many other pleasant things he told us.

The next day at noon ["by the time of the heat"], at the Saṅgha Park, the elder guided us among the rows of saṅgha members assembled there for the noon meal and had us seated among the rows of students.

At that time, you [Atiśa] had gone to the Gold Isles and other sacred places and you had not yet returned. I [however, unaware of this], imagined that somewhere among the rows of seated monks you were bound to be presiding over one such assembly. Also, as I did not understand the language spoken by the others around me, my doubts were not cleared away.

Then, at one point, Vidyākokila, already very old, arrived among the rows. He looked radiant, was ablaze with splendor, and his *entrée* was like the appearance of the World Mountain. To everyone seated nearby I asked:

"This is Lord Atiśa, is it not?"

"Tibetan āyuṣmat, what are you saying? This is the holy guru Vidyākokila, a realized sage truly learned in the works of Candrakīrti. You know, he is Atiśa's guru."

Likewise, when the great majestic lord Nāropa and others, most brilliant from among the oceanlike assembly, stood amidst the rows, each time I pointed them out with my finger and asked:

"Is this Lord Atiśa?" . . . "Oh, this must be Lord Atiśa, no?" . . .

"What are you talking about? This is the great lord and master Nāropa, at present incomparable on Earth! He too is one of Atiśa's gurus," was the only answer that came forth. As I could not see Atiśa anywhere, I started to get depressed, wondering: "But where then could this Lord be? Which one is it [among those assembled here]?" and as nobody around was able to tell me for sure, I was close to being really discouraged. At one stage the king of Vikramaśīla took his seat on the throne specially prepared for him, but not one of the paṇḍitas great or minor did as much as rise from his seat.

Right then, as all the rows of participants had joined the assembly, you, Lord, appeared, and I could not gaze at you enough. To Indians looking at you, you looked Indian; to Nepalis and Tibetans and to the gods, as they beheld you, you looked Nepali and Tibetan and a god alike. Besides the great splendor of your appearance, there was a smile on your face: your robes were smooth, looking as if polished. A great number of small keys were hanging from your waist. You started to walk without a haughty air; your walk was gentle, as you hurried in from outside; and upon your arrival, numerous āyuṣmans in front presented incense fragrances to you. The king in person rose from his seat; and as he got up, so did the assemblies of paṇḍitas and ordained ones. I saw how you took a place above the central row and thereupon I thought: "I can't see the reason why everyone shows him such marks of homage and gets up for him, nor why he has the seat at the head of the row. Is he of that royal family perhaps? This front row seat, if it doesn't belong to some amazing elder, it must be Atiśa's very own!" and so, again I asked:

"Is this Atiśa?"

"What are you saying? This is Vīra Hāsavajra. He is a wandering paṇḍita without any fixed abode."

"And what qualities is he outstanding in?" I further asked.

"His excellent qualities I am unable to assess," he said, and no explanation followed.

Then one day I was reciting the *Heart Sūtra* at one of the gates of the monastery. At the point [in the sūtra] where I said, "Form *ha*, feeling *ha*," other paṇḍitas did not say anything. But once the Lord [Atiśa] was walking by. He smiled and stopped,

"Thank you, āyuṣmat. But that is the vulgar pronunciation. Say, 'form *a*, feeling *a*.' "

I [not realizing that he was Atiśa] thought, "This kind paṇḍita seems special. He is gentle, humble, clear, and whatever he says is spoken with the wish to be helpful. If I cannot invite the Lord [Atiśa], I must invite him [to come to Tibet]."

In the morning, I was saying, "form *a*, feeling *a*," when the Lord smiled and said, "Venerable one, even that comes out sounding harsh. This is the speech of the protector Avalokita, there's nothing wrong with it. It is fine to say, 'no form, no feeling.' " Thus he spoke. As a result, an even stronger faith in him was born in me.

While I was still outside the vihāra complex and had walked to the other side, there he was, giving out the torma foodstuffs and the deities' altar offerings to a great many beggars. I inquired from all the beggars there:

"Is this Lord Atiśa?" and one beggar replied:

"What shaky talk is this? Don't you take Atiśa to Tibet! Don't you ever cut off our daily meal by depriving us of the Lord! In any case, no, this is not Atiśa! The unique and great Atiśa is in a secret place!"

Again the next morning, as Atiśa was giving out food to the assembled beggars, one poor beggar boy had missed out on his share and was now running after him, repeating:

"Atiśa, bāla ho, bhāta ho na, bhāta ho na!" ["Atiśa, there is one child (left, with) no rice, no rice!"], and as I watched the beggar boy running after him, I thought:

"This seems definitely to be Lord Atiśa!" and I was dumbfounded. My eyes filled with tears and I too started to run after him. But next, as I was about to catch up with [him, i.e.,] you at the bridge, there you [Atiśa] stood, telling me:

"*E ma*, āyuṣmat from Tibet, truly, shed no tears! Toward your Tibetan king, ministers, and subjects, I feel badly [for not having come earlier]. It so happens that, while already quite old, I still do have to hold many keys. Even now you should not lose heart. Offer your prayer requests to the precious ones."

Yet as soon as he had spoken, moved by both great hope and utter gratitude, my eyes filled with tears and I could not bring out a word. Thereupon the Lord, aware of my tears, gave me a long discourse, with instructions about how to conceal the plan. At that moment Putawo arrived. Behaving like one quite alarmed, he said [pointing at me]:

"Did he say anything bad?" and so I hid my tears. [There is some apparent confusion here, in that (1) Gya Tsöndrü Sengé first tells Nagtso that Atiśa is not yet back; (2) he then informs him that Atiśa will be back, at the assembly; (3) Nagtso states he was still unaware of Atiśa being away; (4) but then the latter *does* appear, although everyone in Nagtso's reach denies it. Rather than view the above as confused narration, it seems to be written so by design, as if better to evoke Nagtso's nervousness and uncertainty; this builds to the culmination in the scene with the beggar boy who missed out.]

SIGNS AND PROPHECIES OF ATIŚA'S IMPENDING DEPARTURE FOR TIBET

[Atiśa's own divinations and received prophecies are amply treated in his extensive sacred biography. Here it is Nagtso the translator, still speaking in the first person, who requests some omen from Atiśa. The latter sends him to consult a young boy, a dancing yoginī, two children, and finally, in the passage here (which marks the end of the *Itinerary*'s part 1, "The Invitation"), a weaver girl.]

Also, ever since my leaving Tibet, up to right now, miraculous manifestations assisted me in an uninterrupted flow, but whether they meant anything definite I did not know. So each of these questions I addressed to him, further adding a request for soon preparing "the armor" [protective amulets] for our departure. The Lord spoke:

"At the south gate of Vikramala's royal palace there is a weaver girl. Go and ask her." So I went there and as I inquired about these future events, she gave forth a short laugh, then spoke:

"In that Tibet of yours, isn't there one excellent lay practitioner of renown? What's his name?"

"There is this one Genyen Chöphel (Dge snyen Chos 'phel) that we have, one who has reached all three qualities: he is learned, experienced, and goodhearted. He is from central Tibet and resides in Khams."

"And what's his clan?" she asked. I said:

"He is known as Dromtönpa, 'the teacher from Drom.' "

"No, it isn't 'Drom,' it is the upāsika 'Drum' (*'brum*). To start with, he was born up north, in the region of Tsa gyé. Isn't he [the one to become] the heart-son of Atiśa? You know his name, clan, and native land—are you by any chance trying me out, making insinuations with deceitful questions? Having shown [yourself] at all times, throughout the seasons, as a snake, don't you play illusory tiger [with me], as if you were before a blind statue!" [translation tentative]. This she said, and next went on in song:

> Now I start to understand, . . . The solitary man at Nepal Fortress, starting from right then; . . . also the one who helped you out of the bamboo hut; . . . and the boatman, . . . the gatekeeper [boy], . . . the voice within the gate tower [at Vikramaśīla], . . . the Tibetan child in the morning, . . . the ṛṣi in the passage, . . . the beggar boy in the center of town, . . . the boy carrying the crystal arrows, and yesterday's boy and girl, . . . it appears that all of these are Drumtön's miraculous transformations. To anyone with a sufficiently strong faith and devotion, even without being endowed with the miraculous power of clairaudience, it would have been obvious that it was Lord Avalokiteśvara who thus in each of these cases intervened—obvious indeed, unless this person, though born with normal faculties, had suddenly turned deaf and blind. Since you have been in his presence [in the form of the enumerated miraculous transformations], offering him one prayer will bring it about that you won't face any great hardships. Now that you are aware of this and have gained confidence, think: "At all times, in all circumstances, please look at me with your compassion," and this will cure the restlessness of your mind.

[At the end of this long account, I, Nagtso, concluded with these words:]

"Lord Atiśa, today, through the sincere motivation of our prayers to you, please keep us in mind by your great love. Somehow, please arrange it so that you can come, we request," thus we pleaded.

NAGTSO'S FINAL INTERVIEW WITH ABBOT RATNĀKARA

[Following Nagtso's lengthy account of the antecedents to the invitation (part 1 of the *Itinerary*), Atiśa accepts the invitation to Tibet. All the luggage is secretly sent ahead to Mitra Vihāra, somewhere close to the Nepalese Therai. Earlier on (in the sacred biography), Atiśa expressed his wish to visit the Naturally Formed Caitya of Swayaṃbhū in Kathmandu Valley; he now sends Nagtso with a formal request for abbot Ratnākara to take over his duties, during his absence.]

In the morning Nagtso approached the elder Ratnākara and conveyed the request made by the Lord: "Great Elder, in your presence I offer you this request [from Lord Atiśa]: 'I should really show these Tibetan āyuṣmans around the vihāras at the great sacred spots; and we would like to set out carrying offerings for each of these sacred places. Could you, in the meantime, please take over my dharma duties regarding the Buddha's teaching?' "

The elder replied: "Excellent idea! I too would like to see each of these vihāras. So, for a couple of days I would like to follow you, and join your company."

[Nagtso said,] "Hmm, at the conclusion of our visit to a great many of the sacred spots, were you, great elder, to continue with us once we go beyond Mitra Vihāra, the long road might fatigue and utterly exhaust you."

At these words the elder had this thought: "Aha, this time, it seems that he *is* going to Tibet!" and guessing [the real aim of our trip], he addressed Nagtso as follows:

"Tibetan āyuṣman! At first you told me you had come to me as a disciple. Now it turns out that in reality you came to steal my paṇḍita! Paṇḍitas sent out previously to that yak enclosure of yours have fared like the paṇḍita who now on the sly wants to go to the Tibetans: evil people will be spreading rumors, and as a result the blessings for the benefit of beings will have no lasting impact.

"Even now it is in my power to forbid the paṇḍita from going—except that the dharma king of Tibet, this genuine bodhisattva, is dear to my heart. Moreover, a great number of people and a lot of wealth from Tibet have been sacrificed for this specific purpose. And on top of all that, you are my disciple, with a dharma connection existing between us. So, all right, this time, do ceremoniously invite him for a three year period, after which you will accompany him back here. If you fail to do so, know that the sacred [tantric] samaya vow between us will become undone [a grave infraction]."

After he had spoken these words, in Nagtso Gungthangpa's mind the thought occurred: "Taking into account the great distance between India and Tibet, three years counting going there and the return journey will be pretty useless. Even if it depended solely on me to make him stay a *full* three years in Tibet proper, such a length of time would barely suffice to install virtuous qualities in Tibet. If, at the conclusion of the three years, I will have to conduct him back, it will seem that there had never existed all that much of a need to invite the paṇḍita in the first place. If, on the other hand, I fail to accompany him back to India, I will be breaking a sacred oath. Which one is the better course to follow . . . ?" As he remained there absorbed in thought, shedding tears [enough to water] a desert, a young horseman of fair complexion, carrying a crystal staff, suddenly arrived in a great hurry close to him:

"You, dressed like one ordained, what has happened that your mind is in such distress?" After Nagtso had told him, the boy continued:

"As the proverb goes:

> In the world, a teaching that benefits is rare.
> Even more rare is one who cares to listen to it.

If I teach you the thing to do, will you do it?"

"Never before," Nagtso pondered, "did a situation arise for me to offer salutation to someone of that class [of celestial beings]. So this time, I should definitely offer him homage by a full prostration and *then* ask him for advice," and after he had thus bowed down in full prostration, the boy spoke:

As the proverb goes,

To whatever extent moral excellence deteriorates [in the world],
It is never right to offer prostrations to the ordinary body.

Even without your prostration, the benefit would have been gained. Likewise, under the given circumstances, there will not be any downfall from your samaya. If you apply the appropriate skillful means, Atiśa will remain in Tibet for the rest of his life. Tomorrow morning, when about to set out for Tibet, go greet and offer prostrations to elder Ratnākara, request him to accept you in his compassion, further request an "empowerment by his feet," and add the wish: "Even if we are not to meet again, may you retain an excellent health." At that time, the sthāvira will give you the following reply:

"As mentioned yesterday, accompany the paṇḍita back here after three years. Within these three years, virtuous qualities will have been established in Tibet. If no disease or anything else stands in the way of either master or disciple, then please come all the way to Vikramala yourself. Otherwise, send along your disciples instead."

To this you should reply as follows: "I shall certainly do as the guru says. The great request, however, is threefold. Two items therein concern requests to be agreed upon outside your control. One concerns a request to be agreed upon outside my range," after which I was to recite the following: "To the Lord Avalokiteśvara and to [Atiśa] the one foremost in the Buddha's teaching [I ask]:

In accordance with what was said by the great elder,
But also in accordance with Tibetan tradition, please hear this prayer of mine.
Will I accompany Atiśa back to India
Or will he rather stay in Tibet?"

And right away, father [buddha] and [bodhisattva] son [Atiśa, in my vision] will reply:

If I tell you to accompany me back to India, then accompany me back to India;
If I tell you I will stay in Tibet, I will just stay in Tibet.

[Tell the elder:] As long as there is no clear order to act otherwise, I solemnly declare I shall conduct him back to this very India. However, that provision [of Atiśa making up his own mind], you must allow for. Ratnakāra will immediately be most pleased that this word [of Atiśa] might overrule yours, āyuṣman."

The next morning, everything happened exactly that way. The elder further spoke:

"Āyuṣman, this is fine. You must indeed address your prayers to buddha and bodhisattva: how could either say anything wrong? If he says, 'Let us leave,' then leave; and if he does not tell you any different, then accompany him back here.

"Āyuṣman, please understand: in the absence of Atiśa, there is going to be darkness gathering over India. If you ask me how come: many dharma centers have been destroyed, many vihāra complexes are becoming desolate, and many more are the Turuṣka armies that will come. Keeping all this in mind I beseech you, master and entourage, all of you: in order not to bring about such harm, proceed well aware of transmigrating beings [and safely bring him back to India]."

So in this way, due to these words of good luck, all were in high spirits by the time they left.

—9—

The Journey to the Golden Mountain

Matthew Kapstein

During the eleventh century, Tibetan Buddhism entered a period of rapid development and change. The collapse of the central Tibetan royal dynasty had taken place following the assassination of the anti-Buddhist monarch Langdarma (Glang dar ma), probably in 842, and the ensuing power vacuum persisted for a full four hundred years. Local lords vied for ascendancy, and religious authority was no less contested than temporal power. The uncertainties of the age encouraged Tibetan seekers and adventurers to look outside of Tibet for authoritative sources of Buddhist teaching, with the result that throughout the eleventh century we find Tibetan translators and pilgrims journeying to India and Nepal in search of gurus, scriptures, and esoteric lore. These developments were particularly prominent in western Tibet, where the great translator Rinchen Zangpo (Rin chen bzang po, 958–1055) was patronized by the monarchs of the Guge kingdom. There, too, the saintly Indian scholar and adept Atiśa (982–1054) was invited to teach beginning in 1042 (see chapter 8). The careers of these two notable Buddhist monks mark the beginning of what Tibetan historians call the "later spread of the teaching," or the age of the "new translations."

Many of the Tibetans who became inspired by the renewed contacts with Indian Buddhism during this time developed a special interest in the esoteric teachings of Vajrayāna, the "Vajra Vehicle," so called because the primary symbol of this branch of Mahāyāna Buddhism is the vajra, a ritual implement at once symbolizing the diamond-like clarity and unalterability of mind-as-emptiness and its lightening-like brilliance. (The Sanskrit term "vajra" [dorje (*rdo rje*) in Tibetan] literally means both "diamond" and "lightening bolt.") Vajrayāna Buddhism has its own authoritative texts, called tantras, which are primarily manuals of ritual and esoteric lore. The reason that the age of new translations came to be so called was above all owing to the newness of the tantras introduced during this time. Though Vajrayāna Buddhism and the texts of many tantras had been known in Tibet from the eighth century onward, the older translations differed in many respects from these later arrivals.

Among the major topics treated in the tantras is *abhiṣeka* (Tib.: *wang* [*dbang*]), the consecration or "empowerment" whereby a disciple is initiated into a sphere of meditation called a maṇḍala, which is most often represented as a heavenly palace. At the center of the maṇḍala there resides a deity who is the focal point of the initiate's meditation, and who is invoked by means of special formulas called mantras. The central deity may be male, female (in which case she is often referred to as a ḍākinī, a term sometimes also used to describe women who are adepts of Vajrayāna Buddhism), or a couple in union, and is often surrounded by a retinue of divine attendants, arranged symmetrically throughout the maṇḍala. Some of the important tantras that became well known in Tibet during the eleventh century are those of the many-armed deities Guhyasamāja ("Gatherer of Secrets"), Cakrasaṃvara ("Binder of the Energy Centers"), Hevajra ("Hey! Vajra!"), Yamāntaka ("Slayer of the Lord of Death"), and Mahāmāya ("Great Creative Illusion").

The systems of meditation taught in the tantras are referred to as yoga, "union," for yoga is a discipline said to unite the adept with the realization of ultimate reality. This unification of the enlightened mind and the absolute is sometimes symbolized by the depiction of deities as couples in sexual embrace. Besides those types of yoga concerned with the visualization of the maṇḍala and deity and the recitation of the mantra, there are also more advanced disciplines involving visualizations and exercises in which one's body is conceived as a network of subtle channels and energies, the skillful manipulation of which is believed to hasten the adept's progress toward enlightenment and also lead to the acquisition of uncanny, magical abilities: clairvoyance, miraculous flight, the resurrection of the dead, and so forth. Such adepts, who have attained the goals of the esoteric path, are called *siddha*, "accomplished" or "perfected," because they have attained *siddhi*, the mundane or supermundane powers and realizations that are especially cultivated on the path of the Vajrayāna.

Several of the Tibetan traditions of teaching and practice that specialized in the systems of yoga expounded in the tantras came to be known as Kagyü (Bka' brgyud), the "lineages of transmitted doctrine." The most famous of these is the Marpa Kagyü, named for its founder, Marpa Chöki Lodrö (Mar pa Chos kyi blo gros, 1012–1096), one of the eminent translators of the period. Marpa had traveled widely in India, where he became the disciple of the famous siddha Nāropa, who taught him a special system of six yogas that had been formulated by his master, the siddha Tilopa (see chapter 7.) The six yogas are the Inner Heat (Tib.: *tummo* [*gtum mo*]), whereby the adept learns to master the subtle physical energies of the body; the Body of Apparition, through which the illusion-like nature of ordinary experience becomes known; the Dream, in which one achieves the ability consciously to explore the possibilities that are revealed during dreams; Radiant Light, referring to the luminous dimension of the mind; Transference (Tib.: *phowa* [*'pho ba*]), the means to cause one's consciousness to leave the body abruptly at the moment of death and to seek rebirth in a pure realm; and the Intermediate State (Tib.: *bardo* [*bar do*]), which here refers primarily to the state of consciousness in the course of migration between death and rebirth. The first four enable one to attain enlightenment swiftly during this very lifetime, the last two to achieve it at death. These six yogas were transmitted by Marpa to his disciples, of whom the greatest, Milarepa, is famed as Tibet's national poet (see chapter 5, 6, and 11).

It was in this age of spiritual inquiry, experimentation and quest that the figure known to Tibetan posterity as Khyungpo Neljor (Khyung po rnal 'byor), "the yogin of the Eagle clan," was born. Though there is considerable uncertainty about his precise dates, the main period of his activity seems to have been the late eleventh through early twelfth centuries. Originally an adherent of the Bön religion, he converted to Buddhism and became at first a follower of the ancient Nyingmapa school. Like many others of his generation, however, he regarded India as the source of uniquely authoritative Buddhist teachings and so left Tibet to pursue his path in the Kathmandu Valley of Nepal, and in India proper.

During his travels in India he met many masters of the Vajrayāna, some of whom were at that time famed throughout the Tibetan Buddhist world. His foremost teachers, however, were two remarkable women, Niguma and Sukhasiddhi, the first of whom is referred to in his biography as Nāropa's "lady," a term that in this context is usually taken to mean "elder sister," though some say that Niguma had been Nāropa's wife. From Niguma, Khyungpo Neljor learned a system of six yogas that resembles the system taught by Nāropa to Marpa, differing primarily in points of emphasis. The "six doctrines of Niguma," as they are known, continue to be practiced by Tibetan Buddhist adepts at the present time. When Khyungpo Neljor returned to Tibet, he established a monastic center in the valley of Shang, to the west of Lhasa. For this reason, the tradition of his followers came to be known as the Shangpa Kagyü, the "doctrinal lineage of the Shang valley."

The first two selections that follow are taken from Khyungpo Neljor's biography, which was compiled following his death by his four leading disciples. Much of it is narrated in the first person, reflecting the disciples' attempt to record their master's life as he himself had narrated it. Like other Tibetan religious biographies, Khyungpo's is called a *namthar* (*rnam thar*), a term literally meaning "liberation." As this suggests, the central theme in such works is the subject's attainment of spiritual freedom. Namthars are thus illustrative of religious practice and attainment, written usually by authors well-versed in Buddhist doctrine.

The first selection provides a summary of Khyungpo's accomplishments, given in the form of a prophecy by an Indian siddha named Amogha, who, while on pilgrimage in Tibet, visits Khyungpo's parents shortly after their son is born. The five deities mentioned above are here symbolically associated with particular attainments of yoga: Cakrasaṃvara represents the mastery of the energy center governing bodily enlightenment, located in the head; Mahāmāya, that of the speech center, in the throat; Hevajra, the mind center, in the heart; Guhyasamāja, the center governing emanational abilities, below the navel; and Yamāntaka, the source of bliss in the secret center, located in the genitals.

In the second selection we have the remarkable account of Khyungpo's meeting with Niguma. The visionary dimension of Vajrayāna literature is here very much in evidence, and much of the content has to be understood symbolically, as an account of Khyungpo's initiation into the six yogas: the warmth represented by the rivers of molten gold suggests mastery of the Inner Heat, while the teachings of Dream and of Apparition are the explicit focal concerns. The tale is constructed so as to overturn our ordinary conceptions of reality, to introduce us to the luminous and magical realm in which esoteric Buddhist experience unfolds.

Following these extracts from the biography of Khyungpo Neljor is a brief summary of the actual content of Shangpa yogic practice. The text, with some abridgement, is drawn from the writings of a famous nineteenth-century meditation master and author, Jamgön Kongtrül ('Jam mgon kong sprul blo gros mtha' yas, 1813–1899). This important figure was especially well known for his advocacy of an eclectic approach to Tibetan Buddhism known as Rime (*ris med*), avoiding the rigid sectarianism that had become a prominent feature of monastic institutions in Tibet. He was responsible, too, for reviving several rare traditions of meditation and yogic practice, including the Shangpa Kagyü, to whose system of teaching he was personally very much devoted. The modern survival of the Shangpa tradition is due entirely to his efforts and those of his leading disciples. Through the energetic teaching activity of his successor, the late Kalu Rinpoche (1905–1989), Tibetan Buddhist retreat centers where the Shangpa system of practice is emphasized have even been established in the United States, Canada, and France, fulfilling an ancient saying that this teaching would spread throughout the world.

Further Reading

Portions of the following chapter have previously appeared in my article "The Illusion of Spiritual Progress," in *Paths to Liberation*, ed. Robert Buswell and Robert Gimello (Honolulu: University of Hawaii Press, 1992). Full textual citations may be found there. I wish to thank the editors and publisher for permitting their reproduction here.

The Prophecy of Khyungpo Neljor

I was born in a Tiger Year [990?] from my mother's womb,
At which time the Indian siddha Amogha said,
"This emanation of the Buddha will go to India,
Gather the essence of realization of all paṇḍitas and siddhas,
And cause beings to mature and be liberated;
Thus, by various emanations, will he train those who require training.
He will proclaim the doctrine free from limits, the heart of the
  Mahāyāna,

And in the ten directions will proclaim its culmination,
The lion's roar of the coalescence of emptiness and bliss, the teaching of secret tantras.
His body will be Cakrasaṃvara,
His speech will embody Mahāmāya,
And Hevajra his mind;
And while his supreme emanational center will be Guhyasamāja,
His secret center will be Yamāntaka, protector of bliss.
As he arrays such maṇḍalas in his body,
He will really reveal those deities to those requiring training.
Moreover, he will assume the forms of various other deities,
And train innumerable persons difficult to train.
He will live for 150 years,
And when in the end he concludes his career,
He will display varied omens and miracles.
He will then attain buddhahood
In the pure land, Sukhāvatī [the western paradise of Amitābha],
The realm praised by all victorious buddhas;
And there he will turn the Mahāyāna doctrinal wheel.
In the future those who require training, and put their faith in him,
Will reach that buddha realm—
Of this let there be no doubt!"
After he had spoken these words
That guru and siddha
Returned at once to India,
Flying like a bird in the sky.

Khyungpo's Meeting With the Ḍākinī Niguma

Taking with me 500 ounces of gold, I wandered throughout India and asked, "Who, among the accomplished masters, seems to have come face to face with the Buddha himself?" The paṇḍitas and siddhas concurred, "That would be the paṇḍita Nāropa's lady, the ḍākinī of enlightened awareness called 'Niguma.' She abides in the three pure stations [i.e., the eighth through tenth bodhisattva stations (*bhūmi*), from which there is no falling back], and she has really requested instruction in the dharma from Mahāvajradhara himself [the primordial buddha of later Vajrayāna Buddhism]." Asking where she was residing just then, I was told that those of pure vision might meet her anywhere, but that one of impure vision could search everywhere for her without success; for she dwelt upon the pure stations, and her embodied form had become the stuff of rainbows.

Nonetheless, I was told, she sometimes came to the dense grove of the Sosadvīpa charnel ground to preside over the communal feasting of the ḍākinīs. As soon as Niguma's name was first mentioned to me I began to weep: my faith was such that my hair stood on end. Therefore, then and there, I traveled to the Sosadvīpa charnel ground, to the dense grove that was there, and I chanted *namo buddhāya* ["hail to the Buddha!"] as I went along. Then, in the sky, at a height equivalent to that of seven palm trees, there appeared a ḍākinī of dark brown complexion, wearing ornaments of bone, holding a *khaṭvāṇga* [a ritual lance or trident piercing a skull] and *kapāla* [a skull-cup], and appearing at once in various ways, as one and at the same time as many. Seeing her dance, I thought, "This must be the ḍākinī Niguma," and I prostrated myself at her feet and circumambulated her many times. Then I begged her to confer upon me her genuine esoteric instructions. "How do you know," she said, "that I'm no cannabalistic witch! When my circle arrives, you'll be our dinner! You'd better be moving, be quick!" But I persisted in my prostrations, circumambulations, and prayers to receive her instructions concerning the secret mantras. She said, "For the secret mantras of the Mahāyāna you'll need gold. If you've got gold, things may work out." I offered up my 500 ounces of gold, but she just tossed it all into the forest. I thought, "Could she be a cannabalistic witch after all? She's not greedy for gold."

At that instant, the ḍākinī glanced suddenly about the sky, and her circle of innumerable ḍākinīs appeared from space itself. In a moment, some of them built a maṇḍala palace of three stories, some arrayed a maṇḍala of colored sand, while some gathered together the provisions for the feast. Then, late during the night of the full moon, she conferred upon me the empowerment of the Body of Apparition and that of the Dream. When the empowerment ceremony was completed, she said, "Little monk from Tibet, arise!" and in a moment, relying upon the ḍākinī's miraculous powers, we traveled three yojanas [about twenty-four miles]. There, in the sky above a mountain of gold, the ḍākinīs had assembled for the feast, dancing. From the four sides of the mountain four golden rivers descended, and I had to ask, "Where in India is such a mountain as this to be found, or is this too the ḍākinī's magical creation?" To this she said:

> These varied thoughts, full of passion and hate,
> Stirring saṃsāra's ocean,
> Are insubstantial; when you realize that
> All is a golden isle, my son.
> As for apparitional dharmas,
> Like apparitions contemplate them to be;
> You'll become an apparitional Buddha—
> By the power of devotion it will come to be.

And she added, "Now I will bless you. Grasp your dreams!" Having grasped my dreams, I journey to the land of gods and demigods, where a gigantic demigod just swallowed me whole. The ḍākinī appeared in space and said, "Do not try to wake up, my son." It was at that time that she taught me the six doctrines in their entirety.

The Teachings of the Shangpa Kagyü Tradition:
A Summary by Jamgön Kongtrül

Khyungpo Neljor, a learned and accomplished master who was endowed with the "five culminations," received fully the essential wisdom of 150 Indian paṇḍitas and siddhas and so came to be renowned as one unrivaled in his knowledge of limitless approaches to the doctrine. In general, therefore, one cannot make a one-sided estimation of the extent of his teaching. Nevertheless, in accord with the widely renowned traditions of the uniquely sealed lineage of his successors, there are five "golden doctrines" of the Shangpa. [Until seven generations of teachers had passed, beginning with Khyungpo's "grand-teacher," the buddha Vajradhara, his teaching was "sealed" so that it could only be transmitted in full to a single chosen disciple. This "seal" was appropriately broken by the seventh successor, Sangye Tönpa (Sangs rgyas ston pa, 1219–1290).]

1. The roots are the "six doctrines of Niguma."
2. The trunk is the "Great Seal (*mahāmudrā*)."
3. The branches are the "three means for integrating ordinary experience with the path."
4. The flowers are the red and white forms of the ḍākinī Khecarī.
5. The fruit is the realization that body and mind are deathless and without deviation.

These precepts were recorded by Khyungpo Neljor on the basis of the *Stanzas of Indestructible Reality* revealed by the primordial buddha Vajradhara and by Niguma, the ḍākinī of enlightened awareness. So even the meditation topics and the prayers of supplication were never fabricated, altered, or corrupted by the mundane thoughts of ordinary individuals and therefore are like refined gold.

The Six Doctrines of Niguma

With reference to the six doctrines, the *Stanzas of Indestructible Reality* say:

> Matured by the four empowerments, endowed with faith and with vigor,
> Practicing the preliminary meditations upon impermanence, disgust with saṃsāra, and its hazards,
> Whoever strives at this supreme path

Will attain buddhahood within six months, a year, or during this lifetime.

Accordingly, an individual who is spiritually matured by receiving the empowerments of the five tantras that are taught in the *Great Tantra of the Ocean of Jewels*, or of the maṇḍala of Śrī Cakrasaṃvara, and who has received the transmitted blessing of each of the six doctrines and has practiced well the common preliminary meditations, first purifies herself or himself by the meditation called "the purifying enclosure of emptiness formed by the syllable *a*." Then, the six doctrines may be practiced:

1. By the practice of the *path of skillful means*, the warmth of well-being naturally blazes.
2. By the practice of the *apparitional body*, attachment and aversion naturally dissolve.
3. By the practice of the *lucid dream*, the subtle bewilderment that underlies all bewilderment is naturally cleansed.
4. By the practice of the *radiant light*, ignorance is naturally dispelled.

When these four methods are established as the root of one's practice, the afflictions that arise in the bewilderment of the four mundane states of being [waking consciousness, dreamless sleep, dream, and absorption in trance] are removed. The remaining two doctrines, then, are (5) the *transference of consciousness*, whereby buddhahood is attained without having realized it during meditation in this lifetime, and (6) the yoga of the *intermediate state*, whereby the Buddha's body of perfect rapture is realized. These are practiced as appended meditational sequences for those who are lacking in vigor and acumen, whereupon, according to the grades of excellence, mediocrity, or inferiority, one becomes liberated in one or another of the three intermediate states [namely, the time of death itself; the period immediately after death, when one enters into trancelike oblivion; and the period following that, when the disembodied consciousness grows active once more and is subject to intensive hallucinations as it searches for its next place of birth].

The Great Seal

The learned and accomplished master Khyungpo Neljor was exceedingly proud of the *Stanzas of Indestructible Reality* that contain the precepts for contemplating the essential point that is beyond intellectual formulation. Therefore he inserted the paper rolls on which they were written into a small Nepalese amulet box that he wore around his neck. For this reason these precepts came to be known as the *Amulet Box Precepts of the Great Seal*. According to them, one first cultivates tranquility and insight by means of a preliminary practice in which body, speech, and mind come to rest according to their natural disposition. Then, in the main body of the practice, the calling-down of diamond-like pristine awareness causes one to steal a glimpse of the essential point of the teaching. At that, because the four faults then naturally dissolve, all doubts with respect to the nature of mind itself are resolved. In the final practice one learns to sustain the three bodies that have spontaneously emerged. By relying upon the extraordinary means taught to derive the full profit from the practice and to remove obstacles, the Great Seal, which is the doctrinal heart of all sūtras and tantras and the essence of all meditational precepts, becomes fully manifest as the naturally liberating realization of the four bodies of buddhahood.

The Three Means for Integrating Ordinary Experience with the Path

By integrating all phenomena of appearance, sound, and thought with the path, and through the understanding that in actuality they are no different from the guru, the deity, and the apparitional nature of things, one will realize supreme bliss, the unity of clarity and emptiness, in a matter of months or a year. In this way the three bodies are naturally realized.

The White and Red Forms of the Ḍākinī

By means of particularly profound supplications and meditational exercises you may arouse the solar-colored and lunar-colored forms of the Victoriously Transcendent Vajra Woman. When that occurs, the inner heat of the unity of bliss and emptiness blazes up. This results from the alternation of passion and its dissolution in the four energy-centers of the subtle body. On the basis of that you may come to voyage in the space of "supreme coalescence," the domain of enlightened awareness.

The Realization That Body and Mind Are Deathless and without Deviation

The body is set on the path of spiritual freedom through the practice of thirty-two yogic exercises by which deathlessness is achieved. Because your own mind is primordially unborn it is established to be deathless and supremely liberated in and of itself. The bodily mass, which is the fruition of ripening karma, is an assemblage of inanimate matter, devoid of any basis for a determination of birth or death. In fact, if you have confidence based on the realization that the body itself has arisen as a mere mental projection, and that the mind is devoid of birth or death, then bodily form becomes fixed in the Great Seal, the boundless expanse in which there is no erring due to bewildering appearances, as the embodiment of the divine. It is taught that through even some of these precepts the embodiment of coalescence may be attained during this lifetime, and that by merely hearing them one may achieve buddhahood in the conquerors' body of perfect rapture (*sambhogakāya*) during the intermediate state after death. It says in the *Stanzas of Indestructible Reality*:

Those who experience this supreme path in practice,
During this lifetime or during the intermediate state, and at no other time,
Naturally realize the three bodies in the indivisible nature of emptiness and bliss,
And so go forth to journey in the pure space of enlightened mind.

—10—

A Quest for "The Path and Result"

Cyrus Stearns

Among the four major traditions of Tibetan Buddhism, the Sakya (*Sa skya*) sect has certainly received the least attention in modern studies of Tibetan religion and history. Almost nothing has been published in European languages dealing with the distinctive characteristics of this tradition of Buddhist study and meditation. Furthermore, with the exception of studies focusing upon the Mongol period of the thirteenth and fourteenth centuries C.E., there is very little accurate historical information available concerning the Sakya sect.

Strictly speaking, the Sakya tradition began with the founding of the modest hermitage of Sakya in the Tsang (Gtsang) province of southwest Tibet in 1073. The founder of Sakya, Könchok Gyalpo (Dkon mchog rgyal po, 1034–1102), belonged to the ancient Khön ('Khon) family, which has continued to provide leaders for the Sakya order up to the present day.

Although Könchok Gyalpo founded the monastery of Sakya, it was his son Kunga Nyingpo (Kun dga' snying po, 1092–1158), often simply referred to as Sachen ("the great master of Sakya"), who sought out and mastered a vast number of exoteric and esoteric Buddhist teachings, which he then passed on to his sons and disciples. Sachen was in particular a profound master of the esoteric traditions of the Buddhist tantras. Among the numerous transmission lineages of tantra that he received and practiced, the teachings known as "The Path and Result" (*lam 'bras*), or more honorifically as "The Precious Oral Instructions" (*gsung ngag rin po che*), have been passed down to the present day as the most sacred system for spiritual realization within the Sakya tradition.

"The Path and Result" was originally revealed to the great Indian adept Virūpa by the goddess Nairātmyā, the consort of the tantric deity Hevajra. Virūpa summarized these teachings in what are known as *The Adamantine Phrases (Rdo rje tshig rkang)*, which were transmitted orally until the time of Sachen, who first recorded them in writing. "The Path and Result" is thus a system of oral esoteric instruction for meditation based upon the *Hevajra Tantra* and related tantric scriptures. It was passed down in great secrecy from a single master to a single disciple for five generations in India, before being brought to Tibet in the eleventh century C.E. by the Indian master Gayadhara, who taught it to the Tibetan teacher known as Drokmi the Translator ('Brog mi lo tsā ba, 993–1077?). Drokmi was also extremely careful in teaching the tantras, and he gave the full instructions of the path and result to only three of his disciples. The most important of these was Se Khar Chungwa (Se Mkhar chung ba, 1025?–1122?), who likewise gave the teachings to only a few select disciples. It was Se Khar Chungwa's disciple Zhangdön Chöbar (Zhang ston Chos 'bar, 1053?–1135?), also known as Lord Gönbawa (Rje Dgon pa ba), from whom Sachen Kunga Nyingpo finally received the complete teachings of the path and result. Up through the time of Sachen, the masters of "The Path and Result" were lay tantric practitioners, who mostly devoted themselves to meditation in isolated hermitages.

As a young boy Sachen Kunga Nyingpo received many teachings and initiations from his father, the first throne-holder of Sakya, who passed away when Sachen was ten years old. Soon thereafter the master Bari the Translator (Ba ri lo tsā ba, 1040–1111?) was invited to occupy the teaching-throne of Sakya during Sachen's minority, and to serve as his tutor. When he was eleven years old, Sachen, under the direction of Bari the Translator, began a lengthy retreat for meditation upon Mañjuśrī, the divine personification of pristine awareness. Six months into the retreat Sachen was blessed with a vision of Mañjuśrī, who spoke to him these four lines:

> If you are attached to this life you are not a religious person.
> If you are attached to the cycle of existence you do not have renunciation.
> If you are attached to your own goals you do not have the enlightened motivation.
> If grasping occurs you do not have the view.

From that time on Sachen understood all the Buddhist teachings without any difficulty. This instruction is known as "the parting from the four attachments" (*zhen pa bzhi bral*), around which considerable exegetical material has developed in the Sakya tradition. It is regarded as a synopsis of all the teachings of the Mahāyāna and is frequently taught and studied in the Sakya tradition up to the present day.

In the years following his Mañjuśrī retreat, Sachen traveled extensively, studying with many different teachers and mastering an incredible number of exoteric and esoteric teachings of the Mahāyāna and Vajrayāna. The events recorded in the excerpts from the biography of Sachen translated below begin at the end of this period of intense study, when he was in his twenties.

Sachen's father had studied the *Hevajra Tantra* under Drokmi the Translator, and so it was felt that Sachen should also seek out the transmission lineage that had come down through Drokmi. Sachen's relative Dralha Bar (Dgra lha 'bar), usually known as Gyichuwa (Sgyi chu ba), had been a disciple of Salway Nyingpo (Gsal ba'i snying po), one of Drokmi the Translator's other main disciples in the study of the *Hevajra Tantra*. In addition to the *Hevajra Tantra*, Sachen also received from master Gyichuwa a variety of tantric teachings, some of which were passed down through Drokmi's rival, Gö the Translator ('Gos lo tsā ba), and through Mal the Translator (Mal lo tsā ba), who was heir to the teachings of the great Nāropa's disciple, the Nepalese master known as Pamtingpa (Pham thing pa).

It was while still studying with Gyichuwa that Sachen went to meet Lord Khar Chungwa, who was Drokmi the Translator's successor as the lineage holder of "The Path and Result," and first heard of these teachings. Khar Chungwa had also studied the *Hevajra Tantra* with Könchok Gyalpo, Sachen's father, whom he thus referred to as his master. Lord Khar Chungwa did not initially accept Sachen as Könchok Gyalpo's son because Sachen had been born not to Könchok Gyalpo's first wife, who was barren, but to his second wife Machik Zhangmo (Ma gcig zhang mo). This happened some years after Khar Chungwa's stay at Sakya to study with Könchok Gyalpo.

Following the last wishes of master Gyichuwa, Sachen took responsibility for the monastery at Gyichu and prepared to take the vows of celibacy as a Buddhist monk. However, one of Sachen's other masters, known as Nam Khaupa (Gnam kha'u pa), heard the news and forbid him to take the vows. The Sakya tradition is forever grateful to master Nam Khaupa, as he was instrumental in arranging the circumstances that actually led to Sachen's birth, as well as later preventing him from becoming a monk. As a result Sachen's four sons were later born, two of whom, Sönam Tsemo (Bsod nams rtse mo, 1142–1182) and Drakpa Gyaltsen (Grags pa rgyal mtshan, 1147–1216), would succeed their father as leaders of the Sakya tradition. A third son, Palchen Öpo (Dpal che 'od po, 1150–1204), would become the father of Sakya Paṇḍita, Kunga Gyaltsen (Sa skya Paṇḍita Kun dga' rgyal mtshan, 1182–1251), one of the most renowned teachers in Tibetan history.

When Sachen first met Lord Zhang Gönbawa, the master turned him away, saying that Sachen seemed to be a follower of the New Translations (*gsar ma pa*). The master himself said that he only taught some minor traditions of the Great Perfection (*rdzogs chen*), which were based upon scriptures translated in the early period of Buddhism in Tibet. This was a reference to the fact that many Buddhist scriptures, such as the *Hevajra Tantra* and the *Kālacakra Tantra*, were not translated into Tibetan until the eleventh century C.E. Followers of these teachings became known as followers of the New Translations, whereas those who practiced and studied the scriptures translated in the earlier period became known as the Ancient Ones (*rnying ma pa*). There was much competition and disagreement between these two groups. Ironically, of course, Lord Zhang Gönbawa himself was actually the main lineage holder of "The Path and Result," among other teachings, which entered Tibet during the period of the New Translations. When Lord Zhang learned that Sachen was the son of Könchok Gyalpo, who was the master of his own master Lord Khar Chungwa, he was aghast at having rejected him, because of the implied disrespect to one of his spiritual forefathers. After some discussion, he then agreed to give Sachen the teachings of the path and result, as well as a group of eight other instructions known as the Later Cycles of the Path (*lam phyi ma brgyad*). These are profound tantric instructions that have been passed down from such great Indian masters as Dombhi Heruka, Indrabhūti, and Padmavajra.

At the end of the teachings of "The Path and Result" it is customary for the master to give the disciples a prophecy of their future attainment. At this point Lord Zhang stated that Sachen would realize the Great Seal (*mahāmudrā*) in this life if he applied himself to serious meditation. The term Great Seal is used in the tantric traditions of the New Translation period to indicate realization of the ultimate nature of reality. On this occasion Lord Zhang also revealed the significance of a prophetic dream that Sachen had had earlier during his studies with Master Gyichuwa.

Not long thereafter Sachen went into an eighteen-year retreat to meditate upon "The Path and Result." During this period Virūpa is said to have actually come to visit him for one month. Virūpa was flanked by his disciple Kaḥna (Nag po pa), for whose benefit he had composed *The Adamantine Phrases*, and Gayadhara, the last Indian master of "The Path and Result," who brought the teachings to Tibet. Behind Virūpa was Koṭalipa, the author of one of the Later Cycles of the Path, and in front was another great adept named Vinasa. Virūpa bestowed upon Sachen the entire teachings of "The Path and Result," as well as a number of other special instructions that are still taught as part of "The Path and Result" today. Sachen thus received the teachings of the direct transmission (*nye brgyud*) from Virūpa himself, as well as the sequential transmission (*ring brgyud*) he had previously received from Lord Zhang Gönbawa.

At the end of his retreat Sachen taught "The Path and Result" for the first time. At this time he also placed Virūpa's treatise, *The Adamantine Phrases*, in writing for the first time and wrote the first commentary on it, a brief verse summary entitled *The Abbreviated Explication of the Scripture (Gzhung bshad don bsdus ma)*. During his lifetime ten large commentaries were recorded to preserve Sachen's explanations of *The Adamantine Phrases.*

The following excerpts of the biography of Sachen Kunga Nyingpo are a translation of pp. 113.1–116.1 and 118.1–126.2 of *The Expansion of the Great Secret Doctrine (Gsang chen bstan pa rgyas byed)*, written in the middle of the sixteenth century C.E. by the Sakya master Jamyang Khyentse Wangchuk ('Jam dbyangs mkhyen brtse dbang phyug, 1524–1568). This historical survey of the lives of the early masters of "The Path and Result" is one of the latest of the genre within this tradition. It is, however, considered the most reliable of all, being based upon a number of earlier compositions, as well as forming a record of the oral explanations of Tsarchen Losel Gyantso (Tshar chen Blo gsal rgya mtsho, 1502–1567), the main teacher of Jamyang Khyentse Wangchuk, and one of the greatest masters of the path and result. The text translated is 'Jam dbyangs mkhyen brtse dbang phyug, *Gsung ngag rin po che lam 'bras bu dang bcas pa'i khog phub kyi rnam bshad las / gdams ngag byung tshul gyi zin bris gsang chen bstan pa rgyas byed ces bya ba kha'u brag rdzong pa'i bzhad pa ma nor ba ban rgan mkhyen brtse'i nyams len*, in Lam 'bras slob bshad (Dehra Dun: Sakya Centre, 1983), 14:2–155.

Further Reading

Chogay Trichen Rinpoche, *The History of the Sakya Tradition: A Feast for the Minds of the Fortunate*, trans. from Tibetan into French by Phende Rinpoche and Jamyang Khandrao, and from French into English by Jennifer Stott (Bristol: Ganesha, 1983); Ronald Davidson, "The Ṅor pa Tradition," in *Wind Horse* 1 (Berkeley: Asian Humanities Press, 1981), pp. 79–97; Davidson, "Preliminary Studies on Hevajra's *Abhisamaya* and the *Lam-'bras Tshogs-bshad*," in *Tibetan Buddhism: Reason and Revelation*, ed. Steven D. Goodman and Ronald M. Davidson (Albany: State University of New York Press, 1992), pp. 107–32; Dezhung Rinpoche, *The Three Levels of Spiritual Perception*, trans. Jared Rhoton (Boston: Wisdom Publications, 1995); Ngorchen Konchog Lhundrub, *The Beautiful Ornament of the Three Visions: An Exposition of the Preliminary Practices of the Path Which Extensively Explains the Instructions of the "Path Including Its Result" in Accordance with the Root Treatise of the Vajra Verses of Virūpa*, trans. Lobsang Dagpa, Ngawang Samten Chophel (Jay Goldberg), and Jared Rhoton (Singapore: Golden Vase, 1987; reprint, Ithaca: Snow Lion, 1991); Sakya Trizin, His Holiness, and Ngawang Samten Chophel (Jay Goldberg), trans. *A Collection of Instructions on Parting from the Four Attachments: The Basic Mind Training Teaching of the Sakya Tradition* (Singapore: Singapore Buddha Sasana Society, 1982); M. Tachikawa, "The Tantric Doctrine of the Sa skya pa according to the Śel gyi me loṅ," in *Acta Asiatica* 29 (Tokyo: Toho Gakkai, 1975), pp. 95–106.

Sachen's Quest for "The Path and Result"

The elders of Sakya said, "Now, since our ancestral teachings are the scriptures and oral instructions transmitted through Lord Drokmi the Translator, you must be able to receive them in complete depth."

Sachen investigated where he could receive them and, upon learning that Dralha Bar of the Khön family was both a paternal relative and an expert in the scriptures, he went to him at Gyichu in Jang (Byang). Sachen had a dream when receiving the preliminary section of the Hevajra initiation. He dreamed that over a great red murky body of water said to be the sea of existence there were three connected bridges with bridge supports made of kneaded dough. There were many people saying, "Please take me across to the other shore. Please take me."

He took three people across all three bridges. He took seven people across two of the bridges. He took many people across one of the bridges. Then he rested in the sun on the slope of a mountain called Malaya.

The next morning he told the master, who teased him by saying, "With your strength how could you take across more than three people?" but placed extremely great importance in it, and also fully bestowed the teachings.

Sachen received and mastered such teachings as the cycle of Hevajra transmitted from Lord Drokmi the Translator to Salway Nyingpo of Ngari, Hevajra in the tradition of the great adept Kaḥna as transmitted from Lord Gö the Translator, and Cakrasaṃvara as transmitted from [the Nepalese master] from Pamting, which Gyichuwa had received from Mal the Translator.

On one occasion during that time he heard talk that Lord Khar Chungwa was coming to preside over a teaching council at Dok Uk (Mdog dbugs). Many of Gyichuwa's young monks prepared to go to the show. In general the great master Sachen did not enjoy such shows, but because of the great reputation of Lord Khar Chungwa, he wanted to meet him in person and traveled together with them.

Lord Khar Chungwa was seated at the head of the assembly telling a lot of animated stories. He questioned each of Gyichuwa's young monks, and when he arrived in front of the great master Sachen he said, "Who are you, noble son?"

"I am from over at Drom Puk (Grom phug)," he replied.

"One of my masters lived there," Lord Khar Chungwa remarked, "but now he has already passed away. I wanted to visit him but there was no chance. It is said that one called Bari the Translator is there, but I don't have even the slightest wish to go. What is it like there now?"

He replied, "I am the son and heir of your master."

"Don't tell lies, noble son. My master had no son."

The great master was unable to say anything. When the young monks told the story, Lord Khar Chungwa sat for a moment with his eyes squeezed shut, and then said, "If I look at my virtuous deeds [i.e., stock of merit] and the indications in my vital airs, I am about worn out. The saying that the living and the dead don't meet isn't true. The time for meeting has come."

He took the great master onto his lap, held him to his heart and face, and tears filled his eyes. They stayed with their cushions touching together for three days. Lord Khar Chungwa gave Sachen a clear explanation of the internal structure and outline of "The Precious Oral Instructions." Then he said, "This decrepit old man has the teachings, so come quick. If you think 'I can take my time,' I will die."

They returned to Gyichu and the great master planned to go to Khar Chung immediately. When he had finished gathering his things into a bundle, a monk acquaintance called Dönpa Dorje Ö (Ston pa rdo rje 'od) said, "In general, whatever activities a tantric practitioner does are done after asking the master. In particular, from among this many of us monks there is no one he values more than you. It is not right to go without asking the master for permission."

He replied, "I have no suitable gift, so I can't even ask."

Dorje Ö gave him a full piece of silk. Sachen realized that what he had said was true and asked Master Gyichuwa, who said, "Why are you going?"

"To request 'The Precious Oral Instructions,' " he replied.

Master Gyichuwa said, "He is called Se Khar Chungwa the Smooth-Talker. He teaches by gathering up piecemeal the teachings of my master Salway Nyingpo of Ngari (Mnga 'ris). He has no oral instructions at all. Don't go." He didn't give permission.

Sachen thought, "In gratitude for the completion of the scriptures in the presence of Gyichuwa, I will invite him to Sakya, hold a great teaching council, and fulfill his wishes. Then I must go to Khar Chung."

Just when he had finished getting the material goods ready, mainly about three hundred loads of barley, Gyichuwa fell ill and a person arrived to summon Sachen. When he went there, Gyichuwa had already passed away, leaving a last testament that said, "You must take ordination and maintain this establishment of the Khön family."

He completed such things as the funeral services. When he had returned to Sakya and prepared the things for ordination, master Nam Khaupa heard about it and summoned him.

"What is the meaning of preparing the saffron robes?" he asked.

When Sachen told him the story he replied, "Masters are equal, but instead of the dead face of the dead master you must look at the live face of the living master—me. Don't take ordination!"

Sachen did as he was told, and his sons the holy brothers (Trakpa Gyaltsen and Sönam Tsemo) and the others appeared. So this master Nam Khaupa is said to have been very kind to the Sakyapa. Although he didn't take ordination, he did occupy the monastic seat of Gyichuwa.

This great master had intended to go immediately into the presence of Se Khar Chungwa at the completion of Gyichuwa's teaching council, but Se Khar Chungwa also passed away at about the same time as Gyichuwa and Sachen was not able to receive "The Path and Result" from him. Now he examined who was the best from whom to receive "The Precious Oral Instructions." It was said that the two Zhangdön brothers were the best of Se Khar Chungwa's disciples. Between them, the younger brother Ziji Barwa (Gzi brjid 'bar ba) was an expert, but he had passed away. Now the elder brother called Chöbar was living.

Sachen decided to go to him and spoke to master Nam Khaupa, who said, "What will you do?"

"I will request 'The Precious Oral Instructions,' " he replied.

Nam Khaupa said, "The so-called great meditator is a great liar. He doesn't have any oral instructions at all. If you want buddhahood I will teach you a method for realization and you can meditate."

Sachen insisted, "I am certain myself," and was released.

He gave a coat of mail to a man called Apo Gyalpo (A po rgyal po), and both master and servant set off. At an archery field in Ding (Ding), Lord Zhang Gönbawa was sitting with disheveled hair, a bare chest, and wearing a goat skin on top of his lower robe. He was performing yoga and making a lot of haphazard talk.

The great master stopped beside a gully and asked a girl, "Where does the one called Zhang Gönbawa Chöbar live?"

She replied, "I don't know Zhang Gönbawa. If you need Uncle Chöbar, he's over there," and showed him.

He said to her, "Ask him to please come here."

When he came Sachen spread out a white robe he had and said, "Please sit here," but he didn't wish to sit.

Sachen offered prostrations and Zhangdön said, "Aren't you mistaken? You seem like a religious man from far away. Moreover, you seem to be a follower of the New Translations."

"There is no mistake," he replied and offered the coat of mail as a gift.

Zhangdön exclaimed, "Ah! Now what mistake have you made? I have nothing but the food and drink I search for morning and night, so what could I have to loan that you would leave a coat of mail as collateral?" and became alarmed.

"It is not a request for a loan. I am requesting 'The Precious Oral Instructions,' " he replied.

"What are you talking about?" he asked, "Not to mention knowing 'The Precious Oral Instructions,' I've never even heard of them until now. I give explanations of minor teachings, explaining some of the Great Perfection of Tsamunti and of the Brahmin Cycle (*rzdogs chen tsa munti dang bram ze'i skor*). You so-called followers of the New Translations have great suspicions about those. Aren't you suspicious? You should go."

Thinking that if he still insisted it might possibly be given, Sachen said, "It is late for that this evening. I wouldn't arrive anywhere. I request a place to stay."

Zhangdön replied, "I have no house or such fit for a guest. Nor is there any place to stay. You can go or stay. Do what you like!"

Sachen left, not wishing to give a reply.

"And take the coat of mail," Zhangdön said.

"I don't want to take now what I have already offered," he replied.

Sachen did not take it, and Zhang did not take it either, so the coat of mail was left lying in that dry gully. The great master thought, "With the present behavior it could be true he doesn't have 'The Precious Oral Instructions.' Since the one called Nakrong the Translator (Nag rong lo tsā ba) is now in Jaktang (Lcags thang), I will go there and make close inquiry."

He set off to Jaktang and had gotten as far as the point where the road branched when Dönpa Dorje Ö, later also known as Zhang Gyabpa (Zhang Skyabs pa), who was the father of the one called Chosay Öchok (Jo sras 'od mchog), said to Lord Zhang Gönbawa, "Now what? What was the purpose of that one who asked to meet you?"

"He said he needed 'The Precious Oral Instructions,' " he replied.

"And what did you tell him?" he asked.

"I said I didn't know them," Zhangdön said.

Then Dorje Ö said, "When we were staying in Kharchung some of Gyichuwa's young monks came. To one among them Lord Khar Chungwa said, "You are my master's son," took him upon his lap, and his eyes filled with tears. That was probably him. If it was, wouldn't there be damage to your sacred commitments?"

"Oh no!" exclaimed Zhangdön, "There would be. I didn't know. Now you run and see if it's him or not. If it isn't, let him go. If it is, bring him back."

He ran off and caught up to Sachen at the point where the road branched. He told the story and since it was him, invited him back.

Zhangdön said, "I don't want people to be aware of our conversation. We'll meet in private."

He led him to a nearby ravine in Ding and then said, "Who told you I had 'The Precious Oral Instructions'?"

Sachen replied, "I heard it from Lord Khar Chungwa."

"Well then, why didn't you request it from Lord Khar Chungwa himself?" he asked.

"Without Lord Gyichuwa's permission I couldn't receive it," he replied.

Zhangdön said, "It is like the saying [in the *Discourse on the Perfection of Wisdom*], 'some demons appear as abbots and masters.' "

"It wasn't that," Sachen said, "Since Lord Khar Chungwa also passed away at the same time as Master Gyichuwa, if I had gone at that time the teachings of Gyichuwa would have been left incomplete, and I would also not have received the oral instructions of Lord Khar Chungwa. Gyichuwa knew that."

He replied, "I was joking. How could he have been mistaken?"

In brief, it is taught that Lord Gyichuwa knew that it was right for this great master Sachen to be trained by Zhang Gönbawa.

Then master Zhangdön said, "I completely received the oral instructions, but there is no text, and I have never explained them to anyone, so I must also think about them some. And it is not proper to explain them as soon as they are requested. The request must be made at least three times."

He replied, "I requested yesterday and now, so that is two. If I make it three by requesting tomorrow as I leave, would that suffice?"

Perhaps master Zhangdön felt it was necessary to be cautious because Sachen had merely received the internal structure of "The Precious Oral Instructions" from Lord Khar Chungwa. In any case, he replied, "Many great scholars and lesser scholars have now been invited here for a teaching council because of the passing away of the one called Se Dön Dorchung (Se ston Rdor 'byung). It wouldn't be attractive for an old practitioner also to explain the teachings at this place where they are explaining the teachings. This fall I must also collect some gifts for explaining the teachings to some housewives. Come in the spring next year."

Sachen did as he was told. He came bringing an offering of about thirteen ounces of gold for Zhangdön, and a heavy robe for Öchok's father in return for his kindness. But the father had already passed away, so he gave it to Öchok himself.

In brief, this great master fully received "The Precious Oral Instructions" when he was twenty-seven years old. "The Precious Oral Instructions" took four years and the [eight] Later Cycles of the Path took four years, so they were completed in eight years.

Furthermore, this Lord Gönbawa mostly maintained a deliberate behavior of secrecy and didn't even act like he meditated, let alone taught the teachings, except for a few teaching sessions for some housewives. He gave the appearance of passing his time in ordinary activities, such as helping with the work of the local people and collecting all human and dog wastes on the pathways between their places, and heaping it on his own field.

In the springtime, when manure was spread, he would accept the request of every villager who said "Uncle Chöbar, come spread our manure," no matter how many there were.

His wife argued with him, "Are you going to do them all at once, or are you trying to start a fight?"

It is taught that the master satisfied them by manifesting a physical presence at each of their places. In a similar fashion, he would manifest physical presences at the same time during the digging of sod, the harvesting of crops, and so on, but other than everyone just assuming it was him, it appears that no one knew that he was manifesting physical presences.

From among [these kinds of events], when the oral instructions were completely finished he led Lord Sachen to the roof on the occasion of bestowing the prophecy of attainment. He said, "In this Vajrayāna the most essential thing is just to meditate. We were two brothers, and my younger brother made great efforts to study the explication of [Virūpa's] treatise, while I meditated. From among the two of us I had the greater understanding of the treatise. I didn't even meditate that much, but to enhance your confidence I will show you a spectacle."

He put on the goatskin cloak and went outside where there was a large dilapidated basket. He went under it and put the goatskin cloak on top of the basket. After a while many mountain creatures created from different jewels, with various shapes, fur, and colors never seen before emerged from under the basket and covered the entire region of Ding. Again they dissolved one into the other and went under the basket.

Then again countless birds created from various jewels, with different colors and shapes, emerged from under the basket and filled all the area of Ding. They dissolved like before.

Then he manifested in front of the basket, in the center of rainbows and light in midair, the forms of [Avalokiteśvara, Mañjuśrī, and Vajrapāṇi,] the lords of the three spiritual races, having the nature of light. That too dissolved like before.

Then he manifested figures of Lord Gönbawa himself, indivisible form and emptiness, which filled all the valley of Ding.

Then Lord Gönbawa himself went and sat on top of each basket. Infinite lights of various colors radiated from the bodies, transforming all the valley into the nature of light. Finally, they all dissolved one into the other and went underneath that basket. He shook out the goatskin cloak, put it on, and came inside.

He made a prophecy to Sachen: "If you make practice the essential thing, you will realize the Great Seal (*mahāmudrā*) without discarding the body. If you mainly teach, there will appear three disciples who attain the supreme enlightenment, seven who attain [the spiritual level of] patience, and about eighty who become endowed with realization. Do not write these oral instructions in words for eighteen years. Don't even mention the name in conversation. Then whatever you do, whether explain them or write them in words, you will be the owner of the doctrine."

In general, while this Lord Sachen heard fragments of the precious oral instructions from Gyura Agyab (Kyu ra a skyabs), Zhama Könchok (Zhwa ma Dkon mchog), and Drangyul Olka (Sbrang yul 'ol ka ba), they were not complete. It is taught that the first two later became disciples of Lord Sachen.

Sachen then reviewed *The Adamantine Phrases (Rdo rje tshig rkang)* every [day six or seven times], and the extensive path once every month without break.

Previously a monk he stayed with in Gungtang (Gung thang) had resented him and given him poison. While he had been cured when a medicine called Zomo Tsitsi (*bzo mo tsitsi*) was offered to him, again when he was staying at Drongchung (Grong chung) monastery in Yeru (G.yas ru) the residue of that poison arose, and he fell unconscious for about twenty days.

Although the basis of the illness was later cured, he had forgotten all the teachings as a result. He thought, "For the other instructions I can rely upon my companions, books, and so forth, but in regard to 'The Precious Oral Instructions,' the master is not alive, and there are no books and companions. Even though I went to India, it would be difficult to find anyone who knows these instructions."

He went into retreat in the Mañjuśrī Cave of the East Mansion, which is known as the Old Residence. When he made prayers, Zhang Gönbawa appeared in a dream and spoke the oral instructions. Then he made intense prayers, and Lord Gönbawa actually came and completely spoke the oral instructions. He also then recalled those that he had forgotten.

Again he made strong prayers and beheld the face of [Virūpa,] the reverend lord of yoga, whose body was dark red in color with the radiance of ten million suns. His two hands made the ritual gesture of proclaiming the teachings (*dhar-*

macakra mudrā), and with his legs fully crossed, he covered the area of Sakya from Baldrok ('Bal grog) to Möndrok (Mon grog), with the patch of white earth on the mountainside serving as a backdrop.

To the right was the great adept Kaḥna, with his left hand resting in his lap and blowing a horn trumpet held in his right. To the left was Gayadhara, wrapped in the white robes of an [Indian] scholar, seated with his legs crossed and holding a vajra and bell crossed at his heart. To the rear Koṭalipa held a parasol, and in front Vinasa was holding a skull-cup with both hands and offering nectar. These three adepts were each dark blue in color, with hair plaited in a topknot, and wearing a loincloth of white cotton. Sachen beheld the faces of these five, the central figure and his entourage.

[Virūpa] then appeared for a period of one month, sometimes with entourage and sometimes alone. Sachen received the profound path for spiritual union with the master, the common and uncommon protection of Virūpa, Vidvamsana according to the tradition of Virūpa, and seventy-two sets of tantra. In this way, with the direct transmission he actually heard from the lord of yoga, both transmissions were combined in Sachen.

When eighteen years had passed, the bodhisattva Aseng (A seng), who was the son of [Sachen's teacher] Gyura Akyab, supplicated him by saying, "You have 'The Precious Oral Instructions' but you have never even mentioned it to us. You should teach it now."

Since the expiration of the number of years in Zhangdön's command and Aseng's supplication occurred at the same time, Sachen believed that master Zhangdön had arranged the auspicious pattern of events and taught ["The Path and Result"] once to Aseng alone. At his supplication Sachen also composed *The Abbreviated Explication of the Scripture (Gzhung bshad don bsdus ma)*. It is taught that this was the first of all the explications of the scripture in the tradition of this lineage.

—11—

The Yogin Lorepa's Retreat at Lake Namtso

Nālandā Translation Committee

The story that follows narrates events from the life of Lorepa (Lo ras pa), a thirteenth-century Tibetan tantric master of the Kagyü lineage. This episode from his life is presented in *The Rain of Wisdom*, a collection of devotional songs and religious poetry by Kagyü gurus. The stories about Lorepa's life are meant to be both inspiring and entertaining. Much of the narrative is quite serious in tone, telling of Lorepa's fierce efforts to meditate and practice diligently while living in the most austere conditions in isolated retreat; but aside from this inspirational theme, there are amusing anecdotes of the disciples and various helpers, who attempt to emulate Lorepa's lofty detachment and serene confidence without much initial success.

Lorepa belongs to the Drukpa (*'brug pa*), subsect of the Kagyü lineage and in the first song that he sings, he invokes the protection of the Kagyü gurus. All of the Kagyü lineages trace their origins in Tibet back to the lay practitioner, Marpa the translator, but in his song Lorepa also includes the Indian gurus and the buddhas who are considered the source of the Kagyü tradition. For the modern devotee of the Kagyü tradition, this list of enlightened teachers would include more than forty-five gurus, and Lorepa's abbreviated version shows that we are still at an early stage in the lineage's development.

First he invokes the primordial buddhas Samantabhadra and Vajradhara, the mystical sources of the tantras, and symbols for absolute awakened mind in itself. Then we have in succession the Bengali mahāsiddha Tilopa (see chapter 7), his Indian disciple Nāropa (see chapter 9), who in turn taught the first Tibetan, Marpa the translator. Next in the lineage is Marpa's disciple Milarepa, the famous bard and wild yogin ascetic, who mastered the tantric meditation practice of generating inner heat (*gtum mo*) and wore only thin cotton robes (*ras pa*) while dwelling in the mountain caves of Tibet and Nepal. Next in the lineage mentioned by Lorepa is Milarepa's disciple, the doctor Gampopa (Sgam po pa), followed by the two founders of the Drukpa Kagyü sublineage: Lingchen Repa (Gling chen ras pa) and his student Tsangpa Gyare (Gtsang pa rgya ras), who was Lorepa's teacher. The other Kagyü lineage chants, which occur in chapter 27, are written by another subsect, the Karma Kagyü. They are exactly like this list of gurus except that they branch after Gampopa to form a different series of teachers and disciples, apart from the line begun by Tsangpa Gyare.

Lorepa continued the practices of his teachers, and his life-style as a wandering yogin and a religious poet reminds one especially of Milarepa. Lorepa first met his guru Tsangpa Gyare when he was sixteen years old, and two years later he abandoned his family and all worldly activities to devote himself exclusively to his teacher. He studied intensively with the aging Tsangpa Gyare until he died, when Lorepa was twenty-six. Following the death of his beloved teacher, Lorepa practiced for numerous years under extremely harsh conditions, dealing constantly with overwhelming physical and psychological obstacles, but ultimately gaining great realization. The biographies of Lorepa emphasize several points in his life story: his generosity in providing material and spiritual support for other practitioners, the abundant ritual offerings he would regularly make, even to the point of personal impoverishment, and the important monasteries he founded in the later part of his life.

The story of Lorepa's retreat translated here takes place at Lake Namtso (Gnam mtsho), one of the three famous sites associated with Lorepa's life as a yogin. It is one of the largest bodies of water in Tibet, a sort of inland sea, with rocky hermitages situated on its banks and on its islands, which provide an ideal setting for a yogin's solitary retreat. The opening scene describing Lorepa's passage across the lake contains several interesting points. We see a medieval description of a Tibetan coracle boat, fashioned from leather pontoons by the fisherman who promises to help Lorepa. Such vessels are still used today in Tibet as ferries, often manufactured on the spot for the purpose of single crossings of rivers and lakes. Their voyage across the lake on this flimsy raft is a perilous journey, for despite their precaution of setting out on an auspicious day, they encounter rough, stormy weather, enormous waves, and monstrous frogs, all of which terrify the poor fisherman. The fisherman begs Lorepa to protect them from these perils by calling upon the divine assistance of the gods or of his gurus, and Lorepa responds with his invocation to the Kagyü lineage.

After his prayer, Lorepa's teacher Tsangpa Gyare himself appears in the sky, demonstrating the principle of the universality of the guru, the tantric precept that the spiritual teacher is the source of all protection and the truly effective refuge in the world. This visionary appearance is meant to illustrate the proper attitude of a disciple toward his guru for those who practice tantra. That is, the guru is taken to be the all-powerful spokesperson of the phenomenal world: ever present, ever active, the true cause of everything that happens to the disciple on his or her path. In the song Lorepa sings to the vision of his guru, he uses the crossing of the stormy lake as a metaphor for navigating the ocean of saṃsāra, and in evocative poetic imagery he lists six other similes for the unsatisfactoriness of cyclic existence. Saṃsāra is like a flaming fire, into which sentient beings are attracted like naive moths; saṃsāra is like a deep, dark abyss, a pitfall for blind and lost beings; it is like a futile mirage seen in a desert by hot and thirsty beings; and so on. Lorepa's supplication to Tsangpa Gyare as a guide who will protect and deliver them to safety on the "other shore" is heard, resulting in the immediate pacification of the storm; when they reach dry land the fisherman realizes that he was in the presence of a master all along, and he prostrates to Lorepa and asks for his blessing.

Upon arriving at the island in Lake Namtso, Lorepa finds a place that is perfectly conducive to meditation practice. It is unpopulated, except for the presence of the native deities. In the Tibetan worldview these gods and demons are the true proprietors of the land. Specifically this is the palace or earthly headquarters, if you will, of Dorje Küntragma (Lady Vajra All-Renowned, Rdo rje kun grags ma), the goddess of Lake Namtso. She is one of the twelve Tenma (*bstan ma*), native deities who are guardians of Tibet. Originally the Tenma opposed the importation of Buddhism, but through the wrathful magical power of the tantric master Padmasambhava and of the yogin Milarepa, they have been tamed and made protectors of the dharma. So we see Dorje Küntragma peacefully attending Lorepa's lectures, along with the important mountain god Nyenchen Thanglha (see chapter 24) and a host of local deities. This scene evokes the romance of being a solitary yogin. The practitioner on retreat may suffer intense loneliness, but he or she is never altogether alone, for there is a compensatory relationship that develops with the deities of land and water. These subtle beings become the yogin's true society.

In addition to teaching the local deities about the dharma, Lorepa also makes ritual cake or torma offerings to them religiously, even though his meager provisions require that they be much smaller than usual. The size of the torma offering cakes Lorepa makes is supposed to be quite cute and humorous, the size of a small rodent's ear and pellets. Lorepa was famous for taking vows to make particularly elaborate ceremonial offerings to the deities of the maṇḍala and for the benefit of beings. The twenty-fifth day is the time when a religious feast in honor of the tantric deities must be performed. Usually this involves consecrating a full meal and eating it with meditative enjoyment. But so poor and ascetic is Lorepa that his main feast offering, usually a foot-high cake, is merely a bowl of sugar water.

Yet it is clear that both he and the deities were very satisfied by the offerings, and it is no wonder that he has befriended so many. When he decides to leave Semo Island for another island, he encounters an angry scorpion deity who blocks his way with her stingers. In the full version of this story, the argument with the scorpion deity must have been a longer exchange, including an enlightening song. Here, after singing his song about overcoming the obstacles of conceptual mind, Lorepa naturally tames the impulsiveness of the local goddess, who promises to serve him at his new island retreat. This incident reenacts a familiar motif in Tibetan literature, in which the local spirits and earth guardians are tamed, civilized, and converted into protectors of the dharma. We see that Lorepa deserves indeed the honorific title given to Buddhist preachers: "a teacher of gods and men."

The narrative shifts abruptly then to the story of Lorepa's parents going on their pilgrimage to find their son, bringing Gendündar (Dge 'dun dar) with them as their guide. When parents and son are joyfully reunited, Lorepa teaches them some dharma, performs some songs and a few miracles, and then sends them off; but he keeps Gendündar, who becomes his faithful servant during his retreat. For this solitary retreat Lorepa moves into a cave, whose entrance is sealed by Gendündar, and he remains there meditating for years on end. Ordinarily Lorepa and Gendündar would be able to reprovision themselves each year by walking across the ice of the lake. But this is not to be. Quite mysteriously, the lake refuses to freeze over, winter after winter. Trapped on the island, with an ever-decreasing supply of food, Gendündar grows increasingly concerned that they will starve to death. Lorepa seems willing to sacrifice anything to continue his ascetic retreat, and they are reduced to boiling their own shoes for sustenance. In the end it is the universality of the guru in the form of a vision of Tsangpa Gyare that saves them both.

The five wisdom ḍākinīs who assist Lorepa at this point are female principles of enlightenment who bring messages and secret teachings to great yogins. Here the local deities serve the dharma and are ready to help Lorepa at the command of his all-powerful guru. They lay down a scarf, which appears as a path of frozen ice across the lake. Gendündar, accidentally beholding them, is harmed. It is not unusual for the sight of these goddesses to be dangerous. Many local deities were originally demons or gods of particular diseases. Some kill by being seen, some through their noxious breath, some through their penetrating gaze. Others, particularly the ḍākinīs, are messengers of tantric secrets, and the uninitiated may not see them.

When Lorepa and Gendündar reach the shores of Lake Namtso, they are met by three nomad herdboys. It is interesting that when these three boys see Lorepa, each sees him in a different way. This is because the true image of the realized guru is beyond conception, and each disciple sees him according to his propensities and abilities. Amazed at their apparent ability to walk on water, the boys prostrate and request Lorepa to teach them some dharma. The "Song of Five Buddha Fields" sung at this point sounds as if it would be quite interesting, but it has been deleted from this abbreviated account. In fact, throughout this version of Lorepa's retreat we can see places in the text where the tales have been abbreviated or songs have been left out for the *Rain of Wisdom* edition. We do, however, enjoy one last *dohā* or tantric song of experience by Lorepa, the lovely "Song of the Six Encouragements." These songs urge people to practice religion diligently, since everything (one's mind, body, property, wealth, relatives, and children) is impermanent, and only the dharma will bring ultimate satisfaction.

The disciples Lorepa gains on the shore of Lake Namtso follow him north to Uri, where he remains for six years and develops a sizable monastic community. The last paragraph actually is very specific about what kind of practices they are given. They become accomplished in the formless meditation known as *mahāmudrā*, or the "great symbol" or "great seal." This is a meditation practice in which one looks at one's mind directly, without supports or complicated techniques. The outcome of it is that one sees the entire world as being of the nature of mind itself. At that point, things that once seemed solid appear so no longer, but rather seem to carry their own symbolic message. And since the entire world is seen as mind, it is as if the "seal of mind" has been stamped on all of reality. This practice is based on penetrating down to the subconscious mind, the "basis" (Skt.: *ālaya*). It is by observing the basis of mind, its own subconscious, that one can see the phenomenal world being projected by mind. And so the text concludes that his disciples "became realized, establishing confidence in the wisdom of the basis."

The translation below (with some corrections here) appears in *The Rain of Wisdom,* trans. Nālandā Translation Committee under the direction of Chögyam Trungpa (Boulder: Shambhala, 1980), pp. 246–55. It is based upon a text compiled by Mikyö Dorje in 1542, the abbreviated title of which is *Bka' brgyud mgur mtsho* (*The Ocean of the Songs of the Kagyüs*).

Further Reading

The Rain of Wisdom, translated by the Nālandā Translation Committee (Boulder: Shambhala, 1980).

Jetsün Lorepa's Retreat at Lake Namtso

Carrying a pair of shoulder bags full of roasted barley flour, Jetsün Lorepa journeyed to the great lake of Namtso in the north, which surrounds the island of Semo. The ice on the lake had melted, and so he had to stay on the shore where many fishermen were living nearby. Although he had made a strong resolution to practice on the island, since the ice had melted, there was no way to get to the island. So he supplicated the guru and wept.

One of the fisherboys said, "Young monk, why are you weeping?"

Lorepa replied, "I made a vow to meditate on that island, but since the ice has melted, my practice is hindered; therefore, I am sad."

The fisherboy exclaimed, "How wonderful that you have such faith! I will ferry you to the island."

But the boy's father said, "This lake is brackish. There is no water to sustain you during your ascetic practices, and if the lake does not freeze, your two years of provisions will not be enough. There is no history of anyone living there except glorious Galo and the Master Padmākara. This boy is my only son and I dare not send him. I know this lake better and I am stronger than my son. Since you have such great faith, I will take you now, but we both might die. Even so, I have committed evil by killing many fish, and you might liberate me."

They tied three pieces of wood together as a base, and underneath they attached three inflated leather bags. On top of that, they made a latticework of rope and sticks. Then they put the two full bags of roasted barley flour on the raft. The fisherman sat on one side, and the lord of dharma [Lorepa] sat on the other. On the eleventh day, as the stars came out, they launched their raft. At midnight the lake roared and crashed about, making a great tumult. The waves of the lake rose to the height of a man. Lightning flashed in the sky, and a great hailstorm came down. Frogs as big as goat-kids leapt onto the raft.

The boatman became extremely frightened and said, "It is unfortunate that you want to meditate on the island; both of us are going to die. Don't you have someone like the Kagyü gurus to supplicate? Can't you give a command to the local deities?"

With intense yearning and longing, Lorepa made a supplication to the Kagyü gurus, asking for help. He sang this secret song:

> Dharma body Samantabhadra and consort, inseparable from guru Vajradhara,
> Your emanation, guru Tilo, protector of beings,
> Guru Nāropa, free of faults and perfected in virtue,
> From the dharma realm of great bliss, please protect sentient beings.
>
> Teacher Marpa Dharma Intellect (Chos kyi blo gros), kind guru,
> Great lord of yogins, guru Milarepa,
> Guru Physician [Gampopa], who realized compassion-emptiness,
> From the realm of unconditioned luminosity-emptiness, please protect sentient beings.
>
> Omniscient protector of beings, guru vajra-king,
> Supreme heruka, glorious guru Lingchen Repa,
> Lord of the four bodies of the buddha, lord of dharma, protector of beings, honorable Drukpa,
> Please protect sentient beings with your compassion free of concepts.
>
> Authentic lord of dharma who accomplishes benefit for himself and others,
> Kind precious one who mercifully accomplishes benefit for beings,
> Merciful guru, wise in the ways of kindness,
> Please protect sentient beings of this dark age.

Thus, Lorepa supplicated.

From the direction of Semo Island they saw a mass of rainbow light shaped like a pitched tent. In the middle of this, they saw a vision of Tsangpa Gyare in enjoyment body aspect (*sambhogakāya*) holding a vase of eternal life in his hand. Again Lorepa supplicated:

O gurus, victorious ones of the three times and your descendents,
Please hear the lamentations from my heart.

Gurus and hosts of vajra brothers and sisters,
Learned and disciplined meditators who have attained unsurpassable enlightenment,
Decent dharma practitioners who have entered the gate of the teachings,
Please join your minds together and protect sentient beings.

In this terrifying fire pit of saṃsāra,
Please protect sentient beings who are as naive as moths.

In this fathomless and boundless ocean of saṃsāra,
Please protect sentient beings who are fragile as a cobweb.

In this pitch-black abyss of saṃsāra,
Please protect sentient beings who are blind and have lost their way.

In this great prison of saṃsāra without escape,
Please protect sentient beings who are defenseless captives.

In this poisonous pit of great suffering, saṃsāra,
Please protect sentient beings who are blind and mad.

In this futile mirage of great suffering, saṃsāra,
Please protect sentient beings who are hot and thirsty wild animals.

In this deceptive dream and illusion of saṃsāra,
Please protect sentient beings, long tormented through lack of realization.

O protector, lord of dharma, be a refuge for all, both high and low.
Please protect sentient beings with your great kindness and supreme consideration.

Gurus, victorious ones and your descendents, peaceful and wrathful deities throughout the universe,
Oath-bound protectors who delight in the side of the white,
Quell obstacles and the hosts of demons and establish sentient beings in happiness.

You gurus who do not discriminate
Between sentient beings and buddhas,
Please protect sentient beings who suffer!
Pacify obstacles and perfect virtues!
Cause the teachings to flourish and purify the realms!

Through the blessings of this supplication, the chaos was pacified instantly, and they easily arrived at dry land. The fisherman saw that the lord of dharma was the Buddha in person and he prostrated, circumambulated, and requested his blessings.

Before the fisherman returned, the lord of dharma said, "Surrender your mind, heart, and chest to the three jewels, and they will certainly not deceive you. You will meet your son easily without obstacles." The fisherman then easily returned to the other shore.

The lord of dharma inspected the qualities of that place. He saw that the lake was naturally clear and the color of vaiḍūrya gems. As the Sun rose and set, it seemed to rise and set from the depths of the lake. It was the palace of Dorje Küntragma (Rdo rje kun grags ma). In the middle of the island there was a field that was not very large, but flat like the palm of a hand. In the middle of this field, rock formations were piled up like jewels. To the right and left of the field there were hills that looked like the outstretched wings of a vulture. At the south end of the field there was a nāga cave and a maṇḍala cave, clean and clear, naturally pleasant, and giving rise to meditative concentration (*samādhi*). He saw that this was a place for practice, free from bustle and distraction, where experience and realization would increase like the waxing moon. He was very pleased.

Lorepa set aside one-half of a full bag of roasted barley flour for the next year and the other half of the first year's provisions. He made the deity offerings and sacrificial cakes (*gtor ma*) regularly. He made the deity offerings the size of a small rodent's ear, the middle sacrificial cakes the size of sheep pellets, and the one hundred cakes the size of small rodents' pellets. He made the stock of his gruel from the cake water of these. He said that he had never experienced more joy than in that year. For the offering of the twenty-fifth day [of the lunar calendar] the lord of dharma would dissolve a piece of rock-crystal sugar in a small offering bowl and then perform the long Cakrasaṃvara sādhana. He said it was very satisfying.

At that time, both the great Nyenchen Thanglha, in the garb of a young sorceror, and Dorje Küntragma, in the garb of a nobleman's daughter, surrounded by a great assembly of lake goddesses and local deities, came from time to time to listen to the lord of dharma's teachings and songs. Because all the gods and demons enjoyed his songs, they assembled in turns and said, "Yogin, please either sing or expound the dharma." So Lorepa expounded the dharma and sang many songs.

One day he went to view the scenery. He saw that on the far shore the fishermen had placed some fish in heaps and had spread out others. He sang the song of seven compassions.

In the following year, the Dritak nomads who lived on the shore said, "Last year a young Drukpa monk went to Semo Island without many provisions. We should see if he is still alive." Two of them went to see. They heard the voice of the lord of dharma making supplications in his practice cave, and they said, "He has gone mad!"

But as they approached, they saw that, although the lord of dharma had not used more than half of that full bag of roasted barley flour, he looked extremely healthy and his practice was prospering. They were amazed and their faith was aroused. They requested him to leave the island at that time, but he said, "I still have half a bag of barley flour and I will stay here."

Lorepa stayed for a whole year. Then he thought that in the winter, when the ice had formed on the lake, he would go to Shamo Island. However, the local deity manifested as a scorpion. At the entrance to the cave she placed one stinger on the floor and one stinger on the roof and blocked his way. So he sang the song of nine resolutions, ways of transcending conceptual mind.

The local deity then transformed herself into a twenty-year-old maiden, prostrated, and said, "I was not really trying to harm you, but I do not like your leaving! Now that I see that you are not to be diverted, I will serve you during your stay at Shamo Island." Then she vanished, and the lord of dharma went to Shamo Island and stayed there.

Then Lorepa's father and mother went to the refuge of beings, Tsangpa Gyare, who gave them his own attendant, Gendündar, as a guide. Joining together, they all traveled to the north. As there was ice on the lake, they were able to meet with the lord of dharma on Shamo Island. Both mother and father embraced the lord of dharma and cried. As it is said, "Where there is great joy, there are many tears." For several days, he made his parents content by teaching the dharma, singing songs, and performing miracles. He then sent them back to Central Tibet.

Lorepa told Gendündar [to prepare for a solitary retreat, saying], "Live in the eastern rock cave, cook the food, and practice. Now wall up the entrance to my rock cave." The lord of dharma stayed sealed up inside. Each time Gendündar would offer him food, he would eat just a portion of it and leave the rest to dry.

After seven years passed, Gendündar said to the lord of dharma, "The barley flour is completely consumed and ice has not formed on the lake." The lord of dharma gave him the dry food and said, "Make this into a soup; bring it here to me and drink some yourself." He saved the dregs of the soup and left them to dry.

Again Gendündar said, "The dry food is consumed."

The lord of dharma said, "Cook this." He gave him the soup dregs and said, "Make this into soup; bring it to me and drink some yourself."

Later on, Gendündar said, "Again the food is consumed and ice has not formed."

The lord of dharma said, "Shake out the bags and roll it into dough." When it was rolled, there was only as much as the size of a thumb. The lord of dharma performed a feast offering (*gaṇacakra*) and a visualization. He then realized that a local deity had brought the corpse of a deer to the beach, and he told Gendündar that there was something wonderous on the beach. Gendündar went to the beach and cut up the corpse that he found there. He offered some to the lord of dharma and ate a little himself. In this way, they were able to pass the eighth year.

Later on, Gendündar said, "The meat is now consumed."

The lord of dharma said, "Boil my shoes and meditation belt, your shoes and meditation belt, and the flour bags!" and he threw his shoes and meditation belt out to his attendant. Immeasurable suffering arose in Gendündar. He boiled them well and offered them to the lord of dharma.

Later on, Gendündar thought, "These too are finished. If I were to die, that would be sustenance for the guru." He said, "Guru sir, there is a human corpse down on the beach. Is it all right to eat it or not?"

The lord of dharma said, "It is all right."

Then the attendant tied one end of his sash to a bush and the other end around his neck. However, the lord of dharma knew that Gendündar was preparing to drown himself, and he quickly went out to him. The lord of dharma took him by the hand and brought him back up, saying, "Son, it is not necessary to make such a mistake! Although I may die, I have no regrets. For the sake of the dharma, I have practiced asceticism." He then sang the song of the four nonregrets.

That night the lord of dharma dreamt that the refuge of beings, Tsangpa Gyare, was on the beach in a white pitched tent, surrounded by a retinue of many local deities. At dawn the sound of a ritual hand drum (*ḍamaru*) was heard in the sky. The lord of dharma thought, "What is that?" He looked and he had a vision of the five wisdom ḍākinīs.

The ḍākinīs said, "Brother, you have been overburdened for a long time. Now you may go to Central Tibet. We request that you walk on the surface of the ice." Then they vanished like a rainbow.

The lord of dharma said, "Gendündar, get up and see if it is possible that ice has formed on the lake in accordance with the omen in my dream."

Gendündar thought, "Are we going to Central Tibet? It has been nine years since the lake has frozen. Since ice has not formed in the winter months, it is impossible for it to form during the summer!" Nevertheless, since it was the command of his guru, he went and looked. On the lake there was ice, an arrow's flight in width and a cubit in depth. On its surface there was a moderate snowfall, in which lay the footprints of a fox. Intense joy and immeasurable faith and devotion for the lord of dharma arose in him and he said, "Since the ice has formed, please let us be off."

The lord of dharma said, "Go and put the books and personal belongings in the bag and bring them along." They then departed.

The lord of dharma said, "Gendündar, you go first." Just as he reached the shore, Gendündar wondered if the lord of dharma was coming behind him, and he turned around to look. The ḍākinīs quickly gathered up the silk scarf on which they both walked, but since the lord of dharma had not reached the shore, the lower part of his body was immersed in the water.

The lord of dharma said, "If you had not looked back, it would have been better. The sight of the local deities is poisonous; therefore, your life will be short. If I bless you, you will have a long life, but you will not meet with me in the next life. Son, would you like a long life, or would you like to be with me in the next life?"

Gendündar said, "What joy is there in this life? I would prefer the joy of being with the guru in the next life." Therefore, his life was short, but in his next life, he was born as the son of a potter and met with his guru.

The lord of dharma and his disciple were seen coming from the middle of the lake by three herdboys. Each one saw them in a different form, and the herdboys were amazed. When the lord and his disciple arrived on the shore, the herdboys prostrated, offered them their barley flour and leeks, and said, "Both of you, master and disciple, must be accomplished ones (*siddhas*)! What a great wonder that you have now come across the water in this season! We request you to teach the dharma." The lord of dharma then sang a song called "The Five Buddha Fields" for the boys.

The boys said, "If you cross this hill, you will find our camp. Please go there! We will round up our sheep and cattle earlier than usual and come there."

So the master and disciple went toward the large encampment called Kyangpa, but they stayed in a field at a distance from the tents. The attendant asked if he could go into the encampment.

The lord of dharma said, "If you are hungry, eat the flour and leeks. Practice!"

Gendündar replied, "Lord of dharma, even if you will not go, I must go."

"If you must go, do not say that we came from Shamo Island."

When the attendant arrived at the encampment, he found many dogs. There was also a group of young toughs who demanded, "Where do you come from?" Nervously, Gendündar blurted out that he was from Shamo Island. They said, "The lake has not frozen for many years. You must be a bandit chief!" and they beat him.

When Gendündar returned, the lord of dharma asked him if he had gotten any alms. He said, "I did not get any alms—I got a beating!"

The lord of dharma said, "I told you before to stay and practice. Now practice!"

The three boys arrived at the camp at sunset and told their parents about the lord of dharma, and the parents went over and invited them both back to their camp. "Come to our camp, and we will serve you," they said. "Earlier on, we did not realize that you were the attendant of the lord of dharma—please forgive us!"

The lord of dharma and his attendant stayed there about seven or eight days. Then, their patrons again requested the dharma, saying, "For the past few days, you have constantly and naturally taught the dharma to us. But since we are highlanders, we have not understood very much. Therefore, please put the holy dharma into a melodious song."

Then, the lord of dharma sang this song of the six encouragements to practice, which bring impermanence to mind:

This workable mind
Is like mist on white glacier mountains.
One never knows when the mist will disappear, so resort to practice!
It is certain that it will disappear, so resort to the holy dharma!

This illusory body composed of the four elements
Is like a tree root rotting.
One never knows when the tree will fall, so resort to practice!
It is certain that it will fall, so resort to the holy dharma!

This property built up by competitive ancestors
Is like the illusion of a magician.
One never knows when the illusion will be destroyed, so resort to practice!
It is certain that it will be destroyed, so resort to the holy dharma!

These objects of wealth collected through avarice
Are like honey collected by bees.
One never knows who will enjoy the honey, so resort to practice!
It is certain that others will enjoy it, so resort to the holy dharma!

Agreeable and loving relatives
Are like travelers gathered in a marketplace.
One never knows when the travelers will disperse, so resort to practice!
It is certain that they will disperse, so resort to the holy dharma!

These sons of your own flesh
Are like hundred-year-old dotards.
One never knows if they will help you, so resort to practice!
It is certain they will not help you, so resort to the holy dharma!

Thus, the lord of dharma sang. Great faith arose in their patrons. They said, "Let us find out where the precious lord of dharma lives, so that we may practice the dharma."

Later, when the lord of dharma was living at Uri in the north, the patroness known as Karlek, the three herdboys, and a few others came there, cut their hair, changed their names, and became monks and nuns. They requested teaching and received transmission. In particular, they were given the view of the holy dharma of mahāmudrā, and the meditation of emptiness and stainless luminosity. Thus, the play of unobstructed experience arose in them. By doing just this practice, some of them, both male and female, wandered carefree from retreat to retreat and became realized, establishing confidence in the wisdom of the basis (*ālaya*).

—12—

Memories of a Past Life

David Templeman

Tibetan lamas are believed to be reincarnations of former great teachers. In the case of particularly famous and influential lamas, that line of incarnation is often traced far back into the past, from Tibet back to India, often ending (and hence beginning) with a disciple of the Buddha himself. The accounts of those past lives are an important genre of Tibetan literature. What follows is a brief biography of the immediately preceding rebirth of the great scholar Tāranātha (1575–1634), a biography composed by Tāranātha himself, ostensibly from his memories of own past life. Among the many fascinating elements of the biography is that the previous incarnation is an Indian prince rather than a Tibetan, despite the fact that one of Tāranātha's previous incarnations had been identified as a Tibetan. That is, the line of Tāranātha's incarnations begins long ago in India, moves to Tibet, and then moves back to India for one lifetime only, then back to Tibet in the form of Tāranātha himself. This brief Indian interlude is recorded below, in Tāranātha's biography of an Indian prince who lived only to be eight years of age. In this way, a brief gap in the lineage line is accounted for, and the lineage is revitalized by a return to India, which Tāranātha, like other Tibetan Buddhists, regarded as the source of the unadulterated and authentic dharma.

Tāranātha's work about his own immediately preceding incarnation as the young Indian Prince Rāmagopāla is touching for the poignancy of the boy's brief but beautiful life. The work represents the nostalgia Tāranātha felt for India as a sacred land, but the aesthetic form of the boy's short life also exemplifies Tāranātha's conviction that Buddhism transcends the limits of age, locale, family background, and sectarian affiliation.

For Tāranātha, India was and remained a land of marvelous miracles and wondrous events, a place where the very traditions he loved so dearly were still alive and flourishing. Even as a youth, Tāranātha had several visions of some importance that connected him to India. While he was extremely ill sometime before his second birthday, five Indian ācāryas appeared before him in a vision and blessed him, bringing about a swift recovery. After recovering from this illness he discovered that he had some difficulty recalling his previous incarnations. His parents, fearing that the illness had resulted in a state of semi–brain damage, took him to a prominent Tibetan lama, who diagnosed this memory lapse as a harbinger of his future attainment of the clear-light state. Later in his childhood, Tāranātha saw some Indian ācāryas begging, and he fantasized that he might be in Bodhgayā or some such place in India, a country that surprisingly enough he never visited. Moreover, Tāranātha's own *Autobiography* mentions that he not only had many dreams about meeting Indian yogins, but that he actually met Indian siddhas and paṇḍitas fairly frequently in his earlier life, including his own guru Buddhaguptanātha.

How might we approach interpreting Tāranātha's biography of the Indian prince? A reasonable starting point would be to view it mainly as a work concerned with lineage, that ennobling pursuit for absolute authenticity in the received teachings. More specifically, it is a work that examines the semi-lacuna in this long and illustrious chain of rebirths; it is concerned with evincing Tāranātha's own spiritual pedigree, the unbroken lineage of pure and unadulterated teachings reaching back in time to the Buddha himself, or at the very least to one of his close disciples. In Tāranātha's case his lineage starts with the shadowy and mystical figure of Jvālapati (= Jvālanātha), after whom Tāranātha was named. The focus in Rāmagopāla's biography seems to be as much on the siddha Jvālanātha, also referred to as Meghanātha, as on the prince himself, and the reader might question whether the work is indeed a biography of a lineage predecessor or simply another of those works that Tāranātha loved so much, the accounts of the siddha lineages. From this primogenitor sprang a line of realized practitioners that extended from India into Tibet and thereafter into Mongolia, reaching its finale in 1924 in the person of the eighth Jebtsundamba Khutukhtu of Urga. Despite a ban effected on any further reincarnations of the lineage, there is still said to be a Tāranātha lineage extant among the Tibetan refugee community in India to this day as well as one in Mongolia.

As we might expect, Tāranātha had an extremely high regard for his own lineage, and he wrote extensively on several of its major figures and streams of teaching. In his *Autobiography* he reinforces his own place in that lineage when he mentions that several times during his childhood he repeatedly exclaimed, "I am Lama Kunga Drolchok," apparently without ever having heard the name before. Here he was referring to Kunga Drolchok (Kun dga' grol mchog, 1507–1566), the great scholar from Mustang who was the immediate predecessor of the young Prince of Tripurā, subject of the present work. The *Autobiography* also records that some time after his eighth year, Tāranātha admitted that he was "the master of laziness and indolence," in contrast to his previous life as Kunga Drolchok, when he saw himself as quite energetic. It may strike one as strange here that Tāranātha did not mention his immediate prebirth as Rāmagopāla, referring instead to his penultimate predecessor, Kunga Drolchok. It may be surmised that since the young prince only lived to be eight years old, Tāranātha would have had few memories to recall. In any case, he certainly had enough information to write the present work. How much Tāranātha recalled from memory and how much of his previous life he was told by his Indian teacher Buddhaguptanātha—whom he met eight years before writing the present work—remains a question.

As with almost all hagiographical works, the implicit purpose is to link the subject clearly and irrefutably with a great and glorious teacher, one who lived in a time when the purity of the teachings was unquestioned, in an almost mythic perfect time. For Tāranātha, obsessed with India even before his meeting with Buddhaguptanātha, this period became increasingly the glorious age of India, particularly up to the eleventh century. In his case the great and glorious teacher was the mahāsiddha Kṛṣṇācārya from whom his own line flowed. Kṛṣṇācārya was an eleventh-century yogin from Orissa, the location itself giving us another interesting link in the chain binding Tāranātha to Prince Rāmagopāla, as we shall note below. Kṛṣṇācārya was one of the early systematizers of the texts and maṇḍalas of Cakrasaṃvara and was one of the composers of some of the most beautiful spiritual verses in the Indian vernacular, the so-called *caryā* songs. Kṛṣṇācārya opened up many areas of India to Buddhism, combatting the inimical local forces both demonic and religious, and ended his life struggling against a malicious witch in just such a venture. As Tāranātha inherited a great deal of information on the halcyon days of the siddhas of India from his guru Buddhaguptanātha, he was able to find considerable interest not only in the events that surrounded his long-distant predecessor but also in his own personal teacher Buddhaguptanātha, who himself was linked to several great Indian Buddhist yogins.

In many of his works Tāranātha has given us some of the most interesting data on late siddhahood in India extant in either Tibetan or Indian literature; we have inherited these short epithetical accounts of late siddhas as a result of his felicitous meeting with his teacher. Thus Tāranātha's lineal links with the glorious and great Buddhist land of India are quite palpable both in his inheritance of the continuum of rebirths from Kṛṣṇācārya and equally remarkably in those that were much closer to his own time. Although he was not a unique figure in this relatively late period of spiritual inheritance from India, he is certainly one whose teachers are among the most thoroughly documented. All of this wealth of detail on the lives of the great yogins of India suggests that the biography of Rāmagopāla fits into an overall plan of Tāranātha that was primarily focused on the forms of Indian Buddhism that survived well into his own times as exemplified in the lives of both the earlier and later siddhas.

The work translated below may be of considerable importance to historians of Buddhism because it contains a great deal of information on the presence of late siddhahood in India in the sixteenth and seventeenth centuries. The existence of Buddhist practitioners in such a relatively late period of Indian history is a fact often acknowledged by Tibetan historians, who frequently record the activities of Indian Buddhist yogins in their own works, but it is one seldom referred to by other scholars. These wandering yogins appear to have been prevalent in certain areas of India, carrying their direct, practical experience of the dharma, especially in its later forms, into far-flung reaches of Asia.

Besides the spiritual activities of the later siddhas, we also gain important insights into the customs of the era from the detailed information provided in this small work. Tāranātha had gained an encyclopedic knowledge of things Indian apparently without being able to consult Indian texts at first hand. From the very first section of this text we can see that he was familiar (most probably through the oral transmission of his Indian teachers) with some fairly esoteric aspects of Indian history. He knew the early stories of the *Rājmālā*, the record of the dynastic rulers of the tiny state of Tripurā right from its origins as a series of incarnations of the Moon itself. It seems, however, that many of the details in the life of Tāranātha's predecessor must remain tantalizingly obscure.

Nevertheless, this tiny biography has more than history and the preoccupation with lineage as its main interest. It is not wise to dwell too much on what may or may not have been the historical events of the small work—such a pursuit tends to reduce the contents of the biography simply to a search for historical evidence, apparently not Tāranātha's main aim in the work at all. Rather, we should look instead at the *Life* itself and find out what might have been intended for the Buddhist reader in the Tibet of the times. Certainly once the purely historical data and the more contentious aspects (including the antagonism between the proponents of Buddhism and Hinduism) are put behind us, then what we are left with is a gemlike piece of instruction perhaps aimed at the master of Gurmo Palace, Khyenyang (Mkhyen yangs) himself, at whose behest the account was written. Tāranātha's injunctions in the tiny biography concern the fundamentals of statecraft, especially the benefit of keeping firmly to the teachings despite other pressing requirements of governance, the value of performing pilgrimage, and the primacy of maintaining childlike purity in one's intention and actions. Such advice may seem simple, but for a person controlling both land and vassals it might have been rather more difficult to implement.

That Tāranātha wrote such simple and charming pieces of advice is apparent from his *dohā* songs in his *Collected Works*, in which he addresses one in particular to Lady Namkha Gyelmo (Nam mkha' rgyal mo). In it he briefly outlines some rules for proper maintenance of the state, but several of his points are good rules for living, too. For example, he advises the lady to avoid the throng, to eschew arrogance, to cease clinging to things too dearly, to avoid pride and jealousy, and finally to be generous in her largesse to the poor. Interspersed among these timeless pieces of good counsel are the usual Buddhist homilies about the exceptional fortune of attaining a precious human rebirth, the benefits for her in the confession of sins, the dangers of grasping, and the wisdom of abiding by the injunctions of her chosen teacher.

What we cannot fail to see in the biography is the spirit of the young prince as it shines through these few pages. The reader is surely to be touched by the vision of the young lad playing with his games but in reality making offerings to the Buddha, or of him perhaps hand in hand with his father, visiting the holy places of Buddhism. Brevity has its own sense of poignancy, none more so perhaps than in this brief Indian life, a tiny gem caught between those of two great Tibetan masters.

The present text was taken from Tāranātha's *Collected Works*, vol. 12, folios 685–96. It is based on the *Rtang brtan Phun tshog gling* edition, printed in Leh Ladakh in the Smanrtsis Shesrig Dpemzod series, 1982, ed. C. Namgyal and Tsewang Taru.

Further Reading

On the life and works of Tāranātha, see Jonang Tāranātha, *The Origin of the Tārā Tantra*, trans. David Templeman (Dharamsala: Library of Tibetan Works and Archives, 1981); Jonang Tāranātha, *The Seven Instruction Lineages*, trans. D. Templeman (Dharamsala: Library of Tibetan Works and Archives, 1983); and *Tāranātha's Life of Kṛṣṇācārya / Kāṇha*, trans. D. Templeman (Dharmasala: Library of Tibetan Works and Archives, 1989). On Tāranātha's lineage in Mongolia, see C. R. Bawden, *The Jebtsundamba Khutukhtus of Urga* (Weisbaden: Otto Harrassowitz, Asiatische Forschungen, Band 9, 1961). For a general study of Indian Buddhist saints and siddhas, see Reginald Ray, *Buddhist Saints in India: A Study of Buddhist Values and Orientations* (New York: Oxford University Press, 1994); and J. B. Robinson, *Buddha's Lions: The Lives of the Eighty-Four Siddhas* (Berkeley: Dharma Publishing, 1979). A previous version of the translation appeared in *Tibet Journal* 17.4 (1992):36–45.

The Account of Prince Rāmagopāla

Benediction!

Like an auspicious springtime festival, arisen as if by magic,
What is contained herein will be completely victorious over a mind full of aggression or maudlin thoughts. . . .

The wafting odors of great sweetness
Create a wondrous picture everywhere,
So that even the most violent-natured person will laugh in joy
And will smile like the very sun itself.

The wondrous tales, joined together as they are,
Have been fashioned as if by a heavenly maiden.
As for those who follow these many lineages,
These stories will become a veritable nectar for their ears. . . .

> Now, it has been said that
> At a certain time in days of yore,
> There arose by means of a life-bestowing nectar, a divine boy
> To whom I offer every sort of religious sacrifice. . . .

In the lineage of the eastern land of Tripurā a youth of the warrior caste meditated on the deity of compassion, Ārya Avalokiteśvara, for a period of six months. As a result of this, Lokeśvara appeared . . . in a dream before him and asked, "What is it you desire?" The lad begged him, saying, "O, Noble One, both the members of my Lunar caste and myself . . . wish to grasp the reins of temporal power." The Noble One replied, "In the world there are few enough people with real merit. You may become a lineage holder for a period of fifteen generations," and having said that he became invisible. In the morning, in order to pay his homage to the Noble One, the youth made preparations to go to visit the deity Khasarpaṇa, and while there he made his offerings.

Now at that particular time in the southeastern part of India the priestly caste of Orissa were saying, "We were truly happy during the reign of the previous king, but now because of various dissensions we have become most unhappy, and we are searching widely for a new king." They went off into many places looking for just such a person, and finally they abducted that youth of the warrior caste who had come there to pay his homage to Khasarpaṇa.

The Orissan people installed him on the lion-throne and duly invested him. He became known as Āgamarāja. When his lineage had reached the eighth generation, King Mukunda Deva started to exert his considerable power over the lands of Orissa, Gauḍa, southern Bengal, Purī, parts of Bihar, and the land of Kaliṅga. His control lasted for a long time, and with his powerful armed forces he brought under his sway the whole kingdom known as Triliṅga. Most of the population of northern India became his subjects, and he became known as King Hastināātha.

The king's second son, named Rāmabartari, was master of the areas of Magadha, Mathurā, and Prayāg. He had as one of his sons a transformational form of the great yogin Kāṇha, who had promised that by the fearlessness of truth he would receive the rebirth of the holy lama Kunga Drolchok (Kun dga' grol mchog). . . .

On the day that the prince was born in the city of Gayā, a naked, ash-smeared yogin came to the top floor of the palace. Even though he was quite alone he took up the full breadth of the corridor, and he started to perform his own offering ceremony. The king's household priests felt that the yogin was quite impure, and they said to each other, "As for yogins, in the twelvefold classification of beings, both they and their actions are said to be quite abnormal. For such a person to take delight in our performance, which is karmically pure, such as this one is doing is really quite improper. This yogin should not even be permitted here at all." Upon saying those words, all the priests' own sacrificial items became invisible, and the priests began to ask themselves whether in fact the yogin was a human being or indeed a nonhuman spirit. While they were doing this, yet another yogin appeared before them, and the priests supplicated him with the words, "O holy teacher, greetings to you! We pay our homages to you!" and upon hearing those words the yogin became invisible yet again.

At a later time when his father was performing the vast and liberal birth ceremonies attendant upon the prince, the King Mukunda Deva, who had been an exclusive devotee of certain non-Buddhist practices in the past, erected a surrounding wall for eight leagues around the sacred site, motivated as he was by the power of faith. Both inside and outside the walls guardians of the sacred precinct were ordained, and each day horsemen and camel troops were also to be found there on guard.

On the morning of the tenth day, the king himself was seated before the shrine intended for the offerings. While the priests were about to make their offerings and had prepared by making gifts to the Hindu god Nārayāna, there suddenly appeared a yogin holding a skull-cup, who started to wash himself in the vessel intended for the priest's ritual water oblations. The priests took hold of birch switches, and just as they were about to give him a thrashing he uttered the words "*phaṭa ye*!" As those sounds resounded, the entire offertory shrine was smashed to pieces and the brahmin priests were reduced to a state of sheer terror. The yogin then announced to the king, "In another birth your son was of a Buddhist family, and for you to be performing a birth ceremony such as this is entirely improper. In truth, you must now make liberal offerings before a gathering of yogins instead!" At that the king demanded, "Just who is this person?" and the yogin replied, "I am Meghanātha!" and he dissolved into the very earth—so it is said. The king then did precisely what the yogin had commanded, and the child, the prince, was given the name Rāmagopāla. Later on, when the boy attained an age where he could understand the story told above, he came to praise the Buddha and the yogin Gorakṣa continually and exclusively.

Now the royal mother, a woman of the warrior caste named Lakṣmīni, who had gained faith in the Buddha right from the outset, summoned a learned scholar from the western region of Saurāṣṭra. He possessed the three higher trainings and was a veritable mendicant embodiment of perfected buddhahood. As any teacher would have, he encouraged the prince with hymns he sang in praise of the Buddha, and he bestowed on him the empowerments of many of the very highest deities, as well as telling him their secret spells. He also made the young prince recall his many previous incarnations, especially his earlier rebirth as the holy lama Kunga Drolchok in Tibet, where his meaningful words and discourses had caused the lamp of the teachings to blaze. He came to have total recall of them all as even more things were told to him, and even the priests and the Hindus themselves grew astounded. From the mendicant Guptamitra the prince received the instructions on attaining the attitude of enlightened practice, [the *bodhicittotpāda* vow,] as well as the many meaning-levels of those profound teachings. With all these as well as the requisite recitation of words of power and yoga practice, he soon was able to accomplish whatever he desired.

Because he was a prince, he was able to use considerable amounts of money to buy various things for his amusement, and when he played the games that he had bought, it appeared to others as if he were making offerings before actual Buddha images and shrines.

Once while the prince was wandering with a few attendants in various groves near Rājagṛha, he saw a yogin directly in front of a certain tree with three monkeys and a bear, his only assistants in creating spiritual nourishment. At yet another time, while seated in meditation, the prince saw that there was an impediment to the free and unrestricted movement of his psychic winds, and with an excess of faith the prince prostrated himself before the above-mentioned yogin. For as long as it took for the young prince to perform the yogic practices he would not reenter his own city. As for that yogin, he was the true student of the great siddha Oṃkaranātha and was known as Meghanātha, otherwise known as Jvālanātha.

If at this point I were to recount a little of the story of those gurus I would say: In Madhyadeśa, there was a certain boy of the warrior caste who had been without a father since he was quite small and thus was raised in the family of his uncle. Now there was a yogin of a certain lineage who drew near and gave the lad a certain yoginī's creative visualization exercise. Eighteen years passed without the boy uttering even a single intelligible comment. Their minds depressed, the uncle and his wife said to the boy, "You are nothing but a fool! Can the way you are acting be in any way proper?" When they finished telling him off in this way, they exiled him from the land. Feeling deeply despondent, the youth went to live in various places, begging alms and performing the creative visualization of the goddess Vajrayoginī.

After sixteen more years had passed and he was able to produce firm meditational states within himself, he packed up and went far westward to Hiṅgulāja, near the borders of Baluchistan, the abode of the goddess Umādevī, the wife of Śiva. He slept for six months there on top of a stone image of the goddess, while he himself was engaged in a single session of clear light meditation. The goddess Umā became terrified and cried out, "Yogin, *rid dhi de hi ki ni dhi de!*"

To this the yogin replied, "What would a yogin do with the powers he was granted? If you were to offer me the teaching of the most perfected realization (*jñānasiddhi*), I would most certainly accept it!" At this, the goddess replied, "I myself have been granted absolutely no powers like that at all! You will have to go and request them from Gorakṣa himself." After she had said this he went off in search of Gorakṣa. In the western land of Sindh, at the end of a row of countless yogins, he espied one whose face was particularly ugly, and from whose limbs oozed pus and blood. Knowing that this was Gorakṣa, the yogin prostrated before him and begged him for the teachings. The yogin drank a bowl of vegetable stew that had been previously blessed by the master, and he found that he gained complete mastery over all spheres of wisdom. He become a great yogin-master in his own right, one with experience of things as they really are, in all their directness. He also gained a huge following of students, who attached themselves to the doctrines he expounded. Now, it happened that some of his ideas did indeed become mixed up with the fundamental tenets of the Hindus, and many who came after him and who were called by his name, Oṃkara the scholar, were indeed practicing heretical [i.e., Hindu] yogins. At a later time, while causing rain to fall at an unseasonal time, he also manifested simultaneously a magical vision of his body blazing with flames. Thus he became known as Meghanātha ["Cloud Lord"] and also Jvālanātha ["Blazing Lord"].

While the young prince Rāmagopāla was repeatedly paying his respects to the yogin-saint, the latter bestowed upon him the blessings of the very highest deities, as well as the related instructions and the accompanying tantric vows. The teacher said to the lad, "Boy, you must *not* go home! Abide instead in a state of suchness, the state of things as they are." The young prince did as he had been told and his father, King Rāmabartari, said to the teacher, "Restore my child to me right here and now!" To this the ācārya replied, "As for the lad he is *my* child of religion, and as such he is under *my* control." When he had said this King Rāmabartari grew enraged and sent someone to relieve the yogin of his stipend and all other means of livelihood. However, those sent to remove them from him were unable to do so. A thousand cavalry were sent with the same royal order to "Subdue the evil yogin!" but when they drew near him, he merely uttered a few magic spells and all the horsemen were frozen into rigidity, unable to move even the slightest bit. They were all amazed at this and said, "*E ma*, Now we have faith in this mighty yogin!" When their faith developed, they eventually were released from their thralldom. They were summoned before the king and he too was amazed at what had happened; going before the yogin, he prostrated himself, pressed many coins upon him, and begged for his pardon.

Much later on, the emperor, namely, King Mukunda Deva, and the Mughal military commander of Delhi were involved in a power struggle. Mukunda had come a fortnight's march west of Magadha, to the land of Mathurā near Delhi. King Rāmabartari was staying thereabouts with his army of three hundred thousand men, and the great yogin-teacher Meghanātha was also there, moving back and forth between the positions of both army commanders, begging them for alms. Through the power of his truthful words, the dispute died down of its own accord.

Now at the battle site near Delhi there were about six thousand heroic war elephants, with three among them considered to be the main ones. The chief of these royal war elephants was known as Gopālahasti, who was thirty cubits in height and renowned for being able to outperform two hundred ordinary war elephants. The yogin performed the miracle of pressing down with his hands on these three most excellent elephants, and he crushed them. When the holy being Meghanātha had calmed them down again with his magic spells, it was discovered that the cavalry forces of both kings were quite unable to proceed against each other, even though commanded to do so. Each of the armies was held in thrall, and everyone there realized that they were totally incapable of any sort of action. All those who witnessed it were completely amazed at what they had seen.

At yet another time, whenever King Rāmabartari made his midnight offerings to Kubera the god of wealth and to Śiva, he would meet Meghanātha, who would magically appear before him. The yogin would admonish him, saying, "If your family makes its offerings exclusively to the Buddha [as they do], then all these other things that you yourself are doing here [at this shrine] are really quite improper!" Sometime after those encounters, during a time of peace and tranquility, the lower foundations of a certain road in the kingdom gave way and were hurled around as if they were merely handfuls of seed. When Meghanātha and his students [including the prince] arrived as if by magic, everything was once again restored. Thereafter the king, the father of the prince, made his principle offerings to the Buddhists who had demonstrated themselves so mighty in their magic.

Accordingly, the holy one, the prince, went before three different teachers at various times, but at all other times he remained in his palace. In company with his father, he went via various countries to visit eastern and southern Bengal, Orissa, the Jagannātha shrine at Purī, northern India, and the northeastern Himalayan areas. While there he also met Ānandaprajñāroti, the master of the great yogin-saint Ānandabhadra. The prince pondered deeply on the instructions he had received on the correct recitation of the magically potent spells of the noble goddess Tārā, and he became one in whom the later and higher signs of realization were to arise [almost] immediately.

This highest of beings went on pilgrimage to the Buddhist holy places of Rājagṛha, Kukkuṭpāda, Gṛdhrakūṭa, and all the others. Indeed, he visited all the great pilgrimage places of the Victorious One, the Buddha, as well as all the groves and cities associated with the Blessed One's life, as if he were on an amazing, fantastic pleasure trip. He is renowned for being able to accomplish a hundred years worth of fully perfected deeds in just eight short years of his life. As for his transmigration from that particular birth, he is right here now, in the form of this very person [Tāranātha]!

As for those who have preceded me, they have filled me quite spontaneously with whatever virtues I have. Thus I praise the knowledge of their virtue and pray that I may ever cleave to it. In order to be one who follows those noble ones, those teachers who so correctly demonstrate the way, I pray that I will always keep close to their knowledge and always sing its praises. Through my prayers, may those fully perfected beings continue toward the state of the perfectly good, and by the strength of my prayers, may I always stay close to them. . . .

Just as spray arises from the hidden watery recesses of the ocean, so too does whatsoever merit arise that may accrue from these holy biographies spoken of here. May that merit be dedicated, unchanged, for the welfare of all sentient beings! Thus, I, Tāranātha, at the age of twenty-three years, wrote these words at Gurmo Palace, in the Tsang district of Tibet, after the verbal entreaties of Khyenyang, the lord of men there.

Blessings on all sentient creatures!

Rites and Techniques

—13—

A Rite of Empowerment

Richard J. Kohn

The ultimate goal of Buddhism is buddhahood. In the 2,500 years since the Buddha's own enlightenment, countless methods have been elaborated to attain this goal. In the tantric view, one of the quickest ways to achieve enlightenment is to visualize that you have already achieved it. Recent experiments outside the sphere of religion confirm the special power of goal-oriented visualization. Athletes have shown that visualizing victory can be as effective as physical training; cancer patients routinely use visualization to increase their odds of survival. In the tantric meditation known as deity yoga, practitioners focus on their inner potential for enlightenment and visualize themselves as enlightened beings. Such meditation is not a haphazard affair. A specific enlightened being, called a *yi dam* in Tibetan, should be chosen in consultation with the practitioner's spiritual master, or lama. The lama and the *yi dam* are so fundamental to tantric meditation that, along with the feminine celestial spirits known as ḍākinī, they are said to constitute the "three roots" of tantric practice.

Before students can begin a course of meditation on a *yi dam*, they must undergo a ceremonial initiation or empowerment. The *yi dam* invoked in the ceremony that follows bears the lengthy name Union of the Blissful, Lord of the Dance, Great Compassion (*Bde gshegs kun 'dus gar dbang thugs rje chen po*): Lord of the Dance, for short. Lord of the Dance is a form of the popular Tibetan deity Avalokiteśvara, who embodies the compassion of all buddhas. The rituals of Lord of the Dance are part of the secret teachings of Mindroling (Smin grol gling) monastery, which, before it was looted and vandalized by the Chinese in the 1960s, was the largest and most influential Nyingma monastery in central Tibet.

Empowerment is the sine qua non of the tantric experience. Originally it was a private affair: a master would gather a few disciples in an isolated place and initiate them in his favored forms of meditation. In Tibet, private empowerments are still prevalent. However, they have been supplemented by a uniquely Tibetan celebration: the mass empowerment. The largest empowerments—His Holiness the Dalai Lama's Kālacakra initiations—attract hundreds of thousands of people.

The empowerment text below is used in the Mani Rimdu festival performed at monasteries in the Everest region of Nepal. Although popular, Mani Rimdu (*ma ṇi ril sgrub*) is a more modest affair than the Kālacakra: from three hundred to one thousand people attend.

Without formal initiation, a student is not allowed to practice deity yoga. However, not everyone who attends a large-scale public empowerment intends practicing; many come purely for the blessing that the ceremony confers. For those who do intend to practice, there is even some question whether the Mani Rimdu initiation is sufficient. In the words of the text, only "those fortunate ones who apply their extraordinarily sharp powers to the profound meaning with the best of attention" receive "the blessing which empowers them to practice." Normally, those who wish to meditate on Lord of the Dance are sent to the lama for a full, formal initiation. Only a lama can perform the empowerment either as a self-contained ceremony or as part of a more lengthy ritual performance.

Like many Tibetan rituals, the empowerment refers the practitioner to other ritual texts. One passage tersely instructs the officiant to "expel demons; and meditate on the protective circle, distribute and gather up flowers, and clarify the creation of the aspiration"—and each of these is a ritual in its own right. Unfortunately, there is no space here to follow up all these references, as enticing and mysterious as they may be. Additionally, Tibetan texts often use oblique allusions to guarantee secrecy: without complete familiarity with the tradition and the guidance of a qualified master, it is impossible actually to perform the ritual. The translation below respects the tradition's reticence. In cases where the missing material contains no secrets to conceal, but basic Buddhist concepts that are taken for granted, I have supplied them in brackets.

The empowerment affirms its place in the greater Buddhist tradition at the outset. Near the beginning, the officiating lama—the text calls him the "diamond master"—takes time to "give an appropriate religious discourse as an introduction." This brief general lecture starts with concepts common to all schools of Buddhism, such as impermanence and death, and leads up to the reasons a disciple should seek empowerment. But an empowerment is, above all, a guided mystical experience. Nothing could make this clearer than the moment when the lama instructs his disciples to visualize that "the gods of the maṇḍala . . . project from their hearts countless forms—bodies, syllables, and symbols which blaze in a mass of beams of light, which come helter-skelter, like rain and snow, like a blizzard. They enter through [your] pores and fill [your] body to the brim. Bliss blazes unbearably." This vision disarranges the order of the universe as we have come to know it in our day-to-day lives. The ritual mirrors this in a visceral way—by using the sense of smell. Instead of normal, sweet-smelling incense, the participant is told to burn, among other things, cat droppings and soiled clothes. This practice, although on the surface bizarre, has a profound philosophical subtext. If, in emptiness, the realm of absolute truth, all opposites are reconciled, then how can we distinguish the sweet-smelling from the foul?

Obviously, different individuals will be able to realize the ecstatic scenario to different degrees. The text advises the disciple to look for "a sign that [the deities] have come." Such signs, called *pebtak* (*phebs rtags*) in Tibetan, may be internal or external. One lama that I interviewed divided internal *pebtak* into three categories: signs of the body, such as shivering; signs of speech, such as spontaneously singing; and mental signs, such as suddenly becoming very happy. In searching for an example of an external sign, he referred to a meteorological event that occurred during the Kālacakra initiation that the current Dalai Lama performed in Wisconsin. When the ceremony reached the descent of the wisdom beings, the wind kicked up, the sky grew black, and, although no rain fell, a rainbow appeared.

The text lists some of the signs of a successful empowerment:

> The first sign of grace
> By virtue of such an empowerment
> Is that, unasked for, aspiration and respect are born in one's stream of consciousness.
> The second sign of grace
> Is that whatever you turn your imagination to is firm and clear.
> The third sign of grace
> Is that understanding of self-emergent wisdom rises.

The empowerment is also said to confer concrete benefits such as long life and health. These benefits come to all who attend, whether or not they receive the full impact of the ceremony.

The empowerment incorporates philosophical insights as well as mystic experiences. At one point, the lama tells his disciples that "the continuum of ideas that hold things as twofold is broken." One lama explained this gnomic passage in this way: "The Buddha has no thought of me and them. Regarding things as self and other, mine and theirs, is a kind of egoism (*bdag 'dzin*). It is this that is broken."

Despite its startling visionary experiences, the Mani Rimdu empowerment text does not veer off into complete fantasy. It views ritual as a process of energizing the will to bring out one's own highest potential. A runner may, in her mind's eye, see her chest straining to the finish line long before her feet reach it. Imagining that you have already accomplished your goal is a means to achieving it, not a substitute for achieving it. The text recognizes this distinction between perception, imagination, and will. At one point, disciples are enjoined to "will" the deities that they have visualized "to be there as if they were really perceived."

There are many different kinds of empowerment ceremonies. The Mani Rimdu empowerment uses a distinctively Tibetan object called a *torma* (*gtor ma*)—a ritual cake sculpted of barley-flour and decorated with colored butter. Although their origins are unclear, some feel that tormas began as a nonviolent Buddhist alternative to animal sacrifices (see chapter 15). Over the centuries, tormas have become more and more elaborate. Some reach an astounding three stories in height and depict the lives of the saints in high relief of sculpted butter. In the Nyingma system, the elaboration is more a matter of metaphysics than engineering. At first, the torma is considered to be a simple offering; then, it becomes the body of the god. Near the end of a ritual, the lamas explain, the gods melt into the torma as light and it becomes the very substance of spiritual achievement, which the participants, in theory at least, must take into themselves by eating. However, in a large public festival like Mani Rimdu, eating the torma is symbolic rather than real. With a thousand people in attendance, the ritual object would be demolished before the ceremony was over.

The empowerment ritual is a participatory drama and takes the form of call and response. The lama prompts the initiates at each turn, asking questions or requesting them to repeat passages after him. "Imagine something like this," he instructs them, "this very place on earth, purified, becomes the great maṇḍala of omnipresent wisdom." "Repeat after me," he commands, " 'O diamond master, pray consider me!' "

At the end of the text there is a charming disclaimer typical of Nyingma literature. In the colophon, the author Oḍḍiyāna modestly claims that his sublime orchestration of visionary experiences and philosophical precepts was scrawled "by the paw of the thick-headed Oḍḍiyāna."

The translation below is from Oḍḍiyāna, *Thugs rje chen po bde gshegs kun 'dus kyi gtor dbang gi mtshams spyor ngag 'don bdud rtsi'i nying khu zhes bya ba bzhungs so (The Utterance that Is the Essence of Ambrosia: The Annotated Torma Empowerment of Great Compassion Union of the Blissful).* The ritual instructions are rendered in a smaller typeface.

Further Reading

Stephan Beyer, *The Cult of Tārā Magic and Ritual* in Tibet (Berkeley: University of California Press, 1973); Daniel Cozort, *Highest Yoga Tantra: An Introduction to the Esoteric Buddhism of Tibet* (Ithaca: Snow Lion, 1986); Rolf Alfred Stein, *Tibetan Civilization* (London: Faber and Faber, 1972).

The Utterance that is the Essence of Ambrosia:
The Annotated Torma Empowerment of Great Compassion Union of the Blissful

Namo Padmalokeśvarāya!
First bowing with respect to the god of the maṇḍala,
Lord of the Dance, treasure of compassion,
I will set out the essence of ambrosia: the practice
Of the blessing torma empowerment.

The torma empowerment system is the essential meaning of profound path great compassion, Union of the Blissful. It has three parts: the Introduction, the Actual Practice, and the Conclusion.

Introduction

The ordinary empowerment [depends on] awakening the dormant seeds of the karma of previous training [in meditation on Lord of the Dance Great Compassion]. For the profound instructions to be entrusted to you, you must be matured by this essential empowerment. It empowers you to put the profound advice into practice for your own benefit.

When performing it, whether you are using the extensive main maṇḍala [e.g., a sand maṇḍala] or doing it without one, arrange a bouquet of red flowers on a covered shelf a cubit square. In the middle, in a skull or precious vessel atop a tripod, place a decorated red glorious torma, moistened with ambrosia medicine and incense. It should be [in the shape of] four-leveled Mount Meru. Atop it, in the four intermediate directions, there should be buttons (*mtheb kyu*) with balls, each of them surrounding the main torma.

Place a miniature portrait and a red silk canopy on top of it. Set out an extensive circle of offerings and feasts as well.

If it is performed in connection with the basic empowerment [which is a part of the ordinary ritual practice of Lord of the Dance], however large or small the basis of meditation, there is no difference in the meaning of the meditation. A separate "achievement worship" is unnecessary.

On the other hand, when granting just the torma empowerment separately, perform the *[Union of the Blissful] Manual* straight through and create (i.e., imagine) the torma as the god. Finish the worship, praise, recitation, and so forth and offer the feast worship.

Then, wash the disciples with "However born . . . ," etc.; expel demons; and meditate on the protective circle, distribute and gather up flowers, and clarify the creation of the aspiration. After that, give an appropriate religious discourse as an introduction.

Then, do the main empowerment ritual. [The Master says—]

> O teach the empowerment of the blessing torma
> The essence of the heart of the quick path which matures the fortunate!

As was said, having had the profound instruction in [the two stages of tantric meditation] creation and fulfillment entrusted to them, those fortunate ones who apply their extraordinarily sharp powers to the profound meaning with the best of attention are granted this very torma empowerment of the essential meaning, the blessing that empowers them to practice. The Master finishes the things that were to be done and the disciples offer a maṇḍala [a ritual that symbolically offers the universe to the Buddha, his teaching, and the spiritual assembly that practices it].

Having inserted this explanation, offer the maṇḍala.

Then, for the purpose of the prayer, imagine something like this: This very place on Earth, purified, becomes the great maṇḍala of omnipresent wisdom. In it, the diamond master himself sits in the form of Union of the Blissful,

Lord of the Dance, Great Compassion. Pray to him with the powerful longing of unchanging faith. Repeat after me—

O diamond master, pray consider me!
Pray mature the stream of my consciousness
In the Union of the Blissful maṇḍala,
The secret path of every Buddha!

—pray, saying this three times.

Then, in the sky in front [of you], there is the lama and noble Great Compassion indivisible, surrounded by the oceanlike host of conquerors of the three roots [the lama, the *yi dam*, and the ḍākinī]. Will them to be there as if they were really perceived, and think "I go to them for refuge until all sentient beings, myself and others, are in the heart of enlightenment." Repeat after me—

Namo! Until all beings, including myself are enlightened
[I go for refuge to the ḍākinīs,
The lama, Buddha, holy dharma,
The best of congregations and the god of the maṇḍala—
Union of the Blissful].

—go for refuge by saying this three times.

Next think, "Keeping to this path, out of compassion, I will liberate all sentient beings [whose numbers are] vast as the sky. Their behavior continually causes nonvirtuous acts and gains this effect: the sufferings of the six different kinds of life. I will place them in constant bliss."

Repeat after me—

The ocean of existence is hard to cross,
[And beings, as vast as the sky.
So that I may ferry them across,
I give birth to the sacred resolve
To reach unsurpassable, perfect enlightenment].

—generate the aspiration by saying it three times.

Next, the descent of the wisdom [beings] is the achievement that is the basis of blessings. Therefore, disciples should observe the physical essential—sitting straight and erect, the vocal essential—controlling the breath at the mouth, and the mental essential—that the diamond master's heart radiates beams of light that strike the disciple and purify him into emptiness, out of which, like a fish jumping out of water, Union of the Blissful, Lord of the Dance, Great Compassion is born as befits a peaceful/wrathful one. The red letter *hrīḥ* in his heart burns and illumines like a butter lamp. Its light incites the gods of the maṇḍala to project from their hearts countless forms—bodies, syllables, and symbols which blaze in a mass of beams of light, which come helter-skelter, like rain and snow, like a blizzard. They enter through [your] pores and fill [your] body to the brim. Bliss blazes unbearably.

Think this and recite the root mantra, adding *jñāna ābeṣaya a āḥ* to it. Let varied music sound. Bring down blessings by burning the five ambrosias, cat droppings, women's skirts, and gugul [incense].

After you get a sign that they have come, will that "the wisdom beings who shower blessings have become firmly of one taste with the disciple's stream of consciousness," make a cross with the vajra, and make it strong by saying *tiṣṭhavajra*.

If this [ritual] is being done in connection with a main empowerment, then the above need not be done separately [as it would be redundant].

The Actual Practice

With unending powerful longing, take flowers in both hands, join your palms and pray. Repeat after me—

> Union of the Blissful, Avalokiteśvara,
> Treasure of compassion, consider me!
> Bestow the blessing of the body upon my body—
> Pray excite appearance/emptiness bliss!
> Bestow the blessing of speech upon my speech—
> Pray give birth to the ability to know that sound is empty!
> Bestow the blessing of mind upon my mind—
> Pray give birth to nonideational wisdom!

—pray, saying this three times.

Next, the Actual Empowerment.

The torma vessel becomes a great self-emergent spontaneously built paradise. The torma substances sit in it in the form of the gods of the circle of Union of the Blissful, Lord of the Dance, Great Compassion's maṇḍala. Out of [the head, throat, and heart:] the three places on the chief and each of his entourage, come the blessings of the body, speech, and mind diamonds, and every true achievement, [and] body gestures, speech syllables, [and] mental symbols—countless forms that emerge radiating like beams of light whose nature is ambrosia. They dissolve into the disciple's three places [i.e., his head, throat, and heart] and cleanse his body, speech, and mind of every obscuration or propensity to one. The whole inside of the body fills with white, red, and azure ambrosia.

The body which appears to be material, is purified and becomes an immortal body of brightness. Speech spontaneously becomes the melodious sound of the indomitable diamond. The continuum of ideas that hold things as twofold is broken, and the special wisdom of the union of bliss and emptiness is born in the string [of thought].

—will this.

Hūṃ! The torma vessel is the self-emergent palace.
The torma is the Blissful Compassion God.
A shower of blessings and true achievement
Rains from the maṇḍala of body, speech, and mind.
In your unflagging compassion consider [us] with love,
And bestow blessings and great true achievement
Upon the body, speech, and mind of [us] fortunate ones!
Liberate [our] bodies into appearance/emptiness bodies of light!
Make our speech disappear into indomitable sound itself!
Liberate our minds in the dharmakāya's bliss!
O divine host of Blissful Compassion,
Establish [our] bodies, speech, and minds as [your] body, speech, and mind!

Add *baliṃta kāya vāka citta abhiṣīñca hūṃ* to the root mantra, and saying it, place the torma on the three places [head, throat, and heart] on the disciple's body. Think that,

"Finally, all the gods of the torma dissolve inseparably into the disciple."

The torma substance, into which the gods, as light, have melted, is given as true achievement. The disciple enjoys it [i.e., eats it] and says,

sarvasiddhibaliṃta abhiṣīñca hūṃ.

Conclusion

There are three measurements of the heat of grace that arises in connection with an empowerment such as this—

The first sign of grace
By virtue of such an empowerment
Is that, unasked for, aspiration and respect are born in one's stream of consciousness.
The second sign of grace
Is that whatever you turn your imagination to is firm and clear.
The third sign of grace
Is that understanding of self-emergent wisdom rises.

As it says, the actual signs of grace or something similar to them will be born in one's stream of consciousness.

With these [words], the torma empowerment of the essential meaning comes to an end. With a fierce desire to protect and be bound by the vows and disciplines obtained on this occasion, repeat after me—

O chief, whatever you bid,
All that will I do.

—accept this by saying it three times.

Offer a maṇḍala in order to give thanks. Then, think "if I offer everything—

my body, enjoyments and collection of virtue, emanated like the wealth of a universal emperor's empire, pray give me a part of it to enjoy!"

Repeat after me—

> If from now on I offer myself
> To you as a slave . . .

—three times.

The roots of virtue are dedicated to unsurpassed enlightenment.

Then, adorn the end [of the ceremony] with the "Thanksgiving Worship and Praise," the "Plea for Patience," "Remaining Firm," "Gathering In," the "Dedication," and the "Auspicious Omens." If this is done in connection with the main empowerment, [the section above] from "Proclaiming and Adhering to the Vow" [i.e., O chief, whatever you bid . . .] on need not be done separately.

> May the method of empowerment written herein,
> Which brings signs from the points of view
> Of attitude, aggregates, and realms, which vanquishes desire and ideation,
> And which also establishes the three diamonds,
> mature the fortunate one's stream [of consciousness].

So saying, this Essence of Ambrosia: The Practice that Clarifies the Torma Empowerment of the *Inner Meaning of Profound Path Great Compassion, Union of the Blissful*, was requested by the supreme incarnation of Dokam Shechen (Mdo khams zhe chen) Monastery, Pema Sangngak Tenzin Chögyal (Padma gsang sngags bstan 'dzin chos rgyal). In accordance with which, this complete edition of the liturgy was written by the paw of the thick-headed Oḍḍiyāna.

—14—

The Horseback Consecration Ritual

Yael Bentor

Tibetans perform consecration rituals for images, scroll paintings (*thang ga*), reliquaries (stūpas), books, and other sacred objects. It is by means of a consecration ritual that an image or a stūpa is transmuted from a mundane object into the nature of a buddha. As the regent of the fifth Dalai Lama, Desi Sangye Gyatso (Sde srid sangs rgyas rgya mtsho), explained, the enlightened being pervades everything, down to each of the countless particles that make up the phenomenal world. One simile commonly used for illustrating this omnipresence of the enlightened being is the sesame seed and its oil. Although the hard sesame seed may not seem to contain any fluid, after crushing the sesame seeds one may obtain plenty of oil. Another popular simile used to describe the pervasive presence of the enlightened being is space, which abides everywhere; like space, the enlightened being is said to be naturally established everywhere. However, ordinary people whose minds have not been sufficiently developed are unable to see or comprehend this. Therefore, the Buddhist tradition prescribes the consecration of images, stūpas, thangkas, books, and other objects. These holy objects serve to localize the sacred presence of the enlightened being, making it available for interaction with human beings, who worship it, receive religious inspiration from it, and accumulate merit from these activities.

A consecrated image or stūpa is also regarded as a form of emanation body of the Buddha, that form of the Buddha that is visible to ordinary beings. There are three types of emanation bodies: (1) "supreme emanation bodies," such as the historical buddha Śākyamuni, who appeared on Earth to show the way to enlightenment and to teach the dharma; (2) "born emanation bodies," such as reincarnated lamas, like the Dalai Lama; and (3) "made emanation bodies," namely, the images, stūpas, bridges, and other objects ritually created and empowered that concern us here. Much like the other types of emanation bodies, images and stūpas are believed to carry out the enlightened activity of the buddhas. The objects to be consecrated are also considered to be bases or receptacles of the buddhas' body, speech, and mind. Images and thangkas are regarded as receptacles of the body; books, *dhāraṇīs*, and mantras are receptacles of the speech; while stūpas and *tsha tshas* (small clay tablets, in this case in the shape of stūpas) are the receptacles of the buddhas' mind. Buddhist temples and shrines usually contain all three types of receptacles. Here the word "receptacle" will be used as a general term for all objects to be consecrated.

The consecration ritual is almost invariably performed soon after the creation of a sacred receptacle. If the receptacle is a major statue, a stūpa, or a temple, the people or patrons who financed the construction of the religious object may invite a high lama to perform the consecration ritual. If the receptacle is smaller, such as a figurine or a thangka owned by individual householders or monastics, then they may be brought to a monastery for consecration by its abbot, or by an incarnate lama. Larger monasteries usually perform an elaborate consecration rite once a year in order to renew the consecration of the temples and their sacred objects. On such occasions, nearby householders and monastics will often bring their receptacles for consecration or reconsecration. While the proper performance of the ritual procedures is believed to play a significant role in determining the results of the consecration, the religious realization and experience of the lama who performs it are also deemed crucial for the efficacy of the rite. Given two identical-looking receptacles, one consecrated by a monk of no more than local renown and the other by a lama who is widely esteemed, the latter receptacle will be considered superior in power.

The manual translated below contains one of the most popular consecration rituals of the Gelukpa sect, which may be performed for a single receptacle or for a large collection of stūpas, images, thangkas, books, and other objects. Performed either by a ritual master alone or accompanied by an assembly of monks, the ritual may last anywhere from fifteen minutes to a few hours. Since it is suitable for brief consecration practices, this ritual has earned the title "Horseback Consecration," a name that advertises that one can easily perform it while riding past a receptacle without even dismounting one's horse, a feature that may well appeal to the Tibetan nomad. In the vast majority of consecrations, though, this does not occur.

To clarify the manual translated below, it is important first to identify its key ritual actions and their significance, and thus avoid the bewildering effect of the ritual's seemingly endless details. What complicates making any simple summary or interpretation of the ritual is that all manuals in current use draw on a variety of works based on different points of view. Hence manuals, such as the one presented below, present a large variety of concerns. Yet it is possible to identify the basic purpose of the ritual: the transformation of the receptacle into a chosen buddha (*yi dam*). This process relies on the fundamental tantric practice (*sādhana*) in which one first imaginatively transforms oneself into a *yi dam*. The sādhana practice begins with one dissolving one's ordinary appearance into emptiness. Then, emerging out of emptiness, one visualizes oneself as the chosen buddha, a process called the "self-generation," that is, recreating oneself in the form of a buddha. Subsequently, as that buddha, the practitioner dissolves once again into emptiness. Finally, one arises back in the world as an emanation of the buddha in order to help other beings attain enlightenment (see chapter 16). In the philosophical terms of Buddhist soteriology and the bodhisattva path, the dissolution into emptiness consists of wisdom that penetrates emptiness, while the arising back into the world involves the use of skillful means (*upāya*), especially compassion. The practice of dissolution into emptiness ultimately leads to one's own enlightenment, while the return to the mundane world is meant to help others. Expressed in terms of the doctrine of the Buddha's bodies, the dissolution into emptiness ultimately results in achieving the dharma body (*dharmakāya*); yet while in the dharma body one cannot benefit others (who, for the most part, are unable to perceive this body), so one compassionately "returns" to the world as an emanation body.

Similar principles are found in the structure of the consecration ritual, which is, in fact, an application of the sādhana process. The consecration ritual serves as an excellent example of how basic sādhana transformational techniques may be applied to other objects than oneself. To rehearse this fourfold process with reference to receptacles: initially the material receptacle is dissolved into emptiness; subsequently it is generated as one's chosen *yi dam*; following this, the *yi dam* is dissolved once again; and finally it is transformed back into its ordinary appearance as a receptacle, such as a stūpa or image. This appearance seems to be no different from the original one, yet its true nature is regarded as that of the enlightened being. In other words, the material receptacle is initially transformed into the nature of the actual, ever pervasive, nondual enlightened being. Since only a very few advanced practitioners can perceive the enlightened being in such a manner, the process is concluded with a transformation of that nondual enlightened being back into the original appearance of the receptacle. In terms of the bodies of the enlightened being, with this last phase the dharma body "emerges" in the world as an emanation body. According to the Tibetan tradition, ordinary people whose minds are less developed cannot discern any change in the receptacle. But those endowed with yogic perception are capable of seeing consecrated receptacles as if they were the *yi dams* themselves.

Even though the processes described above form the structural skeleton of the consecration, they do not appear in succession during the ritual but are dispersed throughout. It would be useful, therefore, to identify the four basic ritual actions analogous to the sādhana's structure, as they appear in the translation below.

1. (Step 9 below) Visualizing the receptacle away in conjunction with its dissolution into emptiness. This is followed by the generation of the *yi dam* in the space previously occupied by the receptacle. The *yi dam* in this case (as in most other Gelukpa consecrations) is Dorje Jikje (Rdo rje 'jigs byed, Skt. Vajrabhairava), the wrathful form of the bodhisattva of wisdom, Mañjuśrī. While pronouncing outloud the description of Dorje Jikje as given in the manual, the performers visualize him in their minds.
2. (Step 12) Blessing the sense-fields. The head, throat, and heart of the visualized Dorje

Jikje, which represent his body, speech and mind, are marked with the three fundamental seed syllables, *oṃ āḥ hūṃ*, respectively. Through this process the visualized form of Dorje Jikje becomes a suitable vessel for the actual Dorje Jikje and the other deities, called "wisdom beings," which will fuse with their visualized forms (called the "pledge beings") in the following ritual action. The transformation of a practitioner or a receptacle into a *yi dam* is seen also as a transformation of their ordinary body, speech, and mind into the exalted form of an enlightened being's body, speech, and mind.

3. (Steps 13, 15, 16) This process consists of three ritual actions: (a) the invitation of the wisdom beings; (b) their fusion into the visualized *yi dams* so that the two become indistinguishable, nondual, or, as the text says, "one taste" (*ro gcig*); (c) sealing of this fusion by means of initiation. This completes the transformation of the receptacle into the nature of an enlightened being.
4. (Step 21) The nondual buddha whose nature is bliss and emptiness is transformed into the appearance of the original receptacle. Thus the receptacle turns into an emanation body of the enlightened beings as we saw above.

These basic activities of the consecration are accompanied by various additional ritual actions. The consecration begins with preparatory rituals. First (step 1) all the ritual implements and substances are arrayed on a special altar. This is followed by a process of exaltation, which transforms both performers and their implements into the special status necessary for effecting the ritual purpose. In their ordinary worldly form, no person, implement, or substance can take part or be used effectively in a ritual performance. First (step 2), the performers must generate themselves as a *yi dam* (Dorje Jikje in this case), for only in this state can they transform a receptacle into a *yi dam*. No details are given in the consecration manual below because any practitioner would be familiar with this requirement. This process, however, is very similar to the transformation of the receptacle into Dorje Jikje, as discussed above. Next (steps 3–4), all the offerings that will be given to the *yi dam* are also transformed into exalted substances endowed with the three following qualities: (1) their true nature is bliss and emptiness, yet (2) they appear as ordinary offerings and (3) function as objects of enjoyment in a variety of "flavors" for the six senses. One will immediately notice the similarity in structure to the transformation of both the receptacle and the performers. In all these cases the result is an entity whose real essence is nonduality, emptiness, "one taste"; yet at the same time it appears and functions in the world for the sake of others—such an entity is in fact the Mahāyāna ideal.

The following group of ritual actions (steps 5–8) consists of another transformation: empowering the ritual substances so they may effect their purposes. First (step 5), the ritual vase and the water that will be used to bathe the receptacle are generated as an ideal vase, containing water capable of purifying outer and inner impurities. What then follows is the production of a form of "flower power," which will be used in a very interesting subsidiary act of consecration (step 6). In one of the climactic points of this ritual, flowers are scattered on the receptacle.

These flowers are empowered by the potent verse of interdependent origination (*Ye dharmā* . . .): "The Tathāgata has proclaimed the causes of those phenomena that arise from causes, and he also has proclaimed their cessation. So has spoken the great renunciate." This verse, which is thought to contain the essence of the Buddha's teachings, has become a powerful mantra, similar in potency to the *Heart Sūtra* (see chapter 33).

The verse of interdependent origination is inscribed on a brass mirror, on which is placed a small vajra with a five-colored thread wound around it. While holding the end of the thread next to his or her heart, the ritual master recites the verse of interdependent origination one hundred times. The spoken words of the verse are conceived of as traveling through the thread (much like electricity through a wire), charging the words written on the mirror with the activated powers of the verse, as well as with the powers of the ritual master and the buddhas. After removing the thread, bathing water is poured on the mirror, washing the written letters onto the flowers and permeating them with the powers of the verse. When these flowers are scattered on the receptacle at the conclusion of the consecration, the powers imbued in the verse of interdependent origination will be transmitted to that receptacle as well. This is a consecratory method of great importance that occurs as a supplementary practice for the basic tantric process discussed above. This type of consecration, which seems to have originated outside the tantric ritual and is sometimes called sūtra-style consecration, has been adapted and embedded within the complex process of the consecration. Finally, to complete the preparatory phase of the ritual, the substances that will be used in the purification of the receptacle are also empowered, again by means of the five-colored thread (steps 7–8). The mantras uttered here, however, are clearly different, consisting mainly of Dorje Jikje's mantras for ritual cleansing and purification.

Only now do we reach the first step in the basic fourfold structure of the consecration, the imaginative dissolution of the receptacle into emptiness and its generation as the *yi dam* (step 9, described above). This first step is separated from the following one by a long series of purifications and bathings meant to turn the visualized form (the pledge being) into a suitable vessel for the actual wisdom beings. The purifications (step 10) are performed in the presence of the wrathful ones. These are not inferior deities, but emanations from emptiness who use their skillful means to expel any obstructions for the sake of sentient beings, thus reenacting the dual roles of the Buddha's supreme wisdom and compassion. The obstructions they expel vary from harmful spirits to mental impediments, all of which might hinder the consecration. In addition to torma offerings, wrathful mantras, and purification substances, the "act of truth" is uttered for the expulsion of these obstructions. What guarantees the potent efficacy of this utterance is the truth of the lamas, the buddhas, bodhisattvas, protectors, and especially the truth of the main *yi dam* of the consecration, Dorje Jikje. Buddhists have long acknowledged the power inherent in uttering true statements to produce miraculous results.

The bathing of the receptacle (in step 11) functions simultaneously as acts of purification, offering, and consecration. Only rarely do Tibetan rituals involve a reenactment of a myth. This bathing does, however, reenact the early myth of the bath given to the newly born Buddha by the gods Indra and Brahmā. In this context the act of bathing serves to purify and consecrate the "newly born" receptacle. Furthermore, the bathing involves a ritualization of the six perfections of the Mahāyāna bodhisattva (generosity, morality, patience, diligence, concentration, and wisdom). The water used for the bath is to be regarded as embodying each of the six perfections successively, so that one is ritually engaged in their practice while bathing the image, an excellent example of how Mahāyāna ideals are ritualized and rendered into actual substances in this tantric practice. Finally, since this ritual bathing is modeled on Indian standards of luxurious bathing offered in hospitality for a guest, it is likewise concluded with drying and offering perfumes, garments, and ornaments to the "guest," the *yi dam* embodied in the receptacle.

Now we resume with further ritual actions belonging to the basic structure of the consecration summarized above. These include the blessing of the sense-fields (step 12) and the invitation of the wisdom beings, along with an assembly of buddhas, bodhisattvas, dharma protectors, and so forth (step 13). The invitation again reiterates the bodhisattva ideal by recalling the great compassion of the buddhas after their enlightenment. They are requested to emerge from the realm of dharma (*dharmadhātu*) by means of emanated bodies for the sake of liberating sentient beings, just as they had resolved to do throughout their bodhisattva career. Upon their arrival, the invited ones are requested to grant their consent for the consecration (step 14). Once granted, the actual wisdom beings are absorbed into the visualized ones (the pledge beings) and the initiation occurs (steps 15–16). These actions complete the transformation of the receptacle into a *yi dam*. The initiation of the *yi dam* (step 16) may seem out of place here, but it is part and parcel of the sādhana process, which was embedded within the consecration. During the sādhana the excess initiation water on the practitioner's head is conceived as being transformed into a small figure of the buddha Akṣobhya, which seals the initiation within the body. Here a similar process serves to seal the enlightened beings within the visualized ones.

The opening of the eyes (step 17) has been an independent consecration in its own right, known since the beginning of the first millennium in India. Rather than being eliminated, this ritual has been accorded a secondary position in the overall structure of the present-day tantric ritual and assigned a new meaning. In its original form, the Buddhist eye-opening rite seems to have been the method for animating an image and endowing it with an eye of enlightened wisdom. Here the ritual is given a new twist in meaning with the patrons, performers, and sentient beings all aspiring to attain the eye of enlightened wisdom as well. An important new objective complements the main purpose of the consecration, which is to establish enlightened beings in the receptacle; by means of the ritual of eye-opening they are induced to look at the patron and other sentient beings with enlightened wisdom. Hence, the opening of their eyes serves to enhance their enlightened activities, thereby increasing the potency of the tantric consecration. As gratitude for their consent to abide in the receptacle, offerings are made and praise given to the *yi dams* and buddhas (step 18 and 19). The guardians, who are already committed to serving the Buddhist religion, are bound by oath to protect the consecrated receptacle as well (step 20). In the last step of the basic fourfold structure of the sādhana, the enlightened beings dwelling within the receptacle are transformed into the ordinary appearance of the original receptacle, being symbolically transformed into a visible emanation body of the buddhas.

The final ritual action (step 22) is considered to be the climax of the consecration. All the *yi dams*, buddhas, bodhisattvas, and so on who were invited to embody the receptacle are requested to remain available there. The idea of the buddhas and bodhisattvas dwelling perpetually in the saṃsāric world as long as all sentient beings have not achieved enlightenment is one of the basic tenets of Mahāyāna Buddhism. This ritual provides the buddhas, bodhisattvas, and *yi dams* with specific dwelling places in the saṃsāric world, making them accessible for human interaction, inspiration, worship, blessings, and protection. By means of the consecration this rather abstract Mahāyānist ideal becomes more tangible. The request to the buddhas to remain in the saṃsāric world also corresponds to the appearance of the Buddha in a worldly "receptacle," namely, during the entry into the womb of his mother Māyādevī, at the onset of their emanation in the world. Here the parallel between the *yi dam* emanating into a stūpa or images and the Buddha's emanation into his physical body (*nirmaṇakāya*) is evident.

The manual translated below may be found in the collected rituals of the Upper Tantric College (Rgyud stod, vol. 1, pp. 373–83) or in the collected rituals of Stag brag Bsam gtan gling (vol. 3, pp. 454–68). In both cases no author is mentioned. It should be emphasized that the ritual manual is written for an audience of performers versed in the ritual tradition of their school. These performers, who have seen the ritual performed since their childhood, also know by heart a great number of recitations and mantras. Therefore, very often only the first words of each recitation or mantra are provided in our text. One may note also that the instructions to the performers are very laconic. In the translation below, all the recitations and mantras have been completed by consulting other consecration manuals. The parts not found in our text are inserted within brackets. Words and phrases in parentheses have been added by the translator for ease in understanding. The headings and the numbering of the sections were also introduced by the translator. As in the Tibetan text, all the pronouncements made during the performance are given in larger type, while the instructions for the ritual are in smaller type. The translation of the description of Dorje Jikje and the praises made to him are based, in part, on Sharpa Tulku and Michael Perrot, *A Manual of Ritual Fire Offerings* (Dharamsala: Library of Tibetan Works and Archives, 1987), as well as on Sharpa Tulku with Richard Guard, *Meditation on Vajrabhairava* (Dharamsala: Library of Tibetan Works and Archives, 1990).

Further Reading

On images and stūpas, see Loden Sherap Dagyab, *Tibetan Religious Art* (Wiesbaden: O. Harrassowitz, 1977), 2 vols; on consecration, see Yael Bentor, "Literature on Consecration (*Rab gnas*)," *Tibetan Literature: Studies in Genre*, ed. Roger Jackson and José I. Cabézon (Ithaca: Snow Lion Press, 1996), pp. 290–311. For more on the opening of the eye, see Richard F. Gombrich, "The Consecration of a Buddhist Image," *The Journal of Asian Studies* 26 (1966): 23–36. A detailed discussion of tantric initiation can be found in the Fourteenth Dalai Lama Tenzin Gyatso's *The Kalachakra Tantra: Rite of Initiation*, trans. and ed. Jeffrey Hopkins (London: Wisdom Publications, 1985).

The Horseback Consecration Ritual

The recitation manual for the "Horseback Consecration" arranged as it should be performed:

1. PREPARATIONS

One who wishes to perform the consecration ritual entitled "horseback" (should) first prepare (the following ritual implements): bathing implements, a mirror on which the verse of interdependent origination has been written, grain for scattering, incense, (white) mustard, a vajra (wrapped in) a *dhāraṇī* (thread), a brush of *dūrvā* grass, a vase of action in which the supreme vase substances and scented water have been mixed, a drying cloth, a mirror, a bathing basin, the three (postbathing requisites): perfume, garments, and ornaments, (also) eye medicine, eye spoon, etc., offerings and *tormas* for the self-generation, extensive or brief according to the occasion, as well as *tormas* for the obstructions.

2. GENERATION OF ONESELF AS DORJE JIKJE

Perform an extensive self-generation or a brief instantaneous generation.

3. BLESSING THE MAIN OFFERINGS

As for blessing the offerings,
[1] cleanse with water from the vase of action, and cleanse with (the action mantra of Dorje Jikje):

> *Oṃ hrīḥ ṣṭrīḥ* [*vikṛtānana hūṃ phaṭ*]

[2] Purify by reciting:

[Pure] by nature [are all *dharmas*; pure by nature am I].

[3] From the continuum of emptiness *āḥ* (appears); from it arise [very vast and wide skulls inside of which are *hūṃs*. From (their) melting arise water for refreshing the feet, water for refreshing the mouth, water for welcoming, flowers, incense, light, fragrance, food, and music. Appearing as offering substances, their nature is bliss and emptiness. As objects of enjoyment for the six senses, they function to generate special uncontaminated bliss].

[4] The blessing:

Oṃ pādyaṃ āḥ hūṃ
Oṃ āñcamanaṃ āḥ hūṃ
Oṃ arghaṃ āḥ hūṃ
Oṃ puṣpe āḥ hūṃ
Oṃ dhūpe āḥ hūṃ
Oṃ āloke āḥ hūṃ
Oṃ gandhe āḥ hūṃ
Oṃ naividyā āḥ hūṃ
Oṃ śabda āḥ hūṃ.

4. BLESSING THE OTHER OFFERING SUBSTANCES

As for the blessing of the other offering substances,
[1] cleanse with

Oṃ hrīḥ ṣṭrīḥ [*vikṛtānana hūṃ phaṭ*]

[2] Purify by reciting:

[Pure] by nature [are all dharmas; pure by nature am I].

[3] From the continuum of emptiness the offering substances (appear) each ornamented with the quintessence of the first letter of its name. From their complete transformation (appear) inconceivable special offerings, holy substances endowed with the five qualities of sense gratification. They completely fill the whole extent of the Earth and space.

Recite the mantra of the sky treasury three times (while making its) *mudrā*:

Oṃ sarvavid pūra pūra [*sura sura avartaya avartaha hoḥ*]

Bless with the six mantras and the six *mudrās*, recite the power of truth.

5. EMPOWERING THE RITUAL VASES

[1], [2] Cleanse and purify the vase.

[3] From the continuum of emptiness *paṃ* (appears). From it (emerges) a

white precious vase completely endowed with all the essential characteristics (of a vase) such as a large belly, long neck and a downward-pointed beak, filled with essences and water able to purify all the impurities of the inner receptacle.

6. EMPOWERING THE FLOWERS

Recite (the verse of interdependent origination):

> *Ye dharmā [hetuprabhavā hetuṃ teṣāṃ tathāgato hy avadat teṣāṃ ca yo nirodha evaṃ vādī mahāśramaṇaḥ]*

and (the action mantra of Dorje Jikje):

> *[Oṃ] hrīḥ ṣṭrīḥ [vikṛtānana hūṃ phaṭ]*

Place the *vajra* (wrapped in) the *dhāraṇī* (thread) on the flowers.

> The letters (of the verse of interdependent origination) rise up; a radiant blazing ray of light invites all the qualities of existence and peace and all the blessings of the Victorious Ones and their sons. They dissolve in the string of mantras and flowers.

The ritual helper offers the *dhāraṇī* thread (to the ritual master). The ritual master recites about one hundred times:

> *Ye dharmā [hetuprabhavā hetuṃ teṣāṃ tathāgato hy avadat teṣāṃ ca yo nirodha evaṃ vādī mahāśramaṇaḥ].*

Then (the ritual helper) collects the *dhāraṇī* thread and pours bathing water on the mirror. (The ritual master) rubs (the letters written on the mirror) with the brush of *dūrvā* grass and they permeate the flowers.

7. EMPOWERING THE INCENSE

Place the *vajra* (wrapped in the) *dhāraṇī* (thread) on top of the incense. The ritual master (recites) one hundred times:

> *[Oṃ] hrīḥ ṣṭrīḥ [vikṛtānana hūṃ phaṭ]*

8. EMPOWERING THE WHITE MUSTARD

Place the *vajra* (wrapped in the) *dhāraṇī* (thread) on top of the white mustard. Recite one hundred times:

> *Sumbha ni[sumbha hūṃ gṛhṇa gṛhṇa hūṃ gṛhṇāpaya gṛhṇāpaya hūṃ ānaya ho bhagavan vidyā-rājā hūṃ phaṭ]*

Recite three times the hundred-syllable mantra (of Dorje Jikje):

Yamāntaka [*samayam anupālaya yamāntaka tvenopatiṣṭha dṛiḍho me bhāva supoṣyo me bhāva sutoṣyo me bhāva anurakto me bhāva sarvasiddhim me prayaccha sarvakarma suca me cittaṃ śrīyaṃ kuru hūṃ ha ha ha ha hoḥ bhagavan yamāntaka ma me muñca yamāntaka bhāva mahāsamayasattva āḥ hūṃ phaṭ*]

9. GENERATION OF THE RECEPTACLE AS DORJE JIKJE

[1] Cleanse the receptacles with:

[*Oṃ*] *hrīḥ ṣṭrīḥ* [*vikṛtānana hūṃ phaṭ*]

[2] Purify with:

[Pure] by nature [are all *dharmas*; pure by nature am I].

[3] From the continuum of emptiness *hūṃ* (appears). From it (appears) a vajra marked with a *hūṃ*. From its complete transformation (appears) glorious great Dorje Jikje, [his body dark blue in color with nine faces, thirty-four arms, and sixteen legs, standing in a posture in which his right legs are bent and left extended; capable of devouring the three realms, calling out "Ha Ha" with his tongue coiled, fangs bared, having wrathful scowls, next to which, his eyebrows and eyes blaze like (the fire) at the time of destruction (of the world), the yellow tips of his hair bristling upward. He makes the threatening seal at the mundane and supramundane deities, frightening the terrifiers. In a loud cry he roars like thunder "*phaiṃ kara.*" He devours human blood, grease, marrow, and fat, crowned with five dry skulls meant to frighten, adorned with garland of skulls (made of) fifty fresh heads, decorated with bone ornaments, such as a sacred thread of black serpent, a wheel of human bones, (bone) earring, etc. He has a bulging belly, his body naked, his eyebrows, eyelashes, beard, and bodily hair blaze like the fire at the end of time.

His main face is that of a buffalo, black, very wrathful, and endowed with sharp horns. On top of it, in between the two horns there is a red face, very frightening, its mouth dripping blood. Above that is a yellow face of Mañjuśrī, slightly wrathful, adorned with ornaments of youth. At the crown of his head five hair locks are tied. The first face at the base of the right horn is blue, to its right a red face and to its left a yellow face. The first face at the base of the left horn is white, while to its right a grey face and to its left a black face. All the faces are very wrathful, and all nine faces have three eyes each.

Both right and left first hands hold a fresh elephant hide with its head to the right, its hair facing outward, stretched by its left front and back legs. In the first among the remaining right (hands) he holds a curved knife, in the second a javelin, in the third a pestle, in the fourth a knife, in the fifth a lance, in the sixth an axe, in the seventh a spear, in the eighth an arrow, in the ninth an iron hook, in the tenth a club, in the eleventh a *khaṭvāṅga*, in the twelfth a wheel, in the thirteenth a five-pronged vajra, in the fourteenth a vajra hammer, in the fifteenth a sword, and in the sixteenth a small drum.

In the remaining left (hands) he holds a skull filled with blood, in the second the head of Brahmā, in the third a shield, in the fourth a leg, in the fifth a lasso, in the sixth a bow, in the seventh intestines, in the eighth a bell, in the ninth a hand, in the tenth a shroud, in the eleventh a person impaled on a pointed stake, in the twelfth a furnace, in the thirteenth a scalp, in the fourteenth (he makes) the threatening seal, in the fifteenth a flag with three protrusions, and in the sixteenth a fan.

With the first of his right legs he tramples a man, with the second a buffalo, the third a bull, the fourth a donkey, the fifth a camel, the sixth a dog, the seventh a sheep, the eighth a fox, and with the first of the left (legs) a vulture, the second an owl, the third a raven, the fourth a parrot, the fifth a hawk, the sixth a large bird, the seventh a cock, the eighth a swan. He tramples under his feet Brahmā, Indra, Viṣṇu, Rudra, six-faced Kumāra, Vināyaka, Candra, and Sūrya, all facing down.] He stands amidst a blazing mass of fire.

At the heart of the (visualized) pledge being [on a lunar throne appears the (actual) wisdom being as (ever) young Mañjuśrī slightly wrathful, his body yellow colored. His right hand brandishes a sword, his left holds a book at his heart. He sits crossed legged in the vajra position, adorned with the thirty-two major and eighty minor marks (of a buddha). His long hair tied in five knots (on top of his head), and he is adorned with all the ornaments.

At his heart, from *āḥ* arises a solar maṇḍala. At its center, the *samādhisattva*], a dark blue syllable *hūṃ* emanates five rays of light.

10. THE PURIFICATIONS

Bless the offerings to the wrathful ones.

Invitation of the Wrathful Ones

From the *hūṃ* on one's heart a ray of light emanates. It invites to the space in front (of the performers) the entire assemblage of the wrathful ones.

Ring the bell. While making the *mudrā* of *dril stabs* (recite):

Hūṃ. [You are] enlightened wisdom, [a light blazing like the fire (at the end) of the] aeon, [consuming all the dark realms of ignorance and desire; you have overcome all hatred and fears of the Lord of Death. Great Hero, wearing a tiger skin, a mark of a hero, subduer of the enemy, oppressor of the *rākṣasas* who lead astray, the king of knowledge, the wrathful one, may (you) remain here. You are invited for the sake of subduing those who lead astray. May you come for the sake of sentient beings and (partake of) these offerings.] *Oṃ vajra-mahā-krodha-rājā-saparivāra-ehyehi.*

While making the *mudrās* recite:

Oṃ vajra-mahā-[krodha-rājā-]saparivāra pravara-sadkāraṃ arghaṃ pratīccha hūṃ svāhā kamalayestvaṃ (and so forth).

With the appropriate mantras (replacing the name of each offering successively), offer the two waters and the main offerings. Play the cymbals in *slang sil.* While attaching the three seed (syllables *oṃ āḥ hūṃ* to the mantra *oṃ vajra-mahā-krodha-rājā-saparivāra*), make the inner offerings.

Hūṃ. Prostrations [to the assemblage of blazing great wrathful ones who, not abandoning the worldly way of action, appear] from the continuum, the empty nondual essence of dharmas [as the body of the frightening one by skillful means. Prostrations to you who, without wavering from the peaceful continuum of knowledge, possessing voracious fearsome outlook and costumes, a roaring voice that resounds as a thousand thunders, bring under control everything without remainder. Prostrations to you who demonstrate the drama of the supreme knowledge, who carry various threatening weapons in your hand(s), adorned with poisonous snakes, totally overcome the great poisonous afflictions. Prostrations to you who reside amidst a fire like the conflagration (at the end) of an aeon, in the hero posture with one leg stretched and the other drawn back, staring with wide open eyes blazing like the Sun and the Moon, burning a host of obstructions. Prostrations to you whose great ferocity blazes as brightly as the fire at the end of times, whose scowls of wrathfulness seem to emit a thousand lightnings, whose fangs are bare, whose furious voice roars as the sound of thousand thunders, the king of the wrathful ones who subdue a host of obstructions. *Hūṃ.* Prostrations and praise to you who call out the frightening sound of *hūṃ*, who overcome all obstructions without remainder, the god who bestow all accomplishments,] the enemy of the obstructions.

Blessing the Tormas for the Obstructors

By attaching the three seed syllables and *svāhā* to *akāro*, bless the *tormas* for the obstructors.

Summoning the Obstructors

From *hūṃ* on one's heart a ray of light emanates. It summons the assemblage of obstructors which hinder the consecration.

(Offer the *tormas* to the obstructors while reciting) three times:

Oṃ sarva-vighnān [namaḥ sarva-tathāgatebhyo viśva-mukhebhyaḥ sarva-tadkham udgate spharaṇa imaṃ gagana-khaṃ ghṛhana] baliṃ taye svāhā

(Recite) three times:

> *Oṃ sumbha ni[sumbha hūṃ gṛhṇa gṛhṇa hūṃ gṛhṇāpaya gṛhṇāpaya hūṃ ānaya ho bhagavan] vidyā-rājā hūṃ phaṭ*

Then while making the *'byung po 'ur 'ded mudrā* (recite):

> The entire assemblage of obstructors consisting of gods and so forth who stay on the grounds of the great maṇḍala listen! In this place I am performing a consecration ritual; [may you depart from here to another (place). If you transgress my word, with a blazing vajra endowed with knowledge (your) head will be shattered into a hundred pieces;] certainly [the obstructions will be smashed]!

While making the *hūṃ mdzad mudrā* (recite):

> *Namo*! By the truth of the glorious holy lamas, together with the venerable masters of root and lineage, the truth of the *yi dam*, the assemblage of deities of the maṇḍala and [the truth] of buddhas and bodhisattvas, [the truth] of śrāvakas, pratyekabuddhas, dharma protectors, guardians, especially in reliance on the power of truth of the assemblage of deities of the glorious great Dorje Jikje together with his retinue, may the entire assembly of obstructors, whoever would hinder the consecration, be content with these *tormas* and go each to your own place. If you do not depart, with the vajra of the knowledge of the wrathful ones, blazing as fire (your) heads will be shattered into a hundred pieces, no doubt about it!

(Recite):

> *Oṃ sumbha ni[sumbha hūṃ gṛhṇa gṛhṇa hūṃ gṛhṇāpaya gṛhṇāpaya hūṃ ānaya ho bhagavan vidyā-rājā hūṃ phaṭ]*

Play wrathful music.

11. OFFERING BATH

Then assemble the bathing implements and so forth.

> As (the Buddha), who as soon as he was born was bathed by all the deities, likewise, with pure divine water I shall offer a bath.
> *Oṃ sarva-tathāgata-[abhiśekata-samaya-śriye āḥ hūṃ]*.
> This is water whose nature is generosity; it purifies the stains of miserliness. With this water well suffused with the perfume of abandoning which bathes well, I offer a bath.
> *Oṃ sarva-[tathāgata-kāya-viśodhane svāhā]*
> This is [water whose nature is] morality; [it purifies] the stains of immorality. [With this water well suffused] with the perfume of morality which bathes well, [I offer a bath.

Oṃ sarva-tathāgata-kāya-viśodhane svāhā]
This is [water whose nature is] patience; [it purifies] the stains of anger. [With this water well suffused] with the perfume of patience which bathes well, [I offer a bath.
Oṃ sarva-tathāgata-kāya-viśodhane svāhā]
This is [water whose nature is] diligence; [it purifies] the stains of laziness. [With this water well suffused] with the perfume of diligence which bathes well, [I offer a bath.
Oṃ sarva-tathāgata-kāya-viśodhane svāhā]
This is [water whose nature is] concentration; [it purifies the stains of] distraction. [With this water well suffused] with the perfume of concentration which bathes well, [I offer a bath.
Oṃ sarva-tathāgata-kāya-viśodhane svāhā]
This is [water whose nature is] wisdom; [it purifies the stains of] misapprehension. [With this water well suffused] with the perfume of wisdom which bathes well, [I offer a bath.
Oṃ sarva-tathāgata-kāya-viśodhane svāhā]
[(I) offer a bath] with the six rivers, endowed with six exalted qualities, which through bathing purify the six kinds of impurities, may they bathe well.
Faithfully, I offer a bath to the one who is faultless, who is endowed with all the qualities, for the sake of deliverance into that buddha(hood).
Oṃ sarva-tathāgata-[*abhiṣekata-samaya-śriye āḥ hūṃ*].

Drying

[I shall dry] their bodies [with unequaled cloth, clean and well anointed with scent].
Oṃ hūṃ traṃ hrīḥ [*āḥ*].

Offering Scent

[With the best scent whose fragrance permeates] the entire three-thousand-great-thousand-world, [as polishing pure refined gold, I shall anoint the blazing and radiant body of the great sages].

Offering Garments

[For the sake of purifying (my) mind, I offer this precious fine garment varicolored as a] variegated [rainbow, touching it is a cause of bliss, may I be adorned with the best garment of patience].

Offering Ornaments

[Even though the Victorious One, being naturally endowed with the ornaments] of the major and minor marks of a buddha, [does not seek to be adorned with any other ornaments, by offering this supreme ornament of precious substances may all beings obtain a body decorated with the major and minor marks of a buddha].

It is not necessary to use mantras in the (last) three offerings.

12. BLESSING THE SENSE-FIELDS

The deities become marked with white *oṃ* on the head, red *āḥ* on the throat, and blue *hūṃ* on the heart.

13. INVITATION OF THE ACTUAL ENLIGHTENED BEINGS

From *hūṃ* on one's heart a ray of light emanates; it invites the wisdom beings who are similar to the visualized ones together with an assembly of buddhas, bodhisattvas, śrāvakas, pratyekabuddhas, dharma protectors, and guardians to the space in front (of oneself).

Hold incense stick together with the bell.

> [May the protector of each and] every sentient being, [the deity who subdued the frightful Māra with his host, the Blessed One who knows all things as they are, come to this place together with his retinue].
> O Blessed One, [having practiced compassion in numerous countless] aeons, [out of affection for sentient beings, (now that your) intention, (your) great aspiration, is completely fulfilled, it is time to act for the sake of beings as you have maintained].
> Therefore, [for the sake of liberating infinite multitudes of sentient beings, displaying various holy miraculous creations, may you come from the spontaneously arising palace of the] dharma realm [accompanied by your completely immaculate retinue].
> Faithfully (I) invite [the chief lord of all dharmas, similar in color to refined gold, more intensely bright than the sun, peaceful and very compassionate, abiding in a state of concentration and control, endowed with knowledge of the dharmas, free from desire, endowed with a completely inexhaustible capacity. Come hither, come hither, the deity who is the embodiment of peace, who had the supreme birth of a sage Śākyamuni, the omniscient. With offerings I request you to come to this well made reflected image. Having remained here united with the image for the sake of sentient beings,] generously bestow (on us) the best [health, longevity, prosperity, and excellence].
> *Jaḥ hūṃ baṃ hoḥ mahākaruṇika-ātmaka-ehyehi.*

Welcoming

> It is good that the Blessed One has kindly come. We are so meritorious and fortunate. Having accepted my water for welcoming, may you consider me and grant my (request). Welcome, Blessed One, may you come here and be seated. Having accepted my water for welcoming, may you abide here indeed.

[As (the Buddha, who)] as soon as he [was born, was bathed by all the deities, likewise, I shall offer a bath with pure divine water].

Thus recite this (last) verse alone. It is not necessary to recite the mantra (that usually follows it).

[Out of compassion] for me and sentient beings, [through your powers of miraculous creation, as long as I make offerings], may the Blessed One remain (here).
Kamalayestvaṃ.
Welcome, Blessed One, may you come here and be seated. Having accepted my water for welcoming may you consider me too.

Expelling the Obstructions Who Follow the Deities

Then

Oṃ hrīḥ ṣṭrīḥ vikṛtānana hūṃ phaṭ

Thus, having cleansed with water from the (action) vase, expel the obstructors who follow (the invited ones).

Offerings

Make offerings with

Oṃ sarva-tathāgata-arghaṃ-[pūja-megha-samudra-spharaṇa-samaya śrīye āḥ hūṃ]

up until

[Oṃ sarva-tathāgata-] śabda-[pūja-megha-samudra-spharaṇa-samaya śrīye āḥ hūṃ]

14. REQUESTING THE CONSECRATION

Holding incense with the bell (recite):

Out of compassion for us and out of compassion for the disciples and also for the sake of offerings to you, with respect I ask to perform the consecration now, O Blessed One, therefore I am worthy of your kindness. O Vajradhara, now I shall perfectly perform a consecration of a receptacle of body, speech, and mind of Akṣobhya with requisites as much as the patron can afford. Therefore, having held me and my disciples close with compassion, may you together with all the attendants bless the consecration.

Thus recite three times. Then collect the incense sticks.

The deities bestow as they please.

15. THE ABSORPTION OF THE WISDOM BEINGS IN THE VISUALIZED ONES

> *Jaḥ hūṃ baṃ hoḥ* The wisdom beings and the pledge beings become indivisible.

16. THE INITIATION OF THE DEITIES

> From *hūṃ* at one's heart a ray of light emanates; it invites to the space in front of oneself the entire assemblage of the male and female tathāgatas, male and female bodhisattvas, and male and female wrathful ones.

Make offerings with:

> *Oṃ sarva-tathāgata-arghaṃ-*[*pūja-megha-samudra-spharaṇa-samaya śrīye āḥ hūṃ*

up until

> *Oṃ sarva-tathāgata-śabda-pūja-megha-samudra-spharaṇa-samaya śrīye āḥ hūṃ*]

Requesting the Initiation

> (I) request the initiation deities to confer initiation here. Because of this request, the Tathāgatas heed the initiation.
> Those who reside in space, together with the female buddhas such as Locanā, hold parasols, victory banners, etc. over the consecration deity. They dance, sing, and play music. A rain of flowers including saffron falls down. Holding in their hand a slightly slanted white vase filled with the nectar of bodhicitta, they confer initiation. Rūpavajrī and so forth express auspiciousness with melodious auspicious songs. The wrathful ones situated at the four main directions and the four intermediate ones expel the obstructions. As (the Buddha, who) as soon as he was born, [was bathed by all the deities, likewise, I shall offer a bath with pure divine water.
> *Oṃ sarva-tathāgata-abhiṣekata-samaya-śriye āḥ hūṃ*]

Thus recite this one verse together with its mantra.

> Having said this the initiation penetrates the body, and purifies the impurities. The excess water residing at the crown of the head completely transforms and turns into a head ornament of Akṣobhya.

17. OPENING OF THE EYE

Then hold the eye medicine and the eye spoon.

> As the king of the eye healers removes the worldly (eye) film, so the victorious ones remove your film of ignorance.

Oṃ cakṣu cakṣu samanta-cakṣu viśodhani svāhā.
Even though (you) are omniscient, endowed with an eye of enlightened wisdom, free of faults, by reverently opening the exalted eye, may sentient beings, up until the limit of the sky, obtain the eye of enlightened wisdom of the Buddha.
For the sake of achieving actions beginning with pacifying, may (you) look intently on the patron and others with enlightened wisdom.

18. OFFERINGS

[Having accepted this supreme water for welcoming] pure, stainless and pleasing, [(blessed by) mantra which I faithfully offer, may you bestow grace on me].
Oṃ sarva-tathāgata arghaṃ pratīcchaye svāhā

likewise

[Having accepted this supreme water for refreshing the feet, pure, stainless, and pleasing, (blessed by) mantra which I faithfully offer, may you bestow grace on me.
Oṃ sarva-tathāgata]*pādyaṃ*[*pratīcchaye svāhā*
I seek to offer this] best divine flower [to the maṇḍala, consider me compassionately,
O protector, accept this offering.
Oṃ sarva-tathāgata puṣpe pratīccha hūṃ svāhā
I seek to offer this best divine incense to the maṇḍala, consider me compassionately,
O protector, accept this offering.
Oṃ sarva-tathāgata dhūpe pratīccha hūṃ svāhā
I seek to offer this best divine light to the maṇḍala, consider me compassionately,
O protector, accept this offering.
Oṃ sarva-tathāgata āloke pratīccha hūṃ svāhā
I seek to offer this best divine fragrance to the maṇḍala, consider me compassionately,
O protector, accept this offering.
Oṃ sarva-tathāgata gandhe pratīccha hūṃ svāhā
I seek to offer this best divine food to the maṇḍala, consider me compassionately,
O protector, accept this offering.
Oṃ sarva-tathāgata naividyā pratīccha hūṃ svāhā
I seek to offer this best divine music to the maṇḍala, consider me compassionately,
O protector, accept this offering.
Oṃ sarva-tathāgata śabda pratīccha hūṃ svāhā]

Thus make offerings together with the mantras as before, up until "music."

Inner Offerings

Make the inner offerings with

> [*Oṃ*] *hrīḥ ṣṭrīḥ* [*vikṛtānana hūṃ phaṭ oṃ āḥ hūṃ*]

19. PRAISES

> [You are] nondual, extraordinary, [pervasive body. With equanimity to all you are the father of all the victorious ones. Being the realm of dharma you are the mother of all the victorious ones. Being the wisdom being, you are the son of all the victorious ones.
> Prostrations to you, glorious Mañjuśrī, the perfected one. Even though the *dharmakāya* has neither love nor hate, for the sake of taming the poisonous ones of the three worlds without remainder, through compassionate skillful means you manifest as the body of the king of the wrathful ones]. Prostrations to the Frightful One the destroyer of the Lord of Death.

20. BINDING THE GUARDIANS TO AN OATH

> *Oṃ hūṃ traṃ hrīḥ āḥ*

21. TRANSFORMATION OF THE RECEPTACLE

> *Oṃ yamāntaka hūṃ phaṭ*
> Glorious Dorje Jikje dissolves into light. His complete transformation turns into the appearance of each receptacle and its inhabitants.

22. REQUESTING THE DEITIES TO REMAIN FIRMLY IN THE RECEPTACLE

(Recite) three times:

> *Ye dharmā* [*hetuprabhavā hetuṃ teṣāṃ tathāgato hy avadat teṣāṃ ca yo nirodha evaṃ vādī mahāśramaṇaḥ*]

Recite the three verses of auspiciousness:

> [Like a golden mountain endowed with] perfections, [is the protector of the three worlds; the Buddha who has abandoned the three defilements, endowed with eyes wide as petals of lotus. This is the first virtuous auspiciousness of the world. Supreme and immutable, taught by him renown in the three worlds, worshipped by gods and humans, the holy dharma brings peace to all sentient beings. This is the second virtuous auspiciousness of the world. The saṅgha rich in the auspiciousness of hearing the dharma, object of worship for human, gods and *asuras*, the supreme assembly, the basis of wondrous knowledge and glory. This is the third virtuous auspiciousness of the world].

Then

> As all the buddhas from their abodes in Tuṣita heaven entered the womb of Queen Māyā, so may the protector always reside together with the image. For the sake of developing the mind of enlightenment and for the sake of the patron, may you accept these offerings and flowers, etc., my own resources as much as I can afford; may you consider me and my disciples compassionately; may you bless all these; may you agree to abide in this very one.
>
> May all the buddhas and bodhisattvas who reside in the ten directions consider me. As long as the realms of sentient beings vast as the sky are not placed at the level of being in unestablished nirvāṇa, may you firmly remain without passing into nirvāṇa; and particularly, as long as these receptacles of body, speech, and mind are not destroyed by the harm of deeds, earth, water, fire, and wind, [acting immeasurably] for the sake of sentient beings, [may you firmly remain].
>
> *Oṃ supratiṣṭha-vajraye svāhā*

Thus (recite) three times.

> As by seeing the totally good Sugata, there is auspiciousness, by the presence of the Victorious One and his sons here today, may there be happiness and goodness. (You) have subdued the assembly of bad, wicked, and wrong ones, (you) have increased the assembly of the victorious ones and their sons, the knowledge holders. By merely seeing (your) face, warm as the Sun, luminous as the Moon, one obtains supreme bliss. Having generously granted me and sentient beings with (your) warm face, may (you) remain until the end of the aeon. As long as the aeon is not destroyed by fire, water, and wind, for the sake of all sentient beings may you the Blessed One remain.

Recite the hundred-syllable mantra (of Dorje Jikje) three times:

> [*Yamāntaka samayam anupālaya yamāntaka tvenopatiṣṭha dṛiḍho me bhāva supoṣyo me bhāva sutoṣyo me bhāva anurakto me bhāva sarvasiddhim me prayaccha sarvakarma suca me cittaṃ śrīyaṃ kuru hūṃ ha ha ha ha hoḥ bhagavan yamāntaka ma me muñca yamāntaka bhāva mahāsamayasattva āḥ hūṃ phaṭ.*]
>
> O protector, having assumed various forms in accordance with the circumstances, may you act for the sake of all the aims of sentient beings in the worldly realms of the ten directions.

Recite seven times:

> *Ye dharmā* [*hetuprabhavā hetuṃ teṣāṃ tathāgato hy avadat teṣāṃ ca yo nirodha evaṃ vādī mahāśramaṇaḥ*].

Recite verses of auspiciousness of Dorje Jikje.

—15—

An Offering of Torma

Richard J. Kohn

Buddhists have always made offerings to the three jewels: the Buddha, his teaching, and the spiritual community. Mahāyāna Buddhism added vast numbers of bodhisattvas, heros of enlightenment, both human and superhuman, to this list. Offerings, however, were a feature of both Indian and Tibetan religion long before the birth of the Buddha. Tibetans still make offerings to many of the gods of pre-Buddhist Tibet as well as to a host of lowlier spirits. Deities converted by saints of ages past are worshipped as protectors of Buddhism. Many spirits are counted among the "hungry ghosts." Mournful beings, the hungry ghosts wander the world tortured by hunger and thirst, and they are legitimate objects of compassion and charity. The "Three-Part Torma Process" uses an offering called a *torma* (*gtor ma*), a ritual cake found in a wide variety of Tibetan ceremonies, to feed and appease these ghosts and spirits. The Three-Part Torma is often performed as part of longer, complex rituals.

The text was composed by the great seventeenth-century lama Terdak Lingpa Gyurme Dorje (Gter bdag gling pa 'gyur med rdo rje, 1646–1714). It is included in the "Religious Practice" anthology published at his monastery, Mindroling—the leading monastery in central Tibet of the Nyingma or Old Translation School. Gyurme Dorje based his work on material found only in the tantras of the Old School. However, in an early burst of ecumenical spirit—a trend that was not to catch on in Tibet for another century—he arranged his text so that it would "agree, rather than be at odds with, the New Translation School," which is to say the practices of the remaining three sects of Buddhism in Tibet.

Although written in Tibet, the Three-Part Torma is addressed to beings derived from ancient Indian mythology: the directional guardians (Tib., *phyogs skyong,* Skt., *lokapāla*), ghosts or elementals (Tib., *'byung po,* Skt., *bhūta*), and obstructors (Tib., *bgegs,* Skt., *vighna*). The first two groups are supernatural beings, but the third occupies a unique position. Just as certain single-celled organisms are claimed by both botanists and zoologists, the obstructors straddle the border between the supernatural and the psychological. The beings summoned in the

Three-Part Torma are forces to be reckoned with. They are, however, lower in the supernatural order than some of the deities evoked in Tibetan ritual. When major deities are summoned, they must be returned to the transcendental realm by an elaborate, formal process. For the beings of the Three-Part Torma, who inhabit our worldly plane, a quick "begone!"—*gaccha* in Sanskrit—and a small offering cake are a sufficient farewell.

Offerings of food are a staple of religious practice. Buddhist theorists, however, say that there is an even greater gift: religious instruction. In the Three-Part Torma ritual, meditators "Make the gift of dharma" in the standard way. First, they recite the *ye dharma*, a well-known Sanskrit formula that encapsulates the fundamentals of Buddhist philosophy (see chapter 14):

> Whatever events arise from a cause
> the Tathāgata has told the cause thereof;
> and the great ascetic also
> has taught their cessation as well.

They then add in Tibetan—

> This is the Buddha's teaching:
> Do no evil!
> Perform a wealth of virtues!
> Tame your own mind completely!

The obstructors are given some particularly thoughtful advice:

> Everyone fears for his own life!
> Taking your own body as a model,
> Do no harm to others!

The Three-Part Torma is brief and the offering cake small, but the ritual evokes an astonishing number of supernatural entities. Although the text reels them off quickly and casually, we will take a bit of time to introduce them.

The first, the directional guardians, include the major deities of ancient Indian religion. Many of these deities are so old that they were worshipped before Indo-European people migrated eastward and westward to form the basis of Indian and European civilization. Considering that these gods were at one time the bulwark of religious faith from Greece to India, it is almost poignant to see them lumped together with ghosts and a host of miscellaneous obstructive forces—albeit, the text tells us, as their rulers. Unfortunately, we do not have the space to discuss the entire cast of characters. Even books dedicated to the subject of Indian mythology do not explain many of them in detail. A few, however, demand a closer look, some for their importance, some for their obscurity, and some for the unique perspective that our text has on them.

Indra was king of the gods in ancient India. Like Zeus or Jupiter, he "wields a thunderbolt." The Three-Part Torma text identifies him as ruler of the malignant ones, or dön (*gdon*), a class of evil spirits that cause disease. Agni, the ancient

Indian god of fire, is called "king of the *ṛṣi*." This is appropriate enough, since the ṛṣi (pronounced "rishi") are the sages expert in performing the ancient Vedic fire sacrifice of the Hindu tradition. "Big Hand, Who Grasps the Earth" (Sa 'dzin lag pa chen po), also known as "Hand," is one of the few indigenous Tibetan deities evoked in the Three-Part Torma. According to myth, Hand is the lord of the mu (*dmu*), an important class of ancient Tibetan deities. It was Hand who impregnated the Red-Faced Earth-Goddess and gave birth to the seven blazing brothers from a blazing egg—the stern serpent spirits who guard the Buddha's word. The ghosts, or elemental spirits, include members of several other groups: gods, the serpent spirits Tibetans call *lu*, earth spirits, scent-eaters, demigods, mythological eagles, "rotten-bodied ones," and the serpent spirits Tibetans call *docheh*.

Buddhist cosmology describes the gods of ancient India (Skt., *deva*) as living in a series of heavens arrayed above Meru, the mountain in the center of the world. The indigenous spirits that Tibetans knew as *lha* generally inhabited the tops of mountains as well. Tibetans often name their mountains after the gods that live on them. Two famous examples are Chomolangma, the goddess of the mountain we call Everest, and Nyenchen Thangla, the god who gives his name to the Nyenchen Thangla range of northern Tibet (see chapter 24). When the Tibetans heard about *devas* from Indian teachers, they quite naturally grouped them with the benign *lha* that they had worshipped for centuries.

The serpent spirits (*klu, nāga*) live in streams, in underground springs, at the roots of trees, and at the bottom of lakes and oceans. If treated with respect they can be beneficial; if slighted they may cause leprosy and other diseases (see chapter 1). The Tibetans worshipped *klu* (pronounced *lu*) long before they heard of the similar spirits the Indians call *nāga*. Over the centuries, however, the myths have coalesced.

The *yakṣa* are an ancient Indian earth spirit associated with trees and the foundations of buildings. The Tibetans explain that they are very fickle. Sometimes they harm you; sometimes they bestow riches on you. Hence their name in Tibetan: "malefactor/benefactor" (*gnod byin*). The scent-eaters (Skt., *gandharva*) originated in India. Celestial spirits so refined that they need no solid food—they live off the scent of offerings. The contentious demigods (Skt., *asura*) also came from India. They live at the foot of the wish-granting tree that only blossoms—and grants wishes—in the realm of the gods above their heads and out of their grasp. Maddened by envy, they wage constant and futile war against the gods. The Tibetans worshipped the *khyung*, mythological eagles, before they heard of the Indian *garuḍa*. As with the serpent gods, the myths have merged in historical Tibet (see chapter 25).

The "rotten bodied" (*lus srul po,* Skt., *kaṭa-pūtana*) are a class of demons whose putrid smell is said to be an affront to the senses of the gods. They are related to a demoness of Hindu myth who attempted to kill Kṛṣṇa by suckling him with poisoned milk. The *docheh* (*lto 'phye,* Skt., *mahoraga*) are a class of huge subterranean serpents who lie on their sides and rotate in the earth. Lamas explain that their unusual name comes from having a stomach (*lto*) but being "cut off" (*'phye*) at the legs. They are classed among the owners of the soil (*sa bdag*), the supernatural landlords who are the original inhabitants of a place and from whom we borrow the land that we use. It is important to take the *docheh* into consideration before erecting a building—their shifting can shake the foundations of anything built over them. Like the better-known *lu*, the *docheh* are snakes from the waist down. *Drulbum* (*grul bum*, Skt., *kumbhāṇḍa*) are a class of cemetery-dwelling vampire ghouls. The name *kumbhāṇḍa* derives from an anatomical peculiarity: their testicles are said to be shaped like pitchers (*kumbha*).

If facing this army of supernatural terrors sounds like a daunting task, it is! Tibetans, in fact, believe that it is a job for no ordinary mortal. Before facing the obstructors, for example, the participants are instructed to visualize themselves as the fierce manifestation of enlightenment, the Diamond Wrathful One, the blood-drinking great glorious Heruka. As in many religions, the power of the word—of truth itself—is considered to be a potent weapon. Thus, the participants invoke the obstructors "by the power of the true word of the glorious holy lamas." Sometimes, however, gifts and moral suasion are just not enough. The text reminds the participants to "expel any and all [particularly] vicious and coarse-tempered" ghosts "by mustering your diamond wrath and uttering the four-*hūṃ* mantra and by fierce sounding music." Buddhist practice, the lamas say, fulfills both one's own aims and the aims of others. The awesome responsibility of the supernatural struggle is not taken for personal benefit alone, but for the general welfare. Thus, the meditators request the ghosts both to "cure every illness of every sentient being here" and to "cast out all illness" in general.

As its name suggests, the centerpiece of the "Three-Part Torma Process" is offering tormas to the supernatural beings the ritual evokes. The tormas are made of parched-barley flour and decorated with colored butter. Those offered to peaceful deities have sweet-tasting ingredients. Those offered to fiercer beings, the text specifies, are "made of polluted substances like meat and beer." The text employs a number of technical terms peculiar to torma construction. *Tebkyu* (*theb skyu*) are various small pieces of dough affixed to certain tormas. Here, the term refers to a small cup or ledge in front of each torma. *Ting lo* are lamps made of dough. A "handprint" (*chang bu*) is piece of dough squeezed in the first bearing its imprint. A "feast" (*tshogs*) is a pear-shaped torma made of tasty ingredients, such as rice or barley flour, and offered along with other food and drink during a special ritual also called a "feast."

Although often performed in a perfunctory way—the text is commonly read at breakneck speed in the midst of a larger series of rituals—the "Three-Part Torma Process" has moments of genuine poetry. This passage that invokes the ghosts begins this way—

You ghosts who live atop Mount Meru,
And in the happy forests and the abodes of the gods,
And the mountains east and west, and the homes of the Sun and Moon,

And who live on all the mountains,
Who live in the Precious Continent and fill it to overflowing,
And in all the rivers and river valleys,
And in the oceans and ponds, and in the rivulets,
And you who live in the cool mountain springs
And in the cities empty of markets and cattle and gods . . .

Most important of all, the "Three-Part Torma" constantly reminds us that, as it is for many traditional peoples, for Tibetans, nature is not a blank canvas or an empty vessel that we may do with as we please. It is a place vibrant with life, both seen and unseen, that we must approach with respect and with a sense of wonder.

The translation is from Smin gling lo chen Dharmaśri (1654–1717), *Chos spyod kyi rim pa thar lam rab gsal zhes bya ba bzhugs so* (The Sequence of Religious Practices Called "The Elucidation of the Path to Freedom"). Short title: *[Smin gling] chos spyod. ([Mindroling] Religious Practice)*. Xylograph from Rong phu blocks stored at Thub brten chos gling. Ritual instructions are rendered here in a smaller typeface.

Further Reading

René de Nebesky-Wojkowitz, *Oracles and Demons of Tibet: The Cult and Iconography of the Tibetan Protective Deities* ('s-Gravenhage: Mouton and Co., 1956); Wendy Doniger O'Flaherty, *The Origins of Evil in Hindu Mythology* (Berkeley: University of California Press, 1976); Gail Hinich Sutherland, *The Disguises of the Demon: The Development of the Yakṣa in Hinduism and Buddhism* (Albany: State University of New York Press, 1991).

The Three-Part Torma Process

I bow to the Lama and to Vajrasattva!

On the occasion of a large maṇḍala ritual of the Diamond Vehicle, many styles of three-part tormas are spoken of—extensive, middling, or condensed. They should be understood as follows.

[Place] three [tormas] in a precious vessel or other type. The first two [tormas] are the general tormas for the guardians of the directions and the ghosts. They are round and have "buttons." They are white, made of parboiled rice chaff or the like, and are augmented with a feast of pure food and drink.

The third, the obstructors' torma, has lamps made from dough (*ting lo*) and handprints (*chang bu*). It is made of polluted substances like meat and beer.

They are set in a row.

Sprinkle them with pure water. Cleanse them with the diamond malefactor/benefactor gesture and by [the mantra]

Oṃ vajrayakṣa hūṃ

Purify them with the diamond fire gesture and by saying

Oṃ vajra jvalayanala hana daha paca mathabhañjaraṇa hūṃ phaṭ

and

Svabhāva . . .

Think that

From the empty realm comes [the syllable] *bhrūṃ*. From that, a precious vessel, deep and wide. In it, a torma, wonderful in color, odor, taste, and effectiveness, becomes a great ocean of ambrosia.

Bless it on the ordinary level by saying three times,

Oṃ āḥ hūṃ hoḥ

Then, offer the first torma to the ten guardians of the directions. Think that—

The radiance of the [syllable] hūṃ [that I visualize] in my heart invites the guardians of the directions and their entourage.

And grasping the vajra and bell, invite them thus,

O guardians of the directions, powerful guardians of the world,
Wise in the ways of compassion, understanding tutelaries,
Gods and ṛṣis, kings who rule the knowledge bearers,
The races of hungry ghosts, ghouls, and serpents! Masters of the malefactor/benefactors!

You display bodies with each of their powers!
O guardians of the world in the ten directions, if we beg you to stay,
If, worshipping [you] for [all] beings' sake,
We invite you in order to spread the teaching, we pray you come!

Oṃ daśadiklokapāla saparivariye hye hi

Offer them a seat with,

Padmakamalaya staṃ

Make offerings to them with—

Oṃ inḍāya agnaye yamāya nairidya varuṇaya vāyave kuberāya īśnāya ūrdha brahmaya sūrya grihaya adhipataye candra nakṣatra adhipataye adho-prithivibhyaḥ asurebhyaḥ nāgebhyaḥ saparivara arghaṃ . . . and so on.

After [placing] your diamond palms face upward, at the end of the previous mantra [recite]—

Indra . . . etc.

Offer the torma by adding three recitations of:

Namaḥ sarvatathāgate bhyo viśva[mukhebhyaḥ sarvathākhaṃ utgatesparaṇa imaṃ gaganakhaṃ svāhā].

Praise them thus,

Powerful one, god who wields a thunderbolt,
King of gods, master of malignant ones,
I worship, praise, and also salute you,
Eastern quarter, with [your] host of malignant ones!

Fire god who eats what is burned,
King of ṛṣi, demon of the gathered clan of malignant ones,
I worship [praise and also salute you,]
Southeastern quarter . . .

Lord of Death, god who wields a club,
King of the grandmother spirits . . .
I worship . . .
Southern quarter . . .

Virtuous god, far from truth,
King of ghouls . . .
I worship . . .
Southwestern quarter . . .

Water god, who wields a lasso,
King of the guardians of the word . . .
I worship . . .
Western quarter . . .

God who holds the winds and also life,
King who holds all races in his grasp,
I worship . . .
Northwestern quarter . . .

Malefactor/benefactor who bears a club in his hand,
King who protects wealth . . .
I worship . . .
Northern quarter . . .

Powerful one, guiding god,
King of ghosts . . .

I worship . . .
Northeastern quarter . . .

I worship those above—
Great Brahmā and the great planets, the Sun and Moon,
And the planets and constellations.

I worship those below—
The serpent spirits and gods of the Earth,
Big Hand, who grasps the Earth,
And the hosts who know the vows.

Beg them to act, thus—

You of the eastern quarter, host of gods with vajras and your entourage,
Please eat these tormas we offer!
Fire, Lord of Death, Master of Ghouls—far from truth,
Master of Water, Master of Wind, Master of Wealth,
Powerful God—Master of Ghosts,
And great Sun, Moon, and Brahmā above—
All gods and whoever is above the Earth; serpent spirits,
Mountain gods and hosts of the pure—
We offer tormas to each of you in your own individual place!
Eat them with great enjoyment, and then
Rest easy in your individual homes!
If we offer praise and tormas, lamps and respect,
Along with flowers, scents, unguents, and incense to you
And your children, loved ones, friends and courtiers,
Household, soldiers, and battalions,
Drink them and take them well!
Bring our acts to fruition!

Appending

Oṃ daśadik[lokapāla gaccha],
ask them to go.

OFFERING THE SECOND TORMA TO THE GHOSTS IN GENERAL

Invite them—

To you, families of gods, titans
And malefactor/benefactors, *docheh* serpents, *drulbum* vampires,
Sky-soarers and finely feathered garuḍa, rotten-bodied ones,
Scent-eaters, ghouls and malignant ones,
To whatever miraculous beings live on Earth,

To your children and servants and entourage—
I kneel to the ground
And pray to you with folded palms.
Therefore listen and come for benefit.

Oṃ sarva lokapāla ehyahi

Offer them a seat—

Padmakamalaya staṃ

Worship them,

Oṃ deva nāga yakṣa gandharva asura garuda kinara mahoraga manuṣya amanuṣya saparivāra arghaṃ . . . , etc.

Open your diamond palms and, at the end of the above mantra "*Oṃ deva* . . ." offer the torma by adding three recitations of:

Namaḥ sarva [tathāgate bhyo viśvamukhebhyaḥ sarvathākhaṃ utgatesparaṇa imaṃ gaganakhaṃ svāhā].

Commit them to act—

You ghosts who live atop Mount Meru,
And in the happy forests and the abodes of the gods,
And the mountains east and west, and the homes of the Sun and Moon,
And who live on all the mountains,
Who live in the precious continent and fill it to overflowing,
And in all the rivers and river valleys,
And in the oceans and ponds, and in the rivulets,
And you who live in the cool mountain springs
And in the cities empty of markets and cattle and gods,
And in the empty houses and chapels
And who live in cathedrals and in stūpas,
And in the hermit's abode and in the bull's manger,
And who live in the palaces of kings,
And where lanes meet and in the cross-roads,
And who are beside the highway and the solitary tree,
And in the great cemeteries and great forests,
And the homes of lions, bears, and beasts of prey,
And who live in the vast wildernesses where it is right to be afraid,
And you who live in the best of countries,
And you who live in the crowded cemeteries,
Who live there in joy and contentment—
If [we] offer you praise and tormas, butter lamps, and respect,
And garlands, scent, unguents, and flowers,

Receive them, take them well,
And bring our acts to fruition!

Make the Gift of Dharma—

Oṃ ye dharmā hetu prabhavā hetunteṣāna tathāgato hya vadata teṣāñca yo nirodha evaṃ vādī mahāśramaṇaye svāhā

This is the Buddha's teaching:
Do no evil!
Perform a wealth of virtues!
Tame your own mind completely!

Request to go

Oṃ sarva lokapāla gaccha

DEDICATING THE THIRD [TORMA] TO THE OBSTRUCTORS

With the ego of the Diamond Wrathful One, bind them with the *hūṃ*-maker gesture—

Vajra mahāśrīherukoñāhaṃ

Invite them—

Namoḥ! By the power of the true word of the glorious holy lamas—the reverend fundamental [lama] and his lineage, and by the truth of the secret mantras, knowledge mantras, spell mantras, essences (*snying po*), gestures, and the contemplative equipoise (*ting nge 'dzin*) of the Buddha, dharma, and the spiritual community, and by the blessing of the great truth—all classes of obstructors that there may be—come here this instant!

Oṃ ṭākki hūṃ jaḥ

Make Offerings to them

Oṃ guṃkari guṃkari svāhā oṃ pici pici svāhā oṃ guṃ guṃ svāhā sarva bighaṃ grihṇedaṃ arghaṃ . . . , etc.

At the end of the mantra above, "*Oṃ guṃkari* . . . ," give the torma by saying:

Sarva bighānnaḥ . . . , etc.

—three times. With diamond palms and snapping your fingers—

Whoever moves by night—
Ghosts and carnivores
And ghouls who eat raw meat,
And various species of sentient beings
Who live in the thick-trunked trees and elsewhere,
And you and you, we offer you this torma—

Food with meat, beer, radish, parboiled rice, and many fruits!
Be satisfied with this offering
And pacify your harmful thoughts!
And from now on, cultivate
Thoughts of helping us!
Ornament religion and practice it!
Pacify and purify the true vow!
All ghosts—give up punishment!
You are monks and lay-brethren or brahmins.
There is no one who is not afraid of weapons!
Everyone fears for his own life!
Taking your own body as an example,
Do no harm to others!

Oṃ! Whoever you are, be you great or small,
Cast out all illnesses
That cause actual harm to the body,
And then go home, malignant ones!
Since we have thus given
As much worship and respectful service as we were able,
Remain in your vows and,
Fulfill our wishes!
Always remain in your vows
And cure every illness
Of every sentient being here!
Malignant ones, go home!

Say this and make the gift of dharma as before, and [make them] depart by—

Oṃ sarvabighāṃ gaccha

Expel any and all [particularly] vicious and coarse-tempered ones by mustering your diamond wrath and uttering the four-*hūṃ* mantra, and by fierce-sounding music. Cleanse the tormas and throw them out one by one. Furthermore, make this prayer—

Any ghosts who have gathered here
Or live on Earth or else in the sky, wherever you are,
Always love the multitudes of beings,
And day and night, practice only religion!

This three-part torma ritual was excerpted from many textbooks on the [transmitted] word of the early translations, and from *The Torma Ritual Belonging to the Great Ceremony of Nyangter Kagye, the Blissful Gathering (sGrub chen [nyang gter bka' brgyad] bde gshegs 'dus pa'i gtor chog)*, etc. It has been done to agree, rather than be at odds with, the New Translation school. It was composed by the Buddhist lay-brother, the knowledge holder Gyurme Dorje (Śākya upāsaka rig pa 'dzin pa 'Gyur med rdo rje).

—16—

An Avalokiteśvara Sādhana

Janet Gyatso

For All Beings Throughout Space is an example of a tantric sādhana, or "means for accomplishing," as the term is translated in Tibetan (*sgrub thabs*). A sādhana is a meditative visualization technique by which a Buddhist attempts to "accomplish" identification with the Buddha Śākyamuni, or any of the other buddhas, bodhisattvas, or enlightened deities in the tantric Buddhist pantheon. *For All Beings Throughout Space* describes a visualization of Avalokiteśvara, the bodhisattva of compassion, depicted here in his four-armed guise. Avalokiteśvara is well known in Mahāyāna sūtras and tantras as well as in local traditions throughout Asia and appears in a variety of forms in addition to the one described here.

The theory of sādhana meditation is discussed in a number of Sanskrit and Tibetan works. In brief, practitioners imagine themselves as having become a particular buddha figure. This visualized identity is effected in three dimensions of personhood: bodily form, verbal expression, and mental state. It is believed that by visualizing themselves as having the prescribed features of the buddha figure in these three dimensions—as looking like the buddha figure, as chanting its mantra, and as assuming its mental state—the meditator will eventually become that buddha in reality. The assumption is that a person's identity, experience, and existence are self-created, and therefore can be manipulated at will, given the appropriate training and (a universally stipulated prerequisite) a prior receipt of the sādhana technique in a transmission ritual given by a qualified teacher. Another assumption underlying sādhana practice is that the manifest features of the buddha figure so depicted in the text—that is, its iconography, its mantras, and the descriptions of its state of mind—precisely reflect that figure's enlightenment state as such, and thus are efficacious tools to effect the desired transformation from imagined identity to reality. Such a transformation in the practitioner is said to be possible in a single lifetime, a claim that is often made about the efficacy of tantric practice in order to contrast it favorably with the more gradually obtained results of sūtra-based practice, said to require many lifetimes.

Although the theory of sādhana practice would seem to imply that the manifest features of a buddha figure are strictly determined, in fact the many sādhanas extant in Sanskrit and Tibetan for a given buddha or deity figure vary considerably, both in the description of the deity and its mantra and in the visualization technique prescribed. This is due to the nature of the source of the sādhanas, which in many cases is characterized as a vision experienced by the sādhana's author. Since the deity seen in a vision can differ from its normative iconography, so too the sādhana based on that vision can be innovative as well. Such variation is sanctioned by standard Mahāyāna theory, which posits that buddhas and bodhisattvas change appearance at will in order to accord with the varying needs of sentient beings. This theory also made possible the incorporation of local Tibetan deities into Buddhist canons.

The *For All Beings Throughout Space* sādhana is said to be based upon a vision of the bodhisattva Avalokiteśvara (a "direct transmission") experienced by Tangtong Gyelpo (Thang stong rgyal po). This eclectic Tibetan yogin and Buddhist teacher of the fourteenth to fifteenth centuries was also a civic engineer who built over fifty iron-chain suspension bridges in Tibet, western China, and Bhutan. *For All Beings Throughout Space* is universally attributed to Tangtong Gyelpo, but the text is not signed, and there is no independent historical information on its composition; the first commentary on the text that assumes his authorship is written in the early sixteenth century.

Tangtong Gyelpo's interest in public works is reflected in the pithy brevity of the *For All Beings Throughout Space* sādhana, features that distinguish it from other Tibetan Avalokiteśara sādhanas, which tend to be long and complex. Valued for its simple yet suggestive content incorporating the meditation styles of the "inner tantras," the text is perhaps the most popular (and shortest) Avalokiteśvara sādhana in Tibet. It can be chanted by heart by many persons, both lay and monastic, of both genders, from many parts of the country, in all the Tibetan Buddhist sects, and at all levels of society.

For All Beings Throughout Space employs several notable techniques. One concerns the relationship between the practitioner and the visualized figure. Some sādhanas instruct practitioners to imagine the buddha figure sitting in the air in front of them, sending rays of light and blessings into them, but not effecting an identification of the practitioner with the buddha, a technique called the "generation in front"; other sādhanas prescribe that the practitioner imagine his or her mundane body and experience as having dissolved into emptiness and been replaced by a new appearance of the self *as* the buddha figure, called the "self-generation" (see chapter 14). The *For All Beings Throughout Space* sādhana represents a middle position between these "in-front" and "as-self" types of visualization: it begins with a third variation, a visualization of the buddha figure "on top of the head" of the practitioner, but culminates with a full identification of the practitioner with that figure.

The sādhana starts, as is standard in Buddhist practice, when the practitioner "takes refuge" in the Buddha, his teachings, and the community of his followers. The sādhana's author does not supply a liturgy for this initial step, instead allowing practitioners to insert verses of their choice. The sādhana proper commences when the practitioner imagines him or herself to be seated in meditation and surrounded by all beings in the universe. That the ensuing images are seen as occurring simultaneously in the experience of all these beings, rather than being limited to the practitioner, is another distinctive feature of this sādhana.

A lotus flower sprouts out of the practitioner's (and all beings') fontanelle at the top of the skull. Poised above the tips of the flower's petals is a moon-shaped cushion upon which the visualized bodhisattva will sit. Reflecting tantric theories of embryology, the appearance of the bodhisattva is preceded by a mantric "seed syllable," which is thought to encode the enlightenment of the figure that it symbolizes and to be capable of generating the figure itself, just as the seed of parents gives rise to a child. The syllable here is *hrīḥ*, which is often associated with Avalokiteśvara. As the commentaries on the *For All Beings Throughout Space* sādhana explain, the practitioner imagines the *hrīḥ* to be formed of brilliant white light rays that become so intense that they spontaneously reformulate into the full-blown figure of the bodhisattva. The practitioner then focuses on imagining the bodhisattva on his or her head as described in the sādhana. The description is close to the four-armed Avalokiteśvara's traditional iconography. Each element is significant: the white color of his body signifies cool compassion; the lotus held in his hand symbolizes the bodhisattva, whose beauty grows right in the "mud" of saṃsāra; the antelope hide signifies the bodhisattva's compassion for all sentient beings; and so forth. The two "upper" hands here are in the homage gesture; other four-armed Avalokiteśvaras hold a wish-fulfilling gem in those hands. The buddha Amitābha sits on his crown because Avalokiteśvara belongs to the "family" headed by that buddha.

The prayer of praise that the practitioner, along with all sentient beings, sings to the bodhisattva functions as an invocation. The bodhisattva, moved by the sincerity with which the praise is uttered, emits liquid light rays that enter the top of the head of the practitioner and all sentient beings, filling their bodies, dispelling all confusion and bad karma, and transforming the practitioner into Avalokiteśvara. Simultaneously, the light rays spread over the entire universe and turn the environment ("the outer container") into the pure land of Avalokiteśvara, and all beings (the "inner contents") into Avalokiteśvara. While visualizing this sequence, the practitioner repeats the most famous of the Avalokiteśvara mantras, *oṃ maṇi padme hūṃ* (see chapter 2). All the while, the practitioner remains focused upon the empty nature of the mantra's sounds, and of the images being visualized, which are maintained in mind during the mantra recitation period.

At the end of the mantra repetition, the practitioner enters into meditative absorption, endeavoring to set aside all conceptions, including those prescribed by the sādhana itself. Such a contemplative phase is often included in sādhanas, and its description is close to that of other sorts of Buddhist practices, such as insight meditation or Chan sitting, with the exception that it is framed, and evoked, by visualizations preceding and succeeding it.

The final portion of the *For All Beings Throughout Space* sādhana corresponds to what is termed "carryover practices" in certain tantric traditions. Emerging from the meditative absorption and returning to daily life, the practitioner endeavors to continue to see all perceptions of body, speech, and mind as those of the enlightened bodhisattva. All sentient beings, including the self, are to be seen as the bodhisattva; all sounds are understood to be his mantra; all mental phenomena are seen as his mind. The sādhana concludes with the conventional "sharing of merit" that has been gained by performing the practice, here phrased as an aspiration to win enlightenment as Avalokiteśvara in order to help the rest of the world achieve liberation as well.

The translation below is of the *'Gro don mkha' khyab ma*, single-page block print, widely available. The text is published in several collections, including 'Jam dbyangs mkhyen brtse'i dbang po and 'Jam dbyangs blo gter dbang po, eds., *Sgrub thabs kun btus* (Dehra Dun: G. T. K. Lodoy, N. Gyaltsen, and N. Lungtok, 1970), vol. Ga.

Further Reading

For more on the life and accomplishments of Tangtong Gyelpo, see Janet Gyatso, "Genre, Authorship, and Transmission in Visionary Buddhism: The Literary Traditions of Thang-stong rGyal-po," in *Tibetan Buddhism: Reason and Revelation*, ed. Steven Goodman and Ronald Davidson (Albany, N.Y.: SUNY Press, 1992), pp. 95–106. For a detailed study of Tibetan tantric liturgy and sādhana, see Stephan Beyer, *The Cult of Tārā: Magic and Ritual in Tibet* (Berkeley: University of California Press, 1978).

The Direct Transmission of the Great Adept Tangtong Gyelpo, "King of the Empty Plain," Entitled *For All Beings Throughout Space*

[First] take refuge

On the crown of my head
And that of all sentient beings throughout space
Is a white lotus and a moon [-shaped seat].
On top of that is [the syllable] *hrīḥ*
From which [appears]
The precious, noble Avalokiteśvara.
He is white and luminous
And he radiates light rays of five colors.
He is beautiful and smiling
And he sees with compassionate eyes.

Of his four hands,
The palms of the upper two are held together.
In the lower two
He holds a crystal rosary and a white lotus.
Silks and precious ornaments adorn him.
He wears the hide of an antelope across his chest,
And a crown ornamented by Amitābha.
Seated with his two legs in the crossed thunderbolt position,
He leans his back against a pure moon.
He is, by nature, the epitome of all refuges.

Think that I and all sentient beings are praying to him, in one voice:

Lord,
You are unmarred by fault,
And white in body hue.
The perfect buddha ornaments your crown,
And you see beings with compassionate eyes.
I bow to you, Avalokiteśvara.

Recite that three, seven, or as many times as possible.

As a result of this one-pointed prayer,
Light beams radiate out
From the body of the noble one,
And purify defiled karmic appearances and confusion.
The outer container becomes the Land of Bliss.
The inner contents—the body, speech, and mind of beings—
Become the perfected form, teachings, and heart-mind of
Avalokiteśvara.
Appearance and sound turn into indivisible awareness-emptiness.

While meditating on that, recite the six syllables [the mantra *oṃ maṇi padme hūṃ*]. At the end, remain absorbed in the own-state of no-conception about the three circles [doer, done-to, or deed].

My and others' bodies are the perfected form of the noble one.
Voices and sounds are the rhythm of the six syllables.
Memories and thoughts are the expanse of great primal consciousness.

Through the merit resulting [from performing this visualization]
May I quickly come to achieve [identification with] Avalokiteśvara,
And then may I establish every single being without exception in that
state.

—17—

A Fasting Ritual

Roger Jackson

Fasting rituals have been an important element of religious life in Tibetan culture areas for centuries. The collected writings of many of Tibet's greatest lamas include the texts of fasting rituals, and, in more recent times, anthropologists have explored the social and performative dimensions of the rite. In most places, the fasting ritual or *nyungne* (*smyung gnas*) is held annually and draws members of the laity to the local monastery or temple for three days of prayer, prostration, and ascetic practices focused on the great compassionate bodhisattva, Avalokiteśvara or Chenrezi (Spyan ras gzigs). Though there is no solid historical evidence that the type of fasting ritual practiced in Tibetan culture areas originated in India, Tibetans writers do trace the lineage of its practice back to India, and the Tibetan rite clearly combines in it a number of elements that are crucial to Buddhism in India, and elsewhere in Asia.

Socially, the fasting ritual is an instance of a common Buddhist phenomenon: occasions on which laypeople are permitted for a time to participate in the life of their society's most valued religious institution, the monastery or temple. The hallmark of such occasions, whatever their locale or duration, is the assumption by laypeople of some of the vows incumbent upon monastics. In lands throughout Buddhist Asia, laypeople will gather on new- and/or full-moon days (in Tibetan areas, more often the lunar tenth or twenty-fifth days) at their local monastery or temple, observe eight vows (against killing, stealing, lying, sexual activity, using intoxicants, eating after noon, entertainment and ornamentation, and taking an exalted seat), and spend the day praying, making offerings, and listening to religious discourses. The eight vows also may be taken for life by men or women who wish to renounce the world outside the monastic context, or women who wish to live a monastic life but are barred from doing so by the loss of the lineage of ordination. Women also may take for life the same ten vows as a novice monk (the eight listed, with the seventh divided into two and the promise not to handle money added as the tenth). The Tibetan fasting ritual is most closely modeled on the traditions involving lay attendance at monasteries and temples on lunar cycle days; however, it is scheduled less frequently, lasts longer, and is more demanding.

The fasting ritual is also an instance of a phenomenon that is not only Buddhist, but universal: asceticism. Such practices as fasting, silence, and celibacy have found a place in most of the world's religious traditions. Like all ascetic practices, they are aimed at reducing the individual's concern with outer, physical matters and increasing their concern with the inner and spiritual dimension of life. Most traditions believe that by undergoing the hardships involved in ascetic practices, individuals are "purified" and thereby made more capable of the sort of transformation that is held out as the ideal of human life—whether it is described as salvation, nirvāṇa, or living as God or the ancestors may prescribe. Buddhism often has been seen as a tradition that eschews asceticism. The Buddha, after all, tried and rejected the life of extreme austerity, and prescribed for his followers a "middle way" between asceticism and hedonism. It must be remembered, however, that the life of a Buddhist monk or nun was, by the standards of lay life in any culture or era, an austere one: celibacy was required, and while neither fasting nor silence was considered essential to spiritual progress, such practices often were adopted by the great meditators and adepts who have been the tradition's most charismatic and influential figures.

Cultically, the fasting ritual is an instance of the worship of Avalokiteśvara, the compassionate "Down-Looking Lord" who is perhaps the most popular deity of Mahāyāna Buddhism. Avalokiteśvara first assumes textual prominence in the Pure Land sūtras, where he is an attendant of the savior-buddha Amitābha ("Infinite Light"). In the *Lotus Sūtra*, he is described as a great being who hears the appeals of all those in distress and comes to their aid. In a sūtra devoted entirely to him, the *Karaṇḍavyūha*, he possesses his own pure land, on Mount Potala, to which he will bring all those who pray to him or recite his six-syllable mantra, *oṃ maṇi padme hūṃ*. In the tantric tradition, he takes on a variety of forms (often numbered at 108), any one of which a practitioner may ritually serve and contemplatively identify with. Wherever Mahāyāna spread in Asia, Avalokiteśvara followed: he was worshipped in Southeast Asia as Lokanātha, the "Lord of the World," in China, in a feminine guise, as the graceful savioress, Kuan Yin (Guanyin), and in Japan as the multifaceted, powerful Kannon. So important was he in Tibet that he came to be considered the father and protector of the nation, incarnate in the great early kings who promoted Buddhism and in the Dalai Lamas (see chapter 2). Avalokiteśvara also protects individual devotees from rebirth into the various realms of cyclic existence: the six-syllable mantra is often on the lips of the faithful, especially elderly laypeople. The particular form of Avalokiteśvara to which the fasting ritual is devoted is his most elaborate, that with eleven heads and a thousand arms. According to tradition, frustrated by the seeming infinity of beings to save, Avalokiteśvara felt his body and head split apart; his guiding buddha, Amitābha, restored him, giving him a thousand arms and eleven heads, Amitābha's own being topmost. The eleven heads express all moods and see in all directions; each of the thousand hands has in its palm an eye of wisdom, symbolic of Avalokiteśvara's perfect fusion of compassion, discernment, and skill in assisting suffering beings.

The actual historical origins of the fasting ritual itself are obscure. The most common legend of its foundation traces it back to India and tells of a poor, detested Indian woman afflicted with leprosy, who in desperation worshipped Avalokiteśvara in something like a prototype of the fasting ritual. He cured her, and out of gratitude, she took full ordination as a Buddhist nun. It is in remembrance of her that participants in the fasting ritual imagine that the Long Request Prayer at the heart of the rite (section III.E.1) actually is recited by this nun, Lakṣmī. A second legend, related among the Sherpas of Nepal, tells of a group of seven demons who enjoyed feasting daily on humans. One female demon, Adakpalum, had five hundred children, and each of them captured and ate a human being each day. A great lama, Dzichen Rinpoche, managed to capture one of Adakpalum's sons and returned him to her only on the condition that she and her brood desist from cannibalism. They did so, and Adakpalum, having experienced the temporary loss of her son, came to understand how the families of her victims must feel. She repented and convinced her fellow demons to do likewise. Dzichen Rinpoche then prescribed for all of them as a penance three years of continuous practice of the fasting ritual. As a result of observing it purely, the former demons were reborn in Amitābha's paradise, Sukhāvatī, and because the fasting ritual proved so efficacious, it was institutionalized and prescribed for ordinary laypeople who wished to purify negative karma and accumulate merit.

As noted above, the fasting ritual is practiced throughout the Inner Asian area influenced by Tibetan forms of Buddhism, including Nepal, Bhutan, Sikkim, Ladakh, Mongolia, Tibet itself, and, since 1959, in the Tibetan diaspora. The ritual is most often undertaken on an annual basis, in the period preceding the celebration of Wesak, the anniversary of the Buddha's birth, enlightenment, and final nirvāṇa (May–June). Though the rite occasionally was performed by monks in the great Tibetan monasteries, it really is a layperson's practice and so has most often been practiced in smaller monasteries or temples that play a central role in the life of a lay community. Usually, the ritual will be conducted by the local lama or lamas, who often are monks but also (as in the Nyingma tradition) may be laymen; the vast majority of participants are laypeople, and the majority of those middle-aged or older.

The ritual itself formally takes two and a half days, though a day of preparations and a celebratory conclusion may draw the process out for four full days. On the day of preparation, the presiding lama or lamas generally will conduct a ceremony of propitiation to the earth-deities, who are urged to purify the place where the fasting ritual will occur. The lamas also will prepare the ritual altar, replete with water bowls, various offering substances (including specially molded dough offerings called *torma*), and images of the ritual's presiding deity, Avalokiteśvara. If necessary, the lamas may conduct a permission ceremony or empowerment, which will permit those participating in the ritual to visualize themselves as Avalokiteśvara—a quintessentially tantric procedure that requires formal initiation.

The actual fasting ritual begins the next day at dawn with the taking of eight vows. On this day, just one meal (almost always vegetarian) is taken, at noon. Most of the day is spent in three separate performances of the actual fasting ritual (section III), from going for refuge right through to the final dedication of merit. The centerpiece of each ritual session is the chanting of a long "vow prayer" directed to Avalokiteśvara (section III.E.1). As the practitioners recite it (seeing themselves as Avalokiteśvara), they prostrate their bodies fully toward the image of Avalokiteśvara on the altar, as well as toward a visualized Avalokiteśvara they picture constantly before them. The chanting of this prayer while one simultaneously prostrates and visualizes is believed to be especially efficacious in purifying negative imprints and generating merit.

On the second day of the actual ritual, precepts again are taken at dawn, but the strictures on participants on this day will be far more severe: no food at all is to be ingested, and not a drop of liquid is to be drunk—not even, it is said, one's own saliva! Also, apart from the chanting that is done during the three ritual sessions, silence is strictly observed: there is to be no conversation whatsoever. This second day of the ritual is the most grueling, for to chant and perform hundreds of prostrations on an empty stomach is no easy task; also, the elimination of speaking as an outlet adds psychological pressure to the physical duress. It is not unusual for participants to feel weak and highly emotional during the second day. Yet the hardship they are enduring is believed to serve as a powerful purifier, and it is borne stoically, if not always enthusiastically.

Silence and the fast are maintained until the morning of the third day. No precepts are taken, and after a final session of the ritual (in which the obligatory chants and prostrations are lessened), the participants are given a great meal to mark the formal conclusion of the retreat. The celebration often will continue through the day, culminating in an evening offering ceremony accompanied by a ritual feast, at the conclusion of which volunteers and donors will come forward to begin planning for the next year's fasting ritual. It might be noted that although the schedule just described is most typical, on occasion the ritual may cover the entire two weeks prior to Wesak, with pairs of one-meal and fast days following one another again and again. This makes for a retreat whose intensity and difficulty is comparable to that of the austere retreats in Zen monasteries (*rohatsu sesshin*).

In the context of the normative spiritual vision of the Tibetan Buddhist world, the major purposes of the fasting ritual are those already suggested: the purification of negative karma and the accumulation of merit. Given Buddhist assumptions about the infinity of previous rebirths we all have had and the deluded way in which we have conducted ourselves through most of those rebirths, it is axiomatic that we all bear with us in our mindstreams the seeds sown by countless actions motivated by greed, anger, and ignorance. According to karmic theory, each of these seeds must bear fruit and will do so when the appropriate conditions arise. In most Buddhist traditions, however, this rather gloomy prospect is mitigated by the assurance that—short of attaining a full enlightenment that will destroy all previous negative karma—one may delay such fruition through cultivating positive actions and reduce or even eliminate some negative results through sincere repentance and purification. Generally, it is assumed that the more zealous the pursuit of purification, the greater the number of negative seeds that will be destroyed or damaged. Thus, an ascetic discipline like that imposed in the fasting ritual, in which repentance is expressed and penance performed in the presence of a loving and potent deity, is held to be especially efficacious. At the same time, the generation, during the ritual, of positive states of mind (devotion, compassion, some insight into the nature of reality) sows positive seeds in the mindstream, which will bear fruit in this and future lives, delaying the fruition of unpurified negativity, and increasing one's potential to attain the ultimate positive condition, enlightenment itself.

Typically, the normative view of the benefits of the fasting ritual is expressed in terms of its effects on the individual. Clearly, however, there is also a social dimension to the practice, unstated but highly important. On the broadest level, as a collective experience, the fasting ritual provides for the participants a natural sense of community, which ideally will extend beyond the ritual period and find expression in people's ordinary lives. The greater the proportion of a community that participates in the fasting ritual, the greater the ritual's effect on social cohesion will be. The fact that the ritual centers on the worship of the great merciful bodhisattva, Avalokiteśvara, and that one attempts both to receive and to identify with his boundless compassion, only reinforces the potential for its effecting social cohesion: compassion and forgiveness are, obviously, of considerable social value, whatever their "karmic" effects on the individual. A further social function of the fasting ritual is to bring the lay and monastic communities together. Laypeople are permitted for a time to share in something resembling a monastic life-style, and thereby to gain access to the sort of religious power usually reserved for the clergy. Still, the ritual is overseen by lamas, and the attitude laypeople are likely to develop from the experience is perhaps less often one of spiritual self-sufficiency than of gratitude to and a renewed sense of dependence upon the clergy. A further social function that may be performed by the fasting ritual is that of easing the transition to a less active life for that considerable proportion of the participants who are older people. In Buddhist cultures, one form of "retirement"—especially for widows and widowers—is to join a monastery, and the fasting ritual clearly paves the way for this.

Both Tibetans themselves and Western scholars have tended to view Tibetan Buddhism as a "complete" Buddhism, one that weaves together into a single tradition virtually every strand of thought and practice that developed in the Indian Buddhism from which the Tibetans drew their inspiration. Such a characterization may be a bit simplistic, but there is an element of truth to it. From the eighth to the fourteenth century, Tibetans self-consciously appropriated as much of North Indian Buddhism as they could, and they attempted to organize a vast body of material into a coherent, integrated system. The fasting ritual exemplifies this, and we can see in it a subtle integration of the three major "vehicles" of Indian Buddhism: Hīnayāna, Mahāyāna, and the tantric tradition, the Mantrayāna or Vajrayāna, which is itself a subset of Mahāyāna. Also, the ritual reflects a remarkable combination of three approaches to religiousness identified in India, and often seen as equally valuable but incompatible: ritual, knowledge, and devotion.

From the Tibetan perspective, the most important feature of Hīnayāna Buddhism is its promulgation of standards of morality. In particular, the Hīnayāna tradition has contributed to Buddhism as a whole the basic sets of vows to be observed by laypeople and monastics. Lay practitioners generally will observe a set of five vows, against killing, stealing, lying, sexual misconduct, and taking intoxicants; fully ordained monks will observe well over two hundred vows, and fully ordained nuns (who are rare outside China nowadays) will observe well over three hundred. The set of eight vows, which are taken by participants on the two full days of the fasting ritual, clearly fall somewhere in between lay and full monastic vows: they extend lay vows by forbidding all sexual activity rather than just sexual misconduct, as well as by severely restricting usual modes of eating and entertainment; at the same time, they fall well short of full monasticism by their failure to regulate behavior in anywhere near the detail that full vows do (see chapter 20). Though the eight vows taken by fasting ritual participants are regarded as "Mahāyāna" precepts, and the prayer that precedes them (section II) does employ distinctively Mahāyāna terminology, the vows themselves are identical to those taken by "Hīnayānists"; there is nothing specifically Mahāyānist about them, and they remain the most clearly Hīnayāna aspect of the rite.

Tibetan Buddhists are self-consciously Mahāyānist, so it is not surprising that the fasting ritual contains many elements typical of the Great Vehicle. We already have noted that one way of locating the rite in the history of Buddhism is by considering it as a manifestation of the cult of Avalokiteśvara. As noted above, only in Mahāyāna texts and cultures is Avalokiteśvara so important a deity, and only there does compassion receive so central an emphasis in religious rhetoric. Similarly, while the purification of negative karma and accumulation of merit that are immediate goals of the fasting ritual are common to Hīnayāna and Mahāyāna practices, the achievement of complete buddhahood that is the ultimate purpose of the fasting ritual is a uniquely Mahāyānist ideal: in the prayer preceding the taking of precepts (section II), one expresses the hope of achieving "the stage of fully completed buddhahood," and at the conclusion of each ritual session (section III.M), one prays that one may oneself someday "become a greatly compassionate one," equal in knowledge, compassion, and power to the Buddha himself. This sort of aspiration is encountered only infrequently outside the Mahāyāna.

Also, the ritual is framed in a distinctly Mahāyāna way. Though it begins like almost any Buddhist practice with an invocation of the three jewels of refuge, the Buddha, dharma, and saṅgha, the text immediately adds a uniquely Mahāyāna touch by insisting that the practitioner generate the thought of enlightenment, *bodhicitta*, the aspiration to attain the full enlightenment of buddhahood so that one may assist all sentient beings in their temporal and spiritual undertakings (section II). This spirit is supposed to inform every action that one performs, within the ritual or outside it. As the ritual in general and (though it is not stated) each session begins with a distinctly Mahāyānist aspiration, so it concludes with one: the wish that any merit one may have accrued not be selfishly hoarded but, rather, be "dedicated" to the enlightenment of others (sections III.I, III.M, IV). In between the initial aspiration and final dedication, there is much else that is typically Mahāyāna: reference to the nature of the reality as emptiness (*śūnyatā*); active visualization of the deity one worships, Avalokiteśvara; praise of him in the most elaborate terms; and the performance for him of the seven-branch liturgy and various ablutions—all elements of proper ritual (*pūjā*) that Mahāyānists freely adapted from Hindu models.

The tantric tradition of Mahāyāna—known as the Mantrayāna or Vajrayāna—was the dominant style of Buddhism during the period when Tibetans absorbed the religion from India, and the fasting ritual, like virtually any Tibetan practice-tradition, is deeply influenced by tantric conceptions. Perhaps the most crucial of these is the idea that the practitioner must identify with the deity to whom the ritual is directed, in this case by visualizing himself or herself as possessing the body, speech, and mind of Avalokiteśvara. This "preenactment" of the wisdom, form, and functions one will attain at the time of enlightenment is known as "taking the goal as path" and is unique to tantric traditions of meditation. It cannot be practiced without a formal initiation from a lama, whether the initiation be a full empowerment imposing long-term vows and responsibilities upon the disciple or a permission ceremony of more limited scope. The fasting ritual is not only a rite of worship, purification, and merit-making, but a tantric sādhana, or meditative scenario, which involves first reducing oneself and one's environment to a natural state of emptiness; then from that state of emptiness generating the deity both in front of and as oneself; next drawing into the visualized deity, or "pledge being," the actual deity, or "wisdom being," and receiving blessings in the form of light from the actual deity; reciting various mantras of the deity's and performing various ritual movements, including prostrations and hand-gestures (*mudrā*); making offerings of dough-cakes, *tormas*, to transmundane and worldly divinities; and, finally, dismissing/dissolving the visualized deity—though afterward, one is to resume not one's ordinary form, but a simplified version of Avalokiteśvara, with whom one continues to identify (see chapters 13, 14, and 16).

As the fasting ritual reflects an integration of the three vehicles of Indo-Tibetan Buddhism, so, too, does it integrate in a remarkable fashion the three "yogas," or approaches to the divine that have been singled out—and often considered quite separately—in Indian traditions: devotion, knowledge, and ritual. That devotion is central to the ritual is fairly obvious: verse after verse refers to the salvific, purifying powers of Avalokiteśvara, whose intervention is requested repeatedly in the most heartfelt manner. The verses of praise and request, in particular (sections III.E–F), stand as beautiful examples of what might be called Buddhist devotionalism (*bhakti*). Knowledge, on the other hand, is not so obviously a part of the text—certainly, there is little in it that is overtly philosophical. However, the tantric element of the ritual is predicated on the practitioners' ability to reduce themselves to emptiness, then to visualize themselves as Avalokiteśvara while simultaneously being aware of the visualization's empty nature. Also, by seeing themselves as Avalokiteśvara, practitioners imitate his omniscient mind, which has direct knowledge of all conventional and ultimate truths. All this, in turn, requires that one have at least an "imaginative" understanding of the nature of reality, which requires at least a general philosophical appreciation for ultimate truth—hence a certain type of knowledge. Indeed, it is important to remember that normative Buddhism in Tibet is essentially a gnostic enterprise, and that the most passionate devotee or obsessive ritualist must have knowledge of the true nature of things in order to attain the prescribed goal of full buddhahood.

The fasting ritual is, of course, above all a ritual—it is identified by the Tibetan word for rite or ritual, *cho ga.* What does this mean, though? In the most general sense, religious ritual involves the repeated performance of certain prescribed actions, which are believed to narrow the gulf between the human and the divine. In the fasting ritual, the divine that one hopes to effectuate is Avalokiteśvara, and the actions one performs are hallowed by tradition and intensified by repetition. What is more, tantric ritual is repeated, prescribed action that is deliberately integrative of the whole human person. Here, the practitioner's body (through prostration and hand-gestures), speech (through mantra and prayer), and mind (through visualization and contemplation) are all involved in the ritual process.

The fasting ritual, like so many Tibetan ritual practices, is like a fabric in which many diverse strands have been woven together: Hīnayāna discipline, Mahāyāna worship and aspiration, and tantric meditative procedures; passionate devotion, detached understanding of reality, and detailed ritual performance; and, finally, activity by all elements of the participant's person: body, speech, and mind. Tibetan Buddhism may or may not really be "complete" Buddhism, but the fasting ritual provides compelling evidence that, at the very least, it is a complex and many-layered tradition.

The fasting ritual text translated below is entitled the "Nectar-Drop: The Extremely Condensed Fasting Ritual of Eleven-Headed Avalokiteśvara." It was composed by Tuken Chökyi Nyima (Thu'u bkwan chos kyi nyi ma, 1737–1802), a great scholiast of the Gelukpa sect of Tibetan Buddhism. As with many ritual texts, Tuken's involves more than appears on paper. It is, after all, meant to be performed, and while in Tibetan traditions ritual performance is usually keyed to texts, it is by no means enslaved to them. Thus, depending on the circumstances of a ritual performance (the nature and capacity of the participants, the inclinations of the presiding lama), sections may be added or subtracted from the text, without the performance thereby ceasing to be "of" that text. Performances of Tuken's text often will involve changes of ordering (for example, the abbreviated sevenfold liturgy sometimes is recited much later) or the addition of other prayers and practices, most notably: refuge and thought of enlightenment prayers, which will be recited at the outset of every ritual session, prior to consecrating the offerings; the maṇḍala offering of Mount Meru, the continents and various precious substances, which may be added after the seven-branch liturgy; and a four-line version of the vow prayer, which may be recited in lieu of the long one as one prostrates. In addition, Tuken occasionally gives instructions in so sketchy a manner that interpolation is required to follow them; for instance, he specifies toward the beginning of the ritual session that one should "take refuge, generate the thought of enlightenment, and contemplate the four immeasurables." Each of these entails a specific prayer that must be recited, usually three times. Similarly, when Tuken incorporates into his text much material that he has drawn from earlier texts, he will give only the first line; the rest is to be supplied by the practitioner, who is presumed to know it.

In the translation below, prayers given by Tuken in abbreviated form have been spelled out fully; the only other addition made to the printed text is to supply section titles, so that the text's structure may be clearer. Sections that communicate instructions are set apart here in smaller type. Sections that are metrical in the original are broken into poetic lines here, though no attempt has been made to duplicate the original meter. Finally, mantras have been translated to the degree that their syllables have a discernible meaning; untranslatable syllables, such as *oṃ*, *hūṃ*, and *phaṭ*, have been left as they are. The mantras have been translated simply so the reader may get a sense of the mixture of semantic and lexical items of which they are composed; it must be recalled, however, that the power of a mantra resides not in its semantic sense but in the sounds themselves, each of which, and in various combinations, has particular divine associations. That is why Tibetans invariably write and recite mantras in the original Sanskrit, and in most cases have no idea what a mantra's "translation" (or, on occasion, original pronunciation) may be.

The translation is from *Spyan ras gzigs zhal bcu gcig pa'i smyung gnas kyi cho ga shin tu bsdus pa bdud rtsi thigs pa zhes bya ba,* from *The Collected Works (gsung 'bum) of Thu'u bkvan Chos kyi nyi ma* (New Delhi: Ngawang Gelek Demo, 1969), vol. 5, folios 233–46.

Further Reading

An earlier translation appears in *Eleven-Headed Avalokiteśvara's Fasting Ritual Condensed into a Nectar Drop*, trans. Roger Jackson, with additional trans. by John Makransky (Oregon, WI: Deer Park Books, 1989). See also the Seventh Dalai Lama, *Nyung Nä: The Means of Achievement of the Eleven-Faced Great Compassionate One, Avalakiteśhvara*, trans. Lama Thubten Zopa Rinpoche and George Churinoff (Boston: Wisdom Publications, 1995). For anthropological studies of this ritual in the Nepali context, see Christoph von Fürer-Haimendorf, *The Sherpas of Nepal: Buddhist Highlanders* (Berkeley and Los Angeles: University of California Press, 1964), pp. 180–85; and Sherry B. Ortner, *Sherpas through Their Rituals* (Cambridge: Cambridge University Press, 1978), pp. 33–60.

Nectar-Drop: The Extremely Condensed Fasting Ritual of Eleven-Headed Avalokiteśvara

I. AUTHOR'S PREFACE

Having prostrated with my body, speech, and mind to the lotus feet of the kindly guru,
Who is the compassion of all the conquerers gathered into one,
The one with a white lotus who performs as a saffron-clad monk,
I will set down the practice of this fasting ritual.

II. ONE-DAY MAHĀYĀNA PRECEPTS [DAYS 1 AND 2, AT DAWN]

Wishing to perform the fasting ritual of the eleven-faced noble Avalokiteśvara, you should arrange a drawing or actual statue of the body, etc., of the Greatly Compassionate One. Or, if they are unavailable, you should put white points in the center of a mirror, and in front of that put a vase two-thirds filled with pure water. Then, put into the vase the various Action Tantra substances. In front [of the vase] place three rounded tormas and arrange whatever offering is to be received. Then, at daybreak, when the lines of the hand can just be seen, after you have washed well, you should take the one-day Mahāyāna precepts. You should prostrate to the altar, conceiving it as the actual Greatly Compassionate One. First, take refuge [in the Buddha, dharma, and saṅgha], generate the enlightened thought, and contemplate the four immeasurables [love, compassion, joy, and equanimity].

All buddhas and bodhisattvas of the ten directions, with your divine wisdom please pay attention to me. As the previous tathāgatas, the arhats, the fully enlightened buddhas like a divine skillful wise horse, a great elephant, did what had to be done, accomplished all tasks, overcame all the burdens of the five aggregates controlled by delusion and karma, fulfilled all their aspirations by relinquishing their attachments, by speaking immaculately divine words and liberating the minds of all from the bondage of subtle delusions' impression, and who possess great liberated transcendental wisdom, for the sake of all that lives, in order to benefit all, in order to prevent famine, in order to prevent mental and physical sicknesses, in order for living beings to complete a buddha's thirty-seven realizations, and to receive the stage of fully completed buddhahood, I, who am named ____, from now until sunrise tomorrow shall take the eight Mahāyāna precepts just as you have done.

Three times.

From now on I shall not kill, nor steal others' possessions, nor engage in sexual conduct, nor lie. I shall avoid intoxicants from which many mistakes arise. I shall not sit on large, high, expensive beds. I shall not eat food at the wrong time. I shall avoid singing, dancing, and playing music, and I shall not wear perfumes, rosaries or ornaments. As arhats have avoided wrong actions such as taking the lives of others, I shall also avoid actions such as taking the lives of others. May I quickly receive enlightenment and may the living beings who are experiencing various sufferings be released from the ocean of cyclic existence.

To keep morality purely, say twenty-one times:

Oṃ maintain effective morality, maintain, maintain. Being of great purity, lotus-bearing, hold, hold with your hand. Look down continuously *hūṃ phaṭ svāhā.*

III. THE RITUAL SESSION [3 TIMES ON DAYS 1 AND 2, 1 TIME ON DAY 3]

A. Consecrating the Offerings

Instantly I assume the form of the Greatly Compassionate One.

> *Oṃ padmanta kṛta hūṃ phaṭ*
> *Oṃ* naturally pure are all dharmas, naturally pure am I.

I become emptiness. From the state of emptiness comes the syllable *bhrūṃ*. From *bhrūṃ* comes a vast and delicate precious vessel. In it is an *oṃ*. The *oṃ* melts into light. From the light arises drinking water, foot-washing water, flowers, incense, lamps, perfume, food, and music. They are inherently empty. In appearance, they are themselves, but their function is to confer extraordinary undefiled bliss.

> *Oṃ* mouth-water *āḥ hūṃ*.
> *Oṃ* foot-water *āḥ hūṃ*.
> *Oṃ* flowers *āḥ hūṃ*.
> *Oṃ* incense *āḥ hūṃ*.
> *Oṃ* light *āḥ hūṃ*.
> *Oṃ* perfume *āḥ hūṃ*.
> *Oṃ* cakes *āḥ hūṃ*.
> *Oṃ* sound *āḥ hūṃ*.

B. Visualization

> *Oṃ* naturally pure are all dharmas, naturally pure am I.

> I am in the state of natural emptiness that is the inseparability of the dharma-sphere and knowledge.
> In my place and in the space in front of me is a lotus. On it is a moon-seat.
> On the moon is a white *hrīḥ*. From it comes Avalokiteśvara.
> His central face is white, the right is green, the left is red.
> Above those, the central face is green, the right is red, the left is white.

Above those, the central face is red, the right is white, the left is green.
Above those is a dark blue wrathful face. Above that
Is the beautiful face of Amitābha. The two main hands
Are pressed together at the heart. The upper right holds a crystal rosary,
The upper left a lotus. The lower right is in the gesture of supreme giving, the lower left holds a nectar-vase.
The middle right holds a wheel, the middle left a bow and arrow.
The other nine hundred and ninety-two hands
Are in the gesture of supreme giving. In the palm of each
Is a mighty eye that gazes on sentient beings.
Avalokiteśvara is beautifully adorned with jewels,
And is clothed in flowing silk.
His body is a perfect enjoyment body, gloriously blazing with all major and minor marks.
His two feet are placed together. The main gurus of the lineage
And a vast assembly of peaceful and wrathful deities surround him. They are marked at their forehead, throat, and heart
By [*oṃ, āḥ,* and *hūṃ*]. From the *hrīḥ* [at my heart and that of the front visualization], light rays
Invite Guru Avalokiteśvara and his retinue from their true abode,
And they melt into nonduality with me and the front visualization. We are empowered [by initiatory goddesses], then adorned by Amitābha.

C. The Seven-branch Liturgy

1. Prostration

I prostrate to the gurus,
Who are the sum of all the buddhas' bodies,
Whose essence is Vajradhara,
Who are the root of the three jewels.
I prostrate to Avalokiteśvara,
Whose white form is clothed with no fault,
Whose head is adorned by a perfect buddha,
Who looks down on beings with compassionate eyes.
I prostrate with supreme faith,
With as many bodies
As the number of atoms,
To all those worthy of prostration.

Wherever in the world's ten directions
Reside all those lions among humans who come in the three times,
To them all, none excepted,
I prostrate with my body, speech, and mind.
With all the conquerors directly before my mind,

By the force of my prayer to practice the good,
I prostrate to all those conquerors
By bowing as many bodies as there are atoms in the world.
Seated on each atom are buddhas numerous as the atoms,
Each encircled by bodhisattvas;
Thus I visualize each and every dharma-realm filled up with
  conquerors.
With oceans of unending praises of them,
With every sound in an ocean of songs,
I recite the virtues of all the conquerors
And utter the praises of every tathāgata.

2. Offering

From the *hrīḥ* at my heart come offering goddesses with offerings for me and the front visualization.

a. Short Offering Mantra

Oṃ noble lord of the world and your retinue: accept mouth-water
  svāhā.
Oṃ noble lord of the world and your retinue: accept foot-water *svāhā*.
Oṃ noble lord of the world and your retinue: accept flowers *svāhā*.
Oṃ noble lord of the world and your retinue: accept incense *svāhā*.
Oṃ noble lord of the world and your retinue: accept light *svāhā*.
Oṃ noble lord of the world and your retinue: accept perfume *svāhā*.
Oṃ noble lord of the world and your retinue: accept cakes *svāhā*.
Oṃ noble lord of the world and your retinue: accept sound *svāhā*.

To those conquerors I make offerings
Of holy flowers and garlands,
Cymbals, balms, and superior umbrellas,
Superior lamps and holy incense.
To those conquerors I make offerings
Of holy garments and superior perfumes,
Incense and powders equal to Mount Meru,
All superior things specially arrayed.
I visualize for all the conquerors
Whatever offerings are excellent and vast.
By the strength of my faith in practicing the good,
I prostrate and make offerings to all the conquerors.

3. Confession

Whatever sins I have committed
With body, speech, and mind,
By force of attachment, anger, and delusion,

All those I confess.
If you have time, recite the general confession [to the 35 Buddhas].

4. Rejoicing

Whatever merit all the conquerors
In the ten directions, the bodhisattvas, solitary buddhas
And those training and beyond training may have,
In all that I rejoice.

5. Requesting

Those who are the lamps of the world of ten directions,
Who have awakened to the stage of enlightenment and attained nonattachment,
I ask all those, my protectors,
To turn the unexcelled wheel of dharma.

6. Entreating

To those who wish to show nirvāṇa,
I make this entreaty with folded palms:
For the benefit and happiness of all beings,
Remain for as many aeons as there are atoms in a field.

7. Dedication

Whatever little merit I may have accrued
By prostration, offerings, confession,
Rejoicing, requesting, and entreating,
I dedicate for the sake of the enlightenment of all.

8. Abbreviated Seven-branch Liturgy

I prostrate respectfully with my body, speech, and mind to the lotus feet
Of Guru Avalokiteśvara and his retinue.
I present all real and imagined offerings.
I confess all sins accumulated from beginningless time.
I rejoice at the virtues of ordinary and holy beings.
[I entreat you to] remain until cyclic existence is emptied.
I request you to turn every dharma-wheel for the sake of beings.
I dedicate all my and others' virtues to the great enlightenment.

D. Recitation

On a moon-seat at my heart and the heart of the front visualization,
There is a *hrīḥ*. There is a mantra rosary spinning around the *hrīḥ*.
From the rosary emanate divine bodies and infinite light rays,

Which purify the sins, obscurations, and sufferings of the six classes of beings,
Who attain the rank of noble. The conquerors
Are delighted by a cloud of vast offerings.
All their blessings and attainments are gathered into the form
Of light rays and melt into me.
From the fingers of the two visualized deities, myself and that before me,
A stream of nectar falls, filling the vase [visualized earlier].

1. LONG MANTRA

Homage to the three jewels. Homage to the holy gnosis-ocean, to royally arrayed Vairocana, to the Tathāgata. Homage to all the tathāgatas, the arhats, the perfect buddhas. Homage to noble Avalokiteśvara, the bodhisattva, the great being, the greatly compassionate one. It is thus: *Oṃ* hold, hold, be firm, be firm, support, support, make haste, find me, proceed, proceed, go forward, go forward, O blossom, O precious blossom, come, join, remove my mental obstructions *svāhā*.

Twenty-one times or more.

2. SHORT MANTRA

Oṃ jewel-lotus *hūṃ*.

As many times as possible.

3. HUNDRED-SYLLABLE MANTRA

Oṃ lotus being, guard my vows; lotus being, let them be firm. Be steadfast for me, be satisfied, be nourished; be favorable for me. Grant me all accomplishments. Indicator of all karma, make glorious my mind *hūṃ*. *Ha ha ha ha hoḥ*. Blessed one, lotus of all the tathāgatas, do not forsake me, lotus being, great vow being *āḥ hūṃ phaṭ*.

Three times

E. Praises

The wisdom-being of my self-visualization melts into the front visualization. On top of my head appears the nun Lakṣmī, dressed as a renunciate. With her two hands pressed together at her heart, she asks for intercession.

1. LONG VOW PRAYER

Oṃ I prostrate to the protector of the world.
The one praised by the supramundane world.
The one praised by the chief gods, Māra and Brahmā.

The one who is accomplished by the praises of the supreme royal
master.
I prostrate to the supreme protector of the three worlds.
The one with the form of infinite tathāgatas, with a virtuous form.
The one with the crest-ornament of the infinite brilliance of the
tathāgatas.
The one who clears up the ghosts' hunger and thirst by the supremely
generous gesture of his right hand.
The one adorned by a golden lotus in his left hand.
The one shining with a red-yellow garland in his fragrant locks.
The one whose face is beautiful like the brilliant moon.
The one whose lotus-eyes are extremely noble and bright.
The one whose scent is perfect, like that of a snow-white shell.
The one marked by pearls of stainless light.
The one adorned with the beautiful rays of reddish dawn.
The one whose hands are like an ocean of sweetened lotuses.
The one with a youthful face the color of an autumn cloud.
The one whose shoulders are adorned by many jewels.
The one whose palms are young and smooth like the highest leaves.
The one whose left breast is covered with an antelope hide.
The one who is gracefully adorned with earrings and anklets.
The one whose abode is a supreme stainless lotus.
The one whose abdomen is smooth as a lotus petal.
The one bedecked with jewels in a magnificent belt of gold.
The one with a fine cotton garment around his hips.
The one who has crossed the great ocean of the master's supreme
knowledge.
The one who has accumulated many wonderful merits.
The one who is the source of all happiness, who clears up aging and
disease.
The one who has put the three realms behind him and shows the
practice [for attaining the pure land] of Vajrayoginī.
The one who is the supreme living being, who conquers the trembling
host of demons.
The one with lovely feet adorned by golden rings.
The one who liberates beings by practicing [love, compassion, joy and
equanimity].
The one who strides like a proud elephant moving among geese.
The one who has completed the accumulations [of merit] and obtained
the teaching.
The one who rescues beings from oceans of milk and water.

Those who habitually rise at dawn should respectfully
Think of the power of Avalokiteśvara.

If one celebrates him with these supreme epithets,
Then whether one must be born a man or a woman, in that and all future births
One will accomplish what is necessary for transcending the world.

This is to be recited twenty-one times, while prostrating.

F. Requests

O noble Avalokiteśvara, treasury of compassion,
You and your retinue please heed me.
Please quickly free me and mother and father
Sentient beings of the six realms from cyclic existence.
May I quickly arouse in my mindstream
The deep and vast supreme enlightened thought.
With your power, please quickly purify
My karma and defilements, accumulated from beginningless time,
And with your compassionate hands
Lead me and all beings into the pure land of Sukhāvatī.
O Amitābha and Avalokiteśvara,
Please be my spiritual friends in all my lives,
Teach me well the precious good path,
And place me quickly on the level of a buddha.

This should be requested with intense longing.

G. Torma Offering

Oṃ padmanta kṛta hūṃ phaṭ
Oṃ naturally pure are all dharmas, naturally pure am I.

The tormas become empty. From the state of emptiness comes a *bhrūṃ*. From the *bhrūṃ* comes a wide and delicate precious vessel. Inside of it is an *oṃ*. The *oṃ* melts into light. From the light arise tormas. They turn into a great ocean of undefiled wisdom-nectar.

Oṃ āḥ hūṃ

Three times

1. First Torma

Offer the torma to the chief deity—the Greatly Compassionate One—and his retinue, by saying three times:

Oṃ noble Avalokiteśvara and your retinue, please take this torma; take it and eat it, eat it.

Then offer:

Oṃ noble lord of the world and your retinue, please accept mouth-water *svāhā.*
Oṃ noble lord of the world and your retinue, please accept foot-water *svāhā.*
Oṃ noble lord of the world and your retinue, please accept flowers *svāhā.*
Oṃ noble lord of the world and your retinue, please accept incense *svāhā.*
Oṃ noble lord of the world and your retinue, please accept light *svāhā.*
Oṃ noble lord of the world and your retinue, please accept perfume *svāhā.*
Oṃ noble lord of the world and your retinue, please accept cakes *svāhā.*
Oṃ noble lord of the world and your retinue, please accept sound *svāhā.*

I offer this torma of a nectar-ocean
To noble Avalokiteśvara.
Accept it and grant me and all other beings
Superior and ordinary attainments.

2. Second Torma

Oṃ the syllable *a* is first because of the primordial nonarising of all dharmas *oṃ āḥ hūṃ phaṭ svāhā.*

Three times. Then:

Oṃ ḍākinīs and dharma-protectors and your retinue please accept mouth-water *svāhā.*
Oṃ ḍākinīs and dharma-protectors and your retinue please accept foot-water *svāhā.*
Oṃ ḍākinīs and dharma-protectors and your retinue please accept flowers *svāhā.*
Oṃ ḍākinīs and dharma-protectors and your retinue please accept incense *svāhā.*
Oṃ ḍākinīs and dharma-protectors and your retinue please accept light *svāhā.*
Oṃ ḍākinīs and dharma-protectors and your retinue please accept perfume *svāhā.*
Oṃ ḍākinīs and dharma-protectors and your retinue please accept cakes *svāhā.*
Oṃ ḍākinīs and dharma-protectors and your retinue please accept sound *svāhā.*

I offer this torma of a nectar-ocean
To the assembly of dharma-protectors and ḍākinīs.
Please accept it and help me accomplish enlightened deeds,

Those that pacify, increase, empower, and compel.

3. Third Torma

Say three times either "*Oṃ* the syllable *a* . . ." or:

Homage! Seen by all the tathāgatas. *Oṃ* maintenance, maintenance *hūṃ*.

I prostrate to the tathāgata Many-Jewels.
I prostrate to the tathāgata Holy Beauty.
I prostrate to the tathāgata Soft-and-Peaceful-Body.
I prostrate to the tathāgata Free-from-all-Fear.

I offer this torma of a nectar-ocean
To the lords of place and soil.
Please accept it, and without malice
Be my good and steadfast friends.

H. Ablution

Next, pour the water from the physical vase onto the divine image appearing in the mirror:

With a stream of saffron-water nectar I bathe
The lamp of beings, the protector Avalokiteśvara.
May all the stains of beings' two obscurations be cleansed,
And may they have the fortune to obtain the three stainless bodies.

Oṃ the glorious vows from empowerment by all the tathāgatas and the noble lord of the world and his retinue *hūṃ*.

I dry all those bodies by applying
A matchless cloth, clean and fragrant.

Oṃ hūṃ traṃ hrīḥ aḥ purified body *svāhā*.

For the sake of training my mind, I offer jeweled clothes
Exquisite as a rainbow
And the cause of joy to anyone who touches them.
By this may I and others be adorned by the clothing of holy patience.
Because the conquerors are naturally adorned with the major and minor marks,
There is no need to adorn them with further ornaments.
By my offering superior jewel-ornaments,
May I and all beings attain the body adorned with the major and minor marks.

I. Dedication

Through these virtuous actions of mine,
May a buddha quickly arise in this world.

May this buddha show dharmas for the sake of beings
And quickly liberate sentient beings from their manifold sufferings and torments.
In this and all my lives,
May I attain a good [rebirth] realm, a clear mind, and humility.
Respecting great compassion and my guru,
May I remain steadfast in Avalokiteśvara's vow.
O Avalokiteśvara, whatever your form is like,
Whatever your retinue, longevity and world-sphere,
Whatever your superior good signs are like,
May I and all others be only like that.
By the power of offering and praying to you,
Please pacify sickness and poverty
In the world where I and others abide,
And increase dharma and good fortune.

May the supreme enlightened thought
That has not arisen arise;
May that which has arisen not decline,
But only increase more and more.

J. Hundred-Syllable Mantra

Oṃ lotus being, guard my vows; lotus being, let them be firm. Be steadfast for me, be satisfied, be nourished; be favorable for me. Grant me all accomplishments. Indicator of all karma, make glorious my mind *hūṃ. Ha ha ha ha hoḥ.* Blessed one, lotus of all the tathāgatas, do not forsake me, lotus being, great vow being *āḥ hūṃ phaṭ.*

Three times

K. Entreating Forbearance

O blessed one, greatly compassionate, pay heed to me.
When we are beginners, our concentration is dimmed
By the forces of sinking and scattering;
Our recitations are impure and our rituals either excessive
Or deficient. Please, O noble, greatly compassionate one, accept patiently our limited purity;
May we not encounter obstacles.

Om jewel-lotus hūṃ.

Several times.

L. Final Purification

The noble, the Greatly Compassionate One, is a little closer in the space before me, at the head of his retinue. A stream of nectar falls from his body parts. It bathes the outside, inside, and middle of my body and purifies without exception all the illnesses, demons, sins, and obscurations of my three doors, together with the propensities thereto.

Then pour and drink a little of the water used for washing and bathing.

M. Final Dedication

Through this virtue may I quickly become
A greatly compassionate one
And lead each and every being,
None excepted, to his pure land.

N. General Instructions

There are three sessions on both the preparatory and the actual day. Take the one-day Mahāyāna precepts each day at dawn. The rest of the ritual is the same in all sessions. On the preparatory day, make a gold throne that supports the three white substances (curds, milk, butter). Do not eat from bronze vessels, leaves, or the palm of your hand. In the afternoon, take tea without sugar or honey. Apart from that, do not eat suitable (foods for the morning, such as) curds, milk, or fruit. At dawn on the day of the actual fast, you begin to observe silence. Do not eat even a single grain of barley or drink a single drop of water. Except for the precepts, (the ritual) on the third day is as on the day before, but the required recitations are fewer: it is suitable to say the praises merely five or seven times.

O. Special Offering Prayer

On the third day, after ablution, say:

Oṃ vajra muḥ.

The wisdom-being of the front visualization returns to his natural abode. The pledge being melts into me. I become the one-faced, two-armed greatly compassionate one. Atop my head is a white *oṃ*. At my throat is a red *āḥ*. At my heart is a blue *hūṃ*. I am marked by these.

By saying this auspicious prayer, I am adorned.

IV. EPILOGUE

I have arranged this ritual with the intention of benefiting some householders and others of feeble intellect and energy. It is very important for those of forceful intellect, without believing these few words to be the essence, to practice the extensive rituals written by the earlier and later conquerors (Dalai Lamas) and by Panchen Chökyi Gyelpo. Even this abridged ritual should be known in detail from the great texts.

The sādhana of the noble, supreme lotus-bearer,
The treasury of compassion who looks down

Perpetually with a thousand compassionate eyes
On the countless tormented and protectorless beings:
Rightly explained by my holy predecessors, it was a beautiful
Jeweled garland, a brilliant blessing, a mass of blazing light
Set in array. Why, then should one such as I
Add to the rosary his half-baked foolishness?
Nevertheless, in this case, with a respectful heart,
I have composed this brief collection of words
For the benefit of some present-day people
Who are trapped by low intelligence and wavering mind.
Through this virtue, may I and all other beings
Be held at all times by Avalokiteśvara.
May he quickly save us from the worldly ocean agitated by waves of suffering,
And place us in a the bliss of a liberated state.

V. COLOPHON

This is the extremely condensed fasting ritual, called "Nectar Drop." Here in lower Amdo, the rituals found in the collected works of the great paṇḍitas are quite widespread. Still, some people of low intelligence need their mouths to be filled, so—entreated again and again by many great and ordinary monks and laymen, I have sent forth as a stream of water this ritual to be read by the ignorant.

—18—

Food, Clothes, Dreams, and Karmic Propensities

David Germano

One of the most vibrant and controversial traditions of Tibetan Buddhism is an ancient interlinked set of movements known as the Great Perfection (*rdzogs chen*). Centered in the Nyingma sect and the nominally non-Buddhist Bön lineages, over the centuries, it has to some degree served as a locus for ecumenical dialogue in Tibet. Its inception was in the eighth century under largely unknown circumstances, though its subsequent development was clearly a Tibetan phenomenon drawing on diverse strands from such sources as Chinese Chan, Indian Buddhism, Daoism, tantric Śaivism, and indigenous religions. Its controversial nature largely stemmed from its questionable claims of being largely Indic in origin, its strikingly antinomian language, and its creative innovativeness in the context of South Asian Buddhism.

While historically there have been many variants of the Great Perfection in the Nyingma tradition, the most interesting is arguably the Seminal Heart (*snying thig*) movement, which began in the eleventh century and was systematized in the fourteenth century by Longchenpa (Klong chen pa, 1308–1363). The tradition holds itself to be a revelation of hidden lineages brought to Tibet in the eighth century by the great Indian saints Vimalamitra and Padmasambhava, but most evidence points to it instead being a Tibetan reformulation of the Great Perfection from the eleventh century onward. Nyingmas began to incorporate a wide variety of meditative systems (often transforming them in the process) within the Great Perfection under the influence of new Tibetan Buddhist tantric traditions, even while preserving its rhetoric emphasizing the nonnecessity of formal meditative practice in light of all beings' primordial buddha-nature.

One of the clearest summaries of the Seminal Heart is Longchenpa's *The Treasury of Words and Meanings* (*Tshig don mdzod*), which, along with its companion work *The Treasury of the Supreme Vehicle* (*Theg mchog mdzod*), comprises a veritable encyclopedia of Seminal Heart thought and practice. The former's eleven highly structured chapters concern the following topics: (1) cosmogonic background detailing the primordial nonmanifest ground of existence, the initial manifestation of actual worlds, and the liberation of the primordial buddha Kuntu Zangpo (Kun tu bzang po; Samantabhadra; "the All Good One"); (2) the origins and processes of ordinary, distorted cyclic existence (saṃsāra) against that backdrop; (3) the way in which primordially pure buddha-nature as the ground continues to characterize all life within saṃsāra; (4) the difference between buddhas and sentient beings, especially in terms of how they know the world; (5) the nature of the subtle body as the locus of this entire cosmic drama within and as each living being; (6) the theoretical background of the Seminal Heart's transformation of visionary tantric praxis; (7) the relationship between the ground's vast expanse (*dbyings*) and its resonating intelligence (*rig pa*); (8) how one contemplatively attunes oneself to these processes operative in the background of being; (9) the various psychophysical indicators that mark progress in contemplation; (10) the intermediate states (*bar do*) of dying, death, postdeath, and rebirth wherein liberation hangs in the balance; and (11) the nature of the fruit of buddhahood in terms of its styles of presence and modes of knowing.

The eighth topic is thus devoted to contemplation (*nyams su len pa*), a term literally meaning "to take into your own experience," that is, means for bringing one's indwelling primordial buddha-nature into the light of self-awareness. A variety of techniques are grouped under this rubric, ranging from simple directed reveries to complex meditations involving one's body, speech, and mind in intense dramas; they also run the spectrum from highly structured prescriptive techniques to more free-flowing stimulation of normally unconscious and highly individual processes. Longchenpa classifies them under two overarching rubrics: practices "for those with psyches wrapped up in objective reference points," and practices "for those to whose psyches awareness is self-presencing." The nature of this distinction is that the former practices are more structure-oriented in their utilization of codified sequences of acts, concentration exercises, and artificial "reference points" such as alchemical pills, visualized external or internal images, and special viewpoints; the latter practices are more process-oriented in their general emphasis on cultivating spontaneous experiences that reflect what one's own awareness throws up, or "self-presences."

Great Perfection contemplation in the strictest sense is divided into two complementary styles known as the "breakthrough" (*khregs chod*) and "direct transcendence" (*thod rgal*). The former represents a cultivation of one's own naked self-awareness as directed by intensely poetic guided reveries; the latter consists of contemplating a spontaneous flow of light imagery gradually unfolding into visions of vast maṇḍalas of buddhas. Prior to discussing these, Longchenpa presents at length an anthology of the "reference point" practices classified into different groups. Since direct transcendence has its own separate preliminary practices (see chapter 19), and these practices immediately precede the section on breakthrough contemplation, clearly they are intended as being particularly useful for leading one into breakthrough contemplation. In other words, the contemplative states induced through these techniques are both deconstructed and deepened in the guided poetic reveries constituting the breakthrough instructions. Thus they provide a practitioner with the necessary experiential background that renders these poetic precepts more than mere vague evocations of purity, intensity, and spaciousness.

In the present context, we will focus on one such group of practices, namely, the "meditative states of the bodhisattva." This represents a blending of such diverse practices as alchemy, breath yoga, dietary changes, fire yoga (*gtum mo; caṇḍāli*), a wide variety of dream yogas, meditations on radiant light, and poetically thematized contemplation on self-awareness, the nature of experience, and external appearances. These are classified suggestively into four types of meditative states corresponding to our attachment to food, clothes, dreams, and karmic propensities, respectively. This quartet relates to how these preliminary contemplative techniques are focused on energy fixations in ordinary existence in order to undo the resulting blockages. They thus utilize the liberated energy for spiritual concerns: sex (sex yoga), food (involving alchemical practices utilizing herbs, and so on, as well as visualization-energized breathing), clothes (meditations centered around the well-known technique of "mystic fire," whereby internally generated warmth alleviates the need for clothes), dreams (a simple series of instructions enabling one to bring sleep into the contemplative path), and the network of karmic propensities permeating the unconscious (a more general series of exhortations to enter into a state of naked awareness undercutting these propensities' self-sustaining vicious cycle of neurotic conditioning).

Longchenpa begins with a general discussion of the essence of meditation as a simple sitting practice with three key elements: a formal posture and meditative session, unfocused eyes and mind, and releasing breath out into space. The lack of focus indicates that experience should involve a release of focal vision rather than a gaze of mastery or zeroing in, letting go of themes or objects that are typically put in the foreground. This gaze is mirrored by the breath, which instead of being internally penned up is released through yogic "vase" breathing into the far distant spaces that ordinarily constitute the forgotten background of our lives. Even in this simple practice, we can see how the emphasis on posture, gaze, and breath indicates a body-based knowing, that is, that the ways of knowing advocated in these texts must of their very nature involve bodily activities and processes. The practice overall foreshadows breakthrough contemplation, as well as functioning to deconstruct the ensuing emphasis on concentration and techniques.

The Meditative Session Eliminating Attachment to Food

The yogas of food and clothes present techniques for contemplatively generating constant dietary nourishment and warmth without relying on ordinary sources. In addition to the obvious benefits such techniques have in the difficult material conditions of isolated retreat sites in the glacial wildernesses of Tibet, they also represent powerful attempts to come to terms with physical embodiment and the need both to draw energy from a nourishing exteriority (food) and to maintain protective barriers from a disruptive exteriority (clothes).

The three principal yogas of food embrace alchemical practices, which in Tibetan are termed the "extraction of essences" (*bcud len*). All three share the basic paradigm of transforming substances in a ritual and contemplative context into nutritious energy capable of sustaining our biological being. The first set of practices concerns ingesting various juices, meats, stones, herbs, and precious substances (mercury, gold, etc.); the second involves "eating" one's own energized breath; and the third represents a variation on the classic tantric transgressive practice of consuming one's own excrement. It is the second practice that I would like to detail as the "eating winds" yoga.

The Treasury of the Supreme Vehicle (TCD2 164.4–5) specifies that with inhalation one visualizes ingesting the quintessential energies of external appearances via one's nostrils into the flavor channel (the main channel on the right side of the subtle body). This energy overflows the throat wheel of channels, thus revitalizing and sustaining the body. The specific significance of the flavor channel and throat wheel is pointed out in the fifth chapter of *The Treasury of Words and Meanings*, where both are specifically linked to the digestion of food and distribution of the vibrant energy extracted from food throughout the body and mind to replenish one's energy. Thus "eating" winds refers to consuming external energy via visualization-energized breathing:

> You join the upper and lower winds [of the body], pull them into the flavor channel (with inhalation via the nostrils), and imagine the throat wheel is thus filled with the flavor of ambrosia. By means of concealing the earth and water winds [i.e., yellow and blue in color], all appearances become food for you and dissolve within the throat and flavor channel. Through meditating on them as pervaded by the bliss of meditative states, you accomplish the yoga of food.

The constant theme in all these variations of "concealing" winds, or "joining" upper and lower winds, refers to the important yogic technique of "vase breathing." In this practice, the meditator presses down the body's upper currents of energy and pulls up its lower ones, thereby penning them up in a spot around the navel in a "vase." Thus, rather than the winds functioning in diverse ways throughout the body, their energy is restrained and concentrated in a single spot, such that they become "nonmanifest" or concealed.

In his explication of food yoga in *The Seminal Quintessence of the Master* (LYT1 431.2–6), Longchenpa describes two alternative techniques for overcoming food so as to sustain oneself instead on the food of contemplation. In the first, one imagines a blue sky as the nature of all appearances; by inhaling its blueness, one ingests the vibrant quintessence of the space energy at the heart of all appearances. This fills up the body to the point of overflow. One thus directly takes high-intensity energy from the element of space, and through this energy revitalizing and replenishing one's own internal physical elements, one no longer needs to rely on the ingestion and digestion of coarse food to maintain one's life force. Also by concentrating the internal winds within, one conserves and intensifies this energy rather than continually dissipating it:

> In the training on the meditative session cutting attachment to food, for "the extraction of essences," "eating the winds and mind as food," and so forth, one should look at their respective written explanations, while here I will just briefly teach the pith of "eating the winds and mind as food." In the morning you expel the winds' residue three times and then imagine all appearances as the sky. Next as you inhale the wind inwards, you visualize the body's entire interior as being filled to the brim with its blueness. Joining the upper and lower winds, you hold them. Thus your physical and psychic elements are lucent, and you no longer require food.

The second technique involves a visualized yoginī slicing open the upper tip of the meditator's heart, which then fills up with the flow of white and red "enlightening minds" (*bodhicitta*, i.e., seminal nuclei) from her vagina. In this way, the meditator is to consider that his entire body is filled with bliss; again the key point is holding the winds together. Thus again by the power of concentration one derives energy directly from the elements' essences and bypasses the ordinary coarse method of extracting energy from the external elements (ingestion and digestion); the meditator then concentrates these energized winds to prevent the energy's dissipation. In this way one literally lives off meditation and becomes divorced from the various obsessive images ordinarily invested in food:

> Alternatively, at the tip of the heart's upward-facing mouth is a white yoginī of awareness holding a ritual sickle, with which she slices open the heart's tip, such that it becomes filled by the flow of white and red enlightening minds from her vagina. Imagining that the entire body's interior is filled with bliss, the holding of the winds in union is the crucial point. Thus all attachment to food becomes naturally eliminated, and you sustain yourself day and night with the food of meditative states.

In his *The Seminal Quintessence of the Profound* (ZMYT1 333.3), Longchenpa offers yet another version of this practice. This again involves inhaling the core energy of external matter and life forms in the aspect of white and red quintessences and thus directly extracting energy to sustain life from the external world via visualization-energized breathing. In this way one "eats the winds," extracting "nutrition" (quintessential energy) from one's breathing rather than from ordinary food substances:

> Cutting off the flow of the winds' elemental energies is as follows: the meditator crouches down, expels the winds' residue externally, and focuses on visualizing gnostic winds filling the stomach in waves of white and red ambrosial vibrant quintessences. Joining the upper and lower winds, you hold them in. You then slowly exhale externally, and when inhaling internally, all of the environment and its life forms [animate and inanimate] come into the nostrils in the form of white and red quin-

tessences; you thus concentrate on their filling the body up. A blissful, clear and nonconceptual state of contemplation spontaneously arises, and the meditator becomes divested of attachment to food and clothes.

The Meditative Session Eliminating Attachment to Clothes

This yoga is a variant of the classic "fierce woman" (*gtum mo; caṇḍāli*) fire yoga practices, which are famous in the West for its classic exam procedure in which an initiate is expected to utilize contemplatively generated heat to dry wet clothes in the middle of the night while sitting naked on a glacier. Heat's significance here thus ranges from physical warmth to the heat of gnosis burning through all emotionally distorted illusion. While in the present context the practice is supplemented by alchemical ingestion of various substances and visualization of internal colored shapes corresponding to the four elemental energies, the core of the practice is relatively simple. Inside the meditator's body, a triangle of fire at the navel represents solar energy while a white *haṃ* syllable at the crown incarnates lunar energy. Breathing fans the former's passionate blazing upward in hot flames, thereby causing the latter to melt and begin to drip downward in a cooling flow. These drops gradually pervade the body with their orgiastic bliss until the entire body is energized. Clearly this stock sequence of contemplative events is modeled on sexual experience, and in fact it also forms the core of sexual yogic practices. Just as the solar digestive powers are contemplatively distributed throughout the body, the lunar seminal energies are reinvested in the entire body rather than concentrated in the genitals and then lost through ejaculation. In both cases normally autonomic physiological processes are thus contemplatively accessed and fundamentally transformed so as to develop self-sustaining loops of energy flow in the body.

The Meditative Session Eliminating Attachment to Dreams

Having dealt with daytime needs, Longchenpa turns to yogas coping with the darker landscapes that constitute nighttime: sleep, dreams, and their rhythms of consciousness' projection and dissipation closely paralleling the processes of life and death. In that sleep is a parallel process to dying involving the dissolution of self-awareness into a deep state of absorption, one may wonder why and how we dream; in fact this mirrors the wider question of why we think, and the even deeper cosmogonic question of why there is anything rather than nothing. The conventional response is that dreaming, the reconstitution of a dream body within a dreamed landscape, is driven by karmic propensities bound up with the principal five emotional distortions: ignorance, hatred, attachment, jealousy, and pride. During endless lifetimes in saṃsāra, traces of our own actions have accumulated within the base of being (the so-called universal ground), such that in the collapses of dying and sleeping, this web of karmic traces impels the mind to relink with the inner winds and thus reconstitute a provisional body within the intermediate states of postdeath and dreams. In these psychic bodies, everything accumulated within this deep strata comes into play, and thus dreams are a reflection of our karmic latencies. In fact, the texts' description seem to indicate that the ultimate aim of these practices is to reach a moment when the dreams fade away into a continuum of radiant light, a structureless nirvāṇa where all personalized images dissipate into a continual flow. Yet if we were to thus conclude that dreaming is an inherently distorted process that must be eradicated, we would be left bewildered as to why Tibetans put such great stock in the content of dreams—biographers often convert dreamed encounters with deities or teachers into autonomous, free-standing visions.

A constant theme running throughout all these practices is the epistemological value of dreams and illusions. In other words, the ways of knowing and nature of appearances in dreams—their fluidity, the blurring of boundaries, the at times shocking transformations, the confusion between self and other identities—have critical implications for ordinary daytime experience. Precisely the space we generally associate with the loss of reality-awareness, deception, and confusion is, in a troubling reversal, now identified as the only site where we are open enough to have a glimpse of reality itself (in deep sleep) as well as the true nature both of the truth status of appearances and of the relations of external appearances to our own interiority. If the truth is truly out there, then the landscape of a dream is the only one with the revelatory capacity for it to come to light in our experience. Thus rather than illuminate the space of dreams with daylight's solar clarity, these yogas reverse the eliding of boundaries to allow the illusory and intermixing quality of dream experience to filter back into daytime experience. The goal in dreaming is thus the same as in life: to be aware and then to work, or play, within that self-awareness. To become aware in a dream is lucid dreaming, the awareness that we are dreaming even as we dream; in the light of this self-awareness, the movement of dreams no longer has a malevolent edge to it. In line with the traditional tantric notion that the five root emotional distortions stand revealed as none other than the five primordial gnoses, and the Great Perfection's motif that the play of illusion can be both impure and pure, the very activity of dreaming can be seen also to have a pure energy when we look to its deeper nature. Dream yoga thus could be said, in a sense, to be the overcoming of karmic dreams to open the vast new vistas of the dreaming of a buddha, a gnostic dreaming that takes place within "the vast sky of originally pure emptiness."

Thus the most fundamental principle of these practices is lucid dreaming, which is termed "recognizing" or "identifying" one's dreams *as* dreams even while dreaming them. Obviously most of these practices assume a basic capacity in lucid dreaming, without which there could not even be any question of pursuing any practice after falling asleep. Yet beyond this basic function, lucid dreaming also incarnates the key principle of self-recognition (*rang ngo shes*), which constitutes the threshold between saṃsāra and nirvāṇa, between the path of an ordinary being and the path of a buddha. In the dream landscape the manifest truth of this imperative for self-recognition is crystalline in its clarity: the entire dream world with its landscapes and others is a self-referential self-projection, despite which we react with emotions of terror, lust, and confusion as if these projections were autonomous forces. Thus the recognition or recalling of these projections in a moment of lucid dreaming can have a tremendous liberating impact as we suddenly realize our implicit role.

Longchenpa presents two distinct contemplative systems for becoming situated in the night: an eight-phase practice for working directly with dreams, and a four-part meditation on the radiant light that manifests in deep sleep (drawn from *The Direct Consequence of Sound Tantra* and *The Six Spaces Tantra*, respectively). In the former, the first three phases incarnate the essential principles, while the remainder are supplementary and enhancing techniques: recognizing dreams while dreaming (lucid dreaming), learning to work with the consequence process-fluidity of appearances, and abandoning attachment to the truth status of any particular structure so as to let dream self-awareness permeate the daytime as well (the third is itself an effect or qualifier of the first two).

In the first phase, recognizing dreams allows one to eliminate attachment to the dream-appearances, since one is aware of them as dreams, just as one has no attachment to the reflections in a mirror; it also enables one to pursue religious practices while dreaming. During the day, initially the meditator focuses on particular appearances as being dreamlike, while eventually he or she extends that recognition to all emotions and situations such that they are all seen to lack any concreteness or ability to harm. In *The Seminal Quintessence of the Profound* (ZMYT1 336.3–337.1), Longchenpa explains that in cultivating this dream-awareness during the day one is to chant repeatedly "they are dreams, they are magical illusions." He also specifies two ways of taking hold of dreams: the "smooth" way involves recognizing dreams without depending on any particular conditions, while the "rough" way is thinking "they are dreams" under the conditions of the terror experienced in being confronted by an abyss, dog, enemy, or violent water. In *The Seminal Quintessence of the Master* (LYT1 433.1–5) he suggests at night laying down on the right side and focusing on the aspiration "Tonight I will recognize my dreams, and thus train!" He also specifies lying down with the mind focused on a sphere of light at the heart; if that fails to produce lucid dreaming, one should intensely supplicate one's master and generate devotion and pure vision.

With this capacity for continued self-awareness in place, in the second phase one proceeds to work with transforming the particular dream appearances. To maintain a sense of the dreamlike character of all phenomena during the waking day and consider all phenomena as the primordially pure maṇḍala of buddhas involves an extraordinarily difficult "transformation" of ordinary dense phenomena into their pure fluid counterparts. To cultivate this ability, one begins by utilizing mirrors and imagination in a waking state and then proceeds to apply this capacity to the much more vivid and comprehensive transformations possible in a self-aware dreaming state. The daytime practice consists of watching the shifting reflections in a mirror's surface as one places it in front of different objects, which opens one up to a sense of the fluidity and insubstantiality of appearances and induces a feeling of the dreamlike nature of all phenomena. With that basis, one extends it into an imaginative transformation of daytime appearances, more like a waking daydream or reverie rather than a carefully constructed visualization in the generation of a deity in tantric practices. Sustained practice during the day will naturally lead to these transformations occurring during dream-time, where the actual transformation is accomplished much more readily than during daytime vision, given the fluid and unstable nature of dream appearances. While lucidly dreaming, the meditator begins with minor mundane transformations such as horses and elephants (classical examples of what a conjurer conjures up) and gradually moves on to transforming the entire dream world into a pure realm such that all appearances are the deities' bodies. Thus beginning with simple transformations, gradually one gains the capacity to transform the entire dream world into the pure land of buddhas and rainbow-colored visions, a capacity that eventually filters down into ordinary waking perception. Initially during the day, however, it is quite improbable that one can transform or reveal all appearances into divine maṇḍalas, and thus the technique of mirror and imaginative transformation is a powerful means to introduce the fluid and pure nature of appearances. Through training on these transformations, a sense of the primordial purity of all internal and external phenomena is induced, and the meditator overcomes attachment and conditioning by them, seeing that they are no more substantial or solid than reflections in a mirror; during dreams at night it is certain one will reside in pure lands and receive new teachings on the Buddhist doctrines and practices.

Radiant light signifies the luminous emptiness forming the background openness to being that usually recedes in the face of the activity it makes possible. As one becomes increasingly intimate with the dreaming activity, one becomes correspondingly freer from the compulsive marginalization of this background radiance to the mind and appearances, such that radiant light comes to the fore. Thus the dream yoga is complemented with a succinct meditation on radiant light, which *The Seminal Quintessence of the Ḍākinī* (KGYT3 81.5–92.5) presents as threefold: taking hold of radiant light externally during the day (i.e., direct transcendence practice), concealing radiant light within the sheath during the night (a variant of dream/sleep yoga), and all phenomena remaining within sameness in between (a less technique-oriented account of how the practice deepens as daytime and nighttime experiences are integrated).

The Treasury of Words and Meanings, however, focuses on a four-part meditation that stretches across the entire day and night: at twilight the meditator withdraws his or her sensory faculties, at midnight inserts cognitive objects into the vase, at dawn illuminates gnosis, and during the day seals appearances. According to Khanpo Jikphun ('Jigs med phun tshogs), this meditation is done every day for the rest of one's life, in conjunction with the practice of direct transcendence and breakthrough. The twilight "withdrawal of faculties" indicates that the meditator is to gather the senses within as psychic energy is concentrated on interior visualizations of energy flows rather than the normal daytime dispersion of the psyche wrapped up in exterior objects. Then at midnight the meditator focuses energy solely on the luminosity within the heart, with the image of a butter lamp within a vase glowing subtly without emerging externally (just as the heart is the home of awareness's essence where its luminosity is largely latent). Thus at this point all psychic energy is withdrawn from exteriority and brought within into the vase of the heart, where it is inserted and hence no longer shines out externally, like the contraction of consciousness that marks the onset of sleep. At dawn the meditator then allows gnosis to shine back into the exterior field of perception, so that during the day he or she can seal all experiences and appearances with its radiance as well as an awareness of their dreamlike status. Longchenpa explains the rationale of each phase as follows (TCD2 327.6–7): "By contracting the sensory faculties into their abodes at dawn, you block the gateway of psychic activity; by inserting the cognitive objects into the vase at midnight, cognition shines directly within yourself; by primordial gnosis being clearly displayed at dawn, sensations are purified right where they stand; and by sealing appearances during the day, enframing characterizations are subdued."

Within that basic framework, the details of the first two phases in particular vary quite a bit. *The Seminal Quintessence of the Profound* (ZMYT1 343.3–344.1) gives the most simple version:

1. The withdrawal of the sensory faculties into their abodes at twilight: from a sphere of light in the heart, (light) emanates upward and strikes the empty seminal nucleus lamp in the conch-shell house (skull). You thus one pointedly train on this light going upward and downward.
2. The insertion of objects of cognition into the vase at midnight: you focus solely on the light within the heart.
3. The illumination of primordial gnosis at dawn: sitting in the imposing posture of the lion, you focus the mind on a white *a* hovering in the space an arrow's length from the spot between your eyebrows, whereby a sensation of empty radiance manifests.
4. The sealing of appearances during the day: you cultivate the resolution that everything is a magical illusion or dream.

The syllable *a* (at times given as *āḥ* or *aḥ*) figures prominently in these practices as a symbol due to its distinctive nature as the unarticulated sound forming the matrix for all other articulated sounds that form human languages.

The Meditative Session Eliminating Attachment to Karmic Propensities

This is a technique-free meditation leading directly into breakthrough contemplation: it is a poetic inquiry that shapes the empty spaces increasingly inhabiting the foreground of one's experience following the dream yogas. Karmic propensities are closely bound up with dreaming, since they constitute the latent patterns that ordinarily regenerate and reorganize a distinctive life out of the chaos of intermediate states, a process mirrored in the manifestation of dream selves out of sleep's chaotic dispersal of consciousness. Thus the sequence of four yogas begins with the more biological issues of food and clothes, proceeds to epistemological and ontological stances toward self-identity and external appearances in dreaming, and then proceeds to deal with the underlying propensities that continue to generate those stances through endless cycles of collapse and reorganization. Yet this ordering of the karmic propensities is of a particular type: given over to rigid routinization, founded upon a strict separation of interiority and exteriority, maintained by consequent distorting emotional reactions, and bound up with the past, present, and future. Thus time itself is implicated in the rhythms of attachment, aversion, and ignorance. The poetic evocation, however, points to an alternative to this karmic temporal organization in the gnosis of a buddha, suggesting that rigid order is a false response to the chaos of life. Instead, a more complex, flexible patterning is hinted at in a buddha, who inhabits the sameness of the three times, a dynamic regime of intertwining flows devoid of karmic linear delineation of subjects and objects diametrically opposed to each other, forever sealed off into themselves.

The text of the *Tshig don mdzod* is translated from the edition of Klong chen rab 'byams pa's *Mdzod bdun*, published by Sherab Gyaltsen and Khyentse Labrang in six volumes (Gangtok, Sikkim, 1983).

Further Reading

For a traditional presentation of these dream yoga practices, see Namkhai Norbu, *Dream Yoga and the Practice of Natural Light*, ed. Michael Katz (Ithaca: Snow Lion Publications, 1992). For further details on the fire yoga practice, see Geshe Kelsang Gyatso, *Clear Light of Bliss* (London: Wisdom Publications, 1982).

The preceding discussion was principally based on the following Tibetan sources: *Theg mchog mdzod* (TCD), *Bi ma snying thig* (VNT), *Bla ma yang tig* (LYT), *Mkha' 'gro snying thig* (KGNT), *Mkha 'gro yang tig* (KGYT), and *Zab mo yang tig* (ZMYT). The first work is also published as part of the *Mdzod bdun* (see above), while the other five works constitute the massive *Snying thig ya bzhi*, published in an eleven-volume edition by Trulku Tsewang, Jamyang and L. Tashi in New Delhi (1971).

For more precise references, please refer to my upcoming translation of *The Treasury of Precious Words and Meanings* as well as my associated monographs tentatively entitled *Mysticism and Rhetoric in the Great Perfection* and *The Architecture of Absence and Embodied Visions.*

The Meditative States of the Bodhisattvas

My discussion of the bodhisattvas' meditative states is in two parts: a brief discussion of their essence and an expansive explanation of their full extent.

A BRIEF DISCUSSION OF THE ESSENCE OF THE BODHISATTVAS' MEDITATIVE STATES

The Conch Shell Letters describes them thus:

> The meditative states of the bodhisattvas
> Are the cessation of mental craving.
>
> The key points of the body: you sit in the lotus posture
> And straighten up the back;
> You set your hands in the gesture of contemplative equanimity,
> Bend the neck forward slightly,
> And bring the eyes down to the tip of your nose.
>
> The key points of awareness are that while your eyes [gaze]
> An arrow's length away without looking at anything in particular,
> You pull the breath inward and then exhale it extremely far away;
> Your mind thus settles into contemplative equanimity.

The Tantra of Self-Arisen Awareness says:

> The meditative states of the bodhisattvas
> Don't involve concentrating your mind,
> Since they come about naturally or automatically.
>
> With experiential familiarization, you get at the depths of realization
> And divest yourself of any thoughts about food;
> Enjoyed by those abiding on the spiritual levels,
> Neurotic discursiveness is naturally absent.

AN EXPANSIVE EXPLANATION OF THE BODHISATTVAS' MEDITATIVE STATES IN THEIR FULL EXTENT

This involves three sections: (1) the naturally occurring meditative states exist when one's cognitive energy is totally absorbed or distracted into oblivion, such as how it is completely caught up and thus self-absorbed in the eyes of an arrow straightener, the eyes of a hare, or a hawk sleeping in its nest; (2) the meditative states of abiding on the spiritual levels are the individual contemplations corresponding to the ten spiritual levels; and (3) the meditative states with a continual objective reference as support are contrived meditative states, such as the training stage of the four sessions of meditation [described immediately below]. *The Tantra of the Sun and Moon's Intimate Union* explains these further:

The meditative states of the Mahāyāna are as follows:

The naturally occurring meditative states
Settle your body and speech into a pristine state without contrivance.

The meditative states adhering continuously to an objective reference
Suppress provisional manifestations of emotional distortions;

And the meditative states of abiding on the spiritual levels
Spiritually foster your own mental stream.

In the present context I would like to elaborate upon the meditative states that adhere continuously to objective references. There are two harmful influences for practitioners: you accumulate the karma of revolving in saṃsāra's three realms provisionally through the harmful influences of food and clothes, while ultimately it is through the harmful influences of dreams and latent karmic propensities. Thus you must train on the four sessions or phases of meditative states as antidotes to these harmful influences: the meditative session eliminating attachment to food, the meditative session eliminating attachment to clothes, the meditative session eliminating attachments to dreams, and the meditative session eliminating attachment of latent karmic propensities.

The Meditative Session Eliminating Attachment to Food

As described by *The Direct Consequence of Sound Tantra*, this involves (1) the various alchemical extractions of essences, (2) eating the winds as food, and (3) preparations of ambrosial excrement:

I will explain the great amazing wonder
Of such alchemical extraction of essences
Not taught in any other tantras—
Listen up bodhisattvas, masters of the gods!

(1) Via reliance upon precious materials,
Your life span will be equal to the Sun and Moon;
Through a preparation of various stones,
Your body will be impervious to weapons;
Through herbally based preparations,
You will be without white hair or wrinkles;
Through extracting the essences of "juice" preparations,
You become dazzlingly radiant and youthful;
Through flesh-based preparations,
Your body becomes energetic and increases in strength.

(2) Furthermore, I will explain the amazing
Extraction of essences based on winds
Known as "cutting off the elemental energies' flow."

This practice is understood by working with the upper and lower winds—
Through thus skillfully concealing the winds,
Or, alternatively, counting the passage of breaths,
The yoga of food comes to pass.

Such is the alchemical extraction of essences
Based upon the elemental energies.

The tantra continues:

(3) I will explain the amazing extraction of essences
Which cuts off the flow of the body's elemental energies.

By reverse cycling the flow of excrement
You will exhaust your ordinary physical contaminants;
Furthermore, through eating its extracted quintessence
After being boiled within liquid butter
In reliance upon the proper procedures,
The flow of elemental energies will be cut off.

By thus cutting off the flow of the body's elemental energies
Parasites will not remain in the body,
And in the consequent absence of urine, feces, and so forth
Your external and internal winds will also become nonexistent.

The Meditative Session Eliminating Attachment to Clothes

This session involves practices utilizing the winds and profound supporting factors, respectively. The supporting factors are preparations of such things as flesh, herbs, and juices. In terms of the winds, you crouch down and let the winds trickle down within as you inhale, such that the stomach is filled up [as you do vase-breathing]. You then exhale slowly and do so in accordance with a meditative visualization of fire. In this way warmth arises externally in the body so that you no longer need clothes; warmth arises internally in the mind so that neurotic conceptuality gradually dies down and you remain in a nonconceptual state. *The Direct Consequence of Sound Tantra* describes these practices thus:

The yoga of clothes is like this:
You settle in it through the winds and profound supporting factors.

(1) With exhalation and inhalation of the winds,
And via the key point of penning up their movements at your navel,
You visualize fire in a manner that accords with
The particular balance of elements in your body.

(2) With preparations of supporting factors,
You properly prepare a pill or powder

From two, six, seven, or three [substances],
Swallow the pill, and subsequently rub it on your stomach.

At the time of doing these yogas, the alchemical extraction of the four elements' essences is synthesized into a single practice. This is done through relying on preparations of the precious substance mercury and such, the winds of the four elements, and visualizations. You are thus able to actualize the enlightened qualities stemming from food, clothes, and so forth. *The Direct Consequence of Sound Tantra* describes the practice thus:

A practitioner aiming to equalize
The four elemental energies should do as follows:

In accordance with the key points of earth, water, fire, and wind,
Mix them into your body and ignite them with the winds;
Your own body is transformed
By the individual elements, and in cultivating that
You should meditate on the maṇḍala that subsumes the key points.

By becoming optimally familialized with those experiences
The potency of all four elements arrives at equilibrium,
And thus you experience bliss and are divested of fear.

Having thus also accomplished the psychic attainments of both food and clothes,
Your life and riches will be completely perfect.

The maṇḍala that subsumes the key points requires explanation. First off at dawn you eat one pea-sized pill prepared from these four substances: orchids as the extraction of earth energy's essence, mercury as water energy, asparagus as fire energy, and eaglewood as wind energy. Having done this and taken hold of your internal winds [i.e., vase breathing], you visualize a triangular maṇḍala of fire at the navel, a circular maṇḍala of water at the heart, a square maṇḍala of earth at the throat, and a bowlike maṇḍala of wind at the crown. From a downward facing *haṃ* based in the latter's hollow, interior drops of "enlightened minds" [i.e., seminal nuclei] descend, thus pervading the triad of your throat, heart, and navel. In this way heat is stirred up [from the navel] and pleasure descends [from the crown]. Through fixing your mind on the bliss and warmth occurring in this process of the fire's blazing and the nuclei's dripping, you will actualize the supreme of psychic attainments for both clothes and food. As taught by the master Śrīsiṃha, you will accomplish this through deeply felt experience.

The Meditative Session Eliminating Attachments to Dreams

As explicated by *The Direct Consequence of Sound Tantra*, this has two aspects: "examination" and esoteric precepts on meditation:

Carrying the key points of dreams onto the path
Involves preliminary activities and getting down to the key points.

As preliminaries, you must refine body, speech, and mind
Until you have attained the requisite signs of mastery;
Based upon that, you then do examination, supression,
And the identification of your triune karmic propensities
[corresponding to past, present, and future].
Getting down to the key points
Means implementing these practices' main points—
Training, transformation, cutting off, interchanging,
Controlling, thrusting to the key points, penning up, and reversing—
Such that karmic dreams become utterly exhausted
And distorting karmic propensities uprooted.

You will achieve the following results in dependence
On your relative diligence during practices:
It is certain that the superior will eliminate dreams altogether,
The average will recognize them as being dreams [i.e., lucid dreams],
And the inferior will bring about change in their content.

For these practitioners dreams initially become more prevalent:
The superior ones forget their dreams such that they ultimately cease;
For average practitioners dreams become exceedingly lucid,
And then ultimately are recognized as being dreams in the very act of dreaming;
And for inferior practitioners dreams are unclear, and then change [toward a greater clarity]—

Thus all three types arrive in their own way at the practices' optimization. In ascertaining the key points of contemplatively taking these dimensions into your own experience, I will discuss the preliminary activities and then the main practices.

Preliminary Practices

The preliminary activity of "examination" involves the key points of examination, supression, and identifying your karmic propensities. Examination as the first phase entails relaxing quietly in a sunny spot and massaging yourself with an ointment; at night you then lie down on your right side and examine your dreams. Furthermore, if you can't identify your dreams other than briefly, there is the technique of "supression": it is easy to identify them clearly by first focusing the mind on a red *āḥ* at your throat and then lying down without becoming distracted. I will now outline the practice of identifying your karmic propensities. If you dream predominantly of such things as objects you were previously attached to, the series of karmic propensities of those previous attachments will be stronger, and thus the relative difficulty of their transformation is intermediate. If you dream predominantly of current relationships and situations, this is extremely easy to deal with—with three or four days of meditation you can gain experiential mastery. If you dream pell-mell of all three temporal dimensions [past, present, and future]—meeting in places you haven't gone with people you have never met before, and so forth—this is called "the conjunction of the three types of karmic propensities" and is extremely difficult to eradicate.

The Main Practices

The meditation of the main practice involves eight phases: training on dreams, transforming, cutting off, interchanging, controlling, thrusting to the key points, penning up, and reversing. "Training on dreams" means you develop a single-minded aspiration to experience phenomena as dreamlike and then without distraction train on whatever appears during the daytime as essentially being dreams. Having thereby come to recognize dreams as dreams in the nighttime as well, you must exercise yourself in training on everything as a dream. "Transformation" involves observing the different reflections in a mirror, transforming one after another during the daytime, and then transforming all appearances into a deity's body and so forth. You must then also perform such transformations as horses into elephants with your various dream-appearances, finally transforming them into buddha fields and deities' bodies. "Cutting off" entails cutting off your attachment to things' veracity. As during the day you experience them as mere dream-visions, normal appearances are no longer held to be veridical. Having recognized dreams as dreams [i.e., lucid dreaming at night], without exulting even in your capacity to transform and train on dreams, you should think "everything is without truth and impossible to pinpoint." Thus you will cut off the immediate flow of all cravings toward any appearances whatsoever. "Interchanging" will refine your skill. In successive instants you transform manifest appearances into vanished appearances, and vanished appearances into manifest ones; you also do such things as interchange pleasure with displeasure, nonthought with thought, or thought with nonthought.

"Control" functions to stabilize. Having looked to your experiences at that time, you identify them internally without slipping out of that state, and thus meditate. "Thrusting to the key points" integrates you with the dimension of realization. Staying sensitive to how they are free in their very manifestation and free flowing without segmentation, you train undistractedly on all the nightime dream appearances and daytime appearances. "Penning up" continues meditation within that state. Having penned up the mind one pointedly for a lengthy time in this state of training on dreams as being without truth and free in their very manifestation, you meditate. "Reversal" is their resolution within reality. Letting be all your daily appearances, dreams, views, and meditation without fixing the mind on anything at all, you activate their subsiding within naturally cleansed reality, the vast sky of originally pure emptiness.

By practicing thus, at first the most diligent will forget their dreams, the average will have lucid dreams, and the inferior will delight in and be inclined toward their dreams; ultimately the flow of dreams will be cut off for all three. Upon freeing dreams within radiant light, the contemplation of reality will blend day and night together. At that time, your body will become divested of any shadow, and you will see for yourself its minute atomic particles. Thus it manifests devoid of truth like the appearance of a shadow, and after death the intermediate existence [leading to rebirth] becomes naturally cut off. *The Direct Consequence of Sound Tantra* describes it thus:

> The illusory body is refined in dreams,
> While the physical body of one well versed in it
> Comes to resemble a shadow.
>
> Then after death they are able to apprehend as themselves
> The illusory body of the intermediate state.

The Direct Consequence of Sound Tantra explicates training on radiant light in reliance upon sleep in this context:

> When you train in the meditative state of sleep,
> With experiential mastery, external appearances become radiant
> Beyond any distinction between day and night,
> And through this the great radiant light is present.

This involves two styles of meditation; the first is a general meditation upon radiant light. You meditate during the day by expanding awareness's vivid clarity as you zero in on cognition's transparent brightness in accordance with the key points of the body and winds. While laying in the manner of a lion during the night, you rest within the state of identifying the radiant light of the nonconceptual cognition that occurs on the verge of falling asleep. Thus you remain in that very state utterly devoid of dreams and even continue to see nearby appearances, yet remain totally without any selective and discursive thought processes. If you consider this state to be sleep, this is contradicted by your clearly ascertaining individual appearances [visual, auditory, and so on], while if you consider it not to be a state of sleep, this is contradicted by the fact that there is "awakening" from this state. During this time five-hued appearances as well as nuclei, rays, and butter lamp–like appearances are seen clearly, which is termed "the manifest radiant light." Zeroing in on cognition's transparent brightness is "the empty radiant light," as you remain within the triad of bliss, clarity, and nonconceptuality.

The second style is a detailed four-part meditation utilizing the key points of radiant light: withdrawing the sensory faculties into their abodes at twilight, inserting objects of cognition into the vase at midnight, illuminating primordial gnosis at dawn, and sealing appearances during the daytime. First, you meditate while focused on the lamp of the empty nuclei in the conch shell house [i.e., the skull]. Second, you concentrate one pointedly on a white *aḥ* in your heart. Third, with the lion gaze you impell the *a* within the heart into the sky a bow's length away from your crown and focus on it floating there. Finally, [during the day] you meditate by zeroing in on cognition's transparent brightness in accordance with the key points of the body as well as the mind (just as described previously); in postcontemplative awareness you understand appearances as magical illusions and dreams ["sealing"]. *The Six Spaces Tantra* explains these thus:

> During the day you seal appearances;
> During the night in your own resting place,
> In order to optimally take hold of the four times' sameness,
> The practitioner withdraws the faculties' gateways into themselves
> And brings the mind to bear
> On the lamp of the empty nucleus.
>
> When the nucleus itself increases,
> Focus on it as also reflecting your cognition's increase;
> Likewise, when the nucleus becomes minute,
> The nucleus's increasing minuteness
> Should be felt as the increasing minuteness of cognition.
> Through these key points of sleep and dreams
> You can uproot your karmic propensities stemming from previous attachments.

The Meditative Session Eliminating Attachment of Latent Karmic Propensities

Not rejecting on account of what you possess nor actualizing on account of what you lack, not attached to what you possess nor worried about what you lack, not following in the tracks of the past nor laying in wait for the future, and without dressing up present cognitive activity with clothing antidotes, you identify a naked alertness free right where it stands. Appearances are free in and of their very appearance, like a small bird carried away by a hawk; your mind's movements are free in and of their very movement, like the vanishing of a breeze in space; and appearances and cognition are freed into nonduality, like salt dissolving into water. *The Six Spaces Tantra* describes it thus:

> For the individual who does not grasp after the past, does not project forward the future, and lets current cognitive activity be in its own place, all cognition blends into one without temporal divisions. This is termed "the single essence subsuming all into one," while the practitioner is called "the visionary who is aware of the three times' sameness."
>
> Through the method of memory's self-exhaustion, saṃsāra and transcendence are nondually integrated: "the visionary aware of the three times' sameness" terminates memories of the past, supresses memories of the future, and releases memories of the present to vanish of their own accord.

> Also, "the visionary realizing the three times' sameness" does not obsessively continue to focus on experiences of the past, does not projectively focus on experiences of the future, and does not intellectually focus on experiences of the present.
>
> "The visionary realizing the three times' sameness" does not proliferate past dimmed awareness, does not encourage future dimmed awareness, and does not intimately embrace present dimmed awareness.
>
> "The visionary realizing the three times' sameness" does not cling to past hatred, does not hook in future hatred, and does not temper present hatred.
>
> "The visionary realizing the three times' sameness" does not amass clouds of past ignorance, does not pave the way for future ignorance, and does not bring down a torrent of present ignorance.
>
> "The visionary of the three times' sameness" does not respond to the buddhas of the past, does not noisily announce the buddhas of the future, and does not focus directly on the buddhas of the present.
>
> "The visionary of the three times' sameness" extirpates past desire, resolves firmly against future desire, and banishes present desires.
>
> "The visionary realizing the three times' sameness" does not hold tightly to past jealousies, does not mentally contract into future jealousies, and does not get involved in present jealousies.
>
> S/he is referred to as "the great visionary who realizes the nonduality of saṃsāra and transcendence."

The "buddha" mentioned in this passage refers to the presencing of deeply felt contemplation in terms of unusual enlightened qualities.

—19—

The Elements, Insanity, and Lettered Subjectivity

David Germano

Tibetan Buddhist meditative systems are in general characterized by a consistent threefold classification scheme based on the triune nature of every activity: a beginning, a middle, and an end. The technical language used to express this in contemplative systems is the preliminaries, main practices, and concluding practices. This triad can be used to characterize the three phases of a single contemplative procedure, to integrate three intertwined, sequentially dependent contemplative techniques, or to serve as loosely connected rubrics integrating a wide variety of meditative systems. The classic paradigm is the "three excellences," which should be applied in all contemplation: one begins a meditation with the recitation of a refuge prayer and a prayer for arousing an enlightened motivation (*bodhicitta*) as preliminaries; intermediately one implements the main practice without getting trapped in conceptualization or reification; and finally one concludes by dedicating the merit of contemplation to the enlightenment of all living beings. A more tantric reflection of this triad is the initial evocation of emptiness, the intermediate manifestation of envisioned divine images out of that emptiness, and the concluding dissolution of those images back into emptiness.

In Nyingma tantric traditions in general, the classic use of these rubrics to integrate different contemplative procedures from the three vehicles of Indian Buddhism into a six-month-long retreat program can be found in Patrul Rinpoche's nineteenth-century *The Words of My Perfect Teacher* (*Kun bzang bla ma'i zhal lung*). The preliminaries are classified into exoteric outer practices corresponding to the Hīnayāna and esoteric inner practices corresponding to the Mahāyāna and Vajrayāna. The former inculcate basic Buddhist values through guided meditations on six topics: the difficulty of finding an optimal human life, the impermanence of life, the sufferings of cyclic existence, the pervasive karmic law of cause and effect, the benefits of liberation, and the value of a spiritual teacher. Following these meditations are what is commonly known as the "five hundred thousand" preliminaries, named after the standard practice of doing each one hundred thousand times over the course of four to six months: the recitation of a refuge prayer while visualizing a vast assembly of spiritual figures, the recitation of a bodhicitta prayer with the same visualized backdrop, the recitation of the hundred-syllable mantra of the purificatory buddha known as Vajrasattva, the ritualized offering of visualized and material maṇḍalas, and the practice of guru yoga. Having completed these preliminary practices, the practitioner is allowed to continue on to the "main practices," which are themselves threefold in nature: the generation phase, perfection phase, and Great Perfection.

Indo-Tibetan Buddhist tantra itself has had many phases and competing movements, but in later periods it became increasingly standard to summarize contemplative techniques into the two overarching rubrics of generation and perfection phases; the addition of a third element in terms of the Great Perfection is unique to the Nyingma tantric lineages, though parallel developments such as Mahāmudrā can be found elsewhere. The generation phase boils down in essence to deity yoga, the imaginative appropriation of a new subjectivity, self-identity, and body-image as a male or female buddha. This is done particularly through vivid visualizations of the body's exterior in the form of a buddha, though emotional and cognitive identification is also essential; special hand gestures (*mudrā*) and ritualized chants (mantras) are used to support this identification. The perfection phase techniques then come to terms with the body's own reality, in terms of both its interior (symbolic) and its mute space devoid of images (nonsymbolic). Symbolic techniques are subtle body meditations, which use visualization, breathing, and chanting to sense and manipulate the internal flow of energies in the body. The key technique is perhaps the "fierce woman" (*gtum mo*) fire practice, a variant of sexual yogic practices: the crux is the flow of ambrosial seminal nuclei through the four wheels or energy nexuses (*'khor lo*) at the subtle body's center, the concomitant experiences of four degrees of intensifying bliss and the consequent concentration of winds or currents of energy (*rlung*) within the subtle body's central channels. The types of experiences deriving from these processes are summarized as threefold: bliss, clarity, and nonconceptuality. Nonsymbolic perfection phase contemplation, however, involves divestiture of iconic content and other contrivances as one simply rests in the space of the images' dissolution. As such, it can come at the conclusion of the visualizations' dissolution in either generation phase or symbolic perfection phase techniques, or it can be pursued as a free-standing contemplation (in the latter sense, it is often understood as outside of the generation/perfection phase structure—see "breakthrough" below). This thus reflects a continuance of earlier calming techniques and meditation on emptiness, though transformed by its practical and rhetorical context.

The main practices of the Great Perfection itself are twofold: breakthrough (*khregs chod*) and direct transcendence (*thod rgal*). Breakthrough reflects a further development of nonsymbolic perfection phase contemplation as a free-standing contemplation stressing natural vision and breathing in a psychic landscape shaped by stunning poetic rhetoric. Often referred to as meditating on "the nature of the mind" or the "vastness of the sky," the emphasis is on the absence of fixed contemplative techniques as one tunes into a fluid unobstructed embodied awareness. Direct transcendence, however, is an unusual variant on generation and symbolic perfection phase techniques, though the emphasis is on exterior vision in the surrounding space rather than interiorized subtle body meditations. The unusual character of this practice lies in its emphasis on cultivating spontaneous image flow of unpredetermined nature through initial reliance on external light sources. It is explicitly contrasted to the painstakingly contrived visualization of buddhas or maṇḍalas of buddhas in the standard generation and perfection phase techniques. This practice integrates breakthrough contemplation as the necessary state of awareness within which these visionary contemplations must unfold. The main practice begins with an introduction (*ngo 'phrod*) to the direct perception or immediacy (*mngon sum*) of reality, which then forms the heart of contemplation: in direct transcendence one literally sees buddhahood directly with one's own eyes, while in breakthrough contemplation one becomes immersed directly within pristine awareness.

The Seminal Heart tradition of the Great Perfection, however, also has its own internal divisions of preliminary and main practices. Varying classificatory schemes are utilized, but the most common considers the breakthrough and direct transcendence contemplations to be the twofold main practice, while all other contemplative techniques are considered preliminaries. While these preliminaries include the standard range of meditations on impermanence, compassion, the purificatory Vajrasattva, and so on, they also generally embrace two integrated sets of practices that are unique to the tradition (at least in these particular forms). In *The Seminal Quintessence of the Ḍākinī* (KGYT1 289.2ff.), Longchenpa terminologically differentiates the latter from the former by contrasting them as "extraordinary" preliminaries to the "ordinary" sevenfold preliminaries. The ordinary practices are: a visualization practice aimed at seeing all appearances as the guru; the purification practice of maṇḍala offerings; meditating on the impermanence of life; contemplating the karmic law of cause and effect; cultivating the four immeasurable emotions of impartiality, love, compassion, and sympathetic joy; arousing an enlightened motivation; and the purificatory practice of the Vajrasattva's hundred-syllable mantra. The two sets of unique Great Perfection preliminaries are presented in different ways, but the most standard presentation is that of the four yogas of food, clothes, dream, and karma (see chapter 18) along with a triune set of practices I have summarized as the elements, craziness, and subjectivity as letters. The former *tend* to be associated with leading the disciple into breakthrough contemplation, while the latter are generally positioned as preliminaries to direct transcendence. The technical terms for the latter three sets of practices are the yoga of the four elements' sounds (though often presented as involving all five elements), the conduct of differentiating between the domains of saṃsāra and nirvāṇa, and the preliminaries of body, speech, and mind. Before turning to Longchenpa's own exposition of this triune practice, I will briefly summarize them and discuss the precise way in which they serve as preliminaries leading one into the flow of direct transcendence contemplation.

The Yoga of the Five Elements: Dynamic Vision and the Intertwining of Intersubjectivity

The elements yoga involves a type of calming technique utilizing the natural sounds of the Buddhist fivefold classification of material elements into water, earth, fire, wind, and space, as the object of concentration. As preliminaries to the practice, the practitioner goes to a secluded spot where he or she can remain in solitude without distraction, relax body, speech, and mind, make a fire, present a ritual feast offering and sacrificial cakes (*gtor ma*) to the ḍākinīs, and then examine the fire's shapes and colors for omens. The actual practice is then done in any posture that maintains the upper torso's straightness, since it is essential that there is no distortion in its subtle channels and the psychophysical energy flowing through them. Thus, the classical lotus posture is particularly useful, though other postures are equally effective in this case.

The sounds of water, fire, and wind are simply their naturally occurring forms: a waterfall or turbulent stream, a campfire or fireplace, and a windy spot such as a mountain top. The sound of earth is created artificially by a variety of techniques, such as striking wood repeatedly and focusing on the resulting sound (one can create the same sound or various sounds, as one finds effective for concentration). *The Illuminating Lamp* (VNT2 57.4) advocates making egg-sized balls of colored clay and slapping them back and forth between the hands. In either case, the resulting sound is "cool and heavy"; in contrast to the unstable, constantly shifting sounds of water, fire, and wind, this sound is deep, resonant, steady, and relatively distant or nondynamic. In terms of the space or sky yoga, one lies supine on one's back with limbs stretched out flat. While slowly exhaling, one thrusts one's awareness far away into space's empty expanse. Doing this again and again, the practitioner becomes immersed in the experience of the sky's nature, though other than the gentle sound of exhalation there is no coarsely distinct sound of space. This type of sky yoga is also used as an enhancing practice for breakthrough meditation by virtue of its inducing a sense of emptiness, while the posture itself is an auxiliary posture, in direct transcendence practice termed "the posture of sameness primordial gnosis." Whichever element is being practiced, the practitioner is to become totally absorbed in its sounds until he or she seems literally to dissolve within them. Given the way these pervasive sounds tend to fill up the body and mind the moment one turns one's attention to them, this practice yields powerful effects unusually quickly. In this process the mind's grasping and internal chattering gradually subsides, until only a natural flow of experience remains: empty, radiant, and nonconceptual. That experience should be identified as the true nature of the mind and is considered an intuition of the inner pure buddha-nature that characterizes all living beings.

These simple practices link up to direct transcendence contemplation, and the complex system of thought it embodies, in a number of interesting ways. To begin with, unlike more static calming contemplations that cultivate concentration via focus on a still statue, a slightly flickering candle flame (the space an arm's span in front of the meditator), or the relatively placid movement of the breath in and out, the object of focus here is intrinsically dynamic and changing. The quest to find a still place right in the midst of all this dynamic movement perfectly mirrors the nature of direct transcendence contemplation, where the key is to experience a bewildering flow of spontaneous imagery and yet avoid indulging in the investiture of emotional energy into the exterior or exteriorized images. Thus one must balance between remaining in a perfectly still and unfissured circulation of internal energies (the breakthrough) and yet simultaneously and perpetually move beyond it (direct transcendence) to the manifestation of images envisioning one's own being; this sense of balance is first cultivated in the uncanny experiences of stillness found within the turmoil of a roaring waterfall or crackling fire. Another danger of calming techniques is overly rigid control as one becomes fixated on concentrating ordinarily dispersed psychic energies in a mastered and mastering gaze. When the object of that gaze is a passive, perfectly still item such as a statue or even a predetermined visualization scheme, there is an inherent tendency for the gaze's potential aggressive and controlling aspects to be encouraged by the compliancy and inertness of its object. But in these practices we instead find a dynamic, inherently motile object that refuses to be controlled in its constantly changing visual and aural designs, movements that are allowed to take their own course. In these ways, it accords with the Great Perfection's rhetoric of defeating the intellect's demands for control in preference for a body-based spontaneity of image and action. This rhetoric is embodied in the direct transcendence's insistence on waiting in the intense silence of breakthrough for the movement of images to take shape and to resist the impulse to begin to structure that movement intellectually with the forestructuring of preordained visualizations.

Craziness and Naturalness: The Differentiation between the Domains of Saṃsāra and Nirvāṇa

This practice is split into three separate phases correlated with our triune identity as physical, verbal, and mental, reflecting the practical necessity of coming to terms with one's concrete embodied existence beyond mere intellectual analysis. Despite this, it is governed by a unitary principle: the practitioner begins by simply crazily acting out whatever impulse pops up until finally pure exhaustion leaves him or her with no alternative but to enter a state of deep relaxed quiet termed "settling into naturalness" (*rnal dbab*). The quest thus is to begin with the ordinary life-stream muddied with emotionally fueled physical, verbal, and mental waves and proceed to zero in on a calm, natural, pellucid fluidity that is the mind's true nature. The practice opens with a frenetic, sped-up version of life in saṃsāra as the practitioner lets himself or herself go without the normal plethora of restrictions due to personal neuroses and societal strictures, acting out whatever impulse to thought, speech, or physical action comes to mind. The traditional Buddhist world comprises six types of life forms, which also function as psychological states or orientations that humans may find themselves in at any given point: hell beings, starving spirits, animals, humans, demigods, and gods. Thus a large part of this meditation naturally tends to be the imitating of these different beings' thoughts, physical behaviors, and verbal languages in accordance with whatever strikes one's fancy. It is essential that one yields to impulses in immediate and abrupt ways, rather than mentally directing and structuring activities. For example, one jumps and prowls like a wolf, howls like a wolf, and imitates its thought patterns as it thinks about how to track down and capture a sheep; or one pretends to be a mass murderer and then suddenly switches to the outlook of a self-sacrificing saint. While in general this practice is discussed in terms of three distinct categories corresponding to body, speech, and mind, in fact some teachers have students do all three together since otherwise it entails improbable acts like saying things without thinking, and so forth.

In short, one lets oneself go crazy physically, verbally, and mentally in a flood of diverse activity, so that by this total surrender to the play of images and desire across the mirroring surface of one's being, one gradually comes to understand the very nature of the mirror itself. Thus it is important to maintain awareness even as one experiments with opening up one's limitations and defined self, since the goal is not dissolution into insanity, but rather learning how to relax as one overcomes verbal, physical, and mental habitual conditionings. To aid in this maintenance of awareness, periodically when the frantic nature of this process gets intense, one abruptly shout "*phaṭ*" in a fierce tone and looks to the essence of the mind. Until such a sudden glance reveals that one has broken through the defenses to gain an enduring relaxation into the empty nature of the mind, one continues to return again and again to the wild enactments. The overall time period is indeterminate since it all depends on when the practitioner is able to make this differentiation and gain a visceral sensation of the mind's empty, vibrant nature: it can range from three days to three years, though often periods of seven, twenty-one, or one hundred days are mentioned.

At some point, the sudden look into the mind's nature amidst all the crazy activity thus gives way to a collapse into a deep state of relaxation in which the underlying purity of the mind's nature can finally come to the fore, thereby allowing one to differentiate this *transcedence* of oneself out from the ordinary cyclical patterns of distorting activity that characterize life. In the state of quiet relaxation when the body, speech, and mind become exhausted, habitual conditionings and defense mechanisms are relaxed, leaving nothing but to let go into one's own natural state. This settling into naturalness can be done in whatever position is physically comfortable, though in general a classic position in the Great Perfection involves lying on the right side with the right cheek resting on the right palm, and the right elbow tucked into the right side (lying facedown is said to lead to ignorance, lying on the left side to hatred, and lying on the back to desire).

While in theory the moment for settling in naturalness should be guided by personal insight, in practice it tends to be somewhat prestructured: one can do it for three days following uninterrupted practice of the "craziness" for a number of days; alternatively, during the day or morning one can do the impulse-activity and then settle into naturalness at night. In his *The Seminal Quintessence of the Master* (LYT1 165.1, 166.3, 168.2), Longchenpa indicates one does the "conduct" during the day, while at night one lies down on a comfortable bed to settle into naturalness: following physical conduct the body should be perfectly still, following verbal conduct one should be perfectly silent, and following mental conduct one's mind should be perfectly nonconceptual. Either way, the settling into naturalness is done for a number of hours at a time. The commentary on the passage from *The Tantra of the Self Emerging Teaching* (VNT1 182.2–6) cited in *The Treasury of Words and Meanings* provides a more programmed twelve-day schedule that one repeats once a year or as much as is possible given the circumstances: the practitioner begins with three days of physical activity, followed by one day of relaxing the body into its natural state by lying on a comfortable mattress; intermediately practicing verbal activity for three days, followed by one day where one relaxes speech into its natural state by not talking with anyone at all even to the extent of making a gesture; and finally for three more days practicing "differentiation" in terms of the mind, followed by one day during which the mind relaxes into its natural state via ceasing ordinary conceptualization. This preliminary dyad of frenetic activity and settling into naturalness mirrors the dyad of direct transcendence and breakthrough and also prefigures the ultimate end of direct transcendence visions when the visions fade away into nothingness.

The texts themselves refer to both "exoteric" and "supreme" motivations or rationales underlying these practices, which are substantially identical to the explanations given below for the final set of preliminary practices. In *The Treasury of the Supreme Vehicle* (TCD2 201.7ff), Longchenpa explains the practice of physical conduct thus:

> Since when initially the body develops in the embryo, both our speech and mind develop based upon it, it is necessary first to engage in the body conduct. The necessity of this practice is that through it you exhaust the karma of subsequent ordinary embodiment and thus no longer delight in ordinary activities, as well as purify physical negative actions. . . . If you practice this for seven days, eleven days, or half a month, externally attachment to your body is naturally reversed, internally your body becomes calm and subdued, and esoterically it is certain that your [corporeal body] will be freed as a luminously radiant illusory body. Then by relaxing in the body's natural condition for three, seven, or eleven days, your psychophysical components and so forth expand, and your body is unified with the emanation body.

Subsequently (TCD2 202.7) he explains verbal conduct in similar terms:

> In reliance upon thus [giving voice] to these different verbal expressions, you will interrupt the flow of circling within the three realms of saṃsāra. . . . When you diligently undertake this practice for the number of days specified above, the most diligent will be able to [totally] reverse attachment to speech itself, while for more ordinary practitioners realization will dawn that speech and all appearances are similarly aimless and impossible to pinpoint.
>
> The body is our foundation and the mind is the fruit or culmination, while speech is the connection between them; thus the conduct of speech is placed as the intermediate phase here. In this practice the rationales are to interrupt involvement in distorting forms of expression through voicing various sounds of your own and others, to not subsequently be reborn as whichever type of being's speech you give voice to, and to free the cycles of letters.

Finally (204.1) he explains mental conduct:

> Having practiced this for many days, you will no longer cycle through the three realms. . . . Via then settling into naturalness without any further projections or contractions, the basic gateway of ordinary psychic attention is blocked. . . . When you are divested of attachment to both the body and speech, it is appropriate to engage in the conduct cutting the root of the mind. By training on it to the point that it inherently fades away without a trace, you become free of the three realms of saṃsāra.

In *The Seminal Quintessence of the Master* (LYT1 168.2), Longchenpa offers an optimistic outlook:

> With diligent practice, superior practitioners will experience the emergence of the requisite signs in three days; for the average it will take five days; and for the inferior it will take anywhere from seven days onward. If at that time the sky becomes lucent with rainbow colored lights, it signifies you have exhausted your negativities and obscurations with mastery of the yoga; otherwise negativities and obscurations continue to hold sway, and thus you must again exert yourself in the practice.

Earlier in the same text (LYT1 165.2–4, 166.4–5, and 167.5–168.1), Longchenpa specifies the experiential signs marking success in each of the three phases; he also describes how the master will meditate on reality's immediacy in his or her own residence during these practices and periodically go out to a place where all his or her disciples can easily gather to inquire as to what signs have or have not occurred for each—if the requisite signs have not yet occurred for any given person, he or she has them repeat the practice. The signs of physically differentiating between saṃsāra and nirvāṇa are such things as becoming divested of any attachment to the body, feeling like one does not even have a body, not noticing heat or cold, not feeling hunger or thirst, never becoming fatigued, feeling as if one is flying through the sky, and blissful warmth blazing in the body. By repeating the practice until such signs occur, it is certain one will physically accomplish the differentiation. The motivation behind this practice is to pacify physical obstructions, purify negativities and obscurations, free the body into the emanation body (*nirmāṇakāya*), and become nondually united with the unchanging adamantine body of all the buddhas. The signs of verbal differentiation are such things as Sanskrit language, many teachings one never previously knew and melodious songs naturally welling up from within oneself, or the experience of such things as feeling no desire to speak and the supremely blissful dimension of the ineffable. The meditator is to repeat the practice until such signs occur. The motivation behind this practice is to pacify verbal obstructions, purify negativities and obscurations, free the speech into the enjoyment body (*saṃbhogakāya*), and become indivisible with the essence of the adamantine speech. The signs of mental differentiation are that the mind becomes radiant and light, distorting ideation ceases, one experiences a blissful, clear, and nonconceptual contemplative state, and the realization of skylike primordial freedom dawns from within. The meditator is to repeat the practice until such signs occur. The motivation behind this practice is to pacify mental obstructions, purify negativities and obscurations, free the mind into the reality body (*dharmakāya*), and expansively awaken into the essence of the adamantine mind.

Subjectivity as a Vajra, Letters, and Perfectly Intangible: The Preliminaries of Body, Speech, and Mind

The final set of practices is again divided into physical, verbal, and mental phases, which in this case are quite distinct from each other. However, the principle in each reiterates the pattern of activity followed by deep relaxation that characterizes the differentiation of domain practices. Longchenpa says it is best to do each for no less than seven days, acceptable to do each for three or five days, and necessary to at the very least do each for one day, since the introduction of the main practice depends on mastery of the preliminaries (LTY1 372.1). Of the three sets of preliminary practices, these are the mostly widely practiced in contemporary circles and the most emphasized in the classical literature. The reasons for their importance are fairly clear: they do not require special environments such as the other practices do (a windy spot, a stream, seclusion to act crazy in, and so forth); they are neatly packaged along the lines of the much beloved body, speech, and mind rubrics; their streamlined use of visualization invokes the power of tantric imaginal processes in a distinctively Great Perfection style; and the contemplation on the mind is a classic analytical inquiry opening up into breakthrough practice.

The Preliminaries of the Body

In a secluded spot, one assumes the "vajra" posture as one stays relaxed and breathes naturally. This posture involves placing the two soles together in a standing posture as one goes up on the toes, and putting one's two palms together (with a small space between them) above the head but not touching it. In this posture, one visualizes the body image as a three-pointed blue vajra, blazing hot with hundreds of small fire sparks. Its upper three tips are formed by the two hands and head, while its three lower tips are formed by the two legs and genitals. The three lower tips symbolize the three bodies of a buddha (reality, enjoyment, and emanation), the three upper tips symbolize the ground's essence, nature, and compassionate resonance, and the body/vajra's unification of these two ends into a single unity via the waist symbolizes the integration of breakthrough and direct transcendence (KGYT2 336.4). You then hold this posture until finally the legs give out and you collapse helplessly to the prepadded floor; you do *not* decide when to fall, but rather wait until your body's fatigue no longer allows it to sustain itself. The body's deep fatigue blocks the mind's ordinary ceaseless stitching together of experience, thereby ripping a hole within the constructed world through which you can begin glimpse another nature. You thus settle into naturalness by relaxing in whatever posture you happen to collapse in as you fall to the ground (adjusting the posture after the collapse would only foster conceptuality and thought activity, and as such should be avoided). Once conceptuality begins to stir again, you repeat the process. In the Palyul (*dpal yul*) tradition, the meditator is instructed to thrust a white "*a*" from his or her head through the Brahmā's aperture (i.e., at the head's center where hair swirls outward) far away into the sky and then fall back to flat on the back while chanting "*ha, ha, ha*" three times.

Longchenpa in *The Seminal Quintessence of the Profound* (ZMYT1 200.3) identifies the exoteric rationale as reversing attachment to the body, calming obstacles, and purifying the body's negative actions, the latter being the common element in the former two. He describes the ultimate rationale as the body not subsequently entering into the stronghold of the womb, being freed within the emanation body, and becoming nondual with the Buddha's body, the latter being the common element in the former two. This practice's connection to direct transcendence contemplation is similar to the previous practices: the dynamic, motile visualization of sparks flying off a burning hot vajra, the forced exhaustion of ordinary mental processes through viscerally experienced exhaustion, and the tuning into a state of relaxed uncontrived naturalness that is direct transcendence's necessary precursor.

The Preliminaries of Speech

The fourfold practice relating to speech involves the visualization and chanting of the syllable "*hūṃ*." In the standard mantra "*oṃ āḥ hūṃ*" it corresponds to the Buddha's mind and is further identified as the seed syllable of all the buddhas; thus in these practices *hūṃ* symbolizes one's own enlightened psychic energy. As you "seal," "refine your skill," "seek suppleness," and "enter the path" with the use of singular or pluralized *hūṃ*s which are visualized, chanted, and felt, your subjectivity thus undergoes concordant transformations: it is sealed, refined or activated, rendered supple, and finally inserted into pathways.

The first phase is termed "sealing" (*rgyas gdab pa*), since in two steps one seals or authenticates all appearances as illusory by transforming them into *hūṃs*. The initial phase is the sealing of external appearances: sitting in the lotus position with a straight back, the meditator visualizes his or her ground-awareness as a blue *hūṃ* in the heart. From it a *hūṃ* emerges from the right nostril (LYT1 367.1), then two, and then one after another many small *hūṃs* fill up all of the external landscape, such that everything is transformed into *hūṃs*. The meditator visualizes everywhere as filled with luminously radiant pure lands in the form of *hūṃs* radiating with the light of the five primordial gnoses; he or she imagines mountains as large *hūṃs*, forests as small *hūṃs* and leaves as minute *hūṃs*. These visual transformations are accompanied by continual chanting of long melodious *hūṃs* done with the lips and teeth just barely separated (KGYT1 295.1–2). During the entire process the meditator is to maintain awareness of the heart's central *hūṃ*, while gradually becoming convinced that nothing is real; impure vision is transformed into pure vision; the sense that the entire exterior display is a reflection of one's internal pristine awareness also induces a sensation of intimate intertwining expressed by the notion that the world is "self-presencing" (*rang snang*). Longchenpa sums up the significance of the practice thus (LYT1 367.2): "to ensure that at the time of the main practice your inner awareness will not fall under the sway of external appearances."

In the second step the meditator is to seal the internal body and mind by imagining the external *hūṃs* dissolve one by one into the body's interior through the left nostril or all the pores of the skin, such that the entire body is filled with *hūṃs* (LYT1 367.4 and KGYT1 295.3). When the large *hūṃs* (such as of a mountain) enter, one can visualize either the body as proportionately large or the *hūṃ* as entering within a sesame-seed-sized body, which leads to the liberating experience of appearances as indeterminate and awareness as aimless. The meditator may experience an uneasy feeling like an overfull stomach as the *hūṃs* fill up his or her interior, though via this practice he or she is eventually free from awareness being fettered by the physical body (LYT1 367.4). Finally, all the *hūṃs* disappear within the expanse and one relaxes the mind into its natural state. I have been told of oral instructions that one can eventually do the entire process with each exhalation and inhalation: the *hūṃs* manifest externally as all appearances with exhalation and then reenter the body with inhalation.

The second phase is termed "refining skill" or "activating potency" (*rtsal sbyong*) as it further develops the practice by literally interpenetrating, a process that again begins with exteriority and then proceeds to interiority. In terms of external appearances, hand-span-sized blue-black *hūṃs* glowing with the fiery light of the five primordial gnoses (KGYT1 295.5) emanate out via the right nostril from the heart's central *hūṃ* as the meditator repeatedly recites *hūṃ* forcefully and incisively. These *hūṃs* proceed unimpededly through material things with the capacity to perforate them at the mere touch; in their to and fro unimpeded penetrating movement, one imagines that everything one generally prioritizes in the visual field is gradually perforated. Thus in this practice appearances are not transformed but rather riddled with holes, becoming like rainbows in their transparency and intangibility. This explosion of materiality finally culminates in the total eradication of all appearances so that one no longer sees anything at all. The meditator then proceeds to the inner body, as the *hūṃs* pass back and forth directly through the body without returning through the nostrils, such that their perforation eventually destroys the body; it becomes no more than the reflection of the moon in water. As before, this external/internal oscillation can eventually be done with each exhalation and inhalation, such that with exhalation the exterior is shot through with holes and with inhalation the interior experiences a similar fate.

The third phase is termed "seeking suppleness" (*mnyen btsal*) or "seeking out an aid" (*gnyen btsal*): the former term indicates seeking the gentleness or pliability of the mind rather than its usual rigidity and stiffness, while the latter term indicates using a stick as an aid for the visualization as the eyes focus on *hūṃs* winding up and down it, which also functions as an "antidote" to mental rigidity. Focusing on a meditative reference point in front, such as a mountain, tree trunk, or upright stick planted in the ground, the meditator is to emanate out a rope of *hūṃs* from the heart's central *hūṃ* via the right nostril and coil it around the reference point so that it moves on up to its top in a spiraling motion. To develop one pointed mental stabilization, one then focuses attention on the *hūṃ* at the top for an extended period of time, while maintaining an awareness of the garland of *hūṃs* going back to the heart through the nostril. Then the *hūṃs* slowly unwind down the stick, recede back to the nostril, and thus dissolve into the heart's *hūṃ*; one then repeats the entire process from the heart anew, eventually collapsing the entire projection and reabsorption into the space of a single exhalation and inhalation. While concentrating on their movements, the meditator utters melodious drawn out *hūṃs*. The aim behind this phase of the practice is to gain stability in concentration so that wherever one focuses the mind, it takes hold there. As one thus gains control over awareness by shifting its focus point in space at will by training on these "flexible" reference points, awareness becomes more supple such that in encountering the exterior world a fluid mutability is introduced into its perceptions (LYT1 368.4).

The fourth phase is termed "entering the path" (*lam gzhug*): identifying subjectivity with a blue-black *hūṃ* half an arm's length (or whatever is comfortable) in size as one hums a song of long melodious *hūṃs* and begins to travel to places known and unknown. According to Khanpo Jikphun, there are various methods for the initial generation of this subjectivity as a traveling letter: the meditator's own body is transformed into the traveling *hūṃ*, the heart's *hūṃ* increases in size, or a second *hūṃ* is emanated from the heart's *hūṃ*. One's body then literally *becomes* the *hūṃ* rather than a dualistically conceived rider and mount and is considered to be the essence of one's psychic complex of unified winds and mind; one's humming of *hūṃs* matches the rhythms of this *hūṃ*'s movement. The meditator begins by traveling to places he or she knows and is attached to such as towns, dense forests, gorges, or waterfalls, thus bringing these karmic traces to closure as attachment to them is exhausted in the simple fatigue of constant travel. One then proceeds to let the imagination roam free and overcome attachment even to the more unusual spaces of imagination, as one opens up new fields of experience by transporting consciousness into unknown places, including pure lands where one then remains in a state of contemplation. Throughout one continues to consider that as a *hūṃ* one can travel anywhere without limitations. If the mind grows fatigued in these travels, the meditator is to shout "*phaṭ*" and release the traveling to remain nondually where one is. Ultimately, in Longchenpa's explanation, one travels farther and farther away, until finally with the thought that one is going infinitely far away to the limits of the sky, one just lets the visualization go and return to a quiet presence in the body without the *hūṃ* sequentially retracing its steps; this can also be accompanied by a final "*phaṭ*".

The Preliminaries of Mind

This final practice of questioning leads directly into breakthrough contemplation. It is centered in a famous triune practice of observing one's own mind called "origin, abode, and destination" (*'byung gnas 'gro*), which revolves around the temporal structures of past, present, and future. In three successive phases, the meditator is to observe each thought that manifests in the mind's landscape, inquiring as to where it came from, where it endures, and to where it departs when it subsides. The practice thus entails a rigorous quest for the mind, which despite its apparent nearness proves to be deceptively elusive when one seeks to pinpoint analytically its circumstances. In addition to direct introspective observation of particular thoughts, there is also a more analytical directed inquiry into the general nature of thought: how do they arise, how are they in their subsistence, how do they disappear? The meditator begins by examining possible sites of the mind's origination and its nature in its initial origination. Does it originate from external appearances, or is it merely a construction of socializing discourses? In observing a particular thought, one asks whether it is linked to one of the senses (something seen or heard?). Does it originate from the internal psychophysical components or from matter? Analyzing matter itself down to its atoms, one finds its own seeming solidity fades away under scrutiny. Eventually this sustained relentless questioning yields a realization that the mind is unborn, rootless, and empty, thus introducing the meditator to the inner dimension of the emanation body. The examination then proceeds to the mind's current site of endurance and how it might exist substantially as an agent of such endurance. Through a similar type of inquiry seeking the mind's essence within inner, outer, and liminal spaces, one realizes its truth as nonabiding and without support; this serves to introduce the enjoyment body. Finally the meditator turns to the ultimate site to which thoughts fade away and how they function as an agent of that fading: where do thoughts go when they cease? The consequent realization of the mind as unceasing and beyond limitations introduces the reality body, the openness into which all manifestation dissolves.

Via this questioning and the consequent realization that there are no concrete answers to grasp onto, a gap opens up, a sense of openness that prepares the meditator for the symbolic introduction to the skylike nature of awareness. He or she observes the absence of any precise source, abode, or destination; instead, everything arises, exists, and subsides interdependently. When this inquiry thus yields no answers as the mind proves impossible to pinpoint in this way, one's awareness suddenly recedes to the intangible background of the mind, or the emptiness of mind-as-such (*sems nyid*). This then is termed the introduction to the mind's nature, the reality body of experience. The point of this is experientially finding what the wide open space of the mind's nature is really like, and thus as the master gives the symbolic introduction, the meditator suddenly realizes that the true characteristic of body, speech, and mind is none other than the sky. Once this recognition is stabilized, it functions as the initiatory introduction (*ngo 'phrod*) into the main practice. Breakthrough contemplation itself bypasses these more analytical types of conceptual inquiries, though it presupposes their previous utilization to penetrate to the emptiness of the mind.

Relaxation and Revitalization

In *The Seminal Quintessence of the Ḍākinī*, Longchenpa presents these preliminaries in three phases: the "external" (combining the "differentiation" practices with the preliminaries of body, speech, and mind), the "internal" (i.e., the six-syllable-realm meditation), and the "esoteric." The esoteric itself consists of two aspects (KGYT2 349.4–352.3): settling into naturalness and revitalization. In short, following all the frenetic activity shaking up the meditator's energy, he or she lies down and relaxes in a quiet state; this then must be followed by a revitalizing process allowing energy to reorganize into more positive patterns. While other Great Perfection preliminary practices are designed to enable one to enter the experience of the union of inner calm (*zhi gnas; śamatha*) and incisive vision (*lhag mthong; vipaśyanā*), this recedes to the background in the wild activity of the differentiation practice. Thus following this practice one "relaxes in the natural state" to avoid sickness ensuing after all the agitation, as well as to rest in the experience of the mind's ultimate nature that comes to the fore following the exhaustion of ordinary physical, verbal, and mental activities. Longchenpa indicates the meditator is to lie on a comfortable bed divested of thought, speech, or movement, resting in a natural state: still in the nonwavering of the body, quiet in the lack of speech, and nonconceptual in the mind's deep calm. Subsequently settling into naturalness is said to penetrate to the fundamental dimension of the breakthrough (KGYT2 352.6)

Following this relaxation the meditator must revitalize or rejuvenate his or her now purified energies and thus reengage the union of inner calm and incisive vision; in this way he or she brings this union to the fore again, placing it in the path where it sustains the ensuing practices of breakthrough and direct transcendence. Having divested himself or herself of physical, verbal, and mental obscurations preventing the corresponding positive energies' development, the meditator now allows those positive qualities to unfold. Thus after settling into naturalness, one uses a trio of gazes in set postures to revitalize in the reintegration of stillness and movement: first the listener (*śrāvaka*) position stills the body, the posture of a bodhisattva stabilizes that quiet, and then the wrathful stance frees that stabilized energy so that it can participate in dynamic enlightened movement. The listener position refers to the classical lotus position with its seven points; the posture of the bodhisattva refers to sitting in the lotus position with the eyes staring wide open into space; and the wrathful stance signifies a standing posture with one leg extended out front with the heel on the ground and toes in the air, and the other leg drawn in with sole on the ground and knee crooked, while the eyes stare wide open into space as one verbally utters "*ha ha hi hi.*" These three postures are done successively with the time for each phase indeterminate, since each is completed whenever one is able to attain stable meditative union of inner calm and incisive vision within it, at which point one moves on to the next phase. Since usually the wrathful position with its sound "*ha ho hi*" tends to make the mind waver, it is the most difficult and thus is done last; success with it indicates that the meditator's contemplation has become stable enough that he or she can move onto the main practices of the Great Perfection.

The text of the *Tshig Don Mdzod* is translated from the edition of Klong chen rab 'byams pa's *Mdzod bdun*, published by Sherab Gyaltsen and Khyentse Labrang in six volumes; (Gangtok, Sikkim, 1983).

Further Reading

For one of the most popular Nyingma accounts of the standard preliminary processes, see Patrul Rinpoche, *The Words of My Perfect Teacher* (New York: HarperCollins, 1994). For a translation of Longchenpa's own account of such practices as well as an extension into Great Perfection contemplation, see Herbert Guenther, *Kindly Bent to Ease Us* (Emeryville, CA: Dharma Publishing, 1975–1976). For a very loose translation of a late Bönpo work with Great Perfection preliminary practices almost identical to those outlined here, see Shardza Tashi Gyaltsen, *Heart Drops of the Dharmakaya*, trans. Lopon Tenzin Namdak (Ithaca: Snow Lion Publications, 1993). For an interesting autobiographical survey of the Great Perfection, see Namkhai Norbu, *The Crystal and the Way of Light* (London: Routledge & Kegan Paul, 1986). Finally, for an interesting account of practices similar to the "differentiation" in the wildly popular contemporary Qigong movement in China, see John Alton, *Living Qigong* (Boston: Shambhala, 1997).

The preceding discussion was principally based on the following Tibetan sources: *Theg mchog mdzod* (TCD), *Bi ma snying thig* (VNT), *Bla ma yang tig* (LYT), *Mkha' 'gro snying thig* (KGNT), *Mkha 'gro yang tig* (KGYT), and *Zab mo yang tig* (ZMYT). The first work is also published as part of the *Mdzod bdun* (see above), while the other five works constitute the massive *Snying thig ya bzhi*, published in an eleven volume edition by Trulku Tsewang, Jamyang and L. Tashi in New Delhi (1971).

For more precise references, please refer to my upcoming translation of *The Treasury of Precious Words and Meanings* as well as my associated monographs tentatively entitled *Mysticism and Rhetoric in the Great Perfection The Architecture of Absence and Embodied Visions.*

Preliminary Practices for Transcendence

SETTING FORTH THE RELATIONSHIP OF THE PRELIMINARIES TO THE MAIN PRACTICES

Analogically, it resembles how a traveler embarked on a frightening road first reconnoiters the road for concealed sources of danger, following which she or he can proceed onward comfortably without worry. In a similar manner, you first penetrate to the fundamentals of your three gateways [physical, verbal, and mental] via these preliminaries, and thus are able to proceed to the ultimate reaches of the main practice without impediments or obstacles.

It also resembles how someone first takes care of security at a sentry castle in a dangerous border region, and thus is able to stay in the "main residence" with their mind at ease. In a similar manner, you first cut the root of all oscillation between hope and fear or acceptance and rejection via the preliminaries, and then are able to rest at the time of the "main practice" without compulsive exertion driven by your hopes and fears.

Finally, it resembles how prior to farming one must amass the requisite materials, whereby "the main stage" of farming will go smoothly from the seedlings up to the autumn harvest. One must proceed similarly in meditative practice: having first resolved the ground's great spontaneous presence via the preliminaries, you proceed through the four visions' optimization at the time of "the main practice," and consequently attain in your own being the fruit of the All Good One (Kun tu bzang po) reality itself.

THE ACTUAL PRELIMINARIES

This involves three sections: training on the four elements' sounds and realities as the initial guidance on the three bodies of a buddha; training on the conduct of differentiating between the domains of saṃsāra and nirvāṇa as the initial guidance on awareness; and training on the preliminaries of body, speech, and mind as the initial guidance on the mind.

The Initial Guidance on the Three Bodies: Training on the Four Elements' Sounds and Realities

The Direct Consequence of Sound Tantra provides a brief discussion:

The phase of training on the three bodies
Emphasizes the sensual qualities of the elemental energies:
The best way to definitively accomplish it
Is through training on the supreme sounds of earth, water, fire, and wind.

(1) You apprehend the harmonies of the ḍākinīs
In the turbulent noise of water's sound;
When you continually cultivate attunement with it,
The emanation bodies will definitively come to pass.

(2) The cool and heavy sound of earth
Is endowed with the voice of the great Brahmā;
When you continually practice listening to it,
The perfect enjoyment body will definitively come to pass.

(3) Training on the drawn out sound of fire
Reveals the melodious tones of Viṣṇu;
Whomever cultivates listening to it,
Will definitively attain the reality body's enlightened qualities.

(4) The whistling and fierce blowing of the sound of wind
Is the speech of the royal *khyung*'s flapping wings as he soars in the sky;
When you continually concentrate on its recitation,
You are training on the shared exoteric dimension of the three bodies.

The Illuminating Lamp explains these practices more extensively:

(1) To expand on this, in seclusion
You get a fire going with firewood and so forth,
And then sit on a comfortable seat
At a spot two fathoms in distance from the fire.

The key point of the body is that it should be like an animal
As you gaze fully like a lion
By casting your awareness into the fire's center.

You join your own cognitive experiences
To the sound of fire's energy there
In its turbulent roaring, whooshing, hissing,
Humming, crackling, and snapping.

The desired accomplishment will without a doubt ensue
For a fortunate one practicing thus for half a month,
As the visionary becomes endowed with psychic powers.

(2) In practicing on the sound of water
The practitioner does the preliminaries as before;
Then when crops are ripening in autumn yellow,

In an empty place where downflowing water is falling turbulently,
And waves are extremely agitated,
The key point of the body is crouching down,
While the keypoint of awareness is directing it to the middle of the water
As you gaze at its center with an elephant's glance.

If initially your capabilities aren't up to it,
You cover your head up, off where the sound is minimal,
And listen to the degree your endurance allows.

Through meditating thus for three months
You will accomplish the great assurance of self-awareness;
When you listen continually to this sound of water
Having directed your cognitive attention to the ears,
The supreme unborn will without a doubt unfold,
And you will come to understand a wide variety of teachings.

This is a procedure appropriate for revitalizing depressed states.

(3) Those who desire to attend to the sound of wind
Should do the preliminaries as before.

At the juncture of three valleys or on a mountain peak,
You carefully construct a secluded hut
With windows in the cardinal directions.

The yoga itself then involves directing your auditory attention
To whatever direction the wind is blowing.

Through practicing this continually,
The desired accomplishment will without a doubt ensue
For a fortunate one in one month,
As the visionary attains the supreme felt experience.

(4) The sound of earth is heavy and consistent:
Making many types of egg[-shaped clay balls],
You meditate continually on [their sound]
As you toss them back and forth between your hands.

Through meditating thus for six months you will obtain
The definitive fruit of dominion over the elements.

(5) For the sound of space, the visionary
With the right fortune should go to a mountain peak;
The key point of the body is to lie supine,
While you cast your awareness into the sky
As a space soaring khyung,
And exhale your breath again and again.

When you thus remain continually within the sky,
Without a doubt in three years
You will become like a bird in the sky.

When you meditate on these continually,
You will accomplish worldly benefit
And attain the level of the supreme seal.

The Tantric Seed of Experiencing the Esoteric describes the practices thus:

The wonder of it!
For the individual desiring such exoteric signs to emerge
So as to guide other living beings,
The branches of efficacious means to do so are like this;
For these varied exoteric activities and signs,
You must train in first reversing attachment.

Whatever you are able to train on among the practice-phases on the mind,
Through it you tune into the nonconceptual mind.

Via the yoga of their sounds just as they are,
You become experientially attuned to the sounds and realities
Of the four elements of earth, water, fire, and wind,
And thus come to know psychically by means of this yoga
The respective languages of the six types of living beings.

Through the succession of days in a month, seasons, and six aspects of a day,
You know the inherent times of all of their languages.

Whoever understands this with diligent exertion and divested of error,
Will come to understand the flow of the mind,
In future, present, and past just as it is,
And act for the welfare of others with emanations.

If you don't train on this first off,
You will not attain the potency of psychic powers
In planting the seeds of emanations.
Therefore, train on the sounds of the elements.

The Initial Guidance on Awareness: Training on the Conduct of Differentiating between the Domains of Saṃsāra and Nirvāṇa

In the first phase of this triune practice you make the differentiation within your body and in the evening settle into a natural state; then in the second phase you make the differentiation within your speech, and thus settle into a natural state; and finally in the third phase you make the differentiation within your mind and thus settle into a natural state. As explained below, the underlying rationale for each phase is twofold. In the words of *The Tantra of the Self Emerging Teaching:*

> Those of superior fortune who desire to engage
> The thus described ultra-esoteric presence of reality's immediacy
> Must begin with the preliminary practice of conduct,
> In order to initially reverse attachment
> In their physical, verbal, and mental being.
>
> (1) In terms of the body, you must run, lie down,
> Raise up, shake the limbs,
> Circumambulate, and prostrate,
> Whirl the limbs, roll the head,
> And do whatever actions come to mind;
> Dance, do symbolic hand gestures, and make abrupt changes,
> Doing whatever actions you can imagine.
>
> Whoever acts thus
> Cuts off physical attachment within herself,
> And thus differentiation [of the two domains] ensues in all physical states
> Via contemplatively implementing this tantra, O emanation body!
>
> (2) After that, you begin the conduct of speech:
> You should chant mantras, recitations, preaching,
> Utter things existent, nonexistent, and apparent,
> As well as diverse verbalizations of your thought processes,
> Or voice the symbolic cries of various animals
> And the diverse aspects of their languages.
>
> Whoever acts thus
> Cuts off verbal attachment within herself
> And thus differentiates between the domains of saṃsāra and nirvāṇa.
>
> (3) Subsequent to this,
> You should undertake the conduct of the mind
> By acting out various discursive thoughts:
> Likes and dislikes, pleasures and pains,
> Permanence and impermanence, and so forth;
> Reflection on views, meditations, and conducts,
> Religious and irreligious notions, and so forth;
> Desire, hatred, and ignorance,
> Virtue and nonvirtue, and so forth.
>
> Whoever acts thus
> Cuts off mental attachment within herself
> And thus differentiates between the domains of saṃsāra and nirvāṇa.

The Direct Consequence of Sound Tantra describes these practices as well:

The wonder of it! Without making this astounding
Differentiation between saṃsāra and nirvāṇa,
The binding involvements of your body, speech, and mind
In the three realms won't be severed.

Thus I will explain the triune differentiation
Of saṃsāra and nirvāṇa.

(1) In terms of the body, moving and sitting,
Twisting, a variety of yogic exercises,
Flinging out and pulling in your limbs,
And a wide variety of other physical actions are utilized;
First envisioning them through imagination,
The physical behavior and actions of the six types of living beings
Should be mentally identified with and then physically acted out.

Whoever is up to such conduct
Cuts off the flow of subsequent karma through thus undertaking it;
This practice has two underlying rationales
Classified into the exoteric and the supreme.

(2) Having thus optimized the first phase as marked by the appropriate signs,
The practitioner undertakes the conduct of speech.
Because this aims to realize verbal expression's true nature,
You don't repress anything you might say
In a wide variety of sounds and languages.
You thus express all sorts of positive and negative things
In the languages of the gods, serpent spirits, gnomes,
Ethereal spirits, vampires, and Viṣṇu;
In brief, the languages of the six types of sentient beings
Are mentally envisioned and then verbally expressed.

This phase as well has two rationales
Classified as supreme and exoteric.

(3) Having thus reached optimization of that phase
The practitioner must perform the conduct of the mind,
Which involves relying on mental activity's cycling
Projections and contractions around the past, present, and future.

Your mind in its likes and dislikes, nobility and vileness,
Its external examinations and internal reflections on
All the variety of existent and nonexistent things—
The practice is mindful attentiveness to whatever thus pops into your mind.

The cutting off of subsequent births' flow is thus certain;
This phase's underlying rationales are classified as above.

Having completed this practice of conduct
You zero in perpetually on the key points of immediacy,
While with its perfection you no longer enter the three realms of
saṃsāra—
You should thus rely on this extreme exotericism.

The Initial Guidance on the Mind:
Training on the Preliminaries of Body, Speech and Mind

This involves two aspects: the actual preliminaries and settling into a pristine natural state. *The Direct Consequence of Sound Tantra* describes the former thus:

Since the preliminaries of the body
Block the drive fueling ordinary activity,
Assuming the adamantine sceptre posture
And thus refining the body benefits the mind.

Speech: focused on the syllable *hūṃ*,
Via "sealing," "refining skill,"
"Seeking out an aid," and "entering the path,"
You refine speech, thereby benefiting the mind.

The mind: when you analyze the triad
Of the mind's initial place of emergence,
Intermediate dwelling, and final destination,
Such refining of the mind leads to an understanding of its abiding
reality.

The Direct Consequence of Sound Tantra also explicates [the consequent phase] of settling into a natural pristine state:

Via thus yogically tuning into naturalness,
You must settle into a natural state.

These preliminaries' underlying rationale is as follows: the exoteric motivation is to pacify obstacles of body, speech, and mind as well as cleanse evil acts and obscurations, while the supreme motivation is to be freed within the matrix of the Buddha's body, speech, and mind. Thus it is said:

This practice has two underlying rationales
Classified into the exoteric and the supreme.

The underlying rationales and motivations behind the triune settling into a natural state are as follows: through the body settling into its natural state, your psychophysical components, sensory elements, and enlightening minds [i.e., the body's seminal nuclei] expand; through speech settling into its natural state, you remain within an ineffable dimension as linguistically informed discursive thought processes become exhausted; and through the mind settling into its natural state, you liberate the objects ordinary thought is addicted to.

My discussion of the preliminary practices is thus complete.

—20—

The Regulations of a Monastery

José Ignacio Cabezón

According to tradition, Tsong kha pa (1357–1419), founder of the Gelukpa sect of Tibetan Buddhism, composed his commentary on Nāgārjuna's *Mūlamadhyamakakārikās*, the *Ocean of Reasoning*, while he was in residence in a small hermitage outside of Lhasa called Sera Chöding around the year 1409. In the midst of writing this work, one of the pages of the text is said to have flown into the air in a gust of wind. It began to emit "*a*" letters (the symbol of the Perfection of Wisdom) in the color of molten gold. Some of these melted into a stone at the base of the hill and became permanently imprinted on it. Witnessing this, Tsong kha pa prophesied that this place would be the future site of a great center of Buddhist learning, an institution of particular importance for the study and practice of the Madhyamaka doctrine of emptiness. This was in fact the very place where Tsong kha pa's disciple Jamchen Chöje (Byams chen chos rje shākya ye shes, 1354–1435), would found Sera monastery in the year 1419.

The three great monasteries of the Gelukpa sect, Drepung, Ganden, and Sera, are religious universities, centers for the study and practice of Buddhist doctrine. There, some of the monks engage in a twenty-year program of study and prayer that culminates in the degree of geshe. Based on the classical texts of Indian Buddhism and their Tibetan Gelukpa commentaries, the full curriculum included the study of Collected Topics (introductory metaphysics, logic, psychology, and epistemology), Perfection of Wisdom (the fundamentals of the Mahāyāna Buddhist path), Pramāṇa (advanced logic, studied during special winter interterm sessions at a retreat outside of Lhasa, with monks of all three monasteries in attendance), Madhyamaka (the theory of emptiness), Vinaya (the monastic precepts), and Abhidharma (advanced metaphysics). With these subjects and texts as the basis of their curriculum, monks engage in memorization, oral explanation, and study, and especially debate as the chief methods of transmitting Buddhist doctrine from one generation to the next. The text translated below deals with the traditions and customs of one of Tibet's great monastic institutions, the Je (Byes) College of Sera.

The fifth holder of the Sera throne is a particularly important figure because he is credited with having founded the Je College of that institution. This is Günkhyenpa Rinchen Lodrö Senge (Kun mkhyen pa Rin chen blo gros seng ge), a disciple of Tsong kha pa and Jamchen Chöje. Many interesting stories surround the life of Günkhyenpa. According to oral tradition, after he received a hand-blessing from Tsong kha pa, Günkhyenpa had permanently imprinted on his head the palmprint of his hand. According to another well-known tradition, when he first arrived at Sera and visited the main temple, one of the sixteen arhat statues came to life. Moving forward to greet him, it said, "It is good that the great Günkhyenpa has come. How appropriate that you are raising the banner of the teachings here." This legend is perhaps meant to explain why Günkhyenpa, along with a hundred or so followers, abandoned his original monastery at Drepung to establish the Je College at Sera.

Günkhyenpa is one of the most interesting and controversial figures of his day, partly because of his multiple sectarian and monastic affiliations. Born as the son of a Nyingma lama, he is said to have made an oath to him never to abandon the practice of the deity Hayagrīva, a deity with strong historical roots in the Nyingma sect (see chapter 35). Keeping to his word, he eventually made Hayagrīva the tantric meditational deity (*yi dam*) of Sera Je. Although Günkhyenpa wrote several monastic textbooks (*yig cha*) that were used at the Je College in the early days of that institution, these were apparently confiscated in later times by the Tibetan government because they were perceived as not being in complete accord with what had come to be considered Tsong kha pa's ultimate stance concerning the profound view of emptiness.

The early history of Sera is obscure. It seems that initially this monastery contained four separate colleges, which underwent numerous transformations until only two colleges remained, known as Je and Me (Smad). A third Tantric College (Sngags pa) was founded at Sera much later under the patronage of the Mongolian ruler Lhazang Khan, who controlled Lhasa during the early part of the eighteenth century (1706–1717). Hence, from that time until the final occupation of Lhasa by the Chinese in 1959, Sera monastery had three colleges and could boast a monastic population of somewhere between 8,000 and 10,000 monks, making it the second largest monastery in the world (after Drepung). During the final takeover of Lhasa by Chinese forces in 1959, Sera was bombed and many of its temples, libraries, and monastic living quarters were completely destroyed. Most of what remained was either neglected or pillaged during the Cultural Revolution. Today Sera monastery in Lhasa, partially rebuilt, primarily with private Tibetan donations, has a resident population of close to 500 monks (the limit set by Chinese authorities). A "new" Sera monastery in the Tibetan settlement camp of Bylakuppe in South India was founded by monks of the original Sera, who went into exile in India after the overthrow of the Tibetan government by the Chinese. This latter institution, thriving to this day as a center of Buddhist learning, has a resident monastic population of approximately 2,000 monks.

The translation that follows is an excerpt from a work that deals with the traditions of the Je College. The *Great Exhortation* (*Tshogs gtam chen mo*), as the work is known colloquially, is an oral text that was published in written form for the first time only in 1991. Surviving in oral form for hundreds of years, it has been passed on from one generation of monks to the next simply by being recited several times a year in assembly. In the Je College, the oral nature of the transmission of the *Great Exhortation* is expressed by the saying, "a lineage from mouth to mouth, a lineage from ear to ear." The monks of the college consider the work to be of great profundity. Hearing it is said to be equivalent to hearing the complete teaching of Tsong kha pa's magnum opus, the *Great Exposition of the Stages of the Path to Enlightenment* (*Lam rim chen mo*).

As regards content, the *Great Exhortation* is a conglomeration of historical anecdotes, spiritual advice, and the rules and customs particular to the Je College. It belongs to a genre of Tibetan literature known as *cha-yik* (*bca' yig*), documents that deal with the rules and regulations of particular monastic institutions. Although all Buddhist monks and nuns in Tibet follow as their principle discipline the monastic vows as set forth in the Indian Buddhist vinaya tradition of the Mūlasarvāstivādin sect, Tibetan monasteries felt a need to supplement this general discipline with more specific documents that focused on the practical aspects of daily life: the *cha-yik*. The Je College's *cha-yik*, the *Great Exhortation*, is unique in that it is the only one, to my knowledge, that has been preserved orally. The work is composed in a highly honorific and formal style and, typical of oral texts, is quite repetitive. As one would expect of a living oral tradition, the work has become a hodgepodge of information by virtue of having been added to throughout the generations. It gives "the listener" information on such practical matters as the process that novices must follow to enter the monastery, the types and quality of robes and shoes that may be worn and their symbolism, the kinds of rosaries that may be used, and even where monks may urinate. The several discussions that preface the actual *Exhortation* (the last of the six divisions) provide us with interesting historical clues concerning life in the Je College. For example, the clear limitations concerning place, time, and the individual expounding the *Exhortation* are reflective of a historical period in which "advice" must have been plentiful and gratuitous, to the point where those in positions of power must have felt a need to limit and standardize it. Clues such as these make the present work one that is an important source not only for the study of monastic life, but for the study of Tibetan religious history as well. Its eclectic and synthetic character, combining themes and styles from both high and popular cultures, makes it unique in Tibetan "literary" history, and very enjoyable reading.

The present translation is based on a manuscript that would become the first printed edition of the text, published by the Je College in India. Fearing that the work would be lost unless it was preserved in written form, several of the older monks of the monastery compiled a working manuscript. This preliminary version was then circulated more widely until consensus was achieved. Although now existing in a written version, the text continues to be recited by heart at regular intervals in the assembly of the Je College in India, either by the disciplinarian (*dge skyos*) or by the abbot (*mkhen po*).

The passage that follows is a translation of the first third of the text *Byang chub lam rim chen mo dang 'brel ba'i ser byes mkhas snyan grwa tshang gi bca' khrims che mo* (Bylakuppe: Ser jhe Printing Press, 1991). The full title reads "The Great Regulations of the Sera Je College of Learned Scholars, [Composed] in Relation to [Tsong kha pa's] *Great [Exposition] of the Stages of the Path to Enlightenment.*" According to the Mongolian Geshe Senge, the recently deceased abbot of the Je College of Sera in Tibet, the *Great Exhortation* was written down by the Mongolian scholar Janglung Paṇḍita (Lcang lung paṇḍita). Upon searching the indices to the seven volumes of his collected works, however, I was able to find nothing under the title "Great Exhortation." The seventh text in the *ca* volume entitled *Dge' ldan theg chen bshad sgrub gling gi bca' yig chen mo'i zur 'debs dren gso'i brjed byang*, which was missing from Geshe Senge's edition of the collected works, might very well be the work in question. It is possible that Janglung Paṇḍita, who studied at Sera Je, adopted the *Great Exhortation* as the disciplinary text (*bca' yig*) for his own monastery, Ganden Thekchen Shedrupling (Dka' ldan theg chen shes sgrub gling). The present disciplinarian of the Je College in Tibet, who has seen the Janglung Paṇḍita version, claims that it varied considerably from the one used at present. For example, the former is said to have only five major divisions, as opposed to the six major and three minor divisions of the version now recited at the Je College. Until Janglung's work is found, however, we must be content with the Indian edition as the only available one.

The *Great Exhortation*, being the transcription of an oral text, is not an easy work to translate. The text is full of archaisms, honorifics, and formal expressions, and the phrasing is often difficult to render into English. At times one has the feeling that a sentence will never end. When it does the point is often lost in the ceremonial and poetical nature of the language. In my translation I have tried to strike a balance between, on the one hand, capturing the oral flavor of the text and, on the other, creating an intelligible translation. In the interests of the latter, some explanations have been inserted in square brackets. The numerous repetitions, the set phrasings, and the clear evidence of textual layering are of course vestiges of the *Great Exhortation*'s very recent past as an exclusively oral text. This is an aspect of the text I wanted to preserve in translation because it is innate to the text's self-identity.

Further Reading

The most detailed discussion of the *Bca' yig* literature in a Western language is Ter Ellingson's "Tibetan Monastic Constitutions: The Bca' Yig," in *Reflections on Tibetan Culture: Essays in Memory of Turrell V. Wylie*, ed. L. Epstein and R. F. Sherburne, Studies in Asian Thought and Religion, vol. 12 (Lewiston: Edwin Mellen Press, 1990), pp. 205–30. An excellent general overview of the curriculum of the Gelukpa colleges is Guy Newland's "Debate Manuals (*yig cha*) in dGe lugs pa Monastic Colleges," in *Tibetan Literature: Essays in Honor of Geshe Lhundub Sopa*, ed. J. I. Cabezon and R. R. Jackson (Ithaca: Snow Lion, 1995). On the tradition of Indo-Tibetan scholasticism pursued in Tibetan monasteries, see my *Buddhism and Language: A Study of Indo-Tibetan Scholasticism* (Albany, N.Y.: SUNY Press, 1994).

The Great Exhortation

It has been said, from the supremely vast and beautiful vase that is the mouth of the glorious Gendün Gyatso (Dge 'dun rgya mtsho, the second Dalai Lama), who [in his eloquence] brings a smile to the lips of Sarasvatī [the goddess of scholarship]:

> The Je College is the place for the systematic study of the scriptures
> Of the two trailblazers [Asaṅga and Nāgārjuna], of Vasubandhu,
> Guṇaprabha, and Śākyaprabha, [Indian scholar-saints whose works, in Tibetan translation, form the basis for the monastic curriculum.]
> May this assembly increase like a lake in summer,
> And may the three aspects of scholarly activity flourish.

As he has said, [our college] is completely without an equal in elucidating, like the sun, the precious teachings of the Conqueror through the three activities of exegesis, dialectics, and composition and through the three actions of hearing, contemplating, and meditating upon the oceanlike scriptural tradition of the scholars and sages of India and Tibet, like those of the trailblazers Nāgārjuna and Asaṅga.

Lord refuge, great abbot, great Vajradhara, and those who sit before you, the supreme congregation, a disciplined assembly of āryans, a congregation of a multitude of scholars, a precious oceanlike assembly, and also the general assembly of the deities of the maṇḍala that are the play of the blessed one, the great glory, the Supreme Stallion [Hayagrīva], the merest remembrance of whom allows one easily to obtain every accomplishment, both supreme and ordinary, as well as those who have been sworn into allegiance, Ging-nga (Ging lnga), Za (Bza'), Dong (Gdong mo bzhi), Begdze Chamsing (Beg rtse lcam sring), lend me your precious ears.

What is it that I have to say? The white banner, which is renowned under the name of our own "Sera Je College of Renowned Scholars," flies forcefully from Tö, where the air is filled with the sweet aroma of the Dzāti, to Me, where the silk is manufactured. As you are all aware, from today we begin our famous great Summer Doctrinal Session [one of the major periods of study and debate in the monastery's academic year]. So be it. As the first of the series of rules and regulations for this period of time, the disciplinarian must make the assignments for the begging of wood. [It must have been the case in the early days of the college that the monks depended on the wood they received through begging for cooking fuel. This they used especially for making tea that would be drunk during special debate sessions. In the later days, once the college achieved a greater level of economic stability, the practice of begging for wood became a ceremonial one, though these debate sessions never lost the name of the "Begged Wood Debates" (*shing slong dam bca'*).] After that the lord refuge, the great abbot, the great Vajradhara, will give a detailed and extensive exhortation based upon the *Great Exposition of the Stages of the Path to Enlightenment*. If there arises no other urgent business, such as a religious festival, the debate session is then held after the third day, and then I, just as water is poured from one vase to another and a stone is passed from one hand to another, must offer the *Great Exhortation*. This is a fine and old custom. May it never deteriorate but only flourish. So be it.

O field of merit for beings, and even for the gods, unsurpassed earth, source of refuge, O disciplined assembly of āryans, congregation of a multitude of scholars, precious oceanlike assembly, O general assembly of the deities of the maṇḍala that are the play of the blessed one, the great glory, the Supreme Stallion, the merest remembrance of whom allows one easily to obtain every accomplishment, both supreme and ordinary, as well as those who have been sworn into allegiance, Ging nga, Za, Dong (mozhi), Begdze Chamsing, whose power, like the blazing of the flames of lightning, overcomes an entire stone mountain's worth of the demonic hordes of the dark side, lend me your ears for this profound message.

What is it that I have to say? As you are all aware, the time has come for the famous great Summer Doctrinal Session of this white banner that flies forcefully over the three worlds, renowned under the name of our own "Sera Je College of Renowned Scholars." So be it.

The disciplinarian must now offer you a rough outline of the series of rules and regulations to be followed during this period based upon the *Great Exhortation*. These six fundamental divisions are (1) the object to whom the *Great Exhortation* is to be offered, (2) the time during which it is to be offered, (3) the individuals who should offer it, (4) how it should be offered, (5) the stages of listening, and (6) the actual *Great Exhortation*, which is what is to be listened to.

(1) The place where the *Great Exhortation* is to be offered is, for example, as follows. It should be offered only before this kind assembly of masters of the three baskets [of the teachings: discourses (*sūtra*), monastic discipline (*vinaya*), and metaphysics (*abhidharma*)]. If from ancient times there is no example of houses or dormitories bringing [this advice] to each other's doorsteps, how is it possible to do so now? The Great Debate Session, the Great Festival, the *Great Exhortation*, and so forth are all times during which permission to be absent is revoked. This being the case, I am assuming that all of you, the elderly, the young, and the middle-aged, have all come and are present at the assembly.

(2) The time when it is to be offered is, for example, as follows. An exhortation connected to a doctrinal period should be offered in the middle of the doctrinal period and an exhortation associated with a doctrinal off-period

should be offered at the end of the [preceding] doctrinal period. [A "doctrinal period" is the time when the debate sessions are meeting and the full curriculum is in effect. During "doctrinal off-periods" the debate sessions are suspended, and this gives monks the opportunity to devote more time to the intensive memorization of texts.] The exhortations connected with the Great Debate Session, the Great Festival, and Wood Begging are to be given only sporadically. It is not permissible to offer a speech during every assembly, for it will act as an impediment to the study of the doctrine.

(3) The individuals who should offer it are as follows. Only the master [the abbot] and the disciplinarian count. No more than these [two] are necessary. No fewer than these [two] can encompass it.

As for the fact that no more than these [two] are necessary, it is as follows. Even though this college has a faculty of administrators and scholars comparable to the collection of the stars in space, if all of them offer the *Great Exhortation*, some would disclaim what others said, while some would affirm positions that others disclaimed. This being an obstacle to discipline, we say "too many are not necessary." Regarding "too few cannot encompass it," the series of rules and regulations of this college is greater than Mount Meru, deeper than the ocean, more subtle than a mustard seed, finer than a horse's tail hair. Hence, it is difficult for a single person to recite the *Great Exhortation*. What the disciplinarian does not recite, the master must offer with added emphasis, and what the master misses, the disciplinarian must offer with added emphasis. This is what is meant by "too few cannot encompass it." So be it.

(4) Regarding how it should be offered, there are two points to mention: the fact that it should be offered using honorific terms and metaphors, and the fact that it is to be offered just as water is poured from one vase to another and a stone is passed from one hand to another.

(4.1.1) The first point, that it should be offered using honorific terms and poetical expressions, is as follows. "Honorific terms" refers to the fact that it is necessary to offer it using words that express the good qualities of the body, speech, and mind of the saṅgha. This means not only expressing their qualities by using "top hat" (*dbu zhwa*) for "hat" (*zhwa mo*) and using "venerable shoes" (*zhabs lcag*) for "shoes" (*lham gog*), but also that one is not allowed to offer it using ordinary words, that is, saying "you" and "me," or "horse" and "shit," and so forth.

(4.1.2) That it should be offered using metaphors does not refer to [using] the metaphors explained in the Vedic scriptures, but instead to being subtle while offering it. When someone creates a small infraction of the rules of this great and precious college, if such a person is sitting at the head of the row one should look toward the back of it, and if he is sitting toward the east then one should look toward the west. In other words, one should offer [the exhortation] so that others are not aware [of the identity of the perpetrator of the offense], even though one is oneself aware. If that individual does not recognize that [the advice] is being directed at *him*, then during the second exhortation it is necessary to make others slightly aware [of the identity of the person] by referring oneself to those who sit near him in the row and to his housemates. If the individual still does not recognize that it is being directed at him, then on the third occasion one must direct oneself at that very person and say, "*You* have broken such and such a rule," offering [the exhortation] by pointing the finger at him. The reason for offering the exhortation twice [before actually identifying the individual] is that this college is an honorable and compassionate college. Hence, one is not allowed to point the finger from the very beginning. Given that it could harm the reputation of a particular person, it is necessary to offer the first and second exhortations. It is permissible to skip the first two exhortations in the case that one sees, hears, or suspects that one of the four root monastic infractions or the drinking of alcohol has taken place, in which case it is necessary to point the finger from the outset.

(4.2) The fact that it is offered just as water is poured from one vase to another and a stone is passed from one hand to another refers to this. For example, whether it be water or nectar, if one pours it from a gold pot into a copper pot and from a copper pot into a clay pot, what one is pouring is the same in essence. It does not change [according to the receptacle]. Likewise, whether it be the *Great Exhortation* of this college or all of its great rules and regulations, insofar as these rules, which have been passed down in a lineage from mouth to mouth and from ear to ear, have not changed in essence from the time of the great Günkhyen Lodrö Rinchen Sengewa (Kun mkhyen Blo gros rin chen seng ge ba) to the present time, this situation resembles that of the example. And just as the vessels into which it is poured can have different shapes, colors, and prices, etc., the one who is giving the *Exhortation* can have one of three types of mental faculties, sharp, middling, or dull. This is how it is similar to the example. How it is offered like a stone passed from one hand to another refers to this. Whether it is a round stone or a square stone and whether one passes it from the front of the line to the rear or from the rear of the line to the front, there is no change in the shape and nature of the stone. Likewise, the lack of change in the nature of the rules of this precious college is what makes it similar to the example. [This is a claim as to the accuracy of the oral lineage, the point being that the text can and does remain intact regardless of the nature of the individuals who pass it from one generation to the next.] Just as the man who holds the stone in his hand can be good, bad, or middling, likewise, the person who gives the *Exhortation* might be the likes of even Maitreya or Mañjuśrī, or he might simply be like myself, someone who has no innate knowledge of spiritual or worldly affairs, nor any of the good qualities attained through training. This is how it is similar to the example.

(5) The stages of listening have four subdivisions: (5.1) how one should listen to it from the viewpoint of body, speech, and mind, (5.2) how one should listen to it from the point of view of seniority, (5.3) how one should listen to it from the point of view of position, and (5.4) how one should listen to it from the viewpoint of abandoning the three faults of the vessel, which act as

negative conditions, and of relying on the six recognitions that serve as positive conditions.

(5.1) As for how one should listen to it from the viewpoint of body, speech and mind, it is as follows. Body: One should not rest one's back against pillars or walls and so forth. Speech: No matter what kind of profound tantric recitations one may be applying oneself to, one must cease those recitations and listen. As regards how one should listen from the viewpoint of the mind: even if one's mind is equipoised in the nonconceptual samādhi of bliss and clear [light], one must arise from that samādhi and listen. This is not because profound tantric recitations and the nonconceptual samādhi of bliss and clear light are not important, but because these very rules of the monastery and college are even more important; [it is for this reason] that one must cease those practices and listen.

(5.2) As for "how one should listen to it from the viewpoint of seniority," it is as follows. The elders must listen to it as if they were judges. The middle-aged should listen to it to refresh their memories. Novices should listen to it for the sake of learning something they did not know before.

How is it that the elders should listen to it as if they were judges? It should not be the case that, influenced by their like or dislike of an administrator, they say that something is not one of the rules of the college when it is, or that something is one of the rules of the college when it is not. Instead, they should listen as impartial spectators to the law of karma. For example, they should listen as spectators to the law of karma, just as in the realm of embodied beings, the two chief disciples of our teacher [the Buddha] did; and, just as in the realm of the disembodied, the wrathful protector of the doctrine, Chamsing, does. [Tradition has it that some of the Buddha's chief disciples had the ability to discern the karmic actions in the past lives of beings that had led them to their present predicament. This allowed them to perceive a particular situation simply in terms of karmic causes and effects and presumably vitiated the tendency on their part to make judgments concerning the agents involved.]

How is it that the middle-aged should listen to it to refresh their memories? Even if one has previously fathomed all of the rules of this college, and even if one has ascertained them in one's mind, in the meantime one might have gone on a short or long pilgrimage, or one might have gone to visit one's parents in one's native place, in the process slightly forgetting the rules. If this has been the case, then one should listen so as to refresh one's memory of them.

How is it that novices should listen to it so as to learn something they did not know before? Realizing that they have never before heard the *Great Exhortation* of this college, they should listen to it for the sake of learning something they did not know before.

As regards the term "elder," there are two types: those who are elders from the viewpoint of provisional meaning and those who are elders from the viewpoint of definitive meaning. The first refers to those [elder monks] who do not know how to follow the rules of the monastery and college and who do not know how to explain them to others. Even if these individuals have spent one hundred years in the college, they are nonetheless provisional elders and definitive novices. Those who *do* know how to follow the rules and who know how to explain them to others, even if such individuals are only in the lowest Collected Topics class [for monks in their teens and preteens], are nonetheless definitive elders and provisional novices.

Now someone may be an elder from the viewpoint of class or from the viewpoint of years. From the viewpoint of class, someone is an elder if they have reached the Vinaya class or above. From the viewpoint of age, someone is an elder if they have been at the college for more than fifteen years. Someone who is middle-aged can be middle-aged from the viewpoint of class or from the viewpoint of years. From the viewpoint of class, someone is middle-aged if they are in a class between Beginning Scripture [the first subclass in the Perfection of Wisdom class] and Advanced Madhyamaka. From the viewpoint of years, someone is middle-aged if they have been at the college between four and fifteen years. Someone can also be a novice from the viewpoint of class or from the viewpoint of years. From the viewpoint of class, someone is a novice if they are in one of the three Collected Topics classes. From the viewpoint of years, someone is a novice if it has been three years or less since they have arrived at the college.

(5.3) As for "how one should listen from the viewpoint of position," it is as follows. From on high, the lord refuge, the precious abbot, even if he has been residing in the western suite during the doctrinal off-period, during the doctrinal period must listen to the *Great Exhortation* by moving into the eastern suite [which is just above the debate courtyard where the exhortation is given]. From the intermediate level, the abbot's private secretary, the two managers, and so forth must listen to the exhortation from the various windows of the print shop [located just inside from the debate courtyard]. From below, the cook, water bearers, temple manager, teachers, students, and so forth must listen from the two side doors that face each other on both sides of the debate courtyard.

As for "how one should listen to it from the viewpoint of abandoning the three faults of the vessel, and of relying on the six recognitions," it is as follows. One must listen devoid of the three faults: that of a vessel turned upside down, that of the leaking vessel, and that of the filthy vessel. For example, no matter how excellent the food or beverage one attempts to put inside the vessel, if it is turned upside down, nothing at all will enter it. Likewise, it is as if, having come to listen to the exhortation, under the influence of a lack of discipline and of distraction one shows not the slightest interest in listening when the master or administrator offers the exhortation. This is how it is similar to the example.

As for how to listen to it devoid of the fault of the leaking vessel, it is as follows. Even if one puts food or beverage into a leaking vessel, it will not remain there for long. Likewise, it is as if, having come to listen to the exhortation, one does not retain in memory the little that one has managed to ascertain, so that when one arrives at one's quarters and one's teacher asks how the exhortation went today, one has nothing to say in response. This is how it is similar to the example.

As for how to listen to it devoid of the fault of the filthy vessel, it is as follows. No matter how excellent the food or beverage one puts inside a filthy vessel, even if it is divine ambrosia, it cannot be used due to the filth. Likewise, it is as if, no matter how excellent a job the master or disciplinarian does in giving the exhortation, even to the point of giving extensive scriptural citations and reasoning, if one is oneself influenced by an evil motivation, instead of taking it as a method for disciplining oneself, one claims that what is part of the exhortation is not part of it, and so forth. This is how it is similar to the example of the filthy vessel. In brief, just as the Blessed Lord has said, "Dedicate yourself to listening well." It is necessary to listen with a proper motivation.

As for how one should listen from the viewpoint of relying on the six recognitions, it is as follows. The six recognitions are:

1. One should recognize the one who gives the exhortation to be like a doctor.
2. One should recognize oneself as the patient.
3. One should recognize the exhortation to be like the medicine.
4. One should recognize its sustained practice to be like the cure of the disease.
5. One should recognize the Tathāgata to be a holy being.
6. One should have the recognition, "may the doctrinal methods remain for a long period of time."

Alternatively, one can recognize the one who is giving the exhortation as one's master, one can recognize oneself as the disciple, and one can recognize the exhortation itself as the stages of the path to enlightenment. On top of these three recognitions, one can add the last three recognitions [of the previous grouping of six]. But whichever of these two systems of enumeration one adopts, it is important to realize that individuals who are afflicted with a serious illness will liberate themselves of the disease in dependence upon the assiduous application of medicinal treatment that is consistent with the advice of an expert doctor. In this same way, one should have a recognition of oneself as the disciple. One should have a recognition of the person giving the exhortation as one's master, and one should have a recognition of the *Great Exhortation* as the doctrine, the stages of the path to enlightenment. It is also necessary to listen with the thought, "How wonderful it would be if by my assiduous practice of these series of rules and regulations, the precious teachings of the Conqueror, would remain in the world for a long period of time." As the *Bodhicaryāvatāra* says:

> If, being frightened by the possibility of ordinary illness,
> One follows the advice of a doctor,

> What need is there to speak of the need to constantly apply oneself
> When one is afflicted with the illness of the manifold faults such as attachment, etc.?

Hence, it is necessary to listen with a good basis in these nonmistaken recognitions.

(6) As for the actual *Great Exhortation*, which is what is to be listened to, it is as follows: (6.1) the series concerned with the entrance of a postulant, (6.2) the series concerned with the practice of the rules once one has entered, (6.3) the series concerned with taking up the banner of the accomplishments at the end, that is, after having practiced, and (6.4) as an aside, a discussion on asking permission to be absent.

(6.1) As for the series concerned with the entrance of postulants, it is as follows. Postulants are of two types, laymen, who wear white clothing, and branch monks, who come from afar. Let us consider the case of laymen, who wear white clothing. [The layman] must be the kind of person [who is malleable], like a stainless white piece of wool that can take up whatever color one applies to it, be it yellow or red. He must be seven years of age or older, and even if he is seven years of age, he must be able to scare away a crow. [These are the criteria that the Vinaya gives for the time at which a young boy is allowed to take novice vows.] In short, he must be someone who is devoid of the four impediments that act as conditions obstructing ordination [the obstacles to the arising of the vows (e.g., not being human or being a hermaphrodite), the obstacles to the maintenance of the vows (e.g., not having the permission of one's parents), the obstacle to the betterment of the vows (e.g., illness), and the obstacle to the beautification of the one who possesses the vows (e.g., having a crippled or mutilated hand)], and they must possess the five concordant conditions. [It is not clear what these five conditions refer to, although the *'Dul ba'i sdoms* suggests that a series of four concordant conditions refer to the three requisite robes of a monk together with the begging bowl.]

Let us consider the case of branch monks who come from afar. They must be men who have not come after having embezzled funds or offerings from their own outlying monasteries, and who have never had to be even slightly reprimanded by qualified masters and administrators in their outlying monastery. In short, they must not be monks who make the rounds of all the great monasteries as if they were a circular earring [causing havoc in one and moving on to the next], they must not be the type of monk who makes the rounds of the outlying monasteries as if he were shifting through the string of his beads.

Such a person should then be properly examined so as to determine to which house or regional house he belongs. [Sera Je monastery had ten houses and six regional houses. All of the latter were, at least in theory and perhaps in the very distant past, associated with one house, but in recent history all have acted as essentially independent entities with almost the same authority as the houses themselves.] He should then be taken care of well. He should not immediately be pounced upon [by monks of a certain house] like dogs attacking a piece of lung. If someone is a branch monk who belongs to one's own [house], whether he is a king who comes on a throne of gold or a beggar who comes with a stick and an empty satchel, the house or regional house to which he belongs must take care of him well. If I hear that there is a difference in the attention given to a monk based on his economic position, I will not leave it at that, but, calling in the offending parties, I will mete out punishment that will not be light. On the other hand, if a monk does not belong to one's own house or regional house, even if it be a king on a golden throne who should arrive, one is not allowed to take care of him. It is necessary to take care of those who belong to one's own [house], whatever their position, because one never knows how a particular person will in the future be able to benefit the teachings of the Buddha or, in particular, the religious and political status of this college. It is necessary to practice as it is stated in the *Vinaya*: "Caste and family line are not the chief thing; spiritual attainment is the chief thing."

It is necessary for the teacher of that postulant first to present to him a complete set of robes, from the hat to the boots. Let us take the case of the hat. It should be as yellow as possible—black, the color of crows, is not allowed. Moreover, the main portion of hat [called the "lawn"] symbolizes a Buddha field; the threads that stick up from the top symbolize the thousand buddhas [of this aeon]; the lining of the lawn should be white, the lining of the trailer must be blue, and its outer covering should be red—this symbolizes the threefold protectors [Avalokiteśvara, Mañjuśrī, and Vajrapāṇi, respectively]; the twelve lines of stitching to be found in the front part of the trailer represent the twelve branches of scripture; the three blue strings that hang from the trailer represent the three baskets of teachings. Even if one is an ordinary run-of-the-mill monk who possesses no other religious objects, it is sufficient if one makes one's hat an icon and makes offerings to it. No other [icon] is necessary.

Let us now turn to the overcoat. It must have a lotus collar, and it must have been cut [and restitched] at the waist. The lotus collar is necessary because it is an auspicious symbol for one's taking future birth within a lotus in the pure land, with a body that is of the nature of mind. The upper part of the overcoat must be turned inside out and stitched to the lower part of the overcoat, and the symbolism is this. This serves as an auspicious symbol of [the continuity of the teachings, that is, of] the fact that immediately after the teachings of our incomparable teacher, the Lion of the Śākyas, there will arise the teachings of the conqueror, the protector Ajita [Maitreya]. It is necessary to line the inside border of the overcoat with yellow cloth, and this serves as an auspicious symbol for the spread, in all directions, of the teachings of the great master Tsong kha pa, the bearer of the yellow hat, the protector Mañjuśrī himself.

Let us now turn to the vest. It must have "lion shoulders" [symbols of fearlessness]; it must have "elephant tusks" [on the back, symbols of constantly being in the jaws of death]; and it must have the blue thread [lining the arm openings]. It is necessary to have the blue thread so as to remember the kindness of the Chinese monks [who wore blue robes and who helped to reestablish the monastic lineage in Tibet after a period of persecution]. The master, the recognized incarnations, the college's *chos mdzad* [a class of men from aristocratic or wealthy families who enter the monastery as monks and, due to their families' benefaction, are given special status], and so forth are allowed to wear fine wool on the backs of their vests. Everyone else must either wear a vest made of rough wool or else a vest like those worn at the Lower Tantric College.

Let us now turn to the shawl. It is not permissible to wear a fine woolen shawl with full hemming in the summer time, nor is it permissible to wear a finely woven hundred-stitches-to-the-thumb woolen shawl in the winter time.

Let us now turn to the skirt. If one is a fully ordained monk, one must wear a real lower garment [with patches]; if one is a novice, one must wear an "imitation" lower garment [without patches]. Both must have an upper border and a lower border. In short, it is necessary that one's robes be such that they are capable of acquiring the blessing as explained in the *Vinaya*. [Robes that meet the criteria set forth in the *Vinaya* can and must be blessed. Fully ordained monks must keep their robes with them and never sleep apart from them. If they do so, the blessing is lost and the garments must be reblessed.]

Let us now turn to the underskirt. From among the one that is open in the front and the one that loops in a closed circle, the former, which is open in the front, is not allowed. Let us now turn to the shoes. One is allowed to wear only Sangpu (Gsang phu)-like shoes. One is not allowed to wear any of other brands that are in fashion, such as white shoes. What is more, the Sangpu-like shoes symbolize the three poisons of the afflictions. It is necessary to wear only these because they serve as a special auspicious symbol of the fact that our own minds are under the power of the three poisons of the afflictions. One is allowed to fix [broken] soles only with a piece that is spliced at the middle and not with an entire new sole.

Let us now turn to the water receptacle. Gold or silver, etc., are not allowed. It is necessary that the water pot should be made either of copper or of bronze, and for the pot cover to have all of the proper characteristics, such as having an exterior of red wool and a lining that is blue.

Let us now turn to the rosary. One is allowed to carry only those made of the seeds of the bodhi tree or of six-faced bodhi seeds. As an exception, the monks who are engaged in the Hayagrīva propitiation rituals are allowed to carry, discreetly, rosaries made from the likes of 'Bo ti rtse and Rakṣa. One is not allowed to carry anything apart from these, to wit the different rosaries that are in fashion. When one reaches Introductory Vinaya class one is allowed to add one counter [to one's rosary], and when one reaches Abhidharma one is allowed another counter [to help one keep track of all the divisions, subdivisions, and other enumerations that are covered in these two classes]. One is allowed no more than a pair of counters. Also, one must not separate the two counters on one's rosary but must put one beside the other. It is completely forbidden to put turquoise, coral, or other ornamental stones among the beads of the rosary.

Let us now turn to the bowl and flour bag. One must carry a bowl of the Ganden indentation style, and that too must not be of a random size. It should be a bowl the size of that of the general saṅgha, and should be the same size as the bowl of the great chanting leader. The bowl of the chanting leader should also not be of a random size but should be such that it can fit within his five fingers. Let us now turn to the flour bag. It should have the rainbow red and yellow strips. The outer covering should be blue and the inner lining white. This symbolizes the objects focused upon within *kṛtsna-samādhi*. The flour bag should be just large enough to carry one meal's worth of barley flour. The strings for closing the flour bag, for the rosary, and for the hat handle should be made only of stretched musk-deer leather. Cotton strings and so forth are not allowed. The mat should be such that [when placed on the cushions in the assembly] it can protect the property of the saṅgha. In short, the required dress should not be so good that it rivals that of the master and administrators, etc., nor so poor that it is just a series of patches with none of the original material left. One should avoid falling into either of these two extremes.

All of the administrators of this college, the general manager [of the monastery], the main enforcer [of the monastery], the abbot's private secretary, the [college] managers, the housing manager, the treasurers, secretary, and so forth, all have attire that is proper to their station. Some are allowed to wear vests with brocade, some are not. Some are allowed to wear *re zon* shoes, some are allowed *re zon* shoes with brocade on the calves. It is completely forbidden to have shoes with layered leather soles.

After the teacher has made the proper arrangements for the required dress of the student, it is necessary for the house warden first to inform the abbot's household. He must therefore come before either the steward of the abbot's household or the chef and partially unravel his shawl [as a sign of respect]. If they are sitting, he must kneel properly before them and state that there is such and such a postulant who belongs to his house and who is either a branch monk from afar or, if he is not a branch monk, a layman, who wears white clothing, who is a postulant for admission into the college. He must then ask when they can have an audience with the lord refuge, the precious abbot. If [the members of the abbot's household] are standing, then he must partially unravel his shawl and ask hunched over. Moreover, he is not allowed to make a suggestion as to the time, saying, "Can I bring him tomorrow morning?" or "Can I bring him now?" He must be ready to bring him whenever he is told to do so. After the individual teacher has made the proper arrangement for the robes of the postulant, since it is considered the first auspicious symbol for the postulant's entering the doctrinal door of the college and monastery, he [must offer to the abbot] a pitcher full of tea and a ceremonial scarf that is as clean as possible. The butter to be used in the tea should be as delicious as possible and the tea itself as fine as possible so as to insure that the lord refuge, the precious abbot, finds it to his liking. There is a saying that in olden days a ceremonial scarf worth five *kar ma* was to be offered. Be that as it may, since this is the first auspicious act [the student will engage in], he should have a ceremonial scarf that is as white as possible, and if [the postulant] is a layman, who wears white clothing, he should also offer one *tam kar* as a fee for the ritual cutting of the hair. In brief, one should offer the master at least a needle and some thread and [if one is well off] a horse or even an elephant.

Then, an elder monk who has at last arrived at the Vinaya class must bring the postulant and open the entry curtain of the steward of the abbot's household. When they go in for the audience, the postulant must do three full prostrations [extending his body full length], while for the teacher it is permissible to do three abbreviated prostrations. Moreover, it is not permissible for the elder monk to prostrate placing himself in front and the postulant behind. The postulant must do full prostrations so that it can be determined whether or not he has any defects in his limbs.

As soon as the audience is over [the abbot] will offer one cup of tea. Squatting, the postulant should take the cup respectfully with both hands and drink immediately. One is not allowed to set it down. Then, so as to examine whether or not the postulant has any faults in his speech, the lord refuge, the precious abbot, will ask the elder monk, "What is his native place? Where is his home monastery?" and the elder monk must answer. Then he asks the postulant, "What is your home monastery? What is your name?" in response to which the postulant must answer. When the question is being asked of the postulant, if the elder monk answers, this is an indication that the postulant has something wrong with his speech. When the question is being asked of the elder monk, if the postulant answers, it is an indication that he has a disrespectful or slanderous nature. As soon as the tea is finished [the elder monk] must partially remove his shawl, kneel on the floor, and ask permission [for the student to attend assembly], prefaced by a reason. If [the student] is a branch monk from afar [the elder monk] must ask, "Please be so kind as to allow this postulant to attend the tea-assemblies of the college and the tea-assemblies of the monastery discreetly for three doctrinal sessions [approximately three months], until he has prepared [that is, memorized] the threefold special recitations and the ninefold ritual cake offering of this precious college." [These are the ritual recitations special to the Je College that all monks must know by heart before they enter the monastery officially. Until that time, the postulant is allowed to attend communal tea-assemblies "discreetly," which is to say unofficially. It is assumed that the monastic postulant who comes from a branch monastery has already memorized other essential and common texts and prayers. A newly ordained layman is given a more lengthy period of time in which to prepare all of the required texts, as we see in the lines that follow.] If he is a layman, who wears white clothing, [the elder monk] must ask, "Please be so kind as to allow this postulant to attend the tea-assemblies of the college and the tea-assemblies of the monastery discreetly for three years until he has prepared the one-volume *Special Recitations Called 'The Extremely Clear'* that begins with 'Refuge' and ends with the 'Prayer for the Long Life of the Doctrine,' the *Abhisamayālaṃkāra*, the *Madhyamakāvatāra*, the threefold special recitations, and the ninefold ritual cake offering of this precious college."

After the audience with the lord refuge, the precious abbot, is finished they must go, in order, to the disciplinarian of the Great Assembly [the common assembly hall of all of Sera's colleges], to the disciplinarian of the college, and to the house master, tell them that the audience with the lord refuge, the precious abbot, has now been completed, and request, as above, that the postulant [be allowed to attend assembly, etc.]. If the postulant finishes memorizing the *Special Recitations Called "The Extremely Clear"* in one month, then it is not necessary for him to wait three months or three years. He is allowed to attend the debate sessions [immediately].

Prayers and Sermons

—21—

The Sermon of an Itinerant Saint

Matthew Kapstein

Shabkar Tsokdruk Rangdröl (Zhabs dkar tshogs drug rang grol, 1781–1850) ranks among the most revered of popular Tibetan preachers and saints. An adept, pilgrim, and poet, he traveled throughout Tibet during the early nineteenth century, delighting people of all classes—commoners and ordinary monks, as well as incarnate lamas and the highest officials of government—through his wide-ranging activities as a Buddhist teacher and his enormous personal generosity and charisma. His autobiography, from which the selections presented below are drawn, is regarded as one of the masterworks of Tibetan literature.

In these passages, we meet Shabkar around 1820, after he had journeyed thousands of miles from his homeland in Tibet's northeastern region of Amdo (he had been born near the border between the Qinghai and Gansu provinces of modern China) to far western Tibet. There he passed some time dwelling in the vicinity of the great pilgrimage center of Mount Kailash, a mountain sacred to both Hindus and Buddhists. This region is to the north of the Crystal Peak and its environs in western Nepal, places that are also discussed in other chapters of this book (see chapters 5 and 34). During the course of Shabkar's sojourn in the Kailash area, he attracted numerous devotees and disciples from the surrounding regions and so was often asked to deliver religious teachings. Our selection opens with an account of the way in which he came to be associated with great wonders by the local population. Following this he records the contents of a typical sermon delivered to those who attended his teachings, thus providing us with an exceptional record of the content of popular Tibetan Buddhist preaching.

The main themes that are stressed in the sermon are also well-known from texts concerning the stages of the Buddhist path: the unique qualities and rarity of human life, its transitory nature, the workings of karma, and the trials of rebirth. What distinguishes their presentation in Shabkar's autobiography from the similar discussions found in doctrinal treatises are his descriptions of the context for his teaching, the sense of urgency that as a preacher he imparts to his words, and his desire to appeal to Tibetan Buddhists of all sectarian backgrounds. This last aspect is evinced by his quoting not, as is usually the case, only well-known Indian Buddhist scriptures and the Tibetan representatives of just the author's own sect, but also past masters who adhered to several different traditions. For example, he juxtaposes passages from Tsongkhapa and Longchenpa, the leading thinkers of the Geluk and Nyingma sects. Thus, he preaches in a style that Tibetans sometimes characterize as "nonpartisan" (*ris med*).

As Shabkar's account makes clear, the successful Tibetan Buddhist preacher, even if he or she enjoyed no established hierarchical position, could accumulate substantial wealth from the offerings of the faithful. It is important to note that nowhere do we find evidence that Shabkar charged a formal "fee" for his teachings; indeed, this would have been considered unacceptably bad form in Tibet. The forces that encouraged devotees in their generosity were, rather, the strong belief that donations to a worthy religious teacher were a powerful means to gather the positive karma needed to insure a favorable rebirth, and sometimes even success in this life, and the social pressure that encouraged Tibetans to "keep up with the Joneses" by matching the charity of their peers. Extravagant generosity in this context could actually promote the advancement of one's social status, much as "conspicuous consumption" is thought sometimes to do in modern consumerist societies (see chapter 22).

As for the teacher himself, it was generally held to be essential that he or she not simply hoard the wealth received, though undoubtably some teachers and ritual specialists did just that. It was expected, rather, that the charitable gifts offered by devotees would be redistributed by their recipients, contributing to the support of monasteries, temples, and retreats. Shabkar, among other things, became famed as a great supporter of the restoration of the famous Bodhnāth stūpa in Nepal and other religious monuments, and also acquired a reputation as one who made especially generous gifts to beggars and indigents. He exemplified in this way the notion that wealth accumulated through religion was best "reinvested" by continuing to fill one's own karmic store with good works.

Shabkar's account well illustrates, too, the carnival atmosphere that often accompanied public religious teaching in Tibet. For the laypeople, there is always plenty of *chang*, the rich home-brewed barley ale of Tibet, and the sessions of religious instruction are concluded by popular songs and dances. The weighty topics of suffering and mortality, in the traditional religious culture of Tibet, are seldom set in a gloomy atmosphere. They provide, rather, the impetus for living this life well. This means, above all, that one should strive to the extent possible to realize spiritual values, but without altogether neglecting, at the same time, the cultivation of a joyful affirmation of the fleeting goods of this life.

The present translation was originally executed on behalf of Professor Nancy Levine of the Department of Anthropology at the University of California, Los Angeles, in connection with her research in Humla, Nepal. It is based on the original Tibetan blockprint edition of the autobiography, *Snyigs dus yongs kyi skyabs mgon zhabs dkar rdo rje 'chang chen po'i rnam par thar pa rgyas par bshad pa skal bzang gdul bya thar 'dod rnams kyi re ba skong ba'i yid bzhin nor bu bsam 'phel dbang gi rgyal po* (Dolanji, Himachal Pradesh: Tsering Wangyal, 1975), 2 vols.

Further Readings

A complete and thoroughly annotated English translation is available in Matthieu Riccard, trans. *The Life of Shabkar* (Albany: State University of New York Press, 1994).

AN APPARITION AT CRYSTAL PEAK

I formed spiritual connections with all the lamas from all regions who arrived at my hermitage, when I was staying near Mount Kailash, and I established connections with them through the dedication of merit. I worshipped and prayed to the deities of the snow peaks repeatedly. Then, one night during a dream, Lama Dordzin Rinpoche (Bla ma Rdor 'dzin Rin po che, a hermit who lived on the slopes of Mount Kailash) of the snow peak arrived and said, "Now, if you'll come to see the holy places, I will guide you!" He then went off and I followed. We visited a huge palace, as big as the great temple of glorious Sakya (Sa skya, the main seat of the Sakyapa sect), and made of various precious stones. Inside of it was a massive stūpa of taintless crystal, which one could see right through, inside and out. It was transparent and of the nature of light. Inside it were all of the deities of the four classes of tantra, the foremost among them being Cakrasaṃvara, appearing like the images in a mirror, each one clear and distinct. I offered prostrations, performed circumambulations, made offerings, and prayed, whereupon light rays poured forth from the hearts of all those deities and struck me. I dreamed that the excellent pure awareness of bliss and emptiness was born in my body and mind.

Again, one day, while I remained in meditative absorption I had a mystical experience in which many heroes and ḍākinīs appeared in the sky, saying, "We're going to circumambulate the fortress of the deity Cakrasaṃvara." They gathered various items for worship and I saw them doing circumambulations in the sky above Mount Kailash.

Then while I was staying there, patrons who came from near the valley at Crystal Peak asked me to visit their homeland. I responded that I could not come there, but I told them to have faith and pray, and that the blessing of my protection would be just the same as if I were to come there in person. These patrons had such faith that they believed that my words meant that I would travel there miraculously, and so they prayed for this to occur. Accordingly, I repeatedly imagined that I went where they lived and blessed them. Based on such circumstances, one day some woodcutters and herdsmen, whose karma was pure, saw me come flying through the sky from the direction of Mount Kailash, holding white banners in each of my hands. They said that they really saw me alight on the summit of Crystal Peak and plant those banners there and then fly off. When they told the locals of this everyone looked and saw a great white banner on the summit of Crystal Peak, which had not been there before. All of them became most faithful. From that time onward the circumstances allowed for the great spread of the Buddha's teaching in that place.

TRAVELS AND SERMONS IN FAR WESTERN TIBET

Leaving the Snow Peak, Mount Kailash, I went to the neighboring places, Kangzakpa and Parka Tazam, to benefit the inhabitants. In my dreams at night I crossed the ocean in a boat and traversed a great, polluted plain, riding a horse, and so forth. These and other, similar dreams I took to be portents that many goods and riches would come to me. Then I went to Tsegye monastery, Gopa Rinchen's tribe, Nyala Chukpo's tribe, Tochu monastery, and Pretapuri, continuing as far as Khyunglung monastery, where I acted as both a pilgrim and a teacher simultaneously. I had audiences with, and worshipped the venerable monks, and I expounded the doctrine to the patrons. Gopa Rinchen offered me a large tent, worth forty silver *srang*, and five *zho* of gold. [The *srang* is a Tibetan measure of weight, a bit less than half an ounce, and also is the name for a coin of that weight. The *zho* is a tenth part of a *srang*.] And other patrons offered to me gold, silver, clothing, jewelry, and many foodstuffs, riches, and luxuries.

Returning from there, I visited Kepa Serki Chakyip monastery, on the banks of Mapham Yutsho (Lake Manasarovar), and Bönri monastery, Seralung monastery, and Bönmopuk monastery. I distributed tea to the monks, worshipped, and prayed. Then I visited some West Tibetan nomad encampments of the Horpa tribes, and Limi in Rong. Many of the patrons from the Crystal Peak of Rong came there to meet me. I instructed them in the dharma and all apparently turned to religion, for they made many offerings of food and clothing. Afterward, I traveled in stages to Ngöchukpo in the south of Rong, and to the upper, middle, and lower districts of Purang. To many hundreds and thousands of monks, disciples, and lay-patrons I gave the empowerment of longevity, the empowerment of the Great Compassionate Avalokiteśvara, the transmissions and instructions for the creation and perfection stages of meditative deities, and whatever other teachings seemed appropriate.

At first, to make the disciples fit vessels for the doctrine, I would teach them the meditation and mantra of the buddha of purification, Vajrasattva. Then I would bless them, by having these disciples meditate on the guru seated above their heads in the divine form of the buddha Vajradhara. After that, I would give them an ordinary exposition of the doctrine, such as this:

First you all must adopt a refined attitude, as is appropriate for listening to the teaching, by thinking, "On behalf of all sentient beings, our mothers throughout the universe, we must attain the precious stage of unsurpassed, authentic and perfect Buddhahood. By all means, we must attain it swiftly! To do so, let us listen to this profound, true doctrine, taught by this genuine and glorious guru. Then, let us try to incorporate what he teaches us into our own experience." For it says in the *Tantra of the Diamond Peak* (*Vajraśikharatantra*):

> Controlling well all your thoughts,
> Listen with an exceptionally fine attitude!

And in the *Collection of Aphorisms* (*Udānavarga*):

> Abandon sleep, torpor, and sloth;
> And listen with utmost joy!

And in the *Birth Stories* (*Jātaka*):

> As a patient listens to the doctor,
> Listen to the doctrine, doing it homage.

Just so you should listen with a refined mental motivation and a respectful physical deportment.

To continue: At this time, when we have acquired the great ship that is the liberty and endowment of this human existence, we must free ourselves from this terrible sea of saṃsāra. Why do I say this? It is because, owing to the force of some previous virtues we have now met with favorable circumstances and so have acquired precious human bodies. We have all five senses. We can talk and think. We have been taken into the following of spiritual friends. We have encountered the Buddha's teaching. For these reasons we have the ability to practice the doctrine. At a time like this, when we know the means to practice the pure doctrine that will certainly release us from saṃsāra, if we do not practice it here and now, it will be most difficult to acquire such a foundation again in the future, and encounters with the doctrine will become exceedingly rare. As the Buddha has said:

> Though there are many world-systems,
> Birth on the saw-edge of Jambudvīpa is rare,
> And a pure human body is most difficult to obtain.

And in the *Enlightenment of Buddha Vairocana* (*Vairocanābhisambodhi*) it says:

> In this world the omniscient buddhas
> Are as rare as the Udumbara flower:
> These may rarely come forth, or they may not,

Blooming once in five hundred years.
And this way of the practice of secret mantras
Is even rarer than that!

And the venerable, magnanimous Tsongkhapa [1357–1419, founder of the Gelukpa sect] has said:

A human body and the encounter with the teaching
Are frequently not obtained, but now we have them.
Because it is possible now to achieve a great goal,
Consider this well, and gain the essence of human existence!

The all-knowing [great Nyingma thinker] Longchen Rabjampa (Klong chen Rab 'jams pa, 1308–1363) too, has said:

To obtain this liberty and endowment
is a one in a hundred chance.
Beyond that, meeting the doctrine
is like finding a daytime star,
And to encounter the doctrine of the supreme vehicle
is like reaching the end of the world.
So now is the time to practice that doctrine
from the very depths of your heart.

Because they have all thus affirmed it, we must indeed practice the doctrine. If we do not practice it then we are even dumber than the merchant who returns empty-handed from his journey to an ocean isle. We are like corpses without having died. We are like madmen without having been possessed. We are even dumber than someone who uses a jeweled vase as a spittoon or a bedpan. As it says in Nāgārjuna's *Letter of Friendship* (*Suhṛllekha*):

Someone may use a golden urn, decorated with jewels,
To dispose of filth and sweepings.
But one, born human, who does harmful deeds,
Is said to be far dumber than that.

With reference to such persons, who are the worst sort of idiot, let us leave off the discussion of their obtaining the path to liberation and omniscience in the future. Such persons fall into the three evil destinies of the hells, tormented spirits, and animals, and then for many millions of aeons do not even hear the word "happy destiny." As it says in the *Entrance to the Bodhisattva's Life-style* (*Bodhicaryāvatāra*):

By not performing wholesome deeds,
And amassing harmful ones,

For one hundred million aeons
One will not hear the phrase "happy fate."

So, if for the sake of the trivial food and clothing of this lifetime, you amass harmful deeds, and then in future lives do not even hear the word "happy destiny," you have acted as stupidly as one can in this world. It says in the *Entrance to the Bodhisattva's Life-style* (*Bodhicaryāvatāra*):

Having obtained such liberty as this,
If I do not now practice virtue,
There is no greater deception,
No way one could be any blinder.

When such a sinner, who is the worst sort of fool, dies, he seems pitiful to the buddhas and bodhisattvas. The great master Padmasambhava has said:

This liberty and opportunity are exceedingly hard to obtain.
Pity on those who are left empty-handed, dharma-less,
When Death afflicts them with the final illness!

Thus, one must decide how much a person really values this life according to whether or not he or she has acquired some dharma. As Phadampa [an Indian teacher who visited Tibet several times during the late eleventh and early twelfth centuries. His verses addressed to the people of Ding-ri, a town to the north of Mount Everest, are frequently quoted as proverbs.] has said:

Buddhas rarely are found among those who lack diligence,
So accept difficulties, O people of Ding-ri!

If you are unable now, when will you be able?
This is your one chance in a hundred, O people of Ding-ri!

No one can know how much a man or woman values this life.
Don't come back empty-handed, O people of Ding-ri!

Accordingly, during this lifetime, when we have been born in a central, spiritual land, then in order not to enter future lives empty-handed, I pray that you who are energetic and intelligent partake now of the meaning of having this precious human body, by making good use of the genuine doctrine.

If you think that it will do to practice slowly, in a lax manner, it won't. The reason for this is that although we have obtained the precious human body, we will die. We won't remain alive for too long. The Buddha has said:

Where there is birth, there is death.
Where there is growth, there is decline.
Youth is impermanent,
And a youthful complexion is robbed by disease.

This lifetime is stolen by death.
There is nothing at all that is permanent.

And the great master Padmasambhava has said:

If you don't recognize impermanence, the undependability of things,
You'll go on hankering after saṃsāra.
Prettily, you pass your life frivolously,
And waste this liberty and endowment in the way of distractions.
One who is sick, on the verge of death, is like a lamp with no oil left.
When the causes of vitality are finished, one has no power to remain.

Just so, in this interval between birth and death no one has a life that is really free. There is no reason to doubt this, asking oneself, "Is it so? is it not?" As the master Aśvaghoṣa has said:

On earth or in the heavens,
Should you see or hear,
That someone's been born who's deathless,
Then you'd better not be without doubts!

Whether one is as excellent as a spiritual friend, as fine as an earth-ruling king, as rich as a universal emperor, or as poor as a starving beggar; whether one is a newborn babe or an eighty-year-old, there is no one who does not come under the dominion of death. Think about your own countrymen and village-companions, your old parents, your newborn infants, your loving friends: most of them have many plans for this life. But when the demon death arrives they have no power to remain, and off they go to their future abodes empty-handed, without the dharma. And you and I are no different! With each passing year, month, day, morning, and afternoon, we draw closer to the mouth of death, as if we were animals being led to the slaughter. It says in the *Collection of Aphorisms* (*Udānavarga*):

People are just like death-row inmates,
Who with each step approach their own executioners.

And in the *Song of the Girl Sale ö* (*Bu mo Sa le 'od*):

This human body is the result obtained
By the force of a mass of past merits.
The years and months hasten it onward,
It's drawn forward with each meal you eat.
Not sitting still for an instant you near death.
Thinking of this, girl, you'll make yourself miserable.
So better to practice the doctrine, uniquely true and divine.

Though it is certain that we will die, it is not certain when we will die. Even today there are innumerable persons whose complexions are fading, who, this afternoon or night, or tomorrow, will be blackened corpses. They do not think they will die tomorrow. But this body, composed of the four elements, is no more durable than a piece of food that is already being eaten: its breath is insubstantial like steam, and its warmth is merely a spark. At every instant there is some risk. Therefore, if you have the good fortune to practice the doctrine, practice it this year rather than next, today rather than tomorrow. This is no time to wait. As the conqueror Kelsang Gyatso [Skal bzang rgya mtsho, the seventh Dalai Lama, 1708–1757] has said:

> Today he terminates enemies, protects his friends.
> Engaging in conversation, the body feels fine, the mind lively.
> But by the time night falls that body will be devoured
> By the vultures and dogs of the charnel ground. Isn't it so?

And in the *Entrance to the Bodhisattva's Life-style* (*Bodhicaryāvatāra*):

> It is never appropriate to sit comfortably, thinking,
> "At least today I will not die."

And in the *Collection of Aphorisms* (*Udānavarga*):

> It is never certain which will come first,
> Tomorrow or the next life.
> Therefore, do not worry about tomorrow,
> But concern yourself with future life.

When it comes time to die, nothing is of any use but the authentic doctrine: not the house you built for this life, nor your accumulated wealth, nor friends and associates, nor children, wife, servants, and luxuries. It says in the *Play of Mañjuśrī* (*Mañjuśrīvikrīḍita*):

> Parents offer no refuge,
> Neither do friends or relations.
> All of them will abandon you;
> You must pass to the next life alone.

And the great master Padmasambhava has said:

> Even if the King of Physicians [the Buddha] were to arrive in person,
> He would not know how to extend life, when lifespan is exhausted.
> The powerful cannot drag death into court.
> The clever cannot persuade it with deceits.
> The wealthy cannot bribe it.
> Bereft of all food and wealth,
> You must go, like a hair plucked out of the butter.

Just so, when it comes time to die, even the power and might of a universal monarch is of no use. The riches of Vaiśravaṇa, the god of wealth, are of no more value than a sesame seed. Even if you have a great company of parents, friends, relations, and associates they cannot lead you elsewhere. As if you were merely a hair picked out of the butter, you enter the great abyss of the intermediate state (between death and rebirth, *bardo*), not knowing your destination. Without refuge or protection you must go on alone. Such a time will certainly come. And when it does come, that is not all—the bewildering manifestations of the intermediate state are terrifying, beyond conception, inexpressible. When you come to experience them, nothing will be of benefit except the genuine doctrine and the precious guru who is your guide. None of the comforts or friendships of this life can help.

Moreover, owing to the force of past actions and psychological affliction we continuously revolve through the three realms of saṃsāra, and in future lives will find only misery, without a moment of ease. Concerning that: If born in the hells, the torments of heat and cold are unbearable. If born among the hungry ghosts one is afflicted by the pain of hunger and thirst. If born among the animals, one is brought to grief by the pains of being slaughtered, devoured, enslaved, and by that of stupidity. If born among human beings, one will mourn the anguish of birth, aging, illness, and death. If born among the demigods, there is still the suffering of violence and strife. And even if born among the gods, there will be the pain of death and the fall to a lower condition. These and other sufferings surpass the imagination. As it says in the *Sūtra of Mindfulness* (*Smṛtyupasthānasūtra*):

> Hell's creatures are afflicted by hellfire.
> Animals are afflicted by devouring one another.
> The hungry ghosts are afflicted by hunger and thirst.
> Humans are afflicted by the struggle to earn their livelihood.
> Demigods are afflicted by violence and strife.
> The gods are afflicted by shamelessness.
> There is never any happiness in saṃsāra,
> Not even so much as the head of a pin.

And the great master Padmasambhava has said:

> In the six cities of karma, [that is, the realms of the hells, hungry ghosts, animals, human beings, demigods, and gods,] from which there's no release,
> One spins about as in a whirlpool.
> O! Pity the inhabitants of unending saṃsāra!

And Marpa of Lhodrak [(1012–1096), founder of the Kagyü tradition] has said:

> My son [Milarepa]! Think on the sufferings of saṃsāra!
> Even if I had one hundred tongues,
> And could speak for ten million unimaginable aeons,
> I could not even begin to describe

The nature of saṃsāra.
So do not waste the holy doctrine I have taught you!

Just so, one cannot even begin to explain the sufferings of saṃsāra. Therefore, in brief, whether one is born high or low in the three realms of saṃsāra, it is an abode of suffering. Whoever else one befriends, one befriends suffering. Whatever else one experiences, one experiences suffering. Whatever one does, it only leads to suffering. Therefore, like criminals fleeing from the dungeon, we must seek to escape from this saṃsāra that is an ocean of suffering churned by the great waves of karma and psychological affliction and full of the terrifying sea serpents that are the three kinds of suffering: change, pain itself, and the continuous potential for further suffering.

Above and beyond all that, one's own personal liberation will not do by itself. Because all living beings have been the gracious parents of our past lives, we must liberate them from saṃsāra as well. And to free ourselves from saṃsāra and then to liberate other living beings from saṃsāra too, at the outset we must attain the precious condition of authentic and perfect Buddhahood, which is without faults and is endowed with all positive attributes. Concerning the way to attain it, formerly the Buddha taught limitless approaches to the doctrine, but they may be summarized in the words of the *Sūtra of the Rules of Freedom* (*Prātimokṣasūtra*):

Not doing any harmful actions,
You must practice perfect virtue,
And thoroughly tame your own mind.
This is the Buddha's teaching.

Just so, we must abandon harmful actions and achieve virtue. These are the nonvirtuous actions: selfish attachment, hatred toward others, and unknowing ignorance are the three poisons that motivate ten nonvirtuous actions: killing other living beings, taking what is not given, sexual misconduct, lying, slander, harsh speech, prattle, covetousness, injurious thoughts, and perverse opinion. We must abandon these ten—their actual performance, encouraging others to do them, and delighting in their performance—as if they were poison.

Minor harmful actions, too, if not abandoned are like poison entering one's heart, and so will create great suffering. It says in the *Collection of Aphorisms* (*Udānavarga*):

Having committed even minor misdeeds,
The world beyond becomes a great terror,
Leading to greater ruination—
It is like poison afflicting the heart.

Therefore, it is essential that one repent of past misdeeds and bind oneself by vows in the future. For example, one who has consumed poison in the morning may receive an antidote in the afternoon. Just so, the repentance and vows remove misdeeds and make even a sinner fortunate enough to ascend to heaven and to liberation. Therefore, I ask that all of you make great exertions to repent and to take the vows, from now until death.

Now you may ask: Having abandoned unvirtuous conduct, what are the virtues we must achieve? Thinking of all living beings as the gracious parents of our past lives, we should be compassionate to beggars and other unfortunates who come to our doors. We should love those who are unhappy. And we should think as follows: to remove the sufferings of living beings and to establish them in happiness, I must become a buddha. Therefore I will practice the genuine doctrine.

So, with love, compassion, and an enlightened attitude we should protect the lives of other living beings, give generously and without attachment, adhere to our vows, speak truthfully, bring adversaries together, speak gently, praise others' virtues, be content, love others, and believe in the causal principle of karma—these are the ten virtues. Moreover, we should also practice prostrations, do circumambulations, erect images, books, and stūpas, recite the scriptures, give worshipful offerings, recollect the words and meaning of the doctrine, expound them to others, critically examine those words and their meaning, become absorbed in the contemplation of that which is genuinely significant, and so forth. We should practice such positive karma ourselves, encourage others to do so, and rejoice when others have done so. Thus, even if we practice only minor virtues, then just as a pot is filled drop by drop, we will gradually attain Buddhahood. As it says in the *Verse Compendium of Transcendent Discernment* (*Prajñāpāramitāsañcayagāthā*):

> Just as drops of water in a empty pot
> Gradually fill it up little by little,
> So, with an enlightened attitude as the basis,
> Positive virtues gradually lead to perfect Buddhahood.

For this reason, whatever virtues you practice, you should be like the hero who, not faint-hearted, just goes into battle. Be like a ring of fire that just blazes continuously! Be like the Ganges river that flows without ceasing! You will then be happy in this life, joyous in the next. And finally, you will attain Buddhahood.

CELEBRATIONS FOLLOWING THE TEACHINGS

By my earnest preaching of this all the rich desisted from their sins, and vowed never to kill again in the future. Many goats, sheep, yak-cows, and yak-bulls were liberated from the butcher. [A customary way of earning religious merit among Tibetans is to purchase animals destined for slaughter and to set them free instead. Such animals are marked, usually with special ribbons, so that others will abstain from harming them.]

When the local-folk were all assembled, we performed the hundredfold feast-offering and had great banquets, following which songs such as these were sung:

Lord of refuges! Wish-granting gem!
Take your seat on a throne of jewels!
We will offer you song and dance
Before your very eyes.

In the pinnacle of the Potala
The Conqueror [the Dalai Lama] dwells with his sons [the court].
Circumambulate them three times,
And bodily obscurations are removed!

When the Conqueror takes his horse
Over the Turquoise Roof Bridge [a famous monument in Lhasa],
The fish who swim beneath it,
Need not be born in the hells.

This seems so joyous!
The sun has arisen on the snow mountain's peak!
ONE! TWO! THREE! [the dance steps are counted]
This seems so happy!
The lake's surface has become silken!
FOUR! FIVE! SIX!
We've got joy and happiness together!
The leaves have sprouted on a heavenly tree!
SEVEN! EIGHT! NINE!

Along with such songs, there were many dances. Sometimes they danced to this song:

It's fine to have *chang* as your wealth,
For with *chang*, there is no end:
Up to the door's upper portal
The storeroom is filled with barley!

Even if you get a god's body next time,
The offerings you'll get are just water [instead of *chang*]!
So now, when you have a human body,
Be joyous and energetic!

If you think on this world, saṃsāra,
You'll see that it has no real value.
O lord of refuge, wish-granting gem!
Please snip a lock of my hair! [thereby creating an affinity with the community of monks and nuns, whose heads are shaven.]

This seems so joyous!
The sun has arisen on the snow mountain's peak!

And so on. The refrain was just as before.

They sang many other songs, such as one that began, "Earth Goddess! Earth Goddess. . . ." Such activities as I have just described continued over a period of many months, and all the young and old alike became joyously enthusiastic, so that their happiness rivaled the gods. Food, wealth, and riches rained down on me: Dorje Wangchuk of Limi offered fifty *zho* of gold. The rich lady of Lhongö offered fifteen *zho* of gold. The rich man of Logpa, the rich man of Gyashang, the military commander of Kyitang, and the other rich men of Purang offered fifteen, twenty, or thirty *zho* of gold each; and those who were without still offered two or three *zho* of gold each, or whatever clothing, jewelry, wealth, or objects they could afford. Just the gold I was offered came to a whole horseload altogether. Moreover, I received thirty *tamkas* of gold; one hundred big and small silver amulet boxes; five silver maṇḍalas [a special set of ritual objects, used for making symbolic offerings of piles of grain representing a gift of the entire world-system surrounding Mount Meru], large and small; two silver lamps; three trays for offering-cakes; eighty pearl and coral earrings; a bag full of turquoise, coral, and amber headresses; forty-three new silk and flannel robes; ten old ones; twenty-five good horses; and two mules. Also, innumerable persons offered silver *tamkas* and ingots, woolen blankets, cotton cloth, and ceremonial scarves.

—22—

From the Autobiography of a Visionary

Janet Gyatso

Literary theorists have maintained that autobiography is a genre that is largely exclusive to the modern West, but Tibetan literature provides evidence to the contrary. A large number of autobiographies have been written by Tibetans, mostly religious figures, with no known influence from the West. Nor are there significant analogues of this genre in Indian or Chinese literary traditions. Tibetan religious autobiographies were written as early as the eleventh century but have been produced in significant quantity since the sixteenth century, and in great numbers in the nineteenth and twentieth centuries. Such texts are written in a variety of contexts, and with a variety of intentions. Most Tibetan Buddhist autobiographers state that an account of their personal experiences might be instructive to their disciples. They also write about their life experiences in order to demonstrate their own spiritual progress, to contextualize and cast legitimating light on their other writings, and to attract students and patrons.

There are various subgenres of Tibetan autobiography, and it is not uncommon for a single author to write several accounts of his or her life from the different perspectives these subgenres represent. The author represented here, Jigme Lingpa ('Jigs med gling pa, 1730–1798), wrote several autobiographical works, including two "secret autobiographies," a subgenre that focuses primarily upon meditative experiences, visions, and realizations. In contrast, the selections translated below, from Jigme Lingpa's 455-page "outer autobiography," are part of the narrative of his publicly observable deeds—such as childhood events, education, travels, and so forth—although as will be seen, the outer account can reflect on inner thoughts and feelings as well.

Jigme Lingpa was a well-known teacher and revealer of "treasure texts" (*gter ma*) in the Nyingma sect of Tibetan Buddhism. He stayed in retreat from the ages of twenty-eight to thirty-three. During this retreat he is believed to have had several significant visions, which he later committed to writing, entitled "The Heart Sphere of the Great Expanse" (*Klong chen snying thig*). He established a retreat center in central Tibet close to the Yarlung valley where the tombs of the ancient Tibetan kings are located, and he attracted a significant and influential following. His "Heart Sphere" writings remain the most widely practiced meditations and liturgies among adherents of the Great Perfection tradition of the Nyingma. He is the author of a nine-volume "Collected Works," which includes an important study of the Old Canon of Tantras, "The Heart Sphere" cycle, and several original works on early Tibetan history and architectural sites, in addition to the outer autobiography excerpted here.

Autobiographies and biographies of all sorts are extremely popular reading material in Tibet, and an outer autobiography such as Jigme Lingpa's is well known to both lay and monastic readers. Although not the most carefully crafted of his works, it is typical of his subtle and often complex style and is rich in anecdotes and wry humor concerning especially his later life as a sought-after teacher and tantric master. It reproduces much of his correspondence, as well as some of the poems and songs for which he was admired. The song contained in the first selection translated below has achieved fame on its own for its suggestive tantric nuances; it has since been excerpted in a widely used as part of the liturgy of a communal feast (*gaṇacakra*) that takes place at the conclusion of a tantric initiation; it is often sung in Nyingma rituals with a haunting melody.

Both of the selections presented here are of primary interest for the insight they give into the sort of relationship that obtained in Buddhist Tibet between a visionary such as Jigme Lingpa and powerful lay political figures. Such figures would request Buddhist teachings from a master and in return would offer vital economic and political support for the master's projects and community of followers. Autobiographies are especially useful in shedding light on some of the more subtle and complex aspects of such a relationship—for example, the private doubts and cynical attitude we see Jigme Lingpa harboring in both of the following selections concerning these figures' affluent life-styles and the unlikelihood of their developing genuine religious insights—which would not be evident in other sorts of writings and documents.

The first selection concerns Jigme Lingpa's initial meeting with a member of the powerful Yuthok (G.yu thok) aristocratic family, who was an important government official. After granting a few perfunctory ritual blessings and assessing Yuthok's attitude toward religion and ability to develop the faith (or "pure vision") necessary for tantric Buddhist practice, Jigme Lingpa sings a symbolic song that transforms their encounter into a charged moment of bonding between a tantric master and his circle of students. The song merges classical Indic poetic imagery with a distinctively Tibetan longing for warmer climes and constructs an allegory of a special moment of close feelings. The "peacock from eastern India," a stock phrase in Tibetan popular lyrical tradition, would be Yuthok himself. In Tibet the peacock's tail feathers were often worn ornamentally on hats as insignia of official rank, serving as an emblem of beauty, dignity, and noblesse. The reference to the rainbow colored circular design in the peacock's plumage, a conventional symbol for the primordial light-sphere (*thig le*) of Great Perfection meditation, is a direct reference to Yuthok's interest in such practices. The "cuckoo from the leafy forests" is another popular figure in Tibetan lyrics. The bird migrates to central Tibet during the springtime, and its sweet cooing voice is believed to enhance fertility and bring about rain. Here the cuckoo would appear to be Jigme Lingpa himself, the singer of poetry, and the transmitter of the fertile dharma and its "ripening and liberating nectars." Effecting a separation between narrator and author not uncommon in this sort of poetic song, the poet's voice reflects the perspective of his listeners, that is, the gathered disciples, or "vajra brothers," and their devotion to the lama who in this case is the author, Jigme Lingpa himself. The scene is a celebration of these vajra brothers' receipt of a tantric initiation in which symbolic liquids ("liberating nectars") are tasted, and the narrator has a vision of a deity and a lama (whose identities are not specified). The song culminates with a request that the lama bestow upon the disciples an esoteric teaching from the Great Perfection tradition ("the clear light vehicle," attributed to the ḍākinīs, the female buddha/angel/trickster deities) concerning the achievement of a body of pure "rainbow" light.

The second selection recounts Jigme Lingpa's reflections on another meeting with powerful political figures, the king and queen of the eastern Tibetan Khampa principality of Derge (Sde dge). This royal couple had been in correspondence with him for several years, influenced by reports of his virtues from fellow countrymen who had already journeyed to meet him in central Tibet. The couple from eastern Tibet is now on a pilgrimage to central Tibet, reminding us of a similar pilgrimage described elsewhere in this anthology. (See the description of the pilgrimage by Do Khyentse's parents in chapter 3). Jigme Lingpa, aware of the serious burden entailed in hosting such an entourage, takes pains to deflect them away from his own humble retreat center and arranges for their meeting to occur instead at the ancient monastery of Samye (Bsam yas). Even here their demands exceed the resources of the area, and we see Jigme Lingpa objecting strenuously, both on behalf of the local people and in hopes of enlightening the king, in the conventional sense, about the merits of being considerate toward subjects and hosts in foreign lands.

Jigme Lingpa gives a number of major teachings to the couple, including the "eight transmissions," which covers the principal eight tantric deities of the Nyingma, and the "heap of instructions," which concerns the practices of the Great Perfection tradition. He establishes a particularly close relationship with the queen; soon after this incident the king dies, but his queen and her son remain two of Jigme's principal patrons throughout his life. In addition to giving him many other sorts of support, she sponsors and oversees the publication of his "Collected Works" toward the end of his life. Since this collection includes the outer autobiography from which the following passages are translated, Jigme Lingpa's candor in the final lines of the second selection, indicating that he rushed through his teachings to the king and queen so that their party would leave quickly, and coming close to comparing them to barbarians, is noteworthy.

The translation below is excerpted from *Yul lho rgyud du byung ba'i rdzogs chen pa rang byung rdo rje mkhyen brtse'i od zer gyi rnam par thar pa legs byas yongs 'du'i snye ma*, in *The Collected Works of 'Jigs-med-gliṅ-pa Raṅ-byuṅ-rdo-rje Mkhyen-brtse'i-*

'od-zer (1730–1798), reproduced from a set of prints from the Sde dge Dgon chen blocks (Gangtok, Sikkim: Pema Thinley for Ven. Dodrup Chen Rinpoche, 1985), 9:1–502. Selection 1 is found on pp. 210–11; selection 2 is found on pp. 359–62.

Further Reading

For more on the life of Jigme Lingpa, see Steven D. Goodman, "Rig-'dzin 'jigs-med gling-pa and the *kLong-Chen sNying-Thig*," in *Tibetan Buddhism: Reason and Revelation*, ed. Steven D. Goodman and Ronald M. Davidson (Albany, N.Y.: SUNY Press, 1992); and especially Janet Gyatso, *Apparitions of the Self: The Autobiographies of a Tibetan Visionary* (Princeton: Princeton University Press, 1997). To learn more about Tibetan religious and political songs, see Melvyn Goldstein, "Lhasa Street Songs: Political and Social Satire in Traditional Tibet," *Tibet Journal* 7, 1 & 2: 56–57; also Per K. Sorenson, *Divinity Secularized: An Inquiry into the Nature and Form of the Songs Ascribed to the Sixth Dalai Lama* (Wien: Arbeitskreis für Tibetische und Buddhistische Studien Universität Wien, 1990).

During that year, when the Lord of Archery Pawo Wangjuk (Dpa' bo'i dbang phyug, "Powerful Hero") of the Yuthok family was at the hot springs, he came here on a side trip. He arrived with about fifty assistant archers, rivaling [in ostentatiousness] a fourfold army [of infantry, cavalry, elephants, and chariots].

In general, it's hard for anyone to tell what is in the mind of another. But he did seem to be someone who—for a householder—had managed to develop the pure vision to regard the three precious jewels with the highest respect. He said he needed a protection ritual and a blessing, and so I performed them. He had a great liking for poetic songs and insisted I do one, and so I sang this, with the others singing backup:

> On the wishing-tree
> That is the coming together of karma and prayers,
> There has arrived
> A young peacock from eastern India.
>
> The peacock's parasol-wheel has turned
> Toward the direction of the holy dharma,
> And we young ones
> Shall take the path to freedom.
>
> Coming in
> On Queen Spring of Merit's chariot

Is a cuckoo
From the leafy forests of southern Mön [Bhutan].

His tune is sweeter
Than the flute of the celestial maidens on high.
It is the auspicious indication
Of three months of summer warmth.

We vajra brothers and friends here gathered,
Share common karma and prayers,
And have arrived inside the teaching circle
Where the lama is sitting.

A song sung
With feelings of happiness,
Which celebrates the drinking
Of the ripening and liberating nectars,
Has a special meaning.

In the middle of the line
Where we were sitting
In great unmoving bliss,
I saw,
Without meditating on them,
The faces of the deity and the lama.

And I request,
By way of the clear light vehicle
Of the mother ḍākinīs' heart-sphere teachings,
The power-means to accomplish
A dharmakāya rainbow body.

When he was about to go, he said he would take the four initiations. He touched his forehead to mine, tears falling from his eyes. If such a way of perceiving things were to dawn on my disciples, it would help them greatly in their cultivation of experience and realization!

Among the set of offerings he gave me was a large bag of butter. I offered this in Lhasa, and it became my first connection with performing ceremonies there.

During that year the king of Derge planned to come to Central Tibet. I feared that if he came to my own place it would make difficulties for the peasants. So I sent a message with the lamas from Kham who were returning [to Derge]. "When you meet some of the [king's] retainers who are close to him, please give them the message that I will definitely be going to Samye Monastery in the ninth month in order to consecrate a stūpa, so it would be good for us to get together there," I urged them. In due course, representatives of the king reached me and gave me his reply that there could be no better place to meet than Samye. Soon after, the king arrived, and we met at Samye fort. I had to give him many empowerments, transmissions, and permission rites, which I did in the Ivory Chapel, the small room on the middle storey.

Then he wanted forty-five corvée horses in order to go up to the Chimpu Hermitage. Where were the peasants to get them from? They would be ruined. So that the king's seed of merit might actually grow and bear fruit, I sent this message to him:

You, man of power, with the traits of a bodhisattva!
Sentient beings are controlled by karma.
This is an extremely degenerate period,
Especially in this Land of Snows.
Last year there was a bad harvest, famine,
And a variety of plagues.
This year there has been extreme misery
Due to war and taxes.
This area in particular is actually paradise itself,
But the place is small,
And the people are poor in necessities.
Every day they have to move to a different place
And the villages are becoming empty.
Perceiving this bad era,
Your compassion and sadness should increase.

You see the local sacred mountain with your eyes,
But when it is time to go there,
And you climb the long trail of stone stairs,
The distance becomes even longer.

Pay a wage of three silver *zho* for each horse
And breathe a big breath of life into this place, please!

And thus it came to pass that ten corvée horses would do.

The next day while giving the empowerment for the eight transmissions, I told him how pleased I was that he had reduced the number of corvée horses to a smaller amount. And since he might also go to Yarlung, the ancient site of the ancestors and other [pilgrimage spots], I explained to him the source of black so as to fully ripen his white karma, because both he, the master, and his servants were very powerful. He promised to heed me.

The queen was very intelligent, with good propensities, and she comprehended the symbols of the "heap of instructions" in three days. She said that since it is difficult to meet one's guru often, they should linger for a while at Samye. But their staff people were making problems and impositions, so I endeavored to complete the empowerments and the various teachings quickly, in no more than six days. [The king] said that we should make prayers together in the presence of the Lord [Buddha statue] and urged me to set up the "offerings in thousands" precisely, which I did.

In general, even though one's mind is moistened with a renunciatory attitude, if one doesn't have any thought of respecting the local rules and so forth, the "truth of reality" will not [be obtained] through manipulations of hope and fear. But anyway they were not the same as those from other kingdoms that are filled with barbarians and miscreants.

23

A Prayer to the Lama

Donald S. Lopez, Jr.

During this degenerate age in which buddhas do not publicly appear, it is said that gurus compassionately serve as the buddhas' surrogates, leading suffering sentient beings to enlightenment. The guru is thus the representative of the Buddha and, in tantric practice, is to be regarded as inseparable from him. The practice of visualizing one's guru (in Tibetan, lama) as a buddha, a practice called "guru yoga," is therefore a central part of Tibetan tantric practice, and all sects of Tibetan Buddhism have a well-known prayer of devotion to the lama. For the Gelukpas, that work is the "Offering to the Lama" (*Bla ma mchod pa*), composed by the first Panchen Lama, Losang Chö gyi Gyaltsen (Blo bzang chos kyi rgyal mtshan, 1570–1662), the tutor of the fifth Dalai Lama, the Dalai Lama who, with the aid of his Mongol patrons, was able to bring Tibet under his political control.

The text is written in a highly ornate poetic style, filled with allusions and symbols that operate on several levels. To explain each of these fully would require a separate tome (several of which exist in Tibetan). What follows is a general summary of the text, identifying its structure. In the translation, I have added stanza numbers for ease of reference, to which I refer here.

The work begins with obeisance to the lama and then to Vajradhara, the chief tantric buddha for the Geluk, who is said to be able to bestow the boon of buddhahood (as well as the more mundane powers called *siddhis*) in a single instant. In the first stanza, the author (and, by extension, the person reciting the text) visualizes himself as a divine lama. This term (*lha bla ma*) means the lama in the form of a buddha. This is the ultimate goal of the Buddhist path, and its presence at the very beginning of this work is a powerful indication of the tantric nature of this text, since what is said to make the tantric path so much faster than the ordinary bodhisattva path is the practice of taking the goal as the path; that is, imagining to be a buddha now is the most effective technique for actually becoming a buddha in the future. Visualized as the divine lama, the author next imagines rays of light extending in all directions to purify all beings and lands throughout the universe. Next is the recitation of the refuge formula, performed in Sanskrit for extra potency. Tibetans add a fourth source of refuge to their formula, going for refuge first to the lama, then to the Buddha, the dharma, and the saṅgha. The author seeks refuge not only for himself but for all beings, referred to here as "aged mothers equal to space," reflecting the belief that all beings in the universe have been one's mother in a past lifetime. Out of compassion for these "motherly sentient beings," the author promises to achieve buddhahood in order to liberate them all from suffering. The first section of the text, the preliminaries, concludes with the making of offerings to the lama and the three jewels (stanza 8).

The next section of the text (stanzas 9–17) provides a detailed description of what is to be visualized. At the top of a magnificent tree there is a throne supported by lions, where sits one's own lama, dressed as a monk. In his heart sits the buddha Vajradhara, in union with his consort. The lama is surrounded by hosts of buddhas, bodhisattvas, ḍākinīs, and protectors of the dharma. This great assembly is called the "field for the collection of merit" (*tshogs zhing*), those to whom one makes offerings of gifts and praise, thereby amassing a great stock of virtue. At first, these beings are merely imagined to stand arrayed before the mediator. Next, as in other sādhanas (see chapters 16 and 17), the actual lama, buddhas, bodhisattvas, and so forth are invited to come from their various abodes throughout the universe and merge with their visualized doubles, ready to receive the offerings of the meditator. That merging is effected by the recitation of the mantra *jaḥ hūṃ baṃ hoḥ*.

The next section of the text is devoted to an elaborate version of the seven-limbed offering. Since this practice has already been discussed in the introduction to this volume, it will suffice here to note the correspondence of the stanzas: obeisance (18–22), offering (23–37), confession (38), admiration (39), supplication of the buddhas and bodhisattvas to teach the dharma (40), entreaty not to pass into nirvāṇa (41), and dedication of the merit of performing the preceding toward the enlightenment of all beings (42). The sevenfold offering exists in myriad forms in Tibetan literature. The version here is one of the most famous.

The next section of the text (stanzas 43–55) comprises an elaborate series of praises and requests, addressed to the lama in various aspects: he is a monk who maintains the discipline purely (43), he is a master of Mahāyāna doctrine (44), he is a skilled teacher of tantra (45), he is the compassionate guru who teaches those that past buddhas have failed to teach, and so forth. As a result of these requests, the lama merges with the meditator, providing the initiations of Unexcelled Yoga Tantra, transforming the meditator into a buddha (54). Again, we see here the tantric technique of turning the goal into the path.

The path, in fact, remains to be traversed, and the next section of the text (56–85) provides an eloquent survey of the entire Buddhist path. Most of the topics of the "stages of the path" (see chapter 28) are mentioned here, from taking advantage of one's rare rebirth as a human, to the practice of love and compassion for all sentient beings, going so far as to be willing to breathe into oneself all the sufferings of others and breathe out to them all one's happiness and virtue (66,

70). Empowerment to practice each of the six perfections, the "bodhisattva deeds" of giving, ethics, patience, effort, concentration, and wisdom, is requested in turn (72–79), the final perfection, the perfection of wisdom receiving three stanzas of attention. Requests to maintain the tantric vows and for success in the Unexcelled Yoga Tantra practice of transforming death, the intermediate state, and rebirth into the three bodies of a buddha (see chapter 29), come next (80–82). If one is not successful in becoming a buddha in this lifetime, then the lama is requested to transfer one's consciousness directly into a pure land upon death, where one can continue to make progress toward enlightenment (83). Above all, the author asks always to be near the lama, never to be separated, wherever the lama may appear. The prayer ends with a dedication of the merit toward that end.

The text is translated from *Bla ma'i rnal 'byor dang yi dam khag gi bdag bskyed sogs zhal 'don gces btus* (Dharamsala: Tibetan Cultural Printing Press, 1977), pp. 40–74.

Further Reading

For a book-length commentary by the current Dalai Lama, see H. H. the Dalai Lama, Tenzin Gyatso, *The Union of Bliss and Emptiness: A Commentary on the Lama Choepa Guru Yoga Practice* (Ithaca: Snow Lion Publications, 1988).

The Rite of Offering to the Lama

In the language of India, *Gurupūjakalpanāma.* In the language of Tibet, *Rite of Offering to the Lama.* I bow down and go for refuge to the feet of the excellent lama, peerless in kindness. I pray to be cared for with great mercy at all times and in all circumstances.

I bow respectfully at the lotus feet of Vajradhara, a wish-granting jewel, through reliance on whom the supremely desired gift is bestowed in an instant—the three bodies [of a buddha] and great bliss, together with the common attainments.

Having bowed, I will compose a necklace, a beautiful garland of flowers that come from the garden of quintessential instructions of the excellent sūtras and tantras, the supreme method, without a second, for the achievement of all help and happiness for students of good fortune.

Within a state of great bliss, I myself am a divine lama. From my radiant body a mass of light rays extend in the ten directions, blessing environs and inhabitants and transforming them into marvelous forms with the sole quality of infinite purity. (1)

With a great mind of completely pure virtue, I and sentient beings, aged mothers equal to space, from today until the essence of enlightenment, go for refuge to the lama and the three jewels. (2)

Namo gurubhyaḥ. Namo buddhāya. Namo dharmāya. Namo saṅghāya. (3)

Upon becoming a divine lama myself, for the sake of all motherly sentient beings, I will establish all sentient beings in the supreme state of a divine lama. (4)

In this very lifetime, quickly, quickly, I will manifest the supreme state of a primordial divine lama buddha for the sake of all motherly sentient beings. (5)

I will free all motherly sentient beings from suffering and establish them in the place of great bliss, buddhahood. For that purpose I will practice the profound path of divine lama yoga. (6)

Oṃ āḥ hūṃ (three times) (7)

Their entity is wisdom. Their aspects are the forms of inner offering and various substances of offering. Their function is to create the special wisdom of bliss and emptiness [by serving] as objects of the six senses. The clouds of outer, inner, and secret offerings completely fill the reaches of earth, sky, and the space in between, inconceivably pervading everyplace with gifts of excellent substances. (8)

In the vast sky of indivisible bliss and emptiness, clouds of Samantabhadra's offerings gather. In their center is a wish-granting tree adorned with leaves, fruit, and flowers. At the top, on [the backs of] lions is a throne of blazing jewels, on which is a vast lotus, sun, and moon. (9)

My root lama, endowed with three kindnesses, sits there. In essence, he is all the buddhas, in aspect, a saffron-clad monk with one face, two arms, and a radiant smile. His right hand is in the gesture of teaching the doctrine, his left, in the gesture of meditation, holds a begging bowl filled with ambrosia. He wears the three robes, the color of saffron; a yellow paṇḍita's hat adorns his head. (10)

In his heart sits the pervasive master Vajradhara, with one face, two arms, and a blue-colored body. Holding vajra and bell, his embraces his consort Vajradhātu Iśvarī. They delight in the sport of innate bliss and emptiness. They are adorned with jeweled ornaments of many kinds and robed in garments of heavenly silk. (11)

Adorned with the major and minor marks, blazing with thousands rays of light, and sitting in the adamantine posture enhaloed by a five-colored rainbow, his aggregates are the five sugatas, his four elements are the four consorts, his six sources, channels, sinews, and joints are actually bodhisattvas. His hair pores are the 21,000 arhats, his limbs are wrathful protectors, his light rays are guardians of the ten directions and secret yakṣas. The worldly [gods] are his footstools. (12)

Surrounding him in order sit root and lineage lamas, *yi dams*, hosts of maṇḍala deities, and buddhas, bodhisattvas, heroes, and ḍākinīs, surrounded by an ocean of protectors of the teaching. (13)

Their three doors are marked by the three vajras. Hooked light rays from the letter *hūṃ* radiate and invite the wisdom beings from their native lands; they become firmly inseparable [from the imagined beings]. (14)

Source of auspicious marvels and joy and in three times, root and lineage lamas, *yi dams*, and the three jewels together with the assembly of heroes, ḍākinīs, dharmapālas, and protectors, by the power of compassion, come here and remain steadfast. (15)

Although the nature of phenomena is devoid of all coming and going, you manifest everywhere endowed with deeds of wisdom and mercy in accord with the intentions of myriad disciples. I beseech the excellent refuge and protector, along with his retinue, to come. (16)

Oṃ guru buddha bodhisattva dharmapāla saparivāra ehyahiḥ. Jaḥ hūṃ baṃ hoḥ. May the wisdom beings and the pledge beings become nondual. (17)

I bow down at the lotus feet of Vajradhara, the lama whose body is like a jewel, who compassionately grants in a single instant the supreme state of the three bodies, the sphere of great bliss. (18)

[You are] the wisdom of all the infinite conquerors. [You have] the supreme skillful means to appear anywhere in any way that tames, sporting through the dance of the saffron-robed. I bow down at the feet of the excellent refuge and protector. (19)

I bow down at the feet of my venerable lama who has destroyed at the root all faults and their latencies, who is a treasure of measureless jewel-like virtues, the sole source of all help and happiness. (20)

I bow down to the kind lamas who are in reality all the buddhas, teachers of all, including the gods, source of the eighty-four thousand excellent doctrines, preeminent in the midst of assemblies of āryans. (21)

Emanating bodies equal to the particles of a world, I bow down with faith and belief, with an ocean of melodious praise, to the lamas of the three times abiding in the ten directions, to the three supreme jewels, and all that worthy of homage. (22)

To my venerable protector lama and retinue I offer an ocean of clouds of all manner of offerings. (23)

From an ample vase, well-fashioned, bejeweled, and radiant, four streams of purifying ambrosia gently flow. (24)

Beautiful flowers in trees, as blossoms, and beautifully arranged garlands fill earth and sky. (25)

The sky is filled with blue summer clouds from the smoke of fragrant incense, the color of lapis. (26)

Joyous rays from suns, moons, gems, and scores of blazing lamps dispel the darkness of a billion worlds. (27)

Great oceans of scented waters perfumed with the fragrance of camphor, sandal, and saffron swirl to the horizon. (28)

Food and drink having the essences of a hundred flavors, feasts for gods and humans are piled like mountains. (29)

From an endless variety of musical instruments come melodies to fill the three worlds. (30)

Holding glorious sights, sounds, fragrances, tastes, and objects of touch, goddesses of the outer and inner desirable qualities fill every direction. (31)

The four continents and Mount Meru a billion times over, the seven precious substances, the minor precious substances, and so forth, marvelous environs and inhabitants, creating joy for all, a great treasure of all that gods and humans enjoy and desire, these I offer with a clear mind to the perfect supreme field, refuge and protector, treasury of compassion. (32)

For the delight of my venerable lama I offer a joyous grove where thousands of spreading lotuses of offered substances grown from the virtues of mundane existence and peace captivate the minds of all on the shore of a wish-granting ocean of offerings actually arranged and mentally created, and where bloom in all forms flowers of my own and others' virtues of the three doors, the mundane and supramundane, emanating a hundred thousand fragrances of Samantabhadra's offerings, bearing the fruit of the three trainings, two stages, and five paths. (33)

I offer a drink of Chinese tea, having the color of saffron and a fragrant aroma with the glory of hundred flavors, the five hooks and five lamps, and so forth, purified, transformed, and multiplied into an ocean of ambrosia. (34)

I even offer beautiful and magical consorts with the glory of pleasing youth, skilled in the sixty-four arts of love, a host of messengers field-born, mantra-born, and innate. (35)

To you I offer the supreme ultimate mind of enlightenment, great wisdom of innate bliss free from obstruction, spontaneous, beyond expression in word or thought, inseparable from the sphere of all phenomena, devoid of self-nature and elaborations. (36)

I offer many kinds of auspicious medicine destroying the illnesses of the 404 afflictions, and to please you I offer myself as a servant; I beseech you to keep me as your subject as long as space endures. (37)

In the presence of the compassionate one I regretfully confess and vow not to repeat whatever nonvirtuous and sinful deeds I have committed, exhorted others to commit, or which I have rejoiced in, from beginningless time. (38)

Though all phenomena have no sign of self-nature, I rejoice sincerely in white [deeds] appearing as the happiness and joy of all worldly beings and āryans, occurring like a dream. (39)

I pray that a hundred thousand clouds of perfect wisdom and mercy gather and rain down profound and vast doctrines in order to grow, sustain, and increase the jasmine grove of help and happiness for limitless transmigrators. (40)

Though the vajra-body has no birth or death but is the repository of the king, lord of union, I beseech you to remain eternally according to our wishes, not entering nirvāṇa until the end of saṃsāra. (41)

I dedicate the collection of white virtue thus produced so that the venerable lama with the three kindnesses might care for me and so that we not be separated in all my lifetimes and so that I attain the power of a unified Vajradhara. (42)

I beseech the elder, who maintains the vinaya, the source of virtues, great ocean of ethics, completely filled with a mass of gems of much hearing, wearer of saffron, the master who is the second lord of sages. (43)

I beseech the spiritual friend of the supreme vehicle, master of doctrine, representative of the family of the conquerors who, when endowed with the ten excellent qualities, is worthy to show the path of the Sugata. (44)

I beseech the foremost of vajra-holders, with the three doors well-restrained, great awareness, endowed with patience and honesty, without deceit or pretense, knowing mantra and tantra, having the pair of ten principles, skilled in drawing and teaching. (45)

I beseech the compassionate refuge and protector who shows the auspicious path of the Sugata exactly as it is to sentient beings of the ruinous age, unseemly and difficult to tame, who were not restrained by the countless buddhas who have come. (46)

I beseech the compassionate refuge and protector who performs the deeds of the conqueror for the multitude of sentient beings who are without protection or refuge at the time of the setting of the sun of the sage. (47)

I beseech the compassionate refuge and protector, even a single pore of whom is well-praised as a field of our merit greater than all the conquerors of the three times and the ten directions. (48)

I beseech the compassionate refuge and protector. The wheels that adorn the three bodies of the Sugata through an enticing nexus of magical skillful methods guides transmigrators with an ordinary form. (49)

I beseech the supreme lama, essence of the three supremes, whose aggregates, constituents, sources, and limbs are the nature of the five sugata lineages, their consorts, bodhisattvas, and wrathful protectors. (50)

I beseech the protector of primordial union, chief of vajra holders, pervasive master of the hundred lineages, essence of the ten million maṇḍalas arising from the sport of omniscient wisdom. (51)

I beseech you, in actuality the ultimate mind of enlightenment, without beginning or end, completely good, indivisible from the sport of unobstructed innate joy, the nature of all, pervading everything stable and moving. (52)

You are the lama, you are the *yi dams*, you are the ḍākinīs and protectors of doctrine. From now until enlightenment, I will seek no refuge other than you. Hold me with the hook of compassion in this [life], the bardo, and all future lives. Free me from the fears of mundane existence and peace, grant me all attainments, be my constant friend and protect me from obstacles. (53)

By the power of beseeching him three times in this way, from the lama's body, speech, and mind come white, red, and dark blue ambrosia and rays of light in succession and then together. They melt into my own three places in succession and then together, purifying the four obstacles. I attain the four pure initiations and the four bodies. A double of the lama happily melts into me and I am empowered. (54)

By the power of offering and faithful requests to the venerable lama, excellent and supreme field, may you, protector, root of joy and goodness, empower me to be joyfully cared for by you. (55)

Realizing how this leisure and opportunity found just once is difficult to encounter and quickly perishes, empower me to extract the meaningful essence without being distracted by the pointless activities of this life. (56)

Fearing the blazing fire of the sufferings of the three evil realms, I take heartfelt refuge in the three jewels. Empower me to strive with diligence that I may abandon sins and establish boundless collections of virtue. (57)

The waves of karma and afflictions are in violent upheaval. Many sea monsters of the three sufferings attack. Empower me to create a powerful wish for liberation from the great ocean of existence, boundless and worthy of fright. (58)

Abandoning the attitude that sees this prison-like saṃsāra, difficult to bear, as a pleasure grove, empower me to possess the āryans' treasure of jewels, the three trainings, and seize the banner of liberation. (59)

Thinking about how all these destitute transmigrators who were my mothers repeatedly protected me with kindness, empower me to create unfeigned compassion, like a loving mother for her beautiful child. (60)

It is said that in not wanting even the most subtle suffering and in never being satisfied with happiness, there is no difference between myself and others. Empower me to rejoice in the happiness of others. (61)

Seeing that the chronic disease of cherishing myself is the cause of unwanted suffering, empower me to rebuke it and resent it and destroy the great demon of self-cherishing. (62)

Seeing that an attitude of holding my mothers dear and placing them in happiness is the source of boundless good qualities, empower me to hold these beings to be dearer than my life, even though they rise up as my enemies. (63)

In short, through the awareness that discerns the differences in faults and virtues between fools who act only for their own welfare and the lord of sages who worked only for the welfare of others, empower me with the ability to equalize and then exchange self and other. (64)

Self-cherishing is the door of all downfall. Cherishing my mothers is the basis of all that is good. Therefore, empower me for the essence of practices: the yoga of the exchange of self and other. (65)

Therefore, venerable lama of great compassion, empower me so that all the sins, obstructions, and sufferings of transmigrators who have been my mother ripen for me without remainder now, and all my happiness and virtue is sent to others, endowing all transmigrators with happiness. (66)

Though environs and inhabitants are completely filled with the fruits of sin and unwanted sufferings descend like rain, empower me to take misfortune as the path, seeing these as causes for consuming the fruits of evil deeds. (67)

In short, may whatever good or evil that appears be transformed into a path that enhances the two minds of enlightenment. Empower me to cultivate a mind of bliss through the practice of the five powers, the essence of all doctrines. (68)

Empower me to meditate immediately on whatever I encounter using the skillful method of the four applications and to make leisure and opportunity meaningful through the pledges and instruction of mind-training. (69)

So that I may free transmigrators from the great ocean of existence, empower me to be skilled in the aspiration to enlightenment through love, compassion, and the supreme intention, giving and taking magically mounted on the breath. (70)

Binding my mind with the vows of a pure child of the Conqueror to the single path traversed by the conquerors of the three times, empower me to strive with diligence in the practice of the threefold ethics of the supreme vehicle. (71)

Through the instructions for magnifying the wish to give without attachment, may I transform my body, resources, and collections of virtue of the three times into the objects desired by each sentient being. Empower me to fulfill the perfection of giving. (72)

Empower me to fulfill the perfection of ethics by not transgressing even for my life the vows of individual liberation, bodhisattva and tantric vows, accumulating virtues and achieving the welfare of sentient beings. (73)

Though all nine types of beings of the three realms become angry, abuse, accuse, threaten, and kill me, empower me to fulfill the perfection of patience, working for their benefit, responding to their harm without a quarrel. (74)

Even though I must remain in the fires of Avīci for oceans of aeons for the sake of each sentient being, empower me to fulfill the perfection of patience through compassionately striving for supreme enlightenment without regret. (75)

Abandoning the faults of laxity, excitement, and distraction, empower me to fulfill the perfection of concentration through the samādhi of single-pointed equipoise on the nature of all phenomena, empty of true existence. (76)

By the yoga of spacelike equipoise on the ultimate conjoined with the great bliss of pliancy that is induced by the wisdom that specifically understands reality, empower me to fulfill the perfection of wisdom. (77)

Realizing how inner and outer phenomena appear but have no true existence, like an illusion, a dream, or the form of the moon in a still lake, empower me to achieve the samādhi of illusion. (78)

Empower me to realize the meaning of Nāgārjuna's intention: to see that it is not contradictory but complementary that not even an atom of saṃsāra or nirvāṇa intrinsically exists, and that the dependent arising of cause and effect is infallible. (79)

Then, crossing the deep ocean of tantras through the kindness of the helmsman Vajradhara, empower me to hold the pledges and vows, the roots of attainment, to be dearer than my life. (80)

Empower me to purify all stains of the perception and conception of the ordinary through the yoga of the first stage, transforming birth, death, and bardo into the three bodies of a conqueror so that whatever appears is perceived as divine bodies. (81)

Empower me to actualize in this very lifetime the paths of clear light, illusory-body, and union arising from you, protector, setting foot in the eight petals of my heart in the central channel. (82)

If I have not completed the components of the path when death arrives, empower me to go to a pure land by the forceful method of enlightenment, the lama's transference, or through the precepts of applying the five powers. (83)

In short, protector, empower me so that in all my lifetimes I will be cared for by you and not be separated and be your foremost child, grasping all secrets of your body, speech, and mind. (84)

O protector, grant me the good fortune to be the first in your retinue, wherever you manifest buddhahood, attaining effortlessly and spontaneously all my temporary and ultimate needs and wishes. (85)

Having appealed in that way, I request the supreme lama to come happily to the crown of my head in order to empower me and to once again place your radiant feet firmly in the center of the lotus of my heart. (86)

I dedicate the pure virtue of such deeds as a cause for fulfilling every deed and prayer of the sugatas of the three times and their children, that I may uphold the excellent doctrine, verbal and realized. (87)

Through that power, may I in every lifetime never be separated from the four wheels of the supreme vehicle and may I complete my journey on the paths of renunciation, the aspiration to enlightenment, the correct view, and the two stages. (88)

—24—

A Prayer to the God of the Plain

Richard J. Kohn

When a religion moves across borders, there is always a question of how it will respond to its new cultural surroundings, and, conversely, how its new surroundings will react to it. Western religion has traditionally had a strong reaction to foreign gods. The famous episode of the ancient Hebrews worshipping the Babylonian deity Baal is a case in point. Buddhism and other ancient Indian religions were often more flexible when it came to gods other than their own. Many Hindus consider the Buddha to be an incarnation of their god Viṣṇu. Buddhists return the favor by incorporating battalions of Hindu deities into their cycles of worship, from the elephant-headed Gaṇeśa to the blood-thirsty Mṭṛka goddesses.

In the eighth century, the king of Tibet, Tri Songdetsen (Khri srong lde btsen), was intent on establishing the Buddhist monastery of Samye (Bsam yas), Tibet's first, at the foot of Hebo Hill not far from the banks of the Tsangpo River in central Tibet. The forces that favored Tibet's indigenous religion, however, were less enthusiastic. Each day the royal workmen laid the foundation stones; the next morning they would find their work mysteriously scattered over the countryside. Clearly, the king needed a new strategy. He decided to invite Padmasambhava, a great meditator famous for his magical powers. When Padmasambhava arrived in Tibet, rather than rejecting its indigenous gods, he set about converting them into protectors of Buddhism. The saint's biographies recount a series of these supernatural encounters on his way from Nepal to central Tibet. On Hebo Hill, overlooking the site of the future monastery, Padmasambhava confronted the ancient god Nyenchen Tanglha (Gnyan chen thang lha), God of the Plain. God of the Plain is one of the most important Tibetan local deities. He gives his name to the seven-hundred-mile-long Nyenchen Tanglha mountain range of northern Tibet. Tibetans also count him as the special protector of Red Hill in Tibet's capital, Lhasa, on which the Potala palace of the Dalai Lamas stands, as did the palace of the kings before it.

When I first translated this prayer to Tanglha in the early 1980s, I happened to tell a Buddhist monk with whom I was studying that I found its language particularly beautiful. There was one of those long silences that, even cross-culturally, signals a serious mistake. "It's Bön language," he quietly replied. Although scholars in recent years have argued about the precise meaning of this word, for my friend, Bön simply meant the indigenous pre-Buddhist and, more significantly, *non*-Buddhist religion of Tibet: the religion that had opposed the establishment of Samye monastery more than a millennium ago.

In line with its pre-Buddhist origins, the prayer to God of the Plain is a tour de force of indigenous Tibetan literary devices. Some passages are reminiscent of the earliest examples of written Tibetan, the ancient royal stone inscriptions of central Tibet and the manuscripts discovered in the Central Asian oasis of Dunhuang. A few of these ancient patterns are discussed below. If you wish to know more about ancient Tibetan literary technique, the great French Tibetologist R. A. Stein gives an excellent summary in his classic *Tibetan Civilization* (1972, 252 ff.).

Love of spatial orientation, massive use of parallelism, and split lines of verse:

> I create a wisdom palace—may it be not small!
> I set up a lion and elephant throne—may it be not low!
> I spread out the Sun, the Moon, and a lotus as carpets—may their light be not dim!

Concern for a god's parentage:

> To name the body god's father—
> He is Oté Gungyel ('O te gung rgyal).
>
> To name the body god's mother—
> She is the One-Winged Turquoise Bird.

Tanglha's father, Oté Gungyel, is said to have sired eight mountain gods. Like his son, he lives on a mountain bearing his name.

Strong and evocative nature imagery:

> Name the country in which you dwell—
> It is Damshö Narmo ('Dam bshod snar mo).
> A wild throne of shimmering green turquoise,
> Verdant in summer, verdant in winter too.
> The country in which you dwell is delightful to experience.
> You adore it! [It is] the country of the gods!

Riddles—the ancient Tibetan royal chronicles tell us that professional riddlers were among the priests of the ancient Tibetan court:

> In what do you dress your body?
> You dress it in white silk, in white cotton.
> On what mount are you mounted?
> You are mounted on a divine swan-white horse.

Repetition and onomatopoeia:

> Touch high-so-high—to the zenith,
> And defend the low-so-low like a son.
>
> Blessings bank, they bank like clouds.
> Compassion sh-sh-showers like the rain.
> You have the shining vow! Ya la la!

Sounding out the second passage in Tibetan gives a good feel for the rhythms of ancient Tibetan religious verse:

> chinlab trintar tib se tib/ tujey chartar sha ra ra/ damtsik dangden ya la la (*byin rlabs sprin ltar thibs se thibs/ thugs rje char ltar sha ra ra/ dam tshig mdangs ldan ya la la*)

In addition to purely literary devices, the prayer to God of the Plain contains many ancient Tibetan religious concepts and symbols.

> Turquoise—"One-winged Turquoise Bird," "throne of shimmering green turquoise," and so on—has long been the Tibetans' favorite gemstone. Turquoise is linked to the Tibetan concept of humanity and of the divine. As a metaphor, it occurs throughout Tibetan mythology.
>
> The sky-rope (*namtak* [*gnam thag*], *mutak* [*dmu thag*]), in Tibetan mythology, connected the kings to the heavens. The rope symbolizes the king's kinship with the gods. It was down this rope that the kings climbed to earth and began to rule—a literal "divine descent." Once their rope was cut, kings became mortal. This is behind the words "If you contend with anyone/I hope you cut the contender's rope!"
>
> The whiteness of gods: white is considered a sacred color in many parts of the world. In Tibet, the connection is especially easy to understand. The mountain tops—the abode of the gods—are cloaked year-round with snow. The ancient Tibetan kings, who were considered gods, wore white; God of the Plain, the prayer tells us, dresses "in white silk, in white cotton."
>
> Body gods: ancient Tibetans believed that a number of gods and/or souls lived in different parts of the human body. God of the Plain is called the "body god" of King Tri Songdetsen, indicating that he had a special relationship as a divine bodyguard with the king who had invited Padmasambhava.
>
> Religion of gods/religion of men: ancient Tibetans made a distinction between two types of religion, what we might call high religion and folk religion. In this poem, the religion of gods—originally a purely Tibetan concept—is used to refer to Indian religion. The prayer calls God of the Plain "King of the Scent Eaters" (Skt., *gandharva*), an ancient Indian celestial spirit.

The prayer recounts a series of events, but its main purpose is not historical; it is a tool of meditation. A common Tibetan meditation technique is visualizing oneself as one of the spiritual heroes who struggle for the enlightenment of all beings (Skt., *bodhisattva*). A bodhisattva who is meditated on in this way is called a *yi dam*, a "tutelary deity" or "personal deity." Although Padmasambhava is a historical figure, most *yi dam* such as Vajrakumāra ("Diamond Youth"), Cakrasaṃvara ("Bound to the Circle [of Bliss]"), or Guhyasamāja ("Secret Union") are purely symbolic beings. Another way of looking at the *yi dam* is that he or she is the meditator's own potential to become a buddha brought to fruition. In the Buddhist worldview, local protectors are of a lesser order. Bound to serve the good not by their nature but by a vow, they are dangerous and often temperamental. When approaching protectors—be they major or minor—the meditator must hold fast to his divine self-image as the *yi dam*.

What can we say about the origin of this prayer? We know that it was discovered by Rikzin Gödem (Rigs 'dzin rgod ldem, 1337–1408), a fourteenth-century "treasure master" or discoverer of texts hidden by Padmasambhava and others "for the sake of future generations." Tibetans, particularly those in Gödem's Nyingma sect, attribute the text to Padmasambhava himself. However, Western scholars often dispute the authenticity of these "treasures." Whether our text was written in the fourteenth century or the seventh, the literary evidence suggests it is an adaptation of an authentic indigenous prayer.

The prayer casts Padmasambhava in a somewhat different light than his biographies. To be sure, we hear how the saint subdued God of the Plain with his magic powers. What is new here is Padmasambhava's role as an author and editor. In attributing the prayer to the saint, the text implies that Padmasambhava took an indigenous prayer and rewrote it, inserting an account of converting the god to Buddhism. This makes the act of conversion, at least in part, a literary task. We can imagine the saint, perhaps in the hearing of the king and some of his more anti-Buddhist ministers, taking, as the ritual tells us, "a small crystal drum in his hand, and for the sake of future generations saying—

> I am Padmasambhava.
> You are the Great Stern One, God of the Plain.
> The country is the four horns of Ü and Tsang Province (Dbus gtsang).

Even if there were no others present at that moment but the saint and his invisible adversary, a vast audience would appear in the days and centuries that followed—readers of this text and others like it. For them, Padmasambhava's role as a magician who could convert a hostile power to Buddhism with a single stroke was firmly established—be it the stroke of a thunderbolt or the stroke of a pen.

Curiously, even if the events of the prayer only took place in the mythic imagination of a later generation, the literary process is still the same—an indigenous prayer was converted to a Buddhist work by the addition of a few carefully selected words. This, of course, is not meant to diminish the strongly held Tibetan belief that Padmasambhava was a wonder-worker of the first rank. It may suggest, though, that some kinds of magic are so simple that even a skeptical Westerner can understand them.

The translation is from Gter bdag gling pa 'gyur med rdo rje (1646–1714), *The Special Ceremonies for the Followers of the Diamond Defenders of the Faith Manual [Called] "The Playful Ocean of True Achievement," Arranged in One Place, with the Addition, in Their Respective Places, of the Short Prayers for the Steadfast Women [and for] God of the Plain (Rdo rje'i chos skyong rnams kyi las byang dngos grub rol mtsho'i rjes 'brang gi 'phrin las bye brag pa rnams phyogs gcig tu [b]sdeds pa dang skabs so sor brtan gsol bsdus pa thang lha bcas bcug pa bzhugs so)*. Xyl., from blocks stored at Thubten Chöling.

Further Reading

René de Nebesky-Wojkowitz, *Oracles and Demons of Tibet: The Cult and Iconography of the Tibetan Protective Deities* ('s-Gravenhage: Mouton and Co., 1956); Tulku Thondup, *Hidden Teachings of Tibet: An Explanation of the Terma Tradition of the Nyingma School of Buddhism*, ed. Harold Talbott, Buddhayana Series I (London: Wisdom, 1986); Rolf Alfred Stein, *Tibetan Civilization*, trans. J.E. Stapleton-Driver (London: Faber and Faber, 1972).

The Worship Cloud for the God of the Plain

The Master [Padmasambhava] took a small crystal drum in his hand, and for the sake of future generations said this—

> *Hūṃ*! I create a wisdom palace—may it be not small!
> I set up a lion and elephant throne—may it be not low!
> I spread out the Sun, the Moon,and a lotus as carpets—may their light be not dim!
>
> I depend on you as the supreme wisdom god—may you be not far!
> I set you up as the protector of this fragile planet—may your [magic] powers be not small!
> Come here! Pray sit on the Sun-Moon seat!
> Blazing Diamond Energy! *Samayaja jaḥ*!
>
> *Hūṃ*! To name the body god's father—
> He is Otê Gungyel ('O te gung rgyal).
>
> To name the body god's mother—
> She is the One-Winged Turquoise Bird.
>
> To name the body god himself—
> He is Yashu (Ya shud), god of the Cruel Ones.

Name the country in which you dwell—
It is Damshö Narmo ('Dam bshod snar mo).
A wild throne of shimmering green turquoise,
Verdant in summer, verdant in winter too.
The country in which you dwell is delightful to experience.
You adore it! [It is] the country of the gods!

To name your name in the religion of men—
It is Yashu, God of the Plain.

To name your name in the religion of the gods—
You are King of Scent Eaters—He of Five Topknots.

To name your secret name—
It is Diamond Blazing Energy.

In what do you dress your body?
You dress it in white silk, in white cotton.
On what mount are you mounted?
You are mounted on a divine swan-white horse.

You race throughout the three worlds,
Your whiteness blazing light.
Your right hand brandishes a riding crop
That sends the seven mothers to work.

Your left hand tells a crystal rosary.
You recite [your] tutelary deity ['s mantra] in the realm [of your mind].

What emanations do you send?
You send a hundred thousand horse soldiers.
With your entourage of servants and slaves,
Come here! Do your work!

God of all with vows!
Butcher of all without vows!
Demon of all those who eat their vows!
Glory of all yogins!
Friend of us high achievers!

Giver of orders to work,
Who subdues the demon of insanity
And severs the life of the enemy of anger.
Quickly turn your horse!
May his hoof-beats be not heavy!

Grind your weapon sharp!
May its point be not dull!

If you contend with anyone,
I hope you cut the contender's rope!

If anyone equals you in speed and swiftness,
I hope they lose first place!
I hope you drive out anger!
I hope you defend love!

The time has come! *Samaya*!
Remember your vow!
The time has come, King of Obstructors!
Do the deeds entrusted to you!

You! God of the four-horned country, Ü and Tsang (Dbus Gtsang)!
[You] are the body god of Tri Songdetsen (Khri srong lde btsan)—
King of defenders of religion, son of the gods!
You have the vow to which you were bound

By Padmasambhava of Oḍḍiyāna.
Attend now to the acts to which you were charged!
[May] those in future generations at the end of the æon,
The mantra bearers who follow

Padmasambhava of Oḍḍiyāna
And the noble families attached to the divine lineage
Of the righteous king Tri Songdetsen
Touch high-so-high—to the zenith,

And defend the low-so-low like a son,
And defend religiously the four horns of the realm of Tibet!
Circumambulate Samye temple!
Actualize what we yogins think!

If you do not defend and save
The living beings of this final aeon:

First, don't you remember that the secret master Diamond-in-Hand
Will take aim at [your] heart
In the middle of the heavenly highway?

Second, don't you remember that the great powerful Padma Heruka
Brought you under his power
On Samye's Hebo Hill?

Finally, don't you remember that the great glorious Diamond Youth
Gathered all the gods [and] ghouls at the summit
Of Trasang (Bkra bzang), the king of mountains
And gave them orders?

I am Padmasambhava.
You are the great stern one, God of the Plain.
The country is the four horns of Ü and Tsang Province.

Blessings bank, they bank like clouds.
Compassion sh-sh-showers like rain.
You have the shining vow! Ya la la!

We pray you come, stern God of the Plain!
We worship you and your entourage of the great gods of the body
With shimmering cakes, good and long.
We worship you with pure water from the slates and snows.

We worship you with the smoke of sweet-smelling white incense.
We worship you with gold, silver, and the five precious things.
We worship you with pay-in-kind, with silks and satin.
We worship you with incense, sheep, and clean white rice.

Oṃ vajra "plain" *kara mum nyid khu sali amrīta baliṁta khāhi khāhi*

This was revealed from the Red Copper Treasury of Good Copper Rock from the knowledge bearer Gökidemchen's (Rigs 'dzin rgod kyi ldem can) treasure.

—25—

Invocations to Two Bön Deities

Per Kvaerne

Invocations of deities represent an important genre in Bönpo literature. Two such invocations are presented here. The first invocation was composed by the great Bönpo scholar Sherap Gyeltsen (Shes rab rgyal mtshan, 1356–1415) in the monastery of Menri (Sman ri) in Tsang, which he founded in 1405. It is directed to the god Nyipangse (Nyi pang sad), who appears to be a specifically Bön deity. Nyipangse is intimately associated with the land of Shangshung (Zhang zhung), and particularly with Mount Tise (Ti se) (i.e., Mount Kailash), the holy mountain of Shangshung and hence as much a place of pilgrimage for Bönpos as for Buddhists. Nyipangse belongs to the class of deities known as "guardians of the doctrine." This term refers to the tasks to which they have been bound by oath to perform; by nature they are irascible and ambivalent and need to be constantly reminded of their duty. Nyipangse was defeated in battle by a great Bönpo teacher, and subsequently promised to act as the special guardian of "Great Perfection" (*rdzogs chen*) meditation practices of Bön that are believed to have been transmitted to Tibet from Shangshung. (On Nyingma "Great Perfection" practice, see chapters 18 and 19.) Like other "guardians of the doctrine," Nyipangse is variously referred to as a *tsen* (*btsan*), a *gyalpo* (*rgyal po*, "king"), or a *drapla* (*sgra bla*, corresponding to the Buddhist *dgra lha*, "enemy-god," see chapter 26). The name Nyipangse is in the Shangshung language, a Tibeto-Burman language which is only fragmentarily known. *Se* (*sad*) is, however, the Shangshung word for "god"; *nyi* probably refers to "sun" (Shangshung *nyi ri*, Tibetan *nyi ma*) as similar names of other deities, in which atmospheric phenomena are incorporated, are known (e.g., *Da* pangse, *da* "moon," and *Sha* pangse, *sha* "rainbow"). He is depicted as a great king, wearing white robes and white turban, astride a white horse, bearing a banner of white silk. He is said to be able to appear in different forms under different names, "remaining neither here nor there."

While the "guardians of the doctrine" are beings still caught in the web of saṃsāra, another class of deities called *yi dam* are timelessly enlightened beings. Among the major tantric meditational deities (*yi dam*) of the Bön religion, a prominent place is accorded to Trowo Tsochok Khagying (Khro bo gtso mchog mkha' 'gying), "The Wrathful One, the Supreme Lord Hovering in the Sky," addressed in the second translation below. Like other major deities of this type, he manifests himself, surrounded by his entourage, in meditational visions. He has three heads and six arms. His consort is Khala Dugmo (Mkha' la gdug mo), "The Fierce One in the Sky," a form of Sipe Gyalmo (Srid pa'i rgyal mo), "The Queen of the Visible World," one of the chief goddesses of Bön, who in other connections is honored as a "guardian of the doctrine" in her own right. The second invocation is from a text that was discovered as a "treasure" (*terma*) by the Bönpo "treasure-discoverer" (*tertön*) Shenchen Luga (996–1035) in 1017.

For the invocation of Nyipangse, the translation is from *Snyan rgyud bka' srung srog bdag rgyal po nyi pang sad bka' bsgo*, pp. 645–48 in *History and Doctrine of Bon-po Niṣpanna-yoga*, Śata-piṭaka Series vol. 73 (New Delhi, 1968). For the invocation of Trowo Tsochok Khagying, see *Khro bo dbang chen gyi pho nya'i le'u* fol. 1b–4b, text no. 15, in *Zhi Khro sgrub skor* (Delhi, c. 1967).

Further Reading

For an introduction to the Bön religion, with special emphasis on art and iconography, see Per Kvaerne, *The Bon Religion of Tibet* (Boston: Shambhala, 1996), which contains images of both of the deities invoked here, as well as translations of both texts translated below.

Do not forget, do not forget, your former oath do not forget!
Do not pass by, do not pass by, do not relax attention to your oath!
Obediently performing tasks that Welchen Gekhö (Dbal chen Ge khod) gives—
Protector of the doctrine's word, King Nyipangse (Nyi pang sad)!
King of drapla (*sgra bla*), "life-lord," possessing skill in magic power and strength!
A male, white as conch-shell, the height of a spear,
On his body, a garment of white silk flutters,
At his waist, a tiger-sword in a leopard-scabbard clatters,
On his head, a conch-white plait of hair is twisted round,
In his hand, a banner of white silk is displayed.
As for his mount, it is a horse with red harness, prancing about,
As for his entourage, a thousand vassal kings crowding together!
When given a name by the Bön of Shangshung,
He is called Shelgying Karpo (Shel 'gying dkar po), Nyipangse;
When given a name by the king of Phrom,
He is called "life-lord," king of the created world;

When given a name by the Bön of eternal Tazik,
He is called Shelgying Karpo;
When given a name by the *chö* (*chos*) [Buddhists] of India,
He is called Tsangpa (Tshangs pa) [Brahmā] with the conch-white hair-knot;
When given a name by the king of China,
He is called Dapang Sekyigyalpo (Zla pang sad kyi rgyal po);
When given a name by Pugyal (Spu rgyal) Tibet,
He is called the great Kyatrang (Skya trang).
Assuming magic forms now here, now there, he transforms himself into every god and demon;
Remaining neither here nor there, he accompanies the eight classes [of gods and demons].
Performing magic tricks now here, now there, he spreads abroad various magic tricks.
As for dwelling, he dwells on the summit of Mount Meru;
As for quaking, he causes the ten directions to quake;
As for action, he acts as guardian of the doctrine, the word of Bön;
As for realization, he realizes the rites of the adepts who have taken vows.
His emanations have an entourage of further emanations.
Without forgetting your former sacred oath,
We implore you to come like lightning, with magic feet!
We implore you to come with a loving mind, like a mother!
We implore you to come with a longing mind, like a friend!
Enjoy! Every desirable thing, every pleasure and ornament—enjoy!
Eat! The sacred offering-cake of the word—eat!
Guard! The doctrine of everlasting Bön—guard!
Realize! The thought of the adepts who have taken vows—realize!
Praise! The stage of Bön of the triple universe—praise!
Repel! Adverse circumstances and hindrances—repel!
Act! As virtuous, white companion—act!
Increase! Retinue, enjoyment, power—increase!
Bestow! Long life, well-being of cattle, success—bestow!
Remove! Harmful enemies of the doctrine—far away remove!
Liberate! Enemies who break their oath—quickly liberate!
Do not forget, o king, guardian of the doctrine, possessing magic power and strength!
Do not swerve from the word and oath of Welchen Gekhö!
Do not relax, o friend, attention to your former oath!
Do not pass by, fulfill the task you have been set!

Bswo! When the fire of your intense fury blazes up,
The entire universe resounds with thundering cries of *bswo*!

The entire universe resounds with thundering cries of *cha!*
The entire universe resounds with thundering cries of *ha!*
Causing cries of *bswo* and *cha* and *ha* to resound,
We implore you to grasp everything through undefiled concentration!
We implore you to bind everything by means of undefiled mudrās!
We implore you to liberate all beings through undefiled compassion!

Bswo! From the mind immersed in unmoved concentration
Is evoked through mental power the unique and supernatural Supreme Wrathful One!

Bswo! In the central realm of highest truth, in the blazing shrine of the Wrathful One,
Causing furious cries of *ha* and *cha* to resound,
Is the blazing Wrathful One, the Supreme Lord, the God Towering in the Sky.
His majestic form, furious utterly beyond endurance,
Has three faces, six arms, one leg extended and the other one drawn in.

Bswo! The right face is shining white,
The left face is lustrous red,
The middle face is bluish black.
The dark brown hair twists upward.
He entirely subdues the three worlds.
He utterly overpowers the three realms of appearance by his splendor.
He directs the universe upward,
He presses the nine doors of hell downward.
He wears crystal hanging-ornaments of wind,
He has fastened on the lower garment of lightning.
He is adorned with the insignia of a hero, a demon's flayed skin,
His girdle is a serpent, bound around his waist.
On the upper part of his body is a demon's hide,
And on the lower part, a tiger's tattered skin.
Of his six hands, in the upper right
He clasps the banner of victory.
It overcomes the demons and their hosts.
In the middle right hand he displays
The sword of wisdom that cuts off discursive thought.
With it he cuts the roots of the obstructive enemies, birth and death.
In the lower hand he clasps
The axe of thunder and lightning.
With it he splits the obstructive enemies from top to toe.
Of his six hands, in the upper left
He clasps an arrow and a bow, the weapons of the visible world.

With them he strikes the very center of the heart of the obstructive enemies.
In the middle left hand he extends
The magic lasso of skillful means.
With it he rescues from the pit of repeated birth and death.
In the lower hand he clasps
The magic hook of compassion.
With it he rescues from the swamp of hell.
By showing his conch-white teeth,
He extracts the obstructive enemies from the very center of the heart.
By spreading his many fingers,
He hurls weapons at enemies and demons.
By raising his great face towards the sky,
He consumes the host and country of the ogres as his food.
The eight great gods adorn his head,
The eight great nāgas he oppresses with his feet,
The eight great planets he sets in motion with his hand,
The four great kings he sends forth as his messengers.
The lion, elephant, and horse, the dragon and the garuḍa,
The male and female gods and demons he spreads out to make his seat.
The great mother clasps the great father in embrace.
As for his entourage, he is surrounded by a hundred thousand times a thousand.
Causing furious cries of *ha* and *cha* to resound,
When the great one issues from the void
The whole entourage chants as follows:
"Arise, arise, from the void arise!
Come forth, come forth, from your place come forth!
If you harm, you may harm even a god,
If you are wrathful there is neither near nor far.
There is nothing which you do not subdue:
Those who destroy the doctrine of Bön,
Those who revile the rank of Shenrap,
Those who destroy the wealth of the holders of ritual drums,
Those who break their solemn vows,
Malicious enemies who create hindrances—
Without compassion for them,
Subdue them utterly and grind them into dust!
Drive them far away and quickly 'liberate' [i.e., kill] them!"

Bswo! As for the great mother inseparably united in embrace—
From the mind which has the nature of the tranquil sky
The marks of fury of an irresistible thunderbolt arise:
The Fierce One in the Sky, the matrix, the mother of all!

Shining in splendor with the red color of power,
Bluish black, her hair piled up like clouds cleaving the sky,
Her eyes flash upward like two great, irresistible stars,
Her eyebrows move like rainbows in the space of heaven,
From her nostrils whirls the black apocalyptic storm,
In her mouth compassion spreads a turquoise mist,
From her ears the dreadful sound of a dragon's roar thunders forth.
The marks of glory—Sun, Moon, planets, stars—adorn her limbs.
With her right hand, she hurls the great golden thunderbolt at the enemy,
With her left, she offers a heart to the mouth of the father.
Round her neck, a cobra is passed like a bandoleer.
Inseparably she clasps the father in embrace, her mind resolved on skillful means alone.

—26—

A Smoke Purification Song

Nālandā Translation Committee

Among the most popular, widely practiced, and ancient Tibetan public rituals is the *lhasang* (*lha bsangs*), in which prayers to various deities are accompanied by the burning of fragrant substances, most commonly juniper boughs, sometimes mixed with other fragrant woods and incense. Ancient literature suggests that this is a practice that predates the introduction of Buddhism into Tibet but, like so many other rituals, was widely adapted by both Buddhists and Bönpos and became very popular. Indeed, the performance of smoke purifications in the Tibetan diaspora community has become a policy encouraged by the Tibetan government-in-exile since 1959, because it preserves a quintessentially Tibetan practice.

In traditional Tibetan society, smoke purification rituals were practiced in the most humble villages and by the highest officers of the government in Lhasa. Indeed, most state-sponsored rituals in which deities were called upon to provide blessings or protection included smoke purification. In the mundane affairs of life, such as crossing a mountain pass or fording a river, it was common for travelers to say prayers and offer a *lhasang* to insure safe passage and the protection of the local deities. Smoke purification was performed as part of marriage ceremonies and was an essential part of purification ceremonies held atop hills and along riverbanks. The ceremonies were sometimes accompanied by horse races and archery contests. *Lhasangs* are used on Tibetan New Year to bless the famous prayer flags that are hoisted at that time for the dignity and power of the household. They are also used to bless a new home or even a person's store-bought clothes. The object to be blessed and made a personal possession is passed through the smoke of the *lhasang*.

In a smoke purification a column of smoke is created, and then local spirits are invited to descend the smoke cord, much like the sky rope of Tibetan mythology, and enter the home or encampment of the celebrants. An important part of the *lhasang* is the song sung in praise of the deity. The song translated below is a selection from one very long *lhasang* in which the warrior god of Tibet, Gesar of Ling (see chapter 1), is invited to descend the smoke and bless the place. This particular smoke purification was composed by the great nineteenth-century scholar Jamgön Mipham Namgyal Gyatso ('Jam mgon mi pham rnam rgyal rgya mtsho, 1846–1912). His colophon indicates that although he usually writes in the style of classical court poetry, in this case he wrote the *lhasang* spontaneously in whatever sort of language came to mind.

The song makes constant mention of the local deities of Tibet who are honored throughout Tibet—the *drala* (*dgra bla*, literally "above the enemy") and the *werma.* Although *drala* can be translated as "war gods," they are not truly deities of war. Rather, as their name indicates, they are divine principles that protect against attack or enemies, being "beyond aggression." Sometimes they are depicted as tiny soldiers located on key places on the warrior's body. They protect one in life, helping one to overcome obstacles and defeat enemies. They also offer aid in more mundane concerns of attaining social rank and wealth.

The *werma* (*wer ma*) are martial spirits who are depicted wearing armor and blessing the warrior in battle. They were probably originally the spirits of the tips of arrows and represent penetration and determination. But in this case, they seem to stand, like the *drala*, for all the local spirits who infuse the warrior with dignity and confidence.

Here is an excerpt from this long *lhasang* offering. One who practices this smoke offering and purification would have much more to chant, in addition to the performance of various rituals.

Further Reading

On smoke purification, see Chabpel Tseten Phuntsok, "The Deity Invocation Ritual and the Purification Rite of Incense Burning in Tibet" *Tibet Journal* 16, 3 (1991): 3–27. On the warrior gods (*dgra lha*), see René de Nebesky-Wojkowitz, *Oracles and Demons of Tibet: The Cult and Iconography of the Tibetan Protective Deities* ('s-Gravenhage: Mouton and Co., 1956), pp. 318–40.

The Warrior Song of Drala

Kye
Lha ki ki ki and *so so so,*
Father Gesar the king, god of war,
At the time when enemies fill the kingdom,
Lord Dradül [Dgra'dul, "Tamer of Enemies"], don't be idle, don't be idle.
I put my hope in no other protector but you.

A tsi tsi your hosts of troops are awesome.
A li li they are youthful, wearing splendid accouterments.

A ya ya the great men are very mighty.
The powerful father warriors are on the right.

The beautiful maidens, so lovely and perfumed,
Wherever you gaze at them, they are as if smiling.
Wherever I direct my mind, it goes to them.
The lovely mother warriors are on the left.

Above, the white clouds of the gods' domain are brilliant.
In the middle, the stone houses of the human domain are dark and dignified.
Below, the mist of the water spirit (*klu*) domain rises and swirls.
Grasp the mu-cord [of smoke] and come here.

In the midst of this, O king, please take your seat of joy.
In this white country, the gods' valley,
You are the lord of plentiful land and wealth—
King Gesar of Ling, fulfill this.

Hosts of clouds of cleansing ambrosia (*amṛta*) gather and gather.
Drums and melodious music of thunder reverberate.
Lakes of drink, white and sweet, abound.
Good fragrant incense billows.
Flags and banners flutter like flashing lightning.
With love and faith my mind yearns.
If a son does not rely on his father, on whom will he rely?
In the same way, a daughter must rely on her mother.
At this time, show the signs and marks.
Subdue enemies of the eight directions.
Protect friends who are worthy of esteem.

Show your smiling face of deathless ambrosia.
O great White Light of [the letter] *A* of the womb of space,
You soar on top of the great three worlds.
You play joyfully on a small seat of grass.

From within your mind of luminosity, look upon your child.
Please accept my offering of devotion.
From now onward, until attaining the essence of enlightenment,
Be an unchanging protector and *drala* for me!
May your glorious mind and mine mix inseparably.
A la li la li la mo li.

Kye
In the clear space of great emptiness,
Gods of the three roots, the nature of mercy and compassion,
Father Great Lion, on the troops of warriors

Bring down your blessings; be a protector and refuge.
By this cleansing offering of the divine juniper tree,
I offer up to the three jewels, the objects of refuge,
The lord gurus, *yi dams*, and ḍākinīs.

Lord Gesar of Jambudvīpa,
He, at this time, is in the aspect of a general subjugating the enemy.
With pennants on his helmet fluttering in the sky,
With swirling sparks of dharma protectors and guardians,
Pennants flapping with a cracking sound,
Mother ḍākinīs dancing in concert,
His white helmet flashing forth rays of light,
Biting his lower lip in *drala* fashion, he menaces.
The lace of his armor of a hundred thousand flames is impressive.
The armies of *werma* draw up in formation.
Their three weapons, clasped at the waist, shimmer.
The whistle of the blood drinkers shrills.
Horses gallop and canter, racing along.
The lieutenants march in formation.

If there is a warrior *drala*, it is Gesar.
If there is a *werma*, it is Gesar.
If there is a guru for the next life, it is Gesar.
If there is a leader for this life, it is Gesar.
Outwardly, he is the mighty general Norbu Dradül.
Inwardly, he is Avalokiteśvara.
His unchanging mind is Lord Padmasambhava.
I offer and praise the deities—may their wishes be fulfilled.

For me, your child, steadfast in commitment,
Today be [my] refuge, protector, and helper.
Fulfill my wishes in accordance with dharma.
Now, on this very day,
Fulfill my aspiration. . . .

His skillful chestnut steed
Outwardly, manifests as a horse.
Inwardly, he arises as the mind of enlightenment.
He is the emanation of Hayagrīva.
He is elegant, with a rainbow swirling about.
He has the treasure of the gait of swift wind
And the strength of the wings of birds.
He possesses the glorious strength of a snow lion.
His vajra mane flowing right and left
Magnetizes the *drala* of white conch garuḍa.
The vulture-down on the points of his ears

Magnetizes spies of luminous torches.
His forelegs of wheels of wind
Magnetize the *drala* of lord of life.
The four hooves of the steed
Magnetize the *drala* of swift wind.
On the tip of each hair, deities reside.

If you do not protect me, your child, who will you protect?
Accept this purification and warrior drink; increase your power of swiftness.
Miraculously lead me to the place that I desire.
Accomplish my desires.
Arouse the activity of windhorse.
O horse, *pu pu so so cha cha*, increase. . . .

Colophon

In my heart there are many jewel treasures of supreme mind, profound and vast.
In the milk ocean of my speech
Is this poetry, beautiful as a lovely garden of kumuda flowers.
This was not deliberately made pleasing to the ear and arranged properly.
It is the precious warrior song of *werma*,
Fully possessing thousands of blessings and great splendor.
In that way, these vajra words were composed.
This is the thunder that pleases the *drala* and *werma*.

Thus, on the twenty-fourth day of the third month of the Fire Ox year, this was spontaneously composed by lamplight.

Maṅgalaṃ.

—27—

Daily Prayers

Nālandā Translation Committee

A good deal of the religious life of a Buddhist meditator or clergy member is devoted to chanting prayers and performing liturgical practices. For advanced meditators, these chants are a method of using the voice as a contemplative practice. For others, these are simply the daily ritual performances that provide a frame around their more abstract sitting meditation practice. Translated below is a selection of liturgies recited on a daily basis by Tibetan monks, nuns, and laypeople. The list is not meant to be complete, but it gives some idea of the literature of Tibetan Buddhist prayer.

At the end of a prayer or any other virtuous activity, it is customary to dedicate the merit that has been produced with a prayer such as this dedication prayer said by many Kagyüs at the end of a teaching or a ritual performance:

> By this merit may we attain omniscience,
> Defeat the enemy—wrongdoing—
> And free all beings from the ocean of saṃsāra,
> With its stormy waves of birth, old age, sickness, and death.

The first two prayers translated below are traditional aspiration prayers (*smon lam*, literally "wishing path"), chants intended to fashion the practitioner's future karma; it is believed that by taking oaths and uttering sincere wishes, one can control the specific outcome of one's future rebirths. The first of these prayers is the extremely detailed and lengthy aspiration prayer directed toward the hierarchs of the Karma Kagyü lineage, the incarnations known as the Karmapa.

A number of buddhas, bodhisattvas, and historical figures are invoked, some of whom may be identified here. It mentions, for example, Vajrapāṇi, the wrathful bodhisattva of energy, who is believed to have taught many of the original tantric teachings. Vajrasattva is the tantric buddha who represents the essence of tantric reality and the nature of purity. His name means literally "indestructible being." Cakrasaṃvara is one of the chief tutelary deities, a special semiwrathful *yi dam* who symbolizes skillful means. His consort is Vajrayoginī, the red goddess who represents wisdom. Dorje Pernakchen is a two-armed Mahākāla, the "great black one," so called because he wears a black or blue robe and is a special protector of the tantric practitioner. Akaniṣṭha and Tuṣita are two heavens where buddhas dwell and where the Buddha taught before he came to the earth to teach humans. Jambudvīpa, on the other hand, is a poetic term for the earth. It literally means the "Rose Apple Land."

The language is extremely formal and courtly. For example, the verses that pray for the benefit of the saṅgha ask that it be as rich as the god of wealth, Vaiśravaṇa, as disciplined as the monk who preserved the Buddhist monastic code, Upāli, and as compassionate as the bodhisattva of compassion, Avalokiteśvara.

The first part of the chant was written by the eighth Karmapa. He includes a three-stanza poem by his previous incarnation, Chödrak Gyatso (Chos grags rgya mtsho), and then praises Chödrak Gyatso in his final verses. It is interesting to note that this praise of the Karmapas and invocation of them is written without apology by the Karmapas themselves; they believe in buddhahood so strongly that they are willing to serve as the objects of supplication. As heads of the Kagyü lineage they are regarded as living buddhas, as dharma kings leading countless beings toward enlightenment. Thus when ordinary disciples utter aspirations to fulfill their wishes and to be like them, they are planting the karmic seeds that shall one day come to fruition, transforming themselves into complete buddhas.

The second aspiration prayer below is by Choggyur Lingpa (Mchog gyur gling pa), a treasure-finder (*gter ston*) and one of the founders of nineteenth-century ecumenical movement (*ris med*, see chapter 21). He reports in the introduction to the text that no less a being than Padmākara (Padmasambhava) himself, the founder of the Nyingma lineage, composed this chant. His consort Yeshe Tsogyal, herself a famous teacher, is said to have written the chant down on the silken robe of the famous translator Vairocana and then hidden it so that it would not be destroyed during a period of suppression of Buddhism in Tibet. What identifies this text as a rediscovered treasure text are the special marks, called "treasure marks" (÷), at the end of each line. The colophon at the end of the text tells us that it was found by Choggyur Lingpa and written down by his master, the famous nineteenth-century scholar, Jamgön Kongtrül ('Jam mgon kong sprul, see chapter 9). The collection of individuals involved in the production of the document evokes the history of the Nyingma lineage. The founder Padmasambhava, Yeshe Tsogyal, and the famous translator are at one end of a historical tunnel that surfaces in the nineteenth century with the Tibetan ecumenical renaissance in eastern Tibet. At that time great polymaths like Jamgön Kongtrül joined with wild yogins such as Choggyur Lingpa to produce a new synthesis of Buddhist teachings. Traditional political and social relations are combined with religious principles, and the different orders of society—kings, ministers, wealthy patrons, and so on—are all evoked along with their roles in an ideal Buddhist society.

FULFILLING THE ASPIRATIONS OF GYALWANG KARMAPA

Based on these roots of merit in the three times [of the past, present, and future]: through all my births, may I gather together and comprehend all the teachings without exception of guru Karmapa, lord of dharma. Through that, may the state of being of myself and others be speedily ripened. Through all my births, may I become like glorious Vajrapāṇi, and not be kept from essential secrets of your body, speech, and mind. May I become a worthy vessel who hears, sees, and realizes all the hidden life examples of your body, speech, and mind. Through all my lives, may I accompany you like a body and its shadow, not being separate for even an instant. May I please you by fulfilling your fivefold wishes. Having trained in the splendid activities of the two accumulations [of merit and wisdom], may I be able to fulfill this just as you intend. By means of pacifying, enriching, magnetizing, and destroying [the four magical acts that comprise part of the special abilities of buddha activity], may I not be lazy even for an instant in fulfilling the guru's buddha activity. May I fully accomplish the intention of the guru through all my actions of the three gates [of body, speech, and mind]. May I please you by serving you in all nine ways. Whatever I do, whether virtuous, evil, or neutral, may it serve only to please you. May I not do anything to displease you even for a moment. May I be a principal one to accomplish the buddha activity of the guru, lord of dharma. May I be a master who accomplishes the teachings of the guru, lord of dharma. May I be able to pacify all plague, famine, and war of the ten directions. May I fully actualize luminous *mahāmudrā* at the time of death. Without experiencing the intermediate state (*bardo*), may I enter the maṇḍala of glorious Vajrasattva. Having entered into that, may I establish all sentient beings in the state of great Vajradhara by means of Vajrayāna. In sum, may I be just like you, guru, the lord of dharma, the great liberator through being seen, the liberator through being heard, the liberator through being thought of, and the liberator through contact.

> Remembering from my heart the certainty of death,
> Giving birth to genuine devotion in my being,
> Through renunciation, which is the accomplishment of revulsion,
> May the blessings of Joyous Mikyö enter me.
>
> Continually denigrating myself,
> Exposing the faults of others' ignorance,
> Delighting in the misfortunes of others,
> May these not arise in the being of anyone, myself or others.
>
> Through all my births, may the supreme holy master,
> The only holder of the black crown,
> And the essence of *yidams*, glorious supreme bliss,
> Cakrasaṃvara, accept me.

Through all my births,
May I never be separated
From guru Mikyö Dorje,
The *yidam* Vajrayoginī,
The dharma protector Dorje Pernakchen, and so on.

By this merit may all sentient beings without exception realize the vajra mind.
Unifying upāya and prajñā in eternal bliss, may they attain deathlessness,
Proceeding in a vajra way through the inner path.
I dedicate this so that they may attain buddhahood.

That was written by the bhikṣu, the great vajra holder Mikyö Dorje.

May what is established as true and what is proclaimed as true,
The teachings of you, the unequaled teacher himself,
Blaze for a long time in this world realm;
As you have aspired, may this blaze accordingly.

Having completely attained a body in Akaniṣṭha,
You, the regent in Tuṣita, the protector who has attained the ten bhūmis,
Manifest as the future nirmāṇakāya in Jambudvīpa;
May I accomplish your aspiration.

After victorious Maitreya has accomplished his regency,
Beginning with the sixth buddha in the good kalpa
Up to Rochana, you miraculously manifest as nirmāṇakāya;
May I accomplish your aspiration, Karmapa.

That was written by Gyalwang Chödrak Gyatso at the dharma college Tsethang.

May the saṅgha expand and may all the activities
Of exposition, debate, and composition; learning, contemplating, and meditating flourish.
May it be a harmonious community, have long life, freedom from illness, and so on,
And not be impoverished with respect to its may needs.
Unrivaled in wealth even by Vaiśravaṇa,
Mindful of monastic discipline like Upāli,
And benefiting others like the action of Avalokiteśvara—
May the teachings of Karmapa expand.

Thus wrote Mikyö Dorje.

The Karmapa who accomplishes all the buddha activity without exception

Of the buddhas of the three times in the buddha fields of the ten directions
Is renowned as Chödrak Gyatso ["Ocean of Dharma Proclamation"].
May his auspiciousness be present at this time.

Accomplisher of the buddha activity of the victorious ones, who are victorious over the four māras,
Teaching as Karmapa, the essence of the teachings,
Pervading all directions, pervading and continuous,
May he always completely flourish and may this flourishing be auspicious.

May the dharma teachings of the Practice Lineage
The blazing glory of auspiciousness, the ornament of the world,
Flourish west of the kingdom of Tibet, the Land of Snow.
May there be auspicious peace throughout the world.
I supplicate you to bring peace to the world.

By this merit, may we attain omniscience
And defeat the enemy, wrongdoing.
From the stormy waves of birth, old age, sickness, and death,
From the ocean of saṃsāra, may we free all beings.

THE ASPIRATION PRAYER OF CHOGGYUR LINGPA

NAMO GURU⫶ On the tenth day of the monkey month of Rawa in the year of the Monkey,⫶ on the second floor of Samye, in the shrineroom called Yushel, when performing the Vajradhātu maṇḍala, Padmākara composed this aspiration, which was performed regularly for the lord and all his subjects.⫶ Later generations should practice this one-pointedly.⫶

Victorious ones throughout the ten directions and four times, together with your descendants,⫶
Host of gurus, yidams, ḍākinīs, and dharmapālas,⫶
As many buddha fields of you as there are atoms, all of you without exception, please approach⫶
And be seated on a lotus-moon seat in the space in front.⫶

We prostrate respectfully with body, speech, and mind.⫶
We make the outer, inner, secret, and suchness offerings.⫶
In the presence of the sugatas (Buddhas), the supreme beings,⫶
We feel remorse for our host of previous evil deeds.⫶
Regretting present unvirtuous actions, we make complete confession.⫶
Henceforth we vow to reverse these.⫶
We rejoice in all merit and virtue.⫶

We request the host of victorious ones not to pass into nirvāṇa༔
And to turn the wheel of the *tripiṭaka* and the unsurpassed teachings.༔
We dedicate the accumulation of virtue to all beings without exception:༔
May beings arrive at the stage of unsurpassable liberation.༔

Buddhas, together with your descendants, please consider us.༔
These excellent aspirations that we have begun to practice—༔
Just as they were realized by victorious Samantabhadra and his descendants༔
And Ārya Mañjuśrī,༔
So also may we realize them, following their examples.༔

Precious gurus, who are the glory of the teachings,༔
May you pervade everywhere, like the sky;༔
Shine everywhere, like the Sun and Moon;༔
And be always firm, like a mountain.༔

May the precious saṅgha, the foundation of the teachings,༔
Be harmonious and be rich in the three trainings and pure discipline.༔
May the practitioners of the secret mantra, the heart of the teachings,༔
Keep the oath and reach perfect development and completion stages.༔

May the patron of the teachings, the dharma-protector king,༔
Propagate his kingdom and benefit the teachings.༔

The royal ministers, who serve the teachings—༔
May their intellect increase and may they be skillful.༔

May the wealthy householders who provide for the teachings༔
Have prosperity and be without difficulties.༔

May all kingdoms in which faith in the teachings abounds༔
Have happiness, and may their obstacles be pacified.༔

May yogins treading on the path, even we,༔
Have uncorrupted oaths and therefore accomplish their wishes.༔

May whoever has a karmic connection with us, either good or bad,༔
Be accepted by the victorious ones temporally and ultimately.༔

May beings, having entered the gate of the unsurpassable vehicle,༔
Attain the great kingdom of Samantabhadra.༔

Exert yourself in this aspiration during the six times of the day.༔ Sealed with "*SAMAYA*."༔

Colophon

The great treasure discoverer Choggyur Dechen Lingpa, an emanation of Prince Murup, discovered this text publicly, written with Shurma script in Tibetan by the hand of Yeshe Tsogyal using Vairocana's silken outer monk's robe as paper, at the supreme place Kongmo Ogma on Precious Rocky Mountain, which is on the right side of Great Lion Sky Boulder. Immediately thereupon, Pema Karwang Lodrö Thaye copied this properly. May virtue increase!

Meal Chants

The aim of a meal chant is to transform the ordinary activity of eating into a contemplative practice by making the meal a sacred ceremony. In tantric literature, such ceremonies are often called "feast offerings" (*gaṇacakra*). In them food, which is usually an object of grasping, is offered "upward" to the three jewels, to the deities of the maṇḍala, and to other noble beings. It may also symbolically be offered "downward" to beings who suffer in the lower realms of the spirits, hungry ghosts, and hell beings. After a portion of the food has been offered, the practitioners begin to eat. By abandoning any sense of attachment, the eating becomes an egoless act. Meal chants vary greatly in length. Prior to a meal, Tibetan Buddhists may say a short prayer, intended to transform the eating of the meal into a meritorious deed:

> The unsurpassable teacher is the precious buddha.
> The unsurpassable protector is the precious holy dharma.
> The unsurpassable guide is the precious saṅgha.
> To the unsurpassable three jewels, I make this offering.

One of the longer meal rituals is *The Sūtra of the Recollection of the Noble Three Jewels,* used daily in many Tibetan monasteries. The first part is based on the chants and liturgies of the Nikāyas and the Mahāyāna scriptures. The section that begins with the blessing of the food (*oṃ āḥ hūṃ*) introduces the tantric section of the ceremony. Here Sanskrit mantras are used to make offerings to the various orders of beings served through the generosity of the monastic community. The offering to Hārītī is a special case. This is a mother spirit who, as a woman at the time of the Buddha, had five hundred children and who killed animals in order to feed them. The Buddha kidnapped her youngest son and held him as ransom against her actions. Thus they made an agreement that if she ceased to kill, he would have his community feed her and her children in perpetuity. Since then, the offering to Hārītī and her children is a part of the daily Buddhist food ritual. The text includes numerous Sanskrit expressions and long mantras in Sanskrit. Its title asserts that it is a sūtra, a discourse of the Buddha, but actually, as the notes in the text indicate, it is drawn from numerous sources, some Indian, some Tibetan.

The Sūtra of the Recollection of the Noble Three Jewels is followed by a short feast offering composed by the great Nyingma master Jigme Lingpa ('Jigs med gling pa). It begins with the seed syllables of the elements (*raṃ, yaṃ, khaṃ*) and then gives the seed syllables often used to consecrate substances. This practice can be used in longer ceremonies as an offering to purify any violations of vows or ritual laws that may have taken place. It is also used by Tibetans of the Nyingma lineage to consecrate their daily meals into feast offerings. Although quite short, it has the basic form of the extensive feast offerings (*gaṇacakra*) that are done by advanced practitioners on the semimonthly holidays of the male and female buddhas. For example, not only does it dedicate the food to specific enlightened principles, but it asks them for forgiveness of all evil deeds that are committed and violations of one's vows.

THE SŪTRA OF THE RECOLLECTION OF THE NOBLE THREE JEWELS

I prostrate to the omniscient one.

Thus, the Buddha, bhagavan, tathāgata, arhat, perfectly enlightened, the learned and virtuous one, the sugata, the knower of the world, the charioteer and tamer of beings, the unsurpassable one, the teacher of gods and men, is the buddha bhagavan. The tathāgata is in accord with all merit. He does not waste the roots of virtue. He is completely ornamented with all patience. He is the basis of the treasures of merit. He is adorned with the minor marks. He blossoms with the flowers of the major marks. His activity is timely and appropriate. Seeing him, he is without disharmony. He brings true joy to those who long with faith. His knowledge cannot be overpowered. His strengths cannot be challenged. He is the teacher of all sentient beings. He is the father of bodhisattvas. He is the king of noble ones. He is the guide of those who journey to the city of nirvāṇa. He possesses immeasurable wisdom. He possesses inconceivable confidence. His speech is completely pure. His melody is pleasing. One never has enough of seeing him. His form is incomparable. He is not stained by the realm of desire. He is not stained by the realm of form. He is not affected by the formless realm. He is completely liberated from suffering. He is completely and utterly liberated from the aggregates (*skandhas*). He is not possessed with constituents (*dhātus*). His sense fields (*āyatanas*) are controlled. He has completely cut the knots. He is completely liberated from extreme torment. He is liberated from craving. He has crossed over the river. He is perfected in all the wisdoms. He abides in the wisdom of the buddha bhagavans, who arise in the past, present, and future. He does not abide in nirvāṇa. He abides in the ultimate perfection. He dwells on the stage where he sees all sentient beings. All these are the perfect virtues of the greatness of the buddha bhagavan.

The holy dharma is good at the beginning, good in the middle, and good at the end. Its meaning is excellent. Its words are excellent. It is uncorrupted. It is completely perfect and completely pure. It completely purifies. The Bhagavan teaches the dharma well. It brings complete vision. It is free from sickness. It is always timely. It directs one further. Seeing it fulfills one's purpose. It brings discriminating insight for the wise. The dharma which is taught by the Bhagavan is revealed properly in the Vinaya. It is renunciation. It causes one to arrive at perfect enlightenment. It is without contradiction. It is pithy. It is trustworthy and puts an end to the journey.

As for the saṅgha of the Great Vehicle, they enter completely. They enter insightfully. They enter straightforwardly. They enter harmoniously. They are worthy of veneration with joined palms. They are worthy of receiving prostration. They are a field of glorious merit. They are completely capable of receiving all gifts. They are an object of generosity. They are a great object of complete generosity.

The protector who possesses great kindness,
The omniscient teacher,
The basis of oceans of merit and virtue,
I prostrate to the tathāgata.

Pure, the cause of freedom from passion,
Virtuous, liberating from the lower realms,
This alone is the supreme, ultimate truth:
I prostrate to the dharma, which is peace.

Having been liberated, they show the path to liberation;
They are fully dedicated to the disciplines;
They are a holy field of merit and possess virtue:
I prostrate to the saṅgha.

I prostrate to the Buddha, the leader;
I prostrate to the dharma, the protector;
I prostrate to the saṅgha, the community;
I prostrate respectfully and always to these three.

The Buddha's virtues are inconceivable;
The dharma's virtues are inconceivable;
The saṅgha's virtues are inconceivable;
Having faith in these inconceivables,
Therefore, the fruitions are inconceivable:
May I be born in a completely pure realm.

Substances that have been offered to the three jewels and plunder from others—
I have completely abandoned all such impure and perverted nourishment;
This food is in accord with the dharma, free from evil deeds:
May the health of my body flourish.

Then bless the food with:

Oṃ āḥ hūṃ

From the *Caryāmelāyanapradīpa:*

> Divide the food into four parts.
> First, offer pure food to the gods.
> After that, to the dharmapālas and protectors
> Offer elaborate torma.
> Then, eat and drink.
> Give the leftovers to all the spirits.

In that way, or else, as is said in the Vinaya of the holy dharma, divide the food into three parts. First, offer divine food to the gurus with:

> *Oṃ guru-vajra-naivedyā āḥ hūṃ*

Likewise, offer to the host of buddhas and bodhisattvas with:

> *Oṃ sarva-buddha-bodhisattvebhyo vajra-naivedyā āḥ hūṃ*

Offer to the divine assembly of the maṇḍala of *yi dams* with:

> *Oṃ kāma-deva-maṇḍala-naivedyā āḥ hūṃ*

Offer to Mañjuśrī and others—whatever deity you desire—for example:

> *Oṃ mañjuśrī vajra-naivedyā āḥ hūṃ*

Offer to the dharma protectors (*dharmapāla*) with:

> *Oṃ śrī dharmapāla vajra-naivedyā āḥ hūṃ*

Offer divine food to all the spirits (*bhūta*) with:

> *Oṃ a-kāro mukhaṃ sarva-dharmāṇām ādyanutpannatvāt oṃ āḥ hūṃ phaṭ svāhā*

Give one pinch of food to Hārītī with:

> *Oṃ hārīte svāhā*

and one pinch of food to the five hundred sons of Hārītī with:

> *Oṃ hārīte mahāyakṣiṇī hara hara sarva rāyaṇikṣiṃ svāhā*

Give one pinch of food to the spirits who are capable of receiving the select portion with:

> *Oṃ agra-piṇḍa-āśibhyaḥ svāhā*

If one wishes to purify any poison or the like in the food, chant:

> *Namaḥ sarva-buddha-bodhisattvānām oṃ baliṃ te jvāla-baliṃ ni svāhā*

Repeat this eight times; pick up food with the thumb and ring fingers, and eat. While eating, eat with an attitude that sees the food as impure, with an attitude of nonattachment, with an attitude that benefits the masses of different intestinal bacteria, and with an attitude of remaining on the ship that travels to peace and enlightenment. Do not eat with an attitude that increases passion and craving.

In the *Bodhicaryāvatāra* it is said: "One should eat moderately." The way of doing this is explained according to the *Eight Branches:* "Two quarters of the stomach are for food; one quarter is for drink; and one quarter is left empty." Or else, according to the text *Handbook of Food:* "One should have two-thirds for food and drink, and leave one-third empty."

Finally, give a pinch of food to the spirits who are capable of receiving leftovers with:

> *oṃ ucchiṣṭha-piṇḍa-āśibhyaḥ svāhā*

Then, wash the mouth.

Then, purify the gift:

I prostrate to the Blessed One, tathāgata, arhat, the perfectly enlightened Samantaprabhārāja:

> *Namaḥ samantaprabhārājāya tathāgatāya arhate samyaksambuddhāya / namo mañjuśrī kumārabhūtāya bodhisattvāya mahāsattvāya mahākāruṇikāya / tad yathā / oṃ nirālambe nirābhāse jaya jaya labhe mahāmate dakṣe dakṣiṇi me pariśodhāya svāhā*

By saying this dhāraṇī even once, one completely purifies alms as great as Mount Meru. This dhāraṇī is taken from the *Tantra Determining the Discipline* (*'Dul ba rnam par nges pa'i rgyud*).

Then, as is said in the *āgamas:*

> May the royal patron and likewise
> The other sentient beings who are donors
> Obtain long life, freedom from sickness, prosperity,
> And the companionship of eternal bliss.

That and:

> By this generosity one has power over the spirits.
> By this generosity one is free from enemies.
> Generosity is the transcendent friend.
> Therefore, generosity is said to be essential.
>
> Generosity is the ornament of the world.
> Through generosity, one turns back from the lower realms.
> Generosity is the stairway to the higher realms.
> Generosity is the virtue that produces peace.
>
> The prosperity of the bodhisattvas
> Is inexhaustible, filling the whole of space.

In order to obtain such prosperity,
Completely propagate that generosity.

Say these verses of dedication, aspiration, and generosity.

SHORT FEAST OFFERING

Raṃ yaṃ khaṃ
Oṃ āḥ hūṃ
This desirable feast substance is an embellishment of wisdom play.
Lord of the feast, master of the feast, guru vidyādhara,
Possessors of the three realms of the maṇḍala and of the twenty-four sacred places,
Ḍākas, ḍākinīs, oath-bound dharma protectors:
Approach and accept this enjoyable feast offering.
I confess my transgressions, confusions, errors, and corruptions of the oath.
Destroy outer and inner obstacles into the dharma realm (*dharmadhātu*).
Accept the leftovers and accomplish all actions.
Guru-deva-ḍākinī-gaṇacakra-pūjā-ucchiṣṭha-baliṃ te khāhī

Protector's Chants

Protectors are divine principles that are meant to remind the students and so protect them from deceptions and side-tracks in the midst of daily activities. Iconographically they are often represented as wrathful deities and sometimes even local deities who were bound by oath when they met an enlightened Buddhist master. A monastery or meditation center usually chants the liturgies for its protective principles at sundown, although this is not a strict rule. Here is a general request that specifically commands the protectors to serve the ends of Buddhist teachings and community:

CONCLUDING REQUEST TO THE PROTECTORS

Assemblies of oceans of oath-bound,
Accept this gift of offering cakes (*gtor ma*).

May we yogins with our disciples
Obtain lordship, freedom from disease, long life,
Glory, fame, good fortune,
And all great and vast enjoyments.

Grant us the accomplishments (*siddhi*)
Of the pacifying and enriching actions and so on.
Oath holders, guard us.
Support us with all the accomplishments.

May there be no untimely death, illness,
Malevolent spirits, or obstructing spirits for us.
May we have no nightmares,
Ill omens, or bad dealings.

May the world enjoy peace, have good harvests,
Abundant grain, expansion of dharma,
And glorious auspiciousness.
Accomplish whatever mind desires.

Dealing with Death and Other Demons

—28—

Mindfulness of Death

Donald S. Lopez, Jr.

Each of the major sects of Tibetan Buddhism has a famous text that sets forth the practice of all the essential components of the Buddhist path in sequence, from the most basic and preliminary to the most sophisticated and advanced. There are precedents for such works in India; Atiśa's *Lamp for the Path to Awakening* (*Bodhipathapradīpa*, translated in *Buddhism in Practice*) is often mentioned, but Atiśa's work, even with its commentary, is rather short. The longer and more detailed Tibetan works appear to look back more directly to the Tibetan disciples of Atiśa for their prototype, especially a text called the *Great Stages of the Teaching* (*Bstan rim chen mo*) by Drolungpa (Gro lung pa, c. 1100). The many works that follow are part of a genre called the "stages of the teaching" (*bstan rim*) or, more commonly "stages of the path" (*lam rim*).

The most famous of these works is the *Great Exposition of the Stages of the Path to Enlightenment* (*Lam rim chen mo*), considered the masterpiece of Tsong kha pa (1357–1419), the "founder" of the Geluk sect of Tibetan Buddhism. By the time of its composition in 1402 and 1403, literally thousands of Indian Buddhist texts had been translated from Sanskrit into Tibetan. It was clear, however, that it was impossible for any single person to master such a massive corpus of literature, much less put it into religious practice. Tsong kha pa therefore wrote a work that would, quite literally, set forth everything one needs to know to become enlightened, beginning with the most basic Buddhist practice of seeking refuge in the three jewels and ending with a detailed discussion of how to gain profound meditative insight into the nature of reality. In between, every major topic of Buddhist practice is delineated, including the workings of the law of karma, the practice of love and compassion, and the vows of the bodhisattva. The excerpt below is the section on the importance of contemplating death in order to progress on the path to enlightenment. It is typical of the *lam rim* style, highly schematic, with topics being divided into subtopics and sub-subtopics. It is also typical of the *lam rim* style in its extensive citation of Indian texts and the words of the early disciples of Atiśa in support of its points. Despite its rather dry style, this section of Tsong kha pa's text has served as the lecture notes for thousands of sermons by Tibetan lamas over the centuries. Before turning to the translation, it may be useful to summarize Tsong kha pa's arguments and identify some of his presuppositions.

The *Great Exposition of the Stages to the Path of Enlightenment* is structured around a typology, found also in Atiśa, that divides all humans into three categories: those of small, intermediate, and great capacity. The person who seeks happiness within the cycle of birth and death is a person of small capacity. The person who recognizes the transitory nature of those pleasures and seeks rather to be liberated from mundane existence completely, that is, a person with the motivation of the Hīnayāna, is a person of intermediate capacity. The person who feels an empathy for others through a recognition of his or her own suffering and who, unwilling to seek only his or her own freedom from birth and death, strives to eliminate the suffering of all beings is called a person of great capacity, a bodhisattva.

Each person, then, has a particular goal that implies certain practices. Tsong kha pa sees the three capacities not so much as a typology into which all persons may be included, but as a progression through which all beings must pass. Before one can have the wish to free others from suffering, one must have the wish to free oneself. Before one can seek liberation from the cycle of rebirth, one must conclude that the cycle is something to be escaped, that is unsatisfactory. In order to do this, one must overcome attachment to the possible happiness of future lives. Before one can turn away from the pleasures of future births, one must stop seeking the elusive pleasures of this life and perform virtuous deeds that will bring about a happy rebirth in the next life.

In the *Great Exposition of the Stages of the Path*, Tsong kha pa does not set out all the religious practices of persons of small and intermediate capacity. His purpose is to delineate the path of the bodhisattva, beginning with reasons why the Buddhist teaching is worthy of interest and culminating in the achievement of buddhahood. He describes all the practices essential to this process, many of which are practices of persons of small and intermediate capacity. Hence, his text is an exposition not of all the practices of the three persons, but of those practices common to those of small and intermediate capacity that the person of great capacity must perfect in order to, indeed, become a person of great capacity, that is, someone who is not content to seek happiness for himself or herself alone in this world or beyond it, but who strives to free all beings in the universe from suffering.

Tsong kha pa thus begins with the practices of a being of small capacity, a person seeking happiness within saṃsāra. This is not the simple worldling that Atiśa refers to but rather a person that Tsong kha pa calls, "a special being of small capacity," who for the most part does not act for the sake of this life but who seeks the marvels of a high status in the next world and undertakes to establish the causes of such an auspicious rebirth. To put the purposes of this life above those of the present life, Tsong kha pa argues that it is essential that one be mindful of death, contemplating the fact that one will not remain long in this world.

Tsong kha pa's entire discussion of death presupposes a belief that human life, or more specifically rebirth as a human endowed with what he calls "leisure and opportunity," is precious; something difficult to find and, if found, very meaningful. The immediately preceding section of the *Great Exposition of the Stages of the Path to Enlightenment* is devoted to a discussion of this. Leisure (*dal ba*) he defines as freedom from eight conditions of nonleisure: birth as an animal, birth as a hungry ghost, birth as a hell being, birth as a god of long life, birth as a barbarian in a borderland (i.e., an uncivilized area), not having all one's faculties, having wrong views, and birth in an area where the word of the Buddha has not spread. One must be free from these eight impediments in order to make use of the Buddha's teaching. Opportunity (*'byor pa*) refers specifically to being endowed with the five personal opportunities and five other opportunities. The five personal opportunities are being born as a human, birth in a central country (i.e., where Buddhism is present), having all faculties, not having committed one of the five deeds of immediate retribution (patricide, matricide, killing an arhat, intentionally wounding a Buddha, and causing dissension in the saṅgha), and having faith in the Buddhist scriptures. The five other opportunities are the appearance of a buddha, his teaching the doctrine, the doctrine remaining to the present, followers of the teaching remaining, and the people of the area providing spiritual and physical support out of love for others. These essentially include the converse of the conditions of nonleisure while providing a fuller description of the qualities of the place where one must be reborn in order to take full advantage of the dharma. All of this enumeration is intended to suggest how incredibly rare it is to be reborn as a human who has access to the Buddhist teaching, an opportunity not to be squandered on the pursuit of the ephemeral pleasures of the world. Thus, the death that Tsong kha pa considers is not the death of the noble savage or the cultured despiser, but the death that is the end of a life lived within easy access of the soteric dharma, a life but rarely lived and, once ended, unlikely to be encountered again.

As mentioned above, like all works of the "stages of the path" genre, both before and after Tsong kha pa, his approach to the topic of the contemplation of death is highly schematic. He organizes his chapter under four major headings: the faults of not being mindful of death, the benefits of contemplating death, how a mindfulness of death is engendered, and how that mindfulness is cultivated. Tsong kha pa identifies the belief that one will not die as a manifestation of the first of the four mistaken views: (*phyin ci log bzhi*) to perceive the impermanent to be permanent, the impure to be pure, the painful to be pleasurable, and the selfless to have self. He notes the dissonance between the knowledge that everyone will eventually die and the universal conviction that "I will not die today." With such an attitude, Tsong kha pa says, one will concern oneself only with the affairs of this life and will not engage in religious practice. Any attempts at religious practice will be tainted by laziness and procrastination. One will thereby become involved in activities motivated by desire and hatred, pride and jealousy, and will squander this lifetime in the accumulation of causes of sorrowful rebirths.

The benefits of contemplating death are many. Even if one has little understanding of the dharma, should one conclude "I will die today or tomorrow," one's attachment to the affairs of this world will naturally dissipate, one will turn away from sinful deeds, and the wish to take full advantage of this human birth will naturally increase by engaging in those activities that will serve as causes of auspicious birth in future lives. The only time to insure the welfare of oneself (should one have the motivation of the Hīnayāna) or others (should one have the motivation of the Mahāyāna) is this present lifetime endowed with leisure and opportunity. The fact that the majority of humans do not take advantage of this rare opportunity is due to their thinking, "I will not die yet." Tsong kha pa declares that "the presumption that you will not die is the source of all trouble and the antidote to that—mindfulness of death—is the source of all marvels." Thus, it should not be assumed that the contemplation of death is an elementary practice unworthy of those conversant with more profound topics or that it is a preliminary practice to become acquainted with and then abandoned.

In discussing how a mindfulness of death is to be engendered, Tsong kha pa considers the role of fear in the mindfulness of death. The more common fear of death occurs only at the time of death, when the dying person contemplates separation from family and possessions. Attendant with this fear is the sense of regret that one has not made use of this life and that, consequently, one will fall into a dreadful rebirth. This is the fear of death of the person who has not practiced the path. This fear is not efficacious. It is appropriate and useful to fear death, however, if one has not insured a favorable rebirth through the practice of virtue. Since it is possible to accumulate the causes of future happiness now, this fear of death serves to motivate religious practice. If one fears death now and is moved by that fear to take action to establish the causes of an auspicious rebirth in the next life, one can then die without fear. By giving up attachment to one's body, relatives, and possessions now, one can leave them at death without regret.

The main body of Tsong kha pa's chapter is devoted to an exposition of how to cultivate mindfulness of death, considered within the rubric of "the three roots and the nine branches." They are:

I. Contemplation of the certainty of death
   1. The Lord of Death will come and cannot be avoided.
   2. Our lifespan cannot be prolonged and diminishes unceasingly.
   3. There is no time for religious practice.

II. Contemplation that the time of death is uncertain
   4. The lifespan in our world is uncertain.
   5. The causes of death are very many and the causes of remaining alive are few.
   6. The time of death is uncertain because the body is very fragile.

III. Contemplation that at the time of death nothing is of benefit except religious practice
   7. Friends provide no benefit at the time of death.
   8. Wealth provides no benefit at the time of death.
   9. One's body provides no benefit at the time of death.

The first of the three roots, the contemplation of the certainty of death, begins with consideration of the fact that death cannot be avoided, that no matter who one is or where one hides or when one lives, death cannot be escaped, not by strength or wealth or magic. Next, Tsong kha pa observes that the human lifespan is rarely more than one hundred years and that this period dwindles inexorably with the passage of years, months, days, nights, mornings, and evenings. Much of life is already gone and what remains cannot be extended. Here, he presumably refers to the fact that the length of one's life is determined by the power of the past action that serves as the chief cause of the lifetime. When the potency of that action is exhausted, the life ends. Tsong kha pa provides a number of analogies of unrelenting movement to an end, such as sheep being led to the slaughter, moving closer to death with every step they take. In the same way, there is not an instant of our life in which we do not move toward death. Hence, it is wrong to take pleasure in the misconception that we shall remain in this world, just as it would be unlikely that a person who has fallen from a cliff would enjoy his descent to earth. Such examples are to be contemplated repeatedly. Finally, it can be concluded that there is no time for religious practice in the ordinary lifetime for much of our life is consumed by sleep, by the follies of youth, by distractions, and by the decrepitude of old age. An appropriate time for religious practice will not naturally present itself; opportunities must be made.

The second root, the contemplation of the uncertainty of the time of death, Tsong kha pa says is the most important of the three. The first branch stemming from this root is the fact that the lifespan in this world is indefinite. According to the Buddhist cosmology, the universe consists of four continents surrounding a central mountain. Our world is the southern continent, called Jambudvīpa. In the other three continents, Videha in the east, Kuru in the north, and Godānīya in the west, the lifespan is definite. However, in Jambudvīpa the lifespan is indefinite for at one point in the far distant past, the lifespan in Jambudvīpa was measureless, today it is one hundred years, and it is gradually decreasing such that eventually the longest life will be but ten years in length. Furthermore, the indefiniteness of the length of life derives not only from the fact that the general lifespan in the world fluctuates but that in our world death can come during youth, midlife, or in old age without completing the average lifespan of Jambudvīpa.

The next branch is that the causes of death are many and the causes of remaining alive are few. Causes of death include enemies, demons, animals, and imbalances among the four elements (earth, water, fire, and wind) that constitute the physical body. Furthermore, we live in an age characterized by the five ruinations: ruinous lifespan (*tshe'i snyigs ma*), ruinous views (*lta ba'i snyigs ma*), ruinous afflictions (*nyon mongs pa'i snyigs ma*), ruinous sentient beings (*sems can gyi snyigs ma*), and ruinous time (*dus kyi snyigs ma*). Thus, our deeds lack the power to impel a long life, and food and medicine lack the strength to dispel disease. Our tenuous hold on life is further imperiled by the fact that those things upon which we depend for life are unreliable and can easily become causes of death. Food can poison us, friends can deceive us, the roof can collapse on us. Tsong kha pa speculates that there are no causes of staying alive that cannot become causes of death. And because the body is fragile, it can be easily destroyed.

The final root is the contemplation that at the time of death nothing is beneficial except religious practice. Friends are of no benefit because they can neither keep you from going to the next life nor accompany you to it. Wealth is of no benefit because you cannot take it with you. Not even the body can be taken along to the next life. Only religious practice provides a defense against death.

Tsong kha pa concludes his chapter with the observation, drawn from Śāntideva that the happiness of this life is enjoyed even by animals. To enjoy future lives, one must make use of this leisure and opportunity. Hence, one must be mindful of death.

The translation is from Tsong kha pa, *Mnyam med tsong kha pa chen pos mdzad pa'i byang chub lam rim che pa* (Mtsho sngon mi rigs dbe skrun khang, 1985), pp. 98–114. Topic headings have been added by the translator.

Further Reading

Other "stages of the path" texts available in English include Patrul Rinpoche, *Words of My Perfect Teacher* (San Francisco: HarperCollins, 1994); Herbert V. Guenther, trans., *The Jewel Ornament of Liberation by Sgam po pa* (Berkeley: Shambala, 1971); and a commentary on Tsong kha pa's text by Pabongka Rinpoche, *Liberation in the Palm of Your Hand* (Boston: Wisdom Publications, 1991). A full translation of *Lam rim chen mo*, edited by Joshua Cutler, is forthcoming from the Library of Tibet, published by HarperCollins.

Mindfulness of Death

Placement within the Text

The actual explanation of how to take full advantage [of leisure and opportunity] has three parts: training the mind in the stages of the path common to persons of small capacity, training the mind in the stages of the path common to persons of intermediate capacity, and training the mind in the stages of the path of persons of great capacity.

The first, training the mind in the stages of the path common to persons of small capacity, has three parts: the actual training in the thoughts of a being of small capacity, the measure of having created those thoughts, and dispelling misconceptions concerning that.

The first of those, the actual training in the thoughts of a person of small capacity, has two parts: creating an awareness that sets goals in future lives and implementing the means for [achieving] happiness in future lives. The first of those, creating an awareness that sets goals in future lives, has two parts:

mindfulness of death, that is, the contemplation that one will not remain long in this world, and the contemplation of the happiness and suffering of the two [types of] transmigration that one shall undergo in future lives.

Mindfulness of Death

The first of those, mindfulness of death—contemplating that one will not remain long in this world—has four parts: the faults of not cultivating mindfulness of death, the benefits of [such] contemplation, how to create an awareness mindful of death, and how to cultivate mindfulness of death.

THE FAULTS OF NOT CULTIVATING MINDFULNESS OF DEATH

Conceiving the impermanent to be permanent, the first of the four errors, is damaging to efforts to take full advantage of a base of leisure. There are two [types of impermanence], coarse and subtle. The initial source of harm is [a misconception concerning] coarse impermanence, the very conception that you will not die when [in fact] you will. Although everyone knows that death will come in the end, everyone thinks with each passing day, "I will not die today, I will not die today," mentally clinging until the moment of death to the belief that they will not die. If you are obstructed by such an attitude and do not take its antidote to mind, you will go on thinking that you will remain in this life and will continually think only of means of achieving happiness and removing suffering in this life alone: "I need such and such today."

Not analyzing things of great importance, such as future lives, liberation, and omniscience, will keep you from engaging in religious practice. Although you may perchance engage in hearing, thinking, or meditation, it will come to be only for the sake of this life, and whatever virtue you perform will be of little strength. Furthermore, since [your practice] will be involved with faulty behavior, ill deeds, and infractions, it would be rare for those activities not to be mixed with causes [of rebirth] in bad realms. Even if you try to engage in practices directed toward future lives, you will not be able to prevent the laziness of procrastination, thinking, "I will do it eventually," and through passing time in distractions such as sleep, lethargy, senseless talk, and eating and drinking, proper achievement [that comes through] great effort will not result.

If, in this way, you are seduced by the hope that this body and this life will last for a long time, you will create strong attachment to possessions and conveniences. You will hate what prevents you from having these, or, when you fear that you might be prevented from having them, you will be bewildered and confused about their faults, as a consequence of which you will be immersed in strong forms of the afflictions of pride and jealousy, as well as the secondary afflictions, like being [carried away by] the current of a river. As a result, nonvirtuous actions will increase daily, [deeds] such as the ten faulty activities of body, speech, and mind, the [five deeds of] immediate retribution [killing one's mother, killing one's mother, killing an arhat, wounding a buddha, causing dissension in the saṅgha], misdeeds approaching these [in gravity], and the abandonment of the excellent doctrine, [all of] which have the full power to induce strong suffering in the bad realms. Increasingly ignorant of the ambrosia of the doctrine that sets forth well the antidotes to these [nonvirtues], you will kill the life of high status [that is, a good rebirth] and definite goodness, [that is, the attainment of liberation from rebirth] and, having been destroyed by death, you will be led by bad actions into a hot and unpleasant place among the strong and violent sufferings of the bad realms. What could be worse than that? Āryadeva's *Four Hundred* (*Catuḥśataka*) says:

> If one sleeps peacefully
> While subject to [death], the ruler of the three realms
> Who is himself not subject to death,
> What could be more atrocious?

Also, Śāntideva's *Entrance to the Bodhisattva Deeds* (*Bodhicaryāvatāra*) says:

> Not knowing that I must
> Leave everything and depart,
> I committed various sins
> For the sake of friends and foes.

THE BENEFITS OF CONTEMPLATING DEATH

When, for example, someone comes to the conclusion that he or she will die today or tomorrow, it is generally the case that even those who have little understanding of the doctrine see that friends and material possessions will not accompany them, and so will turn away from attachment to them; they will naturally and increasingly wish to take full advantage [of human birth] through [such virtuous deeds as] giving. Just so, if you create an authentic and full-fledged awareness that is mindful of death, seeing that all toiling for worldly qualities such as possessions, conveniences, and fame is pithless, like winnowing chaff, and is a source of deception, you will turn away from bad activities and, through accumulating good actions, such as going for refuge and [maintaining] ethics with constant and intense effort, you will extract the essence from that which is essenceless, like the body, and will ascend to an excellent state and will lead transmigrators to it as well. What, then, could be more meaningful? This [mindfulness of death] is praised with many examples. The *Mahānirvāṇasūtra* says:

> Among all ploughings, the autumn harvest is supreme. Among all tracks, the track of the elephant is supreme. Among all ideas, the idea of impermanence and death is supreme [because] with these one can eliminate all desire, ignorance, and pride with regard to the three realms.

Similarly, it is praised for being the hammer that simultaneously destroys all afflictions and bad activities and for being the great door of entry into the simultaneous achievement of all virtue and goodness. The *Collection of Aphorisms (Udānavarga)* says:

> Understand that the body is like a clay vessel.
> Similarly, know that phenomena are like mirages.
> The poisonous flower [tipped] weapons of the māras are destroyed
> And one passes beyond the sight of the Lord of Death.

Also:

> Seeing aging, seeing the suffering
> Of sickness, and [seeing] a dead body,
> The resolute abandon their prisonlike home;
> Ordinary worldlings cannot abandon desire.

In brief, the only time to accomplish the aims of beings is now, having attained a special leisure [which serves as] a support. The majority of us remain in the bad realms; a few come to the good realms, but the majority [of those] are in unfavorable situations. Therefore, the opportunity to perfect the doctrine is not encountered in those [situations]. That you do not perfect the doctrine properly although you have gained the circumstances allowing practice is because you think, "I will not die yet."

Therefore, the prejudice that one will not die is the source of all trouble, and the antidote to that—the mindfulness of death—is the source of all that is marvelous. Hence, you should not hold that this is a practice for those who do not have some other profound doctrine to cultivate in meditation, or that although this is something worthy of meditation, one's meditation should be minimal at first because it is not fitting to practice it continuously. Rather, you should ascertain from the depths of your heart that it is necessary at the beginning, middle, and end, and cultivate [the mindfulness of death] in meditation.

HOW TO CREATE THE AWARENESS MINDFUL OF DEATH

The fear of death of those who have not practiced the path at all [manifests itself as] the worry that they will separate from their relatives and so forth, [this fear being caused] by their strong attachment. Therefore, [this kind of fear] is not to be cultivated here. Then what is? Nothing of the body, which is appropriated by actions and afflictions, shall survive death, [and], therefore, you are frightened. However, for the time being, there is nothing to be done about it [and so you should not fear it]. Nonetheless, you should be afraid of death if you have not put an end to the causes of the bad realms and have not accomplished the causes of high status and definite goodness with regard to the next lifetime. If you are frightened about that, since there is something you can do to accomplish those, it is within your power not to be frightened at the time of death. If those aims are not achieved, you will be tormented by regret at the time of death, fearing in general that you will not be liberated from saṃsāra and in particular that you will fall into a bad realm. The *Birth Stories* (*Jātaka*) says:

> Though you hold fast, you cannot stay.
> What benefit is there
> In being frightened and scared
> Of what cannot be changed.
>
> Thus, when you analyze the nature of the world
> Humans are regretful [at death] because they have sinned
> And because virtuous deeds were not done well.
> Thus, they worry that sufferings will arise in the future
> And their minds become obscured by the fear that they will die.
>
> However, I do not know of any [deed I have done]
> That would make my mind regretful
> And I have become most accustomed to virtuous deeds.
> Who, that abides [thus] in the doctrine, is frightened by death?

Āryadeva's *Four Hundred* (*Catuḥśataka*) says:

> He who thinks with certainty,
> "I will die,"
> Gives up fear. Therefore,
> How could he fear even the Lord of Death?

Therefore, when you contemplate impermanence again and again, thinking, "I will undoubtedly separate from my body and possessions shortly," you overcome attachment to the hope that you will not have to leave them. Consequently, you will not have the fear of death caused by the mental distress that comes from having to leave them.

HOW TO CULTIVATE MINDFULNESS OF DEATH

This is to be cultivated by way of the three roots, nine reasons, and three decisions. The three roots are the contemplation that death is certain, the contemplation that the time of death is uncertain, and the contemplation that at the time of death nothing helps except religious practice.

THE CONTEMPLATION THAT DEATH IS CERTAIN

This has three [reasons: the contemplation that the Lord of Death will definitely come and therefore cannot be avoided, that our lifetime cannot be extended and diminishes incessantly, and the contemplation of death ascertaining that even when alive there is no time for religious practice.]

Contemplation That the Lord of Death Will Definitely Come and Therefore Cannot Be Avoided

No matter what kind of body you assume at birth, death comes. The *Collection of Aphorisms* (*Udānavarga*) says:

> If all the buddhas, pratyekabuddhas,
> And śravakas of the Buddha
> Abandoned their bodies,
> What can be said about ordinary beings?

No matter where you stay, death comes. The same text says:

> A place to stay that is unharmed by death
> Does not exist.
> It does not exist in space, it does not exist in the sea,
> Nor if you stay in the midst of mountains.

At whatever time, past or future, there is no difference in sentient beings' destruction by death. The same text says:

> The wise should know that all
> Who arise will go [to the next life], leaving this body,
> To disintegrate completely.
> Therefore, they should engage in [pure] behavior and abide in the doctrine.

You are not liberated by fleeing from death, nor is [death] turned away by such things as spells. The *Advice to the King* (*Rājāvavādaka*) says:

> For example, four great mountains from the four directions having a hard and solid core, indestructible, unsplitable, without fissures, very hard, and massed into one, rise up into the sky and destroy the earth and all the grass, trees, trunks, branches, leaves, and all sentient beings, living beings, and creatures are crushed to dust. When these come, it would not be easy to run away, or turn them away by force, or turn them away with wealth, or turn them away with [magic] substances, mantras, or medicine. Great King, in the same way, these four frights come, and it is not easy to turn them away by force or turn them away with wealth, or turn them away with substances, mantras, or medicines. What are the four? Aging, sickness, death, and deterioration. Great King, aging comes and destroys youth, sickness comes and destroys health, deterioration comes and destroys all wealth, and death comes and destroys life. It is not easy to run away from them, or to turn them away by force, or to turn them away with wealth, or to pacify them with substances, mantras, or medicine.

Gamawa (Ga ma ba) said, "We should be frightened by death now. We should be fearless at the time of death. [In fact] we are the opposite; we are not afraid now, but at the time of death we dig our fingernails into our chests."

The Contemplation That Our Lifespan Cannot Be Extended and Diminishes Incessantly

The *Sūtra Teaching Nanda about Entry into the Womb* (*Āyuṣmannandagarbhāvakrāntinirdeśa*) says, "Currently, if [the body] is protected well and happily, [life] at its longest is little more than one hundred years." Just so, the maximum is no more than that. Even though it may be possible [to live that long], the time until [death] dwindles very quickly. A year is consumed by the passage of days; a day is consumed by the passage of day and night. They also are consumed by the passage of morning [and evening]. Thus, the length of life in general is short and, moreover, much of it seems to already be finished. The remainder of life cannot be extended even for a moment; day and night it diminishes without a break. Śāntideva's *Entrance to the Bodhisattva Deeds* (*Bodhicaryāvatāra*) says:

> This life is constantly being lost
> Day and night without pausing,
> And there is nothing coming from elsewhere to extend it.
> Why should death not come to someone like me?

This is to be contemplated with many examples. When weaving, each time no more than one piece [of thread] goes, but quickly [it all] becomes woven. When animals like sheep are led to the slaughter, they move closer to death with every step they take. The water carried by the current of a strong river or the water in a waterfall on a steep mountain quickly disappears. Just so, one's life is quickly spent and gone. The herdsman picks up his stick and the cattle powerlessly follow him home; in the same way sickness and aging lead us powerlessly into the presence of the Lord of Death. One should meditate [on these facts] from many different perspectives. The *Collection of Aphorisms* (*Udānavarga*) says:

> For example, just as when weaving
> One reaches the end
> With thread woven throughout,
> So is the life of humans.
>
> For example, just as those who are going to be killed
> Come closer to the killing place
> With every step they take,
> So is the life of humans.
>
> Just as the strong downward current of a waterfall
> Cannot be reversed,
> So the movement of human life
> Is also irreversible.
>
> Difficult and brief
> And involving suffering,

[Life] disappears very quickly
Like something written on water with a stick.

Just as cattle go home
When the herdsman raises his stick,
So humans are taken to the Lord of Death
By sickness and age.

Even the Great Elder [Atiśa] went to the bank of a river and meditated, saying that the downward flow of the water was good for meditation on impermanence. Also, the *Vast Sport* (*Lalitavistara*) speaks [of impermanence] with many examples:

The three worlds are impermanent like an autumn cloud.
The birth and death of transmigrators is like watching a dance.
The passage of life is like lightening in the sky.
It moves quickly, like a waterfall.

Thus, when there is some certainty from considering what is within, you should apply your understanding to many things for, as it is said, there is no external thing that does not teach impermanence.

When you think about this again and again, ascertainment is created. It will not arise if it is merely [contemplated] partially. Hence, there is no benefit [in doing so]. As Gamawa (Ga ma ba) said, "You say that nothing happened in meditation, but when did you meditate? If it is during the day, you are constantly distracted, and you sleep at night. Do not lie."

Not only must you go to another world upon being destroyed by the Lord of Death at the end of your lifetime, but up to that point, whether you are going [somewhere], walking around, or lying down, there is no time whatsoever when your lifespan is not diminishing. Thus, from the time you enter the womb, you do not remain for even an instant without moving toward the next lifetime. Therefore, since even the intervening life is consumed completely in a movement toward death led by the messengers, sickness and aging, do not take pleasure in the belief that the time of life remains without moving to the next lifetime. For example, when falling off a cliff, it is not suitable to enjoy the time of falling to earth through space. As cited by Candrakīrti in his *Commentary on the Four Hundred* (*Catuḥśatakaṭīkā*):

Hero among men, beginning from the first night
Upon entering a worldly womb,
One proceeds daily, without delay
Into the presence of the Lord of Death.

The *Instructions for Stopping the Four Errors* (*Caturviparyayaparihārakathā*) says:

Do those who fall to earth from the peak of a high mountain
Enjoy happiness in space as they are being destroyed?

> If they are constantly racing toward death from the time they are born,
> How can sentient beings find happiness in the time in between?

These [passages] indicate that it is certain that you will quickly die.

Contemplation of Death Ascertaining That Even When Alive There Is No Time To Practice Religion

Even if it were allowed that you would live the longest time explained above, it is unsuitable [to think] that you have time. Much of life has already passed purposelessly, and from the rest, half will be passed in sleep, and also much will pass purposelessly due to other distractions. Furthermore, when youth has passed, the time of aging arrives, and physical and mental strength deteriorate such that even if you wanted to practice religion, you lack the power to do so. Consequently, there is no chance whatsoever for the practice of religion. The *Sūtra Teaching Nanda about Entry into the Womb* (*Āyuṣmannandagarbhāvakrāntinirdeśa*) says:

> Of that, half is covered by sleep, and ten years in childhood. Twenty years are old age, [of the remaining twenty] sorrow, lamentation, suffering, mental discomfort, and agitation eliminate [much, and] hundreds of types of physical illnesses eliminate [much].

The *Instructions for Stopping the Four Errors* (*Caturviparyayaparihārakathā*) says:

> The longest of human lives is finished in only one hundred years. Of that, the beginning and end are made useless by youth and old age. Sleep, sickness, and so forth destroy all hope without any time [for practice]. When this is the case for humans who live in happiness, how much do the rest have?

Chaygawa (Mched ka ba) said that if one subtracts from sixty years the time lost in [procuring] food and clothing, in sleep, and in sickness, there are not even five years to devote to the doctrine.

Thus at the time of death, the marvels of this life will become memories, like experiencing pleasures in a single dream and then waking up and remembering them. "If the enemy that is death is surely approaching and cannot be stopped, why should I enjoy the deceptive entanglements of this life?" So thinking, you should decide and determine many times that the doctrine must be practiced. The *Birth Stories* (*Jātaka*) says:

> Alas, afflicted worldlings,
> [I] do not like unstable things.
> Even this glory of Kumata
> Will become a memory.
>
> Alas, it is amazing that beings are fearless
> Placed in a realm like this.

They are joyous and act without qualm
[Though] every path is blocked by the Lord of Death.

If, having powerful and harmful enemies of sickness, aging, and death
That cannot be stopped,
It is certain that one must go fearfully to the next world,
I wonder what person in his right mind would find pleasure in this?

The *Letter of Kānika* says:

The unmerciful Lord of Death
Murders powerful beings without purpose.
While [such] murder is sure to come,
What wise person would be relaxed?

Thus, as long as that great impatient hero
Has not flung the frightful arrow
From which there is no escape,
Take heed of your own welfare.

You should contemplate in this way.

THE CONTEMPLATION THAT THE TIME OF DEATH IS UNCERTAIN

This has three parts: [the need to be mindful of death every day, the contemplation that the time of death is uncertain, and the decision that you must practice now.]

The Need To Be Mindful of Death Every Day

It is certain that death will come sometime between today and one hundred years from now; it is uncertain on which day in between it will come. Therefore, we cannot conclude whether or not we will die today, for instance. However, you must assume that you will day and think, "I will die today." For, if you assume that you will not die, thinking, "I will not die today," or, "I probably will not die today," you will continuously make preparations to stay in this life and will not prepare for the future world, in which case, at that time, grasped by the Lord of Death, you must die in sorrow. If you prepare for death every day, many of goals of the next world will be accomplished so that, even if you do not die [today] you will have done well. If you do die [today, the preparation] is particularly important. For example, when it is certain that a great enemy is coming to do you great harm sometime between now and some point in the future, but you do not know which day he is coming, you must be cautious every day. It is like that. If you think every day, "I will die today," or even "I will probably die today," you will act for the goals of whatever world to which you will go and will not make preparations to remain in this world. If this thought does not arise and you perceive that you are staying in this world, you will prepare for this life and not act for the goals of the next world. For example, if you think that you are going to stay someplace for a long time, you make preparations to stay there. If you think that you are not going to stay there, but are going elsewhere, you make preparations for the place you are going. Hence, you must be aware of death every day.

The Contemplation That the Time of Death Is Uncertain

The contemplation that the time of death is uncertain, [leading to] the decision that you must practice now, has three parts: [contemplation that the lifespan in this world (Jambudvīpa) is uncertain, that the causes of death are very many and the causes of life few, and that the time of death is uncertain because the body is very weak.]

CONTEMPLATION THAT THE LIFESPAN IN THIS WORLD IS UNCERTAIN.

In general, the lifespan in Kuru is certain; in the others [excluding Jambudvīpa, our world], although there is no certainty in the sense of whether one will be able to complete one's own lifespan, there is certainty in most cases. However, the lifespan in Jambudvīpa is very uncertain, because originally the lifespan was measureless, but eventually the maximum length will be ten years of age. Furthermore, there is at present no certainty of the occurrence of death in youth, old age, or in between. In this way, Vasubandhu's *Treasury of Knowledge* (*Abhidharmakośa*) says:

> Here it is uncertain; at the end, ten years;
> In the beginning, measureless.

The *Collection of Aphorisms* (*Udānavarga*) says:

> [Among] the many beings seen in the morning
> Some are not seen in the evening.
> [Among] the many beings seen in the evening
> Some are not seen in the morning.

Also:

> When many men and women
> And even the young die,
> What confidence can there be in living,
> [Saying] "This person is young [and so will not die yet]."
>
> Some die in the womb,
> Some at birth,
> Some when they can crawl,
> Some when they can walk.
>
> Some are old, some are young,
> Some are adults,

Going gradually,
Like ripe fruit falling.

Take to mind the cases that you have seen or heard about of teachers and friends who did not reach the end of their lifespan but died suddenly due to external and internal causes of death without fulfilling their intentions. Be aware of death, thinking over and over, "I also am certainly subject to death."

THE CONTEMPLATION THAT THE CAUSES OF DEATH ARE VERY MANY AND THE CAUSES OF LIFE FEW.

There are many sentient and insentient things that do harm to this life. Think carefully of the many ways in which injury is caused by humans and nonhuman demons, the many dangers to life and limb [caused by] animals, and similarly the ways in which harm occurs due to internal disease and external elements. Furthermore, your body must be established from the four elements [of earth, water, fire, and wind]. Since they even damage each other, the elemental constituents becomes imbalanced such that [some] are in excess and [others] are deficient, at which time sickness is produced, robbing [your] life. Hence, since these dangers are innately present within you, [your] body and life are unreliable. Thus, the *Mahānirvāṇa Sūtra* says, "The perception of death is that this life is constantly surrounded by hateful enemies; it decreases every moment without any increase." Nāgārjuna's *Garland of Jewels* (*Ratnāvalī*) says:

[Your life] dwells among the causes of death
Like a lamp standing in a strong breeze.

Also, his *Letter to a Friend* (*Suhṛllekha*) says:

Life is more impermanent than a water bubble
Battered by the wind of many harmful things.
Thus, that one inhales after exhaling and
Awakens healthy from sleep is fantastic.

Āryadeva's *Four Hundred* (*Catuḥśataka*) says:

Since each element lacks the power,
[The body] arises as a composite [of them].
It is entirely unreasonable to say
That there is happiness in these conflicting [elements].

Since this is a time of the rapid spread of the five ruinations, the accumulation of the great power of virtuous deeds [that cause] one to live a long life is exceedingly rare. Also, since the medicinal value of food and so forth is weak, they have little strength to overcome disease. Moreover, those [foods and medicines] we use have diminished power to increase the great elements with easy digestion; they are difficult to digest, and even those digested have little benefit. Furthermore, since there is little support from the amassed collections [of merit] and faulty deeds are extremely numerous, reciting mantra and so forth have little potency, making it difficult to prolong one's life [through mantra].

Even among the causes of staying alive there are none that do not become causes of death. In order not to die, we seek such things as food and drink, shelter, and friends, but even these become causes of death, as in the case of such things as eating too much food, too little food, inappropriate food, or such things as your shelter crumbling, or being deceived by friends. Thus, it appears that there are no causes of staying alive that cannot become causes of death. Furthermore, despite the fact that there are many causes of keeping alive, they are unreliable, for life itself is for dying. Nāgārjuna's *Garland of Jewels (Ratnāvalī)* says:

> The causes of death are many,
> Those of staying alive, few.
> Those too become causes of death.
> Thus, always practice the doctrine.

THE CONTEMPLATION THAT THE TIME OF DEATH IS UNCERTAIN BECAUSE THE BODY IS VERY WEAK.

Since the body is very fragile, like a water bubble, great damage is unnecessary; life can be destroyed by something that is imagined to be harmful, like being pricked by a thorn. Hence, it is very easy to be overcome by any of the causes of death. Nāgārjuna's *Letter to a Friend (Suhṛllekha)* says:

> If not even ash will remain when the physical world—
> The earth, Mount Meru, and the seas—
> Are burned by seven blazing suns,
> What need is there to consider frail humans?

The Decision to Practice Now

At the end of such contemplation, you should decisively conclude many times that since it is does not appear that there is any certainty as to when your body and life will be destroyed by the Lord of Death, you may not assume that there is time but must practice the doctrine now. The *Letter of Kānika* says:

> The Lord of Death, a friend to no one,
> Descends suddenly. Therefore, do not wait
> Saying, "I'll do it tomorrow."
> Practice the excellent doctrine with urgency.
>
> People who say, "I'll do it tomorrow;
> I'll do this [other thing] today," do not have goodness.
> A tomorrow when you are gone
> Is undoubtedly coming.

The lord of yogins, the glorious Jagatamitrānanda, says:

Lord of the Earth, when this borrowed body
Is happy, without sickness or deterioration,
Do the essential things,
Acting so as not to be frightened by sickness, death, or degeneration.
When sickness, age, and degeneration press in,
Though you might think [about the essential things],
What could you do then?

Having contemplated the uncertainty of the time of death, the most important of the three roots, just this will transform the mind. Therefore, work hard at it.

THE CONTEMPLATION THAT AT THE TIME OF DEATH NOTHING HELPS EXCEPT RELIGIOUS PRACTICE

The three contemplations that at the time of death nothing helps except religious practice are: (1) if you see that you must go to another world, no matter how much you are surrounded at that time by loving relatives and friends who have strong feelings, you cannot take even one with you; (2) no matter how many piles of beautiful jewels you have, you cannot take even a particle of one with you; (3) if you have to discard the flesh and bones you were born with, what is there is say about anything else? Hence, think, "It will certainly happen that I must discard all the marvels of this world and, having discarded them, go to another world. Furthermore, that will happen today." Think about how, at that time, only religious practice will serve as a refuge, a protection, a defense. The *Letter of Kānika* says:

When the past actions issuing the fruition
[Of this life] are spent
And you are connected with a new action
And led by the Lord of Death,

Except for [your own] virtue and sin,
All beings turn away,
No one at all will follow you.
Know that and act well.

Also, it is as the glorious Jagatamitra says:

Divine One, no matter what fortune is gained,
When you depart for another world,
Like being conquered by an enemy in the desert,
You are without children or wife,
Without clothing, without friends,
Without kingdom, without palace,
Though you had limitless power and armies,

They will not be seen or heard.
Eventually not even one
Will follow after you.
In brief, if, at that time, you do not even have your name,
What need is there to speak about anything else?

You must be mindful of death, [thinking] that leisure is of great importance, is difficult to find, and even though difficult to find, can easily disintegrate. Having contemplated in that way, if you [still] do not achieve the final happiness of future lives and beyond, [consider the fact that you at least] need a practice that surpasses animals, because they are more effective than humans in achieving happiness and alleviating suffering while [in this life] before dying. Otherwise, although you have found a life in the good realms, it is as if you did not find one. Śāntideva's *Entrance to the Bodhisattva Deeds* (*Bodhicaryāvatāra*) says:

Those who are tortured by [bad] karma
Destroy this marvelous leisure and opportunity which is difficult to find
In order to [acquire] some common trifling thing
That can be had even by animals.

Therefore, although it is quite hard to produce, you must work at it because it is the foundation of the path. Potowa (Bo to ba) [when asked about the philosophical topic of appearance and exclusion] said:

> My appearance and exclusion is just this meditation on impermanence: all the appearances of this life such as intimates, relatives, and possessions are excluded and, knowing that I must approach the next life alone without another, [I] think that I will do nothing except religious practice. Thereupon, a lack of attachment for this life comes about. Until this is created in the mind, the paths of all doctrines are blocked.

Also, Dolwa (Dol ba) said, "Ancillarily, amass the collections, purify obstructions, and entreat the deity and the lama. When you contemplate earnestly and with perseverance, although you think that [an awareness of death] could not be produced in one hundred years, since nothing that is produced remains as it is, it can be produced with hardship." When Gamawa (Ga ma ba) was asked about changing the topic of meditation, he said to repeat the former; when asked about stopping, he said, "Don't stop at all."

Thus, if your mind is able, meditate in accordance with what was explained above. If it is unable, take up whatever is fitting [to you] among the nine reasons and the three roots. Meditate again and again until you have turned the mind away from the activities of the world, which are like adorning yourself in order to be led to a place of execution.

No matter where the topics of relying on a spiritual guide, leisure and opportunity, and impermanence occur in the pronouncements [of the Buddha] and the commentaries, if you recognize them as being intended for their respective practice and sustain them in practice, you will easily find the intention of the Conqueror. You should understand this in other contexts as well.

—29—

A Prayer for Deliverance from Rebirth

Donald S. Lopez, Jr.

Tibetans compose prayers for myriad purposes, but one of the most common is for a favorable rebirth. Death is seen as a harrowing experience, one over which the dying person often exercises little control, overcome as he or she may be by sickness and fear. The time of death is regarded as of supreme importance because it is then that the next lifetime will be determined. According to karmic theory, each person carries a vast store of seeds for future rebirth, any one of which can fructify as an entire lifetime. There are seeds for favorable rebirths as humans or gods, and there are seeds for horrific rebirths as ghosts or hell beings. It is said that one's mental state at the moment of death determines which of these seeds will create the next lifetime. That final mental state in turn is said to depend on one's prior practice. One's habitual attitudes, developed over the course of a lifetime, tend to come to the fore at death; it is difficult for a perennially angry person to become beneficent in a moment as overwhelming as death.

Tibetans therefore go to great lengths to affect favorably the state of mind of the dying person, placing statues of buddhas and bodhisattvas in the room and reading sūtras and prayers. But the preparation for death should begin long before the terminal moments, and there are many prayers that are recited daily whose purpose is to review the stages of death so that they will be familiar when they ultimately arrive. One such work is translated below, with a commentary. The prayer was written by the first Panchen Lama, Losang Chögyi Gyaltsen (Blo bzang chos kyi rgyal mtshan, 1567–1662, who also wrote the *Offering to the Lama* translated in chapter 23). It was quite common for famous poems to receive prose commentaries from later scholars. The first Panchen Lama's poem is commented upon here by Janggya (Lcang skya rol pa'i rdo rje, 1717–1786), a great scholar who served as the teacher of the Qianlong emperor of China.

The poem begins by summarizing some of the instructions on the mindfulness of death provided by Tsong kha pa in chapter 28. One of the chief concerns of the prayer, however, is that one die a good death, a death that is not unexpected or sudden and in which one is not so overcome by pain or regret that one is unable to make use of the opportunity that death provides. According to the systems of Unexcelled Yoga Tantra, death is a potent moment in which the most subtle form of consciousness, called the mind of clear light, becomes accessible. For the Gelukpas, this mind of clear light is not present in ordinary consciousness but remains locked in the center of the chest in something called the "indestructible drop" (*thig le, bindhu*). Hence, not only is death important because one can try to avoid an unfavorable rebirth, but for the person with the proper training, death can be "brought to the path" and used for the immediate achievement of buddhahood. By proper use of the stages of death, the ordinary states of death, the intermediate state (*bar do*), and rebirth can be transformed into the three bodies of a buddha.

The stages of death described here derive from the system of the *Secret Gathering Tantra* (*Guhyasamāja*). In these texts, the process of death is described in terms of eight dissolutions, as consciousness gradually retreats from the senses toward the heart and the physical elements of earth, water, fire, and wind lose the capacity to serve as the physical basis for consciousness. In the first dissolution, the earth constituent dissolves and the dying person loses the capacity to perceive forms clearly. With each stage, there is a sign that appears to the dying person. Thus, with the first dissolution, there is the appearance of a mirage, like that of water in a desert.

In the second dissolution, the water constituent dissolves and the dying person is no longer able to hear sounds. The sign is the appearance of smoke. With the third dissolution, that of the fire constituent, the dying person loses the ability to smell and perceives a sign called "like fireflies," red sparks of light in darkness. The last of the four elements, the wind constituent, dissolves at the fourth stage. The dying person can no longer taste, experience physical sensation, or move about. At this point, the person stops breathing. The sign that appears to the dying person is called "like a burning butterlamp," that is, a sputtering flame.

According to this tantric physiology, during the process of death, the winds (*rlung, prāṇa*) or subtle energies that serve as the vehicles for consciousness withdraw from the network of 72,000 channels (*rtsa, nāḍi*) that course throughout the body. Among all these channels, the most important is the central channel (*rtsa dbu ma, avadhūtī*), which runs from the genitals upward to the crown of the head, then curves down to end in the space between the eyes. Parallel to the central channel are the right and left channel, which wrap around it at several points, creating constrictions that prevent wind from moving through the central channel. At these points of constriction, there are also networks of smaller channels that radiate throughout the body. These points are called wheels (*'khor lo, cakra*). These are often enumerated as seven: at the forehead, the crown of the head, the throat, the heart, the navel, the base of the spine, and the opening of the sexual organ.

By the time of the fifth dissolution, the sense consciousnesses have ceased to operate. At this point, conceptual consciousnesses, known as the eighty conceptions, dissolve. The winds from the channels that course through the upper part of the body have further withdrawn from the right and left channels and have gathered at the crown of the head at the top of the central channel. When these winds descend the central channel to the heart wheel, what appears to the mind of the dying persons changes from a burning butter lamp to a radiant whiteness, described as being like a pure autumn night sky before dawn, pervaded by moonlight. In the sixth cycle the winds from the lower part of the body enter the center channel at the base of the spine and ascend to the heart. This produces an appearance of a bright red color, like a clear autumn sky pervaded by sunlight. Next, at the seventh stage, the winds that have gathered above and below enter the heart center, bringing about an appearance of radiant blackness, like a clear autumn sky in the evening after the sun has set and before the moon has risen, pervaded by thick darkness. Here, it is said that the dying person loses mindfulness, swooning in the darkness into unconsciousness. Finally, in the last stage, the mind of clear light dawns, with the appearance of the natural color of the sky at dawn, free from sunlight, moonlight, and darkness. This is death. The mind of clear light then passes into the intermediate state (*bar do*), which can last up to forty-nine days, and then, impelled by previous actions, finds a place of rebirth. The process of birth into the next lifetime follows a reverse process of the eight dissolutions, with the appearance of clear light changing to blackness, to radiant red, to radiant white, and so forth.

The tantric yogin is able to make use of these stages of death on the quick path to buddhahood. The mind of clear light provides an extremely subtle, clear, and nonconceptual consciousness, which can be employed, indeed, which eventually must be employed, to perceive emptiness and destroy the most subtle obstructions to the attainment of perfect enlightenment. He or she is said to "bring death to the path" by either using the mind of clear light at the time of death or by inducing the process of death on the stage of completion through various practices (such as sexual yoga) that cause the eight signs to appear in sequence. Through growing accustomed to the process of death and by causing the winds to enter and abide in the central channel again and again, the yogin eventually enters the dawn of the clear light eternally with the attainment of buddhahood.

At the successful conclusion of this practice the yogin creates an illusory body (*mehakāya, sgyu lus*), an immortal body made of the most subtle wind and mind, which, upon enlightenment, becomes the form body (*rūpakāya, gsugs sku*) of a buddha, adorned with the major and minor marks. The yogin must still go through the process of death one last time, a final death in which the gross physical body is left behind, the illusory body is left behind, and buddhahood with its truth body (*dharmakāya*) and form body is attained. After making oneself aware of the fact of death over the course of the path and after simulating death on the tantric path, one must die once again, passing through the radiant night of near-attainment to be born as a buddha in the clear light of dawn. If the dying person is unable to make use of death to achieve buddhahood, one may at least be reborn in a pure land where the path to enlightenment may be completed.

This is the background to the Panchen Lama's eloquent poem, with the allusions articulated and amplified in the commentary by Janggya. Following the convention of the Tibetan text, the poem is presented in its entirety first and is then repeated, interspersed with Janggya's comments.

The following is translated from Blo bzang chos kyi rgyal mtshan, *Bar do 'phrang sgrol gyi gsol 'debs 'jigs sgrol gyi dba' bo zhes bya ba dang de'i 'grel pa gten bde'i bsil ba ster byed zla zer zhes bya ba bcas bzhugs so paṇ chen blo bzang chos kyi rgyal mtshan gyis mdzad pa'i don rnams bshad pa lcang skya rol pa'i rdo rjes sbyar ba* (Gangtok, 1969).

Further Reading

On the stages of death, see Jeffrey Hopkins and Lati Rinbochay, *Death, Intermediate State, and Rebirth in Tibetan Buddhism* (Ithaca: Snow Lion Publications, 1980). On the tantric practices described here, see Daniel Cozort, *Highest Yoga Tantra* (Ithaca: Snow Lion Publications, 1986).

PRAYERS FOR DELIVERANCE FROM THE STRAITS OF THE BARDO, A HERO THAT FREES FROM FEAR

by the first Panchen Lama

Homage to the Guru Mañjughoṣa

I and all transmigrators, equal to space
Go for refuge until the essence of enlightenment
To the sugatas of the three times, together with the doctrine and the assembly.
We pray to be delivered from the frights of this [lifetime], future [lifetimes], and the bardo.

This auspicious base [the human body], difficult to find and easy to destroy,
Is the opportunity to chose profit or loss, joy or sorrow.
Thus, empower us to take the essence, great in meaning,
Without being distracted by the meaningless affairs of this life.

What was joined is parted, all that was accumulated is consumed,
The end of height is sinking, the end of life is death.
Empower us to understand that there is no time;
Not only will we die, but the time of death is uncertain.

Empower us to pacify the suffering in which the body is destroyed
By various causes of death when consciousness is about to leave
The four impure elements and the illusory aggregates
In the city of the mistaken conception of subject and object.

Empower us to pacify the mistaken appearances of nonvirtue
When we are deceived at a time of need by this body lovingly protected,
When the enemies, the frightful lords of death appear,
When we kill ourselves with the weapons of the three poisons.

Empower us to remember the instructions of the lama
When the doctors give up and rites cannot reverse it
And friends have lost the hope that we will live
And we do not know what to do.

Empower us to have joy and confidence
When the food and wealth greedily amassed remain behind,
We leave forever friends loved and longed for,
And go alone to a dangerous place.

Empower us to have the strength of a virtuous mind
When the elements of earth, water, fire, and wind gradually dissolve,
The strength of the body is lost, the mouth and nose dry and contract,
The warmth gathers, we gasp for breath, and a wheezing sound occurs.

Empower us to realize the deathless mode of being
When the various mistaken appearances, frightful and horrific,
Occur, specifically mirage, smoke, and fireflies,
And the mounts of the eighty conceptions cease.

Empower us to produce strong mindfulness
When the wind constituent begins to dissolve into consciousness,
The outer breath ceases and coarse dualistic appearance disappears
And there dawns an appearance like a blazing butterlamp.

Empower us to know our own nature
Through the yoga that realizes that saṃsāra and nirvāṇa are empty
When appearance, increase, and attainment dissolve, the former into the latter
And the experiences like being pervaded by sunlight, moonlight, and darkness dawn.

Empower the mother and son clear lights to meet
Upon the dissolution of near-attainment into the all empty,
When all conceptual elaborations are completely pacified
And an experience dawns like an autumn sky free from taint.

Empower us to be placed in one-pointed equipose
On the wisdom of the union of innate bliss and emptiness
As the moon is melted by the lightning-like fire of Brahmā
At the time of the four empties.

Empower us to complete the meditative state of illusion
When, rising from that, we ascend to an enjoyment body of the bardo
Blazing with the glorious major and minor marks
[Made] just from the wind and mind of the clear light of death.

If the bardo becomes established due to actions
Empower us so that erroneous appearances appear purely,
Realizing, with immediate analysis, how the sufferings
Of birth, death, and the bardo do not truly exist.

Empower us to be reborn in a pure land
Through the yoga of the transformation of the outer, inner, and secret
When the varieties of the four sounds of the reversal of the elements,
The three frightening appearances, the uncertainties, and the signs
appear.

Empower us to attain quickly the three bodies
Upon assuming a supreme base of a knowledge bearer of the sky
Or the body of one with pure behavior, endowed with the three
trainings
Completing the realizations of the two-staged path.

A COMMENTARY ON THIS PRAYER, CALLED "A MOON BESTOWING THE COOLNESS OF COMPLETE BLISS"

by Janggya

I bow down to the pervasive lord, the lama Vajrasattva
Through relying on whom the great bliss of union
Is bestowed in this very lifetime.
I will comment upon the profound instructions.

Here, I will discuss, for the sake of easy understanding, the stages of practice of this text, *Prayers for Deliverance from the Straits of the Bardo, A Hero That Frees from Fear*, composed by the Panchen, the all-knowing Losang Chögyi Gyaltsen Bel Zangpo (Blo bzang chos kyi rgyal mtshan dbal bzang po), the lord of the complete teaching who has gone to the highest state of attainment, the keeper of the treasury of all the secret instructions of the foremost great being, [Tsong kha pa]. Initially, one should build one's motivation and purify one's continuum by going for refuge and engendering the aspiration to enlightenment. Perform as before the guru yoga that is connected with the *yi dam* of

Unexcelled Yoga Tantra, such as Bhairava, Cakrasaṃvara, or Guhyasamāja, together with the seven-limbed service and the offering of maṇḍala. The prayers are to be [recited] as it appears below with mindfulness of the meaning through strong conviction regarding the inseparability of one's teacher and *yi dam*. In other contexts, when this is connected with meditation in the circle of a maṇḍala, one may conclude with torma offering of self-generation or may conclude with offering and praise of the [deity] generated in front; since either is suitable, it depends on the context.

The actual prayers are of four [types], the preliminaries, connected with the common path; those connected with the instructions for someone about to die; those connected with instructions for the intermediate state, and those connected with instructions for taking rebirth. The first, [those connected with the common path] comprise the first three stanzas.

Homage to the Guru Mañjughoṣa

This is an obeisance and an expression of worship to the lama and supreme of deities, Mañjughoṣa.

> I and all transmigrators, equal to space
> Go for refuge until the essence of enlightenment
> To the sugatas of the three times, together with the doctrine and the assembly.
> We pray to be delivered from the frights of this [life], future [lives], and the bardo.

[The first stanza] concerns going for refuge. [Going for refuge] is the heartfelt promise that is not broken from now until enlightenment, unwaveringly seeking protection in the place of protection—the tathāgatas of the three times, that is, the buddhas, the dharma, and the saṅgha—for oneself and all transmigrators equal to space from the fears of this life, the next life, and the intermediate state. [Refuge is sought from two perspectives]: a strong awareness fearful of the general and specific sufferings of saṃsāra of myself and all the kind transmigrators, equal to space, and with an authentic awareness that the lama and the three jewels have the capacity to protect us from that [suffering].

> This auspicious base, difficult to find and easy to destroy,
> Is the opportunity to chose profit or loss, joy or sorrow.
> Thus, empower us to take the essence, great in meaning,
> Without being distracted by the meaningless affairs of this life.

The second stanza is concerned with the great meaning of leisure and opportunity and the difficulty of finding them. An auspicious basis endowed with the eighteen qualities of leisure and opportunity, [see chapter 28] whether [considered] from the viewpoint of cause, entity, or example, is difficult to find and the conditions for its destruction are numerous. Hence, it is easy for it to be destroyed, like the flame of a butterlamp in a strong wind. This [basis], attained merely fortuitously this time, is an opportunity to have the independence to choose joy or sorrow; to acquire the profit of high status [i.e., a good rebirth] and liberation for oneself from now on, or to bring about a loss, such as the sufferings of the bad realms. We pray for empowerment to extract the pure essence through practicing the excellent doctrine of the Mahāyāna, having the great meaning, practicing daily with determination, never being distracted by the meaningless affairs of this lifetime, such as praise, fame, and resources, which are insignificant because they are not rare; they are even acquired by animals.

> What was joined is parted, all that was accumulated is consumed,
> The end of height is sinking, the end of life is death.
> Empower us to understand that there is no time;
> Not only will we die, but the time of death is uncertain.

The third stanza teaches about impermanence. Like traders at a festival, the happy gatherings of relatives and dear friends in the end powerlessly disperse. Like the honey of a bee, not only is all accumulated wealth consumed in the end; there is no certainty that one will be able to use it oneself. Like an arrow shot into the sky by a child, one achieves a high rank of glory in the world and in the end one does not escape sinking. This very body that is born complete and is lovingly protected is finally destroyed by the Lord of Death. At that time, being cast as if into an empty wilderness, consciousness must always go on alone. Thus, not only will one die, but the time when one will die—the year, the month, the week—is uncertain. Therefore, there can be no confidence that one will not die even today. Empower us to practice only the excellent doctrine quickly, having understood that there is no time for the limitless affairs which are to be put aside—the appearances of this life—[such as] accumulating and maintaining possessions, subduing enemies and protecting friends.

The preceding has taught the way to train the mind in the prerequisites to the instructions on death. The second group of prayers applies to the instructions for those who are about to die. This has two parts, removing obstacles to the cultivation of the path, that is, engendering the kind of awareness that is concordant with the doctrine, and the actual mode of cultivating the instructions for one about to die. The first is dealt with in four stanzas.

> Empower us to pacify the suffering in which the body is destroyed
> By various causes of death when consciousness is about to leave
> The four impure elements and the illusory aggregates
> In the city of the mistaken conception of subject and object.

If there is a great suffering that destroys the essential [parts of the body] at the time of death, one is prevented from putting the instructions into practice.

Therefore, the first stanza is a prayer for empowerment in order that that [suffering] be pacified. This city of the gandhārvas, the mundane existence of the mistaken appearances of this life, is produced by dualistic conceptions that perceive the apprehended [objects] and the apprehender [i.e., consciousnesses] to be true. Here, the illusory aggregates are composed of the four elements of earth, water, fire, and wind, which are established from the impure factors of blood and semen from one's parents. These aggregates and one's own consciousness are divided and separated through the divisiveness of the pernicious Lord of Death. As that time draws near, empower us to pacify suffering such that it does not happen that the elements are disturbed by the power of various harmful external and internal causes of death, such as sickness, weapons, and poison, and that a fierce disease ceases and destroys the essential [parts of the] body—the winds, constituents, and the channels that are the basis of the life force.

> Empower us to pacify the mistaken appearances of nonvirtue
> When we are deceived at a time of need by this body lovingly
> protected,
> When the enemies, the frightful lords of death appear,
> When we kill ourselves with the weapons of the three poisons.

If one conceives the mistaken appearances at the time of death to be true and comes under the power of fear and dread, one is prevented from meditating on the instructions. Therefore, the second stanza is a prayer for empowerment in order to pacify that. Arriving at an inescapable passage, one is deceived at [this] time of need by the body that is cherished and protected with food, clothing, and wealth, without shunning sin, suffering, or ill-repute, and [mind and body] separate. The enemies, the difficult to withstand and frightening lords of death, that is, the various forms of the lords of death such as the fear of the separation of life from the body and the fear of fear itself appear. At that time, one murders oneself with the weapons of the three poisons—attachment to this body, unbearable hatred of fear and suffering, and the obscuration that conceives whatever appears to be true. We pray that, when we arrive at that point, we be empowered to pacify all the appearances of unpleasant objects created by nonvirtuous misconception and all the mistaken perceptions of subjects that conceive these to be true.

> Empower us to remember the instructions of the lama
> When the doctors give up and rites cannot reverse it
> And friends have lost the hope that we will live
> And we do not know what to do.

Regarding the third, one prays for empowerment in order to have the ability to meditate on the instructions, without being impeded by fear or forgetfulness at that time. The doctors who hope to cure sicknesses give up and various rites do not overcome the fear of death. Relatives, such as one's father and mother, lose hope that one will live; with eyes filled with tears they make arrangements for the funeral ceremonies. One oneself does not know what to do, like someone abandoned by a guide in a frightful place. At that time, abandoning anguish and panic, we pray for empowerment to remember the instructions of the lama, having the confidence to use death on the path.

> Empower us to have joy and confidence
> When the food and wealth greedily amassed remain behind,
> We leave forever friends loved and longed for,
> And go alone to a dangerous place.

Regarding the fourth, all the wealth and possessions, the home and power that one has greedily accumulated and toiled and worried to protect is left as inheritance. Without ever meeting them again, one leaves forever friends loved and longed for, one's father and mother, one's retinue, and students, from whom one cannot bear to be apart from even for a short time. One will be carried powerlessly, alone and without a companion, by the winds of karma to the dangerous place of the bardo where one has never been before and which is unfamiliar, not knowing what frights and sufferings are there. At that time, we pray for empowerment to have a joy and confidence that are agreeable and cheerful, without the slightest panic or anguish, like a child going home, placing confidence in the lama, *yi dam*, and three jewels. That is, one prays for empowerment in order to increase the happiness of the mind, understanding that all of these appearances of the circumstances of death are to be visualized in meditation prior [to death] and are exhortations to the practice of virtue at the time of death.

The second, the actual mode of meditating on the instructions for one about to die, is [dealt with in the next] six stanzas.

> Empower us to have the strength of a virtuous mind
> When the elements of earth, water, fire, and wind gradually dissolve,
> The strength of the body is lost, the mouth and nose dry and contract,
> The warmth gathers, we gasp for breath, and a wheezing sound occurs.

Regarding the first, when the power of the wind that serves as the basis of the physical earth constituent declines and it dissolves into the water constituent, the external sign is that the strength of the body is lost, that is, one says, "I am being pulled down," thinking that one is sinking into the earth. Similarly, when the water constituent dissolves into the fire constituent, the external sign is that the moisture of the mouth and nose dry up and the lips become puckered and so forth. When the fire constituent dissolves into the wind constituent, the external sign is that warmth of the body gathers from the extremities at the heart and one's luster deteriorates. The external sign of the wind constituent dissolving into consciousness is a gasping for breath, and one makes a wheezing sound from [the breath] collecting uneveningly within. Therefore, when those occur, we pray for empowerment not to be moved by nonvirtuous thoughts, but to have the strength of virtuous minds, in general, virtuous minds such as going for refuge and training in the aspiration to enlightenment through giving and taking and, in particular, meditating on one's lama as being inseparable from one's *yi dam* and visualizing oneself and one's environment as the supported and supporting maṇḍala.

> Empower us to realize the deathless mode of being
> When the various mistaken appearances, frightful and horrific,
> Occur, specifically mirage, smoke, and fireflies,
> And the mounts of the eighty conceptions cease.

As the potencies of the physical body begin to disintegrate, appearances occur. There are many frightful and horrific things, such as unpleasant forms and sounds appearing to those who have been nonvirtuous. Various mistaken appearances, such as pleasant forms and sounds, appear to those who have been virtuous. Yogins who have made progress on the path are welcomed by the lama, the *yi dam*, and ḍākinīs, together with amazing visions. Specifically, an appearance like a mirage arises as the internal sign of the dissolution of earth into water, an appearance like smoke as the internal sign of the dissolution of water into fire, and an appearance like fireflies as the internal sign of the dissolution of fire into wind. After that the movements of the karmic winds that serve as the mounts of the eighty thorough conceptions—the forty natural conceptions of appearance, the thirty-three natural conceptions of increase, and the seven natural conceptions of near attainment—grow weaker and weaker and gradually cease. At that time, we pray for empowerment for the ability to sustain the understanding of the profound mode of being, deciding that birth, death, and all of saṃsāra and, specifically, all of these appearance and the mind are mere projections by mistaken conceptions and that ultimately that which is called "death" does not exist even in name.

> Empower us to produce strong mindfulness
> When the wind constituent begins to dissolve into consciousness,
> The outer breath ceases and coarse dualistic appearance disappears
> And there dawns an appearance like a blazing butterlamp.

Regarding the third, then the constituent of the movement of wind becomes very weak and begins to dissolve into the subtle constituent of consciousness. An external sign of this is that movement of the breath ceases and there is no inhalation. As an internal sign, all coarse dualistic appearances such as the aspect of the external object being distant and cut off from the internal apprehending consciousness disappear and an appearance dawns like a blazing butterlamp unmoved by the wind. At that time, empower us so that the aspect of clarity and knowledge, the conventional entity of the mind, will appear nakedly and so that we will produce a mindfulness that thinks, "I know this sign and that sign," when all of those internal and external signs explained above appear and so that earlier [before death] we will produce an introspection that knows whether or not we are performing the meditation that brings [death] to the path of the two stages.

> Empower us to know our own nature
> Through the yoga that realizes that saṃsāra and nirvāṇa are empty
> When appearance, increase, and attainment dissolve, the former into the latter
> And the experiences like being pervaded by sunlight, moonlight, and darkness dawn.

Regarding the fourth, then, at the time of appearance itself the winds dissolve into the appearance of subtle consciousness and there is the appearance of radiant whiteness in utter vacuity, like a clear autumn sky pervaded by moonlight. At the time of increase itself appearance dissolves into increase and there is the appearance of radiant redness, like a clear autumn sky pervaded by sunlight. At the time of near attainment itself, when increase dissolves into near attainment, there arises the appearance of radiant blackness, like a clear autumn sky pervaded by the thick darkness of evening. When the three appearances, the signs of the gradual dissolution of the former into the latter, appear in that way, empower us to have the ability to understand experientially the entity or mode of being of our own mind exactly as it is through the yoga of the special realization that inseparably joins the entities of the object emptiness—the nonexistence of even a particle of that which is established from its own side among all the phenomena included in cycle of mundane existence and the peace of nirvāṇa—and the subject, the spontaneous great bliss that arises through the method of focusing on important points in the body.

> Empower the mother and son clear lights to meet
> Upon the dissolution of near-attainment into the all empty,
> When all conceptual elaborations are completely pacified
> And an experience dawns like an autumn sky free from taint.

Regarding the fifth, then, upon the dissolution of the subtle mind of near attainment itself into the clear light of the all empty, all the elaborations of thought that conceive various objects such as unity and plurality cease and become pacified and an experience dawns like the utter vacuity of a pure autumn sky free from moonlight, sunlight, and thick darkness, the three tainting conditions that prevent the natural color of the sky from coming out just as it is. The manifestation, just as it is, of the entity of the basic clear light, fundamental and spontaneous, is the mother clear light. That same mind, the path clear light, which, through meditating on the instructions of the lama, is generated into exalted wisdom that realizes the subtle emptiness with spontaneous great bliss is the son clear light. The union of those in one entity is the meeting of mother and son clear lights. We pray for empowerment to be able to [have them meet when the clear light of death dawns].

Empower us to be placed in one-pointed equipose
On the wisdom of the union of innate bliss and emptiness
As the moon is melted by the lightning-like fire of Brahmā
At the time of the four empties.

Regarding the sixth, at the time of all four empties and specifically of the all empty, the clear light, the fire of Brahmā that abides at the triangular junction, that is, the fire of the fierce woman, blazes up like lightning, with the speed of lightning by the yogic power of the basic path. By moving up the central channel it melts the moon, the white mind of enlightenment, at the crown of the head which descends through the *dhūti*, thereby engendering the spontaneous great bliss. We pray for empowerment to be placed in one-pointed equipoise without distraction on the exalted wisdom that inseparably joins in entity that [bliss] and the subtle emptiness.

The foremost great being Tsong kha pa said that the king of instructions for the benefit of those who are about to die is the uninterrupted daily practice that combines three things: mixing in the mind again and again, beginning today, the instructions for one about to die, as they were explained above; forcing oneself to think repeatedly, "At death I should meditate in this way"; and strongly beseeching the lamas and gods for the purpose of that. It is similar with regard to the instruction on the bardo below.

The third group applies to instruction on the bardo and is set forth in three stanzas.

Empower us to complete the meditative state of illusion
When, rising from that, we ascend to an enjoyment body of the bardo
Blazing with the glorious major and minor marks
[Made] just from the wind and mind of the clear light of death.

Regarding the first, thus, when the wind and mind of the clear light of death are themselves moved by the wind, that is, when one rises from that meditative equipoise, the wind that serves as the mount of the clear light of death acts as the substantial cause of and the mind of clear light acts as the cooperative condition of a body that blazes with the glory of the thirty-two major marks and the eighty minor marks. It is a clear and unobstructed rainbow body, having a nature of mere wind and mind and not a coarse body of physical flesh and bone. The bardo of ordinary sentient beings comes about in the same way, but this yogin who is able to generate the clear light of death, the basis, into the entity of the example clear light on the path rises in an enjoyment body, that is, an impure illusory body. We pray for empowerment to complete the illusion-like meditative stabilization of such an Unexcelled Mantra path. This [discussion] applies to a single yogin who, in this lifetime, has achieved realization of isolated speech, or below, of the stage of completion.

If the bardo becomes established due to actions
Empower us so that erroneous appearances appear purely,

Realizing, with immediate analysis, how the sufferings
Of birth, death, and the bardo do not truly exist.

Regarding the second, if an ordinary body of the mundane bardo becomes established due to actions that did not [permit] the attainment in this lifetime of the realization of the stage of completion such as that [described] above, analyze well immediately and understand that one has established the bardo and then realize that all the appearances of birth, death, and the intermediate state are appearances of a mistaken mind and realize the way in which all of those sufferings are not true, that is, they are not established from their own side even slightly. Empower us so that all of the mistaken appearances that arise will appear purely, as the sport of bliss and emptiness.

Empower us to be reborn in a pure land
Through the yoga of the transformation of the outer, inner, and secret
When the varieties of the four sounds of the reversal of the elements,
The three frightening appearances, the uncertainties, and the signs
appear.

Regarding the third, thus, at the time of the bardo, the signs of the reversal of the elements come. With the reversal of the earth wind there is the sound of an avalanche; with the reversal of the water wind, the sound of a stormy sea; with the reversal of the fire wind, the sound of a forest fire; with the reversal of the wind wind, the sound of the wind storm [at the end of an] aeon. There are four such sounds. The three frightful appearances are the appearance of hell beings, hungry ghosts, and animals or [they are] the form of lords of death carrying weapons, the sound of their saying "I'm going to kill you!" and one becoming sorrowful and terrified because of that. The uncertainties are such things as the uncertainty of abode, because of not abiding in one place and the uncertainty of companions because one is accompanied by a variety of companions. Various signs appear such as being endowed with the power of magical activity and [passing] without obstruction through mountains, walls, buildings, and so forth. At that time, empower us to be born in a pure buddha land, a special place for cultivating the path of Unexcelled Secret Mantra, having closed the door of birth in impure saṃsāra through the force of the three yogas: the transformation of all the appearances of the environment—the outer—into pure divine mansions, the transformation of all the inhabiting sentient beings—the inner—into *yi dams* in the aspect of father and mother, and the transformation of all the movements of mindfulness and thought—the secret—into the meditative state of bliss and emptiness.

The fourth section applies to taking rebirth and is set forth in one stanza.

Empower us to attain quickly the three bodies
Upon assuming a supreme base of a knowledge bearer of the sky

Or the body of one with pure behavior, endowed with the three trainings
Completing the realizations of the two-staged path.

In dependence upon the instructions of taking the bardo as the path in this way, one takes birth as a supreme knowledge bearer in a special abode caused and assembled by the very forms of outer flying heroes and ḍākinīs. One then completes the remainder of the path and achieves the supreme state. Otherwise, if one takes birth like those endowed with six constituents who are born from a human womb in Jambudvīpa, one should stop the mind of desire and hatred for one's father and mother and view them as *yi dams* in the aspect of father and mother. One enters the mother's womb and, upon being born outside, one takes the body of a monk endowed with three trainings of those with pure behavior and enters into the teaching of the Conqueror in accordance with its stages. Then, one's continuum is ripened by the four pure initiations, the doors of entry into Unexcelled Secret Mantra Mahāyāna. Having kept the pledges and vows correctly, one brings to fulfillment the progression on the paths of the stage of generation and the stage of completion. Having thereby transformed the basic three bodies into the three bodies of the path, one quickly attains, in this very lifetime, the three bodies of a buddha, the effect: the wisdom truth body, the enjoyment body, and the emanation body. Having done that, we pray for empowerment to establish all sentient beings throughout space on the path to ripening and liberation.

Because the meaning of colophon is easy to understand, I will not elaborate. It is said that these instructions should be kept secret from those who are not vessels, such as those without faith, and from those who have not received initiation into Unexcelled Mantra. The explanations above of the instructions on death and the bardo appear to be intended for the profound instructions on the stage of completion. Therefore, regarding the mode of transforming [these instructions] into the king of instructions on death, the practice is to be done daily, as already explained, through causing the meanings of the instructions to appear in meditation, not through merely reciting the words of the prayers but by being mindful of the meaning. If it is practiced in that way, it becomes the supreme method for taking advantage of the basis of leisure and opportunity. I say:

How wonderful it is to explain clearly with few words
The essences of the path of the highest vehicle,
The essentials of the profound thought of Vajradhara,
The basic promise of the kings of adepts.

By the virtue of striving at this,
May I and all transmigrators
Peerlessly uphold and increase

The path of the highest vehicle in birth after birth
And become equal to the vajra-bearing Nāgārjuna.

The elder lama and monk, Chöje Losang Sangye (Chos rje blo bzang sangs rgyas), asked on behalf of one from Mongolia with a youthful mind who is beginning the complete and profound practice that there be made an explanation, condensed and easy to understand, of the meanings of *Prayers for Deliverance from the Straits of the Bardo, A Hero That Frees from Fear* by the crown of millions of scholars and adepts, the omniscient Panchen Losang Chögyi Gyaltsen. The scribe of the learned Janggya (Lcang skya rol pa'i rdo rje) was the lama and geshe Tshultrim Dargye (Tshul khrims dar rgyas), for whom billions of texts have been spoken. By [the merit] of having done this, may the teaching of the conqueror Losang [Tsong kha pa] spread and increase in all directions.

—30—

Dying, Death, and Other Opportunities

David Germano

The history of the notion of an "intermediate state" (*bar do; antarābhava*), a prolonged postmortem intermediary period between death and rebirth, has ancient roots in Indian Buddhism and can even be traced thematically to early Vedic and Upaniṣadic antecedents. The rise of tantrism in India encouraged renewed attention on the intermediate state, given tantra's overall focus on liminal states, death, and inversion. Thus tantric groups began to articulate contemplative techniques mimicking the process of dying, death, and rebirth so as not only to prepare themselves for the opportunities that actual death offered, but also to take advantage of these opportunities in the ritual re-creation of dying and death within life itself, to see the other side of life, and hence life itself, more clearly.

In Tibet, it was the Nyingma that gave the bardo its fullest expression in a series of innovative works that developed from the eleventh to fourteenth centuries in the Seminal Heart (*snying thig*) tradition. First found in *The Seventeen Tantras*, its most famous formulation is in the fourteenth-century revelation of Karmalingpa (Karma gling pa) entitled *The Profound Doctrine of Wisdom's Natural Freedom [in Encountering] the Peaceful and Wrathful Deities* and forever memorialized in the West as *The Tibetan Book of the Dead*. There are three distinctive overarching features: the centralization and expansion of the "intermediate state" within the entire tradition, such that one is never anywhere but a bardo of one type or another; the expansion of the postdeath intermediate state's description to include a striking new phase known as the "reality intermediate state," marked by the systematic unfolding of a series of visions of one's internal buddha-nature in terms of the deity maṇḍalas known as the one hundred peaceful and wrathful deities; and the systematization of a set of associated contemplative and ritual techniques. In addition, the Seminal Heart provides a fourfold typology of intermediate states expanding the triune set of life, death, and the between state: the ordinary or natural intermediate state of this life between rebirth and death, the dying intermediate state, the postdeath reality intermediate state, and the second postdeath rebirth intermediate state.

The description of the second postdeath (or pre-rebirth) intermediate state is heavily oriented toward the individual's impending rebirth and is closely related to previous long-standing Buddhist presentations of how an intermediate state being lives between death and rebirth. In contrast, the postdeath reality intermediate state represents an innovation based upon the tradition's own resolute immersion within buddha-nature practice and ideology. The collapse of dying's ruthless destructuring of our existence momentarily unleashes nothing other than reality itself, that which manifests when all illusions have been ripped away, even those that in life are safely ensconced within the deep structures of the body. This reality is the buddha-nature, latently present during life in a form iconographically indicated by a maṇḍala of fifty-eight wrathful deities in the head and a maṇḍala of forty-two peaceful deities in the heart; all of these deities sequentially appear in reflection to our external vision in the days immediately following death. There are general antecedents in earlier Buddhist sources in the tantric belief that an advanced practitioner can take on the form of his or her *yi dam* during the intermediate state, or that buddhas come from their pure lands to greet devotees at the moment of death. However, I am as yet unaware of any sources that speak of a systematic revelation of in-dwelling deities that occurs for all life immediately following death. The particular set of deities described here is drawn directly from the Nyingma's own Mahāyoga tantric tradition, which is itself based on a core of texts most likely translated from Indian originals in the eighth to ninth centuries. The tradition presents most living beings as terrified by what is unleashed in dying and as fleeing toward much softer, dim lights that represent the return back to rebirth within the familiar, routinized structures of saṃsāra. The entire account of the deeply encoded forms of the deities, their sequential appearances, and the deceased person's reactions to their appearances against the backdrop of the broader issue of the relation between self and other is a powerful drama presented not only in words, but also in "sounds, lights, and rays" (*sgra 'od zer*).

While the contents of Karmalingpa's famed revelation are largely derivative of previous developments in the early Seminal Heart literature, its great virtues lie in the clarity and dramatic power of its ritual narrative of events following death in a usable handbook as well as its bringing together of all these various traditions into a single, well-organized compilation. The various partial translations into English of Karmalingpa's cycle highlight the portions that directly address the deceased person with exhortations that are ritually delivered by an officiating lama. These lectures describe the appearances that confront the deceased person from the initial manifestation of the peaceful maṇḍalas of buddhas to the varied visual appearances that entice her back into rebirth within saṃsāra. At every point the lama urges the deceased not to give himself or herself over to terror in fear of the chaos and otherness, but instead to self-recognize: to recognize the chaos and seemingly fierce process of change as part of who he or she is, to recognize that the figures looming ahead are his or her own projections as in a dream, to recognize the cosmic maṇḍalas of peaceful and wrathful buddhas unleashed by dying as none other than his or her own interior reality reflected across the sky's horizon, and to recognize the interdependent nature of his or her own subjectivity that thus stands self-revealed. These powerful narratives have become justly famous in Tibet and elsewhere for their vivid images and psychological wisdom. However, it is less well known that Karmalingpa's cycle and the Seminal Heart literature upon which he draws also include a variety of associated texts that articulate other fascinating strategies, not only for dealing with the deceased, but also for the dying and the potentially dying. It is this less well known literature that I would like to focus on as we look into how a number of interesting ritual practices and meditative techniques concerning dying and death formed around the bardo ideology in Tibet. This constellation undoubtedly draws extensively on indigenous Tibetan traditions as well as imported Buddhist sources.

The tenth chapter from Longchenpa's *The Treasury of Precious Words and Meanings* is devoted to the intermediate states; his stated intent is not merely to describe the nature of dying and postdeath experience, but rather to explore these processes in relation to the spiritual opportunities they afford us. Thus the tenth chapter is understood as being elaborated for the sake of those people who are unable to attain freedom within this life in reliance upon the contemplative processes previously detailed in chapter 8, but who may yet skillfully utilize the experiences of dying and postdeath to become spiritually awake. Longchenpa's discussion is structured around the standard four intermediate states, which are the principal transitional periods or gaps characterizing our reoccurring cycles of life and death: this life (the period between birth and death), dying (between life and postdeath existence), postdeath (between dying and rebirth), and the period of postdeath experience leading into the next rebirth (between the postdeath visions and actual rebirth in a new incarnation). At every step of the way there remains the possibility of liberation, and thus Longchenpa carefully details each intermediate state's critical phases and unfolding experiences with an eye toward the possibilities of liberation offered to the spiritually acute individual, with the end result being the charting of dying and postdeath experiences. In fact, often discussions of contemplative instructions are presented in the following threefold division: (1) becoming free in this very life for those of superior diligence; (2) becoming free in the postdeath intermediate state for those of average diligence; and (3) becoming free in the natural emanational body pure land (having been reborn there following death) for those of inferior diligence.

Overview of the Dying Intermediate State

Longchenpa's discussion in *The Treasury of Words and Meanings* of the dying intermediate state has two sections: a general overview and a detailed look at a few important particulars. The former section deals with the following seven topics: the reasons for one's eventual death being a certainty, techniques for examining whether or not one is actually dying, techniques for reversing impending death, the appearances at the brink of death, the oral precepts for a practitioner who is dying (i.e., transference of consciousness techniques), the signs of being born in one of the ordinary six types of rebirth, and the purification rituals to be done for a dying or dead person. The latter section focuses on just two issues: the different ways in which an accomplished saint may die in contrast to ordinary death, and the sequential phases in dying as all the body's internal psychophysical elements sequentially dissolve.

The first section is thus practically oriented with a wide variety of pragmatic observations about the physical effects of dying and sketches of relevant ritual and contemplative practices. These practices begin with illness, when it becomes imperative to discern if one is really near the brink of death or only temporarily ill, and the precise identity of the nonhuman spirit responsible for the health disturbances in question. Dying may be an opportunity, but it is not one Tibetans are in a rush to take advantage of if it can instead be forestalled; these techniques are followed by a discussion of rituals for reversing the dying process and thus recovering one's health. However, the remainder of the section is then devoted to issues concerning the dying process once it has irrevocably set in. A brief discussion of the signs marking the physical body's gradual collapse is followed by a detailed presentation of contemplative procedures that prepare one for eventual death, as well as ways in which a spiritually inclined teacher or friend can impart such advice to aid the dying person should his or her own practice not be up to the task. There is then a brief discussion of how various physical signs at death indicate the nature of the deceased's next rebirth in one of the six domains of saṃsāra, while the final topic concerns the purification rituals that can be done by a lama on a dead person to reverse his or her momentum toward such a rebirth.

Signs of Death I: Casting a Shadow in the Sky

As mentioned above, despite the importance of accepting the certainty of eventual death, the tradition is far from passive about accepting a particular time of death and has developed an intricate system of death prognostication. Such technical discussion of interpreting signs of death is part of a much wider phenomenon of Tibetan culture, namely, the vast energy devoted to interpreting signs and omens of almost every conceivable type, including many different divination practices. These particular observations and techniques are utilized to discern whether death is in fact imminent, the number of days one has remaining, and the nature of demonic influences that are possibly at work in one's ill health. The results thus enable one to best choose the type of rituals and contemplations that may have an effect in reversing the process so as to maintain one's present life force. *The Tantra of the Sun and the Moon's Intimate Union* presents three different sets of death prognostication: nineteen straightforward physical observations, projecting one's shadow's afterimage into the sky, and eight poetically titled practices concentrating on visual phenomena. Analogous discussions can be found in *The Treasury of the Supreme Vehicle* (TCD2 413.6–415.7), *The Seminal Quintessence of the Master* (LYT2 187.4–194.6), *The Seminal Quintessence of the Ḍākinī* (KGYT3 340.4–344.5), *The Seminal Quintessence of the Profound* (ZMYT1 404.3–406.6), and *The Seminal Quintessence of Vimalamitra* (VNT2 265.4–273.2).

While many of these signs utilized for divination may seem quite fanciful, it must be remembered that it is presumed the person doing the examination is a spiritually advanced yogin of commensurate psychic powers enabling an optimal performance of the rituals. They are also framed by other religious activities, such as indicated by Mañjuśrīmitra (the text in VNT) when he stresses the need first to amass the accumulations (of merit and wisdom) in reference to one's master and others. In addition, he specifies the signs "are in reference to an ordinary situation, while they are of indeterminate significance in the case of older people whose bodily constituents are simply worn out." He adds that these techniques are for the serious practitioner who is not inclined toward the exoteric elaborate divinatory practices such as throwing a *mo* (using dice or a rosary). Longchenpa further explains that though ordinary people cannot know when death will come, non-Buddhist mystics can obtain some indication through worldly forms of divination, while superior to that are these Buddhist yogic ways of discovering the time of death. One goes to an empty valley devoid of people, a hermitage, a cemetery, a dense forest, or a mountainous province, and there does the examination of one's life's "form" and so forth. Finally, the presentation of these signs is followed in many of the sources by extensive discussions of the means by which one can reverse the dying process and recover. Techniques are described separately for each of the previously discussed signs indicating impending death, including dietary adjustments, medicinal substances, ritual manipulation of effigies, contemplative practices, chanting scriptures, magico-ritual manipulations of assorted substances, and so on. (See Orofino for a translation of one such treatment; also see the presentation of "ransoming death" below and in chapter 33, the principal of such practices.)

The shadow practices are termed "the examination of your life-force's reflection within the sky's expanse," or "examining your life-form, the intrinsic radiation of the (five) elements," and are to be performed in an extremely isolated spot. In either the morning or evening one rises naked, stretches out one's limbs, and picks up a stick, rosary, vase, or vajra (which one continues to hold in the hands); alternatively one can remain dressed. Then when the sky is cloudless as well as especially clear and bright, with one's back to the Sun one visually focuses and mentally concentrates on the heart of one's own shadow, divesting oneself of all distractions—one can use a stone or a stick to help focus. When the eyes begin to numb and the shadow becomes vividly pale white (just as when one stares at something for a long time, such that visual sensations are altered as the object wavers), one abruptly gazes up at the sky and intently inspects the image of one's own body that is projected there. If one sees the body's reflections along with what is held in the hands as completely intact white images against the sky's black background, this indicates the absence of major obstructions to the life force at the moment, such that worries about impending death are unfounded. The black and white appearance of the shadow against the sky is the natural result of prolonged staring at the ground, as will be evident to anyone who attempts this practice; Mañjuśrīmitra instead specifies that the image's natural color will be that of the clothes one is wearing at the time. However if only a partial body image appears, imminent death is indicated, with the particular nature of the missing element corresponding to the particular time period within which one will die. If the item held in the hand is missing, it is called "divorced from the deity you rely on," and one will die in seven years. If the right hand is missing, five years; the left hand, three years; from the right knee on down, two years; from the left knee on down, one year; all of the legs and arms, eight months; the right leg, one year; the head, five months; the right half of the head, nine months; the left half of the head, seven months; above the neck, five months; the neck on up, three months; the upper torso, two months; the bottom half of the body, one month; the right half of the body, twenty nine days; and the left half, twenty one days.

In addition, the shape and color of the image's light indicate, respectively, whether or not the dying process is reversible by rituals "ransoming" death and the nonhuman demonic cause of the disturbance in health. If the shape is square, spherical, oblong, or a half-moon, it is possible; but if the shape is like a wrapped corpse or triangular, it cannot be reversed. In the latter case, one should divest oneself of everything else and focus on nonattachment and refreshing oneself on the crucial precepts. If the image is white and fading out at the middle, it is a sign one is being harmed by serpent spirits and king spirits. If it is black and fading out at the right, the demons and *ma mo* spirits are the culprit. If it is red and fading out at the left, it is fierce deities, one's own guardian deities or spiritual protectors. If it is yellow and fading out in its lower part, it is the serpent spirits, fierce deities, and king-bewitcher spirits. If it is blue and fading out in the legs, it is serpentine spirits or lake medicine deities. If the image is in a murky black, this indicates the *ma mo* and Lord of Death; an indistinct yellowish light is sign of the earth-boss spirits' influence; and a flashing multicolored light is a sign that forces of a variety of demons are at work.

Signs of Death II: Eight Poetic Styles of Diagnosing Death

The third set of prognostic techniques for the signs of death involve fairly simple yet interesting practices that mostly revolve around visual phenomena. They are all given terse metaphoric titles in *The Tantra of the Sun and Moon's Intimate Union.*

1. *Should the link between sky and Earth come to be cut off.* At noon while facing south and crouching down, one places one's elbow on one's knee and straightens the forearm so it is perpendicular to the ground. Then one holds one's hand in a fist to the spot between the eyebrows and unwaveringly looks directly at the part of the arm right below the wrist. If the contemplated arm thus becomes extremely thin (an optical illusion resulting from staring at it), this indicates there is no problem. However, if the arm's appearance becomes totally severed at this

narrowing point, one will die in nineteen days. The upright arm is thus a "rope" connecting Earth and sky in its vertical orientation running through one's field of vision, which further evokes the grounding of one's skylike insubstantial consciousness in the earthy realities of continued bodily incarnation. The image also plays off the ancient Tibetan myth that early kings climbed back up a sacred rope into heaven instead of dying, until a particular king was tricked so that the rope was severed and he became mortal.

2. *If the man riding the white lioness falls off on the slopes of the cosmic mountain.* At sunrise one goes to a pond to the east and stands at a spot between its western perimeter and an earthen mound or high wall built there, gazing at the wall upon which the water's glow reflects. Normally one should see a dual reflection of oneself on that wall: a lower figure from the Sun's rays directly shining down on the wall ("the lion") and a second figure above it from the Sun's rays reflecting off the pond and bouncing up onto the wall there ("the rider"); because of the Sun's low angle at sunrise, these two shadows should be in close contact with each other. If the second shadow atop the first shadow's head is missing, one will die at midday within sixteen days. If the two shadows appear stacked atop each other, everything is fine. Thus the image of a man falling off a white lion going down the slopes of a mountain refers to the absence of this second shadow atop the first shadow's head, while the mountain slope indicates the wall upon which these shadows are reflected. Analogically, the lion represents our biological vitality, which consciousness rides upon down the tricky slopes of a given life leading from birth to death.

3. *If the waist of the wish-fulfilling tree is cut off at the boundary between the mountain and the plains.* This practice involves examination of pulses. If the artery and vitality-channels (*bla rtsa*) of the legs and arms cannot be discerned, one will die in seven days. The vitality-channels are arteries from which the relative length of life can be determined, and whose pulse can be detected between the wrist's lower corner and the ligament there (substitute the ankle for the wrist in the case of the leg). *The Seminal Quintessence of the Master* also refers just to an "artery," which probably refers to a neck artery, since the "wishing tree" is specified as the neck in the eighth practice (see below): the mountain is the head, the plain the body, and the tree the neck at their juncture. Otherwise, the image is based upon the tree being the lifeblood of the land with saps running through it, as well as its providing a residence to many birds and small creatures, shade, and wood for construction and fire; the "mountain and plain" having a multilayered significance. The body's wishing trees are arteries, which bring oxygen and nutrients among other vital factors to the body, granting the greatest "wish" of all—life. Also the image of a border between the mountain and plain connotes the pulse being taken at the wrist, a juncture between the hand and arm. The body is thus imaged as a cosmic landscape in miniature, with magnificent mountains sloping down to vast plains, at the border of which we find flowering trees which fulfill our every wish.

4. *If the film on the ocean's water disappears.* This examination checks whether

the film atop the ocean's water vanishes or not, with the ocean's water being one's urine and the film being a colored vapor arising from it at dawn. The preceding night one avoids fatigue, drinking beer, sexual intercourse, and a lot of conversation. Then at dawn when the Sun arises over the mountain peaks, one urinates within a vessel (such as a bell-metal pan) that is neither white nor black (evidently based on their respective extreme heat-absorbing and light-refracting properties). When one turns toward the east (so that the Sun's rays directly strike the urine) and gazes upon this vessel containing one's urine, if its vapor (resulting from the warm urine in the cold air) within the Sun's rays is purple, *The Seminal Quintessence of the Master* and Karmalingpa indicate there is no immediate problem, while the absence of this purple glow indicates death within fifteen days. Thus the image is of life being a temporary coagulation of form within the immensity of an ocean of energy. Wispy black vapor signifies death within eleven days, vapor flecked with red dots indicates death within nine days, and any other appearance means everything is fine. You can also examine the urine's color to determine what demonic forces have beset oneself by utilizing the correspondences detailed above in the context of the shadow practice.

5. *If the smoke of the spiritual ascetic ceases within the city of earth.* At daybreak one defecates on the ground and look at the excrement. If it is giving off vapor, all is fine; if instead the vapor has red spots or is all together absent, one will die within nine days. Thus "smoke" refers to this vapor given off by the excrement. Since this is done just as the Sun is coming up over the horizon, in Tibetan areas it would still be quite cold even during the summer, and the warm excrement falling to the cold soil along with the cold air and Sun rays would normally result in steam. The time of sunrise is chosen since the intense Sun rays could not yet have heated the ground and air, as well as its being a typical time for bowel movements. The image analogizes digestive process to "filtering" out distortions through spiritual refinement (literally "virtue-purification"), expunging the solid wastes just as virtue expels emotional distortions. "Earth" (*sa*) as the "ground" (*sa*) one defecates on ("the city" for one's excrement) connotes the "spiritual level" (*sa*) where virtue is cultivated within, while "smoke" indicates the heat of its meditative realization engendered correlated to the vapors arising from one's excrement. In addition "earth" connotes the solidity of excrement, whereas the examination of urine above is analogically linked to water based on its liquidity. Finally, mortal life takes place in the city of earth, with smoke indicating the fire of life's vital processes continuing to burn.

6. *If the unchanging Sun sets at the peak of the cosmic mountain.* This involves whether or not one can see the seminal nuclei lamp's light by pressing on one's eyes, a typical practice used to introduce disciples to the esoteric presence of light within them. By pressing on the eye, usually concentric circles of light should appear off to one side, indicating the "unchanging Sun" of one's psychic life that is generally always present. Thus its failure to appear marks the end of our world as we know it, that is, death, while its appearance indicates everything is fine. The mountain peak refers to one's head (the "summit" of one's existence, both

physically and psychically), and in particular to one's eyes, while the Sun refers to the nuclei, or concentric circles, which usually manifest to one upon pressing the eyes. The Sun is termed " unchanging" since in general it doesn't set with regard to the cosmic mountain at the world's center, but rather revolves around it so that it alternately appears and disappears from the various continents arrayed around that mountain—thus its setting at this mountain would mark the end of the world.

7. *If the sound of the ḍākinīs ceases within the inner recesses of the cosmic mountain. The Seminal Quintessence of the Ḍākinī* says one should press one's ear against the ground while lying in the lion posture, while the consequent absence of any buzzing sound indicates certain death in five, seven, or eleven days. *The Seminal Quintessence of Vimalamitra* agrees with the posture but says that hearing the murmuring cries of many creatures indicates all is fine, while the sound of wind indicates death in seven or ten days, and the absence of sound points to death within eleven days. *The Seminal Quintessence of the Master* simply specifies that one stop one's ears up with one's fingers and that hearing the normal sound like a drum roll indicates that all is well. However, if the sound resembles a great wind, one will die within seven or eleven days, and if there is no sound at all, within five days. The cosmic mountain primarily refers to one's own head, the "peak" of one's physical existence, from which one surveys the surrounding world; within it one usually hears the roar of consciousness-driven vitality, that which "dances in the sky" (*mkha' 'gro, ḍākinī*), while its absence indicates the body's internal life-processes are ebbing away.

8. *Should the demonic Lord of Death raise up from the wish-fulfilling tree.* If seven strands or a lock of hair raise upward from the devil's gateway, death is certain within seven days; the devil's gateway refers to the hollow area in the nape's center below the external occipital protuberance. Thus in this context the wish-fulfilling tree refers to the neck, which is like a trunk growing out of the body and flowering into the head. "Devil" (*bdud*) plays off two medical terms: *sdud sgo* (the anterior fontanelle or the depressed area just below the exterior occipital protuberance at the back of one's head) and *bdud sgo* (the exterior occipital protuberance). Thus the tantra has deliberately spelled "synthesis" (*sdud* referring to the fontanelle where the bone planes "come together") or "knot" (*mdud* referring to the protuberance) as the homonym *bdud* (demon or devil) to create the image of the Lord of Death raising up to strike the living down.

Ransoming Death

Certain points in life present severe disruptions in one's flow of physical and psychic energy, the onset of which are indicated by the above portents and signs of imminent death. To reverse this tendency toward disruption and possible termination of one's life continuity, there are certain yogic techniques that may be effective when carefully applied in dependence upon the particular signs that manifest in a given case. A group of the most important ritual practices utilized in thus reversing death and effecting healing involve the ritual manipulation and offering of a dough effigy of the ill person to the demonic forces troubling him or her. These are generally referred to as "summoning the life" (*tshe 'gugs*), "summoning the life-force" (*bla 'gugs*), "ransoming the life-force," or "tricking or ransoming death" (*'chi bslu*). The effigy or ransom (*glud*) used in these rituals probably derives from earlier practices of scapegoats, where living beings were sacrificed as substitutes to placate gods or demons offended by others' transgressions. Thus many of the rituals' details concern making the effigy as attractive and convincing as possible, with the liturgy alternatingly coaxing and threatening as the lama tries to coerce the spirits into accepting the effigy in place of the person. In addition to dough effigies (*glud, ngar mi*, see chapter 33), many other symbolic or real objects go into making the ritual space a convincing and attractive alternative to the afflicted person: tablets (*sbyang bu, byang bu*) with drawings and names of people, the residence, property and so on, perhaps reflecting an earlier notion of spirit tablets; hair, finger nail clippings, worn clothes, and so on of the person in question, often inserted into the effigy; offerings of various types (especially sacrificial cones) to entice the spirits; other types of barley dough offerings shaped into "hand-molds" (*changs bu*) or "buttons" (*mtheb skyu*); and finally the famous magical device known as the "space" (*nam mkha'*) demon trap used in thread-cross rituals (*mdos*).

The "thread cross" was originally a type of demon trap that caught evil spirits (resembling flying insects) in the "space" or cobweb formed by wrapping five colored threads in alluring diamond-shaped patterns around crossed sticks; they range from simple diamond shapes to huge constructions. Beyer summarizes three functions (327–30): as a demon trap, as a scapegoat, and as a supreme offering in its corresponding to the entire universe. His summary is worth citing:

> The demons are fooled or cheated by the visualization and recitation of the practitioner into accepting the portrait as a substitute object of malevolence and are coerced into enjoying their prize in the separate dimension created for them. . . . it requires highly developed contemplative powers to create an entire world. . . . The visualization is imposed upon the public nonreality of the evil spirits, who, once they are trapped, can no longer perceive ordinary appearances but are aware only of the appearances of this new universe; yet this new home is after all filled with a paradise of good things—the substitutes—and there is no lack of humanitarian impulse in their incarceration. Then the thread-cross is carried to a lonely place and left there . . . and "the return of danger" is blocked and a circle of protection visualized to prevent any escape; here the evil spirits remain until the karma that impelled them to their malevolence is exhausted. Thus the three levels of symbolism converge: the malignant spirits are trapped, offered a substitute object of aggression, and transported to another and contemplatively real dimension through the gate of the space that traps them. (330)

In the Seminal Heart tradition, a fairly straightforward version of such a ritual is found in *The Tantra of the Sun and Moon's Intimate Union* as a technique for averting impending death and is cited as such by Longchenpa in *The Treasury of*

Words and Meanings. In addition, *The Seminal Heart of Vimalamitra, The Seminal Quintessence of the Ḍākinī*, and *The Seminal Quintessence of the Master* (VNT2 278.2–287.4, KGYT3 344.5–353.4, LYT2 194.6–203.4) all deal in greater detail with these techniques, discussing the materials in *The Treasury of Words and Meanings* under the rubric of "general" techniques for ransoming death, and then additionally under the heading of "detailed techniques" giving an account of individual practices for reversing death which are applied in relation to the specific signs that one experiences (from the list of twenty discussed in the preceding). I will here present an account of the former discussion combining these texts as well as details found in *The Seminal Quintessence of the Profound* (ZMYT1 (407.1–418.1). The latter text discusses ransoming death in three phases, each to be implemented successively if the preceding one has failed: external techniques for auspicious supporting links, internal life-actualization with alchemy, and the esoteric abiding reality. The first corresponds to *The Master* and *The Ḍākinī Seminal Quintessences*, the second involves using alchemical ingestion of substances along with various visualizations in life-evocation rituals, and the third involves the triad of feast offerings, sky-eating yoga, and meditation on emptiness (including a "cutting" practice where one offer one's own body). In this text, Longchenpa presents this first practice in three parts: the balancing of the elemental energies with wheels (the ritual discussed in *The Treasury of Words and Meanings*), the propitiation of demons with the thread-cross effigies (briefly explained as repeating the preceding three times, and doing such a ritual with individual thread-cross effigies for each spirit who is harming one), and the repairing of the life-form with curative techniques (the above-mentioned individual techniques for reversing death in correlation with the specific signs).

The practice begins with general activities: giving ritual feasts, offerings, and so forth to one's root master, dedicating oneself to the activities revolving around the two accumulations of merit and insight, meditating on the two yogic phases of generation and perfection, doing "life" meditative actualizations, and training in many "supporting links" (*rten 'brel*). In particular, however, the rituals for the supporting links of the elemental energies must be performed, since obviously the danger of death stems from the disorder of the body's elements. Thus the actual ritual takes part in two phases: (1) using drawn maṇḍalas energized through visualization to rebalance one's disordered elemental energies so as to recover health; and (2) an effigy "ransom" in which one convinces the guilty spirits to accept a substitute effigy and thus not just re-create the disease once again within oneself. In *The Treasury of the Supreme Vehicle*, Longchenpa prefaces the tantra's description of the ritual by saying that through the triad of accumulating spiritual virtue toward a special field, making the wheels of supporting links (the elements), and tricking the demons with an effigy, one can reverse momentum from a diminished life force propeling one to an impending death.

(1) On five separate pieces of Chinese paper or a palm tree leaf one draws one circle apiece with four spokes, encircling hoops, and a center. On each wheel one draws one of the respective elements' seed syllables five times (at the center and

four spokes): on the earth wheel one draw five *laṃ*, on the water wheel *khaṃ*, on the fire wheel *raṃ*, on the wind wheel *yaṃ*, and on the space wheel *ae*. The consonants and vowels are drawn as encircling rims around these. The key to reversing death is rectifying the disbalance in one's body's elements; the elements' seed syllables represent their inner energy vibrations, while the Sanskrit alphabet is also symbolic of energy vibrations and is said to be the esoteric dimension of the body's seminal nuclei, namely, its high-energy nuclei of inner elements. Each wheel is then colored in correspondence with the element it represents—yellow for earth, white for water, red for fire, green for wind, and blue for space. Then having generated each of the five elemental deities in the center of their respective wheels, the actual gnostic forces dissolve into the visualized images. Thus one makes offerings to them, praises them, and supplicates them for the reversal of one's dying. One then recites their respective syllables in numbers equivalent to one's own age, consecrates them with the mantra "the nucleus of interdependent origination," and says a benediction. One then imagines the syllables dissolving into the respective deities. At this point, one inserts each wheel into individual new clay vesseles with closable lids and ties them off with five-colored wool yarn.

Then from the effigy-dough, which is a combination of barley dough with types of earth, water, fire, and wood, and breathed on by different species of sentient beings (such as horses and elephants), one makes a human form one cubit in size. This "dough" is generally barley flour mixed with tea and rolled into a ball, which is then eaten in other circumstances—here it is preceded with the pronoun "I" (*ngar zan*), indicating it is to be utilized as one would use clay for making an effigy of the threatened person. Holding this barley dough in front of creatures' mouth infuses it with their breath, such that the potency of their life force is imparted into the effigy (the breath contains life force). Hence the effigy is given force and vitality that will allow it to be accepted by the demons causing troubles as a substitute for one's own life force, which the demons are close to obtaining. In a similar way, the bits of earth, water, and so forth insert the potency of these five elements into the barley dough so as to empower the effigy; one also inserts a drawn *raṃ* in the effigy's eyes, a *yaṃ* in its ears, a *khaṃ* in its nose, a *laṃ* in its tongue, and an *ae* in its heart, thereby energizing the five sensory faculties with the seed syllabic energy of the five elements.

In this way one first brings the elements' pure energy into an activated form through creative imagination and contains that energy in the vases; second, one creates a sculpture of oneself containing within it real bits of the five elemental energies from the living world around one; and finally, with the little bits of paper inserted into that effigy one links that effigy with the pure energy, thereby generating the healing process.

(2) Thus one makes effigies of oneself which are red, yellow, white, black, green, and multicolored, dying them with white earth, red earth, and so forth, equivalent in number to one's own age (some sources specify that one dye them the colors of the five elements). These colors can be correlated to different types of spirits that they will attract: blue-black to demons, red to the fierce spirits,

white to the king spirits, yellow to the infectious spirits, green to serpent spirits, and multicolored to the demons of the dead. These are then arranged in a line atop a mat and so forth, amidst which are scattered a variety of grains and precious materials.

These human forms are adorned with "space," "tablets," five-colored yarn, and the down of an evil omened bird, or with scrapings of precious materials, colored wool, pieces of silk, and many feathers of evil-omened birds (such as an owl) stuck into these effigies. "Space" is the term for the thread-crosses used in these rituals, which in their simplest form consist of two crossed sticks with colored thread wound around their ends to form diamond-shaped "webs," which are referred to as "sky" or "space." They are accompanied by stylized images on small "tablets" (of the person, threatened possessions, and so on), which act as an effigy or substitute for the threatened person or thing.

One's own urine, hair, nail clippings, mucus, phlegm, excrement, and pieces of clothing must be embedded within the effigies, in addition to clothing them with a sleeve or hem/fringes from one's clothing. In front of each effigy, one carefully arranges a sacrificial cone of the corresponding color, "hand-molds" equal in number to one's age (formed by squeezing a ball of dough between one's hands so that it has an elongated form with wavelike indentations), and a "button" (small tetrahedrons formed from pressing the thumb into bits of dough). These diverse shapes of dough are transformed ritually into various associated things that are able to satisfy the demonic spirits.

Etching indentations equal in number to one's age on notched tablets (*khram shing*) of willow and birch, one plants them in the left shoulders of all the effigies. Nebesky-Wojkowitz explains that the "notched tablet" is a hexagon-shaped wooden tablet covered with notches in the form of leaning crosses (544) that is carried as a magic weapon by many Tibetan deities as well as used in Tibetan rituals (358–59). When used as a magic weapon to destroy the life of an enemy, the number of notches should correspond to the number of years of the potential victim's age; in the present case their function is to further coerce or trick the demons into accepting the effigies as a substitute for the otherwise dying individual.

Then one imagines the arrangement of these ritual substances is emptied out with the intonation of *raṃ*, *yaṃ*, *khaṃ*. These are the seed syllables of fire, wind, and water, corresponding respectively to burning, dispersing, and cleansing, the elemental forces that purge these substances into emptiness. Intoning *oṃ āḥ hūṃ*, one then imagines the offerings to possess the five sensual qualities (the best of scents, and so forth) and empowers them to grant all desires, while by chanting the mantra *namaḥ sarva-tathāgatebhyo viśva-mukhebhyaḥ sarvataḥ-khaṃ udgate sparaṇa imaṃ gagana-khaṃ* one increases them until they are equal in extent to the sky. A gloss in the tantra indicates that in empowering these effigies one use "the six mantras and the six seals," which are a standard series of ritual incantations and gestures "used especially in the contemplative generation from Emptiness of ransoms or substitutes" (see Beyer 346). Thus these actions serve to "bless" or "empower" the sacrificial cone and effigy offerings through visualization and recitation, thereby transcending empty ritual and becoming a reality that fulfills its magical function of ransoming one's death.

For the dedication, one imagines the elemental deities along with the "guests"—the eighty thousand types of "hindering demons," the Lord of Death, and the karmic creditors—and offers all this to them. One dedicates it to them by chanting the four lines given below seven times. The "karmic creditors" (literally "lusting for an answer") refers to all those spirits impeled to harm one by virtue of the powerful memory of previous crimes one inflicted upon them in other lifetimes, and who have thus entered one's current life seeking a debt repaid; the hindering demons are a variety of demons who create obstacles, large and small, in one's path throughout life. In this ritual, one invites these demonic forces whose malignant influences have caused this life-crisis to be one's guests—along with the Lord of Death who must be allayed in particular (since after all it is one's death that the ritual is intended to avert)—to whom one makes offerings of the effigy in the hope that they will accept these as a substitute or ransom for oneself, and thus can be "tricked" out of forcing a premature (not karmically necessitated) death. The chant of this mantra, which applies to all ritual interactions with such nonhuman spirits, goes thus:

> Take it away, take it away, O powerful ones!
> May craving, attachment, and addictions,
> Memory, apprehension, thought, and contact
> Be relaxed, calmed, and freed!

After that, one imagines that they have carried away the effigy for one's own welfare, and thus death has been ransomed. One combines the ritual substances together in a vessel and carries them along with the five wheels to the center of a stream, where one leaves them. Thus for up to three years one is free from any possibility of untimely death due to the agitation of internal elements and untimely death due to demonic forces. This rite should be performed once every three years.

Reviving the Dead for One Last Instruction: The Suchness of the Eyes

In case the dying person dies before the lama's precepts have been fully delivered and had a chance to take effect, a special mouth-to-mouth contemplatively energized resuscitation is used to revive the person. Longchenpa (in TCD) outlines three types of precepts to be applied in the process of dying: the most experienced practitioners simply focus on the expanse/awareness, the intermediately experienced do "transference of consciousness," and the least experienced are exhorted and instructed by someone else. In the third case, if the dying person dies before the lama's precepts have been fully delivered and had a chance to take effect, a special mouth-to-mouth contemplatively energized resuscitation is used to revive the person. Longchenpa explains that this precept pertains to cases where the person dies while the oral precepts are being given, or the person's own spiritual tradition is dissimilar (and thus will not know or be prone to heed these precepts), such that even in these cases the person can still be helped by means of these three types of esoteric precepts. *The Treasury of the Supreme Vehicle* explains the practice thus (TCD2 420.1ff):

> When the dying person's external breath has ceased but the internal breath continues, for an instant one must meditatively abide within the wisdom of reality's immediacy. Then one should join one's mouth and nostrils [the "three doors"] to the deceased's mouth and nostrils as the deceased's internal breath is near to cessation, breathe out three times, and inhale three times. In the first breath out, one should exhale while visualizing one's breath as a white *oṃ*; on the second breath out one exhale with one's breath visualized as a red *āḥ*; and on the final breath one exhales, without visualizing anything at all. As for the three breaths drawn inward, one visualizes one's breath as a *hūṃ* and pulls the deceased's cognition as a dark blue *hūṃ* toward one's own awareness. Also in each inhalation one verbally intones *hūṃ* as one forcefully pulls in the lower intestines [along with the dying person's consciousness symbolized by one's visualized *hūṃ*]. Engendering strength in one's own body, speech, and mind, one pulls [that person's psychic essence] into oneself with magnetic force [and thus infuses it with revitalizing energy]. It is certain that at this time the deceased's own hot breath will come into one in a gentle mist [i.e., with one's forceful inhalation the reviving breath is pulled into one's lungs, which is experienced as a gentle warmth in contrast to the usual cold or neutrally temperatured breath one inhales from the external environment. One's own physical, verbal, and mental energies come into play in the breathing, intonation, and visualization, respectively, of these three syllables, which themselves symbolically incarnate the enlightened body (*oṃ*), speech (*āḥ*), and mind (*hūṃ*). In this way one stimulates the triune energy of the dying person with one's own meditatively energized triune energy and enables the dying person to regain consciousness and strength temporarily.]
>
> In this moment the other's eyes will become wide open and alert, and then the body as well will abruptly be able to sit up. When this comes to pass, one displays the eyes' suchness, the manifestation of reality's immediacy: when the eyes open up wide, one has the person look at the introduction to the empty seminal nucleus lamp by pressing the eyes with the thumb and finger, and then one says the following three times: "Precisely this is the radiant light present within one! When it emerges from your body, the reality intermediate state's natural self-presenting manifestation is precisely this and, thus, not other than yourself—recognize it as your own essence!" If the person makes some type of cry or sound of acknowledgment when one says "Do you see the visions? Do you understand the precepts?" that is excellent, and even some type of gesture on the person's part is sufficient to indicate one's words have hit home and the person has understood their import. Thus that person will attain a nonconceptual contemplation within the reality intermediate state and is certain to be expansively awakened.

A fourteenth-century text attributed to the voice of Padmasambhava (KGNT2 182.3–183.3, 186.5–187.3) gives a variant account of this as "a technique for revival if the person's mental powers have deteriorated and their external breath ceased." One needs to revive the dying person's mental powers to refresh his or her memory on the dying-precepts and help focus his or her energies for the spiritual opportunities afforded by dying and postdeath experiences. Here one also joins one's mouth and nose to the dying person's, but the visualization is such that a white *oṃ* comes from one's right nostril, a red *āḥ* from one's left nostril, and a blue *hūṃ* from one's mouth, which are all visualized as dissolving into the dying person's corresponding apertures. Thus one first joins one's right nostrils in the first exhalation, then the left nostrils in the second, and then the two mouths in the third; between the right nostrils flows the wind energy of the adamantine enlightened body, between the left nostrils flows the wind energy of the adamantine enlightened speech, and through the two mouths flows the wind energy of the adamantine enlightened mind of all the buddhas. With the respective visualizations one exhales three times, and thus one's own syllable-empowered breath mixes with the dying person's syllable-empowered breath. As one inhales three times with a long drawn-out breath, warmth emerges in the dying person's body and the eyes open wide. At that moment one must refresh and clarify the person's mind by saying the following three times: "Hey son (daughter) of the family! Don't be attached to the impure appearances and experiences of this life! Don't be fixated on them!" He then goes on to add that one next sticks a bamboo tube or rolled up paper into the person's ear, and he gives a more detailed set of instructions describing the experiences the person will encounter and how to relate to them, which should also be repeated three times to the dying person.

Three Rituals for Purifying Negative Rebirths

We have now reached the end of the process and accordingly the focus shifts to dealing with the already deceased person in the form of his or her corpse or symbolic representation. Skorupski summarizes Tibetan death rituals into four central practices: the transference of consciousness, the recitation of *The Great Liberation upon Hearing in the Intermediate State*, the ritual with an effigy card, and the cremation ceremony. In turning toward the way in which a spiritual practitioner can be of aid once a person is in the last stages of dying or has actually passed away, Longchenpa presents a closely related triad of "purification rituals" for eliminating the possibility of the person being reborn back in saṃsāra: a version of the transference of consciousness, a "corpse purification" using ritually energized ablution of the corpse and the "seven-day juncture" ritual involving an effigy- or name-card into which the deceased's consciousness is channeled.

(1) *The Treasury of the Supreme Vehicle* describes the first practice in detail (TCD2 422.5–423.4). In particular it indicates that it is taught for guiding ordinary people (who are not spiritually trained and thus not able to master the

process of dying on their own) to the higher states of rebirth. One has the dying person visualize a white *a* or egg-sized globe of light in his or her heart and imagine it moves upward (with the symbolic force of the person's consciousness going upward to higher states of rebirth). One oneself as well visualizes the dying person's consciousness in that form and movement, thereby providing additional impetus to the visualization. Then for a short time one chants *a* in number equal to the person's age in conjunction with long exhalations and drawing out the vowel sound. When the dying person's breath starts to rattle and become erratic, by focusing on the crown of the person's head and chanting *a* twenty-one times vapor will waft upward. Even if the person was given to evil during her or his lifetime, this will lead to a higher rebirth, while if she or he was given to intellectualized theory and meditation it will lead to the recognition of reality itself.

If the person evidences signs of a rebirth in hell, then when breath ceases one must imagine the person's consciousness as an *a* at the heart or navel, which dissolves into five-colored light. Through one's own mind concentrating there for a moment, one leads her or him upward through the six states. Leading the dying person progressively upward from the six states of starving spirits, animals, demigods, gods, and humans, one guides her or him to birth as a human and liberation. Thus this is a ritual that brings benefit through the technique of obtaining the "higher" bliss without experiencing the "lower" suffering, higher and lower referring to the six types of rebirth: the lower realms are marked by intense suffering, while the higher realms are characterized by their relative blissfulness and degree of autonomy. In addition, this ritual of sequentially leading the dying person's psyche upward through the six realms of rebirth should be performed if the person dies while the above visualization is being done, although if one is able to complete the initial visualization prior to death, that is sufficient in itself.

(2) *The Treasury of the Supreme Vehicle* (TCD2 423.4–424.6, 426.1–5) gives a detailed commentary on the second practice as well:

> In front of the corpse, you make a two cubit-sized maṇḍala and so forth, sprinkle it with water fragrant with such scents as saffron. Then in the middle of a drawn and attractively colored eight-petaled lotus you place a vase. The vase can be of clay or precious materials, but in either case it should be colored with a white-wash, adorned at the spout [with flowers, peacock feathers, and so forth], and possess a "mantra cord" tied around its neck. Its five colors are symbolic of the five currents of vibrant energy [the five lights are the pure form of the five elements], which are symbolically incarnated by the five buddha-families. Filling the vase with clean, pure water along with the "vase substances" [often enumerated as twenty-five, these are substances one put in the vase for ritual reasons], on its four sides you place a written *a* with cinnabar [bright red] or realgar [red orange].
>
> Within this vase imagined as an inconceivably splendid mansion of five-colored light, you visualize the teacher, the All Good One, as dark blue in lotus posture with hands in the gesture of contemplative equanimity and in sexual union with his white consort. At the compass points with that pair at the center, one imagines the buddhas

of the five families: [one buddha is at the center indivisible or below the All Good One pair and the other four buddhas are arrayed at the four compass points]. Above is the lineage of spiritual masters in this tradition. In that instant inviting the [real deities], they dissolve [into the visualized forms], and then you do the ritual service [of chanting and visualization] of *oṃ āḥ hūṃ svāhā* and *a* one hundred thousand times [thereby empowering or blessing the water within the vase].

[Having thus given rise to the spiritual energy, one now employs it] by chanting "*oṃ a bhya rgya taṃ keṃ*, all of this person's sins and obscurations *śāntim kuruye svāhā*" [the latter three words are Sanskrit for "may they all be pacified!"]. Taking hold of the mantra cord and visualizing yourself as Vajrasattva, you imagine that through light rays emanating from you and coiling around the mantra cord across to the vase, nectar descends from the individual bodies of the masters and deities by force of the light rays striking them. The vase thus fills up with this nectar. Praising those deities with whatever offerings and praises you know, finally through chanting "*a, a*," the gnostic beings depart and you imagine the visualized beings ["commitment beings"] melt into the water. [The visualized beings are termed "commitment beings" since the visualization is a type of visual commitment. Into these visualized forms the actual "deities" then descend in actuality, such that their vibrant energy can be employed or utilized for the ritual, magical, or soteriological purposes for which they were evoked.]

Then you place this vase on the corpse's head and chant *a* in number equal to the deceased's age. Next visualizing that the vase's water is a flow of the five primordial gnoses' water, you give ablution [to the corpse] while chanting *a*. In doing this you imagine that all obscurations are purified, such that by chanting many *a* syllables, it is certain the deceased person's consciousness will be lead away from the rebirth states of hell. Then you hold the vase at the corpse's throat and give ablution while chanting *bhya* in number equal to his or her age, such that he or she is thus lead away from the starving spirits. Then holding the vase above the genitals [the "secret spot"], the deceased is led away from the animal realms through doing this in conjunction with the visualized syllable *rgya* and its recitation. The vase is next held at the armpit, where by chanting *keṃ* and then giving ablution, he or she is lead away from the demigod realms. Then the vase is held at the head, where by chanting *taṃ* and then giving ablution, that person's psyche is lead away from the god realms.

Then by chanting *oṃ āḥ hūṃ svāhā* while holding the vase at the heart and giving ablution, vile human rebirths are purified away; having thus lead the deceased to a precious human body, you guide her or him to a rebirth endowed with the karmic fate of gaining liberation in that very life. Having done these rituals for three, five, or seven days, when the corpse's remains are incinerated or taken away, it is impossible that the signs marking either freedom from rebirth or a distinguished next rebirth as a god or human will not emerge in the sky at that time. . . .

If the person hasn't yet died, you observe those of the six signs that show up and then visualize the corresponding syllables of those rebirth states, pulling them upward with the breath. [Since by doing this the person's psyche is pulled upward,] the vase is not necessary. However following the person's death, the appropriate procedure is

> to visualize those syllables on the corresponding sites of the corpse and lead the deceased's psyche up through the rebirth states via giving ablution with the vase. Furthermore, even if the person has already taken rebirth in some nonhuman state, through force of this ritual's blessings the life span in those realms [hell and so forth] will be as a brief dream—having run its course in a mere instant, a second or a flash, that person will be reborn in a human realm.
>
> One might object that the chief or best of rebirths is that of a god rather than a human, but in actuality this is not the case. If you exert yourself on the support of a human existence, in one lifetime you can attain liberation and thus be able to proceed to ever higher states. On the other hand, the gods eventually fall down from their rarefied states and are unable to obtain liberation. If they cannot even accomplish special ordinary virtue [since their capacities are not a suitable support for initial ordination, full monastic ordination, and so forth], of course there can be no question of them being able to accomplish the inconceivable supreme virtue. Thus although certainly it is a moral offense, killing such a god does not engender the severe karmic culpability of a major transgression and is considered an "expiable transgression," while should you kill a human it entails a fundamental and "self-destructive" root transgression. For these reasons, it is a human body that is said to be "the chief of life forms, or rebirths."

These transgressions are particulars of the monastic code, which classifies moral downfalls or transgressions into five types. While certain transgressions can be overcome through confessing them to the spiritual community and renouncing the object of that transgression, other transgressions are so major that the guilty party is invariably expelled from the monastic community and thus are termed "defeats." Though all killing of life is considered wrong, it is believed there are gradations in terms of moral culpability ranging from the inadvertent killing of an insect to the intentional murder of a human being for selfish reasons. Thus Longchenpa points out that since a god's life is basically devoid of moral value—consisting of "blissed-out" states without benefit to others or possibility of spiritual refinement—killing a god is not nearly as severe in terms of karmic consequences as the murder of a human being, a life form that is of potential great benefit to other sentient beings and that contains the possibility for spiritual growth even from an apparently evil or indifferent start (such as Milarepa).

(3) The "seven-day juncture" ritual, which in its fullest form is performed for forty-nine days following death, is the principal death ritual performed for lay people in the Nyingma tradition. The term "seven-day juncture" refers to the belief that postmortem existence is divided up into phases that last seven days apiece; the corresponding rituals intended to influence that existence thus themselves also often take place in seven-day units. Lauf (74–85, 118–30) briefly describes a classic version drawn from Karmalingpa's *The Profound Doctrine of Wisdom's Natural Freedom [in Encountering] the Peaceful and Wrathful Deities*, which he begins by outlining the ritual's general facets. The lama summons the deceased's consciousness into a name card or table with the deceased's picture and name on

it, which symbolically represents the dead person's consciousness-energy now wandering through the postdeath states. Via this name card, the lama gives the person a series of teachings and empowerments relating to the various experiences of deities and rebirth sites he or she will encounter during the postdeath stay in the intermediate state. These teachings or conversations not only offer a general guide to the person's experiences, but also provide spiritual advice enabling him or her to best use these experiences to become liberated. A large part of this consists of evoking the one hundred peaceful and wrathful deities appearing sequentially after death through words and painted cards, which the deceased is exhorted to contemplate (most of Lauf's book then describes these deities' symbolic significance). The master acts as a guide through this state's confusion, so that the deceased can overcome the various pitfalls and at last obtain enlightenment or at least a positive rebirth.

The central part of the ritual is performed on the sixth day of the reality intermediate state, when the deceased person visually experiences the six buddhas (corresponding to distinctive forms taken in each of the six realms so as to best suit living beings there) appearing along with the maṇḍala of the five peaceful buddhas. Forming part of the overall maṇḍala of one hundred peaceful and wrathful deities, they are understood as emanations of Avalokiteśvara, and thus as corresponding to the emanational body dimension. In the corresponding ritual, the deceased in the form of his or her name-card is sequentially led through each of the six realms represented by their corresponding seed syllables on a cosmic diagram in the following order: the realms of hell beings, starving spirits, animals, demigods, human beings, and gods. As the name card is progressively moved through, and liberated from, these six realms, the lama recites descriptions of each realm's particular sufferings, introduces him or her to the special buddha corresponding to that realm who can offer salvation to its beings, and ritually closes off the realm as a rebirth site for the deceased. In addition, bowls of rice are offered to the buddhas of the six realms, and sacrificial cones are offered to the evil and demonic spirits of the lower, both of which are set out on the maṇḍala in the corresponding place. In this way the deceased is able to depart from each of the six realms and enter the path to enlightenment.

Longchenpa's *The Treasury of Words and Meanings* describes the seven-day juncture death ritual in accordance with *The Tantra of Sun and the Moon's Intimate Union* as performed for either twenty-one or forty-nine days following death in the case that the corpse is no longer present. The ritual is explained in very simple terms as involving the generation of deities within the vase just as in the second practice, performing similar offerings, praises, and recitations, and then doing the following four ritual activities directed toward the deceased through the symbolic intermediary of the name card into which his or her consciousness is summoned: give ablution, show the path, explain doctrines, and finally purify in gnostic fire through burning. The final burning of the card indicates the consumption of the last tie to this incarnation, as well as the transformative fire of gnosis which can yet purify his or her consciousness into an awakened spirit if the master's precepts are heeded. *The Treasury of the Supreme Vehicle* provides further details (TCD2 426.7–431.4), in which context Longchenpa characterizes it as the "nonelaborate version" in contrast to a much more elaborate set of rituals found in *The Self-Emergent Perfection Tantra* (which he does not explain):

> Those who delight in elaborate forms should do the ritual as explained in *The Self-Emergent Perfection Tantra* with the maṇḍala of the six types of beings, recitation of the rebirth environments, transmitting food, and so forth; those who don't need the elaboration should do it with the above ritual. To elaborate on [the latter], the ritual can be performed in superior, average, and inferior fashion in accordance with the extent of the patron's financial means: the inferior is to do the ritual of leading upward through the six types of realms for one day, the average is do it for seven days, and the superior is to perform it for all seven weeks that the deceased may travel through the postdeath intermediate states.

[Thus, actual form of the ritual—whether elaborate or nonelaborate—depends on the officiating lama's inclination, while the length depends on the benefactor's financial resources.]

> In terms of the procedures of the ritual, you first arrange the maṇḍala and vase, generate the deity in visualization as yourself *and* within the vase, invite the gnostic beings [the *real* deities] so that they dissolve into the visualized deities, and do the recitations. Making offerings and praises to them, you must give ablutions to the deceased's name card, explain the causes and effects of karma as well as the many religious doctrines of the Mahāyāna, and teach the purification along the path to the deceased's consciousness as symbolically present in the name card.
>
> You should recite such passages as the following from *The Tantra of the Illuminator's Enlightenment* in order to "explain doctrines":
>
> In this transitory world the omniscient one
> Is like the extremely rare *uduṃwāra* flower—
> Not only rare, but also of uncertain duration
> As, even should he manifest, he will become unmanifest [subsequently].
>
> If the deceased has seen the gateway to these religious precepts [i.e., had some spiritual experience in his or her previous lifetime], you recite these teachings as many times as possible. For "purification along the path," you recite in abbreviated form the doctrines on the postdeath intermediate state, or ordinary exoteric precepts:
>
> Having relied on the fivefold path—
> The path of accumulation, the path of union,
> The path of vision, the path of cultivation,
> And the unsurpassed extraordinary path
> Which is the path of enlightenment divested of obstacles—
> May you traverse the path of the exalted!
>
> Also in indicating the path, you may recite:

May you be born in the Blissful pure land,
Which emerges from the lotus of fictive existence
Undefiled by the stains of the three states of fictive existence,
Just as a lotus is undefiled by the mud it grows from.

["The lotus of fictive existence" refers to an awakened buddha, who emerges up out of the mire of saṃsāra, yet is completely undefiled by it in his splendid unfolding. The pure land is directly manifest from the buddha as his enlightened display, whereby he compassionately manifests this subtle realm providing optimal conditions for sustained meditative practice and realization. Thus these verses indicate the path up out of the mire of saṃsāra for the deceased's wandering consciousness, illustrating how its possible by giving the example of a lotus rising unstained from the mud. Just so, the deceased must be inspired to free herself or himself of fictive existence and ascend to the rarefied purity of the Blissful pure land where spiritual aims can be one pointedly pursued.]

For those deceased who had embarked on this [path of the Great Perfection] during their lifetime [and particularly the direct transcendence practice], the path to the three spiritual bodies must be taught. . . .

[At this point, Longchenpa provides the content of this teaching in a lengthy quotation from *The Self Emergent Perfection*, which is a detailed description of the spiritual realms (with their main buddhas and precepts being taught) as arrayed in the ten directions of the cosmos, and presented as a direct address to the deceased. Thus it is like a type of spiritual tour guide for the deceased, with the ultimate intention of evoking the experience of the three bodies' inseparable identity.]

. . . Having recited that, you dedicate the merit, say prayers of aspiration, and recite a benediction. This ritual is taught especially for those who are disciples of the natural Great Perfection and hence is more profound and in general superior to the corresponding ritual of "seven-day juncture" as explained in the ordinary, exoteric secret mantras. Thus it must be performed with an authentic adamantine master of these doctrines presiding over the ritual as the master of ceremonies.

The text of the *Tshig don mdzod* below is translated from the edition of Klong chen rab 'byams pa's *Mdzod bdun*, published by Sherab Gyaltsen and Khyentse Labrang in six volumes; Gangtok, Sikkim (1983).

Further Reading

For an account of the originations of the intermediate state in Buddhism, see Bryan Cuevas, "Predecessors and Prototypes: Toward a Conceptual History of the Buddhist *Antarābhava*," *Numen* 43.2 (1996). For general background on Tibetan rituals, meditation, and beliefs concerning death, see Glenn Mullin, *Death and*

Dying: The Tibetan Tradition (New York: Arkana, 1986). For a brilliant account of Tibetan ritual, including many death and dying related ones, see Stephan Beyer, *The Cult of Tārā: Magic and Ritual in Tibet* (Berkeley: University of California Press, 1973). For an account of a Nyingma cremation ceremony, see Tadeusz Skorupski, "The Cremation Ceremony According to the Byang-gTer Tradition" (*Kailash*, no. 9, 361–76). For a translation of important parts of Karmalingpa's cycle, see Francesca Freemantle and Chogyam Trungpa, *The Tibetan Book of the Dead* (Boston: Shambhala Publications, 1987). For a detailed discussion of that cycle, see Detlef Ingo Lauf, *Secret Doctrines of the Tibetan Books of the Dead* (Boston: Shambhala, 1989). For a translation of the key Seminal Heart scripture, see Giacommella Orofino, *Sacred Tibetan Teachings on Death and Liberation* (Dorset, UK: Prism Press, 1990).

The preceding was principally based on the following Tibetan sources: *Theg mchog mdzod* (TCD), *Bi ma snying thig* (VNT), *Bla ma yang tig* (LYT), *Mkha' 'gro snying thig* (KGNT), *Mkha 'gro yang tig* (KGYT), and *Zab mo yang tig* (ZMYT). The first work is also published as part of the *Mdzod bdun* (see above), while the other five works constitute the massive *Snying thig ya bzhi*, published in eleven volumes by Trulku Tsewang, Jamyang and L. Tashi in New Delhi (1971), *The Seventeen Tantras of the Great Perfection* (*Rgyud bcu bdun*) of transcendental authorship. Kaneko nos. 143–159; also published separately in a three-volume edition based on the Adzom blocks (New Delhi: Sanje Dorje, 1973). For more precise references, please refer to my upcoming translation of *The Treasury of Precious Words and Meanings* as well as my associated monographs, tentatively entitled *Mysticism and Rhetoric in the Great Perfection* and *The Architecture of Absence and Embodied Visions*.

TECHNIQUES FOR EXAMINING WHETHER OR NOT YOU ARE ACTUALLY DYING

The Direct Consequence of Sound Tantra refers to twenty-one ways of examining whether or not you're dying:

> The signs of death are twenty-one in number:
> Going to a cemetery in an isolated spot,
> You must make offerings and praises to the spiritual master,
> And furthermore satisfy other beings as well
> With food and drink.
>
> Then you must examine the signs of dying,
> In their external, internal and esoteric dimensions.

Although these examination processes are clearly laid out in the esoteric precepts literature, in my extended discussion of them I will instead clarify them as a topic of the tantras themselves to contribute to people's trust and belief in them. According to *The Tantra of the Sun and Moon's Intimate Union*:

I. The intermediate state of dying is examined thus:
You devote yourself to determining the time of death
In an isolated spot or empty valley,
And should these signs evidence in you
It indicates your present embodiment's life is drawing to a close.

(1) If the fingernails and toenails are without luster or color,
Death is inevitable within nine months.

(2) If the whites of your eyes fade,
Death is likewise inevitable within five months.

(3) If the master of death, the Lord of the Dead, Yama, rises up,
Death will be in twenty-one days,
And nothing at all can change it.

(4) If the ankles swell or jut out,
Likewise death will be in one month.

(5) Should you be examining the body of another
When this person is laid up with illness,
If the bases of her teeth are discolored with grime,
She will die in nine days.

(6) Similarly if the nose flattens out,
Within five days he will come to die.

(7) If the limbs keep stretching out and contracting,
Death is inevitable within seven days.

(8) If the eyes are staring unblinkingly,
Within three days he will pass on.

(9) If the eyes' joints go totally awry,
She will die within half a month.

(10) If the cheeks become gaunt,
That person's life will similarly draw to a close
Within nineteen days.

(11) If breath becomes erratic and panting,
Death is certain within six months.

(12) If the nasal septum gets ruptured and twisted,
He will expire in seven days.

(13) If the eye's tear duct is rent,
She will expire within five days.

(14) If flesh is lost from the left cheek,
Within one day he will similarly expire.

(15) If the upper and lower teeth are clenched together,
Death is inevitable within three days.

(16) If a black spot shows up on the tongue,
That person will expire within two days.

(17) If the ears are sticking flatly against the head,
She will die that midnight.

(18) If the sternum's xiphoid collapses inward,
Death is inevitable within half a month.

(19) If the sleep artery [i.e., carotid] is no longer evident,
Death will take place in half a month.

II. When you are doing this for your own sake,

If your reflection within the dimension of space
Changes without stability and fades out,
Your death will be in but a month.

If the four limbs are cut off in this reflection, death will be in four months;
If above them the head is cut off, within three months;
If the upper and lower bodily parts are split in half, death will be within two months;
And if your body appears all balled up, in one month—
You must recognize their respective times.

(1) Should the link between sky and Earth
Come to be cut off,
You cannot last beyond nineteen days.

(2) If the man riding the white lioness falls off
On the slopes of the cosmic mountain,
Death is inevitable within sixteen days.

(3) If the waist of the wish-fulfilling tree is cut off
At the boundary between the mountain and the plains,
You should be examined by an expert.

(4) If the film on the ocean's water disappears,
The stages of these as well should be classified by an expert.

(5) If the smoke of the spiritual ascetic
Ceases within the city of earth,
You will similarly expire within nine days.

(6) If the unchanging Sun comes to set
At the peak of the cosmic mountain,
Within three days you will die.

> Totally divesting yourself of rituals,
> You should examine the presence of your own awareness' nucleus.
>
> (7) If the sound of the ḍākinīs cease
> Within the inner recesses of the cosmic mountain,
> Death will be in five or thirteen days.
>
> (8) Should the demonic Lord of Death raise up
> From the wish-fulfilling tree,
> Death is inevitable within seven days.
>
> Nothing will be of help [in reversing death then]:
> You should thus devote yourself to experientially tuning into emptiness,
> And since emptiness is endowed with a core of radiance,
> Radiance with a core of awareness
> And awareness with a luminous mansion,
> You should also devote yourself to tuning into the four lamps.

TECHNIQUES FOR REVERSING IMPENDING DEATH

The Direct Consequence of Sound Tantra also speaks of rituals of "ransoming" or "cheating" death:

> If the signs are negative, you must undertake to reverse the process;
> If they are positive, supplicate your spiritual master.

In thus explaining the esoteric precepts on techniques for reversing impending death in general and in extensive detail, I will cite *The Tantra of the Sun and Moon's Intimate Union* in order that you trust and believe in these methods as the necessary "back-support" in reversing impending death:

> When such signs show up in the body,
> The rites of ransoming death should be explained
> And that person should undertake the process of reversal.
>
> (1) You first amass the accumulations of [gnosis and merit]
> In relation to your master and spiritual compatriots,
> Pleasing this special field through gifts and feasts;
> Then you can begin these rites.
>
> (2) In order to balance the elements' sounds [in the body],
> You draw the following "wheels"
> On a leaf of a palm tree.
>
> The wheels are of the five elements,
> Each with four spokes, center, and encircling rims;
> In making these five wheels

Of earth, water, fire, wind, and space,
They should be colored differently
In accordance with each individual element's [standard color].

Each wheel's own letter is drawn five times
Within the quintet of its center and four spokes,
And is then further encircled by a rim of consonants.

You make offerings, hymns of praise, confess your sins,
Make supplications for whatever your particular desires are,
And then visualize the corresponding elemental deity at each wheel's center
While chanting the appropriate number of syllables,
Such that they then dissolve within the respective deities.

Then you insert all those wheels
Into individual clay vessels and seal their lids,
At which point you bind the vessels with five colors of threads in the shape of a cross.

You then combine together wood, water, fire, earth,
And the mouth vapor of different species of sentient beings
Mix them into a ball of effigy-dough,
And then shape it into a cubit-sized human form;
Finally you write the elements' five letters on writing paper
And individually insert each piece of paper
Into the corresponding one of the effigy's five sensory organs.

The elements' degeneration is thus checked and restored.

(3) If you have been possessed or seized by demons,
Balls of effigy-dough equivalent in number to your own age
Should be dyed with colors,
And bits of your own bodily secretions and clothes
As well as substances deriving from the elements
Should be mixed in with the barley dough,
Which are then made into human forms.

You should adorn those effigies
With bits of colored yarn, silk, and feathers,
As well as similarly prepare sacrificial cones
In corresponding colors.

The perimeter of these forms is surrounded
With effigy-dough balls in number equivalent to your age;
Empowering these, you intone these words:

"Take it away, take it away, O powerful ones!
May craving, attachment, and addictions,
Memory, apprehension, thought, and contact
Be relaxed, calmed, and freed!"

All these words should be repeated three times
And then the effigies carried to the center of a stream.

Dying's reversal is thus guaranteed
Beyond a shadow of a doubt!

THE APPEARANCES AT THE BRINK OF DEATH

These appearances derive from the contraction of your inner winds and channels in the dissolution process of the individual elemental energies. *The Tantra of the Sun and Moon's Intimate Union* says:

For whomever becomes stricken with physical illness
And subsequently experiences these signs' manifestation,
The time of death has arrived.

Earth dissolves into earth,
And similarly water, fire, and wind
Individually dissolve within themselves,
Such that your body changes in corresponding ways.

By earth self-dissolving within itself,
Your body becomes heavy, cannot take food,
And all its power to rise and move is exhausted.

When water dissolves within water,
Saliva and mucus trickle out from the mouth and nose.

Similarly by fire dissolving within fire,
Your mouth and nose become extremely dry,
And warmth dissipates from your body's extremities.

Similarly by wind dissolving within wind,
Your breath becomes wheezing and forced, your limbs convulse,
And your eyes roll upward.

For whomever these signs emerge,
It is certain that you will not remain long here in life,
But rather pass away to its other side.

THE ORAL PRECEPTS FOR A DYING PRACTITIONER

For those with the fortune and capacity for this tradition, the following oral precepts should be given and applied at this time. If these precepts are already clear within your own psyche, it is sufficient to merely recall and focus on them now [without needing additional oral explication]. There are two sets of key points here—"entering the sphere and abode" and "entering the spiritual bodies and primordial gnoses"—and you can utilize either on the spiritual path as befits your own circumstances.

(1) The first practice is "transference." When the last wind departs [from the body], you visualize your awareness in the form of your master's body [half a thumb in size with five colored light rays] or a white *āḥ* at the heart and imagine it shoots upward, up and away through the Brahmā's aperture. Simultaneously you intone twenty-one *hik* in rapid succession. Your freedom will thus be guaranteed.

(2) The second set of key points is as follows. As you die, you assume one of the three body postures or lay down in the manner of a lion, focus cognition within your eyes, and focus your eyes on the expanse and awareness. By then letting-be without contractions or projections within the range of original purity, you will be free within that very instant. If the expanse and awareness remain unclear, you must then encounter the postdeath reality intermediate state's manifestations with intact and unwavering trust. You will thus recognize reality as your own dimension and freedom will be certain, just as when you entrust a message to a dependable person, he or she will go inside and outside, up and down the village as necessary and deliver the message to the recipient. The *Tantra of the Sun and Moon's Intimate Union* describes these thus:

At this time, you must yourself become intimately acquainted
With the spiritual master's esoteric precepts,
And refresh your memory with these topics.

(1) If at this time vision is inherently clear
For a karmically fortunate person,
It is termed "cognition resting within itself without remaining [in distractions]."

When the single great wind propels your awareness forth
Following the sequential calming of your four inner winds,
The methods of entering the sphere and abode,
And entering the spiritual bodies and gnosis should be taught.

(2) The methods of entering the sphere and abode lies in the precepts
On "residence-transference" and "residence-entrance" of your consciousness:
Training on consciousness mounted upon the winds
You should prioritize increasing familiarization:
Concentrating on pulling in and propeling forth awareness,
Ultimately in death you propel it forth with a *hik*.

You should receive these teachings verbally from your own teacher.

(3) As to the method of entering the spiritual bodies and gnosis,
You must focus awareness thus:
With your body lying in the manner of a lion,
You focus awareness in your eyes
And instantly make space into the path.

If the expanse and awareness are devoid of fluctuation,
You will without a doubt expansively awaken within buddhahood
Without even passing through the intermediate state,
And even your breath in dying will be calm.

(4) Should the expanse and awareness be unclear,
You must focus your mind on the lights as previously taught
In order to take hold of awareness' lighting-up
Within the intermediate state of reality's bliss,
And thus attain the vision of truth.

If those precepts are not clear to you and assurance is lacking, your memory should be refreshed by your master or a spiritual intimate with intact commitments. Indicating immediacy's manifestation, they have you look to its presence and exhort you thus: "Since it is simply your own current awareness manifesting within the intermediate state that is referred to as 'the intermediate state of reality,' recognize it as your own self-presencing!" "Since your own current naked awareness is the site of original purity's freedom, look unwaveringly within its range!" These exhortations refresh your recollection of the dimension of breakthrough and direct transcendence.

If the person dies while these exhortations are being made, you join the sick person's mouth and nose with your own mouth and nose, forcefully exhale and then inhale. Thus the ceased breath is revived and the eyes open wide, at which time you give the person the oral precepts on introducing him or her to the eyes' suchness, the visionary manifestation of the lamps. Those with the sharpest of faculties will become free right then and there via those precepts, while the rest will become free [subsequently] within the postdeath reality intermediate state. Because the radiant light at that moment is like your escort, it aids you; and since reality's radiant light is like your host, it invites and welcomes you. By joining the two at the center, there is no possibility of deviating elsewhere, just as on the fifteenth the Sun's setting and the Moon's rising are simultaneous and hence there is no darkness. *The Tantra of the Sun and Moon's Intimate Union* explains these thus:

Should these not be clear in your mind,
If your own master is present
He should refresh your memory
Of the previously learned esoteric precepts;
If the master is absent, a spiritual brother or sister
Must make things clear.

If you are doing this for another's benefit,
In order to compassionately take care of her
You should join your three "gateways" to hers,
And apply the breath, inhaling and exhaling;
Because you must give rise to physical, verbal, and mental strength in
the person
Through activating the three syllables [*oṃ*, *āḥ*, *hūṃ*],
This should be done along with the breathing by an expert.

By doing this again and again,
Her experiences will be like this:

Should her physical strength be regained,
The previous oral precepts must be delivered;

However if her cognition clears up,
This person will settle into a contemplative equipoise in wisdom;

If her senses' gateways themselves become alert,
Then she should be made to look to the eyes' suchness.

If her mind comes to abide in equanimity,
She will attain a nonconceptual deep contemplation.

THE SIGNS OF BEING BORN IN ONE OF THE ORDINARY SIX TYPES OF REBIRTH

If the dying person is an ordinary being belonging to one of the six types, the sign of her or his impending rebirth in a particular life environment will be as follows. If she or he is a practitioner whose spiritual capacities are [relatively] "inferior," she or he will find respite in a pure field of enlightened emanations at death, which is indicated by warmth gathering at the crown as he or she dies. However, for others this indicates rebirth in a divine [though unenlightened] environment, which is indicated by the right arm simultaneously flopping or waving around. If warmth gathers at the soles, the left leg stamps the ground, and the eyes become blurry and clouded over in the process of dying, it indicates a rebirth in hell. Should warmth gather at the right armpit and she deliriously raves on, rebirth as a demigod is signified. When warmth gathers at the mouth, the body becomes yellowish and the eyes blur, it is a sign of rebirth as a starving spirit. If warmth gathers at the genitals, the dying person makes animal sounds and then becomes mute with his or her teeth locked together while the eyes cloud over, rebirth as an animal is indicated. If warmth gathers at the eyes, speech remain clear, and memory is devoid of deterioration, these signs indicate rebirth as a human. *The Tantra of the Sun and Moon's Intimate Union* explicates them thus:

(1) The external manifestations are like this:

Should the warmth fade away upward,
The dying person will breathe a great sigh
[And find respite within a pure field of emanations];

If the eyes become unclear and clouded over,
She will be reborn within one of the negative rebirths;

If the right arm flops around,
That person will be reborn in a divine environment;

If she deliriously raves on,
Rebirth in the environment of demigods is similarly indicated;
Stamping her left leg on the ground
Is a sign of rebirth in hell;

Her body becoming yellowish and losing its luster
Signifies rebirth in the realm of starving spirits;

Should creatures' noises bubble forth from his mouth,
It is a sign of rebirth in the animal world;

Or if she is mute with her teeth locked together,
It is similarly a sign of rebirth as an animal;

If speech is clear and memory devoid of deterioration,
That person will be reborn in a human environment.

(2) Those external signs are conjoined
With the following internal signs:

When warmth gathers at the crown,
That person will be reborn within a divine environment;

Likewise should the warmth gather at the soles,
Rebirth within a hell environment is signified;

If warmth gathers at the right armpit,
It is a sign of rebirth in the realm of demigods;

Similarly when the warmth gathers at the mouth,
That person will be reborn within the environment of starving spirits;

If warmth gathers at the genitals,
Rebirth as an animal is indicated;

Should warmth gather at the eyes,
That person will be reborn in a human environment.

For whomever possesses such signs while dying,
The corresponding rebirths are certain.

THE RITUALS FOR PURIFYING AWAY THE POSSIBILITY OF NEGATIVE REBIRTH

These rituals are threefold: the purification done while the person is still on the brink of death yet prior to the cessation of breath, the purification performed on the corpse, and the concluding purification.

(1) In the first practice, you visualize a white *āḥ* at the dying person's heart and direct your own mouth toward his or her crown [the desired point of departure for the dying person's psychic energy]. By then inhaling a long, flowing breath and reciting the syllable *āḥ* in number corresponding to the person's age [intoning one *āḥ* with each exhalation], the person's consciousness is gradually pulled upward [toward the higher gateways of departure from the body leading to more positive types of rebirth].

(2) To purify the corpse, in front of it you prepare [as described in other sources] a maṇḍala with a vase in the middle of a drawn four-petaled lotus. Having generated in visualization the buddhas of the five families along with the lineage of spiritual masters within the vase, you make offerings and praises to them. After chanting *oṃ āḥ hūṃ svāhā* as much as possible, you recite *a bhya rgya taṃ keṃ* as well for a hundred times, and with that vase water you give ablution to the corpse's crown, throat, heart, navel, genitals, and armpit—this is "the cleansing of the [rebirth] abodes."

(3) If the "seven-day juncture" ritual is performed as a conclusion [i.e., after cremation or if the corpse is not present from the beginning], it is as follows. Having generated the deity in visualization along with the vase, you make offerings, praises, and recitations like before. Then you give ablution to the name card [representing the deceased], indicate the path and explain the religious precepts to it, following which on the final night you burn the name card. Then you must dedicate this teaching of the path and say prayers of aspiration [for the sake of the eventual enlightenment of the deceased and others]. *The Tantra of the Sun and Moon's Intimate Union* describes these three purification rites thus:

> (1) In order to sequentially lead the dying person away from these rebirth states
> For the sake of spiritually sustaining her,
> Along with contemplation of the syllable *a*
> You conjoin that syllable's recitation [in number equaling her age] to your breath;
> If she has not died yet,
> You should visualize her psyche as an *a*
> Within her body's center, and gather it in
> By breathing with your mouth directed toward her crown.
>
> (2) When the person ultimately dies,
> You should place a vase on the crown
> Of her defiled body,

Purifying her corpse with the syllabic particle *a*
And a flow of gnostic water.
You thus eliminate the possibility of her rebirth in hell,
Such that the signs are similarly [lead away upwards].

For one evidencing signs of rebirth as a starving spirit:
With contemplation of the syllable *bhya*
You intone it seven times with your breath,
Place the *bhya* on her tongue in visualization,
And gather in her psyche's essence by means of it;
Similarly with the vase above her mouth,
You give ablution with a flow of gnostic water.
Having thus eliminated the possibility of rebirth as starving spirit,
That person as well is lead upward.

For one evidencing signs of rebirth as an animal:
You must purify those states
With contemplation of the syllable *rgya*—
Having recited it nine times with your breathing
And sealed her genitals with a visualized *rgya*,
Through thus eliminating her psychic energies there
You repeatedly impel them forth with the winds,
While similarly with the vase above the genitals
You give ablution with a flow of gnostic water.
Having thus eliminated rebirth as an animal,
That person as well is lead upward.

If the dying person evidences signs of a rebirth as a god:
With contemplation of the syllable *taṃ*
You intone it eleven times with your breath,
And thus purify her psyche;
Visualizing the syllable *taṃ* at her crown,
You pull her undefiled consciousness up to her eyes,
While similarly with the vase above her crown
You purify her consciousness with a flow of gnostic water.
Having thus eliminated the possibility of her rebirth as a god,
The dying person attains a human rebirth.

Should the person evidence the signs of rebirth as an demigod:
With contemplation of the syllable *keṃ*
You recite it twenty times with your breath,
And in her right armpit as well the syllable *keṃ*
Should be skillfully placed with visualization
As you give rise to a great equilibrium in her psyche;
Similarly with the vase above her armpit
You give ablution with a flow of gnostic water.

Having thus eliminated her rebirth as a demigod,
That person as well attains a human rebirth.

Having progressively transferred her consciousness upward through the rebirth states
By means of thus spiritually sustaining her,
Even if she has already taken rebirth in a nonhuman state,
Her lifespan in that rebirth will be progressively lessened
And she will thus subsequently quickly attain the bliss of a human rebirth.

If that person is still breathing
When these rituals are thus being performed,
By [applying] the appropriate syllable along with your breath,
Lower rebirths will be purified without any doubt [as you lead her upward].

Should her breath cease,
If you purify the corpse with a flow of gnostic water
From the vase held at her body's appropriate spot,
Success here as well is guaranteed.

(3) If there should be no corpse,
For up until twenty-one days
Following the person's death
You should exert yourself in the ritual on seventh-day junctures
With an emphasis on having genuine contemplation of the visualizations;
Alternatively, it should be done for seven weeks.

At that time, the path [to the spiritual bodies] must be taught to the deceased
And a variety of religious precepts explained.

Whoever has this ritual performed for them
Will obtain the definitive fruit
Without even the slightest doubt.

Some ignorant individuals of slight learning say "such guiding of a deceased person progressively upward through the six types of realms is not tenable—if you are able to guide them, it is sufficient to lead them directly to the buddha field!" If that is so, *The Purification Tantra*'s explanation of the mantra for purifying the negative actions corresponding to the six types of rebirth as well as its teaching of the path to the Blissful pure land would also be untenable, since accomplishing the expansive awakening of buddhahood by itself is sufficient! Even the ascension and purification progressively upward through the stages of the bodhisattvas and heroines would be untenable—if you can ascend, then it is sufficient simply to proceed to the state of expansive awakening without training in those stages!

The following counterobjection may be raised: "Sequentially purifying lower obscurations that haven't been refined away, after that life you will be born in the Blissful pure land and so on." This, however, can be shown to be similar to our own position here. Having purified these lower karmic tendencies with this ritual, the deceased is elevated upward and thus her progressive traversal upward as well is tenable and appropriate. In this way it can be seen that explaining in a single way and claiming no other ways are possible is ignorant—you must understand that the techniques and positions of the immeasurably many categories of religio-philosophic precepts are limitless.

—31—

Cards for the Dead

Per Kvaerne

Tibetan death rituals, both Buddhist and Bönpo, are extremely complex, but basically serve to guide the consciousness of the dead person, often through a succession of initiations, out of the cycle of rebirth and toward final liberation. The death rites of the Bönpo are said to have been formulated by the great teacher Shenrap (Gshen rab) himself. As with Buddhist death rituals, the consciousness of the deceased is believed to pass through several stages after death, at each of which the possibility of liberation exists; if it is not achieved at the first stage, it may be in the next. There is thus an acknowledged redundancy to the rituals, deemed necessary because death is regarded as a time of great crisis during which the opportunities for liberation are easily missed.

The Bönpo death rites have three parts. Immediately after death occurs, a ritual called "transference of consciousness" (*'pho ba*) is performed in which a Bönpo monk attempts to transfer the consciousness of the deceased directly from the cycle of rebirth to the state of liberation. For the next three days and nights, monks recite a text on "liberation from the intermediate state through hearing" (*bar do thos grol*, see chapter 30), which contains guidance for the deceased concerning the deities, both peaceful and wrathful, that it will encounter in the bardo.

Three days after death, a second ritual is performed in which the consciousness of the deceased is led progressively along the path to liberation. This ritual, which lasts approximately two hours, involves displaying various cards (*tsag li*) to a picture (*byang bu*) of the deceased. A portion of this ritual is translated below. This second ritual takes place in the home of the deceased and is performed by a chief monk and two assistants. The corpse is present in the room but is kept behind a cloth screen. The ritual begins with the chief monk making an effigy of the deceased out of dough and offering it as a "ransom" (*glud*) to malevolent spirits that might interfere with the ceremony. The effigy is taken outside and thrown away. Next, the consciousness of the deceased is summoned and asked to reside in a picture of the deceased. After cleaning the picture, the chief monk writes two series of seed syllables on it. The first series of six represent the six realms of rebirth, as a god, demigod, human, hungry ghost, animal, or hell being. The second series consists of the "five heroic syllables," which are antidotes to the rebirth in the six realms.

The next phase of the ritual involves the presentation of various gifts to the deceased. This is effected through the chief monk showing the picture of the deceased a series of cards on which the gifts are depicted. The cards are held up one by one and are then placed on the floor in front of the picture of the deceased, which has been set on the floor in front of the curtain that hides the corpse. The presentation of each card is accompanied by a ritual formula, each of which ends with the statement, "By the power of thus offering and giving, may the two obscurations [to liberation and omniscience] be cleansed and the two collections [of merit and wisdom] be gathered, and may mind itself obtain buddhahood." Initially, all the sensory faculties (sight, hearing, taste, etc.) of the deceased are satisfied symbolically by being invoked in turn, and a series of small, painted cards depicting the object of each faculty (beautiful forms for the eyes, melodious music for the ear, incense for the nose, etc.) are held up in sequence in front of an effigy of the dead person at appropriate moments during the recitation. In this way, whatever craving for material wealth and worldly power that the dead person may have experienced during his or her lifetime is appeased before the consciousness is prepared to receive initiations.

In the following passage, six spiritual qualities (knowledge, wisdom, right view, and so on) with which the deceased must be endowed are invoked. Each quality is symbolized by an animal, to which corresponds an appropriate ritual card. Three are from the ordinary animal world (yak, horse, and sheep), while three are from the realm of mythology (garuḍa, dragon, and lion). The three first are of particular interest as they played an important role in the pre-Buddhist mortuary rituals. These animals, sacrificed so that they might accompany the deceased in his or her existence after death, each had their own function: the sheep was to lead the way to the land of the dead, serving as guide along cliffs and across rivers on the difficult journey of the dead; the horse (which later was to become a common symbol of the mind for both Bönpos and Buddhists) was to serve as a mount for the deceased; and the yak was to enter into combat with spiteful demons and chase them from the path of the deceased. The three mythological animals are associated with the familiar Tibetan triad of the sky (garuḍa), atmosphere (dragon), and the earth (lion). Furthermore, whereas the first set of animals appear to have a strong connection to pre-Buddhist funerary practices, this next set of three mythological animals is associated with Buddhist concepts; they are said here to symbolize right view (*lta ba*), meditation (*sgom pa*), and practice (*spyod pa*).

With the deceased now ritually provided with satisfaction of all material needs and ritually endowed with the mental qualities necessary for progress toward liberation, it is time for the consciousness of the deceased to be led through the stages of the path to enlightenment. The picture of the deceased is shown cards depicting four groups of deities. The first group of four are the "six subduing *shen*" who compassionately manifest in the six realms of rebirth. Next are the "thirteen primeval *shen*" who liberate beings from the bardo and preside over the thirteen levels of the bodhisattva path. The next group of four includes four central Bönpo deities, including the teacher Shenrap. Finally, the deceased is shown a ritual card showing the buddha Kuntu Sangpo (Kun tu bzang po), the "All Good," the essence of all the buddhas.

The deceased, again through the use of ritual cards, is then given four initiations, after which he or she becomes an "unchanging mind hero" (*g.yung drung sems dpa'*), the Bönpo equivalent of a bodhisattva. As such the consciousness of the deceased now passes through the thirteen stages of the path, each symbolized with a ritual card painted with a swastika. These are placed in a row on the floor, and the picture of the deceased is moved forward one card as the qualities of that stage are recited. At the end of the row is a card showing Kuntu Sangpo. Before moving to that card and thereby symbolically becoming one with the essence of all buddhas, the chief monk takes a lighted stick of incense and burns the six syllables symbolizing the six realms of rebirth that he had written on the picture of the deceased, thus indicating its freedom from all future rebirth.

Finally, to bring about the final union with Kuntu Sangpo, the chief monk places his robe over his head and enters a state of meditation in which he unites his consciousness with that of the deceased. Thus identified with the deceased, he then unites his consciousness with Kuntu Sangpo. At this point, the deceased achieves liberation, and when the monk emerges from meditation, the picture of the deceased is burned and the ashes retained to be made into small religious figurines called tsatsa (*tsha tsha*).

The next morning, the third and final part of the death rite, the cremation of the corpse, takes place. Because the consciousness of the deceased is assumed to have achieved liberation by this point, the purpose of the cremation and subsequent offerings, unlike the previous rites, is not to lead the deceased to liberation, but instead affords the family and community an opportunity to accumulate merit by participating in a virtuous ceremony.

The ritual text from which this excerpt is taken was composed by the scholar Sonam Lodrö (Bsod nams blo gros), who was born in 1784 and became abbot of Menri monastery in 1810, after having received them as an auditory revelation from Sherap Gyeltsen (Shes rab rgyal mtshan, 1356–1415), the first abbot of the monastery.

Further Reading

For an illustrated study of the death ritual in which the following is recited, see Per Kvaerne, *Tibet Bon Religion: A Death Ritual of the Tibetan Bonpos*, Iconography of Religions 12.13 (Leiden: E. J. Brill, 1985), which contains an earlier version of the translation.

The divine yak, king of knowledge *(rig pa),* is presented.
In the wide field of the "all-foundation" *(kun gzhi)*
[Roams] the divine yak, king of knowledge-itself *(rang rig).*
On it various ornaments appear, [and] it is loaded with food.
Having proceeded along the path to liberation to the end,
It quickly reaches the field of great happiness,
And having obtained the absolute body *(bon sku)*
Original buddhahood is obtained *(ye sangs rgyas).*

The stallion of the spontaneously existing mind-itself *(rang 'byung sems nyid)* is presented.
In the field of the "all-foundation" of great happiness
—In order that the mind-itself should gradually proceed
Along the "stages" and the "paths"—
The stallion of practice arising from the mind *(sems 'byung spyod pa)*
[Carries] the saddle-rug, the crupper, and the stirrups of the clear light;
It is adorned with the bridle of mindfulness and the halter of watchfulness.
Tamed by the king of knowledge, having in the flash of a moment reached paradise *(mtho ris),*
The highest fruit [i.e., buddhahood] will be obtained.

The divine, magic sheep of wisdom *(ye shes)* is presented.
On the green pasture of the "all-foundation"
[Roams] the divine sheep of knowledge.
Its wool is the clear light; [from it is made]
The rope [for fastening] the load, and the clothes of patience.
Having put on [those clothes], all ignorance,
Actions of the round of birth and death, and obscurations are overcome
And in the sphere of Bön *(bon dbyings)* the fruit
In the form of the three bodies is obtained.

The great garuḍa, king of [right] view *(lta ba),* is presented.
The great garuḍa of knowledge soars in the sky.
With its wide wings it cuts off all error.
The obscurations spontaneously disappear
and original buddhahood is obtained.

The turquoise dragon, king of meditation *(sgom pa)*, is presented.
The great dragon of spiritual vision *(dgongs pa)* soars in midair.
It empties the pit of the round of birth and death, the three planes of existence.
The round of birth and death spontaneously disappears
and manifest buddhahood is obtained.

The great lion, king of practice *(spyod pa)*, is presented.
The great lion of practice stands proudly on the snow-mountain.
When all the darknesses of the five poisons have disappeared,
all suffering dissolves and perfect buddhahood is obtained.

— 32 —

Returning from Hell

Françoise Pommaret

Although the ultimate goal of a Buddhist is to escape the cycle of reincarnations (*saṃsāra*) and enter nirvāṇa, in Tibetan culture ordinary laypeople know that this is an almost impossible aim for them to achieve, and their first priority is to try to avoid "bad reincarnations." It is in this religious context that we can place the genre of texts called "the accounts of people who come back from the netherworld" (*'das log rnam thar*). The *delok* (*'das log*) are people, usually women, who "die" and then travel in the netherworld—hells, and less often paradises. They come back to earth to tell people what they have seen and bring messages from the dead to the living.

The delok's trip has a pattern different from other Buddhist descriptions of descents into hell found in Indian, Tibetan, Chinese, or Mongolian literature, and which involve great saints of Buddhism, such as the Buddha's disciple Maudgalyāyana or Padmasambhava. The latter may be called "savior's stories" because, in these cases, the saint does not "die" but, through his magical power, goes to hell with a definite purpose: to save a person who is close to him (see chapter 7). It is impossible to exclude some influence of the latter stories on the former, but they cannot be considered the same. To find a scheme comparable to the delok stories, one has to turn to China, where examples abound of an ordinary person who dies, goes to hell, and is sent back to earth.

Many of the images employed in Tibetan delok stories reflect the influence of elements that came from classical Indian Buddhism and then spread throughout Asia. The descriptions of the different hells, the judgment of the dead, and the association of each sin with a specific hell are close to Indian models, although the Tibetans have transformed or adapted these elements to their own culture. In addition to the influence of Indian and Chinese themes, Tibetan delok stories were subject to the influence of the indigeneous beliefs of Inner Asia, and particularly the Turco-Mongols, where shamans practiced the trip to the realm of the dead. Indeed, it is highly probable that the ancient pre-Buddhist Tibetans knew about this practice from their contacts with the Turco-Mongol populations. The birth of the delok phenomenon is certainly due to a confluence of beliefs from different populations, including the ancient Tibetans.

One may well wonder whether the delok have any historical reality or if they are merely an imaginary product of religious literature. Several textual elements clearly indicate the actual historical existence of people called delok. Their biographies usually give details of their birthplace, their parents' names, and their social background, although very often they omit the year of their birth and the year of their delok experience. While the biographical narratives actually provide only a little insight into the lives of the delok, they strongly emphasize the delok's desire to practice religion from a young age. Delok are also mentioned in the historical literature, albeit rarely, which provides valuable historical clues. Added to the information from the biographies, they make it possible to conclude that delok were indeed historical persons and to date both the first occurrence of the phenomenon and the earliest appearance of the biographies. Buddhist delok are attested to in the literature as early as the twelfth century, and thirteenth-century biographies of two Bönpo masters of the twelfth century describe them as having a similar experience. This convergence makes it possible to say that the twelfth century marks the appearance of the delok in Buddhist and Bön literature.

From their biographies it is known that the great majority of the delok came from the Nyingma and Kagyü milieux, which are allegedly less dogmatic than the Gelukpa. Between the twelfth and fourteenth centuries, these two religious sects underwent intellectual transformations that determined the formation of the delok literary genre. One of the dominant aspects of the delok stories is the place given to the cult of Avalokiteśvara, the bodhisattva who saves beings. The delok claim to be his incarnation, and their accounts are frequently punctuated with *oṃ maṇi padme hūṃ (hrīḥ)*, his mantra formula in six or seven syllables, which when recited is believed to save one from the realms of reincarnation (see chapter 2). The erection of prayer-flags carrying the *maṇi* formula is one of the most popular ways of helping the dead to be liberated from bad reincarnations. The religious storytellers who recite this formula, known as *maṇi pa*, also play the role of saviors of the dead in these texts. Their popularity, as well as that of the *maṇi* formula, was spread in the thirteenth century, largely by the great Nyingma "treasure-discoverer" (*gter ston*) Guru Chöwang (Chos dbang, 1212–1273). Interestingly enough, he was himself a "savior saint," as he went to hell to liberate his mother. The delok stories thus belong to the context of the soteriological cult of Avalokiteśvara that developed at this time.

However, the texts that certainly had the most immediate influence on the delok accounts were those in *Bar do thos grol* genre, the "Liberation in Intermediate State through Hearing." These texts are included in a large Nyingma collection called "The Peaceful and Wrathful Deities According to Karmalingpa" (*Kar gling zhi khro*). Karmalingpa was a "treasure discoverer" of the fourteenth century who is credited with the discovery of this collection. These texts deal not only with the intermediary state of passage between two incarnations, the *bar do*, but also the peaceful and wrathful deities and the whole liturgy of death rituals. A comparison between the *Bar do thos grol* texts and the delok texts reveals numerous thematic parallels. Yet, whereas the *Bar do thos grol* are ritual texts, with theoretical explanations set forth in an allusive and elusive literary style that is difficult for the ordinary layperson to understand, the delok texts are full of concrete examples and images, written in a popular style. Here is the raison d'être of these texts. Far from being an esoteric teaching written by and for the literate elite, the delok biographies are a religious teaching for the common people. The two fundamental notions of Buddhism, karma and reincarnation, were developed in the Tibetan context in order to be easily understood by each and every person. It is known that, as early as the Dunhuang manuscripts (seventh to ninth centuries), there was a conscious tradition to adapt abstract notions in a didactic and simple way. The delok biographies continue in this tradition of "teaching for the people."

What better way to convey to an uneducated person the abstract notion of karma than to use concrete examples taken from daily life in which he or she can see that an action brings about a retribution or a reward? Strong images strike a chord in people and remain imprinted in their memory. The delok accounts carefully detail the sinful actions of daily life, the physical relationship between sin and punishment, or between virtue and reward, and finally, the rituals that must be performed to earn merit. Some sinful actions are those that anyone may commit every day. Some involve the transgression of interdictions found in many societies: prohibitions against adultery, lying, robbery, breaking of religious vows, or mistreatment of another human being. Others, however, are related solely to Buddhism, or more particularly to Tibetan culture, and are intimately linked to the lives of Tibetans.

The vocabulary of delok accounts is simple. The use of everyday words makes the narrative easily comprehended by ordinary people. Moreover, stock phrases such as "when I was in the country of the human beings . . .", which open all the speeches of the people whom the delok meets, are frequent. The descriptions of the Lord of the Dead, his attendants, and the tortures endured in the hells are basically the same, with only minor variations, in all narratives. These stock phrases do not belong, however, solely to delok narratives. They find their origins in other texts, be they canonical or related to other genres of the vernacular literature. Nevertheless, the way they are pieced together, the stylistic homogeneity, as well as the mixture of religious teachings and simple wording contribute to make the style of delok narratives unique and specific.

The set pattern of the texts, with some variations, deals mainly in stereotypes that do little to depict a delok as an individual. This pattern can be divided into distinct sequences, which will be now examined. To illustrate each sequence, translations of various texts will be given, which are representative of both the content and style of delok accounts. Because of the great length of delok stories, it is not possible to provide a full translation here. However, from the excerpts below and the summary of a complete delok story at the end of the chapter, the reader should gain a clear sense of the genre.

Most delok narratives follow a standard sequence, which can be summarized as follows, after which each of the elements of the sequence will be discussed in more detail.

Prayer

1. Presentation of the delok: name, parents' names, place of birth
2. Preamble to the journey in the netherworld
    - Forewarning dream (optional; episode found only in some narratives)
    - Sickness that leads to a quick and unexpected death
3. The delok becomes aware of his/her death
    - Visualisation of an animal corpse (optional)
    - Indifference of the family members (optional)
    - Departure of the conscious principle from the body
4. First contact with the netherworld
    - Entry of the conscious principle into the bardo
    - First encounter with the attendants of the Lord of the Dead
    - Appearance of a mentor or guide (optional)
    - Crossing of a large bridge (optional)
5. Description of the netherworld
    - First encounter with the Lord of the Dead (optional)
    - Journey through the eighteen hells and the realm of the hungry ghosts; meeting with the damned, who explain the reasons why they are enduring such torments and who give messages for their families
    - Meeting a family member (optional)
    - Scenes where the damned are freed by a *maṇi pa* or a lama (optional)
    - Journey into other realms of reincarnation (optional)
6. Meeting with the Lord of the Dead
    - Arrival before the Lord of the Dead
    - The witnessing of several judgments
    - Judgment of the delok and message of the Lord of the Dead for the living
7. Return to earth
    - Reentry of the conscious principle into the body
    - Delivery of messages from the dead for their families, delivery of the message of the Lord of the Dead, and exhortation to practice religion
    - Colophon (optional)

The narrative always begins with a short prayer. Then, in the first sequence the delok is introduced to the reader or the audience by his or her name, the names of his or her parents and his or her birthplace. For example:

> In Bhutan, in the eastern region of Tashigang, in a place called Pakri sangdün (Phags ri gsang gdung), there was a man named Sonam Döndrup (Bsod nams don grub), and a woman called Tsewang Gyelmo (Tshe dbang rgyal mo) who had all the signs of the ḍākinī Yeshe Tsogyel [Ye shes mtsho rgyal, the Tibetan consort of Padmasambhava]. They had a daughter called Sangye Chözom (Sangs rgyas chos 'dzom) who was an incarnation of the bodhisattva Avalokiteśvara. (SC, p. 5)

The second sequence is a preamble to the trip to the netherworld. It usually describes the delok's premonition dream, then the sickness that leads to his or her sudden death. Often mentioned at this point are his or her previous religious links or the intense desire that the delok has to devote his or her life to religion.

The forewarning dream occupies a long section in the narrative of Sangye Chözom (SC, pp. 5–8), but most narratives have much shorter dream sections. The narrative of Karma Wangzin (Karma dbang 'dzin) says: "The fourth day of the Monkey month . . . Guru Rinpoche [Padmasambhava] appeared surrounded by a rainbow and holding in his hands a vase of long life and a skull full of nectar. . . . Next to him the goddess Tārā was standing in the form of an eight-year old girl" (Karma, pp. 7–8). Some delok do not have a forewarning dream at all; in fact, they just fall sick and die, as in the case of Lingza Chökyi (Gling bza 'chos skyid): "After being sick for sixteen days, having had my horoscope read, having taken medicine and having had all sorts of rituals performed, I did not feel better and my state worsened. I thought I was now going to die. When I was a little girl, I had thought of becoming a nun but my parents and my brothers did not allow it. . . . My head and my whole body suddenly became dizzy" (LC 1b–3a).

Most often the delok do not realize they are dead and the third sequence deals with the gradual realization of their state. The delok need some outside intervention to comprehend fully that they are no longer alive. This sequence typically includes one or two events that help the delok to understand that he or she is dead. He or she first is confronted with the corpse of an animal and then notices that the family does not pay any attention to her or him, does not give her or him anything to eat, but makes food offerings to the corpse of the animal. The delok is overwhelmed by grief and suddenly realizes that she or he is no longer alive. In a third episode, the delok is thrown out of the world of the living and into the bardo, the intermediate state between death and rebirth.

Not all narratives follow the pattern of this third sequence exactly. For example, while the narrative of Sangye Chözom mentions only the episode of the animal corpse, Karma Wangzin's narrative relates only the grief episode. Karma Wangzin feels she is rejected: first by her husband and her servants, who do not offer her tea and do not answer her questions; then, by her own mother, who keeps going around a stūpa without even looking at her. She finally realizes she is dead because her body does not have any smell and she does not make any noise while walking.

In all narratives, it is these first three sequences that contain most of the life details about the delok and serve to identify the narrative as that of a particular delok. They are also often the most touching of all the sequences, especially the grief episode.

The fourth sequence describes the first contact of the delok with the netherworld. It begins with the entry of the consciousness of the deceased (*nam shes*) into the bardo, which is depicted as a country. The delok faces the attendants of the Lord of the Dead, Yama Dharmarāja, who frighten her or him. It is at this instant that, in some narratives, a ḍākinī or the *yi dam*, the protective deity of the delok, appears. She or he will be the delok's guide throughout the trip into the netherworld. Then, in most narratives, the delok must cross a bridge over a large river. This bridge is the landmark indicating the entrance to the country of the dead. In this transition sequence, the delok leaves the world of the living and enters the world of the dead. The order of the episodes—entry of the conscious principle into the bardo, encounter with the attendants of the Lord of the Dead, appearance of his or her ḍākinī or *yi dam* who will be the guide, crossing of the bridge—may vary according to the narrative, and one or more of the episodes might not even be mentioned.

From this fourth sequence onward, the ensuing sequences do not always follow each other in the same order and are more or less developed according to the narrative, or even different versions of the same narrative.

The fifth sequence is devoted to the journey into the hells and into the hungry ghost (*yi dvags*) world, which is generally considered a category of hells. The hungry ghosts are, for the Tibetans, people who have been misers during their life and now suffer from thirst, hunger, and cold. Tortures endured by people who are damned are described in great detail, and the sufferers explain the reasons for their punishment. Among them are found people whom the delok knows, and sometimes one of his or her family members. Sangye Chözom is thus called by a man who is going to be thrown into a big cauldron:

> Alas, alas, girl with good karma, listen to me. As it is said you are going back to the human world, here is what you should say on my behalf: "I am from the region of Tashigang (Bkra shis sgang) in eastern Bhutan. My name is Tsering kar chung (Tshe ring skar chung). My mother's name is Tashi Chözom (Bkra shis chos 'dzom). For my salvation, she should have the texts of the *Diamond Sūtra* and the *Attrition of Sins* copied one thousand times. She should offer one hundred butter lamps many times to the temples. She should erect a big prayer-flag inscribed with the excellent six-syllable formula *oṃ maṇi padme hūṃ*. For the purification of my sins, she should make a ritual of attrition of sins, of merit transfer, and a blessing prayer. If you, my mother, really love your child, you will accomplish these actions for my benefit and I will be reborn in the human world. If you do not do them, I will not be liberated from this cauldron for one hundred years." Girl, give my message on earth. (SC 52–53)

According to the narrative or even different versions of the same narrative, three episodes can be added to this fifth sequence. They are:

1. A first encounter with the Lord of the Dead, who sends the delok to tour the hells and paradises, and tells her or him to come back to see him afterward. This episode is found, for example, in the narratives of Sangye Chözom.
2. An episode where the delok witnesses a *maṇi pa* freeing human beings. There are particularly extensive accounts of this in the narratives of Lingza Chökyi, Karma Wangzin, and Sangye Chözom.
3. Although most delok visit only hells and the realm of the hungry ghosts, some also travel to other realms of reincarnation. Thus, Sangye Chözom tours the animal realm

> (which is here equated to a hell) and the paradises of the buddhas and the bodhisattvas. (SC 97–99, 152–76)

The sixth sequence is devoted to the meeting of the delok with the Lord of the Dead and can be divided into four episodes: the arrival of the delok before the Lord of the Dead, the witnessing of several judgments, the judgment of the delok, and finally, the message the Lord of the Dead gives to the delok for the living. This message can be summarized as an exhortation to accomplish good deeds and not to commit any sins for fear of the terrible punishments the delok has just witnessed.

While the narrative of Nangsa (Snang sa) does not give any lengthy descriptions of hells, it does summarize in a few lines her death, her tour of the hells, and her arrival before the Lord of the Dead:

> At this very instant, the conscious principle of *a lce* [an honorific term given to women of noble extraction] Nangsa came out of her like a hair that is pulled out of butter. After she wandered in the bardo of existence, the attendants and especially the one who had an ox head led her to the Lord of the Dead. Men who had accomplished good deeds were walking on the white road leading to liberation and the paradises, a road that was like a white cloth. Men who had committed sins were led to the black road which went down to the eighteen hells in the three bad realms of reincarnation. In the hot hells, *a lce* Nangsa saw that, standing on a hot iron ground, beings were boiled in a stream of burning lead and that they were enduring numerous types of suffering by heat. In the cold hells, she saw that beings were placed under huge glaciers and were enduring many other tortures which were causing them unbelievable suffering. *a lce* Nangsa was very frightened by what she saw, and as soon as she arrived before the Lord of the Dead, she joined her hands and said . . . (*Snang sa 'od 'bum rnam thar*, pp. 62–63).

Most of the narratives do not provide such concise accounts, but in this sixth sequence, great importance is given to the judgments that the delok witnesses. Sangye Chözom saw, among others, the judgment of a peasant who had committed a great many sins.

> Abundant tears were rolling down his face and the man said: "*Oṃ maṇi padme hūṃ hrīḥ*. Alas, Lord of the Dead, listen to this dead man who begs you for attention. I am from the earth, the southern continent. The name of my place is Kurtö (Skur stod) and my name is Tandrin Punsok (Rta mgrin phun tshogs). When I was in the country of men, I had to commit many sins to obtain food and clothing. I have killed twenty pigs to feed myself. I have also killed many birds, wild boars, goats, and sheep. I insulted the lamas who live high up the valley. I have made bad use of my power over the villagers. When seven foreign traders came to my village, I robbed them to feed my children. I have committed numerous other sins. I do not recall the sins I have committed in the second part of my life. When a *maṇi pa* arrived in my village, the villagers gathered to recite *maṇi* and I went too. This *maṇi pa* described at length the existence of the fears you experience in the bardo, the retribution of

> sins and the reward for good deeds from the narrative of the delok Lingza Chökyi. Extreme regret for my sins was then born in my mind. I wondered what I should do to expiate them. I offered gifts and helped the *maṇi pa*, just to create links between us. I also helped monks. I made some food offerings to the yogins who came by begging. Those are the only good deeds I ever did. I came here after having accumulated a great number of bad black actions. I am not protected by the three jewels [of the Buddha, the dharma, and the saṅgha]. I have no support from the ḍākinī and the protective deities. I do not have the merits of having recited many *maṇi*. Do not send me down to the eighteen hells, great Lord of the Dead, but please have mercy upon me," and he was repeating "Alas." I saw him prostrate thrice. (SC 140–41)

After having witnessed several judgments, the delok appears before the Lord of the Dead to be judged. Here is a short extract of Karma Wangzin's judgment:

> The Lord of the Dead told her: "When you arrived here, did you look attentively at the counting of the good and bad actions? Have you seen the terror that my attendants inspired? Have you understood the meaning and the consequences of good and bad actions? Do you know why I am the Lord of the Dead? A long time ago, Lingza Chökyi went back to earth because there had been a mistake in her name and her family. But a woman from Dartsedoe (Dar rtse mdo) called Samten, a woman from a Bönpo lineage from Kham called Yungdrung Wangmo, and you too, you will go back to earth although there have been no such mistakes in your case. . . . And here is the reason: In a previous life, you met Vajravārāhī. Because you obtained from her all the teachings and initiations, the power of this ḍākiṇī has not disappeared through seven human generations. As you had the power to benefit human beings, you were born to lead them on the path of liberation. As for your present birth, here is the explanation of how you obtained it. In a previous life, you were born as a wise elephant in India. After that birth, you were reborn as a woman at Khoting (Mkho ting) in Lhodrak (Lho brag). When you were very young, your parents took you on pilgrimages; you prostrated in front of the holy images and you went round the temples. You offered butter lamps and food and you recited numerous prayers. Then the treasure-discoverer Nangtsewa [Snang rtse ba, a disciple of Sna tshogs rang grol, 1494–1570] who was from U rgyan Rinpoche's [Padmasambhava's] lineage arrived. You made offerings to him and you requested him to be compassionate. . . . Now, because of the power of a previous vow and the benefits of your actions, you will go back into your corpse and you will greatly benefit human beings." (Karma, 211–15)

After judging the delok, the Lord of the Dead gives her or him a message for the living. This message can be summarized by the two sentences that the Lord of the Dead says in the narrative of Karma Wangzin: "Human beings who try to do virtuous deeds should be sent to the paradises. Those who have accumulated sins should be sent to the hells" (Karma, 220). This message usually constitutes a relatively large part of the narrative, but its length varies according to the text. The last part of the message always concerns the delok. Here is part of the message found in the narrative of Sangye Chözom:

And the Lord of the Dead again added: "Girl, when you go on pilgrimages to all the mountains, big and small, and when you visit the place where the delok Karma Wangzin lived, all the people will come and ask you to tell them about what happens in the bardo. Among these people, to those who are predestined, you must explain everything without hiding anything. You must exhort the people to practice religion. Your lama will tell you the same thing as me. You must go to the fortress of Punakha (Spu na kha) where the seat of the Bhutanese government is situated. Among the lords and the people, young and old alike, some will revere you and have faith in you. Others will insult you and give you evil looks. At that time, people will say various things about you. You must explain everything to them without hesitation. Great benefit for the people will result from your action.

"As for the duration of your life and the difficulties you will meet, here they are: You will have a problem when you are thirty years old; but at that time, your death will be postponed and you will come back here only when you are fifty. You will not fear my attendants, and we will meet again like a father and his child. Then you will be reborn on earth in a 'hidden and blessed country.' Your name will be Dechen Wangmo (Bde chen dbang mo). When you finish converting the people of this country, you will be reborn in the country of Uḍḍiyāna, the land of the ḍākinī. Do not eat fish, pork, or eggs anymore. You must grasp my speech perfectly! Now, as they are ready to burn your corpse, you must go back to earth immediately." (SC 182–89)

The seventh and last sequence of the narrative is always relatively short. After having received the message of the Lord of the Dead, the delok returns to earth to narrate his or her experience, to deliver the different messages, and to exhort people to practice religion. The return of the conscious principle to the corpse takes place very rapidly. The delok regains consciousness, and the cloth that was covering her or him falls off. Not surprisingly, this terrifies the person who was looking after the corpse. The family is called, and the people of the village assemble. Some believe and accept the delok experience, while some think the person is a trickster or a demon. Finally, the delok is recognized as a holy person and relates his or her experience throughout the country. The following relates the return of Sangye Chözom:

As I was thinking I had to go up, a green wind blew and carried me up. In an instant I arrived at my village, Zachugang (Za chu gangs). A woman who was coming to fetch water passed by and we walked a while together. I did not recognize my corpse as it was like the corpse of a pig. As I was thinking I did not know what it was, I lost consciousness and it was as if darkness was falling. My body moved a little and a man who was there checked to see if there was any heat in my heart. My heart was warming up. The seven women who were looking after my corpse started screaming: "The girl is back!" And they started crying and moaning. My mother then arrived. One by one, she took off the clothes that were wrapped around my body and shouted: "Daughter, are you back?" She took my hand and started crying and moaning too. At dawn on the seventh day of the seventh month, all the villagers assembled and they said: "The girl is back from the country of the dead." They came to see me and everybody was talking at the same time. My parents and my family gave me all kinds of food and drink. But, as my body and my mind had been separated for seven days, my throat had dried up and I could not even drink water. The pious people who were there asked me where I had gone during these seven days. Many women, full of faith, looked at me and cried. Some people were jealous and became angry. People who had good karma prostrated themselves in front of me and were circumambulating me. As for the sinners, they did not believe a word of what I was saying, and these demons said that I was not telling the truth. But all the people assembled around me begged me to relate to them what happens in the bardo. (SC 190–92)

Delok narratives may end with a colophon that provides information about the author and date of the text, but, unfortunately, most of them do not; this makes historical research into the narrative and the delok very difficult.

Ethnographic research has shown that a few delok still exist today in peripheral regions, far from centralized powers. This research has led to the discovery that they do not travel to the netherworld only once, as the biographies let us suppose, but at regular intervals during "séances," which occur on auspicious days of the month. In fact, delok are akin to shamans, but shamans who have been Buddhicized in such a way and for such a long time that they have lost the memory of their shamanistic origin.

To bring together the foregoing analysis and description, let me conclude with a summary of the story of the delok Sangye Chözom.

The excellent biography of the venerable delok Sangye Choezom (Sangye Chözom), incarnation of Avalokiteśvara. The story of her visit down to the hells and up into the paradises during seven days is related here.

Delok Sangye Choezom was born in a tiny village in the Tashigang region of Eastern Bhutan. Her father and mother were farmers. In the Year of the Dog, when she was twelve, a man appeared and announced: "This girl has all the signs of a ḍākinī, and in a previous life, she was the delok Karma Wangzin." Later, Sangye Choezom was forewarned in a dream that she would tour the hells.

In that same year, she fell sick and thought she was dying. Her parents told her that if she wanted to come back from the netherworld, she could, as they would keep her body for fifteen days. After that, if she had not come back, they would cremate her. Her conscious principle left her body. When she saw her body as that of a pig she cried, but her tutelary deity (*yi dam*) came to meet her and reassured her. He told her to follow him. While going through various frightening places, her *yi dam* explained to her the meaning of what she saw. He explained that something that might look frightening did not frighten those who knew the deeper meaning. For example, threatening mountains were the paradises of the five buddhas for those who recognized them. For those who did not, they were the first intermediary state (*bar do*).

When she started touring the hells with her *yi dam*, she met people who were paying for their sins by undergoing terrible sufferings. On each occasion, her yi dam explained to her what they had done when they were in the human world and that these torments were the retribution for their actions. Sinners first identified themselves by name and the place they came from and described the actions that had brought them to this state. Then they told her to give messages to people on earth and to tell their families the kind of rituals or prayers that should be done on their behalf so that they could gain merit and be reborn out of these hells.

Later, she arrived at the palace of the Lord of the Dead where she saw all his terrifying attendants, who had animal heads. The Lord of the Dead told her that she had to tour the hells and paradises, to attend the judgment of the dead, and then return to earth to describe what she had seen to the human beings. Therefore, with her *yi dam*, she continued to travel through the hells and meet suffering people, each of whom described what they had done on earth, repented and gave messages for their family. She also met a *maṇi pa*, a religious man, who had the power to deliver sinners from their torments because he had propagated the six-syllable formula of Avalokiteśvara throughout his entire life. Finally, Sangye Chözom met her maternal uncle who also gave her a message for the family.

Suddenly she was called to attend a judgment by the Lord of the Dead. Petrified with fear, Sangye Chözom saw a sinner explaining the bad and good actions he had performed, and pleading not to be sent to the hells. The Black Demon prosecuted the man while the White God tried to defend him. His actions, in the form of black and white pebbles, were weighed by an attendant who had a monkey-head. As the scale was more heavily weighted with black pebbles, the Lord of Death admonished the man, who was sent to the hell corresponding to his sins.

Then Sangye Chözom saw a religious man arrive before the Lord of the Dead. This man described all his virtuous actions and, while the Black Demon tried to prosecute him, the White God spoke in his favor. The dominance of his good deeds was confirmed by the weight of the white pebbles, as well as by the mirror of existence into which the Lord of the Dead looked for confirmation. The man was sent to one of the paradises. Before leaving, he gave a message to Sangye Chözom exhorting humans to perform virtuous actions.

After the judgment, Sangye Chözom traveled with her *yi dam* to two of the paradises. There, people were happy and engaged in religious activities. Her *yi dam* explained to her the kinds of activities on earth that led to these good rebirths. Suddenly, Sangye Chözom was reminded by a yogin that she had to go back to earth, otherwise her body would be cremated. Once more, she met the Lord of the Dead who gave her a lengthy message for human beings, exhorting them to avoid bad actions and do virtuous deeds. He also forewarned her of the slanders she might encounter once she started telling her story but encouraged her not to pay any attention to them. She was then quickly sent up on earth where, after losing consciousness, she was reintegrated back into her body. Once she had come back to her senses, she related her story to all the people and gave the messages from the dead to the living.

Further Reading

See Françoise Pommaret, *Les "Revenants de l'au-delà" dans le monde tibétain* (Paris: Presses du CNRS, 1989), and "Les Revenants de l'au-delà (*'das log*) dans le monde tibétain: sources littéraires et tradition vivante," *Tibetan Studies: Proceedings of the 5th Seminar of the International Association of Tibetan Studies, Narita 1989*, Narita Shinshoji (1992): 673–86; also, Lawrence Epstein, "On the History and Psychology of the *'Das log*," *Tibet Journal* 7. 4 (1982): 20–85.

Abbreviations

SC — *Sangs rgyas chos 'dzom rnam thar*, Thimphu, n.d.
Karma — *Karma dbang 'dzin rnam thar*, Thimphu, n.d.
LC — *Das log Gling bza 'chos skyid rnam thar, Two Visionary Accounts of Returns from Death* (Dolanji, 1974).

—33—

Exorcising Demons with a Buddhist Sūtra

Donald S. Lopez, Jr.

The *Heart Sūtra* is perhaps the most famous of all Buddhist texts, chanted daily in Buddhist temples and monasteries throughout East Asia and Tibet, renowned for its terse expression of the perfection of wisdom, the knowledge whereby buddhahood is achieved. In part because of its brevity (it is only about one page long in translation), in part because of its potency (as the quintessence of the Buddha's wisdom), the *Heart Sūtra* has been put to a wide variety of ritual uses. What follows is a translation of a text that demonstrates the most common use to which the *Heart Sūtra* is put in Tibet, as part of a rite for (literally) turning away demons (*bdud bzlog*), rendered here loosely as "exorcism." The work is entitled *The Procedure for Repelling Demons Based on the Heart Sūtra, the Summation of the Vast, Intermediate, and Condensed Mothers* (*Yum rgyas 'bring bsdus gsum gyi don bsdus shes rab snying po'i sgo nas bdud bzlog gi rim pa*). The *Heart Sūtra* is described here as "the Summation of the Vast, Intermediate, and Condensed Mothers." The perfection of wisdom (*prajñāpāramitā*) is anthropomorphized in Indian Buddhist literature as the mother of all the buddhas because it is this wisdom that gives birth to buddhahood. This wisdom is thus depicted iconographically as a goddess. The perfection of wisdom also refers to the texts in which this wisdom is proclaimed, a large genre of Indian Buddhist sūtras named most commonly for their length. Hence, in the title of our ritual text, the "vast mother" is the *Perfection of Wisdom in One Hundred Thousand Stanzas*, the "intermediate mother" is the *Perfection of Wisdom in Twenty-five Thousand Stanzas*, and the "condensed mother" is the *Perfection of Wisdom in Eight Thousand Stanzas*. The *Heart Sūtra* is said to be the essence of all of those texts.

The ritual text is attributed to Kumārabuddha, who states in the colophon that his work is based on a handbook by one Ugarwa of Gyijang (Dbu dkar ba of [s]Kyi ljang). The ritual set forth in the text is prescribed as a cure for a wide range of calamities, misfortunes, dangers, and afflictions, including epidemic, possession by demons, sick livestock, loss of wealth or property, dying under a bad star, false accusations, and bad dreams. The assumption in each case is that a malevolent force has intruded into the human domain. That force must be brought under control and expelled, to return to its proper realm.

The text begins with two histories, one which it calls the history of the lineage and the second, the history to inspire belief. The first is simply a lineage list of the transmission of the practice, designed to establish the Buddhist pedigree, beginning of course with the perfect Buddha, and then moving to Avalokita, Mahākaruṇa, a Nepalese paṇḍita and translator, and then eventually to Atiśa (982–1054), who brought it to Tibet and transmitted it to his disciple, Drom ('Brom ston pa, 1005–1064, see chapter 8), finally reaching Kumārabuddha. The other history, the history to inspire belief, comprises two stories illustrating the efficacy of the exorcism ritual. In the first story, the ritual is used to defeat an evil magician. In the second story, the ritual is used to exorcise a malevolent spirit of an evil king or unethical lama, known simply as "the king" (*rgyal po*), which I translate below as "spirit king."

The remainder of the text is devoted to instructions for the performance of the rite of exorcism. The person performing the rite (whom we will call the officiant) first places either a painting or statue of the Buddha in the center of a white cloth and arranges offerings in front of it. To the east (that is, in front of the Buddha image), he places seven images of dough stamped with the impression of the divine demon Māra, in the form of a white human on a white horse, with flowers in his right hand (the flowers of desire that Māra shoots at his victims) and a noose in his left. Behind the images of Māra the officiant places a line of seven draught animals, seven dogs, (all made of dough, but perhaps substitutes for actual animals that would have been sacrificed in the pre-Buddhist period), seven thin tubes of dough (*chang bu*), seven small pieces of meat, and seven buttons of dough (*mtheb kyu*). In the south he places seven images of the Demon of the Afflictions (*nyon mongs, kleśa*) in the form of a yellow human on a yellow horse. In his right hand is a sword, in his left a noose. In the west, the officiant places seven images of the Demon of the Aggregates (*phung po, skandha*) in the form of a red human on a red horse. In his right hand is a spear, in his left a noose. In the north, the officiant places seven images of the demon who is the Lord of Death in the form of a black human on a black horse. In his right hand is a club, in his left a noose. For each of the others, the officiant also lays out the five rows of draught animals, dogs, etc. He then prepares individual offering bowls for the Buddha and the four demons with something to eat and three kinds of torma.

It is then necessary to prepare the *ngar mi* (usually translated as "effigy" but read literally either as "powerful human" or as "human as I [am]") of the person who has commissioned the performance of the rite, the patron (*yon bdag*). The officiant makes a dough statue of the patron having first had the patron breath on and spit on the dough. The effigy is then dressed in a garment made from clothing belonging to the patron and is placed in front of the Buddha image with its face turned toward the Buddha and its back toward the officiant. In this position, the effigy stands as both a substitute and a protector for the patron, acting as his surrogate before the demons.

The officiant then visualizes himself as the Buddha, seated in the midst of the four demons. This is a position of both danger and power, from which the long process of exorcism is executed, with the officiant, as the Buddha, playing the role first of host to the demons, then as the agent who enters into a contract with the demons, and finally as their conqueror. Here, the officiant visualizes himself as Śākyamuni Buddha, adorned with the major and minor marks. Instead of sitting in the middle of a maṇḍala, he is surrounded by a retinue, with Avalokiteśvara on the right and eight bodhisattvas (among whom Avalokiteśvara appears again) and eight śrāvakas on the left. As in other sādhanas, the visualized pledge beings fuse with the actual wisdom beings. The meditator next visualizes the goddess Prajñāpāramitā at his heart, seated on a moon disc, surrounded by buddhas and bodhisattvas. Moving to an even smaller scale, the meditator imagines that there is a moon disc in the center of her heart, upon which stands the letter *āḥ*. At an even more minute level, the officiant is instructed to visualize the letters of the *Heart Sūtra* standing upright around the edge of the moon disc at the goddess's heart, not simply the letters of the mantra, but the entire sūtra, for as we will see below, the entire sūtra functions as a mantra in this ritual. The letters of the sūtra radiate both light and their own sound, serving as offerings to the buddhas and bodhisattvas, who in turn alleviate the sufferings and purify all those gathered for the performance of the rite (and all sentient beings) as the officiant contemplates the meaning of emptiness.

The officiant is then instructed to recite the *Heart Sūtra* as much as possible and then make the standard offerings of ablution, flowers, incense, lamps, perfume, food, and music, with the appropriate mantras followed by verses praising Śākyamuni and Prajñāpāramitā. He or she then moistens the images and offerings with water and invites the four actual demons to come from their abodes, the four formless absorptions (*gzugs med khams, arūpyasamāpatti*), and dissolve into their molded images. The four demons are presumably said (in this text) to reside in the form formless absorptions because they are invisible.

The same mantra is used to invite the demons that is used to cause the wisdom beings, the actual buddhas and bodhisattvas, to merge with their visualized doubles (the pledge beings) to bring the beneficent deities into the presence of the meditator. Here, however, something else seems to be at work. The four demons are believed to be invisible, perniciously invading the human domain undetected but for the harm they inflict. In order that the demons to be placated and turned back, they must be made visible and brought into physical presence. Hence, dough images are made for them, which they are then invited to enter and animate.

The text then provides the *Heart Sūtra* in full, with the instruction that it is to be repeated nine times. After each set of nine repetitions, the officiant claps and turns one of the seven rows of demons, draught animals, dogs, tubes of dough, pieces of meat, and buttons of dough so that it faces outward. The sūtra is then recited nine more times and another row is turned, until the seven rows in the east have all been turned around, requiring sixty-three recitations of the sūtra.

The same procedure is repeated for the demons in the other three directions, such that the sūtra must be repeated 252 times to complete the process. The four demons and their retinues have been turned away (*bzlog*) from the Buddha by the power of the *Heart Sūtra* so that they now face outward, toward the effigy of the patron.

The officiant is instructed to say different things depending on whether the rite is being performed for a sick person, to destroy an enemy, and so forth. If the rite is being performed to destroy an enemy, the officiant is instructed to say, "By the power of the words of truth of the noble three jewels, may our enemy so and so today be summoned, liberated [i.e., killed], and his flesh and blood eaten by the gods and demons of the world. May his consciousness be led into the dharmadhātu."

Offerings of food and the torma are then made to the demons, with requests that they refrain from further harm. The demons, now residing physically in their dough images and facing toward the officiant, are further brought under control by bringing them into a social relation, the position of the guest, to be offered hospitality, in the form of food and gifts, by the officiant, acting as host. For example, to the divine demon Māra the officiant is instructed to say, "I offer this biscuit, endowed with a hundred flavors and a thousand potencies to the assembled armies of the child of gods. May it turn into enjoyments, their exhaustion unknown, that agree with their individual thoughts. Having delighted and satisfied them all, I pray that all of the harm unleashed by the four demons will be cast aside."

The gift to be offered to the demons is the *ngar mi*, the effigy of the patron. First, the person whom the effigy represents cleans the effigy with water that has been in his or her mouth. The officiant then blesses the effigy. The *ngar mi* is called a ransom (*glud*) and is repeatedly praised; it is described as being superior to the patron of whom it is a replica. This is the key moment in the ritual, in which the demons, in attendance at a feast as guests of the officiant, in the form of the Buddha, are asked to participate in an exchange. In return for releasing the patron from their power, they will be given something of greater value, the *ngar mi*. This does not seem to be a case of confusing the demons into thinking that the *ngar mi* is the patron; rather, the officiant's task is to convince the demons that the *ngar mi* is more desirable than the patron. The assumption, of course, is that they cannot but agree to the bargain.

Once the offering of the effigy has been made to the demons, the next step is the dispatching of the demons and the removal of the torma. The demons, as guests, have been fed and offered a gift. It is now time for them to depart. Here the demons are both cajoled and threatened, invited to return with the gifts they have received to their palaces in the formless realm. The patron, in order to save himself, gives up something of himself by pressing precious substances into the body of his effigy. This is what allows the officiant to deceive the demons into accepting the effigy, believing the mannequin of dough to be more desirable than his human double. The offering of the effigy is thus a gift given in order to receive;

in effect the demons and the patron (with the officiant acting as his agent) enter into a contract, agreeing to release the patron from their power in return for their taking possession of the *ngar mi*. The demons are to understand that any breach of this contract carries with it a penalty; should they not keep their part of the bargain and return to harm the patron, the officiant, through his surrogate, the Buddha, will visit them with punishment.

The next step is to take all of images and offerings (with the exception of the Buddha image) to a safe distance and then place them facing away from the place where the rite was performed. The location, however, depends on the purpose for which the rite is performed. For example, if the rite is for the welfare of a sick person, they are to be put in a cemetery. If a horoscope predicts that danger is approaching as a result of the "fourth year executioner," the inauspicious year that occurs four years after one's birth animal in the twelve-year cycle, or as a result of the "conjunction of the seven," the ill fortune that results from a relationship with someone seven years apart in age, they are to be placed in the direction the harm [is predicted] to come from. If it is for bringing happiness, they are placed either above or below a crossroads. If a curse is being deflected, they are placed the direction of the curse. If one is making a curse, they are placed in the direction of the enemy. If one has been harmed by the spirit king, they are placed at the base of a temple or a stūpa. If one has been harmed by a female devil, they are placed outside the town. If one has been harmed a nāga, they are to be placed at a lake or a spring. "In brief, it is said that wherever harm comes from, deliver it there."

Before going, however, it is important to make an offering of golden elixir (*gser skyems*) to all the other demons who might do harm. The offering of the elixir (usually beer) is a long section of the rite, after which everything is carried away as music is played. According to the text, it is not necessary for the officiant to carry the torma to the appointed place, unless he is placing a curse on someone or unless the purpose of the rite is "very important." The text does not specify who should go under ordinary circumstances, but we know from other sources that a person of low social class, such as a beggar or a corpse cutter, would be hired for the purpose.

The rite then concludes with a blessing, calling upon the five buddhas and a sixth deity, perhaps suggesting the chtonic concerns of the exorcism ritual, the goddess of the earth. The usual offerings, prayers, and dedications are then made, with the officiant reminded to keep in mind throughout that both officiant and patron are by nature empty. The text concludes with a final testimony to the rite's potency. There is then a concluding dedication which ends with the words, "By coming under the power of the four [demons] in this existence, one is bereft of happiness and tormented by millions of suffering. Until one attains the vajra-like samādhi [the final moment of meditation before the achievement of buddahood], this rite is an amazing method of exorcism."

One of the fascinating things about this ritual is that it contains elements that scholars identify as part of pre-Buddhist Tibetan religious practice, most notably the creation of the dough effigy of the patron and its use as a "ransom" offered to demons in exchange for their promise to desist from harm. At the same time, the work is structured like a standard Buddhist sādhana (see chapters 14 and 16), with the most recited Buddhist sūtra in Tibet, the *Heart Sūtra*, functioning as little more (or less) than a long mantra. It is in such contexts that the lines that appear to divide Buddhist and Bönpo seem to fade from view.

The translation is from a badly worn blockprint from the Library of Tibetan Works and Archives in Dharmsala, India, a photocopy of which was kindly provided to me by Hubert Decleer. This edition contains no information on the place or date of publication. A more easily accessible Geluk version with the same title is found in the fourth volume of an eleven-volume set, published in India, of ritual texts of the Rgyud smad tantric college, entitled *Gsang chen dpal ldan smad rgyud grva tshang gis nyams bzhes chos skor gyi rim pa*, pp. 309–31. In the Tibetan text, instructions to the officiant appear in small print, while the actual words to be recited appear in large print. That convention is retained in the translation below.

Further Reading

For an analysis of this ritual and of the *Heart Sūtra*, see Donald S. Lopez, Jr., *Elaborations on Emptiness: Uses of the Heart Sūtra* (Princeton: Princeton University Press, 1996). For discussions of related exorcism rites practiced in modern Nepal, see Sherry B. Ortner, *Sherpas through Their Rituals* (Cambridge: Cambridge University Press, 1978), pp. 91–127; Stan Royal Mumford, *Himalayan Dialogue: Tibetan Lamas and Gurung Shamans in Nepal* (Madison: University of Wisconsin Press, 1989), pp. 140–64; and Vincanne Adams, *Tigers of the Snow and Other Virtual Sherpas* (Princeton: Princeton University Press, 1995).

The Stages of Repelling Demons Based on the Heart Sūtra, the Summary of the Vast, Intermediate, and Condensed Mothers

Bowing to the lama, inseparable from [the goddess] Prajñāpāramitā, who lacks utterance, thought, and expression, I write the *Heart Sūtra*'s repelling of demons.

This has two parts, the history and the actual practice. The first has two parts, the history of the lineage and the history to inspire belief. The first is: the perfect Buddha, Avalokita, Mahākaruṇa Ratnamati, [Dharmakīrti of] Suvarnadvīpa, Atiśa, the virtuous friend Dönpa (Ston pa), Potowa Rinchensel (Bo to ba rin chen gsal), the translator Jungne Dorje of Donglo (Stong lo [Tshul khrims] 'Byung gnas rdo rje), Ugarwa of Gyijang (Kyi ljang Dbu dkar ba), and the great scholar Kumārabuddha.

Regarding the second, the lineage was received by Ugarwa of Gyijang. He made the *yi dam* for it and had faith in it. In that country were Ugarwa of Gyijang and someone called Gulo (Ku lo). Gulo was performing black magic of [deities] such as red and black Yama and red and black Mun pa whereby he freed [killed] many people with his power. One day, Ugarwa of Gyijang offered Gulo something to drink, gave him some clothing, and advised him, "Your power works quickly, but afterward there will be certain [negative karmic] fruitions." [Gulo] was hurt by what he said and became enraged and swore an oath, "You will not live [another] week." Gulo left. Then, because Ugarwa practiced this [rite], in a week Kulo's own power turned on him and he died. Then he surpassed [everyone] in repelling curses.

Furthermore, a Chinese named Patso (Pha 'tsho) was harmed by the spirit-king. An astrologer made a horoscope and said, "If you perform a ritual with the corpse of a young child, place it in a clay pot and get rid of it in Ü (Dbus), it will help. He did that, and took it to Ü where it was purchased by Geser (Dge ser) in Phan yul. The spirit king harmed Geser and all of his horses and donkeys were destroyed. The spirit king appeared to Geser, who asked him, "Whom do you fear?" "I fear Ugarwa of Gyijang; I fear no one else." Geser tricked him saying, "Tell me where he is and I will kill him. Then you will fear no one." He explained the story and gave him directions. Geser went to the place of Ugarwa and told him what had happened. He was given this very sādhana and with it Geser repulsed the demon. From that point on, the harm of the spirit king was pacified and [Geser] was able to use his mind for the dharma. Then the spirit king returned to the Chinese Patso. Patso said, "Whom do you fear that you have come back?" "I have come fearing Ugarwa of Gyijang and Geser; up until now I have been staying at Geser's place." Patso said, "I will go to Ü again. You guide me. The two of us will go to Geser's place and will stay there." Geser and Patso met and he explained to him what had happened before and gave him an auspicious gift. He asked for the method of getting rid of the spirit king and was given this. By practicing it he was freed from the harm of the spirit king. In the same way, if one makes effort at this, whatever you wish for, such as the supreme achievements, will be quickly attained.

Second, the actual practice of the text has two parts: the preliminaries and the actual. First, place either a painting or statue of Munīndra [Śākyamuni Buddha] in the center of a white cloth. Arrange offerings in front of it. To the east [that is, in front of the buddha-image] place seven [images of dough stamped with impression of] the divine demon [Māra] [in the form of] a white human and a white horse, in the right [hand] are flowers and in the left a noose, [behind that a line of] seven draught animals, seven dogs, seven thin tubes of dough, seven small pieces of meat, seven balls of dough. Similarly, in the south [place] seven [images of] the demon of the afflictions [in the form of] a yellow human and a yellow horse. In his right hand is a sword, in his left a noose. In the west [place] seven [images of] the demon of the aggregates [in the form of] a red human and a red horse. In his right hand is a spear in his left noose. In the north [place] seven [images of] the demon who is the Lord of Death [in the form of] a black human and black horse. In his right hand is a club, in his left a noose. For the other, place the draught animals and so forth as above. Spread a black cloth below them [around the white cloth]. Prepare in the individual offering bowls [for the buddha and the four demons] something to eat, a beautiful red flower torma [a dried torma decorated with butter in the shape of petals], a white torma, and a red torma [in the shape of a triangle]. Having clothed an adorned *ngar mi* [a dough statue of the patron which the patron has breathed on, touched, and had his saliva mixed with], turn it facing away [from you and toward the buddha-image]. Place the image of Munīndra, etc., facing you. Through starting with the mind of refuge, think with great faith and aspiration that you are not different from Munīndra. Say:

What is before me is unobservable. Therefore, it becomes emptiness. From the nature of emptiness [appears] a cushion of jewels, lotus, and moon [upon which sits] the chief of teachers, the complete and perfect Buddha Śākyamuni. His body is gold, with one face and two arms. His right hand touches the earth, his left is in the gesture of equipoise. On his head is the crown protrusion. He is adorned with the thirty-two auspicious marks and eighty auspicious minor marks, like wheels on the soles of his feet. He emanates boundless light and beams of light. A retinue appears; the pledge and wisdom beings nondual. He is attended to the right by the noble Avalokiteśvara and to the left by the eight dear bodhisattva sons and the eight supreme śrāvakas, such as Śāriputra. At the heart of the chief on lotus and moon is the great mother surrounded by her sons, the buddhas of the ten directions. At the heart of the great mother is a moon maṇḍala. At its center is the letter *āḥ*. At the edge appear the letters of the *Heart Sūtra*. They radiate beams of light together with their own sound, making an offering that delights the conquerors and their children. All the blessings and powers gather and touch the primary ones, I and those protected, as well as all sentient beings, purifying all sins and obstructions and pacifying all sickness, demons, and obstacles; the meaning of the eighteen emptiness is created in your mind.

Recite the *Heart Sūtra* mentally as much as you can. The blessing according to the general offering is: *Oṃ vajra amṛta*, etc. *Oṃ sarva tathāgata arghaṃ praticcha puja megha samudra spharaṇa samaya hūṃ* [the offering of water] and so on [for the other six offerings of foot washing, flowers, incense, butter lamps, perfume, food] through *śabda* [music]. Pray for the desired aim, praise him with either the extensive or brief praise, such as [the praise of Śākyamuni]: When you, best of bipeds were born . . . [you took seven steps on this great earth and declared, "I am supreme in this world." It was then that the wise bowed down to you.] and [the praise of Prajñāpāramitā]: The inexpressible, inconceivable . . . [perfection of wisdom, unproduced, unceased, the nature of space, the sphere of the wisdom of specific knowledge. I bow down to the mother of the conquerors of the three times.] Then moisten the images and offerings with water and invite the four demons to dissolve into their own forms. With them appearing clearly in front of you say this: O white divine demon and hosts of white demons, abiding in the realm of nothingness, hosts of divine demons and your emanations. When I, the mantra holder, invite you to your excellent form here [on] the seat prepared, I beseech you to come here for just a little while and abide in your form. *Jaḥ hūṃ baṃ hoḥ*. They dissolve and are nondual. O yellow demon of the afflictions, abiding in the realm of neither existence or nonexistence. Afflicted sentient beings wander in saṃsāra. Assembled army of demons of the afflictions, so that the afflictions of sentient beings might be removed, when I, the mantra holder, invite you, I beseech you to come here for just a little while and abide in your form. *Jaḥ hūṃ baṃ hoḥ*. They dissolve and are nondual. O red demon of the afflictions, you abide in the realm of limitless consciousness, innate like the shadows that arises from the four gatherings. Assembled army of demons of the aggregates, when I, the mantra holder, invite you, I beseech you to come here for just a little while and abide in your form. *Jaḥ hūṃ baṃ hoḥ*. They dissolve and are nondual. O black demon Lord of Death, who separates sentient beings from life, abiding in the realm of infinite consciousness. Assembly of demons of the black Lord of Death, with your hosts, retinue, and servants, when I, the mantra holder, invite you, I beseech you to come here for just a little while and abide in your form. *Jaḥ hūṃ baṃ hoḥ*. They dissolve and are nondual. O assembled army of demons of the four demons, in order that the patron may remove the four demons, abide to enjoy supreme offerings; today accept this excellent offering of these patrons. I beseech the four demons, their retinue and servants to turn away.

Then the *Heart Sūtra*:

In the language of India, *Bhagavatīprajñāpāramitāhṛdaya*. In Tibetan, *Transcendent and Victorious Essence of the Perfection of Wisdom*. One section. Thus did I hear. At one time the Bhagavan was residing at Vulture Peak in Rājagṛha with a great assembly of monks and a great assembly of bodhisattvas. At that time, the Bhagavan entered into a samādhi on the categories of phenomena called, "perception of the profound." Also at that time, the bodhisattva, the mahāsattva, the noble Avalokiteśvara beheld the practice of the profound perfection of wisdom and saw that those five aggregates also are empty of intrinsic existence. Then, by the power of the Buddha, the venerable Śāriputra said that to the bodhisattva, the mahāsattva, the noble Avalokiteśvara, "How should a son of good lineage who wishes to practice the profound perfection of wisdom train?" He said that and the bodhisattva, the mahāsattva, the noble Avalokiteśvara said this to the venerable Śāriputra, "Śāriputra, a son of good lineage or a daughter of good lineage who wishes to practice the profound perfection of wisdom should view things in this way: form is empty; emptiness is form. Emptiness is not other than form; form is not other than emptiness. In the same way, feeling, discrimination, conditioning factors, and consciousnesses are empty. Therefore, Śāriputra, all phenomena are empty, without characteristic, unproduced, unceased, stainless, not stainless, undiminished, unfilled. Therefore, Śāriputra, in emptiness there is no form, no feeling, no discrimination, no conditioning factors, no consciousness, no eye, no ear, no nose, no tongue, no body, no mind, no form, no sound, no odor, no taste, no object of touch, no phenomena, no eye constituent up to and including no mental consciousness constituent, no ignorance, no extinction of ignorance, no aging and death up to and including no extinction of aging and death. In the same way, no suffering, origin, cessation, path, no wisdom, no attainment, no nonattainment. Therefore, Śāriputra, because bodhisattvas have no attainment, they rely on and abide in the perfection of wisdom; because their minds are without obstruction, they have no fear. They pass completely beyond error and go to the fulfillment of nirvāṇa. All the buddhas who abide in the three times have fully awakened into unsurpassed, complete, perfect enlightenment in dependence on the perfection of wisdom. Therefore, the mantra of the perfection of wisdom is the mantra of great wisdom, the unsurpassed mantra, the mantra equal to the unequaled, the mantra that completely pacifies all suffering. Because it is not false, it should be known to be true. The mantra of the perfection of wisdom is stated thus: *gate gate pāragate pārasaṃgate bodhi svāhā.* Śāriputra, bodhisattva mahāsattvas should train in the profound perfection of wisdom in that way." Then the Bhagavan rose from samādhi and said, "Well done" to the bodhisattva, the mahāsattva, the noble Avalokiteśvara. "Well done, well done, child of good lineage. It is like that. Child of good lineage, it is like that; the practice of the profound perfection of wisdom is just as you have taught it. Even the tathāgatas admire it." The Bhagavan having so spoken, the venerable Śāriputra, the bodhisattva, mahāsattva, the noble Avalokiteśvara, and all those surrounding, and the entire world, the gods, humans, demigods, and gandharvas, admired it and praised the speech of the Bhagavan.

At the end of each of the nine times, clap your hands and perform the repelling as follows: Each row of seven images and substances in the east which was offered on a black base is placed facing outward [one row at a time each time the sūtra is recited nine times]. Do that until the seven in the east are complete [that is, until the sūtra has been recited sixty-three times]. Do the same for the three in the south, west, and north. When expelling a sickness, demon, enemy, or obstacle, adapt the words and the visualization accordingly. Folding your hands, say:

Namo. I bow down to the lama. I bow down to the Buddha. I bow down to the dharma. I bow down to the saṅgha. I bow down to the great mother, Prajñāpāramitā. Through bowing down to them, may these, our true words, be effective. Just as in the past the lord of gods, Indra, contemplated the profound meaning of the perfection of wisdom and, through reciting the words, repelled all opposing forces such as the sinful demons, so in the same way, may I also contemplate the profound meaning of the great mother, the perfection of wisdom, and through reciting the words repel all opposing forces such as the sinful demons and (specifically, if there is a sick person, say the name) for this so-and-so, may those obstructing demons who led in the disease in the beginning, who took up residence [literally, "build a nest"] in the middle, and who provide no benefit in the end all now be repulsed [clap], destroyed [clap], pacified [clap], and completely pacified by the performance of this repulsion of demons with the *Heart Sūtra* and by the words of truth of the noble three jewels. May he be freed from the 84,000 types of obstruction and the conditions of discord and harm and by the good fortune that brings harmony and all that is marvelous, may there be happiness and goodness here today.

With regard to bad omens, follow the procedure above, and say: [May] all bad omens in the day and bad omens in dreams at night, and, in particular, this such and such bad omen [be destroyed by] the noble three jewels, etc., as above. If you are making power [in order to destroy] say [instead]: By the power of the words of truth of the noble three jewels, may our enemy so and so today be summoned, liberated [i.e., killed], and his flesh and blood eaten by the gods and demons of the world. May his consciousness be led into the dharmadhātu. In the same way, use your reasoning to adapt it for other situations. If there are three people who can recite the *Heart Sūtra*, [recite it] nine times, with each person doing three. This is known as "repulsing with nine *Heart Sūtras*."

Regarding the offering of food to the deities and the moistening with water, bless it with *oṃ āḥ hūṃ* and say seven times *nama sarvatathāgata avalokite oṃ sambhara sambhara hūṃ*. After saying the names of the four tathāgatas and bowing down, say: I offer this biscuit, endowed with a hundred flavors and a thousand potencies to the assembled armies of the child of gods. May it turn into enjoyments, their exhaustion unknown, that agree with their individual thoughts. Having delighted and satisfied them all, I pray that all of the harm unleashed by the four demons will be cast aside. Having offered the biscuit in front of the children of the gods, say: Just as the treasury of the sky has everything so may I act with my own power, lacking the annihilation of resources, without striving, and without being in danger. Then say the words of truth, By the power of my thought . . . and dedicate it. In the same way, moisten the beautiful flower torma with water. Bless it with the three syllables [*oṃ āḥ hūṃ*] and say the mantras, etc. Say the names of the four tathāgatas as above, and then say: I offer this beautiful flowered torma endowed with a hundred tastes and a thousand potencies to the assembled armies of the demon of the afflictions, etc., up to the point of offering the torma in front of the demon of the afflictions and speaking the power of truth as above. Also, bless the white torma, say the mantras and the four names as before and then say from: I offer this white torma endowed with a hundred flavors and a thousand potencies to the assembled armies of the demon of the aggregates. May it turn into enjoyments, their exhaustion unknown, that agree with their individual thoughts, etc., to the offering in front of the deity of the aggregates, to the expression of the power of truth and the dedication as before. Also, having moistened the red torma with water, say the mantras and the four names, etc., as before and then say: I offer this red torma with a hundred flavors and endowed with a thousand potencies to the assembled armies of the demon of the Lord of Death. May it turn into enjoyments, their exhaustion unknown, that agree with their individual thoughts. Having delighted and satisfied them all, I pray that all of the harm concocted by the four demons will be cast aside. Then offer the torma in front of the images of the demon of the Lord of Death and say: Just as the treasury of the sky has everything, so may I act with my own power, lacking the annihilation of resources, without striving, and without being in danger. Then say the words of truth, By the power of my thought . . . and dedicate it as before.

Next, ablution of sickness, etc., with an effigy. The sick person, etc., cleans the ransom effigy with water from a pot etc. [the water being spit out by the sick person] Bless it saying: From the nature of emptiness, *oṃ āḥ hūṃ svāhā*. The effigy arisen from melting [of those letters] comes to have all of the aggregates, constituents, and sources complete, is endowed with the qualities of the desire realm and has a treasure of wealth of resources whose exhaustion is not known. *Oṃ āḥ hūṃ. Oṃ sarva bidapūra*, etc. Then moisten it with water and [say] the three letters and say the mantra *sambhara* seven times or three times and say the four names. After that, say:

Hūṃ. This beautiful effigy of a human I offer today as ransom for the patron. As to its cause, it is established from jewels. It is adorned with types of the colored silk. Its ornaments sway. I have put turquoise in his mouth and I send gold in his hands, [all] offered to hands of the four demons. [If the patron] meets them in a pass, they turn around on the pass; [if he] meets them in a valley, they turn around in the valley. His skill in speech is clarity, his skill in movement is supple. What is greater than the beautiful fillet on his head? His auspicious body is adorned with ornaments; this auspicious person has great power. I have no attachment to him [and offer him freely]. In order to purchase the lord of offering [from the demons], I send this ransom today. May it remain as ransom for the great lords of ransom [i.e., the demons]. This is a ransom for his eight collections of consciousness, five elements [earth, water, fire, wind, space] and his [twelvefold] dependent origination, a ransom [for] his constituents and sources, a ransom for his six collections of sense organs. A great person of grain with clothes of the five types of precious substances [gold, silver, turquoise, coral, pearl]. In his right hand a bannered spear that turns back the battles of saṃsāra, in his left a pliant rope. His right foot is wisdom—copper, his left foot is great method—iron. I offer such a great person made of dough as a ransom for this owner of the offering to the assembled armies of the four demons together with their retinues. Because this ransom is more auspicious than the person [the patron], this beautiful ransom is received by all the assembled armies of the four demons. May they now prepare to go to their own abodes. Do not break the words of the three jewels. At the request Indra, the king of gods, the bhagavan Śākyamuni summoned the four demons and gave them a ransom. Remember your promise to follow his instructions; do not harm those assembled here. Go, demons, to your own abodes. By satisfying the demons with the ransom, may harm by the four demons be pacified. Just as the treasury of the sky has everything so may I act with my own power, lacking the annihilation of resources, without striving, and without being in danger, etc., and dedicate it with: By the power of my thought, etc.

Make offerings [of the ransom] into the maṇḍala of the four demons as before. At this point, if there is a sick person, this is also the traditional technique for transferring sickness. Then, the dedication and sending away of the torma. Having expressed the power of truth, say: *Hūṃ*. I am the bhagavan Śākyamuni. I am the great and glorious Guhyapati. I am the antidote to demons and obstructions. Great demons, gods, nāgas, evil spirits of the night, hungry ghosts, flesh-eaters, demonic lady of disease, may you not transgress my words. By receiving this ransom torma, the sickness, demons, and impediments of myself and the donor, lord of the offering, are pacified, the grip is broken, the bonds are released, the knots are loosed, the repression is lifted. If the deeds that are requested are not established, the punishment [decided by] the Sugata in the past is that [you] sentient beings will be reborn in the hells again and again and will experience great suffering. Therefore, may we not be harmed. Four demons, prepare to return to your abodes. The true and infallible words of the Buddha are achieved accordingly and bliss is attained. I and the patron, lord of the offering, are freed from the four great demons and the impediments, sickness, and demons are quickly pacified; the aims of our intentions are achieved.

Then, the dispatching of the four demons. Assembled armies of the four demons do as you have been instructed and go to your abodes in the four realms. Demon child of gods and your assembly of white, go to the abode of nothingness. Yellow demon of the afflictions, go to limitless consciousness. Red demon of the aggregates, go to abode of neither existence or nonexistence. Lord of Death and your assembly of black, go to the realm of limitless space. Demon son of gods, demon of the afflictions, demon of the aggregates, demon Lord of Death [all of whom] arise from the obstructions to omniscience and the afflictive obstructions, assembled demonic armies of the four demons, receive this sacrifice of torma. Completely abandon the intention to do harm and mischief to the patron, lord of the offering, and myself. Remain in your respective beautiful palaces, endowed with a mind of bliss; do not harm those assembled here. Go blissfully to your own abodes. *Samaya prabeśaya phaṭ*. Take [the images and offerings from their positions and place them] a little outside [the town] and [carefully] place them facing away. If the [rite is for the] welfare of a sick person put them in a cemetery. Similarly, if a divination [predicts] an enemy [as a result of] the "fourth year executioner" [the inauspicious year that occurs four years after one's birth-animal in the twelve-year cycle] or [as a result] of the "conjunction of the seven" [the ill fortune that results from a relationship with someone seven years apart in age], offer them in the direction the harm [is predicted] to come from. If it is for bringing happiness, offer it either above and below a crossroads. If you are reversing a curse, in the direction of the curse. If you are making a curse, in the direction of the enemy. If you have been harmed by the [spirit] king, at the base of a temple or a stūpa. If you have been harmed by a female devil, outside the town or below three valleys. If you are causing rain and have been harmed by a nāga, place them at a lake or a spring. Harm by a local god in his direction. In brief, it is said that wherever harm comes from, deliver it there.

At this point there is the ceremony for offering the golden elixir. To the numberless lamas, *yi dams*, divine maṇḍala, to the *yi dam*, the rare and sublime *yi dam* and all that is worthy of offering, I wish to give this offering of golden elixir, an ocean of desirable qualities. I act to perform the deed [that will accomplish] my desired aim. To the white ḍākinīs of the three abodes, the excellent protectors who guard the directions together with their hosts I wish to give this offering of golden elixir, an ocean of desirable qualities. I act to perform the deed [that will accomplish] my desired aim. To all eight groups, such as that of the proud chief, the primary object, who abide in this direction I wish to give this offering of golden elixir, an ocean of desirable qualities. I act to perform the deed [that will accomplish] my desired aim.

Then hold it all in your hand, moisten it with water and recite the repelling of ferocity of demons and female devils and take them [to the place].

Bhyoḥ. Sole mother, lady of pestilence together with your retinue, in left hands of each of you is an x of a demon. If an x [meaning death] should fall on the patron, officiant, or those surrounding, please erase the x. Sole mother [Dpal ldan lha mo] in your left hand are the dice and black and white fortune telling stones of a demon (*btsan*). When I and the patron, the lord of the offering, cast our fortunes, separate the black and white dice now. Having gathered the red lots [with the names of those you will harm], remove ours now. In your left armpit is the black bag of disease tied with five hundred snakes. The many spirits are then released [from the bag]. Cast out the army of spirits now. In order to purchase the lord of the offering the repelling of demons is offered. I am not mistaken in making the offering. Receive it and revel in delight. Repel the ritual weapons of Buddhist and Bön priests now. Repel nāgas, plagues, and curses now. Repel enemies, brigands, and thieves now. Repel evil gossip now. Repel the loss of property and animals now. Repel the death of family members now. Repel epidemics and fever now. Repel false accusation of the innocent now. Through the repelling rite of the *Heart Sūtra*, may all classes of disrupting harm be repelled right now. Through blessings together with the repelling by the *Heart Sūtra*, evil fortune [connected with] earth, water, fire, and wind are repelled. Through the formation of the ransom effigy, offerings, and so forth, evil omens are pacified in my land. I pray that loss [due to] sickness and epidemic be repelled. Thus, wherever there is danger, may all the damage of the four demons be repelled to their own abode by the compassion of the three jewels, the blessings of the *Heart Sūtra*, and my power as a mantra-holder. May they be turned back right now. *Samaya prabeśaya phaṭ*.

Say this forcefully, carry them away and make music forcefully. If you are doing it in the extensive form, recite the *Heart Sūtra* nine times. At the end of that, do each of the repellings [as above, "*Namo* . . ." and clap your hands]. Do this in conjunction with saying the words of truth three times. [If] you are making a curse or it is very important, go to the place yourself at the time of offering. From the beginning of the [rite for] repelling the witch given above, carry it and go there. From the repelling of the witch to the golden elixir and torma, chant the repelling with the *Heart Sūtra* up to three times and offer. Imagine that the separation, the achievement of repelling [described] above enters into yourself, the protected ones, and the wheel of protection. If the sickness is very important they should wear white clothing. Seat them on a white carpet facing toward the east and make music. Scatter flowers and say the words of blessing:

Hūṃ The good fortune from the center, the good fortune of Vairocana, the good fortune of an auspicious body, *Jaya*! bestow them on this patron today. By this good fortune may he have happiness. *Hūṃ*. The good fortune from the east, the good fortune of Vajrasattva, the good fortune of stability, *Jaya*! bestow them on this patron today. By this good fortune may he have happiness. *Hūṃ*. The good fortune from the south, the good fortune of Ratnasambhava, the good fortune of the granting of all wishes, *Jaya*! bestow them on this patron today. By this good fortune may he have happiness. *Hūṃ*. The good fortune from the west, the good fortune of Amitābha, power, wind, fame, and good fortune, *Jaya*! bestow them on this patron today. By this good fortune may he have happiness. *Hūṃ*. The good fortune from the north, the good fortune of Amoghasiddhi, the good fortune of spontaneous deeds, *Jaya*! bestow them on this patron today. By this good fortune may he have happiness. The good fortune from the downward direction, the good fortune, the good fortune of the earth goddess Ḍṛḍa, the good fortune of life-bearing grains, *Jaya*! bestow them on this patron today. By this good fortune may he have happiness. May good fortune arise in the day, *la la*; may good fortune be stored up at night, *li li*. By whatever good fortune occurs in the three times, may we be happy here today.

Say whatever extensive or abbreviated verses of good fortune that you know. After that, make an offering to the image of Śākyamuni. Recite the hundred syllable [mantra] and "excess and deficiency" [to correct any errors in the recitation]. Ask for forgiveness. The retinue melts into light and dissolves into the main figure. Recite a prayer [for the teacher] to remain steadfastly and scatter flowers. Ask for sublime and common feats. Seal it with the dedication of the roots of virtue with prayers. Seal it by not observing yourself or the object of protection. You must definitely seal it through not observing yourself or the object of protection. The benefits of doing so are inconceivable and inexpressible. Specifically, harm resulting from evil spells cast by Buddhist or Bön priests, the working of a curse, destroying an enemy who harms with disease, the spread of an epidemic that moves up gradually into one's country, sickness and accident befalling animals, having the spirit-king in the home, dying under a bad star [and thus bringing ill fortune to one's family], false accusation, abusive people, children who do not grow up, diminishment and loss of wealth, bad omens and bad dreams, rough years and horoscopes, evil spells, etc., one is immediately freed from these by doing this repelling. As long as one lives, when you repeat it one, three, or nine times in proportion to the size of obstacle, there is no doubt that it will eradicate the obstacle. Thus is the essence of the minds of the scholars and adepts of India, the *yi dam* of the glorious Atiśa, and the unerring practice of geshe Dönba, Potowa rinchensel, Rimö sung dorje, Ugarwa of Gyijang, and so forth. This work, called, "Repelling Demons and Eradicating All Obstacles with the *Heart Sūtra*," was written by the scholar Kumārabuddha according to textbook written by Ugarwa of Gyijang and ornamented by the lineage of those who saw it practiced. May all transmigrators be victorious in battle with the four demons and have the good fortune to quickly attain the rank of the omniscient Buddha, king of doctrine. May the banner of undiminished good fortune be planted. May sentient beings with method, refuge, purity, and certain entry into the Mahāyāna repel the deeds of the deceptive demons. By coming under the power of the four in this existence, one is bereft of happiness and tormented by millions of suffering. Until one attains the vajra-like samādhi, this rite is an amazing method of repelling.

[Through] the magic of printing, the forms of the letters appear immediately, without tiring the fingers [by copying]. The [text] comes from the cell of those who made the offering for the printing, the monk Jamyang Wangyal ('Jam dbyangs dbang rgyal), endowed with faith, charity, and wealth, and the monk-official of the Potala Losang Loden (Blo bzang blo ldan). Through the merit [of printing the text], may all transmigrators such as ourselves quickly attain omniscience which conquers the four demons and in the meantime may all sickness, demons, and obstacles be quelled. *Sarvamaṅgalaṃ.*

—34—

Turning Back Gossip

Matthew Kapstein

The religious life of Tibet embraces a wide range of ritual practices whose origins are clearly indigenous. Among them are important rituals of the Tibetan state, such as those concerned with the state oracles and protective deities, that have developed over the course of centuries as solemn rites of national significance. On a more humble scale, daily observances such as the offering of the fragrant smoke of burnt juniper to the gods and spirits of the local environment are performed in virtually every Tibetan household (see chapter 26). Rituals of these types have long been incorporated within the Buddhist religion in Tibet and have been reformulated over the centuries to accord, more or less, with Buddhist doctrinal norms.

A particularly important and broad category of ritual practice is devoted to the expulsion of various types of evil forces. The manner in which such rituals have been adopted for Buddhist use has been extremely uneven, varying according to both geographical region and sectarian difference. Throughout the country, however, monks or lay priests associated with village temples had to be proficient in these practices in order to minister to the common troubles, fears, and complaints of the populace. Because this grass-roots priesthood frequently adhered, at least nominally, to the Nyingmapa sect, or sometimes to the Bön religion, a veneer of conformity with the normative teachings of these traditions was often given to the exorcistic rituals intended for village use. Often, for instance, the Nyingmapa versions of the rituals in question are presented as the instructions of Padmasambhava.

The ritual that is presented here concerns the exorcism of "malicious gossip" (*mi kha*). In small and isolated communities it is clearly of great importance that cooperative and harmonious relationships be maintained to the extent possible. Even under relatively favorable circumstances, however, this proves to be a difficult thing to accomplish. Discrepancies of wealth and worldly success, disputes over privileges or prior agreements, and a thousand and one other circumstances may lead neighbors, friends, and even siblings to begin to cast aspersions upon one another, and eventually to fall out. Consider what might take place if the crops of all but a few farmers in a given community be afflicted with blight. Some may suggest that a special twist of fate, or a supernatural power, brought about the unusual success of the lucky households. Perhaps some magical ability was involved. Perhaps a curse was brought down on the less fortunate neighbors. It is not difficult to imagine that the amplification through gossip of what were at first relatively innocent innuendos might soon endanger the social fabric of the community. The exorcism of gossip therefore addressed an important communal and psychological need. It attempted to promote mutual healing and forgiveness by attributing gossip and its pernicious effects to a demonic agent, the "gossip girl" (*mi kha bu mo*), who was not a member of the community at all, but rather an alien and unwanted presence within it. By identifying her origins as lying far outside of the community, demonstrating that her evil influence worked on human and animal alike, and creating an effigy whereby she could be visibly expelled, this ritual, in effect, served as a public disavowal of gossip and all of the terrible effects it was thought to have had on the household or village that sponsored the rite.

Presented as the work of the great eighth-century culture hero Padmasambhava, the ritual as we have it here attributes a Chinese origin to the "gossip girl," a feature that is shared with certain other Tibetan accounts of social ills. For instance, the condemnations of tobacco use that were widely circulated after the mid-nineteenth century attribute the origins of the tobacco plant to a cursed daughter of Chinese demons. The attribution of gossiping, smoking, and other negatively valued behavior to China reflects, to some extent, the degree to which the Tibetans felt themselves to be threatened by the powerful neighbor that often sought to dominate Tibetan affairs. After gossip spread to Tibet, the text goes on to say, its pernicious influence affected even the animal world: by praising and thus calling attention to the positive attributes of various species (the lion's mane, the vulture's quills, etc.), just as human gossip often focuses on achievements that arouse some element of envy ("how did *she* get so popular?"), the gossip girl ultimately destroys all those she commends.

The text begins with the mantra of Guru Padmasambhava and here serves to invoke his presence in connection with the performance of this ritual, and also to authenticate the ritual as an aspect of his teaching. The formula *Hūṃ hūṃ! Bhyo bhyo!* in the second line is specifically connected with exorcistic ritual and is used to dispel evil or polluting influences from the surroundings. Because gossip may attach to any of our possessions, the ritual goes through the main features of the household, expelling gossip from each in turn. Indeed, the entire historical fate of Tibet is related here to gossip's influence. Its final expulsion, however, falters on an apparent paradox: how can one get rid of something disembodied, and hence, presumably, ubiquitous? Padmasambhava, the master exorcist, resolves this difficulty by providing the gossip girl with an effigy and commanding her to identify herself with it. In village ritual performance, the effigy is actually to be removed from the village and destroyed at a safe distance, the spiritual equivalent, perhaps, of the removal of the dangerously polluted waste we at present find so difficult to discard.

The version of the ritual given here, called *Turning Back Malicious Gossip*, was collected by Nancy E. Levine of the University of California, Los Angeles, and Tshewang Lama of Khor Gompa in Humla District, northwestern Nepal, during the course of anthropological fieldwork in ethnically Tibetan communities of Humla. The manuscript is often very irregular in spelling and grammar, so that its interpretation is sometimes uncertain. In editing this translation for the present publication, I have aimed to facilitate the reader's understanding and so have avoided lengthy discussion of many of the difficulties that would be of interest to specialists alone. Explanatory notes are provided in the body of the translation in square brackets.

Further Reading

For a detailed study of the Nyinba community of Humla, readers are referred to Professor Levine's study, *The Dynamics of Polyandry: Kinship, Domesticity and Population on the Tibetan Border* (Chicago: University of Chicago Press, 1988). For a useful overview of Tibetan folk religious practices, see Giuseppe Tucci, *The Religions of Tibet*, trans. Geoffrey Samuel (Berkeley: University of California Press, 1980), pp. 163–212.

HERE IS CONTAINED *THE TURNING BACK OF MALICIOUS GOSSIP* COMPOSED BY MASTER PADMASAMBHAVA.

Oṃ āḥ hūṃ badzra guru padma siddhi hūṃ!
Hūṃ hūṃ! Bhyo bhyo! Turn back! Turn back!
Carnivorous daughter of malicious gossip!
Blood-drinking daughter of malicious gossip!
Red-mouthed daughter of malicious gossip!
Red-eyed daughter of malicious gossip!
Red-nosed daughter of malicious gossip!
You know all the news like a jack of all trades.
You do all sorts of things that ought not to be done.
You make the healthy sick in all sorts of ways.
You cause everything unspeakable to be said.
Daughter of malicious gossip, listen to me!

Girl with black, grimy, tangled hair,
When you first arrived, where did you come from?
You came from the borders of Tibet and China,

Where malicious gossip afflicted the Chinese,
So that the Chinese king sent you to Tibet.
Many Chinese demons then afflicted our tribes.
In the country called Yarlung [south of Lhasa, the seat of the ancient Tibetan empire],
Auguring evil, malicious gossip struck;
The horses got all the horse-ailments there are,
The people got all the human-ailments there are,
And the boys and girls were gradually made sick.
That was retribution for their meeting with you, malicious gossip!
May they now run to my enemy,
O evil-auguring, malicious gossip,
And overturn your scandalous accusations!

Malicious gossip, on the path on which you approached,
You met with the [snow] lion of the upper glaciers,
To whom, malicious gossip, you said,
"For the happiness of the lioness and her cubs,
The turquoise mane suffices, just to roam in the upper glaciers!"
[The so-called "snow lion", an auspicious national symbol of Tibet, is always depicted in Tibetan art with a bright blue-green mane.]
Three days passed after that,
And the lioness and her cubs were buried in an avalanche.
That was retribution for their meeting with you, malicious gossip!
May they run now to my enemy,
O evil-auguring, malicious gossip,
And overturn your scandalous accusations!

Malicious gossip! on the path on which you approached,
You met with the deer of the upper meadows,
To whom, malicious gossip, you said,
"For the happiness of the doe and her fawns,
The pointed horn suffices, just to roam in the upper meadows."
Three days passed after that,
And the doe and her fawns were slain by a predator.
That, too, was retribution for their meeting with you, malicious gossip!
May they run now to my enemy,
O evil-auguring, malicious gossip,
And overturn your scandalous accusations!

Malicious gossip! on the path on which you approached,
You met with the vulture of the upper cliffs,
To whom, malicious gossip, you said,
"For the happiness of the white-tailed vulture,

Sharp feathers suffice, just to roam about the upper cliffs."
Three days passed after that,
And the white-tailed vulture fell into an abyss!
That, too, was retribution for his meeting with you, malicious gossip!
May he run now to my enemy,
O evil-auguring, malicious gossip,
And overturn your scandalous accusations!

Malicious gossip! on the path on which you approached,
You met with the willow-grove's quail,
To whom, malicious gossip, you said,
"For the happiness of the quail and her chicks,
A sweet voice suffices, just to circle amongst the willows."
Three days passed after that,
And the pale, speckled quail were slain by a Hor-pa tribesman [from the north of Tibet].
That, too, was retribution for their meeting with you, malicious gossip!
May they run now to my enemy,
O evil-auguring, malicious gossip,
And overturn your scandalous accusations!

Malicious gossip! on the path on which you approached,
You met with the fish of the upper lake,
To whom, O daughter of malicious gossip, you said,
"For the happiness of the fish and her spawn,
A bright eye suffices, just to swim in the confines of the lake."
Three days passed after that,
And an outcaste hooked the fish.
That, too, was retribution for their meeting with you, malicious gossip!
May they run now to my enemy,
O evil-auguring, malicious gossip,
And overturn your scandalous accusations!

That describes how malicious gossip behaves;
Now, this is how malicious gossip emanates:
Sometimes she dwells on a mountain-top.
"I am Mount Meru," she says.
Sometimes she dwells on the ocean's shore.
"I am the lake's medicine queen," she says.
Sometimes she dwells in the midst of the sky.
"I am the eightfold group of gods and demons," she says.
[Tibetan deities and demons are often listed in groups of eight; in this context, the expression implies "all the worldly gods and demons."]

Sometimes she dwells beneath the red rock.
"I am the *tsen* [*btsan*, malevolent local spirit] who lives beneath the red rock," she says.

Sometimes she dwells at the top of the mansion.
"I am the superior paternal deity!" she says.
Sometimes she dwells in the home's inner recesses.
[In Tibetan belief the house is a sacred realm,
the abode of ancestral and protective divinities.]
"I am the god of the treasury!" she says.
Three brother-gods of the treasury, arise!
May you run now to my enemy,
Evil-auguring, malicious gossip,
And overturn her scandalous accusations!

Sometimes she dwells by the hearth.
"I am the god of the hearth!" she says.
Three brother-gods of the hearth, arise!
May you run now to my enemy,
Evil-auguring, malicious gossip,
And overturn her scandalous accusations!

Sometimes she dwells at the head of the stairs
"I am the stair-god!" she says.
God of the stair, great rafter, arise!
May you run now to my enemy,
Evil-auguring, malicious gossip,
And overturn her scandalous accusations!

Sometimes she dwells in the interior court.
"I am the god of the courtyard!" she says.
Three brother-gods of the interior, arise!
May you run now to my enemy,
Evil-auguring, malicious gossip,
And overturn her scandalous accusations!

Sometimes she dwells behind the door.
"I am the god of the portal!" she says.
Four Great Kings, please arise!
[These four kings of Indian Buddhist mythology rule the four cardinal directions and are regarded in Tibet as the guardians of doorways.]
May you run now to my enemy,
Evil-auguring, malicious gossip,
And overturn her scandalous accusations!

Now concerning malicious gossip's past emanations [earlier in Tibetan history]:
At first, in glorious Samye,
In the king's fortress, the uppermost shrine,
The king, Tri Songdetsen (Khri srong lde btsan),
Was afflicted with the malicious gossip of all the black-headed Tibetans.
The prince, Mutri Tsenpo (Mu khri Btsan po),
Was afflicted with the malicious gossip of all the youths.
The master Padmasambhava
Was afflicted with the malicious gossip of all the gods and demons.
The preceptor Bodhisattva [i.e., Śāntarakṣita]
Was afflicted with the malicious gossip of all the monks.
The great translator Vairocana
Was afflicted with the malicious gossip of all the translators.
The monk Namkhai Nyingpo (Nam mkha'i snying po)
Was afflicted with the malicious gossip of the whole religious community.
Nanam Dorje Düjom (Sna nam Rdo rje bdud 'joms)
Was afflicted with the malicious gossip of all the masters of mantras.
The royal queen Margyen (Dmar brgyan)
Was afflicted with the malicious gossip of all the women.
The wealthy patrons
Were afflicted with the malicious gossip of the whole populace.
All gods and men subject to Tibet
Were afflicted with the malicious gossip of all nations,
With the malicious gossip of corporeal men,
With the malicious gossip of incorporeal gods and demons,
With the malicious gossip of whatever exists,
With the malicious gossip of whatever doesn't exist.

Daughter of malicious gossip, listen here!
First you became nine demon-sisters in China.
[Nine is a prominent magical number in indigenous Tibetan cosmology and is here associated with malignant powers or practices.]
Second you became the nine demonesses.
At last you became the nine gossip sisters.
But whatever you become, now you are turned back!
You have no place at all to stay here.
Malicious gossip, do not stay! Malicious gossip, go away!

Go away to the east, malicious gossip, where your path is revealed!
As soon as you go there from here,
There is a plain gathering beings from all about.
It is the maṇḍala of three plains gathered together.

It is the assembly of a million *the'u rang* spirits.
[The *the'u rang* are minor harmful spirits,
associated primarily with disease and misfortune during childhood.]
Do not stay there! Go even farther away!

As soon as you go farther that way,
There is a mountain gathering beings from all about.
It is the maṇḍala of three mountains gathered together.
It is the assembly of the male and female vampire spirits.
Do not stay there! Go even farther away!

As soon as you go farther that way,
There is a river gatherings beings from all about.
It is the maṇḍala of three rivers gathered together.
It is the assembly of the male and female water-spirits.
Do not stay there! Go farther away upland!

As one goes upland from there,
In the place called Kongyül to the east [an "upside down land" thought to be a center of sorcery],
Malicious gossip appears as a god.
Malicious gossip appears as a nāga.
So that which augurs ill here is trapped for good luck there.
Malicious gossip, you have no place to dwell here.
Malicious gossip, do not stay! Malicious gossip go away!
Go where you appear as a god.
Go where you appear as a nāga.
Go where you will be trapped for good luck!
Malicious gossip, do not stay! Malicious gossip, go away!

The daughter of malicious gossip said,
"Great Master, listen to me!
Padmasambhava, listen to me!
For me to go and not to stay here,
I, malicious gossip, need a body in order to go!"

To this the great master said:
"Daughter of malicious gossip! listen up!
If you, malicious gossip, have no body in order to go,
Let this hollow straw be malicious gossip's body.
Malicious gossip, associate yourself with this body and go away!
If malicious gossip's body needs a head,
Let this red clay pot be malicious gossip's head!
Malicious gossip, associate yourself with this head and go away!
If malicious gossip's head has no brain,
Let this watery mash be malicious gossip's brain!

Malicious gossip, associate yourself with this brain and go away!
If malicious gossip's head has no hair,
Let this black pig-hair brush be malicious gossip's hair!
Malicious gossip, associate yourself with this hair and go away!
If malicious gossip has no ears with which to hear,
Let these radish and turnip slices be malicious gossip's ears!
Malicious gossip, associate yourself with these ears and go away!
If malicious gossip has no eyes with which to see,
Let these little black peas be malicious gossip's eyes!
Malicious gossip, associate yourself with these eyes and go away!
If malicious gossip has no nose with which to smell,
Let this red pot-handle be malicious gossip's nose!
Malicious gossip, associate yourself with this nose and go away!
If malicious gossip has no blabbering mouth,
Let this hot red pepper be malicious gossip's mouth!
Malicious gossip, associate yourself with this mouth and go away!
If malicious gossip has no teeth with which to chew,
Let these hollow cowrie shells be malicious gossip's teeth!
Malicious gossip, associate yourself with these teeth and go away!
If malicious gossip has no tongue with which to speak,
Let a small red smear be malicious gossip's tongue!
Malicious gossip, associate yourself with this tongue and go away!
If malicious gossip has no heart with which to think,
Let this triangular buckwheat grain be malicious gossip's heart!
Malicious gossip, associate yourself with this heart and go away!
If malicious gossip has no hand to stretch out,
Let this ginseng root be malicious gossip's hand!
Malicious gossip, associate yourself with this hand and go away!
If malicious gossip has no clothes to wear,
Let these black shreds of cloth be malicious gossip's clothes!
Malicious gossip, associate yourself with these clothes and go away!
If malicious gossip has no belt with which to bind,
Let this twined mule-tether be malicious gossip's belt!
Malicious gossip, associate yourself with this belt and go away!
If malicious gossip has no feet to stand on,
Let these goat-bones and sheep-bones be malicious gossip's feet!
Malicious gossip, associate yourself with these feet and go away!
If malicious gossip has no boots to wear,
Let these cloven hoofs be malicious gossip's boots!
Malicious gossip, associate yourself with these boots and go away!
If malicious gossip has no hat for the head,
Let these tatters and shreds be malicious gossip's hat.
Malicious gossip, associate yourself with this hat and go away!
If malicious gossip has no horse to ride,

Let this black and white rodent be malicious gossip's horse!
Malicious gossip, associate yourself with this horse and go away!
If malicious gossip has no knife to carry,
Let this tempered iron blade be malicious gossip's knife!
Let this red copper blade be malicious gossip's knife!
Let this dull wooden blade be malicious gossip's knife!
Malicious gossip, associate yourself with this knife and go away!
If malicious gossip has no arrow and bow,
Let this briarwood arrow and bow be malicious gossip's bow and arrow!
Let this bamboo arrow and bow be malicious gossip's bow and arrow!
Malicious gossip, associate yourself with this arrow and bow and go away!
If malicious gossip has no food to eat,
Let these raw vegetables be malicious gossip's food!
Let these garlic-bulbs, onions and turnips be malicious gossip's food!
Let these radish slices and turnip slices be malicious gossip's food!
Let these left-over meat-bones be malicious gossip's food!
Let these leftover grains from the ale-mash be malicious gossip's food!
Let these discarded tea-leaves be malicious gossip's food!
Let this salt, soda, and butter be malicious gossip's food!
Let the leftover food and drink be malicious gossip's food!
Let the dregs of what has been drunk be malicious gossip's food!
Malicious gossip, associate yourself with this food and go away!
If malicious gossip has no wealth to hoard,
Let broken goods and cracked wooden bowls be malicious gossip's wealth!
Let scraps of gold, silver, copper, and iron be malicious gossip's wealth!
Let clippings of silk and clippings of cloth be malicious gossip's wealth!
Let all sorts of grains be malicious gossip's wealth!
Let white and red woolen yarns be malicious gossip's wealth!
Malicious gossip, associate yourself with this wealth and go away!
If malicious gossip has no palace to stay,
Let this gnarled yak-horn be malicious gossip's palace!
Let thread-crosses (*nam mkha'*) and spirit-traps (*rgyang bu*) be malicious gossip's palace!
Malicious gossip, associate yourself with this palace and go away!
If malicious gossip has no paths on which to depart,
Let the path of dung, the path of *chang* be malicious gossip's path!
Let the way of ashes that have vanished be malicious gossip's path!
Let the twisted path of demons be malicious gossip's path!
Let the black demoness reveal malicious gossip's path!
Malicious gossip, associate yourself with this path and go away!

Go away having taken the ritual substitutes and talismans,
[which are offered to the evil being that is exorcized
as symbolic substitutes for the victims of gossip],
Representing the patron along with his household, wealth, and servants.
Daughter of malicious gossip, do not stay! go away!
Carry off the bodily ailments of these patrons
From the roofs of their mansions and down to the plain below,
For the 360 days there are in the twelve months of a [lunar] year.
Carry off their mental distress!
Carry the scandal from their mouths!
Carry off evil-conditions and accidents!
Carry off the lord's Gongpo spirits! [Gongpo (*'gong po*) spirits are thought to afflict adult men and are associated with arrogance and hubris.]
Carry off the curse-bearing talismans!
Carry off the malicious gossip from the four continents!
Malicious gossip, do not stay! malicious gossip, go away!"

Do not stick around the walls of our mansion!
Do not stick around the people above [who live in upper story]!
Do not stick around the cattle below [who live in the lower story]!
Do not stick around our watchdog!
Do not stick around the men of the house!
Do not stick around the household's women!
Do not stick around our little children!
Do not stick around the fields that we sow!
Do not stick around our dairy's yogurt!
Do not stick around our fermented chang!
Do not stick around our gold and silver!
Malicious gossip, do not stay! malicious gossip, go away!

—35—

Hail Protection

Anne C. Klein and Khetsun Sangpo

The practice of hail protection incorporates numerous aspects of Tibetan religion and culture. A social practice as well as a meditative one, it also involves the visual and prognostic arts. The following discussion draws from a traditional Tibetan text detailing the rituals involved in protecting an area from hail, and from Khetsun Sangpo's commentary on that work. This format seemed best suited to conveying the hail-protection practice as a whole, as well as the cultural tensions it embodies. No textual excerpt could provide this. At the same time, the present selection is not altogether different in kind from the primary text translations found elsewhere in this volume in that it adheres closely to the oral and written material from which it derives, following an abbreviated outline of the written text made by Khetsun Sangpo. His ordering does not always strictly follow the order of the text but is devised to bring a bewildering array of subtopics into a comprehensible format. The final section includes material elaborated by Khetsun Sangpo in discussion but not specifically included in his outline.

Khetsun Sangpo Rinpoche is a Nyingma lama, best known among Tibetan scholars for his thirteen-volume series on Tibetan history. However, in the three years prior to his departure from Tibet in 1960, Khetsun Sangpo was in charge of protecting an area south of Lhasa from hail. In 1990, after I had known him for over fifteen years and studied several classic Buddhist texts and practices with him, it finally occurred to me to ask about the hail-protection practices that had occupied his early years. He agreed to explain them, and after careful reflection he decided to base his discussion on the *Tent for [Holding Off] Ferocious Fire and Water, the Instructions for Guarding against Hail through Secret Accomplishment of Hayagrīva* (*Rta mkhrin gsang sgrub gyi sgo nas ser ba bsrung ba'i gdams pa me rlung 'khrugs pa'i gur*).

Hailmaster traditions are linked with the earliest forms of Buddhism in Tibet, coming almost exclusively from the Nyingma and, occasionally, Kagyü sects of Tibetan Buddhism. The rich descriptions of the spirits associated with hail, together with careful elucidation of the substances that injure them, very likely derive from the pre-Buddhist period.

Mahāyāna Buddhism is famous for its intention to help all beings without exception. However, because hail is understood to be brought by malevolent spirit-figures, some of whom are figures in the retinues of bodhisattvas, it becomes the business of the hailmaster to prevent these spirits from accomplishing their goals. In doing so, sometimes he must harm them. This violation of the Mahāyāna spirit was obviously uncomfortable for Khetsun Sangpo, and he spoke of hail prevention as a dirty business, something he was glad to be out of.

> If you ask how was it that I became a hailmaster, was this something that I had aspired to do for a long time? Not at all. It was not something that I wanted, but the circumstances fell out that way and I became a hailmaster quite against my wishes. [In fact, though his own father was a hailmaster, Khetsun Sangpo in his early youth went to study with scholars and meditation masters rather than follow his father's trade.] Because, after all, hailmasters are involved with harming and making trouble for beings who bring hail. This is quite a sin and I have no wish at all to be involved in this kind of nonvirtuous activity. In effect, the hailmaster understands himself to be making war on various spirits, ghosts, and others involved with the bringing of hail. Of course, these are not beings who have form like we do—humans make war with people who have form like ourselves—but this is a war on unseen beings.

He acknowledged my surmise that the nonvirtue of hail prevention might be mitigated if the hailmaster was motivated mainly by a wish to protect the crops and livelihood of persons in his area, but he doubted that this was often the case. More often, he emphasized, hailmasters were motivated by money. Indeed, those who succeeded in protecting their areas from hail were well paid and politically powerful. Khetsun Sangpo expressed his sense of good fortune that he had never needed to engage in the fiercer techniques of hail protection.

Despite this tension between the goals of hail protection and normative Mahāyāna Buddhist sensibilities, the practice of stopping hail is intimately related with orthodox Buddhist tantric practices. That is, in preparing to become a hailmaster one learns to identify with one's own personal deity, or *yi dam*, through traditional practices of recitation and visualization, preceded by the Mahāyāna cultivation of refuge and compassion (see chapters 13, 14, and 16). One chooses a deity based on one's own predilections or one's connection with a lama. Any *yi dam*, male or female, in whom one has faith can be a basis for hail protection, but it should be a fierce one.

The explanation of the hail-protection practice has two main parts: (1) the prior (and higher) activities, which are aimed at accomplishing enlightenment; and (2) various latter (and lower) activities specifically associated with hail protection. In brief, the higher activities involve gaining enlightenment, that is, becoming a buddha oneself, whereas the lower activities, including that of actually preventing hail, pertain to the purposes of this life. The former are crucial for becoming a hailmaster.

The prior activities comprise well-known forms of tantric practice. Khetsun Sangpo condensed them into the four activities of (1) empowerment *(dbang)*, (2) training in ritual practice *(phyag len la mkhas par sbyangs)*, (3) accomplishing recitation and establishing oneself as a deity *(lha'i brnyan sgrub)*, and (4) augmentation *(kha sgong)*. These are methods for acquiring the realizations of the stages and the paths, including the traditional Buddhist accumulations of virtue and wisdom. Properly performing these is the basis for the rest, and thus temporally and spiritually prior to what follows. As Khetsun Sangpo explains: "Why emphasize these prior activities? They are associated with achieving buddhahood, and our condition is such that unless we gain some enlightenment ourselves, it is impossible to help others."

Empowerment accomplishes two things: it plants the seed of the capacity to prevent hail, and it grants permission to read the texts and perform the ritual practices that "ripen" these seeds. To receive an empowerment is to be initiated into a relationship with one's *yi dam*, the figure whose being one takes on during meditation proper and, also, during the act of protecting an area from hail. Once initiated, practitioners are empowered to accomplish, emulate, and experience themselves as the deity to whom they have already been introduced. Training in these practices constitutes the second and third of the prior activities: gaining skill in the ritual practices associated with the deity, and accomplishing the recitation and establishment of oneself in the form of the deity, that is, training in the classic tantric stages of development and completion.

Khetsun Sangpo explained the second activity, "gaining skill in the ritual practices of the deity," in this way:

> Traditionally, Buddhist practices are divided into those having to do with method and wisdom; here in tantra the stages of development and completion correspond to method and wisdom. What is the method? We take our ordinary sense of what we look like, our sense of ourselves as flesh and blood, and put it aside. Instead, we think that our body is the body of the enlightened deity associated with our practice. We practice developing a clear appearance of ourselves as the deity, and if we become accustomed to this sufficiently, it becomes possible to have this experience visually. Not only this, but we imagine that the entire world which we inhabit is itself a maṇḍala mansion, made of light. Everyone we meet, then, is a male or female deity. But such visualization is not sufficient. We also need to understand it to be empty, as discussed in Madhyamaka and other texts. For this reason we practice the stage of completion, the second stage of tantric practices, especially associated with the wisdom of emptiness. With the stage of generation as the method and the understanding of emptiness applied to the stage of completion as wisdom, we can enter into the profound path.

The third prior activity is "approaching the deity through recitation." The word for recitation *(brnyen)* also means "to approach" or "come close." One recites the mantra or sound associated with a particular enlightened being and, in this way, both approaches and becomes like that figure. The first and highest of the three levels at which recitation can be accomplished requires one to continue recitation practice until there arise signs of having achieved the deity *(brtags bsnyen)*. Of such signs the best and most difficult to achieve is the experience of a direct meeting with that deity. Other signs include nectar emerging from ritual sculptures *(gtor ma)* made of butter and barley; or liquid in offering vessels bubbling up as if boiling. The second level of accomplishment is to recite innumerable, almost uncountable, numbers of the deity's mantra *(grangs bsnyen)*. The power one gains is a function of this number. The lowest level of accomplishing the practice of recitation is to recite one hundred thousand repetitions for each syllable of the mantra *(las rung)*.

Performing these practices carefully is said to make activities such as the stopping of hail possible, an enterprise that involves combat against beings associated with hail. According to Khetsun Sangpo, if you can clearly and with an unwavering mind visualize yourself as, for example, Hayagrīva, then worldly deities cannot harm you. Even if you have not understood emptiness and thus not fulfilled the practice of the stage of completion, your own strong visualization causes these worldly spirits to see you as the fierce and powerful Hayagrīva, not as an ordinary an human being. Therefore one is protected, since they would never attempt to harm Hayagrīva.

Once the recitation facilitating emulation of the deity is complete, one undertakes the fourth and last of the prior practices. Peaceful augmentation *(kha sgong la zhi ba'i skyes bsrog)* involves thirteen substances offered to the deity by placing them in fire. These are firewood, melted butter, wheat, beans, shelled barley, unshelled barley, rice, grass roots, kusha grass, sesame, yogurt mixed with tsampa, the other twelve substances mixed together, and the juice made by chopping up beetle-nuts. Except for the firewood, which is in effect their means of delivery, these substances are forms of human food that can also be food for deities. Offering in this way is a peaceful activity.

Once the prior activities have been completed, it is possible to begin any of a variety of activities, including the hail-protection practices that are our focus here. The prior activities are the root of all the functions they make possible.

For hail protection, the various latter activities are five: (1) making ritual artifacts, (2) preparing mantra-empowered pills, (3) meeting the law-enforcer, (4) walking the protected area, (5) during the summer retreat, actually undertaking the activities that will protect an area from hail. These techniques are passed from father to son. In Tibet there were almost no women who worked to prevent hail. In the 1950s a hailmaster passed his skills on to Khetsun Sangpo, his son-in-law, rather than to any of his seven daughters. Still, says Khetsun Sangpo, "these methods would work for anyone who had the ability, woman or man, American or not, and anyone who had that ability would be respected."

There are an enormous number of complex rituals and items associated with this practice. All must be learned with detail and precision. Someone destined for the activity of protecting against hail generally trains in it from childhood and does not engage in any other kind of study. Tibetans consider the training of a hailmaster to be much like that of a Tibetan doctor: both must memorize the names and functions of innumerable herbs and elements and be able to identify them.

The first activity after augmentation is the making of a triangular stand out of birchwood *(shing stag pa'i byang bu)*. On this is attached the figure of one's *yi dam*, at whose heart is placed a circle inscribed with certain mantras and designs. Such a circle is not part of ordinary tantric practice. A second mantra is written on the figure's back, as is often done with Tibetan thankas. In this case however, the mantra is incorporated into a phrase that includes the name of the place to be protected; for example, the writing on the back of the figure Khetsun Sangpo made while staying in Texas is entirely in Tibetan except for the English word "Houston." This ritual object must be made by the hailmaster himself, who will have trained in the intricate designs and mantras required. Khetsun Sangpo observes that, "Of course, there are some inadequate persons who really don't know how to do all the drawings and so forth properly, but there are also those who are very well trained. It is important to make great effort to do everything correctly since success depends on this."

Next, one makes a traditional figure in the shape of a dagger known as a *phurba* and places mantras at two points on the figure; in addition, a scented packet is tied around its neck. Although *phurbas* are most commonly made of metal, for the purpose of protecting from hail one must use a *phurba* made from a red-hued wood known as *acacia catechu (seng ldeng gi phur pa)*. This is a tree that bears a three-pronged leaf; when its bark is peeled back, its color is pure yellow. Thread is wound around the *phurba* as well as the hair of a great lama or a great tantric practitioner, and these also are attached to the top of the *phurba*, fastening the packet of spices and other contents. Later the *phurbas* will be set up inside each of the four huts on the protected property.

Next, one empowers certain substances with mantras that are held very secretly. The substances involved in this practice and the use made of them is not, as in burning the thirteen substances, a case of offering something nice to the deities, of pleasing them or helping them in any way whatsoever. This is a case of making trouble for such beings, harming or hurting them. In this connection it is also the hailmaster's job to examine the astrological situation and learn whether the stars indicate things will go well or not, and which types of beings are involved with the hail on any particular occasion. Thus, the arts of astrology and divination are also part of the hailmaster's education.

There are sixteen substances considered to be antidotes that interfere with beings associated with hail. From these substances one will make pills within which are placed certain fierce mantras. The pills are then empowered through ritual recitation during the hailmaster's twenty-seven-day retreat.

These sixteen antidotal substances are an evocative list, suggesting mysterious but poetically resonant connections among the items it contains:

1. Antidote for the earth demon is earth from a place struck by lightening.
2. Antidote for the earth deity is water from melted hail.
3. Antidote for the earth deity leaders is earth from a place where there has been fighting (e.g., rubble from a house hit by a cannon).

4. Antidote to the *tsen* (*btsan*) is powdered copper.
5. Antidote to the mother nāgas is a wool-like aquatic grass plucked from very still water.
6. Antidote to the father *srin* is black sulphur (very bad smelling).
7. Antidote to the *dmu*-demons (who also cause dropsy by casting an evil eye on one) is soil from a rushing stream.
8. Antidote to the *lha srin* is the fangs of a musk deer or, if one cannot find this, the fangs of a mad dog.
9. As an antidote to [the worldly] Dorje Legba (Rdo rje legs pa) one needs the flesh of a weasel (*sre mong*).
10. As an antidote to demons (*bdud*) one needs the flesh of a hopoo bird. One puts mantras in this flesh, which prevents the demon from doing harm. This flesh does not help or feed the demon in any way; it has a bad smell which turns the demon around. Khetsun Sangpo noted that it is a sin to kill a hopoo bird for its flesh, but difficult to obtain otherwise. "That's the business of a hailmaster. Sometimes one inherits these items from one's father."
11. As an antidote to the four female spirits (*srid mo*) one needs acrid black earth.
12. As an antidote to the female servant nāgas one needs the *spru ma* flower, which the dictionary defines as "a hellebore which cures plague, fever, worms and leprosy."
13. As an antidote to the worker deity group one needs earth from a place where a person has been killed.
14. As an antidote to Yama one needs earth from a crossroads.
15. As an antidote to the *tīrthikas* (non-Buddhists) one needs *grogs shing*—a kind of small clinging plant (not moss) or lichen that can grow on trees or, in Tibet, on doorways.
16. As an antidote to *bhin ya ka* one needs earth from a place where there has been fighting.

Pills are made from these substances for later use in preventing hail. In commenting on the secrecy that has prevailed regarding these substances and the mantras that empower them, Khetsun Sangpo observes:

> Except for the *māntrika*—a father and the son to whom he passes this knowledge—Tibetan people do not know these things. They are kept secret because this kind of power does not depend on substances, or on people, but is derived from the power of mantra. This is completely different from, for example, publishing explanations about how the body works—looking at the cells and so forth, or printing diagrams of these. If such things are not kept secret their power dissipates, just as when you carry a candle it lights the room, but if you give it to someone else you are in darkness. Even the rosary used for mantra recitation should not be seen, it is kept hidden under the sleeve. In this way the customs of Tibet and modern Western countries are completely different.
>
> The thirteen substances offered to the deity as food are not at all secret, nor is the peaceful augmentation through fire offering. But the sixteen antidotes are secret because they are intended only to harm, not to help, their recipients.

> Still, if things are published and not really understood [and the assumption seems to be that they will not be, for Khetsun Rinpoche did not object either to speaking of them publicly or publishing their names], their power does not dissipate.

The hailmaster stays in retreat for twenty-seven days while he empowers these articles and makes pills from the mantrically empowered substances. Gathering all these substances as well as the other ritual articles may entail some difficulty; however, as already indicated, the hailmaster often inherits most of what is needed. Making the pills involves two activities: blackening them in a fire fueled by wood that was initially blackened when used to burn a corpse, and placing them in musk water. Mantras are then positioned inside the pills as one recites a related mantra. The mantra within the pills is written with blood extracted from many beings on a poisonous paper made from a particular bad-smelling wood. Afterward the hailmaster keeps these with him when he walks and guards the area under his protection.

Prior to the hail season, a meeting between the hailmaster and the local law-enforcement officer takes place in the third month of the Tibetan year. It is customary for the hailmaster to write out the rules to be enforced, and for the officer to act as a sort of spy, keeping his eye on the people of the area. Anyone who disobeys the rules is reported to the hailmaster, who may then decide to send hail to descend on the offender. Under such circumstances, the hail is considered the fault of the law-breaker, not the hailmaster, because the officer will have documented that this person did in fact break the law. In other words, the likelihood of hail destroying crops bears some relationship to the actions or karma of the people in the area. From a Tibetan perspective, if the people in an area are involved in war, theft, and so forth, the deities are more likely to send hail. Khetsun Sangpo observes:

> In this sense [in preventing hail] the hailmaster is interfering with the cause and effect of karma. There is a lot of quarreling about this in Tibet. People complain about the hailmaster, saying, "What happened, you were supposed to protect us from hail and you didn't do it." He responds, "Look, I did my part, I stopped the hail, but you are behaving badly and this makes my work similar to trying to plug a leak in a wall with many, many holes. If you behave like this, what can I do?"

After concluding his meeting with the law-enforcement officer, the hailmaster makes his rounds of the area under protection. At this point, then, following whatever length of years it might have taken to emulate fully his protector deity in accordance with the prior activities, the practitioner has spent twenty-seven days in retreat empowering the antidotal substances with mantra. Now he turns his attention to the local terrain, the area that will be under his protection. This area is marked with stone dividers or, less commonly, with wooden fences.

Some time prior to his twenty-seven day retreat he established four huts in the four directions of the property. He now proceeds to each of these, or at least to one of them, carrying the birchwood stand, the *phurba* or ritual dagger, and various other substances such as cedar, which will be offered as food for the deities. It is not that when they eat these their power becomes less, but that they accept this food as a plea not to send hail. If the assigned area is large, it might take two to three days to complete the walk; it may also be of a size that can be walked in a single day.

Now he also places two stone circular plaques known as "reversing discs" (*zlog 'khor*) in each of these four directional points, facing outward. These are decorated with specific designs and mantras. Two other plaques, known as "protective discs" (*srung 'khor*), are also placed there, facing inward. These are inscribed with their own appropriate mantras. Then, with the new crops in the ground, the actual three-month summer retreat for preventing the summertime hail will begin.

There are various methods for preventing hail or altering its course. Peaceful methods include recitation of the mantra of Śākyamuni Buddha and burning *tsang* (cedar) for offering and using the offering vessel (*gser skyems*). Semiwrathful methods involve visualizing oneself as Hayagrīva, with one's flames destroying the hail clouds. Very wrathful methods involve placing substances known as epidermal flakes from a black stallion (*rda bon bdug pa*) in a fire, or using poison pills and a slingshot.

There are other methods as well. One can make a frog out of clay and harden it in the fire. In an opening at its underside one places an enormous number of mantras and other things as well. When hail is imminent, the frog is pointed at the hail cloud. A clay turtle can be used in the same way. There are also methods for trapping the hail-bringing deities underground, or for dispossessing deities of their power. This is done by burying different substances.

During the summer hail season, while in retreat on the highest point of the property he protects, the hailmaster spends his time looking at the skies and analyzing his dreams to determine whether or not there will be hail that day. If hail is indicated, he takes appropriate measures very early in the morning. For example, if the Sun shines through two layers of cloud in a particular way, this is an indication of hail. Or, if one looks not so much at the clouds but at the light coming between them, and if the Sun's rays come very straight in a small opening between the clouds, this is also a sign of hail. If there is one set of clouds over another, and if the Sun is able to get out from between them, hail will come. If two layers of clouds are vertically placed one in front of the other, and if there is space between them for the Sun to shine, this too is a sign of imminent hail. Or if we see the blue sky between the two layers of clouds with the sunlight pouring out horizontally between them, hail is imminent.

One can also judge the likelihood of hail by the clouds themselves. When rain clouds come, they cover the sky from both sides. For this reason rain is much more difficult to prevent than hail; one can target one's energies better on the far more localized hail clouds. These are immediately recognizable. They move like bubbles rising in water, like roiling water, not in a straight path. When one does the practice, one can immediately see the cloud disappear and it cannot hail. Hail is said to occur only in the afternoon and is particularly likely to come on the fourth, eighth, eleventh, fifteenth, eighteenth, twenty-second, twenty-fifth, or twenty-ninth days of the lunar calendar because the earth demons walk about on these days.

As already suggested, it not sufficient just to know that hail is on its way, one must be aware of which kinds of beings are bringing it. Indeed, there is a two-volume text on this subject written by Lelung Shebe Dorje (Las lung shes ba'i rdo rje), a Gelukpa who was a student of Terton Lingba (Gter ston gling pa) and then became a Nyingma during the time of the fifth Dalai Lama. One can understand which types of beings are involved either through watching the clouds or through observing dreams.

To receive signs in a dream, one says a certain mantra before going to sleep, holding some water in the palm of one's hand as one repeats one round on a rosary, and then drinking the water one has thus empowered with this recitation. The dreams do not simply predict hail, but indicate which types of beings are connected with it. For example, if one dreams of sheep eating the crops, this is a sign that nāgas will send hail. If one dreams of a yak, this indicates the demons will send hail, for the demons are something like the lords of the yak. If one dreams of a Tibetan stag *(gsel ba)*, an animal with ten or twelve points on each horn, this indicates that the female demons known as *mamo* will send hail. If one dreams of a horse eating the crops, this indicates that the *tsen* will send hail. If one dreams of a cow eating crops, this also indicates that certain kind of *tsen* that lives in the rocky places of a mountain will send hail. If one dreams of small bugs harming the crops, a kind of *yakṣa* will send hail. If one dreams of a frog and snake eating the crops, this indicates that other kinds of nāgas will send hail. (There are many kinds of nāgas, each kind has a different set of figures associated with it.) If one dreams of a woman cutting the crops, this indicates that the *mamo* deities will send hail. If one dreams of a person wearing white clothing walking alone in the fields, this indicates that the chief of the deities will send hail. If one dreams of a great deal of snow, the deities will send hail. If one dreams of the cabins that one has placed on the four directions on one's land, then one of the eight groups of deities will send hail.

In analyzing clouds, reddish and blackish-yellow clouds in the east that alternately disappear and return is a sign of hail to be sent by *tsen.* In the east, three clouds that look like white felt indicate that female deities known as the Tsomen *(tsho sman)* are angry and want to fight; because of their anger, they will send hail. If in the southern sky at morning there are three brownish-black clouds in the shape of sentient beings, it is the demons who will send hail. If there are clouds shaped like the weapons of the *go cha khyon*—very early tribes in Tibet who carried arrows and other weapons, this indicates that the angry *mamo* will send hail suddenly, without the people knowing it is coming, like a thief moving in secret. A cloud in the north in the form of an alertly sitting monkey means that a king of deities *(dkor bdag)* will send hail. A bluish or reddish cloud like a coiled snake in the middle of the sky indicates that the nāgas will send hail. Depending on where the cloud lies and what the particular signs are, matters enumerated in great detail in various texts, one determines what spirit or figure is likely to be associated with the hail approaching that day, and one responds accordingly. Depending on the type of figure involved, one might be able to use peaceful means, such as simply making an offering to dissuade them from sending hail. Or one may have to have to use harsher methods, such as visualizing oneself as a very fierce figure with flames coming out of one's body, and these flames, then, can burn the arms and legs of the would-be hail-bringing figures. Or one can use the fierce method of putting in fire things that will smell very badly to these figures. In short, there are a number of different methods one can employ, from rather peaceful to very, very fierce. Khetsun Sangpo observes:

> If one takes measures as soon as the cloud appears, even a yogin who is not very powerful can be effective. But once the hail has begun, only someone with great power can send it away. If one is careful from the beginning, it is easy.
>
> I spent four years in the monastery learning the practices of a hailmaster and three in the field. I was very young, I had a very limited mind, I had no power at all, but on seeing the clouds of hail and so forth I did the peaceful offerings and there was never any hail. I was in my twenties at the time, just a child.

The text summarized above appears in the *Collected Works of Thu' 'bkwan blo bzang chos kyi nyi ma* (1737–1802), vol. 7 (Ja), edited and introduced by Ngawang Gelek Demo, with an introduction by Gene Smith. It comments on another text, the *Iron Tent House Guarding against Hail (Ser bsrung gnam ljags gur khang)*, a work from the *Northern Treasure (byang gter)* by Rig 'dzin rgod gyi ldem phru can (also known as Rig 'dzin dngos grub rgyal mtshan, 1337–1408). This latter work is considered a *terma* (recovered treasure) from the time of Songtsen gampo (c. 640).

Further Reading

For more on Tibetan astrology, divination, and dream analysis, see Norbu Chophel, *Folk Culture of Tibet* (Dharamsala: Library of Tibetan Works and Archives, 1983).

—36—

A Prayer Flag for Tārā

Donald S. Lopez, Jr.

Prayer flags are a ubiquitous feature of the Tibetan landscape, designed to promote good fortune and dispel danger. They are colored squares of cloth, usually about a foot square, imprinted with a prayer or mantra. These flags are then attached to poles or to the rooftops of temples and dwellings, or are strung from the cairns found at the summits of mountain passes. The wind is said to carry the benefits beseeched by the prayer imprinted on the fluttering flag, both to the person who flies the flag and to all beings in the region.

The prayer translated below was printed on a yellow piece of cotton cloth, 11 by 14 inches in size. The prayer on the flag is one of the most widely recited in Tibetan Buddhism, the prayer to the twenty-one Tārās. Its translation could easily be placed in the preceding section on "Prayers and Sermons" but is included here, in the section of death and other demons, for two reasons. First, Tārā, whose name means "Savioress," is known for her miraculous powers to deliver her devotees from all forms of physical danger, dangers that in Tibetan Buddhism often take the form of demons. Second, this prayer would seem to provide an auspicious sentiment upon which to close the volume.

Tārā was born from a lotus blossom that sprang from a tear shed by Avalokiteśvara, the bodhisattva of compassion, as he surveyed the suffering universe. She is thus said to be the physical manifestation of the compassion of Avalokiteśvara, himself said to be the quintessence of all the compassion of all the buddhas. Because buddhas are produced from wisdom and compassion, Tārā, like the goddess Prajñāpāramitā ("Perfection of Wisdom"), is hailed as "the mother of all buddhas" despite the fact that she is most commonly represented as a beautiful sixteen-year-old maiden.

She is often depicted as one of two female bodhisattvas flanking Avalokiteśvara: Tārā, the personification of his compassion, and Bhṛkutī, the personification of his wisdom. But Tārā is the subject of much devotion in her own right, serving as the subject of many stories, prayers, and tantric sādhanas. Like Avalokiteśvara, she has played a crucial role in Tibet's history, in both divine and human forms. She was the protective deity of Atiśa, appearing to him at crucial points in his life, advising him to make his fateful journey to Tibet, despite the fact that his lifespan would be shortened as a result. She took human form as the Chinese princess who married King Songtsen Gampo, bringing with her the buddha image that would become the most revered in Tibet. In the next generation, she appeared as the wife of King Tri Songdetsen and consort of Padmasambhava, Yeshe Tsogyal (Ye she mtsho rgyal), who, in addition to becoming a great tantric master herself, served as scribe as Padmasambhava dictated the treasure texts (*gter ma*). Later Tārā is said to have appeared as the great practitioner of the *chö* (*gcod*) tradition, Majik Lapdön (Ma gcig lap sgron, 1062–1149). Indeed, Tārā has promised aeons ago when she first vowed to achieve buddhahood in order to free all beings from saṃsāra to always appear in the female form.

She has many iconographic forms, the most common being as Green Tārā and as White Tārā, propitiated especially to bestow long life. She has numerous wrathful forms; especially famous is Kurukullā, a dancing naked yoginī, red in color, brandishing bow and arrow in her four arms. In tantric maṇḍalas, she appears as the consort of Amoghasiddhi, the buddha of the northern quarter; together they are lord and lady of the action (*karma*) lineage. But she is herself also the sole deity in many tantric sādhanas (see chapter 27 in *Buddhism in Practice*), in which the meditator, whether male or female, visualizes himself or herself in Tārā's feminine form.

But Tārā is best known for her salvific powers, appearing in the instant her devotee recites her mantra, *oṃ tāre tuttāre ture svāhā*. She is especially renowned for her ability to deliver those who call upon her from eight fears: lions, elephants, fire, snakes, bandits, prison, water, and demons, and many tales are told recounting her miraculous interventions. She can appear in peaceful or wrathful forms, depending on the circumstances, her powers extending beyond the subjgation of these worldly frights, into the heavens and into the hells.

Apart from the recitation of her mantra, the prayer below is the most common medium of invoking Tārā in Tibet. It is a prayer to twenty-one Tārās, derived from an Indian tantra devoted to Tārā, the *Source of All Rites to Tārā, the Mother of All Tathāgatas* (*Sarvatathāgatamatṛtāra-viśvakarmabhavatantra*). According to some traditions of commentary on the prayer, each verse refers to a different form of Tārā, totaling twenty-one. According to others, the forms of Tārā are iconographically almost indistinguishable. The famous Tārā chapel at Atiśa's temple at Nyethang (Snye thang) contains nearly identical statues of the twenty-one Tārās. (For a beautiful eleventh-century stele depicting the twenty-one Tārās, see Rhie and Thurman, p. 124). The prayer is known by heart throughout the Tibetan cultural region, recited especially by travelers to protect them in their long journeys on foot and horseback across mountains and plains. The final stanzas of the prayer (generally not recited by Tibetans) promise that one who recites the prayer with faith in Tārā will be free from fear, the sins that cause rebirth as animal, ghost, or hell being destroyed. The person who calls the prayer to mind will be immune to all poisons and fevers. If one wants a child one will have one; indeed, all desires will be granted, no hindrances will stand in the way, and buddhahood will be achieved.

The prayer is filled with allusions to the Indian cosmology and pantheon, demonstrating that Tārā's powers extend throughout the universe, from the heavens to the underworld, that she has dominion over all worldly gods and demons. There is insufficient space to identify all the allusions here; they are treated in some detail in Wilson (1986). Indeed, it might be argued that it is superfluous even to translate the words on a prayer flag. Those who raise them often cannot read them, the very shapes of the letters bearing sufficient symbolic power.

The prayer flag has in its center an image of Tārā approximately two inches square, set within a single-line frame. The prayer itself appears on the flag as if on a sheet of paper, with lines breaking in the middle of the flag to accommodate the picture of the goddess. Like all prayer flags, this one was made from a wooden blockprint, in which a craftsman would have carved the prayers and the picture of Tārā, in relief and backward, after which the block would have been inked and the piece of cloth laid across it. A roller would have then been applied to transfer the words and picture onto the cloth. As with other prayer flags, the names of four protective animals of the four directions appear in the corners of the flag: in the upper right-hand corner "lion," in the upper left-hand corner "tiger," in the lower left-hand corner "*khyung*" (the mythical Tibetan eagle), and in the lower right-hand corner "dragon." As with many prayer flags, after the prayer, there is brief statement of the benefits that will accrue from its flying. In this case, it gives a hint as to the purpose for which this flag was made: "May the lifespan, merit, power, energy, glory, and fame of the person born in ____ year increase!" The person who flies the flag is to write in the name of the year in which he or she was born.

The translation is from a prayer flag acquired by the translator at Tashilhunpo (Bkra shis lhun po) monastery in Tibet in 1985.

Further Reading

On Tārā, see Stephan Beyer, *The Cult of Tārā* (Berkeley: University of California Press, 1973), and Martin Wilson, *In Praise of Tārā: Songs to the Saviouress* (London: Wisdom Publications, 1986). The latter contains an extensive commentary on the prayer. For several color plates depicting various form of Tārā, see Marilyn Rhie and Robert A. F. Thurman, eds., *Wisdom and Compassion: The Sacred Art of Tibet* (New York: Harry N. Abrams, 1991).

Namo Ārya Tāraye
Homage to the Treasury of Compassion, the Noble Avalokiteśvara
Oṃ. Homage to the Exalted Noble Tārā

Homage. Tārā, swift heroine, her eyes like a flash of lightening. Born from the blossoming from the tear on the Protector of the Three Worlds' face. (1)

Homage. Her face a hundred full autumn moons amassed, blazing with the light of a thousand gathered stars. (2)

Homage. Her hand adorned with a water-born lotus, blue and gold. Her sphere is giving, effort, austerity, peace, patience, and concentration. (3)

Homage. Crown of the Tathāgata, her deeds conquer without end, much accompanied by the children of the Conqueror who have attained perfection. (4)

Homage. She fills desire, direction, and space with the letters *tuttāra hūṃ*, pressing down the seven worlds with her feet, able to summon all [beings]. (5)

Homage. She is worshipped by various lords: Indra, Agni, Brahmā, Marut; she is praised by hosts of ghosts, risen corpses, gandharvas, and yakṣas. (6)

Homage. With *traṭ* and *phaṭ* she destroys the strategems of opponents, pressing down with her right foot drawn in and her left foot stretched out, blazing with raging fire. (7)

Homage. *Ture* most horrific, she destroys Māra's hero, with the frown of her lotus face she slays all foes. (8)

Homage. She is adorned at her heart with her fingers in the mudrā symbolizing the three jewels, adorned with wheels of all directions, raging with her gathered light. (9)

Homage. She is joyous, her shining crown emits garlands of light, laughing the laugh of *tuttāra,* she subdues Māra and the world. (10)

Homage. She is able to summon all the hosts of guardians of the earth; with the letter *hūṃ,* frowning, trembling, she frees the destitute. (11)

Homage. Crowned with a crescent moon, all ornaments blazing; from Amitābha in her piled tresses, light is always created. (12)

Homage. Standing amid a blazing circle, like the aeon-ending fire; surrounded by joy, right leg stretched out, left drawn in, destroying the enemy troops. (13)

Homage. She strikes the surface of the earth with the palm of her hand and beats it with her foot; frowning, with the letter *hūṃ*, she subdues the seven underworlds. (14)

Homage. Blissful, virtuous, peaceful, her sphere is the peace of nirvāṇa; perfectly endowed with *svāhā* and *oṃ*, she destroys all sin. (15)

Homage. Surrounded by joy, she vanquishes the body of the enemy; she liberates with the knowledge [mantra] *hūṃ*, arrayed with the ten-syllabled speech [of her mantra]. (16)

Homage. *Ture*, by stamping her foot, her seed is the letter *hūṃ*'s form; trembler of Meru, Mandara, Vindhya, and the three worlds. (17)

Homage. Holding in her hand the deer marked [moon] in the form of the lake of the gods; by saying *tārā* twice with the syllable *phaṭ*, she dispels all poison. (18)

Homage. She is attended by the king of the hosts of gods, by gods and kinnaras; her joyous splendor dispels the disputes and nightmare of armored ones. (19)

Homage. Her two eyes shine with light of the sun and full moon. By saying *hara* twice with *tuttāre,* she dispels the most terrible fever. (20)

Homage. Endowed with pacifying power arrayed with the three realities, she is the supreme *Ture*, destroyer of the hosts of demons, risen corpses, and yakṣas. (21)

This praise of the root mantra and the twenty-one homages.

Oṃ tāre tuttāre ture svāhā. May the lifespan, merit, power, energy, glory, and fame of the person born in ____ year increase!

INDEX

The index includes names of historical figures, deities, and titles of works mentioned in the Introduction and the individual introductions to each of the chapters. Place names, schools, sects, and concepts are not indexed. Phonetic equivalents of Tibetan names are cross-referenced to the transliterated forms, which are alphabetized by the first letter in the Tibetan transliteration. English translations of titles of Tibetan texts are cross-referenced to their Tibetan forms.